AF411498

WEST OF CENTER

WEST OF CENTER

ART AND THE COUNTERCULTURE EXPERIMENT IN AMERICA, 1965–1977

ELISSA AUTHER AND ADAM LERNER, EDITORS   FOREWORD BY LUCY R. LIPPARD

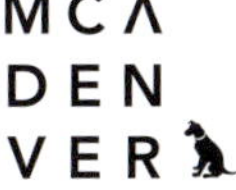

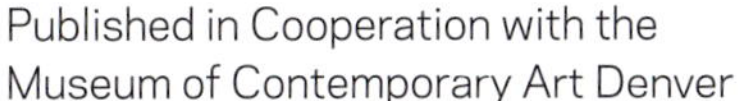

Published in Cooperation with the
Museum of Contemporary Art Denver

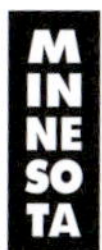

University of Minnesota Press
Minneapolis London

MCΛ
DEN
VER🐾

This book was published on the occasion of the exhibition *West of Center: The Counterculture Experiment in America, 1965–1977,* organized by the Museum of Contemporary Art Denver.

Exhibition Schedule
Museum of Contemporary Art Denver   *November 10, 2011 – February 19, 2012*
Scottsdale Museum of Contemporary Art   *September 29, 2012 – January 6, 2013*

Funding for the *West of Center* exhibition is provided by the Western States Arts Federation, a State Arts Agency, and the National Endowment for the Arts. The Museum of Contemporary Art Denver would like to further thank the citizens of the Scientific and Cultural Facilities District for their support.

An earlier version of chapter 5 was published as Julia Bryan-Wilson, "Handmade Genders: Queer Costuming in San Francisco circa 1970," *Octopus: A Visual Studies Journal* 4 (Fall 2008). Chapter 9, "Expanded Cinema in Los Angeles: The Single Wing Turquoise Bird," copyright 2011 by David James; an earlier version was published in *Millennium Film Journal,* nos. 43/44 (Summer/Fall 2005). An earlier version of chapter 13 was published as Jennie Klein, "Goddess: Feminist Art and Spirituality in the 1970s," *Feminist Studies* 35, no. 3 (Fall 2009): 575–602. An earlier version of chapter 15 was published as Scott Herring, "Out of the Closets, Into the Woods: *RFD, Country Women,* and the Post-Stonewall Emergence of Queer Anti-urbanism," *American Quarterly* (June 2007): 341–72.

Published by the University of Minnesota Press
111 Third Avenue South, Suite 290
Minneapolis, MN 55401-2520
http://www.upress.umn.edu

Library of Congress Cataloging-in-Publication Data
West of center : art and the counterculture experiment in America, 1965–1977 / Elissa Auther and Adam Lerner, editors ; foreword by Lucy R. Lippard.
p.   cm.
ISBN 978-0-8166-7725-2 (hc: alk. paper)
ISBN 978-0-8166-7726-9 (pbk.: alk. paper)
1. Art and society—West (U.S.)—History—20th century—Exhibitions. 2. Counterculture—West (U.S.)—History—20th century—Exhibitions. I. Auther, Elissa. II. Lerner, Adam. III. Museum of Contemporary Art/Denver. IV. Scottsdale Museum of Contemporary Art. V. Title: Art and the counterculture experiment in America, 1965–1977.
N72.S6W48 2012
709.73´09046—dc23   2011031743

Printed in Canada on acid-free paper

The University of Minnesota is an equal-opportunity educator and employer.

18 17 16 15 14 13 12   10 9 8 7 6 5 4 3 2 1

CONTENTS

ix **Foreword** Memory as Model
Lucy R. Lippard

xvii **Introduction** The Counterculture Experiment: Consciousness and Encounters at the Edge of Art
Elissa Auther and Adam Lerner

PART I. COMMUNAL ENCOUNTERS

3 **Chapter 1** How to Build a Commune: Drop City's Influence on the Southwestern Commune Movement
Erin Elder

23 **Chapter 2** Collective Movement: Anna and Lawrence Halprin's Joint Workshops
Eva J. Friedberg

43 **Chapter 3** The Farm by the Freeway
Jana Blankenship

57 **Chapter 4** San Francisco Video Collectives and the Counterculture
Deanne Pytlinski

PART II. HANDMADE WORLDS

77 **Chapter 5** Handmade Genders: Queer Costuming in San Francisco circa 1970
Julia Bryan-Wilson

95 **Chapter 6** Libre, Colorado, and the Hand-Built Home
Amy Azzarito

111 **Chapter 7** Craft and the Handmade at Paolo Soleri's Communal Settlements
Elissa Auther

129 **Chapter 8** Pond Farm and the Summer Craft Experience
Jenni Sorkin

141 **Chapter 9** Expanded Cinema in Los Angeles: The Single Wing Turquoise Bird
David E. James

163 **Chapter 10** Paper Walls: Political Posters in an Age of Mass Media
Tom Wilson

PART III. CULTURAL POLITICS

185 **Chapter 11** The Print Culture of Yolanda M. López
Karen Mary Davalos

209 **Chapter 12** The Countercultural "Indian": Visualizing Retribalization at the Human Be-In
Mark Watson

225 **Chapter 13** Goddess: Feminist Art and Spirituality in the 1970s
Jennie Klein

241 **Chapter 14** The Revolution Will Be Visualized: Black Panther Artist Emory Douglas
Colette Gaiter

255 **Chapter 15** Out of the Closets, Into the Woods: The Post-Stonewall Emergence of Queer Anti-urbanism
Scott Herring

PART IV. ALTERED CONSCIOUSNESS

287 **Chapter 16** Naked Pictures: Ansel Adams and the Esalen Institute
Suzanne Hudson

307 **Chapter 17** Techniques of Survival: The Harrisons and the Environmental Counterculture
Amanda Boetzkes

325 **Chapter 18** Countercultural Intoxication: An Aesthetics of Transformation
Mark Harris

345 **Chapter 19** Everywhere Present Yet Nowhere Visible: Chögyam Trungpa Rinpoche and Dharma Art at the Naropa Institute
Bill Scheffe

361 **Chapter 20** Signifying the Ineffable: Rock Poster Art and Psychedelic Counterculture in San Francisco
Scott B. Montgomery

385 **Acknowledgments**

387 **Contributors**

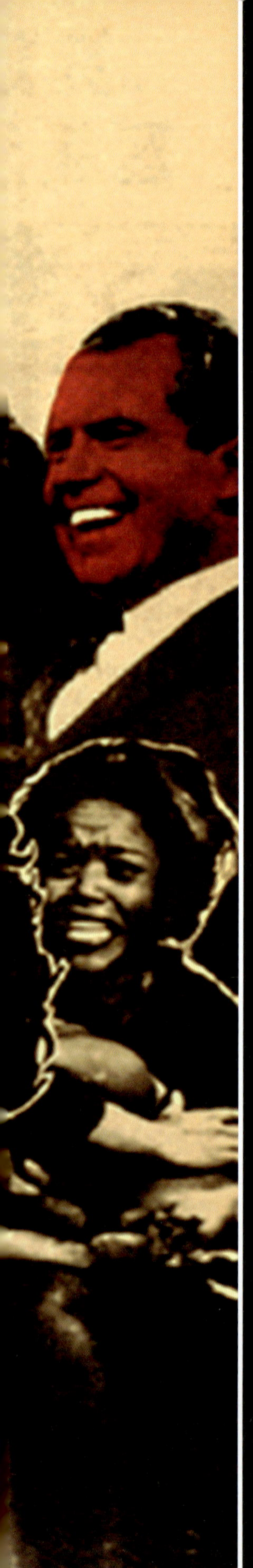

FOREWORD

MEMORY AS MODEL

Lucy R. Lippard

West of Center exponentially expands common knowledge about the arts in the 1960s and '70s—at least to a then-die-hard New Yorker—and offers forgotten models for action today. Reading it, I realized how much I had missed by being (as we presumed) "at the center" in those decades, while many of the things I cared most about had been happening on the "edges." Gotham City was in many ways as provincial as New Mexico, where I have ended up, which was another kind of youthful hotbed. (Unlike the avant-garde, the counterculture embraced provincialism.) In the interest of full disclosure, and contradicting the maxim "If you remember the sixties, you weren't there," I do remember appearing in a book on the Beats from the late 1950s, when I was living sort of communally in the East Village, and in the 1960s lecturing in a plastic minidress, dancing under strobe lights, and so forth—despite being a workaholic, a mother, and turning thirty in 1967. My experience of western liberation, however, was zilch, aside from hitchhiking across the United States in the 1950s, a 1972 trip to New Mexico where my "countercultural" experience was Shalako at Zuni and other Pueblo dances, and some rapid lecture trips to the West Coast. On my first trip to Los Angeles in 1966, I was overwhelmed by the extent that shiny, laid-back California differed from grungy and hyper New York.

I'm not sure it is productive to emphasize obvious distinctions between the avant-garde and the counterculture. It was not an era of either/or but of often unquestioning inclusivity. If New York had a handle (and a triumphant grip) on the avant-garde, having only recently wrested the title from Paris, the counterculture swirled out of control all around us. It was the sea we swam in, surrounding our little island in Lower Manhattan, providing a necessary antidote to, or escape from, the earnest seriousness of New York's Left politics and art-world politics. Minimalism and conceptualism were usually seen as the cerebral products of the East Coast, while finish fetish and light art characterized the experiential West Coast versions. At the same time, boundaries were blurred. Abstract op art, merged with art nouveau, fueled the psychedelic poster; conceptualism was in part inspired by the art/life experiments of Allan Kaprow and artists' books of trademark Californian Ed Ruscha. (Around 1969, Robert Smithson and Nancy Holt made *East Coast/West Coast,* an often witty improvisational video about the bicoastal gulf, with Holt playing an arrogant eastern conceptualist and Smithson a stoned, Nirvana-seeking westerner.) There was also a good deal of cross-pollination, since many artists were shuttling back and forth between the coasts (and Europe). Conceptualism, in turn, made common cause with the counterculture with its antiobject, anticonsumerism, and performative, dematerialized forms.

The antiwar and antiracism movements, then feminism, tried hard to act within the guidelines suggested by Mario Savio during the free speech movement in 1964: "Now we've got the freedom within to be responsible." (See Julia Bryan-Wilson's recent book *Art Workers: Radical Practice in the Vietnam War Era* for an account of our successes and failures.) I remember the exhilaration of being in a huge crowd belting out "Here Comes the Sun" at an antiwar protest in D.C., and the adrenaline rush (better than drugs) of being arrested and spending the night in jail for the cause. Artists could get away with mayhem in those days of new ideas, new contexts, new forms, though few tried. I was told to get my politics out of the art magazines and "go write for the *Berkeley Barb*." (It's hard to write about those days without descending into reminiscence.) Politics and culture, each with multiple branches, ran parallel, meeting at odd vortices. The Art Workers' Coalition had several factions, but the split I recall best was between the more-or-less Marxist minimal/conceptual artists and the countercultural, often anarchist denizens of a Lower East Side that had changed since I lived there in a cold-water flat among Russians and Puerto Ricans for $18 a month. We all questioned and defied both authority and capitalism. We all espoused guerrilla street art and actions. But there were always rifts between the arts and hard-core politics. The political Left was under the illusion that we could overthrow the dominant culture rather than simply change its level of tolerance for "different" lifestyles. Cultural radicalism was often marginalized, as Elissa Auther and Adam Lerner observe, seen by the New Left as apolitical and artistic lunacy. (This distrust of even the most committed activist artists by politicos has not yet been overcome.)

But enough about the center. Decentralization was, and still is, a far more significant concept, built into the new event-oriented genres of public action that were beginning to spread around the country, extending the urge to work "in the gap between art and life," as Robert Rauschenberg put it, far further afield than he had imagined. San Francisco, even from across the country, was acknowledged as the pulsing heart of the counterculture. Scott Montgomery describes concerts there in the 1960s as a passage, "like Alice down a rabbit hole into a new realm of reality and cognition. . . . Within this vortex of seemingly ever-shifting sound and vision . . . [one became] part of an organically cohesive culture outside the confines of normative, straight America." The regional arts that emerged in this period—including music, video collectives, light shows, vernacular architecture, and underground comix—have since crossed the borders into "art."

If the New York Art Workers made some inroads in institutional criticism and reform, San Francisco's Diggers were out there, throwing themselves at the actual barriers between art and life. As one Drop City denizen remarked, "Digging a ditch carries no less status than erecting a sculpture; in fact the individual often discovers that he *[sic]* is happier digging a ditch, *sculpting* a ditch." Social energies were being recognized as art. The French situationists, by way of Guy Debord's influential *Society of the Spectacle,* cut a swath through 1960s theory, though not as great as Marshall McLuhan's *Understanding Media* and its catchphrase "the Medium is the Message" (or "massage"), which also sparked some prairie fires. And, later, when it was translated into English, Ariel Dorfman and Armand Mattelart's *How to Read Donald Duck,* with its analysis of Disney comics

during the heady days of underground comix, also provided a sharp blade
with which to dissect mainstream culture.

"Personal transformation . . . as the key to revolution," as Auther and
Lerner put it, sometimes meant psychedelic drugs and spiritual exploration and navel gazing rather than politics, until feminism introduced "the
personal is political" (and its corollary "the political is personal") and
consciousness was raised rather than expanded. Acid intellectuals, some
of whom were artists and poets, and the growing popularity of Buddhism
(especially in Boulder, Colorado), led to a new kind of spirituality that
became one of the counterculture's significant contributions. Children
of the Beats, we all tuned in to Gary Snyder's poetry, which offered a voice
that transcended generations and called for a reassessment of our relationship to nature.

Until recently, concern for nature (aka the "environment") was regarded
by the urban Left as a suburban enterprise, politically significant but
somewhat irrelevant to eastern city dwellers, for whom tar beach (sunbathing on rooftops) was the norm. Rural communes were rarely on our
radar (though Linda and Dean Fleming, cofounders of downtown Manhattan's Park Place Gallery, also pioneered western communes). Nevertheless, Rachel Carson's *Silent Spring,* published in 1962, and the *Whole
Earth Catalog's* alluring lessons in self-sufficient sustainability nagged
at all of us as we wheatpasted among the skyscrapers. Berkeley, nested
between the Bay and the hills, certainly lent itself to more reciprocity
between nature and culture. This is where Helen and Newton Harrison
(based in San Diego) came in. They brought ecology to the art world or,
as Amanda Boetzkes points out, they brought "the earth back to technology"—as opposed to the attractive but potentially reactionary back-
to-the-land movement. At the same time, the Harrisons also looked
back to the origins of technology as tools and techniques fundamental
to human society, creating an ecological conceptualism—grand schemes
for watersheds and whole countries—whose importance was only fully
recognized in the 1990s.

"Art is Culture is Nature," pronounced artist Bonnie Sherk, whose literally groundbreaking *Crossroads Community (The Farm)* in San Francisco's
Potrero district introduced the notion of the "life-frame" (preceded by
the Diggers' invitation to get liberated by stepping through a giant yellow
picture frame, the Free Frame of Reference, and succeeded by Agnes
Denes's 1982 *Wheatfield—A Confrontation* on New York's Battery Park
landfill and by Future Farmers' recent Victory Gardens in San Francisco).
A rural vision superimposed on a rundown urban industrial area under
a freeway (where Sherk once temporarily placed palm trees, a cow, and a
hay bale to startle passing drivers), *The Farm,* as Jana Blankenship points
out, was a "mini-ecosystem" and life theater, offering a multicultural,
"nonhierarchical environment where all life forms are integral participants."
The disappearance in 1987 of this last holdout for 1960s ecotopia makes
me retrospectively sad in this time of diminished hopes.

Another nostalgia-inspiring moment came with the workshops run by landscape architect Lawrence Halprin and dancer Anna Halprin in the Bay Area, described by Eva J. Friedberg. Though couched in terms *(the Human Creative Process)* that might not fly today, their experiments in movement in space, which eventually morphed into the broader field of city planning, have myriad heirs who may or may not know their lineage. We felt the reverberations of the Halprins' architecture/dance collaboration in New York in Yvonne Rainer's task-oriented dance and her own influence on the art world. The Halprins' awareness of landscape and body features also recalls the performance/sculpture collaborations of Joan Jonas and Richard Serra in the early 1970s.

One of the Halprins' "Experiments in Environment" workshops built a village of driftwood "with structures you could live in, all related to each other," an idea that has not lost its appeal over the decades. They were probably aware of Bernard Rudofsky's seminal writings on vernacular architecture, along with Buckminster Fuller's geodesic domes and their offspring—from "zomes" to "earthships" to Samuel Mockbee's brilliant Rural Studio in Hale County, Alabama, where a chapel made of truck windshields recalls the Drop City windows made of car windshields. Found, recycled, and "liberated" materials became a trademark of the new architectural resourcefulness, producing buildings that cost as little as $10 and a rash of self-sufficiency manuals. By the early 1970s, some 750,000 people were said to be living in thousands of communes all over the country. Amy Azzarito tells the lively story of the pains and pleasures of hand-built homes at the Libre community in Colorado, which has survived to this day, now serving mostly as summer homes, though the land is still communally owned. These stories ring a bell for me, since the ingenuity involved in all of these ventures had urban parallels in early (illegal) loft living in New York, which I eventually traded for living off the grid on solar in semirural New Mexico.

In today's climate of wishful "greening," Paolo Soleri's 1970 description of the automobile is prescient: "5,000 pounds of metal using 6 gallons of poisonous fumes to transport 150 pounds of flesh who wants to buy one pack of cigarettes. That is absurd." If decentralization was one major obsession of the times (remaining particularly relevant for those of us supporting regional arts), Soleri raised the equally important counterconcept of communal (or not) clustering, almost a reurbanization, which makes less impact on the environment and leaves as much open land as possible (valuable to those of us opposing suburban sprawl). "Dispersal is antagonistic to life," he said. "Density is . . . the only morphology that can give us a lively existence."

I sometimes miss a sense of context, of landscape and place, of western identity and its responses to the counterculture in these accounts. For instance, why was Trinidad, Colorado (also known as the capital of sex changes), chosen as the site of Drop City and its unfortunately dubbed art, Droppings? Why (aside from a sometimes warm climate) was the

Southwest the chosen land for many escapees from uptight eastern culture? Sometimes places were "discovered," as youth took to the road in the tracks of Jack Kerouac or *Easy Rider*. Erin Elder notes that land was not only cheap, but the Southwest "resembled a kind of nowhere, a place to explore and experiment outside of rules, institutions, and watchful eyes." Yet it was, of course, already inhabited, and this new wave of colonization was not always welcome. What was the impact on those who already lived in or near these places? (We have no accounts from neighbors.) Local communities were often ignored or antagonistic to the communards' invasions. Yet the Southwest also led the way in experimental architecture. A national conference on the subject called ALLOY was held in an abandoned tile factory in La Luz, near Alamagordo, New Mexico, in 1969.

Scott Montgomery addresses the "new REALLY Wild West" and photographic references to the Gold Rush (a psychedelic pun), nineteenth-century costuming, and especially Native Americans as models for an idealized "precolonial Utopia." Mark Watson takes up the tribalization theme and its political aesthetics, focusing on the legendary "Pow-Wow" or Human Be-In at Golden Gate Park in 1966. The poster for this event featured a historical photograph of a Native man along with supposedly Native symbols evoking technology and drug culture. The "Indians" were always imagined, and simply part of the primitivist package that was more popular, and more contextualized, in the West, where the poverty of reservations was more visible and historic guilt trips more relevant than in the East. (Students at Sonoma State College "surrendered" to local Indian tribes, who wisely accepted no captives.) Cree singer Buffy Sainte-Marie compared the appropriation of Native cultures to vampirism, not so far-fetched.

Lakota scholar Vine Deloria Jr. saw techno-tribalization as empowering Native people and destroying stereotypes, while his son, Phil Deloria, perceived the pastiche of Indians and technology as a "dissipation of meaning" in a "mystical drug-hazy place where 'nothing is real.'" The name of the light show collective Single Wing Turquoise Bird, Los Angeles's "premier light show" in the late 1960s and early 1970s, according to David E. James, also evoked all kinds of western and Native clichés, as did Burton Gershfield's prototypical film *Now That the Buffalo's Gone* (in which Plains Indian imagery was "transformed into solarized red or amber monochrome"). Ultimately, as Watson observes, quoting Gary Snyder, countercultural tribalism was "in fact more similar to the European gypsies—a group without nation or territory that maintains its own values," a global village. (The declared autonomy of countercultural ground was commemorated in 1990 by Mark Brest van Kempen, who won the commission for a free speech movement monument in University of California, Berkeley's Sproul Plaza—a small circle, marked by an inscription on marble: "This soil circle and the air space extending above it are not part of any nation and are not subject to any entity's jurisdiction.")

Even though I lived through the sixties and I remember them, *West of Center* is a cornucopia of fascinating new information, such as Suzanne Hudson's essay on Ansel Adams's connections to Esalen and Jenni Sorkin's gendered and cultural analysis of the prototypical Pond Farm crafts experiments ("somewhere between summer camp and boot camp") with its emphasis on "self-sufficient rural living," disposable art, and its connections to Black Mountain College. I knew little about the art of the West Coast Black Panthers, and I hadn't heard of the marvelous 1970 feminist speech bubbles pasted onto public advertisements in San Francisco ("Hello Men! I'm a picture of a woman that doesn't exist, but my body corresponds to a stereotype that you have been conditioned to desire"). Ant Farm's Truckstop Tour and the "liberated paper" *Kaliflower* were also unfamiliar. A mini-essay on fashion could be drawn from Scott Herring's chapter (the only one to address class) on *RFD* and *Country Women's* "critical rusticity"—the visual styles of neoprimitivist antifashion gay and lesbian collectives rejecting "metronormativity"; Scott Montgomery's reference to "grandma's attic chic"; and Julia Bryan-Wilson's piece on handmade camp as genderfuck collage, "where grit and glitter meet." Another rich vein is mined by Deanne Pytlinski's discussion of alternative exchanges of information, strategies to circulate ideas that predicted the Internet, including community video collectives (and I'd add public access television).

I would have liked to see more on the politics of sexual liberation in this book; *Womanhouse* and the Woman's Building in Los Angeles would have been vital candidates. (Judy Chicago's *Butterfly Atmosphere* is mentioned in regard to light shows, but feminist performance, especially the media-savvy work of Suzanne Lacy and Leslie Labowitz, also played a significant role.) Nevertheless, two major women artists are discussed in depth, Bonnie Sherk and Yolanda M. López. Karen Mary Davalos points out that López's radical Chicana/o poster and print work documented the diversity within the Latina/o community by montaging images drawn from the daily life of the barrios with those of Chicano politics, home-based in the Mission District and local vernacular, representing her own community and its solidarity with Third World struggles. Like Asian American activist Betty Kano and Native American Jean LaMarr— both of whom also became leaders in their multicultural art and feminist communities—López did not sign her political cultural contributions, her posters, buttons, and flyers; relative anonymity was a countercultural trademark, though unpopular in the art world, where names mean everything. The story of encounters and collaborations among Third World activist artists, white artists, and countercultural participants has yet to be fully told, although I noted with interest a reference to a University of California, Berkeley, Ph.D. dissertation by Jason Ferreira titled "All Power to the People: A Comparative History of Third World Radicalism in San Francisco, 1968–1977."

Throughout this book, I was constantly reminded of how much I remain

influenced by those times, those passions. And I am certainly not alone.
The 1960s and early '70s were a testing ground for many experiments that,
fifty years later, remain even more urgently in play. The countercultural
spirit of community and collectivity was rehabilitated in New York's Lower
East Side and South Bronx in the late 1970s and early '80s and, along
with issue-oriented arts, is making yet another national comeback today.
Climate change demands a resurrection of environmental sensitivity
and improvisation. Those of us who have lived both then and now—older,
wearier, perhaps a bit wiser—keep returning to the hope of effectively
fusing art and life and politics. If naïveté and idealism eventually gave
way to cynicism and reaction, temporarily felling those utopian dreams,
the desire for the unachievable never dies. It provides something to
brainstorm about, something to long for, something to work for, something that cannot yet be put behind us.

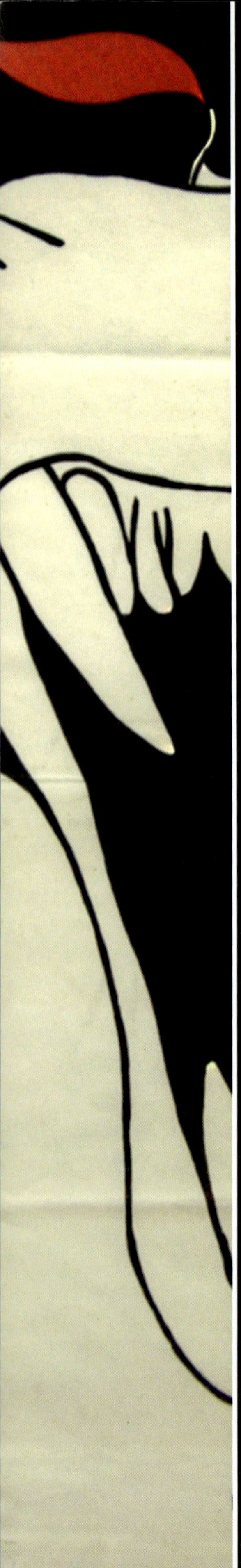

INTRODUCTION
THE COUNTERCULTURE EXPERIMENT: CONSCIOUSNESS AND ENCOUNTERS AT THE EDGE OF ART

Elissa Auther and Adam Lerner

In the summer of 1968, the young East Coast architect Chip Lord traveled to the San Francisco Bay Area to participate in a two-week workshop called "Experiments in Environment," organized by Anna and Lawrence Halprin. He was so transformed by the experience, he wrote a letter to the Halprins telling them that "the workshop was a catalyst, was an education, was a trip into my future, was an art form, was a lifestyle, was a freestylelife race, was groove."[1]

"Experiments in Environment" involved a series of experiences situated in Marin County, California, and the city of San Francisco, including blindfolded nature walks, kinesthetic movement instructions, and light installations. Alongside Lord, architects, dancers, educators, therapists, and sociologists partook in these exercises, aimed to cultivate their sense of self-awareness and creativity through the exploration of space, movement, and collaborative action. The final, communal project, held on the coast of Sea Ranch, involved building "a city out of driftwood, with structures you could live in, all related to each other" (see Eva J. Friedberg's chapter on the Halprins). Anna, a modern dancer, and Lawrence, a landscape architect, worked together to produce the hybrid program that combined her radical, task-oriented approach to modern dance and his interest in sensitizing designers to natural and human-made environments. Lord traveled to the Bay Area for the two-week workshop but he stayed there indefinitely, cofounding the artist's collective Ant Farm, which set in motion its own chain reactions of creative investigations.

The story of Chip Lord's participation in "Experiments in Environment" perfectly encapsulates the scene that *West of Center* aims to recover. It is a story that glorifies collaboration, disallowing any one individual to determine the outcomes. It is about active participation, requiring participants to immerse their entire bodies into the art rather than remain spectators. It is about indeterminate processes, not static objects. It is about hybridity and the evisceration of professional genres like art, architecture, dance, education, and psychology. It tells about personal transformation and freedom as ideals of creative endeavor. It is about finding that freedom in the West. It is utopian. As Lord describes it, it is about mixing art and life into something called "lifestyle," and about discovering something new, something that inspired new terms to describe it, like *freestylelife race*. It is *groove*. It is about interrelated networks of people who all bought in to more or less these same ideas and possibilities for the future. It is a panorama of cultural radicalism that expanded the idea of art into a much larger effort to enact alternative social, political, and ecological systems. These are the attributes of the countercultural experiment of the 1960s and 1970s that the essays in this volume attempt to recount.

The story of "Experiments in Environment" not only paints a picture of the counterculture's utopian endeavor but also suggests how the countercultural enterprise related to the ambitions of the avant-garde art world centered in New York. With an emphasis on spontaneity, process, and genre crossing, the Halprins' workshops bear a similarity to the avant-garde's Happenings and Fluxus performances. Lawrence Halprin even used the musical term *score* to describe their workshop exercises, emphasizing a connection to avant-garde forms, which utilized the same language. The Halprins had ongoing interactions with the central players of the New York avant-garde, including John Cage, Merce Cunningham, Allan Kaprow, and La Monte Young, which reinforced this creative dialogue between the Bay Area experiments and the center of the art world. However, the Halprins went much further than their New York counterparts in seeking to impact the lives of their participants. While the New Yorkers were primarily focused on transforming art, with the hope that art might ultimately transform society, the Bay Area couple sought to transform lifestyle directly. This distinction between "Experiments in Environment" and the Happenings and Fluxus performances reveals the contrast between the broad project of the counterculture and the narrower aspirations of the avant-garde. Not to deny the utopian threads running through the New York avant-garde, the Halprins' workshops speak to the distinct countercultural objective of direct, personal, and social transformation.

The unfortunate fate of the counterculture is that its story doesn't blend well with either the narrative of the New York avant-garde or the political histories of the 1960s. While its commitment to social transformation divorced it from the histories of the avant-garde, its emphasis on culture and lifestyle alienated it from political histories of 1960s radicalism. The New Left was blind to the political potential of projects such as "Experiments in Environment," seeing cultural radicalism as nothing more than a form artistic lunacy.[2] Meanwhile, projects like "Experiments" were largely ignored in histories of art because, among other factors addressed below, the Halprins prioritized society at large over the art world. The obscurity of the Halprins' workshops within both histories of art and histories of 1960s radicalism is generally representative of the treatment of the visual and performative practices of the counterculture. The dismissal of "Experiments" reveals the double whammy suffered by countercultural enterprises: to the art world, they were viewed as non-art, and to scholars of the sixties, they were considered apolitical. Both factions were unable to see the importance of the counterculture as the source for new forms of art, political expression, and the intertwining of the two, a formation with significant legacies in contemporary art and culture.

In what follows, we address this dense constellation of issues with the aim of bringing countercultural artistic practice into critical focus, examining the obstacles that have led to the marginalization of the counterculture in the history of art, and initiating scholarly debate on the subject of alternative visual and performative practices of the 1960s and '70s.

DEFINING COUNTERCULTURE

While the projects enacted under the rubric of the counterculture have
suffered from neglect, the word itself has suffered from abuse. In the mid-
1990s, the historian Theodore Roszak lamented the reduction of the
term *counterculture* by neoconservatives to an "all purpose pejorative"
that stood for "little more than an adolescent outburst."[3] Roszak helped
popularize the term with his 1969 study *The Making of a Counter Culture:
Reflections on the Technocratic Society and Its Youthful Opposition.*[4] Later,
he listened to far right political leaders turn his positive label into the
name for a malady in American society, as when Representative Newt
Gingrich described the counterculture as the opposite of "American
civilization." To Gingrich and other conservatives, "the long pattern of
counterculture belief . . . had contributed to a thirty-year pattern of
social and moral decay" in the United States.[5] Gingrich—like many others
in the 1980s, 1990s, and beyond—used the term to evoke a lifestyle of
drugs, sexual promiscuity, and certain kinds of clothing and music that
painted a picture of self-indulgent hippies. While this image served
his political purpose, it also contributed to the current confusion about
the historical meaning of the term and its legacy. The inheritance of the
counterculture is certainly a set of beliefs that Gingrich rejects, including
"environmentalism, feminism, the rights of gays, American Indians and
ethnic minorities."[6] However, Gingrich's use of the term as a catchall
category for the enemy suggests that the specificity of countercultural
forms of activity of the 1960s and 1970s has been lost.

The origins of the term *counterculture* reside in a scholarly essay published in 1960 by the sociologist J. Milton Yinger.[7] The broader context
of Yinger's research was juvenile delinquency and social deviance. He coined
the term *contraculture* to describe group behavior in which conflict is
central and many of the group's values are "specifically contradictions of
the values of the dominant culture."[8] He distinguished this from "subculture," a form of group behavior with its own internal norms that, however unique, are neutral with respect to dominant society's values. As
opposed to a subculture, a mere subset of dominant society, such as a
religious or professional affiliation, a contraculture was an oppositional
movement with distinct norms and values generated out of its conflic-
tual interaction with dominant society. Significantly, a contraculture
sought to transform the norms and values of the dominant society and,
if successful, replace its host as the dominant culture. Yinger derived
the term *contraculture* from the sociologist Talcott Parsons's passing use
of the term *counterculture* in his 1951 study of subcultures, *The Social
System.*[9] Roszak returned to Parsons's use of the term in *The Making of a
Counter Culture,* which became a best-selling book.

Roszak also defined the counterculture as "radically disaffiliated" from
the mainstream norms and values of society, and he recognized its aspi-
ration to "alter the total cultural context within which our daily politics
take place."[10] The enemy of the counterculture was, in Roszak's view, the

authoritarianism operating overtly or covertly at every level of life in the name of technical expertise—from the rationalizations proffered in support of the Vietnam War and nuclear armament, to the reorganization of the workplace around the goals of efficiency and modern management, to the paternalism of the state that infiltrated the bedroom. As opposed to the class- and labor-oriented political objectives of the historical American Left, Roszak characterized the counterculture as more than "merely a political movement."[11] It was also a "cultural movement," for it "strikes beyond ideology to the level of consciousness seeking to transform our deepest sense of the self, the other, the environment."[12] Roszak's characterization of the counterculture, as both cultural and political, organized around a "personalist style" and directed toward liberation from the alienating forces of technocratic domination, highlighted it as a form of cultural radicalism wherein personal transformation was embraced as the key to revolution.

While Roszak made a case for defining the countercultural project as both cultural and political, it was more common for critics and observers of the 1960s to distinguish between a "political" or activist movement— the New Left—and an "apolitical" formation—the counterculture. The former focused on the structural transformation of the nation's political system, while the latter embraced cultural radicalism as the path toward social and political change. The different orientations of the New Left and the counterculture toward social and political change are neatly encapsulated in the oft-repeated description of Merry Prankster Ken Kesey's appearance at an October 1965 antiwar protest in Berkeley. Todd Gitlin's rendition of the event is representative:

The organizers of Vietnam Day, the round-the-clock antiwar teach-in on the Berkeley campus, invited no less a guru than Ken Kesey, who showed up in Day-Glo regalia, sized up the crowd and the bombastic speakers as some kind of ego-clamoring fascist rally . . . whereupon he honked a chorus of "Home on the Range" with his harmonica . . . and told the fifteen thousand antiwarriors the only thing that would do any good was to "look at the war, and turn your backs and say . . . Fuck it." This was not what the organizers wanted to hear on the verge of a march into fearsome Oakland to confront the army base.[13]

Many accounts from the period and after register Kesey's speech with disapproval, and this condemnation is based on a failure to understand the new terms of discussion presented by the counterculture. Kesey's performance is more than often criticized as a mere "stunt," but it was actually a critique of the political form adopted by leaders of the New Left. Instead of representing a division between political activism and an apolitical lifestyle, it stands for the division between leftists and hippies over how to best foment social change. The conflict between politicos and freaks, to use the parlance of the day, was over different forms of politics. Leftists dismissed cultural radicalism because the leftist understanding of radical change was restricted to conventional forms of political protest. Therefore, Kesey's behavior was not so much misguided but incomprehensible to the protest organizers (although evidently, not to those in the audience who followed his order and proceeded to turn their backs to the stage). The organizers of the rally dismissed Kesey's appearance as a diversion of attention from the political project of the New Left to undermine the power of the military.

The suspicion with which Kesey's gesture of refusal (or any other countercultural gesture for that matter) was received by leftists in the 1960s and 1970s obscured not only its challenge to conventional politics and forms of protest but also its unique synthesis of politics and culture. On both points, there are special consequences for the visual and performative expressions of the counterculture, which were also regularly written off at the time and in retrospective histories of the 1960s as irrelevant to politics, and within art histories of the postwar period, if considered art at all, as a minor development outside the dominant story of modernism. In the studies of both art and politics, a narrative about "the death of the sixties," recounting the rise and decline of the counterculture, continues to devalue its projects and achievements.

ANTI-DISCIPLINARY POLITICS AND CULTURAL RADICALISM

The death-of-the-sixties narrative is an all-too-often repeated story about the period. It goes from optimism and youthful exuberance to self-indulgent excess, violence, and mayhem, ending in regret and embarrassment. This story is detailed by Peter Braunstein and Michael William Doyle in their introduction to their important reassessment of sixties cultural radicalism, *Imagine Nation: The American Counterculture of the 1960s and '70s*. They describe it as an "Iliad-like narrative," wherein the counterculture is reduced to a series of "big moments" that typically include, among others, Albert Hofmann's discovery of LSD and Allen Ginsberg's performance of *Howl*:

Ken Kesey and the Merry Pranksters tripping on acid rediscovering America, this time from west to east, aboard their "magic bus" [named *Further*]. . . . Leary chanting "Turn on, tune in, drop out," sampled onto the Beatles' "Day in the Life"; [and] the flowers, the music, the vision that was (but in actuality, wasn't) the Summer of Love in San Francisco, 1967. This stroboscopic light show will then draw to an abrupt close with the mandatory montage of the counterculture's "dark side"—someone shooting up speed or having a bad trip, the Manson Family murders, and finally the Altamont concert-debacle—all ritualistically invoked as mutually-reinforcing tombstones.[14]

One might append to this scenario the commodification of countercultural values and lifestyles by major corporations in the 1980s. The story of self-indulgent excess finds its rightful end when large corporations master the ability to market to those interests. Nike's advertising slogan

"Just Do It" is a prime example of a company transforming the spontaneity and directness of the counterculture into a call for individual consumption. The ease with which corporate America appropriated the counterculture for its own purposes also contributed to its dismissal by the New Left and scholars of the 1960s.[15] By this account, the legacy of the 1960s is consumerism.

In her expert theoretical study of the counterculture, *Anti-Disciplinary Protest: Sixties Radicalism and Postmodernism,* Julie Stephens examines the obsession with the apparent failure of sixties cultural radicalism. For her, this narrative of failure buries the legacy of countercultural artistic practice or aesthetic radicalism. She argues that the dismissal of the activity of the Merry Pranksters, the Diggers, and other countercultural groups engaged in the creative reimagining of society serves the purpose of privileging the conventional forms of sixties radicalism: "Only those actions which were extensions of a traditional revolutionary perspective and aimed to convulsively overthrow State power come into view."[16] By contrast, the impact of the "psychedelic wing" of the movement, the people that Jerry Rubin called "Marxist acidheads," is either "marginalized, ignored altogether or relegated to the status of an amusing curiosity."[17]

In reassessing the political contribution of the badly maligned cultural segment, Stephens describes their activities as a form of "anti-disciplinary politics." In contrast to commentators and scholars who dismissed Kesey's engagement with the crowd at the Vietnam Day event as apolitical, Stephens views his appearance and speech as a critique of the conventional, "disciplinary politics" that structured the activity of the New Left. For her, the politics of the counterculture resided in its "language of protest which rejected hierarchy and leadership, strategy and planning, bureaucratic organization and political parties and was distinguished from the New Left by its ridiculing of political commitment, sacrifice, seriousness and coherence."[18] Disabling the "political/anti-political" dualism that subordinated the creative ferment of the counterculture to the activism of the New Left, her adoption of the term *anti-disciplinary* also disallows the mutual exclusivity of culture and politics, since the activist and the hippie were both engaged in forms of cultural-political activity. In her analysis, the counterculturalists were participating in new forms of cultural-political address that involved embracing utopianism, rejecting the hierarchy within collectives and between artist and audience, and promoting the illegibility or irrationality of public spectacles, performances, and other organized communal encounters. By eliminating long-held distinctions, Stephens opens up a space for a critical analysis of the distinctive styles, rhetoric, and aesthetic conventions of countercultural practice examined in *West of Center.*

MODERNIST ART HISTORY AND THE COUNTERCULTURE

Just as the counterculture altered the terms of politics, making it unrecognizable to conventional activists, so too did it alter the essential

INTRODUCTION

conditions of art, making it unidentifiable to traditional art practitioners and art historians. What was "Experiments in Environment"? What category does it belong to? Art, architecture, anti-disciplinary politics? For Chip Lord, it was all of the above and more. He was demonstrating more than appreciation when in his letter to the Halprins he created such a long list of terms to describe the workshop. He was attempting to depict the multiplicity and hybridity of a new cultural invention: "The workshop was a catalyst, was an education, was a trip into my future, was an art form, was a lifestyle, was a freestylelife race, was groove." It was this *and* that *and* that—everything all at once without hierarchy. His exhilaration is about the possibility of a new hybrid form of activity that cannot be categorized.

Lord's open-ended description of a new type of practice is what we in this book are—less colorfully—referring to as the visual and performative expressions of the counterculture. Of the practices discussed in this volume, the majority openly flouted disciplinary boundaries, stressed participation and process over the production of discrete objects, blurred distinctions between artist and audience, rejected ideology and conventional political behavior, and embraced irreverence, contradiction, parody, and play. In many instances, it is difficult or impossible to distinguish between the practice of art and the conduct of lifestyle. The essential characteristics of the workshops of Anna and Lawrence Halprin suffuse other counter-cultural projects ranging from the "life acting" of the Diggers to the spectacle of the Trips Festival to the design and construction of geodesic domes at the southern Colorado commune Drop City. These practices—along with the counterculture's psychedelic and spiritual wings, from the expanded cinema light shows of the Single Wing Turquoise Bird collective to Chögyam Trungpa Rinpoche's philosophy of dharma art—demonstrate both the aesthetics of cultural radicalism and the priorities and characteristics of anti-disciplinary politics.

Just as Julie Stephens's study questions the entrenched theoretical frameworks that devalue cultural radicalism, *West of Center* addresses the narratives, boundaries, and assumptions that have led to the marginalization of countercultural practices in the history of art and visual culture. A strange fact about the counterculture is that it occupies such a large part of the public imagination of the 1960s and 1970s but such a small part of the corpus of scholarly research into the period. This volume builds on the few existing art historical investigations of the counterculture.[19] The subject is otherwise largely ignored because its activities have not been viewed as relevant to the history of art. Readers cannot find countercultural practices discussed in the major surveys of art of the postwar period. They also, curiously, cannot find them in studies that address the art world's relationship to the volatile political context of the 1960s, including Thomas Crow's *The Rise of the Sixties: American and European Art in the Era of Dissent, 1955–69* and Francis Frascina's *Art, Politics and Dissent: Aspects of the Art Left in Sixties America.*[20]

Crow's book *The Rise of the 1960s* is instructive in explaining how the counterculture is addressed in the field of art history. The book stands out from other treatments of the period for its nuanced interest in the international political context surrounding art in the 1960s. In fact, the point of the book is that art of the period did not stem from a few exceptionally creative minds but grew out of various geographically specific political and social struggles. Crow's interest in the specific geographies of these struggles leads him to include many artists typically omitted from the history of art, and he does credit Anna Halprin for her foundational influence on the dance-based performance art of the New York avant-garde. The problem is that the struggles always remain context, never the text itself. Crow demonstrates remarkable historical sensitivity noting connections between, say, the civil rights movement and Happenings. However, he doesn't acknowledge that the civil rights movement might have spawned its own art. He makes politics visible within the history of art, but he doesn't have eyes to see the work of Black Panther artist Emory Douglas or Chicana rights artist Yolanda López. Crow decenters and contextualizes art history but maintains a traditional sense of what counts as art, which doesn't include the art of the counterculture.

Crow's treatment of countercultural artistic practices suggests that the counterculture is not considered unimportant but that it is simply not seen as part of art history. Curator and art historian Anne Rorimer's analysis of the period provides insight into the reason that the field ignores the subject of the counterculture. Her book *New Art in the 60s and 70s: Redefining Reality* provides a sophisticated study of a wide range of artists who redefine art by disavowing the notion that a work of art is a self-contained object. For Rorimer, the counterculture figures so prominently in the history of the period that she mentions it in the very first sentence of the book. She says that a "defiant counterculture" is generally how "the period of innovation examined in this book is remembered outside the history of art."[21] This approach seems to be typical of art historians who do not dismiss the counterculture but simply consider it outside the history of art. There is no prejudice. It is simply defined a priori as a subject external to the purview of discussion. The countercultural scene that Rorimer conjures is the backdrop for innovations in the field of art history. It never enters the realm of possibility that the communards of Drop City were engaged in such a radical rethinking of the art object that they imagined the entire society they were building as a form of art.

The counterculture was defined as beyond the history of art because there was never a category within the narrative of contemporary art history that could contain it. It is not surprising that when the counterculture is discussed in art history, it is considered as an element of other histories, such as protest art, identity politics, or video art. In their essay "Facture for Change: US Activist Art since 1950," Jennifer González and Adrienne Posner consider the postwar history of activist art, exploring a range of artists who are largely ignored within the history of art.[22] They discuss Harry Gomboa Jr., for example, a student protestor who became a radical artist, staging agitprop theater at U.S. draft offices in the early '70s with his collaborators in the group Asco. González and Posner trace an important legacy of more or less informal practices that used the language of art to achieve social ends. A particular strain of countercultural art is unearthed by the history of activist art, which was largely untold until a generation of scholars like González and Posner came along.

Building on this research, it is now necessary to develop an art historical category for the broader counterculture. What story connects Asco's street theater to the ecological art project known as *Crossroads Community (The Farm)*? They both integrated theater into larger public spheres. They were both interested in direct social change. They both believed in acting in the realm of society at large. The reason that the story of the counterculture as an entity has not been told in the history of art is that there is no history of hybridity. There is no category for the uncategorizable, no history of art on the border of nonart. If there were such a category, it would undoubtedly tell an interesting story, which would help explain a great deal of what is taking place in contemporary culture.

The first generation of scholars and curators to give art historical attention to the counterculture has largely seen it through the lens of psychedelia. *Summer of Love: Art of the Psychedelic Era,* a major exhibition organized by the Tate Liverpool in 2005, which traveled to the Whitney Museum of American Art and elsewhere, presented the psychedelic aesthetic in art, music, film, architecture, graphic design, and fashion.[23] This exhibition demonstrated the wide diffusion of an aesthetic sensibility both in and out of the art world. David Rubin's recent book *Psychedelic: Optical and Visionary Art since the 1960s* traces the legacy of the psychedelic aesthetic from the 1960s to the present, part of a revival of interest in the period.[24] These studies demonstrate how the psychedelic aesthetic came to represent a certain drug-related fusion of the world and the imagination, and the power of that aesthetic as a unifying flag of countercultural identity. These important books and exhibitions create the impression that the subject of the counterculture is receiving its overdue consideration.

Paradoxically, the attention given to the subject of psychedelia is consistent with the need for further study of the multiple, hybrid practices of the counterculture. The psychedelic style, though more than a surface effect, was only one dimension of the larger, artistically oriented, socially based countercultural movement. Los Angeles–based Single Wing Turquoise Bird created psychedelic light shows, but they also lived communally and performed for mass public gatherings and a Black Panther's event. Which is the artwork? The gender-queer performance troupe the Cockettes embraced an outrageously decorative sartorial style, when they wore clothes at all, but costuming was only one element of their art and lifestyle that, in total, amounted to a complete explosion of sexual, gender, family, and economic norms. The art of the Cockettes was the total picture of their performances, relationships, living arrangements, and sexuality—their "freestylelife race."

Understanding the psychedelic aesthetic is an important part of grasping the counterculture and its legacy.[25] The psychedelic lens makes the counterculture visible to art historians because it places it alongside other broad stylistic movements. It is raised to the level of art nouveau. The next step is to study what else there was of the counterculture beside its style. The psychedelic aesthetic is a visible signifier of a lifestyle. What art was embedded in the set of living practices as a whole? With psychedelia as a starting point, it is now necessary to examine the art of the counterculture as coterminous with the holistic, revolutionary aspects of the movement.

The psychedelic perspective opens the way to examining other important practices of the period. Studies of the psychedelic aesthetic include certain kinds of homespun practices, but the scholars in this volume extend this investigation to examine the general importance of craft in the period, which didn't always partake of the psychedelic style. Light shows were attractive to counterculturalists but so were Paolo Soleri's earth-cast ceramic and bronze bells. Some hand-built architecture may be explored through the lens of psychedelia, but the impulses motivating that architecture connect it to a wider range of practices that are not as easily visible through such a lens. Psychedelia is not the best viewpoint for understanding the importance to the counterculture of making things by hand. It is also not well suited to seeing how art functioned as a catalyst or an education, to borrow again the language of Chip Lord. It misses the workshops of Anna and Lawrence Halprin, for instance. It might also not see that the Drop City commune, with its Buckminster Fuller—inspired dome architecture, involved a cosmology that was the hard-edge equivalent to psychedelic amorphism. The lens of psychedelia is well suited to see the groove but not so much the freestylelife race and all the rest.

What is most interesting about countercultural practices is precisely the way that they burst through existing paradigms of art and design. This is the reason that it is ultimately the fault of the counterculture that it was not included in art history surveys. This was never their intention. The art of the counterculture is the process, product, and remainder of endeavors to reimagine something no less than modern society at large. It is a series of attempts to recast current understandings of the relationship between art and life, work and leisure, individual and society, material and spirit. The art of the counterculture is often invisible to art historians, not because art was only a minor part of the counterculture movement but because the entire movement can be seen as a kind of art.

Because the art of the counterculture and the movement of the counterculture were virtually the same, the central features of the genre are in conflict with traditional methodologies of visual analysis. The emphasis on participation, duration, encounter, and the submergence of the aesthetic into the everyday that characterizes the visual and performative expressions of the counterculture runs counter to the methodologies of modernist art history predicated on the formal analysis of discrete objects. Relevant here is Grant Kester's examination of this conflict in regard to contemporary artists and artists' collectives whose work embraces a dialogic practice in which form is determined through direct action. Such work shares with the practices discussed in this book several priorities, including the desire to challenge conventional systems of knowledge and politics and positively transform participants through "the creative facilitation of dialogue and encounter."[26] The consequences he observes for contemporary artists and artist collectives can be extended to countercultural artists of the 1960s and '70s whose practice is also generally regarded as aesthetically immaterial:

When contemporary critics confront dialogic projects, they often apply a formal . . . methodology that cannot value, or even recognize, the communicative interactions that these artists find so important. The results are not surprising: dialogical works are criticized for being unaesthetic or are attacked for needlessly suppressing visual gratification. Because the critic gains no sensory stimulation or fails to find the work visually engaging, it is dismissed as failed art.[27]

The application of a formal methodology to artistic projects whose express purpose is to avoid the production of discrete objects is akin to treatment of cultural radicalism in histories of the New Left, wherein countercultural activity is measured against and held accountable to an orthodox definition of political activism wholly absent from the intentions of say, the Diggers or the Yippies. In response to one scholar's dismissal of Abbie Hoffman's activism as an incomprehensible gag, Julie Stephens points out, "It implies that the Yippies would have been more fully 'political' if they had embraced more conventional definitions of politics—precisely the thing they were resisting in the first place."[28]

Kester isolates a number of additional norms and assumptions that contribute to the resistance against dialogic practices and that also play a factor in the meager reception of the counterculture. One issue that plays a prominent role is the avant-garde's commitment to forms of irrational communication designed to shock the viewer out of "perceptual complacency,"[29] an orientation that functions as the gold standard in the valuing of an artist's critical or oppositional stance toward mainstream culture. We are all familiar with the names applied to such forms of shock—Kester's list includes the sublime to *l'amour fou* to disidentification—which result in "a kind of epiphany that lifts viewers outside the familiar boundaries of a common language, existing modes of representation, and even their own sense of self."[30] The artists and artist collectives Kester examines, however, are committed to forms of rational communication whether through group discussion, debate, or one-on-one dialogue.

Although such encounters "unfold through a process of performative interaction,"[31] they are not designed to create immediate, startling revelations in the participant.

Likewise, the artists of the counterculture jettisoned the practice of creating discrete objects in favor of practices that were durational, performative, experiential, and built on communal encounter, practices that also appear in the work of the artists and artist collectives examined by Kester. However, a central feature distinguishing the art of the counterculture from the contemporary forms Kester examines is its rejection of rational communication, a rejection that connects the visual and performative expressions of the counterculture to an avant-garde tradition that relishes the irrational, the nonlinear, paradox, and frivolity. These elements manifested themselves in several ways, including the rejection of the hierarchical distinction between leaders and followers or artist and audience; the circulation of images and texts that appear indiscernible, seemingly flippant yet unsettling theatrical actions; and other communal encounters—especially those involving hallucinogenic drugs—as beyond rational explanation. The theatrical display that surrounded Abbie Hoffman's proposal to "levitate" the Pentagon as part of the October 1967 antiwar march embodies several of these elements. Gathered in a parking lot near the Pentagon, the group was composed of hippies in full regalia, many dressed as witches, wizards, or jesters. The psychedelic band the Fugs, who dressed as Hindu gurus, provided music. Ecstatic dancing and chanting to the sounds of finger bells and cries of "Out, demons, out!," "Money made the Pentagon—melt it for love," and "Burn the money . . . burn it, burn it" also permeated the sound space. Circulating among the crowd and the many onlookers was a flyer that declared in the name of every god, from Isis to Buddha, the reclaiming of the "pentacle of power" for humankind. A public exorcism of the Pentagon ensued. The bizarre energy and visual spectacle of the event and the discomfort it reportedly created in the military police assigned to patrolling its borders aptly illustrate the countercultural preference for public street actions that upended the convention of issuing a simple, easily identifiable message.

The Diggers, an anarchist collective established in 1966 made up of former members of the guerrilla theater the San Francisco Mime Troupe, offer another excellent example of the counterculture's critique of rationality. The Diggers practiced what they called "life acting," a form of prefigurative politics in which one lived the revolution by acting it out, thereby experiencing it as reality. In December 1966, the Diggers orchestrated the action called "The Death of Money and the Birth of the Free" on Haight Street in San Francisco. They described their street actions as a form of consciousness-raising "social acid," and "The Death of Money" funeral procession went as follows:

The burial procession. Three black shrouded messengers holding staffs topped with reflective dollar signs. A runner swinging a red lantern. Four pall bearers wearing animal heads carry a black casket filled with blowups of silver dollars. A chorus singing "Get Out of My Life Why Don't You Babe" to Chopin's Death March. Members of the procession give out silver dollars and candles. . . . Street events are rituals of release. Re-claiming of territory (sundown, traffic, public joy) through spirit. Public NewSense.[32]

The Diggers would go on to distribute free food in the panhandle of Golden Gate Park (a performance-like ritual that involved passing through a wooden portal, the Free Frame of Reference, to receive a meal), free clothing, furniture, appliances, tools, and so forth through the Free Store; publish flyers, newsletters, proclamations, and posters through the Free Press; and establish the Haight-Ashbury Free Medical Clinic. But free, as the passage above suggests, meant more than just free of charge or the opposite of money. It was extended in all Digger actions to encompass freedom, liberation, spontaneity, and release from disciplinary constraint and rationality, and thus the basis of a new form of political rebellion.[33]

The social-political-aesthetic-economic actions of the Diggers, like other endeavors of the counterculture, differentiate them from the historical avant-garde. Despite the shared aesthetic of irrationality or shock, the Diggers were too much a part of life to ever be considered part of the avant-garde. Certainly, the avant-garde embraced the art-into-life credo. However, this project was not meant to be realized. The art-into-life credo amounts to the avant-garde's conceptual paradigm that never intends to result in the actual disappearance of the category of art into life. The Diggers, like other projects of the counterculture, are unabsorbable into the avant-garde precisely because on some level they fulfilled the dream of the avant-garde. This is partly why the counter-culture has suffered from a lack of critical attention and why this collection of essays is needed at this time.

THE WEST

In addition to the long list of reasons why the mainstream of art history has not incorporated the aesthetics of the counterculture, one needs to add the fact that the counterculture was largely a regional movement. Thomas Crow's emphasis on regional centers of art and politics is meant to correct the bias of a field that tends to ignore regional differences. Contemporary art history is dominated by the avant-garde, and, for most scholars, if the avant-garde is one thing, it is international. Its locus in New York City serves only to reinforce this connection with other world cities. By contrast, the counterculture was a movement centered largely in the American West, as much as it attempted to reenvision society at large. San Francisco became its hub, serving as an alternative to New York as a site of creative activity. But the phenomenon was also rural and nomadic, and the broad open West was an important character in the story of the counterculture. When leftist intellectuals Gene and JoAnn Bernofsky departed New York in 1965 to help form the commune Drop

City in southern Colorado, they were giving up on the possibility of changing society by working within historical institutions. The West, as it has always been seen in American fantasies, was a place open to new possibilities and freedom. For the Bernofskys, it was a place where it would be possible to "build a civilization from scratch."[34]

The Bernofskys' interest in the West as a place to start a civilization should not be interpreted to mean that the West was a tabula rasa. Instead, it suggests that the West was a place with a history of believing that it is possible to build a civilization from scratch. Historian Andrew G. Kirk argues that in selecting northern California as the home for the influential publication the *Whole Earth Catalog* countercultural guru Stewart Brand "joined a long line of real and fictional western visionaries who chose the West as the stage for their utopian plays."[35] In the 1960s and 1970s, California was not just the West Coast, as it is today. It was the West, a place saturated with a history of utopian dreams. Kirk aligns Brand with the characters in Ernest Callenback's 1975 popular science fiction book *Ecotopia,* which portrayed hippie environmentalists enacting an "old fashioned western dressed in counterculture clothes."[36] In other words, the gun-toting-cowboy fantasy of the West was not so different from the fantasy of the West that attracted so many counterculturalists. Hippies and cowboys were part of the same self-perpetuating mythos of the West as a platform for freedom, mobility, self-determination, and antiauthority.

The anti-institutionalism of the counterculture thrived in an environment free from a dense network of established institutions, a condition characteristic of the West at the time. This open environment nurtured the independent sensibility of the counterculture. This combination of a nonfiltering environment and a free-floating experimentation explains both the originality and relative obscurity of countercultural practices. Kirk points out that Brand was sometimes criticized for his western bias, and, rather than denying his prejudice, he defended a particularly western way of thinking: "We're an idea magazine and ideas are loose on the West Coast. No one complains that the *New Yorker* is overly regional in outlook."[37] The looseness of the West opened the possibility for ideas to take shape that didn't fall within received categories of politics and art. The counterculturalists were not opposed to the categories, but they moved in and out of them with relative ease. When the Diggers created performances in the streets, they moved loosely through the categories of theater, Happenings, protest, and life. This explains why their actions are not easily codified as any of these. The indefinite nature of their practice, fed by a specific environment that cultivated ambiguity, explains why they were never defined within any particular tradition, including a tradition of avant-garde art. Established institutions and disciplines have a natural bias against incorporating ambiguous practices.

This collection of essays centers on the West. Even though elements of the counterculture can be seen throughout the country, its essential nexus was western. This is not so much because of the student protests at Stanford and Berkeley or even because of iconic events like the Summer of Love in San Francisco. Rather, the counterculture is fundamentally western in part because the entire complex of activities that comes to define the counterculture has its center of gravity there. Mapping out the communes, festivals, collectives, light shows, spiritual centers, and ecological art projects, the density is clearly in California, Colorado, New Mexico, and their neighboring states. The Woodstock Festival was in New York, but the Trips Festival, the Human Be-In, the Monterey Pop Festival, and all of Ken Kesey's Acid Tests, to name only the most recognized events, were in the West.

Beyond the numbers, the counterculture is a western phenomenon in a more essential sense. That is where it found its home, where it blossomed. This is literally visible in the case of one participant, George Edgerly Harris III. He was the young, blond pacifist gently placing flowers in the rifle barrels of National Guardsmen at an antiwar protest in Washington, D.C., in one of the most iconic photographs of the 1960s. Born in Bronxville, N.Y., Harris is pictured in a turtleneck sweater, looking like a college student, who might just go sculling in the Potomac after the protest. That was East Coast Harris, where the norms and codes of civil society are still in place. But he was on his way to San Francisco, where he would join Irving Rosenthal's famed Kaliflower commune, drop acid, change his name to Hibiscus, and lead the Cockettes. There, he himself became the flower, donning satin and sequins, a floral headpiece, and glitter in his long beard—even when he wasn't performing bawdy, show tunes—inspired acts for packed audiences at the Palace Theater. His communal home with the Cockettes was encrusted with glittering fabrics, costumes, and knickknacks. In San Francisco, Hibiscus's life would become his art and politics and vice versa. The counterculture had its spiritual home in the West. Its emergence is symbolized by Hibiscus's move across the country. It was a move from boundaries to near boundlessness recalling Stewart Brand's suggestion that things are looser in the West.

CONTEMPORARY ART

What is the relationship between the counterculture and recent contemporary art? To answer this question, it is necessary to tease out the connection between the counterculture in the West and the avant-garde art world centered in New York. Since the counterculturalists were mostly distinct from the avant-garde, we would expect to see little connection between the counterculture and contemporary art, which continues the avant-garde tradition. But signs of the counterculture seem to be everywhere visible in contemporary art practice. These signs point to ways that some countercultural practices were ultimately not very different from the avant-garde but were alternative ways of realizing similar sensibilities. They also suggest that there is a strong need to revise our understanding of the sources for contemporary art. Category ambiguity is a significant characteristic of art of the past ten years, and the avant-garde of the 1960s and 1970s only goes so far in providing a historical foundation for those hybrid practices. The fluidity of recent contemporary art can be better understood if the legacy of the avant-garde is joined by the tradition of the counterculture.

Several countercultural practices discussed in this collection of essays do not reject the avant-garde but take it to a point beyond recognition. These counterculturalists were actually the most enthusiastic followers of the avant-garde's call for the integration of art into life. This is the story of Drop City, whose founders began by practicing a kind of conceptual and performance art they called Drop Art. Inspired in part by Allan Kaprow's Happenings and John Cage's experiments in chance operations, they would drop objects off buildings and watch the effects on the street below. The commune they formed later was a work of Drop Art writ large, a total integration of art into life. Similarly, Bonnie Ora Sherk created a surreal, pastoral scene, complete with a cow, on the breakdown lane of the James Lick Freeway as part of a series of art projects she called *Portable Parks*. She then went on to cofound *The Farm*, an art and urban agriculture community, manifesting the connection between nature and culture as an ongoing social practice. She transformed the activity of making art into the work of perpetuating a lifestyle. Fayette Hauser was a painter, who integrated realistic and abstract elements into her canvases, before she herself became part of the *tableaux vivant* of the Cockettes.

Though some counterculturalists imagined themselves continuing the avant-garde tradition, others were drawing from alternative sources. Emory Douglas and Yolanda M. López were too interested in using art to communicate powerful messages to their constituencies to join the avant-garde in its exploration of the definition of art. Dharma art and goddess-inspired art were clearly drawing from nonwestern spiritual traditions and ancient practices. The Cockettes were responding to musical theater, while video art collectives were responding to television. The Diggers were an outgrowth of the San Francisco Mime Troupe, which invoked a European tradition of art, but not the avant-garde tradition.

There are some art practices discussed in this book that preceded the counterculture but became affiliated with it—more and less willingly— as the counterculture swept through its environs. Paolo Soleri's settlements in Arizona became a countercultural mecca, even though Soleri's utopian vision derived from an older modernist foundation. Counterculturalists saw their own values mirrored in the communal living arrangement, the handmade craft work connecting them directly to the earth, and the vision of a new and better civilization. Similarly, Pond Farm was a residential craft workshop in northern California that can trace its roots to the Bauhaus. Though it was not born out of any hippie interest in emancipation or groove, it shared with the counterculture a belief in the authenticity of making by hand. Even Ansel Adams, who developed his aesthetic sensibility two generations before the youth of 1960s, finds his way into this collection. There is nothing loose about Adams's photography, but there is more to the artist than the style of his pictures. One point of this volume is that the counterculture was not about a particular style. It was not about psychedelia. It was about an ethos that integrated art practices and life activities. It was about reforging modern civilization through individual actions and local practices.

That is the attitude that gathered together older and newer artistic endeavors. It is not surprising that so much contemporary art shows signs of the countercultural attitude. It can be seen as foundational for a certain kind of hybridity in today's art. It is particularly evident in the growing number of artists who join together to operate as nonprofit entities, moving fluidly between the roles of artists, educators, researchers, designers, and community activists. This category ambiguity is especially found on the West Coast, in such creative entities as the Center for Land Use Interpretation, Future Farmers, Machine Project, and others. It is related to another trend sometimes referred to as a "pedagogic turn in contemporary art," which was the subject of a 2009 conference at the Museum of Modern Art, in New York.[38] In this trend, artists and educators use the idiom of contemporary art to instigate social transformation. Signs of the counterculture are also visible in the embrace of craft and handmade production in contemporary art. A growing number of artists are drawn to traditional craft materials, from ceramics to fiber. However, it is significant that many of these artists did not inherit these methods through the tradition of avant-garde art. Rather, the counterculture had its impact in the arena of culture at large, with young artists picking up on a Do It Yourself, or DIY, style through youth and music culture in general. The DIY ethos visible in so much contemporary art worked its way from the counterculture to punk rock to the indie culture that pervades many art schools today.

ORGANIZATION

West of Center is divided into four sections, each of which explores a distinct aspect of the historical, social, and aesthetic dimensions of countercultural artistic practice. The essays gathered together in Part I, Communal Encounters, brings together a diverse array of objects and practices that illustrate the collective and dialogic orientation of artists associated with the counterculture. Taking many different forms, these projects—including video collectives, urban farming, commune building, and creative movement workshops—emphasize lifestyle as an art form. As contributor Erin Elder argues about the dome builders of the southern Colorado commune Drop City, "built by hand with scrounged materials, Drop City was not only a place to make art, but—through a creative reinvestment in daily activities—it was a place to *be* art." Each of these projects speaks to the distinct countercultural objective of direct, personal, and social transformation.

The essays comprising Part II, Handmade Worlds, address the significance of the handmade artifact in the counterculture, confounding, in the case of Paolo Soleri's architectural settlements Cosanti and Arcosanti in Arizona or the light shows of the Los Angeles–based expanded cinema collective Single Wing Turquoise Bird, art-world hierarchies and boundaries separating fine art from craft, architecture, or design. Several essays in Part II extend the discussion initiated in the previous section regarding art as lifestyle and the transformative power of communal encounters. The costuming of the gender-queer theater known as the Cockettes and potter Marguerite Wildenhain's radical pedagogy at Pond Farm are two such examples, and they highlight the significant role craft played in the creation of countercultural identity.

Part III, Cultural Politics, challenges the reduction of cultural radicalism to an apolitical outburst by demonstrating the fusion of politics and culture. These essays also demonstrate the considerable overlap between "disciplinary" and "anti-disciplinary" modes of political action. As opposed to histories of the 1960s that acknowledge only those who sought to effect political change through mainstream legislative channels or structural transformation as legitimately political, the artists, images, and events examined in Part III demonstrate that practices devoted to consciousness raising and personal liberation, the imagining or actual creation of new forms of community, and the cultural feminist critique of patriarchy were important forms of political action in the period.

Part IV, Altered Consciousness, brings together another diverse group of essays that focus on artistic practices meant to elevate consciousness through environmental activism, meditative strategies and philosophies of self-realization, drug-induced enlightenment, and the visual language of the multimedia event. Whether spearheading "new ways of conceptualizing and inhabiting the planet" (see Amanda Boetzkes's chapter), recognizing new potentialities of human existence (the chapters by Suzanne Hudson and Bill Scheffel), or imaging a "new, alternate world order" (Scott Montgomery's chapter), these essays address the shared determination of countercultural artists to reach a higher state of consciousness through art and cultural expression.

The essays comprising *West of Center* examine work that reflected a new artistic identity rooted in the creation and organization of scenarios, sites, events, and networks, and openly solicited participation and involvement, and was experienced by makers, viewers, or participants as integrated into life. What unites this diverse group of practices and artists is the view that what counts as legitimate politics need not be limited to legislative action and other conventional forms of political activism, and that the assumption that art and aesthetic experience, broadly defined, were valuable forms of knowledge with important political dimensions.

This volume does not aim to be all-inclusive. Instead, this collection attempts to reach out to diverse and scattered elements of the movement and tie crisscrossing threads through them. It seeks to piece together samples that give a new sense of the shape and color of the broad fabric. There are many important elements excluded or underincluded. A more comprehensive study of the art of the counterculture would include, in general terms, a sustained analysis of film, poetry, literature, clothing, music, and other aesthetic practices. Together, these accounts would have woven a more geographically diverse picture of the counterculture than that of the current volume. There is also a bias in the selection of essays away from some of the more commonly known examples of the counterculture aesthetic, such as the Merry Pranksters, the Diggers, and Ant Farm, even though they are mentioned extensively in the introduction and throughout the collection. Essays were not selected with the intention of either establishing a countercultural canon or dismantling an existing one. Rather, this volume attempts to balance the need to portray an ample picture of the counterculture with an interest in encouraging new research on the subject. How could this volume even attempt to be comprehensive? It's the counterculture after all.

As a final note, it needs to be said that the editors of this volume came of age in the 1980s, between the youth culture of today and the counterculture of the 1960s. As the next generation, we've been told more than a few times that we can't understand the 1960s since we weren't there. We read into this admonition a characteristic attitude of the counterculture, which valued immediate, lived experiences above all else. That is partly why, unlike many conceptual artists on the East Coast, the individuals discussed in this volume did not keep lasting records of their activities and did not preserve many of the original objects they made. That is the authenticity of the counterculture, and it is precisely what attracts so many young artists to it today. It is also probably what first attracted us to the subject and resulted in so many scholars of our generation contributing to this collection. We are interested in the counterculture not only because we see strong traces of it alive today in the generation that succeeds us. Ultimately, we believe that we are all interested in the counterculture because in its fluidity—its this *and* that *and* that—we find something beautiful and revolutionary that wants to be understood.

NOTES

1. Chip Lord, letter to Anna and Lawrence Halprin, 5 October 1968, Anna Halprin archive, San Francisco Museum of Performance and Design, box 11, folder 6.

2. On the subject, see Julie Stephens, *Anti-Disciplinary Protest: Sixties Radicalism and Postmodernism* (Cambridge: Cambridge University Press, 1998); and Brent Whelan, "'Further': Reflections on Counter-Culture and the Postmodern," *Cultural Critique* (Winter 1988-89): 63-86.

3. Theodore Roszak, "The Misunderstood Movement," *New York Times*, 3 December 1994, A23.

4. Roszak, *The Making of a Counter Culture: Reflections on the Technocratic Society and Its Youthful Opposition* (Garden City, N.Y.: Doubleday, 1969).

5. Newt Gingrich, quoted in Frank Rich, "Gingrich Family Values," *New York Times*, 14 May 1995, sect. 4: 15.

6. Roszak, "Misunderstood Movement," A23.

7. J. Milton Yinger, "Contraculture and Subculture," *American Sociological Review* 25, no. 5 (October 1960): 625-35.

8. Ibid., 629.

9. Talcott Parsons, *The Social System* (Glencoe, Ill.: Free Press, 1951).

10. Roszak, *Making of a Counter Culture*, 5.

11. Ibid., 49.

12. Ibid.

13. Todd Gitlin, *The Sixties: Years of Hope, Days of Rage* (New York: Bantam, 1987), 209.

14. Peter Braunstein and Michael William Doyle, eds., *Imagine Nation: The American Counterculture of the 1960s and '70s* (New York: Routledge, 2002), 7.

15. One source of "Just Do It" is the title of Jerry Rubin's *Do It: Scenarios of the Revolution* (New York: Simon & Schuster, 1970). The assumed connections between the failure of cultural radicalism and commodification are problematic. On the practice of dismissing the counterculture by virtue of its assimilation to mainstream culture through corporate co-optation, see Stephens, *Anti-Disciplinary Protest*, chapter 4.

16. Stephens, *Anti-Disciplinary Protest*, 3.

17. Ibid.

18. Ibid., 4. For examples of the overlap of the New Left and countercultural styles and political ideals, see Stephens, 28 ff.

19. Relevant studies include Christoph Gruenenberg and Jonathan Harris, eds., *The Summer of Love: Psychedelic Art, Social Crisis and Counterculture in the 1960s* (Liverpool: Liverpool University Press, 2007); Bradford D. Martin, *The Theater Is in the Street: Politics and Performance in Sixties America* (Amherst: University of Massachusetts Press, 2004); Peter Selz, ed., *Art of Engagement: Visual Politics in California and Beyond* (Berkeley: University of California Press, 2006), which includes an informative chapter on "Countercultural Trends" and an overview of the California context for the emergence of the counterculture on the West Coast; Margaret Crawford, "Alternative Shelter: Counterculture Architecture in Northern California," in *Reading California: Art, Image, and Identity, 1900-2000*, ed. Stephanie Barron, Sheri Bernstein, and Ilene Susan Fort (Berkeley: University of California Press, 2000); and Felicity D. Scott's complex analysis of Drop City in *Architecture or Techno-Utopia* (Cambridge, Mass.: MIT Press, 2007). Also of value are the individual essays on guerrilla theater, underground comix, and film included in Braunstein and Doyle, *Imagine Nation*. Henry M. Sayre acknowledges countercultural events such as the first Be-In of 1967 as a source of performance art and its political orientation in his *The Object of Performance: The American Avant-Garde since 1970* (Chicago: University of Chicago Press, 1989).

20. Thomas Crow, *The Rise of the Sixties: American and European Art in the Era of Dissent, 1955-69* (New Haven, Conn.: Yale University Press, 2005); Francis Frascina, *Art, Politics, and Dissent: Aspects of the Art Left in Sixties America* (Manchester: Manchester University Press, 1999).

21. Anne Rorimer, *New Art in the 60s and 70s: Redefining Reality* (London, Thames & Hudson, 2001), 7.

22. Jennifer González and Adrienne Posner, "Facture for Change: US Activist Art since 1950," in *A Companion to Art since 1945*, ed. Amelia Jones (Oxford: Blackwell, 2006), 212-30.

23. See Christoph Grunenberg, *Summer of Love: Art of the Psychedelic Era* (Liverpool: Tate, 2005). Exhibition catalog.

24. David S. Rubin, *Psychedelic: Optical and Visionary Art since the 1960s* (Cambridge, Mass.: MIT Press, 2010).

25. See also Barry Mile's *Hippie* (New York: Sterling, 2005); and Alastair Gordon, *Spaced Out: Radical Environments of the Psychedelic Sixties* (New York: Rizzoli, 2008).

26. Grant Kester, *Conversation Pieces: Community and Communication in Modern Art* (Berkeley: University of California Press, 2004), 8.

27. Ibid., 11.

28. Stephens continues: "Many later commentators on the sixties assess the era in terms of whether or not certain protests were properly planned or particular groups had clear enough political goals. Questions of organization and strategy are applied to the very groups which promoted anti-organization and anti-strategy." Stephens, *Anti-Disciplinary Protest*, 32.

29. Kester, *Conversation Pieces*, 12.

30. Ibid.

31. Ibid., 10.

32. *The Digger Papers* (San Francisco: Diggers, 1968), 3. For additional descriptions of this event, see Gitlin, *The Sixties*, 222; and Martin A. Lee and Bruce Shlain, *Acid Dreams: The CIA, LSD, and the Sixties Rebellion* (New York: Grove Press, 1985), 170.

33. For an extended discussion of the various countercultural connotations of the word *free*, see Stephens, *Anti-Disciplinary Protest*, 42-47.

34. Gene Bernofsky, phone interview with Erin Elder, 17 October 2006.

35. Andrew G. Kirk, *Counterculture Green: The Whole Earth Catalog and American Environmentalism* (Lawrence: University Press of Kansas, 2007), 158.

36. Ibid., 156-57.

37. Stewart Brand is quoted in ibid., 158. We recommend Kirk's incredibly insightful and well-written book to anyone interested in the environmentalism of the counterculture and its legacy.

38. The conference "Transpedagogy: Contemporary Art and the Vehicles of Education," organized by Pablo Helguera, took place at the Museum of Modern Art, New York, on 15 May 2009.

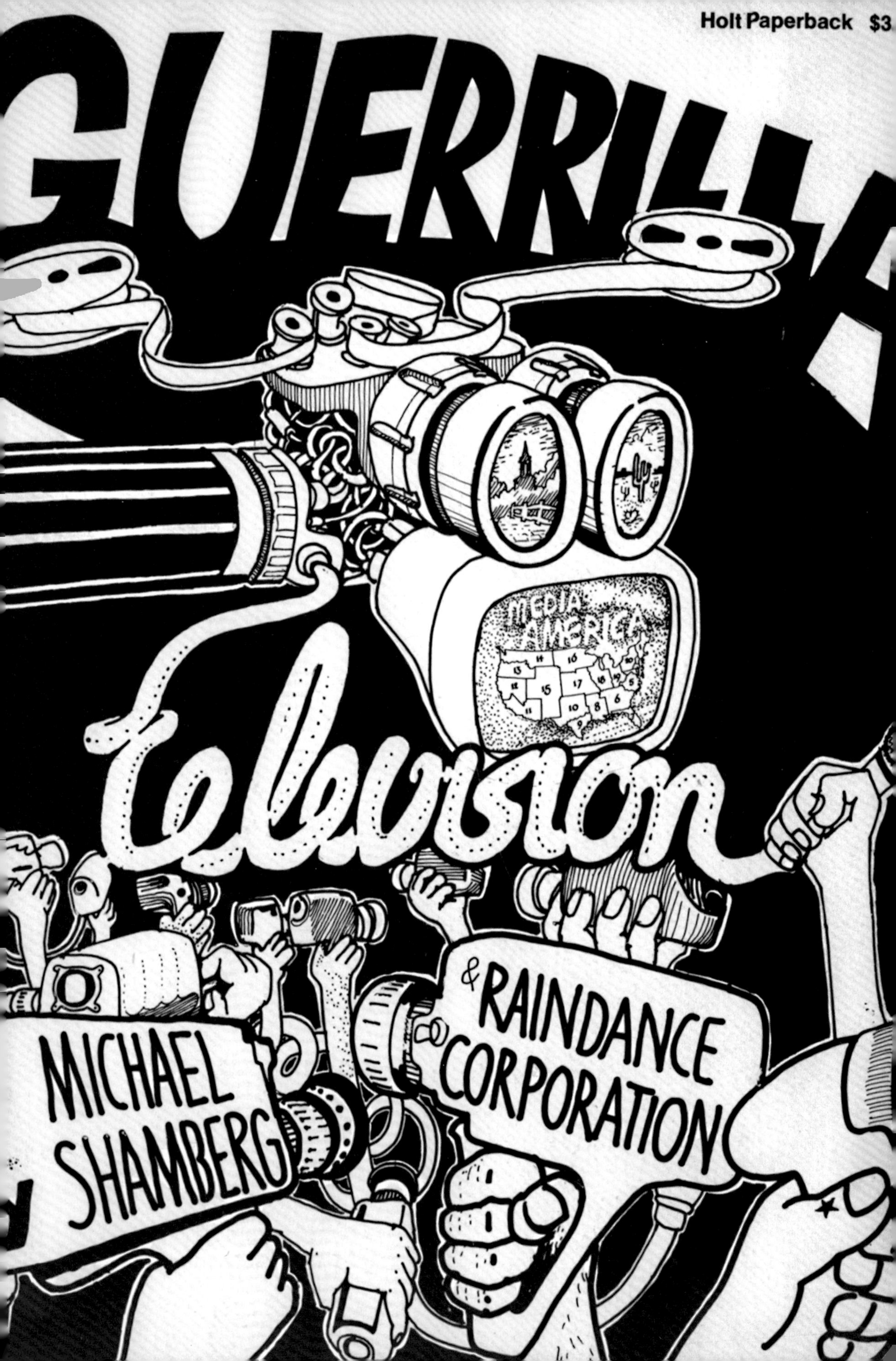
Holt Paperback $3.
GUERRILLA
MEDIA AMERICA
Television
MICHAEL SHAMBERG
& RAINDANCE CORPORATION

PART I

COMMUNAL ENCOUNTERS

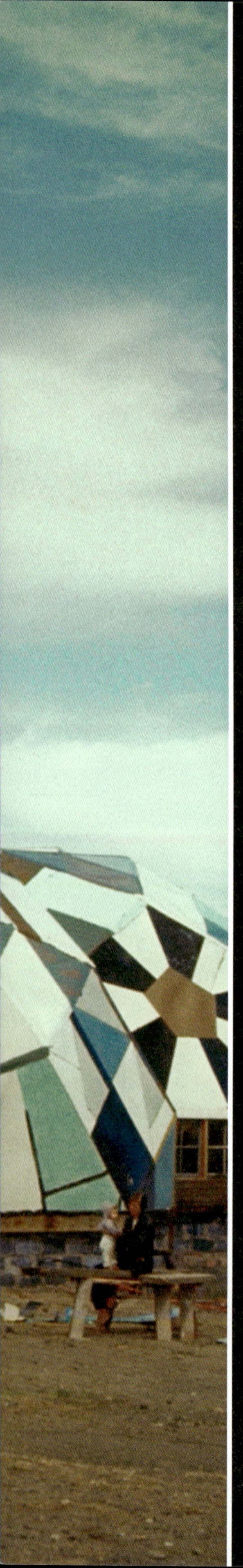

CHAPTER 1
HOW TO BUILD A COMMUNE: DROP CITY'S INFLUENCE ON THE SOUTHWESTERN COMMUNE MOVEMENT

Erin Elder

Just north of Trinidad, Colorado, near the exit for El Moro, is a long flat expanse of tumbleweeds and dirt, leftover snow patches, and barbed wire tangles. Between the Sangre de Cristo Mountains and a chain of flat-topped mesas is an emptiness, a deep breath of silence on the Colorado—New Mexico border. Every trace of Drop City has been swept clean. The total lack of ruins, signage, or lingering communards make it difficult to locate exactly where, from 1965 to 1973, there stood a vibrant community experiment that invested in applying art to every aspect of daily life and that sparked a movement of commune building that came to define the American counterculture.

Drop City was founded on dreams of "building a civilization from scratch," and a shared desire to "do something more than hang a painting, to create a kind of input."[1] Over the course of eight years and on an arid six-acre goat pasture, Drop City produced a miscellany of structures, sculptures, paintings, experimental films, performances, and a type of art called "Droppings." Built by hand with scrounged materials, Drop City was not only a place to make art, but—through a creative reinvestment in daily activities—it was a place to *be* art (Figure 1.1). As it became a counterculture way station, thousands of young people flocked to southern Colorado to learn about new architectural forms, to spin out on psychedelics in an otherworldly setting, to leave their jobs and families in exchange for proverbial free love, free drugs, and free rent. Drop City was the pioneering front of the hip commune movement of the sixties and through shared technology, space, and praxis, "turned on" a new generation of commune builders.

Communalism is an essential component of American rural life, a tradition that has seen a variety of cycles, styles, and core values since the seventeenth century. Although communes have never been part of the dominant paradigm, it's nothing new to the United States. Drop City was simply at the forefront of the most explosive manifestation of communitarian idealism that, between 1965 and 1975, produced "at least 2,000" rural communes and attracted upwards of a million young people.[2] American communal history turned a major corner with the establishment of Drop City. Commune scholar Tim Miller writes:

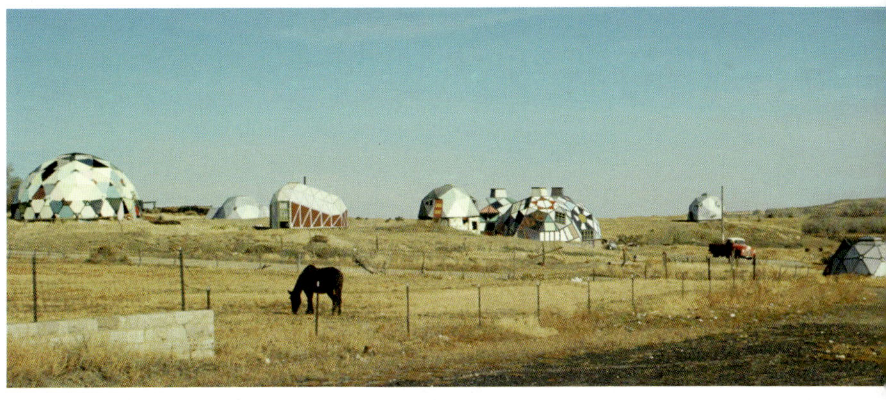

HOW TO BUILD A COMMUNE

Drop City brought together most of the themes that had been developing in other recent communities—anarchy, pacifism, sexual freedom, rural isolation, interest in drugs, art—and wrapped them flamboyantly into a commune not quite like any that had gone before. Drop City thus represents the point at which a new type of commune building had definitively arrived.[3]

Not only was Drop City one of the first open-land, anarchic communes, but also it was the first to stake a claim on the American Southwest as an outpost for a burgeoning counterculture. Drop City established a way of life that combined colorful dissent with do-it-yourself technology, shared physical labor, and outrageous homes built from trash, and this set of enacted principles, in many ways, became the vernacular for the southwestern commune movement. When Timothy Leary toured the Southwest in 1967, he referred to the communes collectively as "drop cities"; others have described Drop City as "the first capital of the outlaw nation."[4] Drop City was clearly the precedent for hundreds of thousands of disgruntled youth who aimed to create a new communal existence beyond the margins of straight society.

In the end Drop City was rumored to host a methamphetamine factory, a vicious round of hepatitis, and possibly even a murder. Drop City was shut down in 1973 by the local health department; the remaining inhabitants were evicted and the land was sold to finance other projects. This brand of kaleidoscopic ruin was not an uncommon ending for the rash of communes that broke out across the Southwest and may account for the ways in which their legacy has been ignored or oversimplified.

As one commune builder has said, "the counterculture occupies a historical niche somewhere between a pernicious social virus and an amusing Halloween costume."[5] While several recent attempts have been made to redress these generalizing trends by unpacking the sixties' contributions to civil rights, the environmental movement, sexual and religious freedoms, health food and agrarian practices, and the cultivation of the American Left, there remains a void in scholarship around the communes of the Southwest. I aim to address some small corner of this void by looking at Drop City as the vanguard of a significant commune building movement. With special interest in temporary spaces for alternative cultural production, this paper examines how notions of consciousness expansion, the network, and the southwestern landscape came to bear on the conceptual and physical manifestation of Drop City and its neighbor communes.

What interests me most about Drop City is how an expansive perspective on art, trash, and everyday life created a particular kind of space that in turn influenced a burgeoning of cultural alternatives. Drop City was both intentional and experimental; grounded by the realities of human survival, it was wildly improvisational in its address of those basic needs. As half-baked as it may have been, the notion of the Dropping gave this artists' collective a reason and a context to create a vibrant alternative to the society they sought to resist. Unlike some other communes *art* was the impetus and the frame that allowed the Droppers to risk everything they had in a long-term, communal experiment. As Dropper Bill Voyd said in 1969, "The only thing that will allow each of us to create his or her Utopia is praxis."[6]

In this essay I analyze the Droppings as a particular frame of reference that motivated the Droppers in what I call an expanded practice. I touch on various aspects of scrounging as it pertained to Dropper architecture, lifestyle, and their patchwork of ideological underpinnings. Later, I introduce notions of expansive building exemplified by the Droppers' relationship to development, the network, and the American Southwest. Clark Richert, one of Drop City's founding members, has said, "We really saw ourselves as artists and we saw Drop City as an on-going work of art."[7] Statements such as this invite a deeper consideration of commune building as art practice and the commune as a cultural form. Although there is not space here for an in-depth argument, I would like to suggest that, given the number of southwestern communes built between 1965 and 1975, this might be regarded as a legitimate art movement with significant influence on contemporary art practice.

DROPPING ART

Clark Richert and JoAnn and Gene Bernofsky were close friends in Lawrence, Kansas, in the early 1960s. Richert and JoAnn met in art class at the University of Kansas, and when she left for a nine-month trip to San Francisco, Gene moved into Richert's second-story loft overlooking what they called a "bourgeois" thoroughfare—Massachusetts Street—in downtown Lawrence.[8] Here is where Droppings, or Drop Art, was born.

During their studies and on return trips to New York, Richert and the Bernofskys encountered the avant-garde practices of such artists as Allan Kaprow, John Cage, and others who taught at Black Mountain College in North Carolina. Through such encounters, they understood Happenings as spontaneous, bizarre, interactive, open-outcome events that were affecting audiences not only in New York and Europe, but also in Lawrence. They shared Kaprow's conviction that the Happening, as a new art form, "couldn't be confused with paintings, poetry, architecture, music, dance or plays. As residues of a European past, these old forms of art had lost their artness . . . by overexposure and empty worship. Happenings are fresh."[9] In support of this desire for fresh forms, Richert and Gene Bernofsky created their own mutation of Happenings called Droppings.

One time they dropped painted pebbles out of their loft window onto passersby below, watching the reaction from their second-story vantage. Another time, they connected an iron and ironing board to a downtown parking meter. On the sidewalk in front of a "bourgeois" hotel, they left an immense breakfast on an elaborately set table, free for anyone to sit and eat.[10] They "dropped" art into an unwitting situation, intending to reframe reality through sudden disruption. Droppings were a form of playful entertainment but were also grounded in a formal art intention to actively disregard distinctions between art, perception, and daily activity.

It seems that early Droppings were little events, largely unpublicized, and often unnoticed. They were primarily a means of testing the artists' working methods and also the abilities of the public to respond to a given situation. The situations were part intentional construction, part volatile investigation. They were at once uncertain and assertive, pointless and poignant. The Droppers sought to create sudden opportunities for momentary changes in perception, but often their work went unobserved and was unwittingly woven into the banal fabric of everyday life. Given their disgust with a complacent and privileged mainstream, Droppings were a humorous way to play off of the "shittiness" of this offensive population. Sometimes audiences "got it," and other times the Dropping fell flat in a puny splatter. Those who interacted with or reacted to the Droppings transformed the work. For those who embraced these bizarre experiments with equally unpredictable responses, the Dropping became something else—it became a medium, a kind fertilizer transformed by the creation of a momentary community.

The Droppers had a love-hate relationship with the New York art world and despised the object-driven market that dominated it in the early 1960s. Yet New York was erupting with new art strategies that evoked participation, chaos, and a general breakdown of the assumed order of things. Exposed to concepts of "unarting," the Droppers joined a movement to dematerialize art by "taking the art out of art, which in practical terms meant discarding art's characteristics. . . . leaving art *is* the art. But you must have it to leave it."[11] This notion of leaving art in order to expand its potential for engaging daily life is key to understanding the shift from Droppings to Drop City.

BECOMING THE DROPPING

While developing a context for their art-and-living project, the Droppers played with ideas of how to expand their experience of Drop Art, how to literally inhabit it. Based on everything they knew to be true of Droppings, it was possible to *become* the Dropping through a collective commitment to living with alternative and undefined situations. Like a Dropping, Drop City would be intentional but unscripted—a spontaneous experiment with open-ended outcomes. In retrospect Gene Bernofsky recalls, "We wanted to enter into the Dropping, *become* the Dropping. We were dropping ourselves onto this land to see what we would do with it."[12]

At Drop City art making would certainly make up a large part of everyday life, but the making of a *place,* and the *habitation* of that place—these would comprise this expanded Dropping. The place would be a refuge from suburban life and a studio for art production. It would be a situation around which to create community, but most important, it would be an intentional experiment with the unknown.

The Droppers approached every bit of life as if it could be art. Work could be art. Food could be art. Trash could be art. Becoming the Dropping threw everything into question, and as a result everything could be viewed, critiqued, created, destroyed, or remade. In his seminal work *The Critique of Everyday Life,* French sociologist Henri Lefebvre discusses how the ambiguous realms of art bring everyday life into view as "a question of discovering what must and can change and be transformed in people's lives. . . . It is a question of stating critically how people live or how badly they live, or how they do not live at all."[13] Similarly, the Droppers believed that art could be the ends and means for a reconsideration of the daily life that mainstream culture had all but taken for granted.

In becoming the Dropping a certain totality was levied on the lifestyle, architecture, and atmosphere at Drop City. Like others of twentieth-century utopian art movements, the Droppers "aim not just at the integration of art and life, but of all human activities. They have a critique of social separation and a concept of totality."[14] The Droppers would override specialization, transcending the boundaries of an oppressive, compartmentalizing dominant paradigm by learning to build and participate on every level of their new society. Nothing escaped the realm of art practice. Diet, fashion, relationships, decisions, and time: all were on the drawing board. As Dropper Bill Voyd wrote, "The works of art we envisage are total, vast."[15]

The Dropping was a context for thinking about a total artwork that encompassed every element of daily life. Through this expansive notion of the Dropping, they were able, as Kaprow advocated, to "unart" art—yet they were able to take it much further than Kaprow would have imagined possible. At Drop City lifestyle was cultivated as art; acting out an alternative reality was in fact the project at hand. But why not simply create a new way of living; why frame it as a Dropping? In building a civilization from scratch, did it matter if distinctions relating to art and performance got lost along the way, and how did this art frame give meaning to what the Droppers were doing?

The Droppers were not alone in their framing or naming of such expansive practice; they had contemporaries who likewise aimed to remake society through similar types of discursive lenses. As an extension of their theater background, the San Francisco Diggers served free food in public parks, opened a number of free stores, and created numerous happenings, parades, and performances. Their work was contextualized by the Free Frame of Reference, often symbolized by empty yellow wooden frames and the declaration "It's Free Because It's Yours." During many Digger events, the public was asked to step through a large golden frame, a gesture that invited a "free perspective; a point of view one could assemble oneself."[16] While the Free Frame of Reference was unnecessary to the project of revolutionizing urban life in San Francisco, it was a tool that invited art-like intentionality and criticality from both the Diggers and their community.

Less of a public construction, Bonnie Sherk employed the Life-Frame as a way of positioning her performances and the *Crossroads Community Farm* as something between art and life, something both avant-garde and perplexing. For Sherk, the Life-Frame was a means of "expand[ing] the concept of art to include, and even be life" but also of using real situations to push the limits of established art conventions.[17] The point is not whether the notion of the Dropping makes Drop City art; rather, it's remarkable how the Dropping (like the Free Frame of Reference and the Life-Frame) was a discursive mechanism that launched this collective of artists into critically and aesthetically engaged countercultural activities.

VISUAL THINKING

The image of the lens is also illustrative of how film technology was changing notions of consciousness at Drop City and far beyond. Gene Bernofsky was a filmmaker and his 16mm Kodak Ciné camera was constantly rolling. He talks about the camera as a tool, comparing its function to that of a hammer or saw; the camera was used to "build a film."[18] The camera was communal property; anyone could use it. Filmmaking was a spontaneous activity, something to do in the moment, something to do every day. Through the cinematic practices of focusing, cropping, and editing, film was another way that art became a means to look, imagine, and construct differently.[19] The films were not documentaries or dramas; they were not necessarily made to be viewed and oftentimes were combined with lights, music, motion, and other elements in which the film was just one small part of a multisensory experience. These expanded Droppings were part of the midsixties movement that amplified the legacy of Happenings on a festival scale, creating what were known as Be-Ins or Love-Ins.

Drop City was one of the many places where film was produced collectively for wholly new and expansive means. Media was becoming more accessible to amateurs; for instance, the Sony Portapak was introduced in 1967 and was the first individually operated video camera. As a result of such emergent film technologies, miles and miles of footage were being shot in the sixties. The camera kept rolling, capturing and framing every moment as art, paving the way toward what experimental filmmaker Stan Brakhage has described as "moving visual thinking."[20] In his 1970 book *Expanded Cinema*, Gene Youngblood discusses the impact of the electronic media age on this new generation: "When we say expanded cinema, we actually mean expanded consciousness. . . . [It] isn't a movie at all: like life it's a process of becoming, man's ongoing historical drive to manifest his consciousness outside of his mind, in front of his eyes."[21]

This link between consciousness expansion and technology was fueled, in part, by widespread LSD experiments. As curator Will Bradley states, in describing the filmmaking practices of the sixties, "acid was seen by artists as a technology in itself," and film technologies were oftentimes developed to "manipulate the cinematic image space in response to their drug experiences."[22] LSD stimulated a temporary synesthesia during which "shape becomes color, which becomes vibration, which becomes sound, which becomes smell, which becomes taste, and then touch, and then again shape."[23] Across the country, cameras and drugs (often combined with music, lights, mirrors, objects, and other contraptions) were perception tools that helped create consumable media that evidenced this new mystic mindscape. Influenced by Marshall McLuhan's claims that "the medium is the message," these artists aimed to produce media that communicated, not so much by way of content but through the characteristics of the media themselves.[24]

DOME HOMES

The way that founders of Drop City critiqued the midsixties status quo built on McLuhan's notion of the medium; to put it simply, their concerns were more about society's form than about its particular issues. While the international political climate was certainly unsettling, the Droppers were more troubled by the suburban communities exploding across America in rigid configurations of tract homes and strip malls, and by young people yielding to the pressure of mundane jobs, families, and a routine existence. The collective had little interest in gridded neighborhoods, urban plans, standardization, and uniformity; they sought to restore a raw and immediate relationship to materials, space, their bodies, and the environment through the act of building. The Bernofskys' main objective was to work, to create, but they wanted to do it without being employed. Therefore, they made a commitment to reject the commodifying "American ideal" that sought to enclose them. To enact this rejection, it was important that they "stop using sidewalks, stop using buildings, and create a new life."[25] This revulsion against American conventions, therefore, had to be expressed through the very practices and forms that made Drop City.

Ground broke at Drop City in the summer of 1965, and dome building was the order of the day. After attending Buckminster Fuller's recent lecture in Boulder, Colorado, the Droppers were inspired; they saw domes as the medium with which to create their new civilization and immediately set out to duplicate his geodesics using scrap materials. In describing their interest in domes, Dropper Bill Voyd has written, "we were held together by a common feeling that the whole structure of American society was rigid and oppressive, that the only way to physical and spiritual freedom lay outside the established system."[26] Domes presented an alternative to the planned, mass-manufactured, and unoriginal housing developments spreading across America.

Without constricting corners or load-bearing columns, domes were inhabitable sculptures made of multitudinous triangles and crystalline forms. The many parts of a dome were equally essential; every stage of construction was important and handcrafted, yet domes didn't require bulldozers, trucks, or heavy machinery and could be completed with simple hammers, saws, drills, and nails. Drop City was one of the first collections of amateur-built domes and gained much attention; especially after receiving Fuller's Dymaxion award in 1966, visitors came from far and wide to learn about domes and dome building. After an extended stay at Drop City, one dome builder imagined that "soon domed cities will spread across the world."[27] With its experimental buildings and open-door policy, Drop City tested a new technology that soon became the architectural vernacular of the counterculture.

BUILDING A CIVILIZATION FROM SCRAPS

Trinidad, Colorado, was founded as a railhead and mining town, but by the time the Droppers entered onto the scene labor had moved elsewhere leaving the region in a constant state of economic depression. Then home to eleven thousand people, the town was a harbor for low-income and immigrant laborers who were collectively some of the poorest in the state. When the Droppers moved onto their six-acre plot of land, no one blinked an eye, as Trinidadians were accustomed to seeing scrapped-together shelters and ragtag attempts at creating a new life.[28]

With very little money and a commitment to voluntary poverty, the Droppers were faced with the creative challenge of building homes with found materials. The Droppers found that Trinidad was home to many demolition experts from Mexico and learned to scrounge by watching these professional demolitions, recovering what the Mexican crews didn't take. They were proud to use "the junk that the junkers junked"[29] and found immense possibility in living off the garbage of a consumer economy. A 1967 Dropper manifesto-like contribution in Boston's underground newspaper *Avatar* recalls this early moment:

We have discovered a new art form: creative scrounging. We dismantle abandoned bridges by moonlight. We are sort of advanced junkmen taking advantage of advanced obsolescence. Drop City was begun without money, built on practically nothing. None of us is employed or has a steady income. Somehow we have not gone hungry . . . things come to us.[30]

Resourcefulness was as much a learned practice as it was embedded in each of the founding Droppers' upbringing. In fact, a working-class background might distinguish the Droppers from other commune builders in their generation. While many sixties-era communes were created by disaffected suburban youths who were fueled by private trust funds,[31] Droppers started with $1,000. They had no cushion, no backup, no privileged life to return to after a foray into the wilds of the counterculture. A lack of financial backing fostered the kind of commune that was created at Drop City, allowing them little choice but to build their new life—not necessarily from scratch but, in fact, from scraps.

The Great Pumpkin Dome (1965) was the first structure to appear on the dusty plot of land. It was made with salvaged two-by-four timbers, the measurements of which proved to be slightly inaccurate, thus lending the structure an immediate idiosyncrasy. The eighteen-foot-diameter wooden skeleton was covered with chicken wire and tarpaper, which were held in place by painstakingly applied layers of donated bottle caps and stolen cement.

Before winter hit, the Droppers built the Kitchen Dome (1965), a slightly larger dome in the Fuller style, augmented by a quasi-A-frame entrance. The timber frame and plywood skin were eccentrically warped when unexpected rain fell before the dome was sealed with tar. Adding to the gritty funk of the Kitchen Dome was the inventive insertion of car windshields as windows. With the completion of the second Drop City building, a peculiar aesthetic stood testament to the Droppers' scrounging practice and their laissez-faire approach to architecture. Neither building cost the Droppers more than $200.

Within the first year, Drop City's population swelled to fifteen to twenty adults. Housing became a pressing need and depended on everyone pitching in with daily building, not unlike the barn raisings of agricultural communities. Work was not mandatory but was very much a part of the place. According to one Dropper, "The greatest impact of communal life upon the artist is the realization that all community activity is equal, that digging a ditch carries no less status than erecting a sculpture; in fact the individual often discovers he is happier digging a ditch, *sculpting* a ditch."[32] Cooperative labor, resource sharing, and scrounging shifted from necessity to lived manifesto and became central to Drop City's identity.

During that first year at Drop City, word of the commune began to spread and soon drew the attention of Steve Baer, who was teaching in the architecture department at University of New Mexico in Albuquerque. Baer was fascinated with polyhedral structures and needed space and a workforce to experiment with his latest inventions, so he approached the Droppers, offering his designs in exchange for Dropper labor. At Drop City Baer introduced "zomes," four of which were eventually constructed. The zome is a dome-like system that involves fewer parts and is more forgiving than Fuller's geodesics. Fuller domes require total accuracy, whereas zomes allow for spontaneity and additions, alterations and mistakes. Zomes encourage experimentation and chance and are always unique in their final manifestation. The geometrics of the Fuller domes were freed up by Baer's new mathematics and authenticated by the Droppers' amateurism and low-budget building practice (Figures 1.2 and 1.3).

Baer's mutant constructions introduced new materials and, therefore, a new form of scrounging. His 1968 *Dome Cookbook* gives instructions for building a zome with car tops, readily available and acquired for twenty cents apiece.[33] Harvesting car tops required an intense and dangerous form of physical labor, yet Droppers traveled to junkyards all over Colorado and New Mexico, chopping car tops in the blazing sun. One Dropper recalls:

It was dangerous; razor-sharp axes skittering off the steel, slicing at legs. When you hit one of the roof supports an incredible jolt travels up the axe's handle and paralyzes your wrists and hands. Jagged steel edges catching clothing, tearing flesh, hands stiff, clenching, clenching. After chopping for an hour if you try to open your hands the fingers insist on closing into fists again. Blisters, blisters on top of blisters, bone weary. . . . And the thumb smashes. . . . It hurt so bad, so bad. But the next day we were at it again. We measured progress on the Complex in thumb smashes.[34]

Droppers made no distinction between scrounging, stealing, or receiving gifts from the "Cosmic Forces." In his 1971 memoir, Peter Rabbit describes the "Great Work" of building Drop City: "It's all free, it all flows from the Cosmic Forces, all energy comes from the same place and it's free."[35] Dropper mysticism expanded the notion of communal into a much larger realm—that of spirit and time—and in doing so enacted an anticapitalist agenda of truly free exchange.

At moments this concept of the Cosmic Forces explained serendipitous good fortune (like encountering a pile of bricks at an abandoned ware-house), and other times it resulted in Robin Hood–style thievery. A favorite story of cosmic favor involves scoring the final shingle for the Complex (1967), a triad of adjoining domes; it was stealthily chopped in the dark of night from a brand-new golden Cadillac parked outside a roadside motel. As Peter Rabbit likes to say, "the shitmobile turned con-vertible overnight."[36] More than spontaneous mischief, this and other

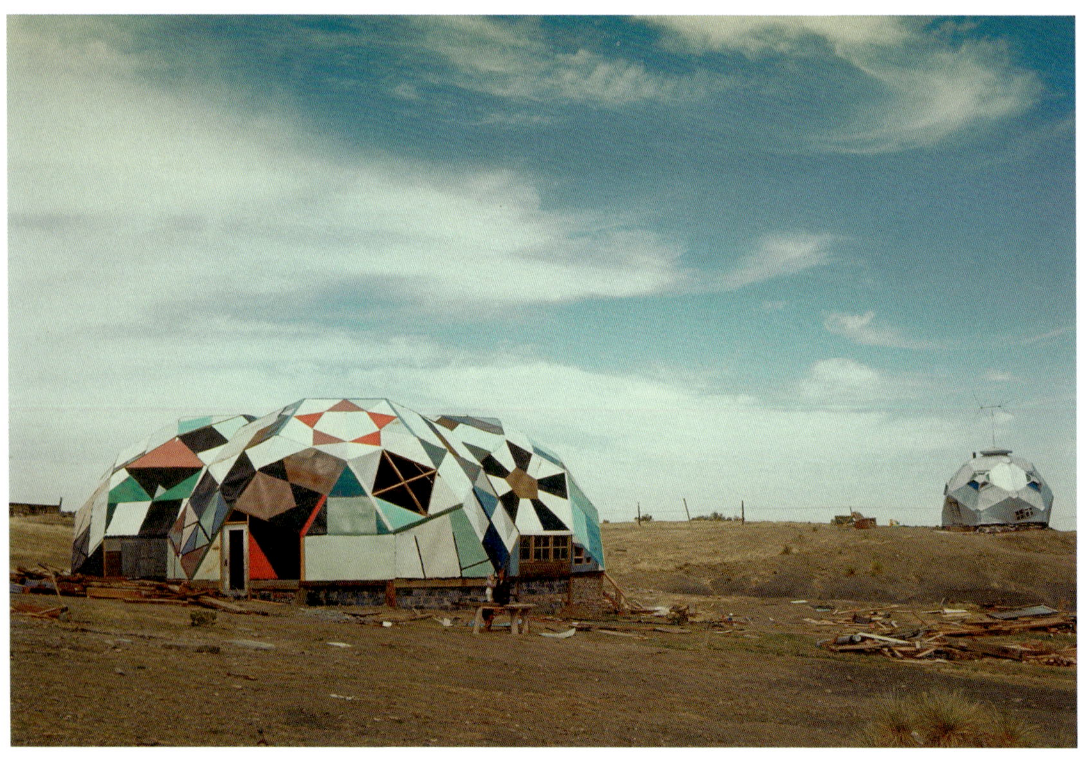

     HOW TO BUILD A COMMUNE

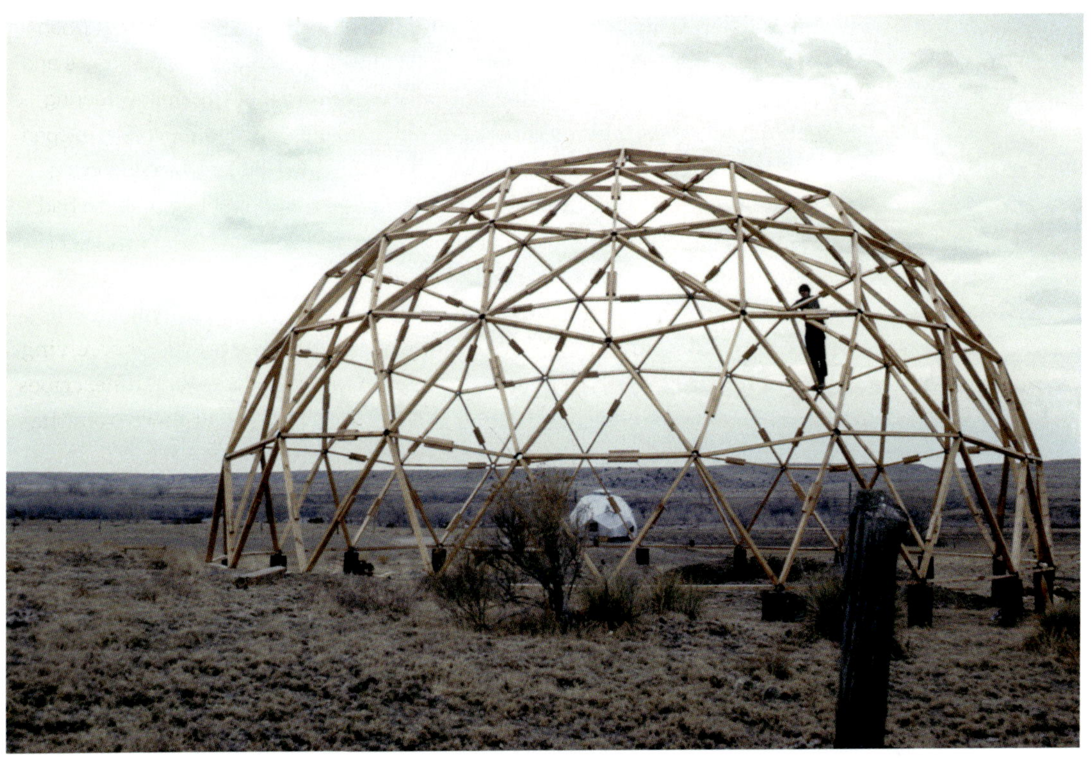

Dropper acts of material reclamation demonstrate the truly radical program under way throughout America in what has been called the "free movement."

In her book *Anti-disciplinary Protest,* Julie Stephens compares the tactics employed by various sixties countercultural groups in rethinking economic exchange, money, and the distribution of wealth. She quotes a Digger who declares, "Money, like God, is dead" and references Jerry Rubin urging people to burn their money. She makes a distinction between the traditionally Left demonstrations in which resources are reallocated and those acts of sixties counterculturalists—by dubbing everything free or a provision of the Cosmic Forces, money was essentially destroyed, its value undermined entirely.[37] Therefore, this was not about socialist economic rearrangement, but about a different economy of value and exchange altogether. Abbie Hoffman once claimed that "the free thing is perhaps the most revolutionary thing in America," as an attack on founda-tional capitalist notions of ownership, property, and value.[38] In this way, the Cosmic Forces were part of this radical "free" movement as much as they were a justification for Droppers in building a civilization from scratch.

POST-SCARCITY RICHES

In his 1971 study *Post-scarcity Anarchism,* political philosopher and ecolo-gist Murray Bookchin claimed that "in the very act of refusing to live by bourgeois strictures, the first seeds of the utopian lifestyle are planted. Negation passes into affirmation within the rotting guts of capitalism itself. 'Dropping out' becomes a mode of dropping in—into the tentative, experimental, and as yet highly ambiguous, social relations of utopia."[39] Drop City was one of the first communal efforts to enact this refusal and was a living display of utopian self-sufficiency. Like hunter-gatherers, Droppers collected what they imagined was provided for them and brought it back to the community to be dispersed as needed; this was true not only of building supplies but also of food, fiscal income, and clothing. Any money—earned from occasional outside work, from the sale of artworks, from child support, even alimony—was collected in a communal fund. A single closet housed all clothing; books were passed around; drugs were shared. Even cars at Drop City became part of the public domain. Sexual relations and sleeping quarters were some of the very few things that Droppers attempted to keep private. The Droppers survived for a short while on government commodities and at times ate the same stuff sold to pig farmers for slop. Supplemental food was scrounged from the local Safeway dumpster; eggs were stolen from neighboring chicken farms. The Droppers made statewide news with their initial enlistment and also their later dismissal from the Las Animas County food stamp program.[40] In 1967, one Dropper told a reporter from the *Denver Post* that Droppers "won't seek meaningless employment just to feed themselves."[41]

Drop City perched on the edge of parasitic dependence and self-sufficiency, relying on the production of waste and, therefore, on consumer society's continued surplus. Although they considered themselves free of capitalism and hierarchy, the Droppers depended on prosperous mainstream America's bountiful trash pile and food stamps in order to survive.

While often stereotyped as dropouts and leeches, the communes required some form of money and made innovative stabs at fiscal self-sufficiency. The Anonymous Artists of America played rock and roll in the bars of nearby towns like Walsenburg, Colorado; the Reality Construction Company set up an adobe brick cottage industry; many others had gardens or small farming operations, published newsletters and books. In the early years, Droppers subsidized their existence through commodity exchange; they sold art objects and actually solicited financial support. Their first monthly newsletter was called *Send Us All Your Money* and listed reasons that readers should do just that.[42] Their underground comic *The Being Bag* (1966)—the first of its kind—was created with the intent of selling subscriptions nationwide. Even Drop City's collective work of art, *The Ultimate Painting* (1966), a giant, spinning, circular painting (Figure 1.4), was shown at the Brooklyn Museum with a price tag of $60,000.[43] The Dropper bulletin that appeared in a 1967 issue of the *Boston Avatar* stated, with an address to which donations could be sent:

We want to use everything, new, junk, good, bad, we want to be able to make limitless things. We want TV videotape recorders and cameras. We want computers and miles of color film and elaborate cine cameras and tape decks and amps and echo-chambers and everywhere. We want millionaire patrons. We want the most up-to-date equipment in the world to make our things. We want an atomic reactor.[44]

Over the years, the collective took their Droppings on the road in hopes of making money. Visiting community colleges and other youth enclaves, they attempted to "turn on" audiences and make a bit of cash. With the completion of the Theater Dome in 1967, Droppers began organizing Droppings on-site that were open to the public. Inspired by the Be-Ins in San Francisco and Central Park, Drop City began marketing itself in alternative newspapers as a stopover between coasts and for their 1967 Joy Festival promised ninety-six hours of "mind-blowing freak out."[45]

During Drop City's middle years hundreds of young people flocked to the commune for a night, a weekend, or a year at a time. By 1967, their open-door policy was irreversible, thanks in part to a *Time* magazine cover story, and the Droppers were forced to shift their focus from art making to the provision of care and entertainment for accumulating dropouts.[46] This stream of visitors bankrupted Drop City's delicate subsistence and led to the community's eventual demise. The Droppers' parasitic practice could not support itself and the onslaught of hippie pests; the trash pile was not that plentiful. And so Drop City was abandoned to the dropouts, and it subsequently crumbled.

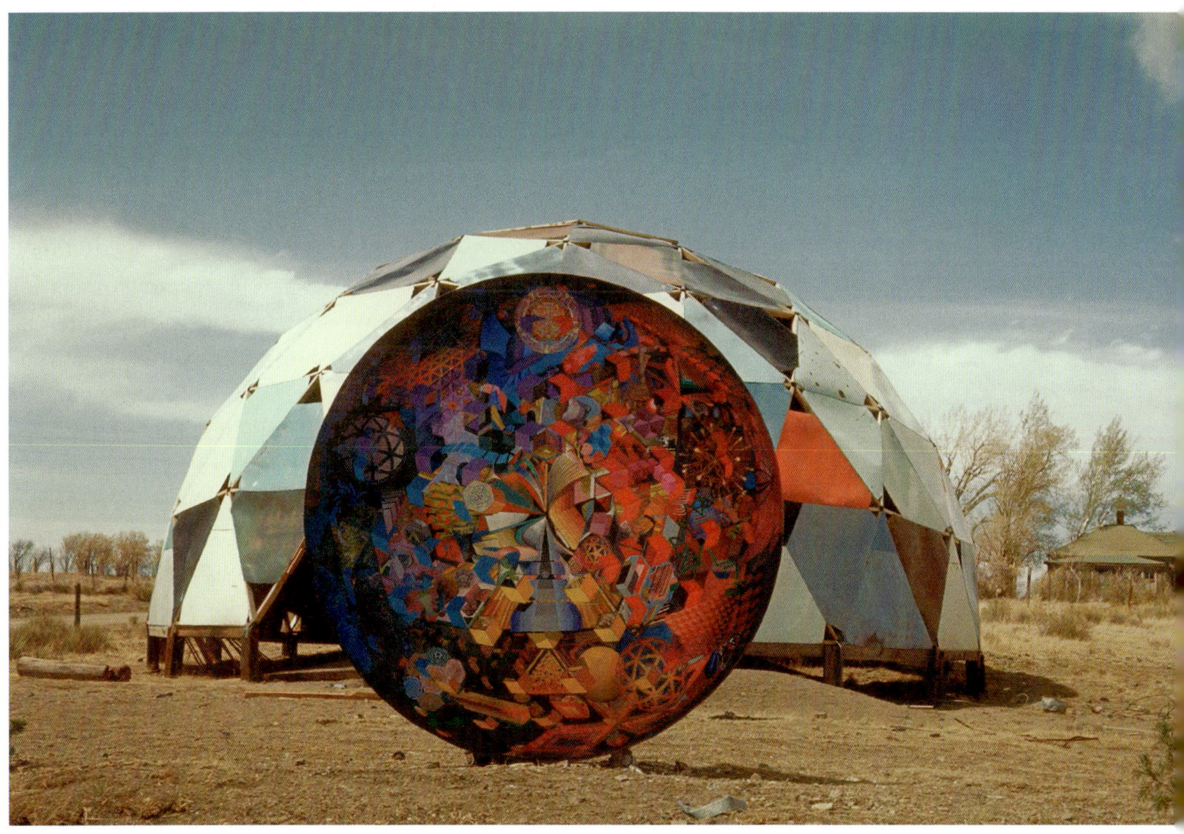

   HOW TO BUILD A COMMUNE

NEW FRONTIERS

After the Summer of Love, many of the urban countercultural centers had deteriorated into a squalid haven of drugs and depression. As the Beatles' George Harrison remarked, "You know, I went to Haight-Ashbury, expecting it to be this brilliant place, and it was just full of horrible, spotty, dropout kids on drugs."[47] With the escalation of race riots and violent protests across the country, cities lost their appeal for many counterculture seekers. As one rural commune dweller said, "A lot of us used to live in the Haight-Ashbury. You had to shoot speed just to survive in a scene like that. . . . The city is doomed. Those who can get it together on the land will be the survivors."[48]

"The key issue . . . is LAND," proclaimed Timothy Leary, and for the thousands of hippies and counterculturalists that relocated to the Southwest, this was certainly true.[49] Not only was land inexpensive, but it also resembled a kind of nowhere, a place to explore and experiment outside of rules, institutions, and watchful eyes. The Southwest was and still is home to the most advanced yet secretive experiments by the U.S. military industrial complex; indeed, it is a proving ground for a variety of large-scale experiments. Many believed that the "Outlaw Area" envisioned by Stewart Brand was to be found in southern Colorado or northern New Mexico where Native Americans, Latinos, Hispanics, cowboys, and spiritual mystics lived close to the earth and with fifty-mile vistas. It was widely believed that there were no more frontiers, and that open space must be claimed in the hinterlands for the "Underground States of America."[50] As New Age pioneers, commune builders carved out what they believed to be a better reality through homesteading acts that brought them together as community and also back to the land.

Returning to the essentials of daily life was seen as revolutionary to many sixties-era communards. One could change the world by making her own candles or growing her own food. Scrapping the system, dropping out, or "starting from scratch" was—although often mundane, quiet, slow, even naive in its manifestation—seen as fundamental to a new world order. These were not necessarily the same sixties radicals who were marching in the streets or bombing police and prison buildings. As one commune builder asks, "How many people here could build a car? How many could refine gas? Could you take care of yourself on the lowest, simplest level? Before we go solving the world's problems I think it's important to know right where we are on this ground."[51] For this brand of radical, the revolution started at home on a very micro level.

By starting with a primitive goat pasture and by building Drop City themselves (there were no contractors or subcontractors), the Droppers implemented basic, do-it-yourself building technologies. By revisiting the nuts and bolts of everyday life, Droppers learned to survive through improvisation. If nothing else, they learned how to drive a nail, how to stretch a can of beans, how to provide shelter for oneself, how to make decisions without a leader. While these small initiatives do not neces-

sarily constitute a new society, they are foundational activities and, therefore, a place to start. As the philosophy of the Situationists illuminated,
"the modern world must learn what it already knows, become what it
already is, by means of a great work of exorcism, by conscious practice.
One can escape from the commonplace only by manhandling it, mas-
tering it, steeping it in dreams."[52] Drop City evidenced an imaginative
reinvention of daily life and was a testing ground for the technologies
and ideologies that influenced back-to-the-land practices that proliferated
in hundreds of hip communes in the late sixties.

OFF THE GRID AND ON THE NET

With the formation of Libre, New Buffalo, the Lower Farm, Five Star,
Morning Star East, the Hog Farm, the Lama Foundation, and up to twenty-
some other communes, the Southwest became a set of tourist destinations for the comparative witness of hippies in action.[53] As the number
of communes grew, a sense of an emergent counterculture gained momentum. The circulation of ideas—especially about construction technologies and tips for newcomers living in the desert—was paramount to
creating a somewhat united "civilization."

Information exchange was aided by the development of the nation's
interstate network (which was completed in the late 1960s), encouraging
road trips and cross-country travel. Richard Fairfield, publisher of the
Modern Utopian, a journal founded to report on the commune movement,
was one of many onlookers who visited Drop City and the southwestern
communes as a firsthand witness, creating a literature and a living network of people and practices.

Ideas were shared through extended visits, newsletters, video collectives, public events, and traveling sideshows. There was a certain non-
chalant but earnest approach to information sharing among the sixties
counterculture. For instance, when Drop City neighbors Linda and Dean
Fleming left the area with commune member Peter Rabbit to found Libre
in 1968, Clark Richert gifted them with dome-building plans scrawled
on a piece of scrap paper. With little more than an equation and a map
of interlocking triangles, the Libreans established their new communal
site with a geodesic dome on their land.[54] In many such cases a notion
or philosophy, even an architectural design, was half-communicated, half-
understood, and half-implemented, yet this partial transmission often
proved to be just enough with personal innovation filling in the gaps.

Underground magazines and newsletters like the *Whole Earth Catalog*
and the *Modern Utopian* aimed to encourage grassroots connectivity by
linking people, ideas, products, and places. Publications like Baer's *Dome
Cookbook,* the infamous *Anarchist Cookbook,* and Antfarm's *Inflatocookbook* introduced new technologies and articulated in aesthetic terms the
counterculture's foundational worldview.[55] Providing "access to tools"
through do-it-yourself instruction manuals—often with hand-drawn
diagrams and personal insights—these grassroots information networks

were as dedicated to style and methodology as they were to content. As is stated in the first issue of *Radical Software,* the voice of the video collective Raindance, "Our species will survive neither by totally rejecting nor unconditionally embracing technology—but by humanizing it; by allowing people access to the informational tools they need to shape and reassert control over their lives."[56] Through collaborative zome building, latrine digging, and the creation of multimedia artwork, the Droppers tested a variety of technologies and modified or humanized them to suit their needs. As an experimental art center and counterculture refuge, Drop City did not have the most sophisticated equipment, but it gave open access to a steadily growing toolbox of situations, techniques, collaborators, and perspectives, which, in turn, cultivated other temporary nodes in a growing web of possibility.

One event that sought to share this toolbox of people and ideas was the ALLOY conference, organized by Steve Baer with Barry Hickman, March 20–23, 1969. It was a weekend event conducted at an abandoned tile factory near La Luz, New Mexico, between the Trinity bomb site and the Mescalero Apache reservation and was framed as a conference on new building technologies. Participants were welcomed from a variety of local and national communes and the *Whole Earth Catalog* was invited to report on the weekend's events. Discussion at ALLOY ranged from concrete to cardboard to 3M tape to dope to evolution to magic. It entertained questions like, "What sort of research do we do to use the technology in order to improve our minds?" Interestingly, the article that appeared in the *Last Whole Earth Catalog* evidences the complexity of this media moment, the various ways that information was reported and received, and the vagaries associated with building a new society.[57] The seven-page spread is a smattering of photographs and unattributed quotes. Very little of the information in the article is useful or cited, and the piece functions more as testament to the fact that something happened, that people attended, and that a particular spirit was in the air. This manner of stylistically relaying incomplete information is perhaps exemplary of the moment's priorities. Although inspired by the idea of an information network, the connections being made were primarily social, ideological, aesthetic. Baer and Fuller may have imagined the Droppers as leaders of a design science revolution, but in the end their major contribution was not scientific or mathematic—it was cultural.

ART OF THE OUTLAW AREA

Since the 1960s, the art world has seen a proliferation of practices, institutions, spaces, and participants who have taken the rhetoric of the counterculture into the microcosm of art and then back out into the realm of daily life. Today, artists plant gardens, produce newspapers, operate free universities, organize protests, design shelters and alternative economies, and they call it art practice. This wave of art that curator Nato Thompson has described as "participatory, embodied, tactical, interventionist, community-based, didactic, relational, social, and dialogical" is interdisciplinary in nature and baffling in its analysis, as it is often process oriented and does not necessarily produce an object.[58] Continuing the project of merging art and life, recent art and artists attempt to activate passive spectatorship through the physical and collaborative participation of audiences and through the construction of situations that produce new social relationships and thus new social realities.

Nicolas Bourriaud, contemporary art curator and critic, claims that "the role of artworks is no longer to form imaginary and utopian realities, but to actually be ways of living and models of action within the existing real, whatever scale chosen by the artist."[59] He describes this living model as "a set of artistic practices which take as their theoretical and practical point of departure the whole of human relations and their social context, rather than an independent and private space."[60] I would argue that this notion of expansive, interdisciplinary, and collectively produced art was exactly the project under way at Drop City and its neighboring southwestern communes. The influence of the counterculture on contemporary art practice is deserving of a closer look, yet it is clear that the work of a vanguard of artists associated with participatory or relational aesthetics closely resembles the do-it-yourself, self-determined, open-ended, utopian, and expanded practices developed during the 1960s at places like Drop City.

Drop City lasted seven years—a short time by society's standards, but long lasting as an artwork. It was a collaborative, open-ended experiment initiated by artists who aimed to revolutionize everyday life and, through both its successes and failures, cultivated a vernacular for the communal counterculture. While Drop City may not be a model for future societies or even for communal living, it was a proving ground for forms of architecture, for scrounging practices, and for expanded notions of art. With its open-door policy and connection to emergent networks, Drop City was essential in developing the relationships and information that, in turn, built the southwestern communes that came to define an essential element of the American Left.

It is projects like Drop City that effectively blur the boundaries between art practice and lived experience, that create interstitial, momentary testing grounds for new possibilities. The creation of these "temporary autonomous zones" is essential if art is to remain vibrant and culture wild and free.[61] As art and life continue to merge in fascinating ways, it is worthwhile to recall Drop City as a provocative social and physical experiment that proved that life in America can be lived differently.

NOTES

1. Gene Bernofsky, phone interview with the author, 17 October 2006.
2. Timothy Miller, *The 60s Communes: Hippies and Beyond* (Syracuse, N.Y.: Syracuse University Press, 1999), xviii–xix. Miller cites a 1970 *New York Times* article as the widely quoted authority on this number. He goes on to outline other speculations (ranging from one thousand to fifty thousand communes), arguing the difficulty of quantifying this sudden phenomenon composed of oftentimes short-lived communal experiments.
3. Ibid., 31–32.
4. Alastair Gordon, *Spaced Out: Radical Environments of the Psychedelic Sixties* (New York: Rizzoli International, 2008), 145–53.
5. Roberta Price, email correspondence with the author, 5 November 2009.
6. Bill Voyd, "Funk Architecture," in Paul Oliver, ed., *Shelter and Society* (New York: Praeger, 1969), 156.
7. Quoted in Gordon, *Spaced Out*, 151.
8. G. Bernofsky, interview.
9. Allan Kaprow, *Essays on the Blurring of Art and Life*, ed. Jeff Kelley (Berkeley: University of California Press, 1993), xxviii.
10. G. Bernofsky, interview.
11. Kaprow, *Essays on the Blurring of Art and Life*, xxix.
12. G. Bernofsky, interview.
13. Henri Lefebvre, *Critique of Everyday Life, vol. 2: Foundations for a Sociology of the Everyday*, trans. John Moore (London and New York: Verso, 2002).
14. Stewart Home, *The Assault on Culture: Utopian Currents from Lettrisme to Class War* (Stirling, Scotland: AK Press, 1991), 5–6.
15. Quoted in Gordon, *Spaced Out*, 170.
16. Ted Purves, *What We Want Is Free: Generosity and Exchange in Recent Art* (New York: SUNY Press, 2005), 34–35.
17. Will Bradley, "Let It Grow," *Frieze* (October 2005): 189–90.
18. G. Bernofsky, interview.
19. Ibid.
20. David E. James, *Stan Brakhage: Filmmaker* (New York: Temple University Press, 2005).
21. Gene Youngblood, *Expanded Cinema* (New York: Dutton, 1970), 41.
22. Will Bradley, *Radical Software; or, The Post-competitive, Comparative Game of a Free Culture* (San Francisco: CCA Wattis Institute, 2006).
23. Gordon, *Spaced Out*, 20.
24. Marshall McLuhan, *Understanding Media: The Extensions of Man* (New York: McGraw-Hill, 1964).
25. G. Bernofsky, interview.
26. Quoted in Oliver, *Shelter and Society*, 160.
27. Quoted in Gordon, *Spaced Out*, 190.
28. "Values in Conflict 'No Right to Be Poor' Colorado's Drop City," *Colorado Heritage* (n.d.), 16.
29. Peter Rabbit, *Drop City* (New York: Olympia Press, 1971), 20.
30. Albin Wagner (Peter Rabbit), *Boston Avatar*, 4–18 August 1967, 7.
31. Dolores Hayden, *Seven American Utopias: The Architecture of Communitarian Socialism, 1790–1975* (Cambridge, Mass.: MIT Press, 1976), 321.
32. Quoted in Oliver, *Shelter and Society*, 158.
33. Steve Baer, *Dome Cookbook* (Corrales, N.M.: Lama Foundation, 1968).
34. Rabbit, *Drop City*, 45.
35. Ibid., 148.
36. Ibid., 46. Although this story is part of Drop City mythology, its truth has been a subject of debate by many Droppers.
37. Julie Stephens, *Anti-disciplinary Protest: Sixties Radicalism and Postmodernism* (Cambridge: Cambridge University Press, 1998), 42–47.
38. Quoted in ibid., 43.
39. Murray Bookchin, *Post-scarcity Anarchism* (Edinburgh: AK Press, 2004), viii.
40. Morgan Lawhon, "Drop City Places Art over Hunger," *Denver Post*, 6 August 1967.
41. Ibid.
42. Rabbit, *Drop City*, 148.
43. G. Bernofsky, interview.
44. Albin Wagner, "Drop City: A Total Living Environment," *Boston Avatar*, 4–18 August 1967.
45. "Drop City Joy Festival," *Burning World Review* (June 1967): 4.
46. "The Hippies," *Time*, 3 July 1967.
47. *The Beatles Anthology*, DVD, directed by Bob Smeaton (Los Angeles: Capital, 2003).
48. Richard Fairfield, *Communes USA: A Personal Tour* (Baltimore: Penguin, 1972), 170.
49. Quoted in Miller, *The 60s Communes*, 92.
50. Gordon, *Spaced Out*, 139–46.
51. Stewart Brand, ed., *The Last Whole Earth Catalog* (Menlo Park, Calif.: Portola Institute, 1971), 116.
52. Raoul Vaneigem, *The Revolution of Everyday Life* (1967), http://library.nothingness.org/articles/SI/en/pub_contents/5.
53. Fairfield, *Communes USA*.
54. Linda Fleming, interview with the author, San Francisco, 21 February 2007.
55. William Powell, *The Anarchist Cookbook* (n.p.: Lyle Stuart, 1970); Antfarm, *Inflatocookbook* (Sausalito, Calif.: RIP Press, 1970).
56. Bradley, *Radical Software*.
57. Brand, *Whole Earth Catalog*, 111–17.
58. Nato Thompson, "The Creative Time Summit: Revolutions in Public Practice," New York, 23–24 October 2009, 3. Program brochure.
59. Nicolas Bourriaud, *Relational Aesthetics* (Paris: La Presses du réel, 2002), 13.
60. Ibid., 113.
61. Hakim Bey, *TAZ: The Temporary Autonomous Zone, Ontological Anarchy, Poetic Terrorism* (Brooklyn: Autonomedia Anti-Copyright, 1985).

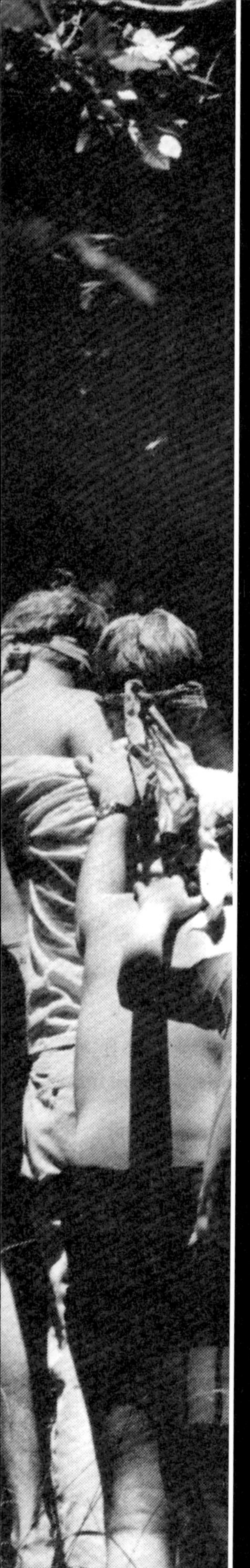

CHAPTER 2
COLLECTIVE MOVEMENT: ANNA AND LAWRENCE HALPRIN'S JOINT WORKSHOPS

Eva J. Friedberg

Young artists today need no longer say, "I am a painter" or "a poet" or "a dancer."
They are simply "artists." All of life will be open to them. They will discover out
of the ordinary things the meaning of ordinariness. They will not try to make them
extraordinary but will only state their real meaning. But out of nothing they will
devise the extraordinary and then maybe nothingness as well. People will be
delighted or horrified, critics will be confused or amused, but these, I am certain,
wil be the alchemies of the 1960s.

—Allan Kaprow, "The Legacy of Jackson Pollock"

An environment is in fact simply a theatre for action and interaction to occur.
The physical features may be programmed but the activities . . . are not. The
real interaction is like a "happening" in that the events and their sequences are
non-programmed but occur as a result of the constraints by the environment.

—Lawrence Halprin, *Notebooks 1959-1971*

According to Allan Kaprow's rendering of the legacy of Jackson Pollock, the artist of the mid-1950s and 1960s was entering into uncharted territory. Instead of working within the confines of conventional form and media, Kaprow encouraged the unbound artist to "become preoccupied with and even dazzled by the space and objects of our everyday life."[1] This call was received by artists working across the art world, and one can arguably include husband and wife collaborators Anna[2] and Lawrence Halprin among the liberated about whom Kaprow spoke. Though trained in seemingly disparate fields—Anna in modern dance and Lawrence in landscape architecture—their educational backgrounds and artistic orientations provided them with the permission to feed off of and nurture the intersections of their separate arts.[3] In 1966 their increasingly intertwined practices led the couple to collaborate on the creation of two workshops that took place in the summers of 1966 and 1968 that combined dance, sensory exploration, design, architecture, and theories of creativity. The workshops, the topic of this essay, were important contributions to the counterculture of the 1960s and its distinctive approach to the blurring of art and life called for by Kaprow.

By the time Kaprow's essay was published in 1958, the Halprins had been living in San Francisco for more than a decade. And while they may have been geographically marginalized from the center of the avant-garde world of Kaprow and other New York–based performers, they were connected to the era of Happenings and expanded theater by way of their own experiments in dance and architecture, which similarly drew on alternative creative processes and everyday experience. In addition, while they claimed to have valued the isolation that their location provided for them, they developed and maintained cross-country professional and personal relationships with such East Coast–based artists as Merce Cunningham, John Cage, La Monte Young, and Kaprow. As their work received recognition, they began to forge friendships and intellectual relationships with other avant-garde artists of the time and also began to influence a new generation of future artists and designers throughout the United States.[4]

As Jeff Kelley notes in his introduction to Kaprow's anthology *Essays on the Blurring of Art and Life,* the artists of Kaprow's generation "wanted a 'new concrete art' to replace the old abstract order," which was represented by the taste and critical writing of formalist critics such as Clement Greenberg.[5] The values inherited from the "proscriptive climate enforced by formalist art critics" were open to challenge in this period, allowing for the emergence of new audiences, mediums, and artistic forms.[6] For Kaprow and others, the incorporation of everyday experience into art was central to challenging the formalist privileging of the autonomous, rigorously self-referential art object promoted by formalism. On this point, Kelley elaborates on Kaprow: "For him the modernist practice of art is more than the production of artworks; it also involves the artist's disciplined effort to observe, engage, and interpret the processes of living, which are themselves as meaningful as most art, and certainly more grounded in common experience."[7] As I demonstrate in this essay, both of the Halprins were interested in pushing the boundaries of their own artistic practices, and their experiments in this regard represent a distinctive, particularly literal carrying out of Kaprow's theorization of art into life that characterized many countercultural projects designed to transform the individual and subsequently society at large.

THE FOUNDING OF A PARTNERSHIP

In the decade leading up to "Experiments in Environment," Lawrence Halprin established his architectural practice in San Francisco through a steady flow of commissions from private residences to public buildings, including schools, churches, and hospitals. Anna had opened a studio in the city where she taught dance and choreographed her own work.[8] In their daily life they continued to share an ongoing exchange of ideas, concerns, and explorations into artistic practice. "In their early years together," recalls Anna's biographer, Janice Ross, "the Halprins were very open about the stimulation and insight each gained from the other's work."[9] Lawrence was heavily influenced by Anna's experiments in dance, which increasingly incorporated task-based movements and improvisation, and she in turn benefited from Lawrence's growing interest in the movement of bodies through gardens and city space. Both artists found a shared interest in the actions and movements of everyday life. For Anna, dance was a method to discover these movements and to celebrate them, while for Lawrence, environmental design helped build the "stage set" for these actions to take place. The Halprins' 1966 and 1968 summer workshops, "Experiments in Environment," integrated the improvisatory, communicative, participatory, and collaborative elements of their cross-fertilized practices.

For four weeks during these two summers, various workshop leaders, including the Halprins, led the participating architects and dancers through a series of exercises situated in three outdoor locations: on the coast of Sea Ranch in Sonoma County, in the woodlands surrounding Mount Tamalpais in Marin County, and in urban San Francisco.[10] The workshop themes of kinetic environment and community supported the objectives of triggering environmental and physical self-awareness, served the Halprins' professional interests, and provided participants with an innovative method to explore their creative potential. The workshops were covered by professional journals such as *Progressive Architecture* and *Dance Magazine* and in the local California press, which, in contrast to these journals, presented the projects as oddities of the Bay Area countercultural movement.[11]

Through an analysis of the workshops themselves, I frame the activities of "Experiments in Environment" within the larger world of the avant-garde, including the intermedia experience-based performances, or Happenings, of Kaprow; Fluxus performances; the Judson Dance Theater;

and John Cage's "chance music" and accompanying performances.[12] The
elements of such event-based performance work included indetermin-
ancy, tasks, event scores, the nontraditional art environment, and the
participatory audience. In addition to incorporating many of these elements,
the Halprins' workshops demonstrated their own identification with—
and interpretation of—countercultural art and politics of the 1960s.
Their location in the San Francisco Bay Area during this time was significant to their artistic embrace of participation and community beyond
that imagined or carried out by Kaprow and other members of the avant-
garde. Furthermore, they felt free to integrate, in a characteristically
California modality, the influences of nature, spirituality, and ritual into
their work, concerns largely absent from the work of their New York—
based peers in the art world.[13]

THE FINE SENSE OF DANCE

From the early days of his career Lawrence cared deeply about the social
and environmental responsibilities inherent to the practice of landscape
architecture. Projects completed during his tenure as a young landscape
architect in the firm of Thomas Church between 1945 and 1949 were
formative to his understanding of the potential of the landscaped environment to influence social relationships and human interactions. Through
his commissions for private residential gardens, Lawrence began to
put his ideas about the social dimensions of landscape architecture
into practice.[14]

Anna's experiments in dance and movement impacted Lawrence's
conceptualization of the movement of people through his built designs
as "performance." In 1949 he contributed an article, "The Choreography
of Gardens," to *Impulse Dance Magazine,* an annual published by the
Halprin-Lathrop dance studio established in 1948. Lawrence's article
included a self-reflective statement on the current state of his work,
and a description of his ideas about contemporary landscape architecture
theory and its relationship to dance. In it he claims that his gardens
are "like stage sets for a dance in that they are designed to determine
the movement of the people in them."[15]

In "Choreography" Lawrence contrasts the stage-set theory of garden
design to formal garden design characterized by static composition and
thus lacking "any real sense of participation."[16] He proposed that a garden
flows "easily in patterns of terraces and paths, varying its texture of
paving underfoot, and its foliage backgrounds, and fences" so that it can
"influence people's movement patterns through its spaces taking on the
fine sense of dance."[17] "Choreography" not only revealed the exchange of
intellectual ideas between Anna and Lawrence about the way nature and
design influenced human behavior, but also that they were beginning to
think about art and the creative process as taking place in a wider arena—
now expanded outside of their individual fields and into the spaces of
everyday life. Lawrence concluded in the article that "everyday surround-

ings have tremendous importance in their influence on our emotional
lives," and that

> the art process must be a total and continuing experience rather than compart-
> mented into museums, theatres, and symphony concerts. If the kinesthetic sense
> is satisfied at a dance concert and left dormant during the week we are only half alive.
> But if it can be cultivated and encouraged in our daily lives in garden and house . . .
> our lives can be given the continuous sense of dance.[18]

In this passage, Lawrence's emphasis on art as a "total and continuing
experience" marks his practice (and, as we shall see, the Halprins' collaborative workshops) as an attempt to collapse the boundary between
art and life. As opposed to the embrace of art into life by the avant-garde,
approached as a conceptual goal and largely carried out through the
gallery or museum setting, the art form that results from the collapse
of boundaries in Lawrence's work (as well as Anna's) is more accurately
defined as lifestyle in the sense that it was directed toward changing
people's everyday lives by way of a heightened consciousness of the body.
In contrast to Kaprow's call to artists that began this essay, the Halprins'
concerns addressed not only the artist but a much wider and more inclusive audience, from children to the elderly, professional to amateur,
educated to unskilled, across the economic scale. All, in their view, could
benefit from the exploration of one's creative capabilities through the
incorporation of aesthetic experience into everyday existence.

Anna's experiments in dance, especially her search for an organic
movement, intersected with Lawrence's interest in fostering the "natural"
activity or movement of the user. Finding herself moving further and
further away from her modern dance training, she began to seek new
sources of inspiration for her practice, including improvisational technique. Anna called the use of improvisation "organic choreography" and
opposed it to "representational choreography," and she utilized it as a
tool to generate new material and a radical style of dance unfettered by
the history and conventions of modern dance.[19] As she explains, experiments with improvisation in her classes and workshops were meant to
activate the "subconscious" stages of human movement. In a 1962 interview with Yvonne Rainer she elaborated on these early exercises: "The
purpose of the improvisation was not self-expression. I was trying to get
at subconscious areas, so things would happen in an unpredictable way.
I was trying to eliminate stereotyped ways of reacting. Improvisation was
used to release things that were blocked off because we were traditional
modern dancers."[20] Often times, in order to push her dancers toward
new discoveries, Anna would put them in defined situations or locations,
combining improvisation with her growing interest in the natural or
built environment. In a public outdoor improvisation, *People on a Slant,*
her dancers performed on the sidewalk near their Union Street studio
attempting to keep their bodies straight against the incline of the hill as

they ascended it.[21] The dancers played with gravity and the sensations experienced from pulling their body in the opposite direction of force. Anna later commented on this attempt: "I was trying to break down patterned movement, to find actions uncontaminated with dance."[22] These movements that had not been "contaminated with dance" were everyday motions, tasks, and actions. In an attempt to undo the historical processes that had estranged dance from natural or repetitive everyday movement, Anna's dancers participated in a type of free association.

During studio exercises Anna began to assign her dancers tasks in order to help them become acutely aware of their bodies. These tasks might have included opening and shutting a door, picking up an object, or interacting with other props and dancers. Anna had a background in anatomy that helped her dancers think about the body's construction in correlation to the movements they discovered from completing these tasks. As Anna elaborated to Rainer in the 1962 interview, "Doing a task created an attitude that would bring the movement quality into another kind of reality. It was devoid of a certain kind of introspection."[23] Through these task exercises Anna and her dancers began to ritualize and explore common movements. Historian Janice Ross calls this exploration of movement "urban ritual," both ordinary and sacred at the same time.[24] Arguably, however, task movements were less about making the body sacred, and more about making evident the very ordinary movements of everyday life as worthy of exploration through dance.

Based on a similar interest in everyday passage through space, Lawrence's gardens were designed to engage the body. From geometric manipulations of pathways that directed movement to open platforms, which created spaces for spontaneous interactions, Lawrence's gardens were experimental playing fields for the user/performer. While they continued to experiment with new processes for generating movement, both Anna and Lawrence also explored new possibilities for spaces for performance. Anna moved her dancers into the theater aisles, out onto the street, and even onto the ceilings of event spaces, while Lawrence directed the movement in his gardens to take place dynamically throughout the entire space. In his *Notebooks* Lawrence observes: "An environment is in fact simply a theatre for action and interaction to occur."[25] Together they recognized how their respective practices were based on similar disciplinary relationships between performer-spectator and designer-user, which they aimed to revolutionize.

Avant-garde artists such as the Dadaists had experimented with adopting public space as the stage for performance in the early twentieth century, and thus Anna's decision to step out from the confines of the proscenium arch in traditional theater space was not unprecedented. However, for the Halprins understanding the environment as a "theatre for action" meant more than simply relocating the practice of theater (or dance) into the open air. Rather, it suggested that the activities of everyday life could be experienced as artful, as a reflexive exploration of one's relationship to the total environment. Ideally, such an exploration could lead to "free[ing] oneself from 'choices' already predetermined by ideology and social convention."[26]

The Halprins' articulation of the space of everyday life as theater not only brings the question of aesthetics to the realm of the ordinary but also demands that we reimagine the relationship between designer and user, or choreographer and audience. The designer becomes the choreographer and the user the performer; and the status of audience ideally disappears entirely. For the Halprins, this collapse of boundaries—between disciplines, artist and audience, and art and life—through participation was the ultimate goal of their collaborative practice. In reworking the traditional power relationships between audience, performer, and choreographer, traditional aesthetic relationships such as that between artist and audience can also be understood as a set of power relations that the Halprins, like their East Coast peers, were investigating. Such relationships had been under scrutiny by the New York avant-garde for some time. In John Cage's most famous piece, 4'33", instead of a traditional musical composition, the audience is treated to four minutes and thirty-three seconds of "silence."[27] A cough from the audience, the rustling of a jacket, or the scraping of a chair, instead, becomes the musical performance. In a performance of his compositions *Water Walk* on the television show *I've Got a Secret,* Cage's use of unusual instruments such as a water pitcher, a radio, and a bathtub brought some audience members to nervous laughter.[28] Undoubtedly, these instances where the audience affects the outcome of the piece have significance for the disciplinary structure of traditional performance methods in a number of different mediums and what it means for them to be challenged.

Art historian Branden Joseph has considered the work of Cage in this regard with implications for the work of the Halprins. Joseph argues: "To disarticulate [performer and spectator] as necessary, bi-univocal relations meant that neither performer nor audience member had to be subservient to the will of another; they could instead work from their own centers, not by doing whatever they want, but nonetheless without being 'pushed,' as Cage put it, in any one direction."[29] Joseph's interpretation of Cage's work with audience and performer here is useful for understanding how the Halprins similarly questioned power relations in their work, especially his suggestion that the disarticulation of traditional audience-performer relationships was "political." He continues: "The breakdown or problematizing of formal and disciplinary distinctions was [for Cage, an avowed anarchist] . . . an unavoidable *political* question. Indeed it was a directly political question" because for him the enforcement of an artist's idea was an "imposition of power," which rendered aesthetic form as politics.[30] The Halprins' cross-disciplinary work, which also problematized formal and disciplinary boundaries, contributed to the larger art world's questioning of the status of the work of art as certain or knowable. However, the political context that framed the Halprins' dissolution of boundaries between practices or the hierarchical relations between artist and audience was quite different from that informing Cage's questioning of medium specificity and its implications for artistic practice. For the Halprins that context was the cultural radicalism of public protest in the Bay Area in the 1960s.

Cultural historian Bradford D. Martin has recognized the confluence of public performance and politics in the 1960s in his definition of public performance as a "self-conscious, stylized tactic of staging songs, plays, parades, protests, and other spectacles in public spaces where no admission is charged and spectators are often invited to participate, and it conveys symbolic messages about social and political issues to audiences who might not have encountered them in more traditional venues."[31] San Francisco of the 1960s was an epicenter of such public performances. In addition to antiwar rallies, the Bay Area was host to the public performances of the guerrilla theaters the San Francisco Mime Troupe and the Diggers, and other forms of participatory encounters including Be-Ins, Acid Tests, and rock concerts. As Martin argues, such groups and events redefined the use of pubic space and broadened the definition of activism to include "more symbolic, but also more immediate ways of 'doing politics' than conventional political protest."[32]

Likewise, the Halprins' work politicized the performance of the everyday through the disciplines of architecture and dance. Lawrence's plazas such as the Auditorium Forecourt Plaza in Portland, Oregon, built in the 1960s, used platforms, waterfalls, and terraces to engage the user in a multisensory environment. The plaza, with its powerful cascading fountain, invigorated the user and encouraged forms of participation with his or her environment that were unorthodox at the time (for example, bathing in the fountain, climbing, or welcoming public gatherings within its confines). This type of open-ended design echoed the countercultural call for liberation from the regulation of social interaction as a method for achieving social change. Anna's work, which similarly sought to release or loosen the body, also carried political implications in the way it called into question social roles played out through the body or prohibitions surrounding its display, especially in the case of nudity.

SCORING THE SELF AND THE NATURAL ENVIRONMENT

The Halprins shared a belief in the transformative power of nature in the liberation of the self. Certainly, their day-to-day surroundings—their home in Marin County, Anna's outdoor dance studio in the woods on their property, and their time spent at Sea Ranch on the Sonoma Coast—had a profound effect on their conceptualization of a "natural" or organic artistic practice. Beyond their immediate surroundings, however, the search for the natural and its relationship to actual nature has been characterized by many present in the Bay Area in the 1960s as being "in the air."[33] In addition to a rising interest in participatory politics, the decade also witnessed the birth of the modern environmental movement, and many members of the counterculture actively participated in a search for decontaminated possibilities of urban living. In a world bombarded with warnings about chemical weapons, nuclear annihilation, increased pollution, and rising urban crime and violence, members of the counterculture combined political and social concerns with ecological ones. Motivated at least partially by these realities, artists of the counterculture bound together a desire for "eco-utopia" and an exploration of the subjective self.[34] Complementary to the decontamination of the external environment, the subject would look internally toward a proper cultivation and care of the self. The Halprins' introduction of collaborative creative workshops in the summers of 1966 and 1968 provided opportunities for young artists to experiment in ways that were designed to transform the self, much like Michel Foucault's theory in *Technologies of the Self*: "Permit[ting] individuals to effect by their own means or with the help of others a certain number of operations on their own bodies and souls, thoughts, conduct, and way of being, so as to transform them in order to attain a certain state of happiness, purity, wisdom, perfection, or immortality."[35]

The sexual liberation of the 1960s and the use of the body as a means of political performance and protest can be understood as a historical undoing as well as a revolutionary method for redefining the self. In the 1960s and 1970s artist bodies and activist bodies reversed the structure of "biopolitics" and power that Foucault introduced in his work on technologies of the self. Rather than being the source of attack and manipulation, the body became a tool and a method for achieving individual transformation that had the potential to effect social change. For the Halprins, their collaborative practice shaped through the exercises of self-knowledge and cultivation of individual creativity led to a liberation from the institutions of art, conventional artistic practice, and the separation of everyday life and politics.

An important technique to achieving this self-liberation was the Halprins' use of scores. A score was a way to guide movement through time and space. It was a written directive, like the notes on a musical score, that could guide the creative process. While it seems paradoxical that it would be necessary to devise a system or language to help liberate natural and creative processes, this was in fact what their scores were meant to achieve. As Lawrence explained in 1969:

I saw scores as a way of describing all such processes in all the arts, of making process visible and thereby designing with process through scores. I saw scores also as a way of communicating these processes over time and space to other people in other places at other moments and as a vehicle to allow many people to enter into the act of creation together, *allowing* for participation, feedback, and communications.[36]

However, before he began writing scores for human interaction and self-liberation, Lawrence first observed the "ecoscore," which he witnessed in the natural environment. Ecoscores, such as the path of a creek that winds its way over rocks and sandbars and eventually carves itself into the landscape, helped him to eventually write scores for the built environment, and then for human processes. This trajectory of the development of scores as originating in natural processes is significant to the Halprins' adoption of scores in order to transform the self, exemplifying the importance of ecological processes to influence human creative practice and social change.

Initially for Lawrence, scores were a way to observe, experiment with, and design the environment. Based on his observations of the wildlife surrounding his home in Marin County, he made countless sketches of the intimate relationships between water, rock formation, and plant life. These sketches often served as the reference point for the scores that he would compose for his landscape architecture projects. In 1965 he published an article in *Progressive Architecture* calling this method "Motation."[37] Through the use of symbols, lines, and diagrams he proposed the new language of Motation as a method to score movement through time and space. In a score written for a fountain in Fort Worth, Texas, the relationship to a musical piece is striking (Figure 2.1). The sheet is divided into bars as on a musical staff. The bottom three staffs show the parts to be played by the separate components of the fountain. Following the score in time (reading from left to right), one can observe the directions written for each system of water jet, which specifies instruction on three sensory levels: aural, light, and visual. A legend on the left assigns different symbols to corresponding empirical observations for changes in the water's character, action, and surface. These include a range of characteristics from rushing water, increased force, to still, calm, and quiet streams. The top-most staff includes the final combination of

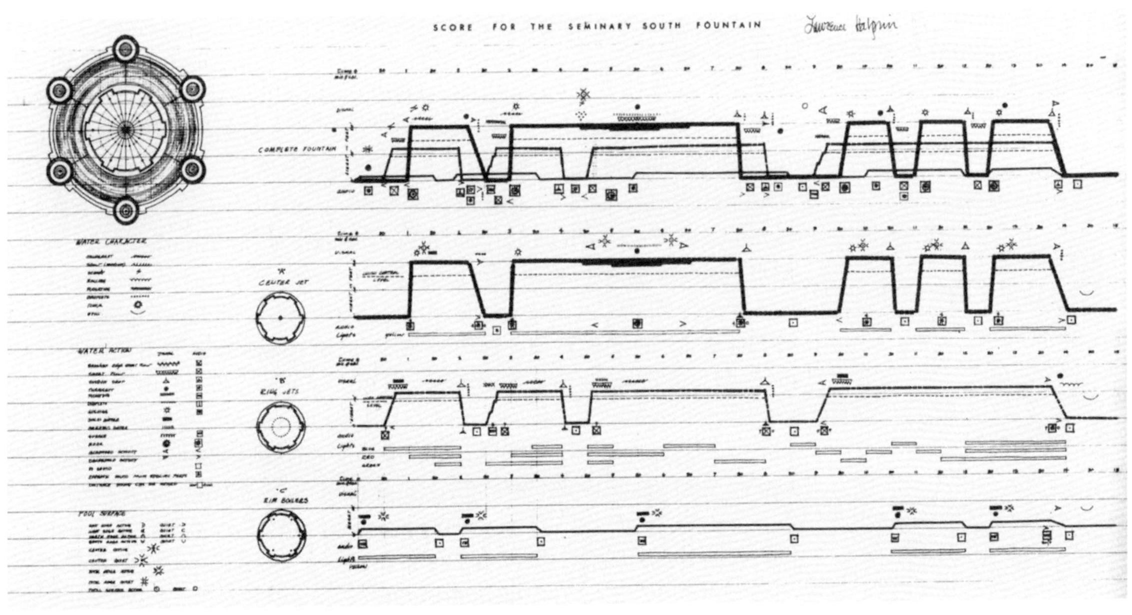

     COLLECTIVE MOVEMENT

all three performances into the final merged sequence. The result of the score was a comprehensive directive for the performance of this fountain. In this particular example, the object to be scored was a fountain; however, it was not long before Lawrence began utilizing Motation for the purpose of scoring human movement, as seen in the "Experiments in Environment" workshops of 1966 and 1968.

EXPERIMENTS IN ENVIRONMENT

As reported by *Dance Magazine* in November 1966, the Halprins decided to work together for "both choreographic and architectural reasons."[38] Anna explained that "she became interested in collaborative activity because of the recent work she [had] been doing in avant-garde dance and in that hybrid theatrical form known as the 'happening.'" To Anna, Happenings usually brought together a number of different artists from different backgrounds and mediums, but she felt that what transpired often tended to be "a mishmash." The problem, she believed, was that the artists "may not always be aware of the nature and possibilities of each other's arts." By contrast, the Halprins' summer workshops, which, like Happenings, were an effort to explore the creative process between individuals with different practices, experiences, and backgrounds, strove to meaningfully connect dance, movement, design, and architecture through the exploration of "a new range of experience."[39]

The twenty-nine dancers and fifteen architects who participated in the 1966 workshop were guided by an interdisciplinary faculty that included, along with the Halprins, architect Charles Moore, geographer Richard Reynolds, composer Morton Subotnick, cinematographer Joe Ehreth, light artist Patrick Hickey, and graphic designer Barbara Stauffacher. Together, they took turns leading exercises that comprised the heart of the workshop.[40] The variety of landscapes and environments used for these exercises (Sea Ranch, the woods of Marin County, and San Francisco) were central to the workshops, and exercises in dance and movement were designed to help the participants intensify their sensory experience of these spaces and sites. This aspect of the project was communicated through the workshop's public announcement as an essential offering: "Through bodily participation in the environment, we will investigate the mutual effect each has on the other" (Figure 2.2).[41] Another announcement from the Lawrence Halprin and Associates firm explained: "The workshop will deal with experiments in perceiving the environment. It will have no set goals. Any results will be in relation to individual responses and discoveries. Courses will not be given in the usual sense, but several areas of experimentation will be dealt with."[42] The focus was mainly physical; for the dancers, the aim was to explore how activities, objects, and space could influence their own movement, and for the architects, the goal was to free their bodies and intellect from convention and traditional design practice at the drafting board in order to encourage a "heightened spatial awareness."[43]

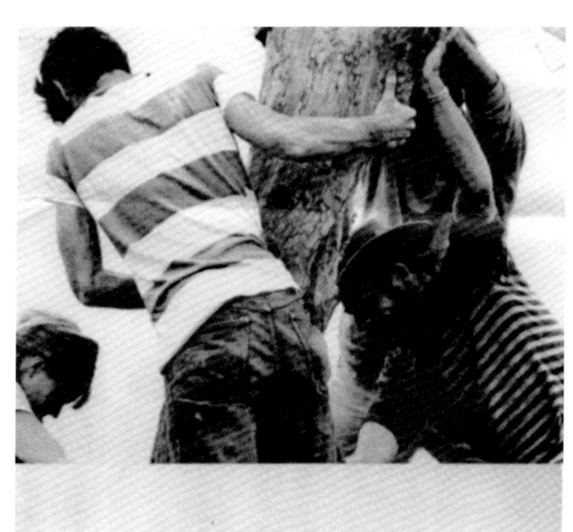

ANN AND LAWRENCE HALPRIN
ANNOUNCE
SECOND JOINT SUMMER WORKSHOP
EXPERIMENTS IN ENVIRONMENT
SAN FRANCISCO BAY AREA
20 DAYS
JULY 1 - JULY 24
FOR DANCERS AND
ENVIRONMENTAL DESIGNERS
INFORMATION AND APPLICATIONS
DESIGNERS WRITE
HALPRIN SUMMER WORKSHOP
1620 MONTGOMERY STREET
SAN FRANCISCO, CALIFORNIA 94111
DANCERS WRITE
HALPRIN SUMMER WORKSHOP
15 RAVINE WAY
KENTFIELD, CALIFORNIA

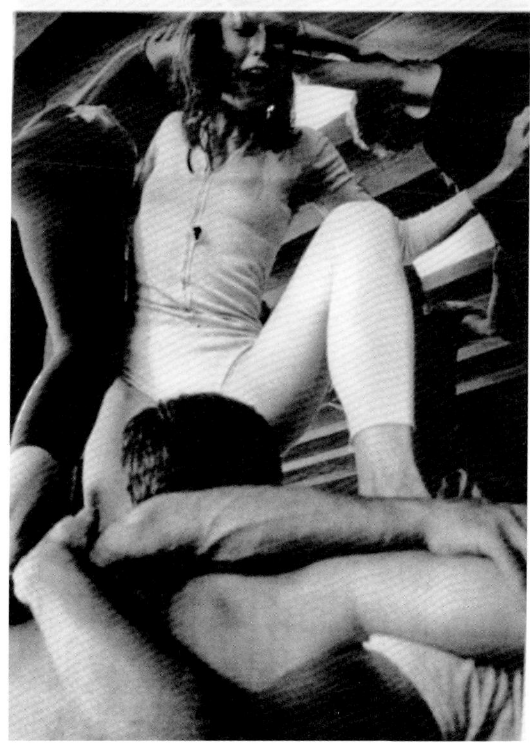

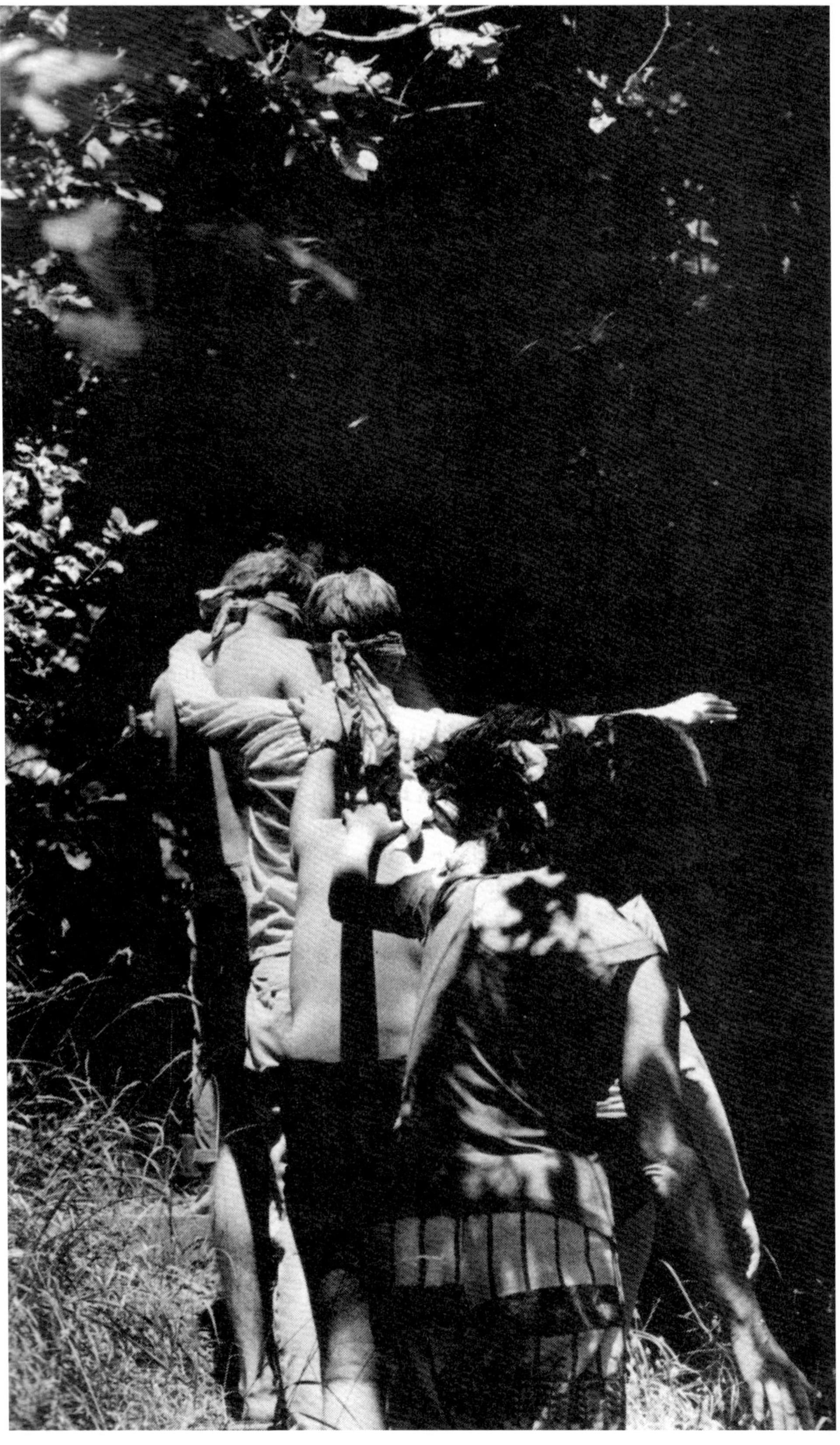

The series of exercises that the dancers and architects participated in were designed specifically to activate their latent senses, and those of the first week were planned to help the participants (especially the architects) become more comfortable with their bodies and facilitate group interaction. Activities included blindfolded nature walks, exercises in stretching and kinesthetic movement, and experiencing "light Happenings" choreographed by Hickey. The participants were also given a set of parameters, or scores, to help guide their experiences but not to determine them. For example, a blindfolded exercise asked that participants take turns leading one another without using their hands. The instructions became even more specific as the workshop progressed—"use back to back contact," or "lead your partner by cheek, then leg"—as each successive limitation contributed to the overall performance score and guided participant experience. Later, another exercise included a similar score (a blindfolded nature walk) but was performed in a different location, altering the ways and the intensity of how the scores were activated (Figure 2.3).[44]

Later exercises required increased interaction and collaboration among the participants and included building a village out of driftwood (led by architect Charles Moore) and an extensive observation and redesign of San Francisco's Union Square. The driftwood village event instructed the participants to "build a city out of driftwood, with structures you could live in, all related to each other." Participants were given a fifty-yard area from the cliffs of Sea Ranch to the oceanfront in which to create their villages, and they constructed a variety of needed community buildings, including a site for rituals, two lookouts with one facing toward the water and another on the cliff looking out over the city (Figure 2.4). Lawrence recalled in his notebook that without the concerns for resale value or other public opinion, each building that emerged was a personalized expression. "The direct response," he wrote in the workshop booklet, "gives enormous insight into the person's interior desires and personality—his interests and attitudes."

Another key exercise, the Union Square analysis and redesign, entailed participants making individual observations of the San Francisco urban plaza. They silently explored, took notes, listened, and "became aware of all the activities of this extremely urban space."[45] Through this experiment each individual carefully observed and recorded the performances taking place in public space: "Middle-aged ladies in tight girdles hard to walk; upper-middle-class tourists, the men in blue jackets and cameras and the ladies walking ahead in white summer suits pointing . . . Japanese girl in such high heels she can hardly stand on them."[46] The following day the participants gathered to redesign the square, a challenge that began with a consideration of the public functions of the space and advanced to find the appropriate process and design to enhance those needs.

One unnamed architect and participant quoted in Burns's *Progressive Architecture* review referred to these activities as "action architecture through movement."[47] A review in the *Los Angeles Times* stated that the participants "argued about preconceptions, how to prevent committee

Scores for Driftwood villages 1 & 2

SCORE 1

SCORE (S)	RESOURCES (R)
1 - Contact the Environment of this beach 2 - Alter the Environment 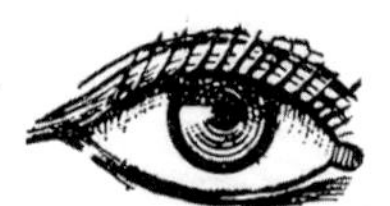	1 - Limiting factors : ~~driving of~~ 2 - 35 People 3 - Materials — driftwood, water, sand, cliffs, wind, seaweed 4 - MOTIVATION : According to individual needs & interests.

SCORE 2 (S) — RESOURCE (R)

SCORE 2 (S)	RESOURCE (R)
1 - Start from the beginning 2 - Build a new environment as a community working together as a group 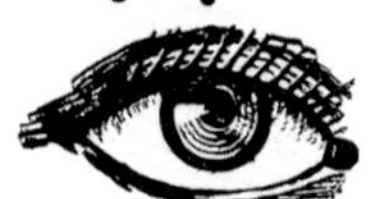	1 - Limiting factor - physical environment of driftwood village 1 2 - Same group of people 3 - Materials - same 4 - MOTIVATION — ⓐ giving up old structure is part of the way of finding new ones ⓑ whatever you do must include your awareness of its impact on the whole group.

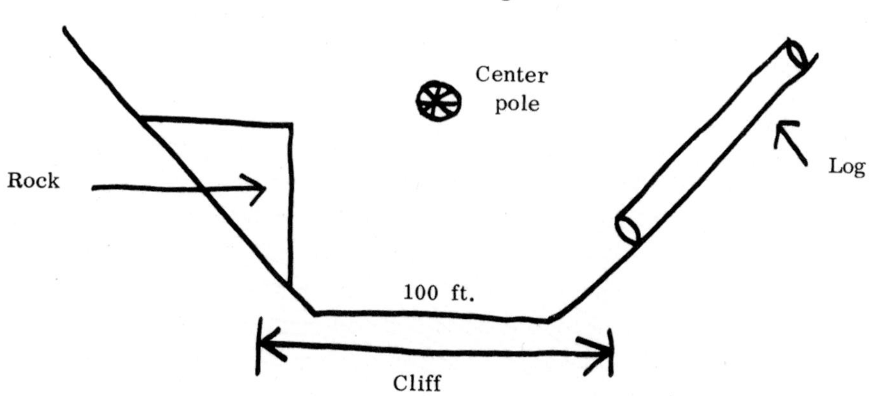

Figure 2.4

Lawrence Halprin, scores for Villages 1 and 2, "Experiments in Environment," 1968. Lawrence Halprin Collection, the Architectural Archives, University of Pennsylvania.

effort from adding up to less than the sum of the individual contributions."[48] Many of the participating architects agreed that the workshops gave them new insight into the possibilities of architectural practice. Participant Robert Holden added that the workshop taught him that "one's first responsibility is to one's own senses. Through the full utilization of these, one can create spaces that will evoke the reactions of others." Peter Van Dine observed that "it put the human as an individual back in the spaces of architecture."[49] Lawrence concluded that the most successful events of the workshops were those where the emphasis was not on a product and participants were free to explore the possibilities of the creative process. As Michael Kirby points out in his discussion of the predecessors of New Theater, "The act of painting rather than the completed composition had become the creative focus."[50] It recalls how one workshop participant described the activities as "action architecture."

AFTERIMAGE

I conclude with an image that seems to crystallize the conjunction between the loosening of the body, the designing of space and built environments, and the shaping of new alternative communities in this era.[51] In a photograph of the 1968 Driftwood Village, three men stand on a hand-built platform somewhere relatively deep in the intertidal zone on the western end of their communal village (Figure 2.5). As they struggle to keep their balance, barefooted and standing on top of thin logs, it appears that they function as the final element of this architectural structure. Another log rises from their hands acting as a flagpole or coat rack for their bundle of discarded clothes. The foamy tide rushes below them, as they set this final piece in place. Whether the wave is flowing in or out at the moment the shot was taken is impossible to tell. The natural curve of their legs and the arch of their backs add a perfect second tier to this pyramid, this viewing platform, this communal reclamation of a piece of uncontaminated territory.

Through the Halprins' workshops these young architects had ignited an active design process through a communal participatory encounter, a hallmark of the period's cultural radicalism. It reconsidered sensory exploration and one's relationship to nature as integral to creativity and rejected the formal restrictions elaborated in conventional modernist architectural training of the period. For the exercise, the architects shed the interior of the studio, pens, drafting paper, and models in order to become the structure. The three of them together as a community become a necessary element toward the completion of the platform. Represented by the discarding of their clothing are the governing roles that they have shed—architect, inhabitant, choreographer, dancer, performer, spectator. The tension between the solidity of the structure, the dynamic nature of the human body, and the ebb and flow of the ocean exemplifies the fluidity and thrill of discovery fostered by the intermedia experiments of the 1960s.

      COLLECTIVE MOVEMENT

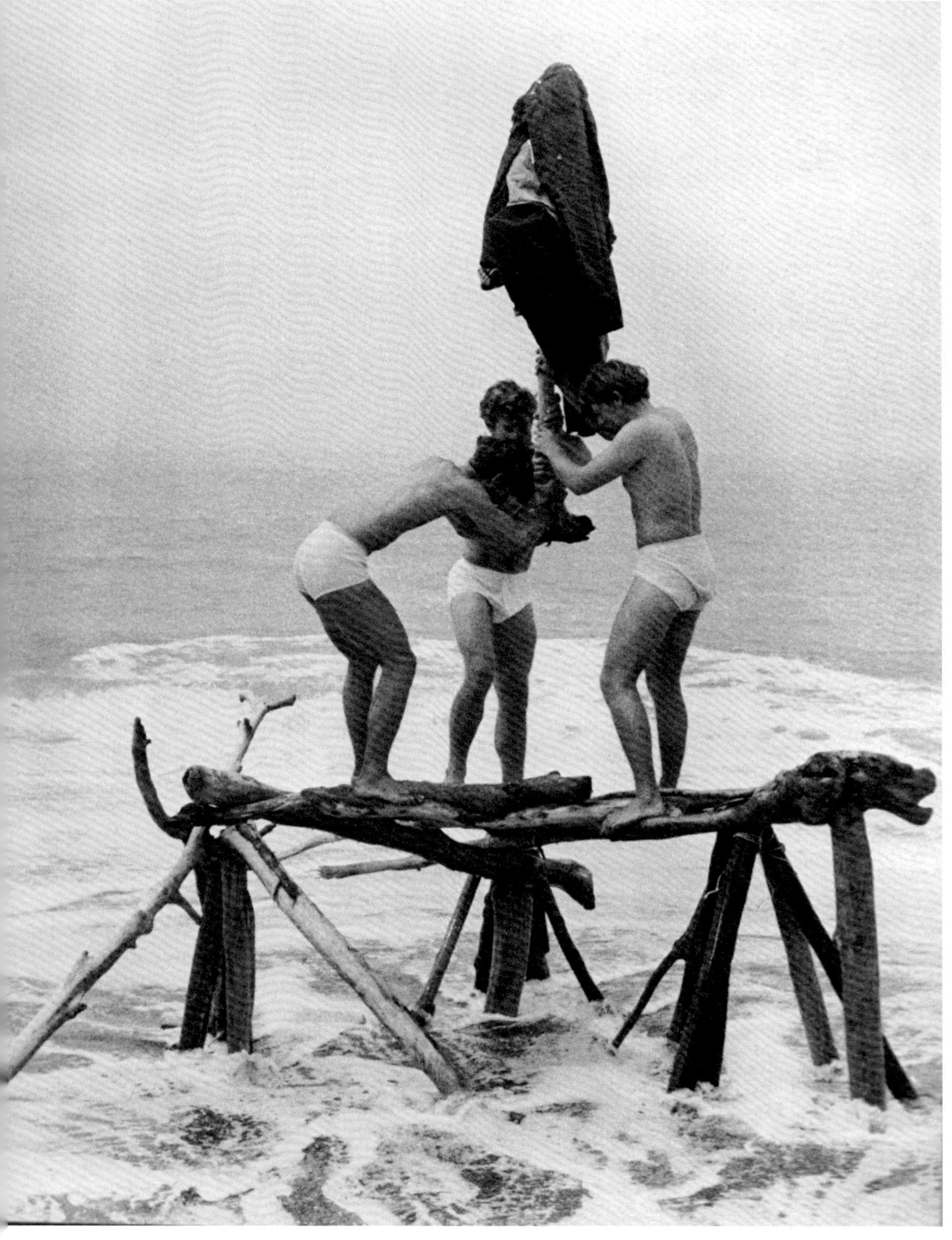

NOTES

1. Allan Kaprow, "The Legacy of Jackson Pollock," in *Essays on the Blurring of Art and Life,* ed. Jeff Kelley (Berkeley: University of California Press, 1958), 7.

2. Or Ann, as she called herself until 1972. Anna is a modified version of her birth name, Hannah.

3. Anna attended the University of Wisconsin in 1938 where she studied modern dance under the mentorship of Margaret H'Doubler. She was also influenced by the modern dance techniques of Ruth St. Denis and Isadora Duncan, which she began studying as a teenager. Lawrence received a B.S. in botany and horticulture at Cornell University and then an M.S. from the University of Wisconsin in horticulture. He received a B.L.A. from Harvard Graduate School of Design where he studied with British landscape architect Christopher Tunnard and Bauhaus architects Walter Gropius and Marcel Breuer, all of whom he credited with having a strong influence on his work. On Halprin's relationship to Gropius and his time at Harvard, see Eva J. Friedberg, "Action Architecture: Lawrence Halprin's Experiments in Landscape Design, Urbanism, and the Creative Process" (Ph.D. diss., University of California, Irvine, 2009), chapter 1.

4. Noted participants of Anna's summer dance workshops included Yvonne Rainer, Simone Forti, and Trisha Brown who later participated in the Judson Dance Theater of 1962-1964. See Sally Banes, *Democracy's Body: Judson Dance Theater, 1962-1964* (Durham, N.C.: Duke University Press, 1993); Carrie Lambert-Beatty, *Being Watched: Yvonne Rainer and the 1960s* (Cambridge, Mass.: MIT Press, 2008); and Janice Ross, "Atomizing Cause and Effect: Anna Halprin's 1960s Summer Dance Workshops," *Art Journal* 68, no. 2 (2009). Ant Farmer Chip Lord attended the Halprins' joint summer workshop of 1968 and noted it as having a seminal impact on his artistic career. In a letter dated 5 October 1968, Lord writes to Anna and Lawrence, "The workshop was a catalyst, was an education, was a trip into my future, was an art form, was a lifestyle, was a freestylelife race, was groove." Anna Halprin archive, San Francisco Museum of Performance and Design, box 11, folder 6.

5. Kelley, ed. *Essays on the Blurring of Art and Life,* xiv.

6. Ibid., xx.

7. Ibid., xii.

8. Lawrence started his own practice in 1949 after working with Thomas Church for four years. Anna opened a studio with Welland Lathrop in North Beach in 1946.

9. Janice Ross, *Anna Halprin: Experience as Dance* (Berkeley: University of California Press, 2007). Ross's biography of Anna Halprin is an excellent source for details on Anna's professional and personal life at this time.

10. In 1963, Lawrence Halprin developed the master plan for the seaside community of Sea Ranch. The Halprins owned a second home there (designed by Moore, Turnbull, and Wurster), and throughout their careers Sea Ranch was an important backdrop to their artistic and intellectual lives. On the subject see Friedberg, "Action Architecture," chapter 2.

11. A 1968 *San Francisco Chronicle* headline read "A Strange Experiment in Learning to Feel," while of the 1966 workshop Art Seidenbaum of the *Los Angeles Times* referred to Lawrence Halprin as a "Moses of modern megalop" and claimed that even "cosmopolitan San Francisco found this a strange tribe." See Donovan Bess, "A Strange Experiment in Learning to Feel," *San Francisco Chronicle,* 23 September 1968; and Seidenbaum, "City Rising Out of Driftwood," *Los Angeles Times,* 13 August 1966.

12. Janice Ross discusses the Cagean connection to Anna's summer dance workshops in *Anna Halprin: Experience as Dance* and her "Atomizing Cause and Effect." Here I hope to broaden this argument to include the joint summer workshops and to also bring Lawrence's landscape architecture theory and practice into this discussion, which has often been sidelined.

13. Ross, *Anna Halprin,* 79-80.

14. Halprin articulated many of these ideas in his earliest published writing. See Lawrence Halprin, "Landscaping a Small Plot," *Sunset* (November-December 1949); Thomas Church and Lawrence Halprin, "You Have a Gold Mine in Your Backyard," *House Beautiful* (January 1949). His comparison to the garden as a stage set was a continuation of ideas that he began in an early piece appearing in *Sunset Magazine,* "Good Theater in the Garden" (1947).

15. Lawrence Halprin, "The Choreography of Gardens," *Impulse 2* (1949): 31.

16. Ibid.

17. Ibid., 33.

18. Ibid., 33-34.

19. Ross, *Anna Halprin,* 87.

20. Yvonne Rainer and Anna Halprin, "Yvonne Rainer Interviews Anna Halprin," *Tulane Drama Review* 10, no. 2 (Winter 1965): 143. The interview took place in 1962 but wasn't published until 1965.

21. Anna Halprin, *People on a Slant,* San Francisco, 1953.

22. Quoted in Ross, *Anna Halprin,* 126-27 (phone conversation between Halprin and Ross, 24 September 2003).

23. Rainer and Halprin, "Yvonne Rainer Interviews Anna Halprin," 147.

24. Janice Ross, "Anna Halprin's Urban Rituals," *Drama Review* 48, no. 2 (2004): 49.

25. Lawrence Halprin, *Notebooks 1959-1971* (Cambridge, Mass.: MIT Press, 1972), 25.

26. Richard Cándida Smith, *Utopia and Dissent: Art, Poetry, and Politics in California* (Berkeley: University of California Press, 1996), 444. For a good genealogy of New Theater and experiments with untraditional theater spaces, see Michael Kirby, "The New Theatre," in *Happenings and Other Acts,* ed. Mareillen R. Sandford (London: Routledge, 1995).

27. John Cage, *4'33",* New York, 1952.

28. John Cage, *Water Walk,* Milan, 1959.

29. Branden W. Joseph, "The Tower and the Line: Toward a Genealogy of Minimalism," *Grey Room* 27 (Spring 2007): 62.

30. Ibid., 58-80.

31. Bradford D. Martin, *The Theater Is in the Streets: Politics and Performance in Sixties America* (Cambridge: University of Massachusetts Press, 2004), 4.

32. Ibid., 6.

33. This idea has been communicated to me through a number of interviewees, including Marc Treib (e-mail correspondence, August 2008) and Yvonne Rainer (interview with author, December 2007).

34. For more on the idea of "eco-utopia" in relation to the work of Lawrence Halprin, see Friedberg, "Action Architecture."

35. Michel Foucault, *Technologies of the Self* (Cambridge, Mass.: MIT Press, 1988), 18.

36. Lawrence Halprin, *The RSVP Cycles: Creative Processes in the Human Environment* (New York: George Braziller, 1969), 1.

37. Lawrence Halprin, "Motation," *Progressive Architecture* 46 (July 1965): 126-33.

38. Jack Anderson, "Dancers and Architects Build Kinetic Environments," *Dance Magazine* (November 1966): 54. The quoted passages in the next three sentences are also from this article.

39. James Burns, "Experiments in Environment," *Progressive Architecture* (July 1967): 130-37.

40. "Experiments in Environment" booklet (Summer 1966). Anna Halprin archive, San Francisco Museum of Performance and Design, box 11, folder 6.

41. Ibid.

42. Workshop announcement, 28 March 1966. Anna Halprin
    archive, box 11, folder 6.
43. Burns, "Experiments in Environment."
44. Almost all the descriptions of the workshops held during
    "Experiments in Environment" as presented here come from my
    own piecing together of the scores as recorded by the workshop
    leaders, photographs taken of the events, and notes taken by both
    participants and faculty.
45. Burns, "Experiments in Environment," 135.
46. Ibid.
47. Ibid.
48. Seidenbaum, "City Rising Out of Driftwood."
49. Holden's and Van Dine's comments are quoted in Burns,
    "Experiments in Environment," 137.
50. Kirby, "The New Theatre," 45.
51. On the loosening of the body and its relationship to the counter-
    culture, see Sam Binkley, *Getting Loose: Lifestyle Consumption
    in the 1970s* (Durham, N.C.: Duke University Press, 2007).

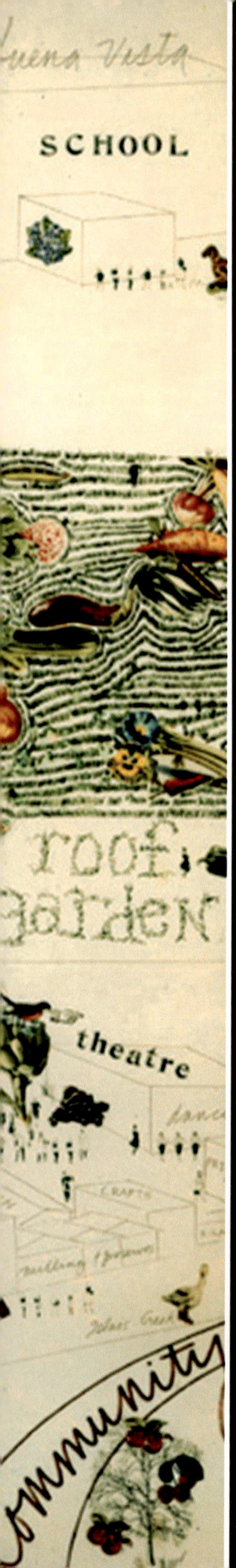

CHAPTER 3
THE FARM BY THE FREEWAY

Jana Blankenship

Liberation of nature is the recovery of the life-enhancing forces in nature, the sensuous aesthetic qualities which are foreign to a life wasted in unending competitive performances: they suggest the new qualities of freedom.

—Herbert Marcuse, *Nature and Revolution*

I saw . . . total integration as a new art form—a triptych (human/plant/animal) within the context of a counter-pointed diptych (farm/freeway) (technological/non-mechanized), etc.

—Bonnie Ora Sherk, cofounder of *Crossroads Community (The Farm)*

The present-day Cesar Chavez Street Freeway Interchange that passes over the Mission neighborhood in San Francisco is a tangle of asphalt and vacant lots, where cars, skateboarders, and the homeless coexist in liminal urbanity. This transitory space was once a place of productivity where life grew and roots deepened under the name *Crossroads Community (The Farm)* (Figure 3.1). From 1974 to 1987, the derelict spaces underneath and beside the freeway sprouted corn stalks, vegetable gardens, and fruit orchards, supported goats and other animals, engaged children, and housed circuses. *Crossroads Community,* affectionately known as *The Farm,* was one of San Francisco's earliest community cultural spaces organized around the ecological principles of living in harmony with nature. Distinctively, *The Farm* brought together people, animals, plants, and educational resources, heralding a new form of ecological thinking in line with countercultural ideals of the period. While postmillennial San Francisco is a city where urban farming thrives, in the 1970s the concept of a farm by the freeway with the express purpose of connecting people, animals, and plants to each other was not an ordinary sight but, rather, a revolutionary project.

In 1974, artist Bonnie Ora Sherk in collaboration with Jack Wickert cofounded *The Farm* on the patchwork of seven acres beneath the freeway described above.[1] With the help of the community and other supporters they turned two large warehouses and several expanses of concrete and abandoned open space into a site-specific installation, consisting of farmland, a community center, a school without walls, and a human and animal theater with the mandate to provide "an enriched series of [agricultural and ecologically progressive] environments within the context

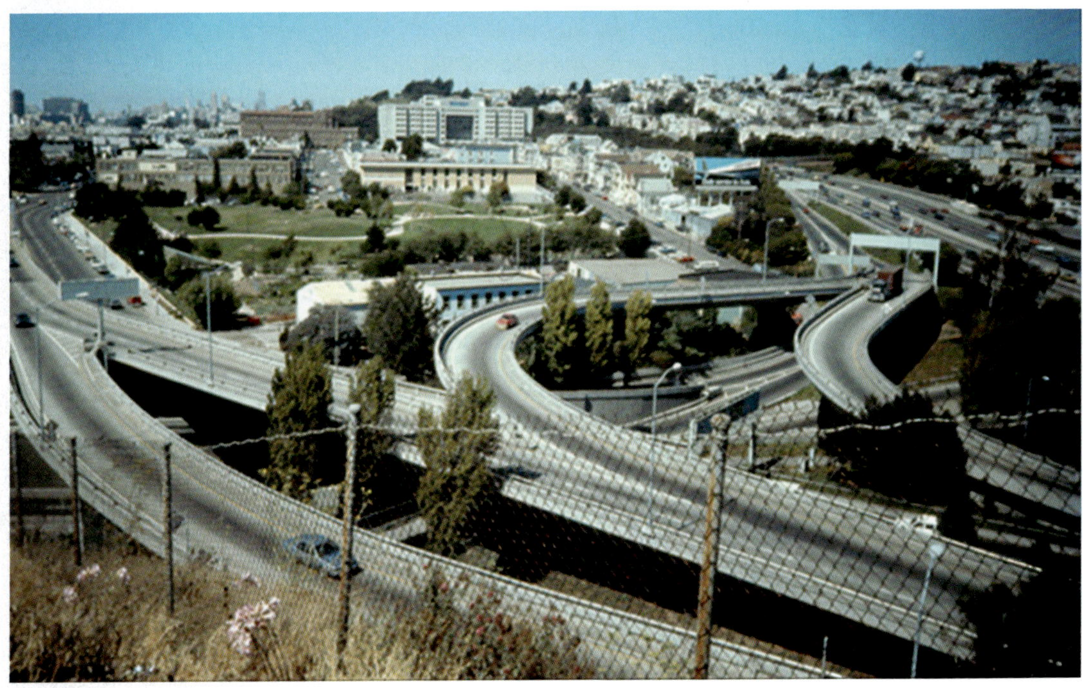

     THE FARM BY THE FREEWAY

of art" for the urban public.[2] Over the course of *The Farm's* existence, the San Francisco Mime Troupe, Make-a-Circus, the Jones Family Company, and Pickle Family Circus, among others, took up residence there, as did numerous artists, poets, dancers, neighborhood residents, volunteer gardeners, and barnyard animals. In Sherk's words, which reflect the diversity of *The Farm's* community and the activity that took place there, *The Farm* was "a play, a sculpture and a sociological model . . . [along with] elements of plumbing."[3] In 1981, Lucy Lippard hailed *The Farm* as "the most ambitious and successful work of ecological art in this country," yet it still remains relatively unknown today even in the San Francisco Bay Area.[4]

The Farm sought to create a radical ecological model that facilitated nonhierarchical interactions, a cornerstone of countercultural organization and activism embraced by cultural radicals from the Diggers to Jerry Rubin's Yippies. Everyone who entered *The Farm* or lived there—plant, human, or animal—was seen as an integral part of the ecosystem. For Sherk, this embrace of nonhierarchical organization reflected her concept of the "life frame," whereby performance could become a microcosm for exploring alternative modes of existence.

Sherk's solo work as a performance artist led to her conception of *The Farm.* In her 1970 piece *Sitting Still I,* part of a series of performances in which Sherk inserted herself into derelict locations around the city, she dressed in a formal gown and occupied an armchair abandoned in a shallow pool of water and trash off the side of the James Lick Freeway, the location of the future Army Street interchange.[5] Sherk sat motionless amid the urban landscape facing her "audience"—the cars that sailed by on the freeway and a group of warehouses and open spaces in the distance, the future site of *The Farm.* The same year, Sherk also created a series of surreal living tableaux in the heart of San Francisco, pastoral scenes juxtaposed against the roaring freeway titled *Portable Parks I–III.* In one of the *Portable Parks,* Sherk collaborated with artist Howard Levine, placing 400 feet of sod, picnic benches, a dozen palm trees, and a cow on the breakdown lane of the James Lick Freeway.[6] This work and the others in the series were demonstration pieces meant to draw attention to the urgency of preserving nature against the ever-expanding commercial development of the city.[7] In addition to highlighting the relationship between urban and natural environments, *Portable Parks,* like *Sitting Still I,* merged Sherk's interests in theater and ecology.

It was during another performance—one in which Sherk explored her concept of "cultural costumes"—that she met her future collaborator Jack Wickert. Wickert, a musician, taxi driver, and member of the San Francisco Mime Troupe, encountered Sherk in 1973 at Andy's Donuts, a twenty-four-hour diner on Castro Street, where every Saturday night for a year she "performed" as a short-order cook and waitress during the graveyard shift. In the early morning hours of one of her shifts, Sherk initiated a conversation with Wickert, one of her customers, about her desire to start an urban public project and, in turn, his need for a performance space. In the words of Sherk, which held appeal for Wickert, too, "I was looking for a space where different kinds of artists and also nonartists could come together and break down some of the mythologies and prejudices between different genres, styles and cultural forms. All of this had to be connected with other species—plants and animals."[8]

At the time of this encounter, Sherk lived across the street from the defunct Borden's Dairy and the patchwork of parcels of land and warehouses surrounding it near the almost completed Army Street Freeway Interchange.[9] Wickert had grown up in the projects on Potrero Hill in San Francisco and spent his childhood nights playing in the same warehouses scattered amid this industrial wasteland. After meeting at the diner, they walked the site, exploring the land underneath the freeway and sharing ideas about its possible transformation. Together, they posed the question, What can we do with this field of concrete and warehouses? They answered with a most unlikely idea: create a farm.

Sherk's *Original Drawing for Crossroads Community (The Farm)*, a collage consisting of drawing in colored pencil and pasted cutouts, is a map of the human, plant, and animal theater she envisioned as *The Farm* (Figure 3.2). According to this vision, a verdant park replaced the empty field of concrete, and the site's two warehouses and adjacent parcels of land were transformed into a barn, theater, the Crossroads Café, roof garden, vegetable rows, and fruit orchards. The collage is layered with numerous humorous vignettes that play with scale—a pig eats an enormous head of lettuce; diminutive adults in the garden are posed against a giant head of garlic, a bunch of carrots, and an eggplant; children at the neighboring Buena Vista School play with a huge dog; and trees hang heavy with oversized fruits—illustrating Sherk's vision of a nonhierarchical environment where all life forms are integral participants. Here Sherk imagines *The Farm* as a gesture of possibility, where city and country come together to create an unorthodox yet productive site where all work together to find—in sociologist Herbert Marcuse's words—"a life of reduced labor, of creative labor, of enjoyment."[10]

COUNTERCULTURAL CONTEXT

A myriad of revolutionary projects appeared in California in the early 1970s that sought to challenge and/or expand the concepts of community and art. In the words of Joan Holden, a member of the San Francisco Mime Troupe and an active participant in *The Farm*, within the atmosphere that spawned these projects and others of the time "everything seemed possible; it seemed possible to re-create society."[11] The re-creation of society, the promotion of nonhierarchical relations, and the emphasis on ecological activism central to *The Farm* were key elements of numerous countercultural projects. In conception and form, *The Farm* drew on three projects in particular: the guerrilla theater of the San Francisco Diggers, the Los Angeles–based project *Synapse Reality* by Aviva Rahmani, and the Berkeley-based demonstration site, the Integral Urban House.

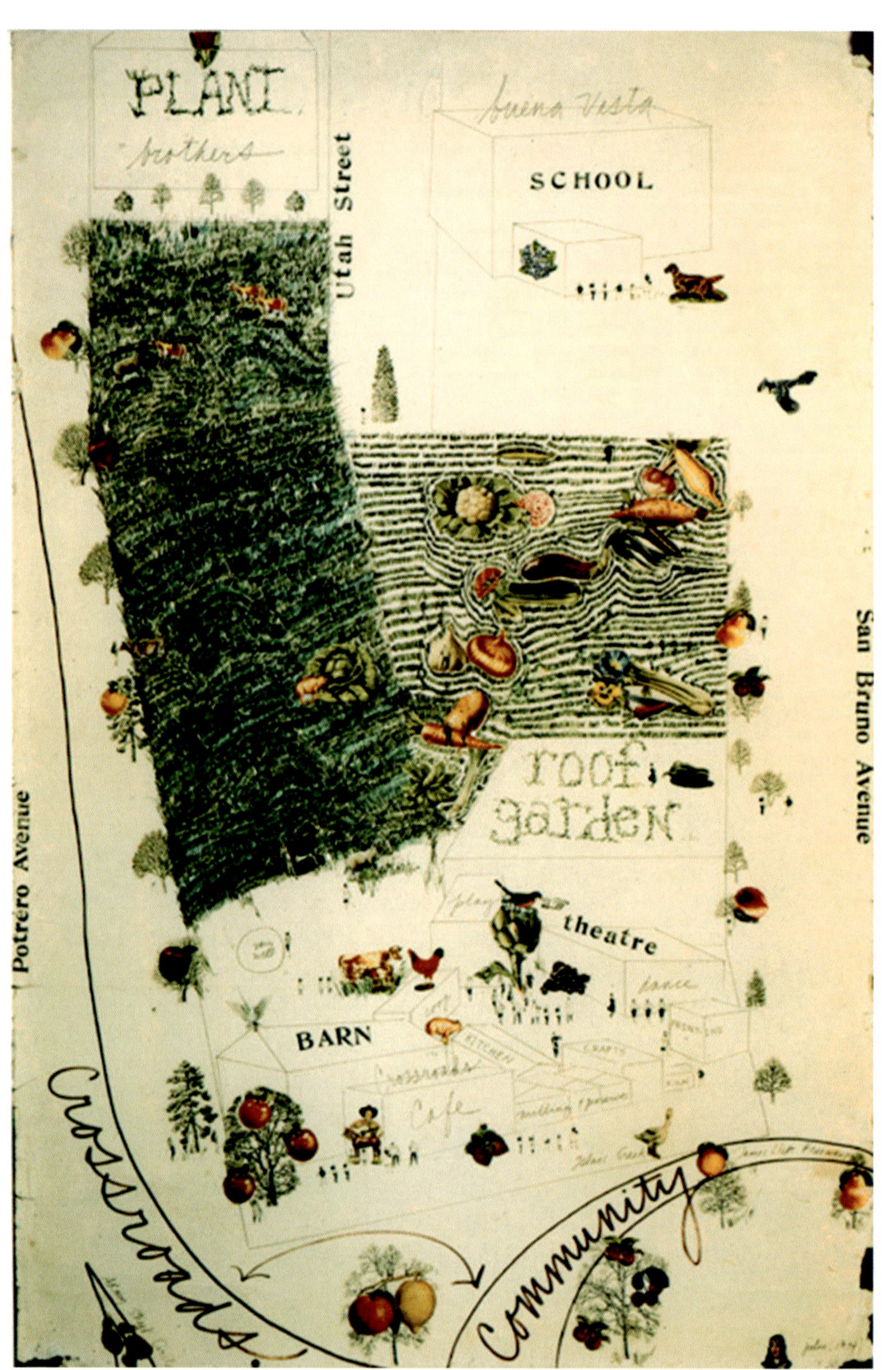

PLANT
brothers
Utah Street
buena vista
SCHOOL
San Bruno Avenue
Potréro Avenue
roof garden
theatre
dance
BARN
KITCHEN
CRAFTS
Crossroads
Cafe
Crossroads
Community

The San Francisco Diggers, an offshoot of the San Francisco Mime Troupe, brought political theater to the streets of San Francisco in the mid-1960s.[12] The Diggers conceptualized their practice as a form of "life acting," in which a new reality, if it could be acted out, was embraced as real. In addition to their guerrilla theater practice, the Diggers also created the utopian Free City project, which encompassed the operation of free stores, a free daily food service, communal housing, a free printing press, and a free health clinic. Individuals participating in the free food service, which took place outdoors in the panhandle of Golden Gate Park, were required to walk through the Free Frame of Reference, a large yellow, wooden picture frame that encouraged one to shift his or her perceptions of life conceived anew outside the cash economy. The goal of transforming individual consciousness through the melding of performance and politics emblematized by the Diggers was embraced across the counterculture. Jerry Rubin proclaimed that "the role of the revolutionary is to create theatre which creates a revolutionary frame of reference. . . . We create reality wherever we go by living our fantasies"; this is an apt expression of this priority, as was Sherk's concept of the "life-frame" conceived to foster and enact an alternative social and ecological life system at *The Farm*.[13]

While Sherk's earlier performances such as *Portable Parks I–III* were temporary works of theater and ecological sculpture, *The Farm* sought to create a more sustained model in hopes of investigating and cultivating the individual's relationship to community, plants, animals, and natural processes under the umbrella of art and ecological transformation. The microcosm of *The Farm* reflected the potential for social change that Herbert Marcuse saw in ecological action: "The emancipated senses would repel the instrumentalist rationality of capitalism while preserving and developing its achievements and through environment (medium) for the human being as 'species being'; free to develop the specifically human faculties: the creative, aesthetic faculties."[14] This was not only a physical manifestation but also a conceptual premise for the reevaluation of art and society. Explaining her goals for the *The Farm*, Sherk stressed that "I'm trying to expand the notion of what art is. . . . Take the rabbit, burrowing tunnels. She's an incredible architect."[15] In the life-frame, each element, from grass to chicken to child, became part of the sculpture.

A second conceptual influence was Aviva Rahmani's *Synapse Reality*, which he described as "an exploration into ecological systems as raw material for art making, primed by research into behavioralism and environmental stability."[16] Rahmani had been a student of Marcuse's while he taught at the University of California at San Diego from 1965 to 1969. In 1968, she founded the street theater troupe, American Ritual Theatre, whose members were also performers in *Synapse Reality*. In an old Spanish villa on the campus of the University of California, San Diego, men and women lived together, shared household chores, created artwork, grew vegetables in the gardens and greenhouse, collected fruit

          THE FARM BY THE FREEWAY

from orchards, and lived with animals, including a miniature goat and horse. A central element of *Synapse Reality* was Rahmani's conceptual symphony *Stay Wait Look Listen* (1974), a series of spontaneous and planned performances based on musical forms that explored the relationships among people, animals, the earth, and indigenous cultures. In the conflation of art and life enacted in *Synapse Reality,* Rahmani and her fellow participants sought to challenge gendered stereotypes, hierarchical relations of power within and without the home, and dependence on the food industry through the creation of a self-sustaining environment. Rahmani's description of the work of American Ritual Theatre as "a sculpture . . . [made up of] people within an environment letting the environment dictate what happens" is echoed in Sherk's description of *The Farm* as a life-scale, site-specific performance sculpture that is both collaborative and an "environmental transformation."[17]

Across the San Francisco Bay, Bill and Helga Olkowski, two members of the ecological research nonprofit the Farallones Institute, bought a Victorian home in Berkeley in 1972 and converted it into a model of urban sustainability complete with orchards, gardens, chickens, rabbits, fish, composting, recycling, and solar-heated hot water.[18] Called the Integral Urban House, it functioned as not only a communal living space but also an ecological demonstration home with the structure and its residents "performing" the principles of sustainable living for the public.[19] Like Sherk, the founders of the Integral Urban House considered their project to be "a mini-ecosystem in which rabbits, chickens, fish, honeybees, plants, microbes, and people interact in a flourishing example of interrelated self-reliance."[20] Despite their different audiences of a green building and an alternative art space, respectively, both the Integral Urban House and *The Farm* were urban homesteads that served as experiments in communal encounter and living how-to manuals for the public interested in restoring a harmonious connection to nature.

WORK ON *THE FARM*

The creation of an urban farm was no easy task. In addition to the strenuous physical labor involved in its creation, its realization required extensive negotiation with the city of San Francisco and private landowners. The reclamation of the land and buildings that became *The Farm* was a feat Wickert described as "hammering, sawing, digging, picking, carrying, lugging, toting, hauling, sweeping, mowing," and vegetable beds, flower gardens, and orchards were designed and planted with labor and donated materials by Sherk, Wickert, gardeners Vicki Pollack and Jeff Brown, and adults and children from the surrounding neighborhood. But the work of creating *The Farm* also included Sherk and Wickert coleasing a 1.5-acre concrete lot complete with several dilapidated buildings and working with Huey Johnson at the Trust for Public Land to negotiate the acquisition of the remaining adjacent lots with the city of San Francisco. In addition, between 1974 and 1975, Sherk collected thousands of neighbors' signatures in support of *The Farm,* leading to the city's purchase in 1976 of the last remaining 5.5-acre lot with the stipulation that it would be developed into a park.

As president and director of the nonprofit organization *Crossroads Community (The Farm),* Sherk applied for and received grants from public and private sources in support of the project, including the National Endowment for the Arts, the Comprehensive Employment and Training Act (CETA), and the California Arts Council, among others. *The Farm* also received funding to hire art teachers, gardeners, and other educators, and the nonprofit formed a managing board that brought together artists, dancers, actors, residents from the surrounding neighborhoods, and interested members of the business community. Under this diverse leadership, *The Farm* developed as a thriving hive of activity that is difficult to fully encapsulate.

Of the two warehouses on *The Farm* campus, one was converted into a farmhouse, and the other into a theater. The latter, the Barn Theater complex, was further subdivided into two performing spaces, a human theater on the first floor occupied by the Jones Family Company, Tumbleweed, Pickle Family Circus, and Make-a-Circus, complemented by an animal theater housed at ground level (Figure 3.3). Another theater program residing in and around this complex, The Raw Egg Animal Theatre (TREAT), was founded by Sherk as an experience for schoolchildren that was part classroom and part life-frame. TREAT was an indoor and outdoor environment composed of bales of straw, trees, a stage, mirrors, wooden fences, small houses, and domestic animals, including cats, pigs, goats, rabbits, sheep, ducks, geese, and chickens. In this space children

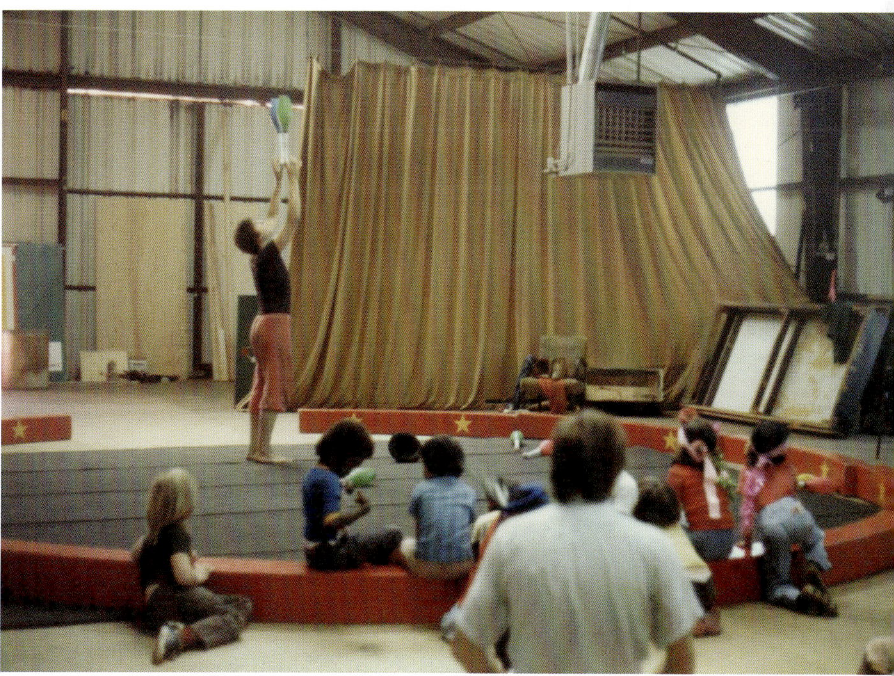

THE FARM BY THE FREEWAY

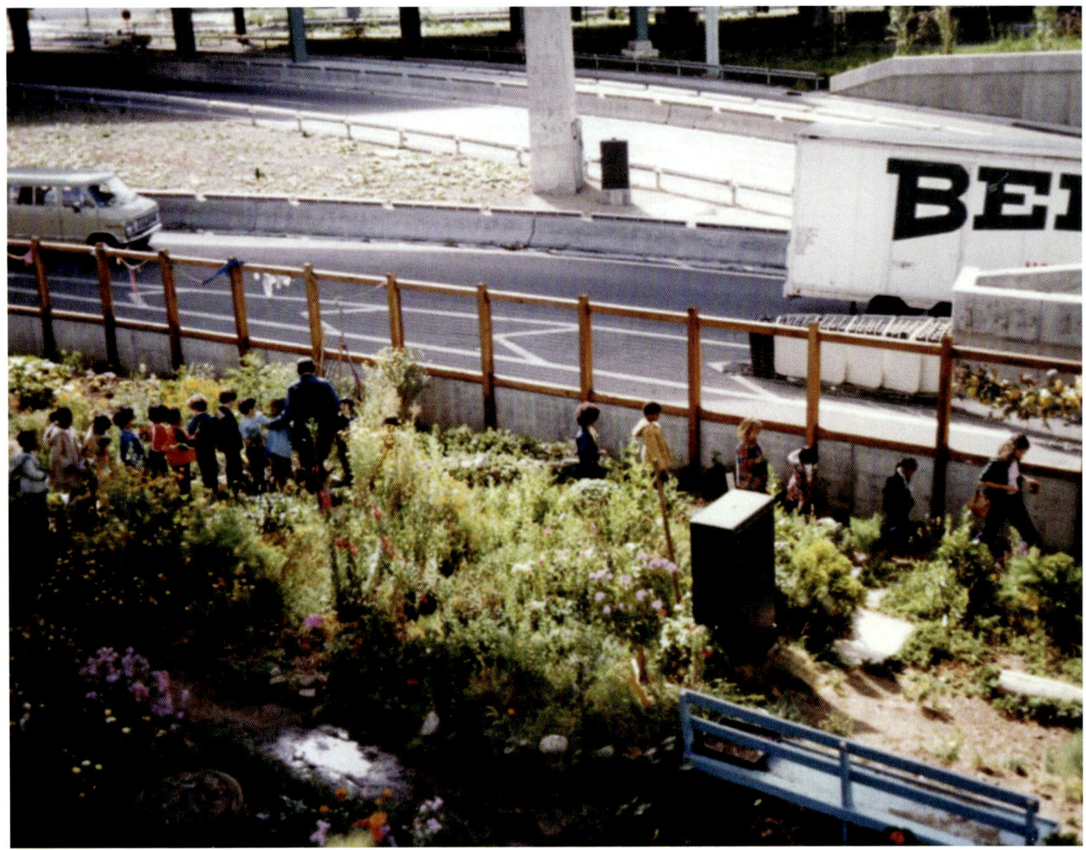

(as well as adults) and farm animals were both students and performers, interacting with each other in an open setting.

Vicki Pollack, one of the lead teachers at TREAT, explained that the program tried to "give children real experiences and expose them to as many things as possible" by using *The Farm* as a classroom where artists, musicians, dancers, and ecologists acted as instructors.[21] Children performed acts of their own creation on the theater stage for an adult audience and could learn about biology firsthand by witnessing the life cycles of plants and animals (Figure 3.4). Interspersed with the miracles of birth and growth were harsh lessons about animal behavior, exemplified by a litter of baby bunnies killed one night by city rats.

In this environmental performance, hierarchies were leveled in efforts to help children, adults, and animals experience and learn from each other. This ideal is reflective of director Jerzy Grotowski's idea of the theater as a laboratory. He describes the role of theater as a "fight . . . to discover, to experience the truth about ourselves, to tear away the masks behind which we hide daily. We see theatre—especially in its palpable, carnal aspect—as a place of provocation, a challenge the actor sets himself and also, indirectly, other people."[22] This radical vision of theater as a form of self-discovery and consciousness raising through the removal of barriers between individuals—and, in the case of *The Farm*, other species—

as a goal shared by many countercultural performance groups in the 1970s, including the San Francisco Mime Troupe, the Diggers, Rahmani's American Ritual Theatre, and New York's the Living Theater, among others.

Residing in the structure adjacent to the Barn Theater complex, referred to as the Farmhouse, was another experimental performance circle known as the Reinhabitory Theater. Its members, made up of the founders of the Diggers, including Peter Berg, Judy Goldhaft, and Peter Coyote, studied animal behavior in TREAT and translated these observations into their own actions. On the vision behind this unusual practice, Coyote explains: "Our organizing principle was to use 'stories' from our bioregion, both ancient and new. Our perspective would be 'multispecies'—telling the tales from the points of view of all local species, not just humans."[23]

The main floor of the Farmhouse was converted into a domestic space with a kitchen, a living room, and an open space for workshops and community gatherings. The kitchen was the hearth of *The Farm,* where people gathered to break bread and hatch plans. The Farmhouse also housed an International Parlor, an exhibition and performance space, and a group of darkrooms.[24]

In the basement of the Farmhouse, a state funded preschool operated that utilized TREAT as part of its curriculum. In addition to the preschool, more than a hundred children per week from more than seventy-five different schools in San Francisco and the greater Bay Area shared this "school without walls" with animals, made art, planted vegetables, and maintained the gardens. Throughout *The Farm's* tenure, a variety of nonprofit research groups would use rooms in the Farmhouse for their operations, including a center run by the group Earthwork to research and distribute information on agribusiness and nutrition.[25] At night, poetry readings and musical and theatrical performances took place in TREAT, the Barn Theater, and the Farmhouse.

Outside, the land was developed into a working farm with a greenhouse. Yet the grounds were not initially suitable for gardening as the soil was contaminated with lead and other toxins. With the application of compost and new soil, the trees, fruit, and an assortment of vegetables flourished, creating an otherworldly landscape that included a field of corn growing by the freeway. Children and neighbors partook in gardening the land and making scarecrows; festivals punctuated the arrival of spring and the fall harvest (Figure 3.5).

The Farm also offered a variety of workshops and educational programs. The bimonthly *Farm Calendar* from March–April 1979 advertised a "Care and Feeding of Edible Landscapes" class, free and open to San Francisco residents. Other programs included artists' presentations, festivals, pageants, lectures, exhibitions, dancing, acting, Native American powwows, music rehearsals and performances, preschool education, and programming for elementary schoolchildren. The calendar was also marked with neighborhood holiday events and hoedowns and encouraged readers to share their knowledge through teaching at *The Farm.*

THE DEMISE OF THE FARM

The Farm was a locus for experimental theater that promoted interspecies dialogue and understanding during its tenure. It was a place where people of all ages congregated to learn about ecology and food production and participated in the creation of a vision of life in harmony with nature. In addition, it was a working farm, a school, an artists' collective, a community center, an art gallery, and a club. While diversity of people, species, and ideas was one of the strengths of *The Farm,* its diversity of intention was part of the project's undoing. The ever-evolving vision and expansion of the project eventually created rifts in its leadership and between *The Farm* and the city of San Francisco.

In 1980, the city announced its decision to reclaim one of *The Farm's* lots and turn it into a self-enclosed neighborhood park. The parks department's plan included running drainage pipes for the new park through *The Farm,* effectively destroying it. Sherk submitted her letter of resignation to the board upon this decision, registering her regret that "we will be wiped out. . . . We've been told we'll have to move out while they bulldoze 30-foot swaths through our growing areas."[26] Sherk's plan for the city park (to be designed in exchange for a long-term lease on part of *The Farm's* city-owned acreage) had been to sculpt it out of natural resources and recycled materials, creating sloping hills, meadows, community gardens, windmills, and a pond fed by the land's underground creek. This plan would have integrated the park into *The Farm* complex. Instead, the parks department opted to create a more traditional urban

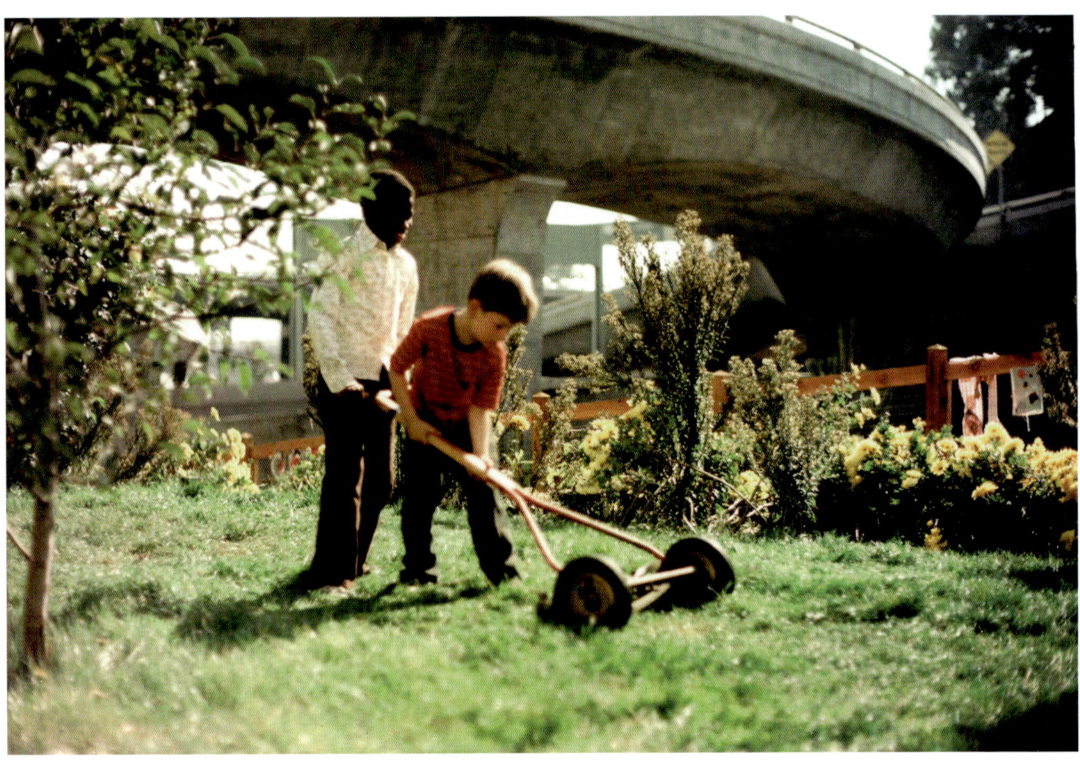

     THE FARM BY THE FREEWAY

park separated from its neighbor by a fence. Named La Raza Park, the plan eventually incorporated Sherk's plan for community gardens, which still thrive today as Potrero del Sol.

After Sherk's departure, *The Farm* continued under a steady succession of directors who oversaw its transformation into a notorious live-music punk rock venue. In 1987, after years of trouble with the landlords, the last of the farmers were evicted. Sixty animals were dispersed to nearby farms, and a space that nurtured many forms of life and aspects of community for thirteen years became vacant again.

The field of corn by the freeway, the elaborate scarecrows, the children's pageants, the experimental theaters, and punk rock concerts all juxtaposed against the cacophonous freeways present a fantastic image caught in time. When *The Farm* disbanded, many of those involved hoped that it would be revived in a different location. While this never happened, the momentum and ideas that were explored at *The Farm* were reinvested back into the community, fostering additional local organizations. *Farm* supporter and participant Jack Davis helped found the Neighborhood Arts Movement as well as SOMArts, which he directed for twenty years. Another Farm community member, René Yañez, established the Galería de la Raza and the San Francisco Arts Commission Gallery. Farm gardener and educator Vicki Pollack cofounded the Children's Book Project, a continuation of her work with underserved populations. Jack Wickert continued to perform with the San Francisco Mime Troupe and joined the boards of several other local art nonprofits. In the 1980s, Sherk began to work on *A Living Library (ALL),* her ongoing project for transferable educational and ecological community centers framed by art that she describes as "an international network of interactive life frames."[27] While the stage has shifted, Sherk's current practice poses the same question she asked more than thirty years ago at *The Farm:* "If we are to continue on this planet and grow as conscious beings we must attain a more spiritual and ecological balance within ourselves and among larger groups and nations. How can we do this?"[28]

The Farm was an amalgam of elements—part theater, part politics, part education—and one of the most unusual examples of countercultural art activism that attempted to create an alternative vision of an ecologically sensitive and meaningful relationship between human, animal, and plant life in an urban setting. It was a product of its moment, rooted in utopian ideals and the expanded practice that pervaded the counterculture. As Sherk says, she wanted *The Farm* to provide a platform to creatively explore and rethink how "we relate to ourselves and each other, with those in the surrounding communities, and with different life forms, in the hopes of experiencing a richer humanity and a possible, positive survival."[29] Despite the impossibility of its long-term survival, *The Farm* was a groundbreaking project that prepared the city soil for similar projects, setting a seminal historical precedent for the lively profusion of urban agricultural and environmental artistic projects that are steadily being adopted into the landscape of San Francisco and other cities.[30]

The boundaries between art, culture, and nature collapsed temporarily for many who entered *The Farm* by the side of the freeway. About his experience there, novelist Ernest Callenbach wrote in 1976, "The Farm is a little piece of Ecotopia here among us now—a sort of 'center that can hold'—a place for things to happen freely but with biological purpose and coherence."[31] While the utopia was an ambitious vision with a center that did not ultimately hold, *The Farm* created a legacy for practices that continue to help shift social and ecological paradigms in the Bay Area and beyond.

1. The collective property address was 1499 Potrero Avenue.
2. Bonnie Sherk, "The Farm" (1980): 2. Mission statement.
3. Bonnie Sherk, "An Alternative to Alternative Arts Spaces," poster, 1979.
4. Lucy R. Lippard, "Gardens: Some Metaphors for a Public Art," *Art in America* 69 (November 1981): 146.
5. The water that had collected came from the belowground Islais Creek, the same source that fed *The Farm* and Sherk's current project *A Living Library*, which is also located on top of the Islais Creek Watershed.
6. Sherk and Levine were the first artists to win the San Francisco Museum of Modern Art's Society for the Encouragement of Contemporary Art (SECA) Vernal Equinox Award. This award was created to provide artists the opportunity to develop public projects with conceptual frameworks outside of the museum.
7. Sherk created three *Portable Parks* in San Francisco during June 1970: one on the breakdown lane of the freeway, one on Maiden Lane in Union Square, and one beneath the freeway. Each ecosystem was erected in the early morning and disbanded at nightfall, except for *Portable Parks III* on Maiden Lane, which lasted for two days.
8. Sherk as quoted by Linda Frye Burnham, "Between the Diaspora and the Crinoline: An Interview with Bonnie Sherk," *High Performance* (Fall 1981): 61.
9. The seven acres of unoccupied land was owned by six different entities, both public and private.
10. Herbert Marcuse, "Herbert Marcuse," *Liberation* 17, no. 6 (September 1972): 12.
11. Joan Holden quoted in *The Farm*, DVD, directed by Kathy Katz and Mike Kavanagh, produced by Jack Wickert (Shaping San Francisco, 1990).
12. On the Diggers, see "The Post-Competitive, Comparative Game of a Free City," in *Art and Social Change: A Critical Reader*, ed. Will Bradley and Charles Esche (London: Tate, 2007), 152.
13. Jerry Rubin, as quoted by Richard Schechner, "The Street Is a Stage," in *Radical Street Performance: An International Anthology*, ed. Jan Cohen-Cruz (New York: Routledge, 1998), 197.
14. Herbert Marcuse, "Nature and Revolution," in *The Continental Aesthetics Reader*, ed. Clive Cazeaux (New York: Routledge, 2000), 259–60.
15. Katy Butler, "A Farm Flourishes beside the S.F. Freeway," *San Francisco Chronicle*, 18 March 1977, 17.
16. Aviva Rahmani, "Practical Ecofeminism," in *Blaze: Discourse on Art, Women and Feminism*, ed. Karen Frostig and Kathy A. Halamka (Newcastle, UK: Cambridge Scholars, 2007), 319.
17. Aviva Rahmani, as quoted in "Troupe at Synanon Plans Non-Smooth Performance," *San Diego Union*, 29 December 1968, E-7. Bonnie Sherk is quoted from an e-mail message to the author, 25 November 2008.
18. The Farallones Institute was founded by Sim Van der Ryn in Sonoma County in 1969 with a mandate to investigate sustainable gardening, water conservation, and green building.
19. The house was open to the public for tours on Saturdays and a publication, the *Integral Urban House*, designed as a do-it-yourself instruction manual, was published in 1979.
20. Julie Reynolds, "The Integral Urban House," *Mother Earth News* (November/December 1976): 1.
21. Vicki Pollack quoted in *The Farm*, DVD. Pollack, a former San Francisco Digger, was hired with CETA funds to be a school gardener.
22. Jerzy Grotowski, *Towards a Poor Theater* (London: Methuen, 1969), 212.
23. Peter Coyote, *Sleeping Where I Fall* (Washington, D.C.: Counterpoint Press, 1998), 328.
24. Sherk also called the International Parlor the Tea Room To Be, as she hoped it would eventually become an elegant tearoom.
25. Caroline Drewes, "The Farm," *San Francisco Examiner*, 6 August 1980, E-1.
26. Maitland Zane, "Growing Threat to S.F. Farm," *San Francisco Chronicle*, 9 October 1980, 5.
27. Bonnie Ora Sherk, "The Creation of a Living Library: An International Network of Life Frames," *Leonardo* 24, no. 2 (1991): 223. Currently, there are three *A Living Library & Think Parks* in San Francisco and one in New York.
28. Bonnie Ora Sherk, "Position Paper," presented at the Center for Critical Inquiry First International Symposium, San Francisco Art Institute (November 1977).
29. In December 1976, Sherk curated an exhibition called *The Farm/ An Environmental and Social Process* at the Atholl McBean Gallery at the San Francisco Art Institute. The exhibition was a combination of installations, performances, lectures, and reflections that raised awareness about *The Farm*. Sherk's words here are taken from the November 1976 invitation to the exhibition.
30. Some of the ongoing ecological projects framed within an artistic context that are taking place in San Francisco are Rebar's annual Parking Day, Amy Francheschini's Victory Gardens 2007+, Robyn Waxman's growing FARM project at the California College of the Arts, and Amber Hasselbring's ongoing Mission Greenbelt Project.
31. This was Callenbach's answer to Sherk's question in 1976, "What is *The Farm* to you?" His quote was included on her "An Alternative to Alternative Arts Spaces" poster from 1979.

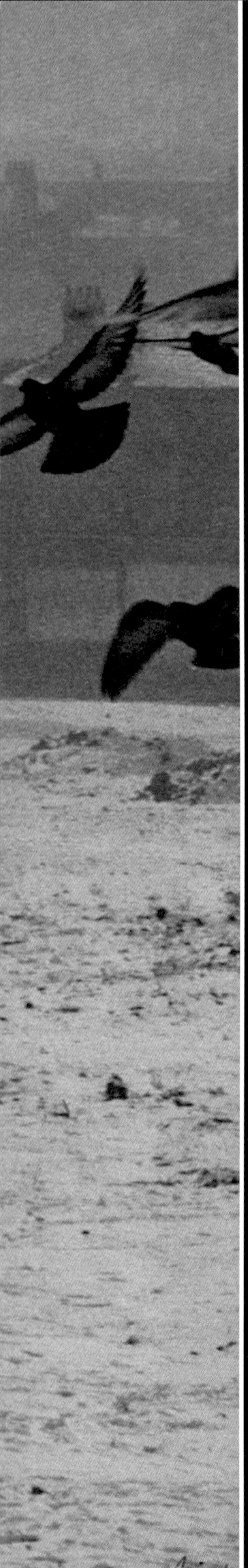

CHAPTER 4
SAN FRANCISCO VIDEO COLLECTIVES AND THE COUNTERCULTURE

Deanne Pytlinski

Artists' adoption of portable video cameras in the late 1960s was an attempt to interrupt broadcast television's one-way flow of information with their own counterimages. In many instances, the goal of liberating the mind from control by the mainstream media through decentralization was coupled with the desire for deeper and more authentic forms of interpersonal communication, an objective closely aligned with counter-cultural values of communal encounter. It is no surprise that many video collectives took shape in San Francisco, as a hub of countercultural activity, and that their emergence relative to video art in California has been of interest to curators and historians of late.[1] However, little research investigates the relationship between these collectives of the late 1960s and early 1970s to the ideals and practices of the counterculture of the same period. This essay examines this relationship by looking at video collectives' embrace of collectivity, their do-it-yourself ethos, and their promotion of alternative social patterns. The video collectives examined here include Ant Farm, Media Access Center, Optic Nerve, Video Free America, and TVTV, all of whom collaborated with one another, a pattern of collectivity that countered the phenomenon of the individualistic art star and aimed at empowering the individual consumer of mass media.

Video collectives were extremely diverse in their structures and purpose, so it is difficult to generalize about their relationship to other kinds of countercultural activity. On the level of collectivity, however, the groups examined here shared countercultural values of communal encounter, nonhierarchical organization, and open membership. Here the comparison is not to communal living per se but, rather, to the embrace of collective labor. In addition, one of the challenges of documenting the early video collectives of the late '60s and early '70s is that members often moved from one circle to another, making for fluid intersections between the various groups, a feature not uncommon among counter-cultural formations. Historian Timothy Miller has pointed out that one of the characteristics of communes of the sixties, as distinct from ear-lier examples of intentional communities in the United States, was their open membership, which facilitated the creation of flexible networks of participants.[2]

The sharing of information and equipment went hand in hand with this fluidity of membership and was part of the "culture of tools" cel-ebrated by video artists associated with the counterculture who wanted to subvert the commercial interests of broadcast networks. The *culture of tools* to which I refer characterizes a collective fascination with the building and reengineering of early video equipment among many practi-tioners of the late 1960s and early 1970s, connecting them to the larger do-it-yourself tool-making ethos of the counterculture.[3]

The first cameras widely available to the personal consumer were inexpensive compared to broadcast equipment, but still out of reach for most individuals. Thus the sharing of equipment, postproduction facilities, and technical expertise organized much of the activity of the

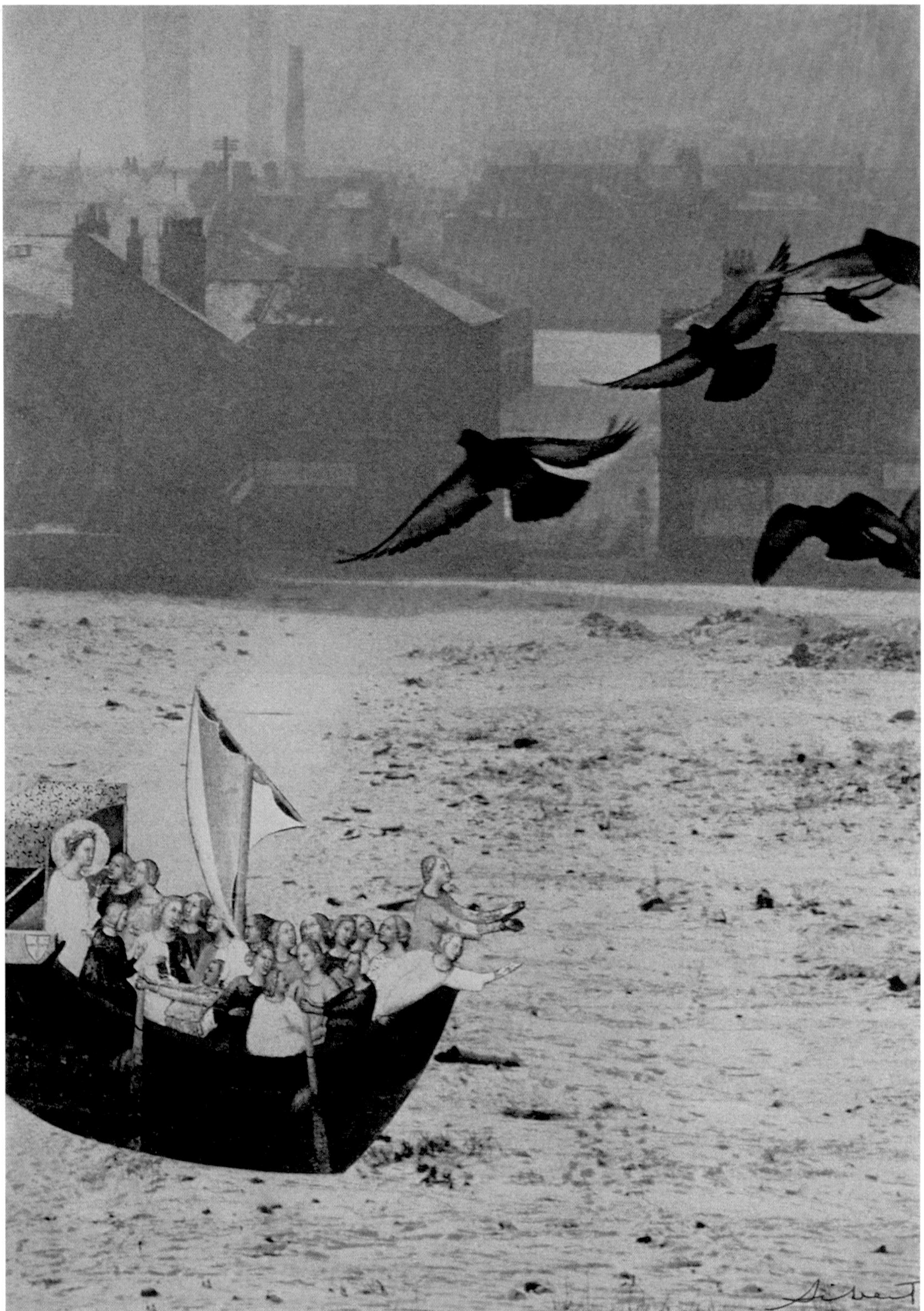

text also contained many references to a more spiritual future based on eastern religions and earth-centered spirituality. Speaking about her early photocollages, Sibert recounts the way she associated her imagery with a spiritual quest: "I began to do very surrealist collages in which disparate elements are juxtaposed, to bring a new psychic landscape. It really is an attempt to reorder the world, or just an attempt to show the contradiction in the world, and how it never had a seamless quality of meaningfulness."[16] One collage shows a boat with the Virgin Mary at the helm, leading her "pilgrims" into an unknown frontier, adrift on a river of an urban environment with smokestacks and an industrial wasteland in the background, asking, "Where is our salvation? Where is our redemp-tion? Where is our purpose?" (Figure 4.3).

When speaking about her pursuit of spirituality, Sibert calls herself a "spiritual wanderer" who was looking for "first of all my own identity and then secondly, the relationship of myself to the world." While few video collectives in the San Francisco Bay Area experimented with rural communal living, Sibert and Wendy Apple, another TVTV crew member, had come from such a collective called Amazing Grace Media in Bearsville, New York, prior to joining TVTV.[17] Sibert associated collective living with that exploration of her relationship with others and with the earth, as imaged through video: "The idea of a communal, or collective organism that we could form, was almost a natural offshoot of that era we were in, of the history of that counterculture. It seemed very predictable because it had been something I had been yearning to do for a long time—to live collectively."[18] Timothy Miller argues that the communards of the 1960s were rejecting a system of greed and materialism in the United States, and certainly Sibert's experience—of looking for meaningful relationships in collective life—is typical and informed her and her peers' outlook on how commercial television alienated people from one another, a situa-tion that could be relieved by a more conscious media ecology.[19]

The Media Access Center's embrace of video technology contributed to countercultural ideas about uniting video with alternative education to empower students, ideas that were well represented in *Radical Software* and *Guerrilla Television*. The group's focus was on making video tech-nology accessible to students and helping them use it to break from the authoritarian conditioning of the traditional classroom and the com-mercial stranglehold of film and television.[20] Fundamentally, Media Access Center distinguished videotape from both film and television, and cen-ter members encouraged students to develop stories based on their own interests and perspectives rather that those imposed by institutions.[21] The tapes produced were the result of many workshops with primarily high school students, including those at Palo Alto–based Pacific High School, the alternative school structured around experiential learning. One such tape made by students of Pacific High, *Juvenile Justice*, took the form of a rap session about their interactions with law enforcement, especially in relation to drugs. Countering the public service announcements that might warn against supposed dangers of drugs, the students interviewed each other about "why they take drugs, parents about why they think their kids take drugs and law enforcement officials about why they enforce the law."[22] For Media Access Center the decentralization of information unleashed by *Juvenile Justice* and other tapes like it was a form of self-empowerment that subverted the control and authority of traditional education because "it allows students to generate their own knowledge. Portable video equipment extends to the whole environment and thus invalidates the school itself as a place of learning."[23] It was proposed that putting cameras into the hands of young people would be more educational and ultimately more transformative than traditional forms of education. In his essay "Meta-Manual" in *Guerrilla Television,* Shamberg scrutinizes educational programming for television. *Sesame Street,* for instance, was criticized for pretending to use television as a hip educational tool but instead reinforcing the one-way communication of broadcast television. Instead of intelligent viewers, Shamberg asserts, *Sesame Street* was about acculturating children to watch television and become consumers. Further, he says, the program never criticized the medium of television by challenging the hierarchical relationship between producer and viewer.[24]

Similar to the way Media Access Center promoted a hands-on learning approach to video, the video collective Ant Farm proposed that both architecture and media could be created by materials at hand with skills taught ad hoc from one person to another. Their architectural and video practices decentralized what had formerly been institutionalized and proposed instead that direct access would bring users together in new relations. In a 1971 collaboration with members of Media Access Center, Ant Farm brought their mobile television studio, the Video Media Van, to a demonstration in San Francisco against an initiative to limit high-rise architecture. In a flyer announcing the upcoming demonstration, Ant Farm promoted the media van, stating that they would be recording local political candidates and the mayor discussing the issue from both sides and that the unedited results would be shown to the audience as an example of information feedback: "This is free public information and we are moving it your way."[25] They claimed that immediate playback of the video would allow attendees to comment on the speeches and view themselves as a part of the event. This suggested that the information would not be mediated through pundits or news anchors, and that viewers would have a direct encounter with the speakers and be free to make up their own minds.

The Video Media Van had been outfitted for Ant Farm's Truckstop tour in 1970, an open-ended event that involved taping their movement across the country and their visits to colleges and other venues where they demonstrated their experimental inflatable architecture. In addition to the publication of their *Inflatocookbook,* which detailed their designs for mobile, temporary, inflatable structures, their published essays in

Radical Software, and their tapes documenting their journey, the tour
was meant to bring their ideas into direct contact with the public with
whom they would interact on an unmediated, localized level. One of
the tapes preserved from the Truckstop tour is *World's Longest Bridge*
(1970), which consists of one long shot as the media van rolled across
the bridge spanning Lake Pontchartrain outside of New Orleans. The camera mostly records the road ahead of the van, the water on either side
of the road, and the sky with clouds that take up nearly half of the frame.
Occasionally, the camera pans around the van, and we see the driver
(Hudson Marquez), Doug Hurr wearing earphones, and the equipment
lining the walls of the mobile video unit.

Ant Farm was not the only video collective to outfit a vehicle as a
mobile television unit. On the East Coast, Dean and Dudley Everson
created the Fobile Muck Truck, and the collective Videofreex had their
Media Bus. Part of the romance of video's portability was its perceived
ability to enter into the world and produce immediate imagery as events
happened. The countercultural theme of the road and direct recording
of encounters had its roots in the Beat poets' stream-of-consciousness
writing, and the spontaneity was meant to contradict the artificiality
of the Establishment's highly polished journalism. Arguably, the ultimate
countercultural example here is Ken Kesey and the Merry Pranksters'
psychedelics-inspired cross-country journey on their bus called Further,
a trip that was also recorded, on film.[26] As Chip Lord states in a 2004
interview with curator Constance Lewellen, the Truckstop tour and the
building of the media van were inspired, in part, by the *Whole Earth
Catalog* and reflected "a larger theme in the counterculture of nomadics,
constantly moving around but somehow making community out of that
process."[27] Mobility was often discussed throughout the video literature
as characteristic of alternative media, and it was positioned in opposition
to the stasis of bourgeois life and broadcast news. In the edited version
of Ant Farm's tape, flutes and drumming accompany the long, monoto-
nous journey, giving it spiritual, even meditative overtones as if the technocratic aspects of the paved landscape and electronic equipment could
be mitigated and repackaged through associations with ancient cultures.

Media vans belonging to various video collectives were represented
in *Guerrilla Television.* In an illustration (Figure 4.4) designed by Ant
Farm that included a photo purporting to represent the Everson's Fobile
Muck Truck and a drawing of Antfarm's tricked-out video van with its
multiple sunroofs is an image of a campground for "cybernetic nomads,"
complete with tepee and television viewers sitting amid monitors and a
videographer taping the entire scene.[28] The nomads are situated far away
from the central power structures of the urban broadcast stations, and
they simultaneously produce video and screen it. One of the monitors
displays a road stretched ahead of the camera, a scene reminiscent of
Ant Farm's Truckstop tour. There is a neoprimitivist element at work in
the image illustrated by the grassy meadow campground surrounded by

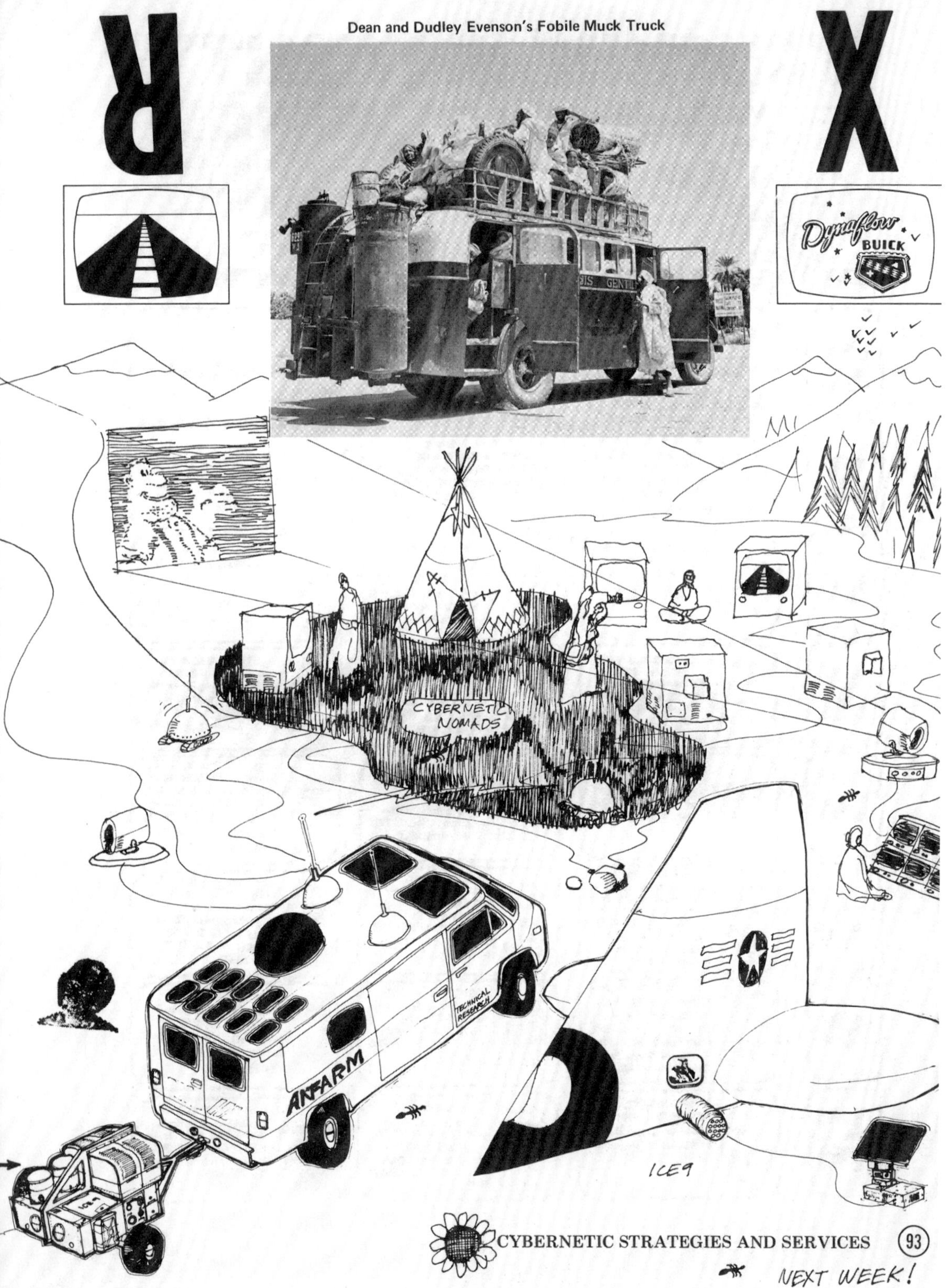
Dynaflow
BUICK
CYBERNETIC
NOMADS
TECHNICAL
RESEARCH
ANFARM
ICE9
CYBERNETIC STRATEGIES AND SERVICES
93
NEXT WEEK!

mountains. As Philip Deloria has observed, references to tepees were a kind of free-floating signifier of both openness and a perceived indigenous connection to the land, and using those signifiers helped members of the counterculture who embraced technology, like the Ant Farmers, to position video as a soft technology amenable to a nonhierarchical society.[29]

Optic Nerve was another San Francisco–based collective committed to the idea of a decentralized media as necessary to a true democracy. Their most well-known endeavor, their critique of the 1973 Miss California pageant titled *Fifty Wonderful Years,* was made at the height of media attention surrounding the women's liberation movement and the protest of the 1968 Miss America pageant organized by the feminist group New York Radical Women (NYRW) still fresh in viewers' minds. As Debra Michals has shown, the era's demonstrations against beauty pageants had much in common with the street theater techniques of media-savvy counterculturalists, as when NYRW crowned a sheep as Miss America to highlight the objectification of women, or through their use of vivid visual symbols such as the "freedom trashcan" into which many signs of gendered oppression, such as girdles, cosmetics, and (possibly) bras, were thrown.[30] When Optic Nerve taped the Miss California pageant, the pageant organizers were very aware of the criticisms coming from the women's liberation movement regarding the pageant industry, and their responses to that criticism is one of the themes of the tape. Optic Nerve refrained from making obvious editorial statements from a master narrator and instead allowed the contradictions of the pageant to reveal themselves through interviews with organizers, participants, and footage of press conferences with mainstream journalists. Those contradictions include pageant rhetoric about representing the young women who participate as "natural women" juxtaposed against various makeup sessions and training exercises where the participants learn to walk in a stylized manner that minimizes natural mobility and standardized their bodies' visual appeal. In the face of early 1970s consciousness raising about women's sexuality, the organizers maintain a concern for preserving the young women's "integrity," a containment that is nonetheless rejected by the participants in behind-the-scenes interviews with Optic Nerve's female interviewers, in which they openly discuss their desires and bristle at the restrictions imposed on them by the pageant.[31]

The coaching of Miss California participants about questions concerning the exploitation of women raised by feminists is repeatedly demonstrated throughout the tape. The young women's internalization of patriarchal codes of femininity is one of the most devastating aspects of the videotape. Optic Nerve, however, also captures the way the mainstream journalists hypocritically acknowledged the feminist challenge but then absorbed and neutralized its impact by valorizing the controlled, demurely deflective responses by the dutiful competitors. Toward the end of the tape, when male reporters ask the pageant's winner how she responds to feminists who criticized the pageant as outmoded and exploitive of women, the winner artfully rebukes the criticism, even pointing to Optic Nerve's cameras saying that local public television station KQED is putting together a documentary that she apparently thinks will expose the fallacy of the feminist critique. Optic Nerve's cameras keep rolling, however, after the broadcast news cameras and lights are shut off, and the viewer witnesses those apparently objective news reporters—all male—approach and flirt with the pageant winner with talk of how wonderfully she managed their penetrating questions and apologies for their networks who "want us to ask . . . questions [that are] controversial." What is perhaps most revealing is how unnerved the pageant winner appears, not at the feminist challenge but at the unwanted attention being paid to her off-camera by the journalists. Her level of discomfort rises as she tries to negotiate their advances and gracefully extract herself from the suddenly threatening public space of the conference room, embodying the ultra-visibility and objectification that marked the very point of second-wave feminists' critique.

While Optic Nerve's *Fifty Wonderful Years* focused on the beauty pageants and thus normative gender standards, other collectives like Video Free America used decentralized media to tape stories about people whose lifestyles did not conform to the standards of mainstream middle-class America. Like the underground radio from which it derived its name, Video Free America aimed to facilitate communication about subjects that were ignored or misrepresented by mainstream media. In the *Continuing Story of Carel and Ferd,* Arthur Ginsberg and Video Free America taped the lives of Carel Rowe, an actress and sometimes director of pornography, and Ferd Eggan, a young gay man addicted to drugs. The pair planned to marry and allowed the cameras to record their lives as they consummated their union and traveled to the Midwest to visit Eggan's parents and "get clean." In this era where homosexuality was just beginning to be represented in media—but almost always as a menacing perversion—and *Playboy* constituted the press's idea of pornography, Video Free America's alternative approach began with allowing the participants to speak for themselves. Ginsberg explains that they began the documentary spontaneously one day after talking to Rowe: "You probably would never do that with film. You wouldn't roll three hours of sync footage without knowing why you were doing it."[32] Being able to respond to a situation immediately and figuring out what to do with the footage later were significant to Ginsberg, since such processes would be cost prohibitive in film, which required development and nonsynchronous sound, eliminating the possibility for immediate feedback. As Ginsberg, Rowe, and Eggan recount, however, the resulting tape is as much about how the presence of the cameras intrude on the couple's relationship as how their subjectivities are constructed through the interaction with media. Most of the video involves Carel and Ferd addressing the camera and speaking about their experiences, their relationship to each other, and their relationships to others, including other sexual partners. In its original format, the footage was displayed not linearly but, rather, across eight monitors using two channels, and it often mixed live shots of the audience with recorded footage. In many cases, Rowe and Eggan were present at screenings, so that they commented on the footage and interrupted its transparent transmission. These experimental techniques were pursued in order to call attention to the medium itself and break the seduction of the narrative in a reiteration of Brechtian motifs, as acknowledged by Ginsberg.[33]

While decentralization of the media and direct access might be presumed to imply an unproblematic notion of truth, in fact the tapes produced by collectives like Video Free America usually demystified the power structures behind the media and problematized the codes of objectivity in television. The fact that media could be used to exploit its subjects was one of the reasons guerrilla television advocates wanted to decentralize its access. Guerrilla video tried to expose the biases of the media and foster free speech by underrepresented parties. As Wendy Apple of TVTV says, "There was no counternarrative on television. There was always the voice of God-narrator, or an anchor, to make news serious. Obviously, a lot of other stories, women's stories, subjective stories, diaries, personal histories, other political points of view, art, were not on television."[34] For TVTV, this situation often called for attention to the use of media spectacle by political parties and other ideologues. In their works *World's Largest Television Studio* and *Four More Years,* about the Democratic and Republican national conventions of 1972, broadcast journalists covering the conventions came under public scrutiny as their jockeying for dramatic stories and the political parties' manipulation of the media became the story itself.

In 1973, TVTV produced another documentary called *Lord of the Universe,* which turned its cameras on an alternative religious group embraced by many former members of the counterculture in order to expose how much the organization utilized media to support its own message. The tape's subject was the Divine Light Mission, headquartered in Denver, Colorado, whose devotees believed their sixteen-year-old guru, Maharaji Ji, to be the incarnation of God.[35] Like other tapes by TVTV, it exposed the hypocrisy behind a hierarchical organization, particularly by juxtaposing the gaudy spectacle of the guru's festival, called Millennium '73 at the Houston Astrodome, with the devotees' fervent and honest spiritual thirst. Interviews with the devotees and their critics shot in black and white are juxtaposed with the oversaturated hues of color tape used for Maharaji Ji, capturing the sparkle of his elaborate gold crown and the LED signs that display celebratory images of fireworks behind his static, seated body.

One of the most notorious of the Maharaji's followers was former Chicago Seven defendant and member of the counterculture Rennie Davis, whose appearance in the piece contextualizes it as a critique of the counterculture. Footage from a tape made by Raindance in 1971 of an antiwar

   SAN FRANCISCO VIDEO COLLECTIVES

demonstration shows Davis speaking against the war in Vietnam and gets juxtaposed against his blissfully enthusiastic statements about the metaphysical power of the guru to bring about world peace, a divide between traditional forms of political protest and the psychedelic or spiritual branches of the New Left that had long separated the ideals of the countercultural from antiwar activists. Davis's statements were played back for his former colleague Abbie Hoffman, who appears in the video as a cynical counterpoint to the guru's followers and especially to Davis, stating provocatively that "if this guy is God, he's the God America deserves."[36]

Highly visible members of the counterculture had explored eastern religions such as Zen Buddhism and Hindu-influenced alternative religions, including Allen Ginsberg and other Beat poets. Miller points out that the growth of alternative religions based on eastern philosophies was impacted by the repeal of the Asian Exclusion Act in 1965, which allowed many spiritual leaders from India and elsewhere to bring their teachings to the United States.[37] Elon Soltes, a member of TVTV, had a family member who had joined the Divine Light Mission, and Megan Williams spoke of how there was a certain kinship with the devotees of the guru. As recounted in Deirdre Boyle's study of TVTV, "the guru followers were people their own age and, like them, had been through a lot of communal experiences only to emerge and find there was no support for them anymore."[38] Given these sympathies, TVTV planned to allow for a dialogue with the Divine Light Mission to emerge, and the production notes encouraged crews to show footage to devotees to generate "feedback." What emerged on tape, however, was a view of just how slick and artificial Millennium '73 was, and the vacuity of its spectacle.

As in other tapes by TVTV, the preparation and behind-the-scenes view of the show and audience response are the focus of their documentary about the Divine Light Mission. They show the Maharaji Ji and his mother handling questions from broadcast journalists with canned responses. The guru's brother is shown leading a glitzy band that played clichéd examples of popular sixties music to capture the attention of the organization's youth members. Devotees of the Maharaji Ji claimed that the leader gave their lives a sense of meaning in a sea of mediocrity and that the visual displays captured by TVTV were perceived by them to show the power and beauty embodied by the "Holy Family." TVTV's exposé of the organization's financial profit made off of followers, who often lived in impoverished communal arrangements, was seen by one devotee as "slanderous."[39] In contrast to Boyle who suggests that the entire counterculture and its apparent failure were the object of TVTV's criticism, it seems more likely that what TVTV exposed was a hierarchical, hypocritical religious organization that had exploited empty symbols of the youth movement toward its own financial gain. This is more of a continuation of TVTV's early countercultural perspective, as noted by Jody Sibert, than an abandonment: "[TVTV] was mostly going to the source . . . of power, infrastructures that held power, economically, politically, culturally, and that started with the conventions in Miami, Republican and Democratic, and went on to *demystify*—a favorite word in those days—to demystify the power of the guru, the cult, of advertising, and so on and so forth."[40]

The critical positions taken by TVTV in *Lord of the Universe* and the tapes about the political conventions, by Optic Nerve on the Miss America pageant, and Video Free America on marriage and drug addiction are all in keeping with a countercultural politics that involved questioning social and political forms of authority, especially those that restricted individual freedom. The video producers do not ridicule participants who are looking for meaningful connections in their personal or spiritual relationships. But they do reveal contradictions in the rhetoric of the organizations that aim to manipulate their audiences through exploiting the media. Guerrilla media, as used by counterculture participants, resisted the consolidation of power and one-way social/political power systems.

Accounts of Michael Shamberg's transformation from guerrilla video practitioner to Hollywood producer of enormous stature rehearses a similar narrative of former Yippie Jerry Rubin's move to Wall Street investor, trajectories that are often held up as examples of the "death of the sixties."[41] The overemphasis on Rubin's presumed sellout supports a false binary between the idealism of the sixties and the supposed soullessness of the eighties. Such pessimistic accounts of the sixties, including the presumed naïveté of the early video activists' utopian beliefs in a decentralized media, mask the very real successes and influences of the period's social transformations, particularly in the realm of civil rights reform, women's rights, environmentalism, and peace activism that continue to inform political activism today.

Most of the video collectives discussed here continued through the end of the 1970s, but the groups dissolved or changed membership so dramatically that they became entirely different entities. The legacy of collectivity and video, however, did not disappear, and community media, guerrilla documentaries, and politicized collectives continue in San Francisco and elsewhere.[42] Taking video equipment into communities and on the road depended on the collaboration of crews, leading to collective forms of practice and labor that continue to frame guerrilla video today.

NOTES

1. The Long Beach Museum of Art recently donated all of its video archives to the Getty Museum, which presented an exhibition and catalog of early video art including several collectives in 2007. Pacific Film Archives at Berkeley has also published major catalogs and took part in a touring exhibition of the work of the video collective Ant Farm in 2007.

2. Timothy Miller, "The Roots of the 1960s Communal Revival," *American Studies* 33, no. 2 (1992): 79.

3. My use of the term *tools* is indebted to Andrew Kirk's phrase *tool freaks* to describe soft technology enthusiasts who patronized the *Whole Earth Catalog*. Andrew G. Kirk, *Counterculture Green: The* Whole Earth Catalog *and American Environmentalism* (Lawrence: University Press of Kansas, 2007), 43. Kirk's chapter, "Thing-Makers, Tool Freaks, and Prototypers," examines how do-it-yourself tool making related to the counterculture and greatly informs this part of my study.

4. Sweeney's video art of the period is notable for its use of feedback and synthesizers. His media collective was called Electric Eye prior to 1970, when, with the addition of Arthur Ginsberg, they changed their name to Video Free America.

5. *Whole Earth Catalog* (Menlo Park, Calif.: Portola Institute, September 1970), 55. Media Access Center's members included Shelley Surpin, Richard Klettner, Pat Crowley, and Allen Rucker. They had many collaborations with members of Ant Farm and, later, TVTV.

6. *Radical Software* was published by the collective Raindance Foundation and was primarily edited by Beret Korot and Phyllis Gershuny of that group. It included essays by individual artists and the myriad of video collectives across the United States and Canada. Michael Shamberg was one of the members of Raindance and a contributor to *Radical Software*. Shamberg also wrote most of the book *Guerrilla Television* (New York: Holt, Rinehart, and Winston, 1971), published as issue 6 of *Radical Software*. Shamberg and Allen Rucker had both been students in communications at college in St. Louis before Shamberg moved to New York and Rucker moved to San Francisco to attend graduate school at Berkeley. In San Francisco, Rucker met the members of Ant Farm. Rucker and Shamberg's continuing relationship materialized in many exchanges of information between San Francisco and New York before Shamberg and his girlfriend, Megan Williams, also of Raindance, moved to San Francisco in 1972. As one example of this cross-continental exchange, issue 10 was edited by Media Access Center and designed by Ant Farm.

7. The term *video guerrilla* was adopted by Raindance members Michael Shamberg and Paul Ryan in reference to video practitioners who adopted the tool as a way to produce alternative tele-vision. Shamberg used *guerrilla* in the title of his book *Guerrilla Television*. As a military term referring to soldiers working in the margins using ad hoc methods of spontaneity, the term was deployed in the context of demonstrations against the Vietnam War to evoke the image of video practitioners as countercultural "soldiers" fighting against all-powerful media conglomerates.

8. Peter Braunstein and Michael William Doyle, "Introduction: Historicizing the American Counterculture of the 1960s and '70s," in *Imagine Nation: The American Counterculture of the 1960s and '70s*, ed. Braunstein and Doyle (New York: Routledge, 2002), 10.

9. Shamberg, *Guerrilla Television*, 29.

10. Kirk, *Counterculture Green*, 55. Theodore Roszak criticized what he called an "elitist managerial" approach to problem solving on the part of technocrats who he believed substituted a faith in technology for political change. Roszak, *The Making of a Counter Culture: Reflections on the Technocratic Society and Its Youthful Opposition* (Garden City, N.Y.: Doubleday, 1969), 11.

11. Marshall McLuhan, *Understanding Media: The Extensions of Man* (New York: McGraw-Hill, 1965), vi.

12. Paul Ryan, "A Genealogy of Video," *Leonardo* 21, no. 1 (1988): 40.

13. Elsewhere I have drawn comparisons between *Guerrilla Television* and *Radical Software* and McLuhan's popular books such as *The Medium Is the Massage* (New York: Random House, 1967), which makes extensive use of photomontage and bold graphic juxtapositions. See Deanne Pytlinski, "Utopian Visions: Women in Early Video Art" (Ph.D. diss., City University of New York, 2006), 94–95. With Ant Farm's knowledge of both the New York video publications, which heavily depended on McLuhan, and the nearby Portola Institute's *Whole Earth Catalog*, a stylistic synthesis of the two sources seems logical.

14. Issue 4 of *Radical Software* had also been designed by Ant Farm. Their relationship to Shamberg and Raindance has been discussed by Felicity Scott in *Living Archive 7: Ant Farm. Allegorical Time Warp: The Media Fallout of July 21, 1969* (New York: Actar Barcelona, 2008).

15. On the counterculture's embrace of the tribal see the essay by Mark Watson, "The Countercultural 'Indian': Visualizing Retribalization at the Human Be-In," in this volume.

16. Jody Sibert, telephone interview with the author, 12 October 2007. The next several quotations from Sibert are also from this interview.

17. Amazing Grace Media existed from approximately 1970–73. While living in Bearsville, Sibert and Apple also participated in an all-women's group called the Women's Video News Service, which made a documentary from women's perspectives of the Democratic National Convention in Miami in 1972. This was the same convention filmed by Shamberg and members of TVTV.

18. Sibert interview.

19. Timothy Miller, "The Sixties-Era Communes," in *Imagine Nation*, ed. Braunstein and Doyle, 341.

20. While some of Media Access Center's tapes made with students were apparently available for exchange in 1971, they appear to no longer be extant. In many ways, for this group the process was more important than the finished product, as they worked mainly to empower communities to use video for their own purposes. There is a good description of the work with the Scripps High School Video Workshop by Pat Crowley and Shelly Surpin of Media Access Center in *Radical Software* 4 (Summer 1974): 6, available at www.radicalsoftware.org.

21. Shamberg, *Guerrilla Television*, 46.

22. Ibid., 61.

23. Ibid., 22.

24. Ibid., 7.

25. Quoted in Constance Lewellen and Steve Seid, *Ant Farm 1968–1978* (Berkeley: University of California Press, 2004), 52.

26. Paul Perry, *On the Bus: The Complete Guide to the Legendary Trip of Ken Kesey and the Merry Pranksters and the Birth of the Counterculture* (New York: Thunder's Mouth Press, 1990).

27. Chip Lord quoted in Lewellen and Seid, *Ant Farm*, 55. Stewart Brand had started the Whole Earth Truck Store in 1968 prior to publishing the first *Whole Earth Catalog*; see Kirk, *Counterculture Green*, 47.

28. Shamberg, *Guerrilla Television*, 93. The photograph representing the Everson's Fobile Muck Truck incongruously shows not the Eversons or their truck but, instead, a group of Arabian nomads atop a loaded-down bus. The use of found photographs from popular magazines for humorous effect was common in Ant Farm's designs.

29. Philip Deloria, "Counterculture Indians and the New Age," *Imagine Nation*, ed. Braunstein and Doyle, 159f.

30. Debra Michals, "From 'Consciousness Expansion' to 'Consciousness Raising': Feminism and the Countercultural

Politics of the Self," in *Imagine Nation,* ed. Braunstein and Doyle, 42.

31. Sherrie Rabinowitz and Lynn Adler were two of the women involved in Optic Nerve. Other members were Jules Backus, Mya Shore, Bill Bradbury, John Rogers, and Jim Mayer.

32. Arthur Ginsberg, "Echo in the Tube," reprinted in *California Video: Artists and Histories,* ed. Glenn Phillips (Los Angeles: Getty Research Institute, 2008).

33. Ibid.

34. Wendy Apple, telephone interview by the author, 12 April 2005. Apple's name is often spelled Appel in early documents. She has spelled her name both ways and currently prefers Apple. Following her preference, I use Apple.

35. Divine Light Mission published a magazine called *And It Is Divine,* which contained many stories promoting the teachings of the guru. Stories and imagery that parallel concerns of the counterculture were abundant, even including a few articles about women's rights and ecology. The inside cover photograph of volume 2, issue 1 (June 1974) is particularly interesting for its use of the photograph of the earth taken on the Apollo 8 moon mission that was widely circulated and discussed in the early environmental movement, including the *Whole Earth Catalog.* Issues of *And It Is Divine* are preserved in the Western history/genealogy section of the Denver Public Library's central branch.

36. Hoffman and the Yippies were known to use media strategically and had been interested in the guerrilla television movement since 1969. The group Videofreex, members of which also worked with TVTV, had taped several members of the Chicago Seven. See Parry Teasdale, *Videofreex: America's First Pirate TV Station and the Catskills Collective That Turned It On* (Hensonville, N.Y.: Black Dome Press, 1999), 15, 28–30. TVTV would also tape Hoffman later in 1974 after he went into hiding. See Deirdre Boyle, *Subject to Change: Guerrilla Television Revisited* (New York: Oxford University Press, 1997), 128–38.

37. Timothy Miller, *America's Alternative Religions* (Albany, N.Y.: SUNY Press, 1995), 8.

38. Boyle, *Subject to Change,* 82–83.

39. Caroline Bromley, "Letters from Caroline" (1980), unpublished manuscript belonging to Denver Public Library.

40. Sibert, interview. Sibert's comment about advertising is a reference to *Adland,* a TVTV tape from 1974.

41. On such narratives used to dismiss the political value of cultural radicalism, see Julie Stephens, *Anti-Disciplinary Protest: Sixties Radicalism and Postmodernism* (Cambridge: Cambridge University Press, 1998).

42. Curators Josh MacPhee and Dara Greenwald organized the exhibition *Signs of Change: Social Movement Cultures 1960 to Now* at Exit Art in 2008 to demonstrate this legacy. See Greenwald's essay on video collectives in *Realizing the Impossible: Art against Authority,* ed. Josh MacPhee and Erik Reuland (Oakland, Calif.: AK Press, 2007).

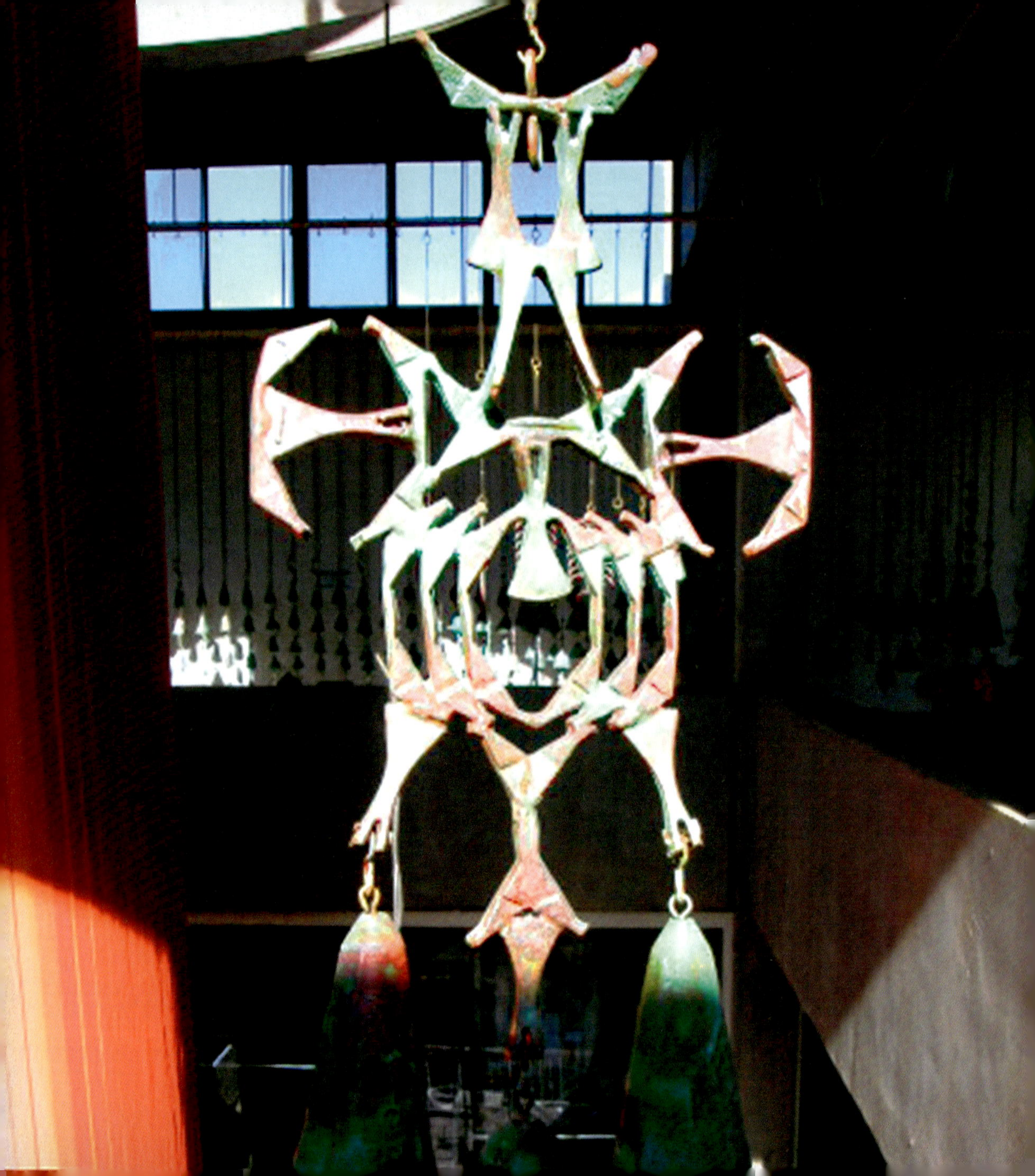

PART II
HANDMADE WORLDS

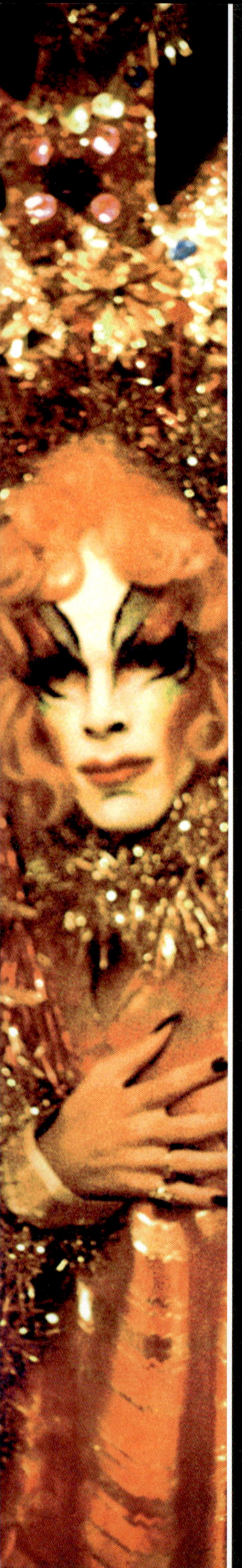

CHAPTER 5
HANDMADE GENDERS: QUEER COSTUMING IN SAN FRANCISCO CIRCA 1970

Julia Bryan-Wilson

In 1974, Alexandra Jacopetti's book *Native Funk and Flash: An Emerging Folk Art* chronicled the reemergence of traditional craft techniques within alternative, hippie subcultures in California.[1] Among its colorful pages, which included documentation of intricate embroidery, hand-carved woodwork, and a macramé children's park, are photographs of what the book refers to as "Glitter Boys"—gender-bending performers who were affiliated with the San Francisco—based groups the Cockettes and its offshoot the Angels of Light, in the 1970s. These collectives were equal parts experiments in communal living, theater troupes, and active promoters of radical new modes of queer and feminist self-fashioning. Category-defying in every sense, the Cockettes and the Angels of Light were known for their outrageous performances wearing handmade outfits both in the theater and in the street. One vivid picture from *Native Funk and Flash* features Pristine Condition ("known as Prissy to her friends"), bedecked in a pink dress with cascading tiered sleeves, a large headdress of gathered fabric and silk flowers, and an apron appliquéd with cloth designs (Figure 5.1). Scraggly threads drip

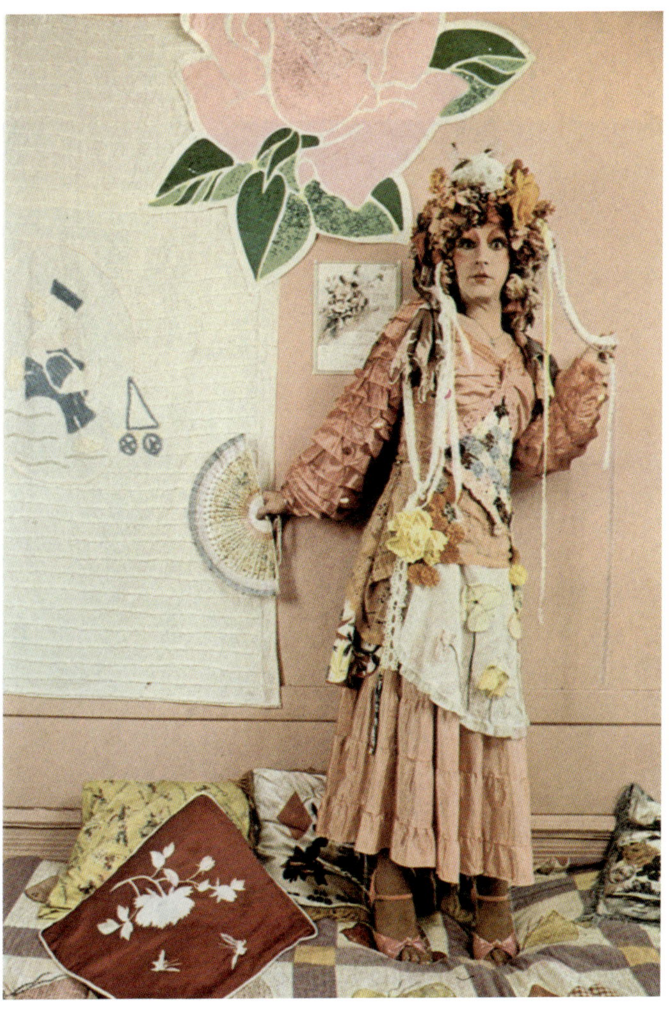

   HANDMADE GENDERS

Figure 5.2

Roger Arvid Anderson, *Goldie Glitters in Pearls over Shanghai*, 1972. Palace Theater, San Francisco, California. Courtesy of the artist. Copyright 1972 Roger Arvid Anderson.

from the skirt's uneven hemline. A diamond-shaped piece of crocheted material—perhaps repurposed from a bed covering—is affixed to the bodice, and the ensemble is festooned with long, ragged streams of old lace. The overall effect, with Prissy perched in pink high heels on a quilt and framed by a light-pink wall decorated with a giant rose, is one of fantastic excess.

Yet it is a form of excess marked not by wealth but by thrift: outfits such as these were made from scavenged materials and trash-picked treasures and relied on the ingenuity of scarcity to achieve their distinctive glamour. As the caption for Prissy's photograph states, "As she

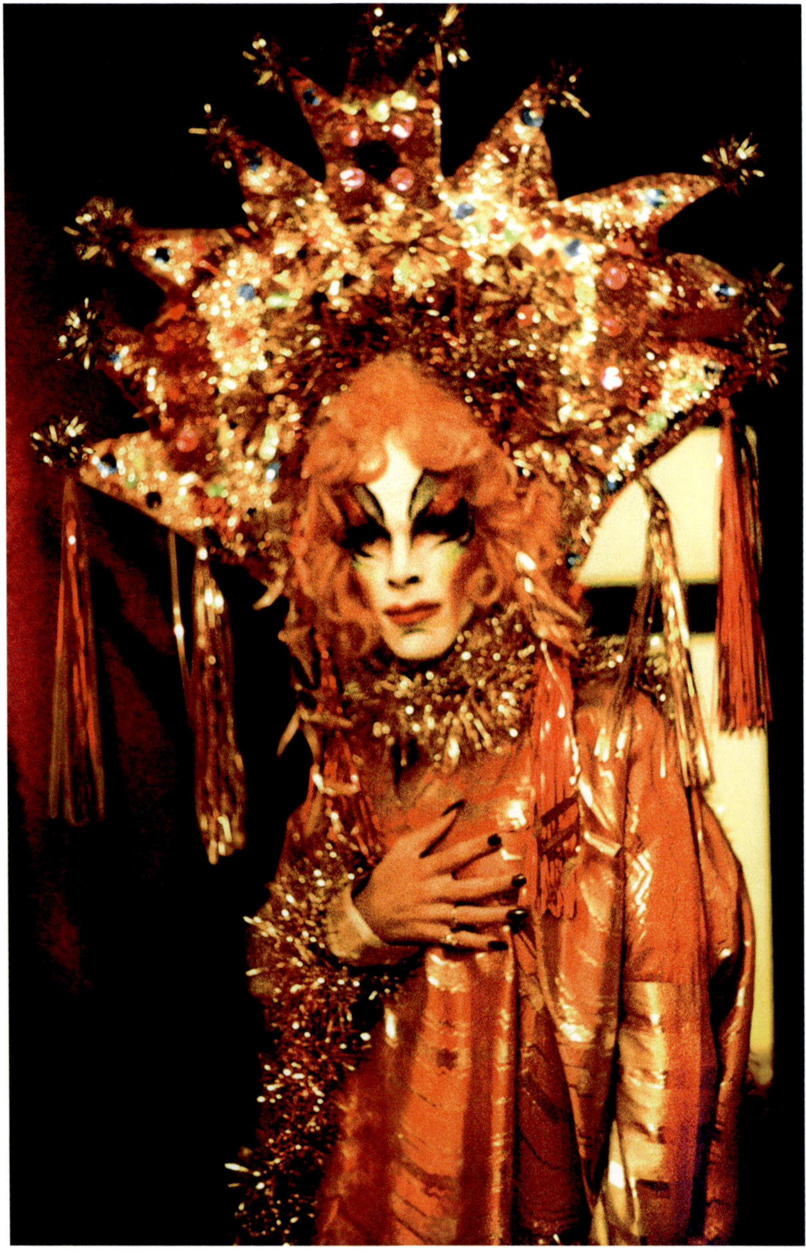

hitched up his dress, s/he said, 'I'm a firm believer in safety pins!'"[2] Such text not only points to the thrown-together, impromptu style that was integral to the Glitter Boys, it also underscores their fundamental gender indeterminacy. Within this one brief sentence, three gendered terms are used in rapid succession in reference to Prissy—first female *(she)*, then male *(his)*, then bigendered *(s/he)*. It is as if no one singular phrase could encapsulate the ever-morphing identities Prissy is taking up, playing with—or perhaps, *putting on*—as with the exaggerated head-dress and bright-red eye shadow.

In this article, I investigate the handmade costumes of the Cockettes and the Angels of Light to propose that the upsurge in crafting in the late 1960s and early 1970s overlapped in provocative ways with a simultaneous emergence of gay and feminist culture in northern California in the post-Stonewall era. These garish get-ups could be situated within long-standing traditions of *drag* and *camp;* within the academy these two dense, related, but distinct terms have been productively circulated, debated, and revised by thinkers such as Susan Sontag, Esther Newton, and Judith Butler.[3] Butler's work in particular reminds us that the notion that gender might be like a metaphoric change of clothes—worn and then discarded at will—is highly problematic, as it disregards the punitive, regulatory force of the law to maintain and uphold normative gender conventions.

In the historical moment I am examining, however, actual outfits *were* part and parcel of a utopian vision in which smashing those conventions seemed entirely possible. I focus on the specific material practices that went into constructing these garments and ornamentations, and how the Cockettes and Angels of Light, like many in the California alternative craft movement, aligned handmaking with countercultural world-making—both as an individualist practice of differentiation and a larger, if somewhat inchoate, communalist project.[4] In the spirit of the patchworked craft of these rough-edged costumes, what follows is somewhat loosely woven, pieced together from archival research, oral histories, and theoretical speculations.

SCRAPS OF HISTORY

The Cockettes were born in San Francisco on New Year's Eve 1969–1970 and lasted for a little more than two years, staging regular theatrical extravaganzas at the Palace Theater that garnered an avid cult following.[5] These performances, lavishly embellished by their flamboyant, gender-bending costumes, showcased irreverent parodies of Hollywood musicals and integrated solo numbers, music, group revues, and dance as they flaunted their general disregard for traditional codes of sexuality (Figure 5.2). Though they included a diverse assortment of characters, such as soon-to-be disco celebrity Sylvester, the Cockettes circulated around one primary charismatic figure, Hibiscus, who wore glitter in his long beard, lipstick, and innovated in his dress style with evocative sartorial flair

     HANDMADE GENDERS

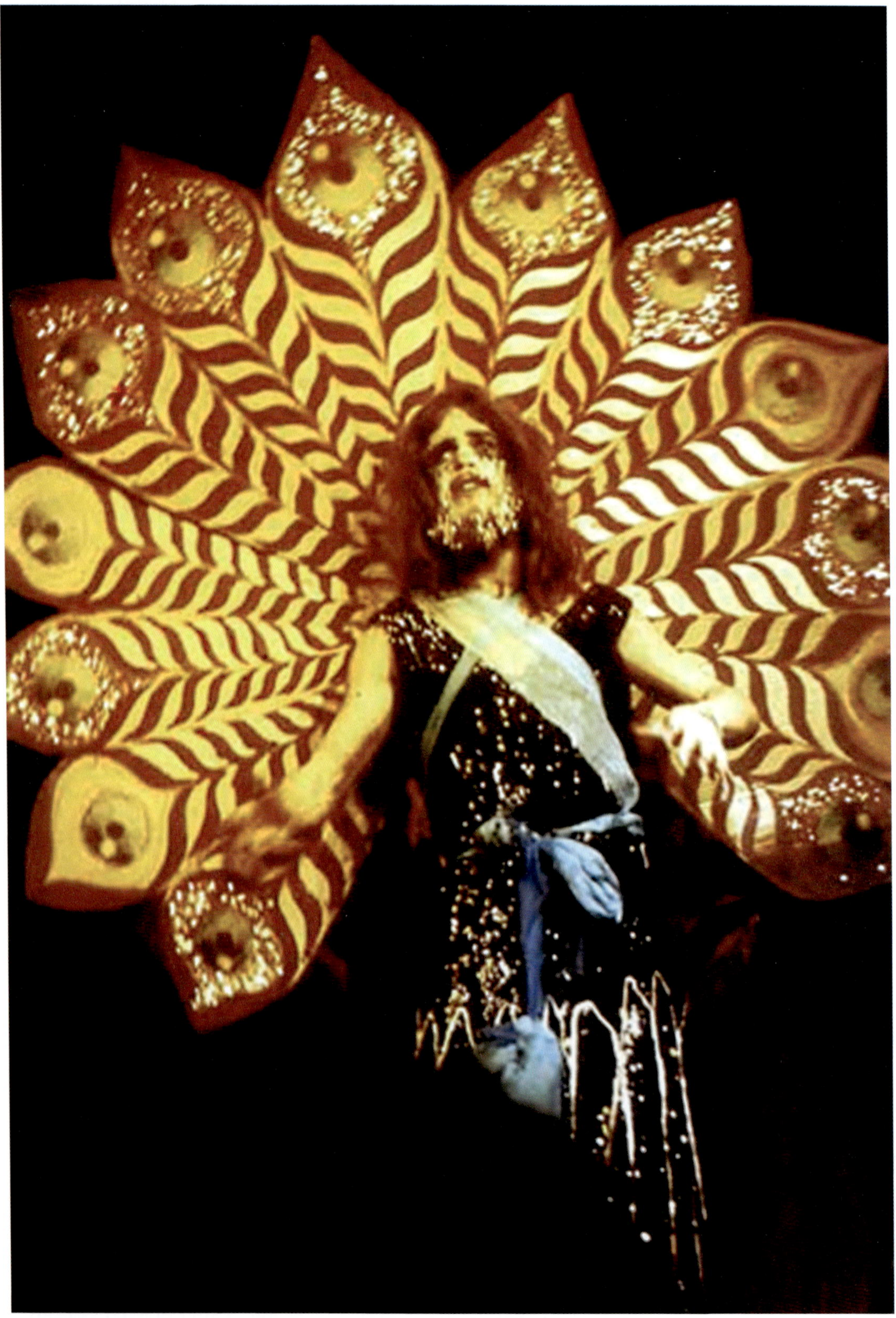

(Figure 5.3). Here Hibiscus is transformed into a luminous peacock, in a costume designed by fellow Cockette Martin Wong, with flame-colored cardboard feathers arrayed around the upper torso to augment and enhance a glitter-encrusted face.

Anarchic in both spirit and practice, the Cockettes made little distinction between stage and street or between public and private as they wore their fantastical regalia as much in everyday life as they did at the Palace Theater. Audience member and poet Allen Ginsberg noted: "Their productions were transvestite-glitter-fairie-theatre masques. Transsexual dressing is a gay contribution to the realization that we're not a hundred percent masculine or feminine, but a mixture of hormones—and not being afraid of that natural self which the hormones dictate. The Cockettes brought out into the street what was in the closet, in terms of theatric dress and imaginative theatre."[6] Ginsberg's remark highlights the crucial role of the imagination in attempting to forge a space for fluid sexual openness—or what we now call *queerness,* though that was not necessarily the term used to describe them at the time. Hibiscus was a touchstone for a nascent neologism—*genderfuck.* Encompassing a wide spectrum of queer and assertively nonnormative sexualities, the term *genderfuck* was first used in reference to phenomena like the Cockettes in a 1974 article in the magazine *Gay Sunshine.*[7] For those affiliated with the Cockettes, the theatrical outfit that "comes out of the closet" (never has that wardrobe metaphor been so appropriate) was one that had been lovingly emblazoned with feathers, broken-apart jewelry, beads, glitter, and detritus from the street. Venturing far outside purely gendered frames of reference, these costumes blended animal/human/machine/myth, as papier-mâché horse heads sprouted manes of rubber dildos and flowing, biblical robes were worn with headdresses of fresh calla lilies.

In 1971, an ideological rift led to the formation of a splinter group, the Angels of Light, which was dedicated to free performances and was active throughout the 1970s. Several of the Cockettes became Angels of Light members; in contrast to the tenuous, ad hoc organization of the Cockettes, the Angels established many tenets of collectivity, lived together in a communal house on Oak Street that had no doors, espoused the eradication of private property, and shared all their resources. The Angels' group house was part of a larger social movement toward alternative living that was in full bloom across the United States in the 1970s.[8] Thus, while there are important distinctions to be made between these two groups, I am primarily interested in the common ground they did share—namely, their investment in and pioneering of handcrafted clothing worn both at home and in their theatrical presentations. Both believed they embodied the revolutionary edge of a new society that began with such crafting. As former Angel Beaver Bauer recounts, "How we lived and what we made were part of what we wanted to see the world become."[9] By all accounts, the communal Angels' group house had its personality clashes, logistical problems,

  HANDMADE GENDERS

Figure 5.4

Models from the Years Ahead
Fashion Show, San Francisco,
1973. They model Billy Bowers's
clothes or their own ensembles;
Wally is in a self-made outfit at
far right, bottom. Photograph
copyright Wendy Mukluk.

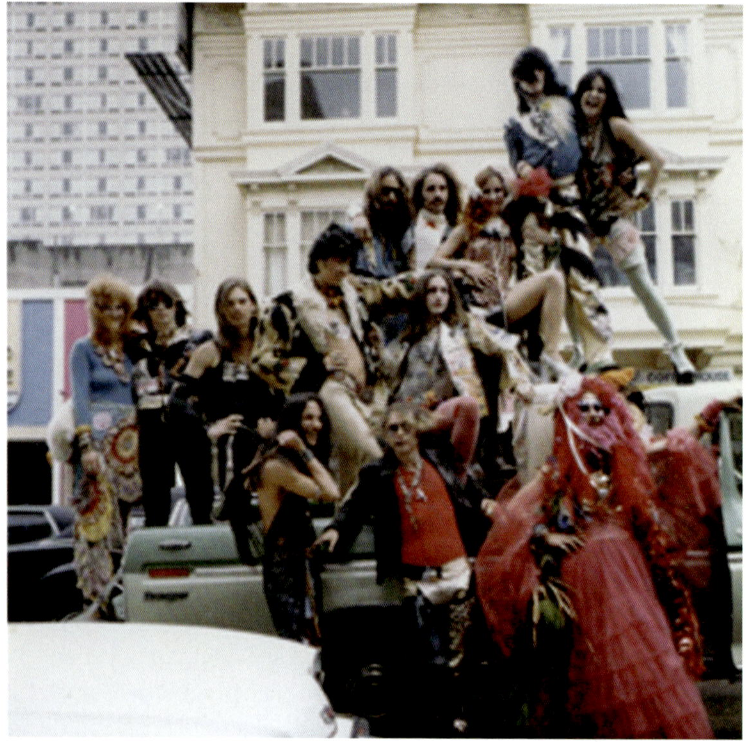

and petty in-fights, but it was also an attempt, however compromised, to create an idealistic, projective space—the world of what-if.

As a photo from the 1973 Years Ahead Fashion Show demonstrates, both the Cockettes and the Angels were defiant about nonconformity and self-fashioning on many axes, not least gender (Figure 5.4). Here a Cockette named Wally—pictured at the far right—is adorned from head to toe in hot pink and red. Sporting a feather boa, a bird perched atop a red wig, a beard died pink, and a flowing gown trailing swaths of sheer material, this ambiguously gendered figure is a vision of extreme fashion confection. Such costumes were not always recognizable within the usual rubric of drag's gender inversion. In an interview in 1980, Hibiscus recounted: "Instead of dressing in drag, I was dressing more as gods. We were all creating mythic figures."[10]

FINDING AND MAKING

The aesthetic of this San Francisco queer counterculture put a great emphasis on dazzle: you were to make a stunning first impression with an overload of eye-catching detail and leave a trail of spangles in your wake. A ruling mantra was that "glitter covers a multitude of sins."[11] These sparkly surfaces were built up by hand using glue, staples, and whatever was available—in the Angel's group house, there was only sporadic access to one used (frequently broken) sewing machine. Former Angel Jessica Copen recalls many drug-fueled all-nighters gluing rhinestones into place.[12] Since everyone was in charge of their own costumes, and skill sets varied widely, many improvised their methods of crafting with little care for how things "should" fit the body. In fact, especially in the beginning years, there was an overarching disregard for the natural shape of the figure.[13] For example, the red outfit from 1973 turned Wally's human form into a bright pyramid of color and texture, a living statue. This disregard for pattern or precedent, combined with a sense that anything at all—from taffeta to tattered curtains—might be used as potential material, promoted experimentation. Within the space of the theater, too, the sets were cobbled together from castoffs and found objects such as painted sheets, cutout cardboard shapes decorated liberally with ubiquitous glitter, and lights stuck in coffee cans.

Many of their base garments were recycled, either dumpster-dived, stolen from costume shops, or found in cheap thrift stores, where used clothes from the 1930s and 1940s were still prevalent. Vintage boas, velvet gowns, and grungy ripped-up castoffs alike all became part of communal "drag rooms" where piles of other fabrics, scraps, and possible accessories were stored. Occasionally, they would make a pilgrimage to Lew Serbin's Dance Art Company, a boutique of "party beads, marabou feathers, strips of sequins, and boxes of turquoise and emerald rhinestone. Located downtown on Powell Street, the place housed more fantasy clutter than a Hollywood five-and-dime and was revered in our circle as a holy shrine."[14]

Because they either had to make their outfits themselves or beg/barter with someone else to do it, they learned quickly how to take shortcuts and to create the most effect from the least expense. Adrian Brooks's memoir *Flights of Angels: My Life with the Angels of Light* recounts the minimal means that they lived on; few had jobs, and they survived primarily from a collective fund of pooled welfare checks: "In 1973, San Francisco reveled in the Glitter Age, its prevailing style coming from retro fashions found in thrift stores or salvaged from 'free boxes.' . . . a new culture was inventing itself."[15] No one found it paradoxical that the new was being refashioned from the old; they relied on the anachronistic as well as the futuristic, borrowing especially heavily from art nouveau—its sweeping organic lines as well as its orientalizing tendencies.

Many came to the Cockettes and the Angels with no background in craft or sewing at all; Bauer reports having previously only made an apron in her Ohio middle school home economics class that was, she told me, "a tragedy."[16] Learning by making on the spot, she went on to create some of the Angels' most memorable outfits, such as the costumes for the 1978 production *Sci-Clones* (Figure 5.5). Here the space aliens wear gowns of transparent shower curtains and extraterrestrial helmets fashioned from plastic champagne flutes found at Community Thrift for an effect that was equal parts Aubrey Beardsley drawing and Fritz Lang's *Metropolis*.[17] In another example of reusing surprising materials, Bauer took from a garbage pile a wad of the sticky material that

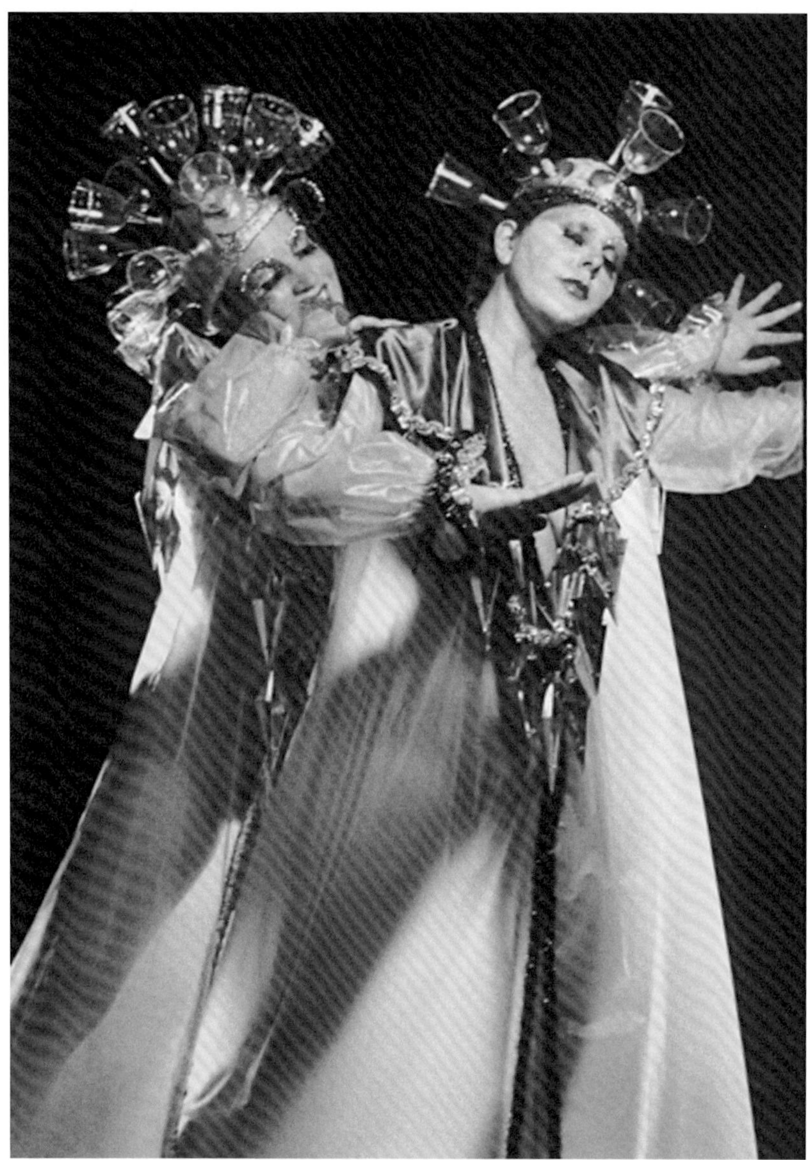

Figure 5.5

Beaver Bauer and Jessica Copen in *Sci-Clones,* an Angels of Light show, 1978. Photograph copyright Daniel Nicoletta.

goes under rugs to keep them from skidding to make an elaborate frog outfit complete with psychedelic patterning. The bubbly texture of the industrial material perfectly suited her character's reptilian skin. Bauer transformed trash to become a resplendent creaturely princess, fully upending the legend of lowly frog that turns into a prince.

Indeed, queer drag and craft are closely aligned, parallel practices: historically, drag queens and kings alike (as well as transgendered folks who aim to pass "seamlessly," to invoke a sewing metaphor) have had to stitch and make their own clothes, or at least to significantly tailor garments. Larger shoulders, poorly scaled sleeves, ill-fitting crotches, or the simple desire to amp up a garment and make it one's own: alterations for nonnormative bodies (whether too big, too small, or otherwise "wrong") necessitate a kind of skilled invention, design sense, and improvisational cunning that, like artisanal knowledge and tradition, are often learned by doing and passed down through mentorship, example, and demonstration. Here the logic of crafted production—and of re-production—is not hereditary but is instead managed within the queer kinship of shared affiliation and activity.

CRAFTING SELVES

None of these outfits was ever considered purely *theatrical,* taken in its most basic definition to mean "destined for the stage."[18] Ensembles were not exclusively meant for performances but were assembled to be worn around town—for instance, as the Cockettes stood on the street corner and passed out handmade flyers promoting upcoming shows. Yet even when at home popping popcorn or making dinner, they elaborately enrobed themselves *for themselves* and for each other (Figure 5.6). They were interested in creating personas unveiled first at home or on the street, and later rehearsed and integrated into a show—itself an "urban carnival" in which the viewers were as richly attired in rhinestones as the performers.[19] As their own best and first audience, they dressed to outdo and impress each other, as well as to command attention within the colorful tapestry of San Francisco. The outfits were understood as outward manifestations of their mutable inner lives. There was little investment in an "authentic" or stable self; instead, "what resonated deep beneath the glitter," as one memoir puts it, was a constantly shifting "spirit."[20] Distinctions about natural versus artificial were dissolved and made irrelevant within the living theater that the Cockettes and the Angels of Light attempted to embody.

If, as Sontag writes in "Notes on 'Camp,'" "the essence of Camp is its love of the unnatural: of artifice and exaggeration," then these outfits might not be properly called camp—some saw them instead as the sincere manifestation of complex internal landscapes.[21] For instance, on the stage, masks and costumes were used to obviate the division between reality and fantasy, but they were also charged with the special power of psychic illustration. Especially in the early years of the Cockettes and,

     HANDMADE GENDERS

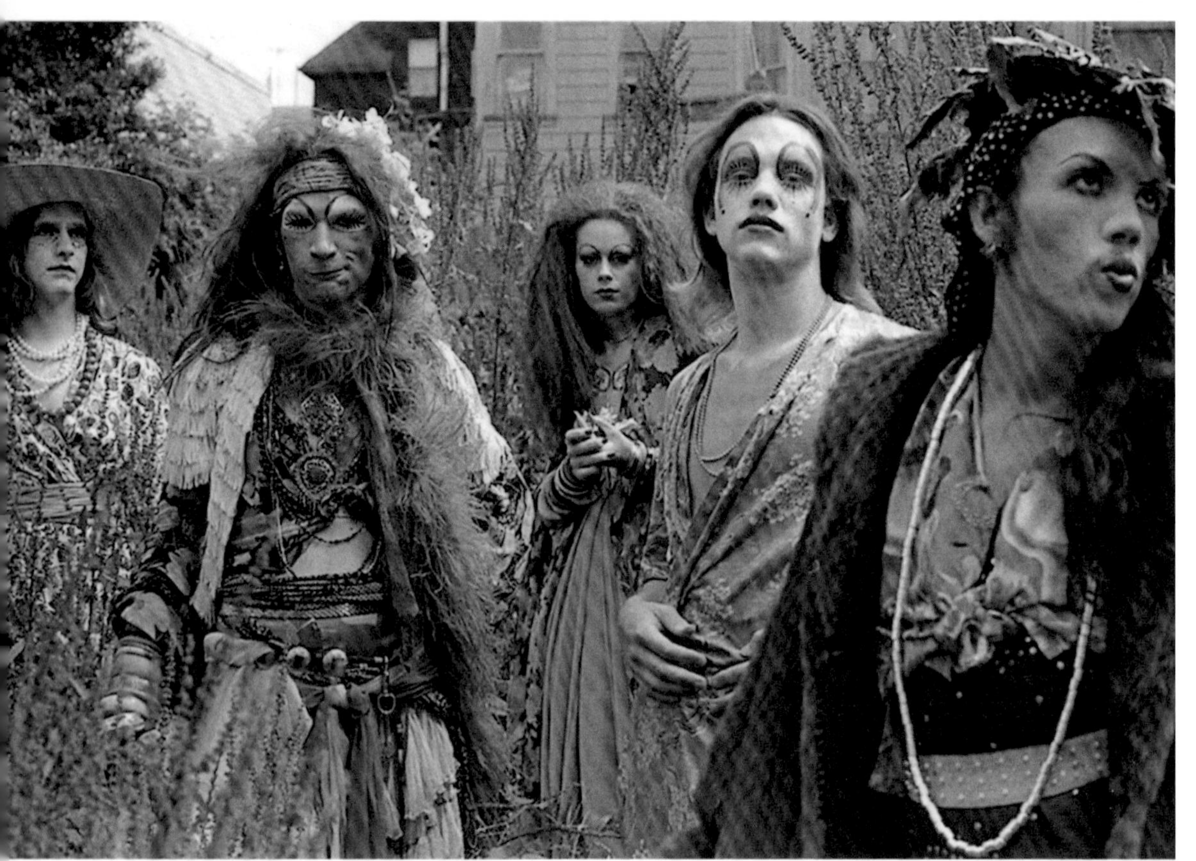

later, the Angels, the shows were only loosely scripted, and everyone more or less designed their own costume based on who or what they wanted to become that day. Because they were invented by each person for each show, individual outfits gave form to each distinctive personality. By extension, they were meant to embolden the spectator to see a range of possibilities for how life could be lived at its most extreme and imaginative. "We believed," states Bauer, "in the transformative power of our masks and outfits and costumes, to change us but also to change the people who saw us."[22] Such crafting was a social sphere; members would together scavenge, staple, and hand-sew their outfits. As productions became more organized and coherent in later years, the Angels also made preliminary sketches to unify the design themes and would develop these concepts communally.

What is more, for some, the *process* itself of handmaking was a forceful means of individual expression and communication. For instance, after a drug-induced episode of psychosis in which she became unable to speak, Cockette Fayette Hauser invented her own complex visual language of crafted scraps. "I was collaging myself together," she recalls.[23] This nonverbal sign system, pieced together from colorful fabrics, was not necessarily readable to others, but had a logic through which she was able to communicate with herself. As Pam Tent (aka

Sweet Pam) recounts, "her mind was so fragmented that assembling her drag became her only focus"—a kind of psychological puzzle to help her put herself back together.[24] In other words, crafting drag was not about dissembling (or falsity) but about assembling an earnest, if provisional, self. The knowing archness that is a hallmark of drag does not quite fit in the case of Hauser, who used it as a route to some sort of fugitive authenticity.

FOLK, FLASH, FEMINISM

Let me return to the appearance of the Glitter Boys within the specific context of Jacopetti's book *Native Funk and Flash*. This series of photos is notable, and not only because of the book's casual, unassuming incorporation of radically undefined gender identities within what is an otherwise fairly heteronormative framework. Jacopetti chronicles the revival of traditional folk arts by mostly San Francisco—area crafters, including everything from chunky, neoprimitive jewelry to stitched-together dolls to hand-decorated or "flashed" denim shirts, with a decided interest in showcasing finely done work, emphasizing the time, care, creative inspiration, and effortful labor of the hand—what we have come to think of as "craftsmanship."[25] Her inclusion of Prissy's dress therefore legitimizes it as *craft*—though with some significant disclaimers. Though she celebrates these raw, lively outfits, Jacopetti's explanatory captions also state: "So here's the art of costuming, not craftsmanship, and the use of common elements like patchwork pieces and old doilies. It's all joined with a fantastic ability to achieve an effect, rivaling the scary shamans of past times for sheer outrageous impact."[26]

The book thus make a distinct differentiation between these hodge-podge, safety-pinned concoctions and the intricate, precise work she discusses in the rest of the book—Prissy's costume is heralded for the lack of finesse, its *disregard* for skill. Though the book draws a line between "costuming" and "craftsmanship," in fact, some of the outfits documented here were early designs by Cockette Billy Bowers, who went on to be a legendary fashion designer, heralded for his handcrafted work using nontraditional materials that was featured in Italian *Vogue* and *Women's Wear Daily*.

The resurgence of folk art that Jacopetti records, including hand-thrown ceramics, leather tooling, and woodworking, was broadly connected to the concomitant growing environmentalism in the late 1960s and early 1970s, as well as seen as a path to a "gentler" lifestyle.[27] In this, it was linked to a countercultural politics of anticommercialism and a rejection of mass production that would pave the way to living with more integrity.[28] While these ideals were not so far from the utopian dreams of the Cockettes and Angels, there were also significant divergences. The costumes they devised broke with the imperative to make as much as you could by hand when they freely incorporated cheaply made consumer goods like plastic glasses. Their craft practices and politics were much more heterodox, and due to the pressures of putting shows together quickly and with very little money, they were unabashed about using whatever they could find (or steal).

The upsurge in the 1970s of traditional textile techniques (sewing, embroidery, quilting, knitting, crocheting) was also intimately related to the feminist reclamations of previously denigrated "women's work."[29] In fact, feminism is vital to this story—not least because it motored much of the return to craft within both the art world and the hobbyist countercultural movement. (It is worth nothing that in 1972, the Feminist Art Program's *Womanhouse,* which featured some work based on conventional women's craft, opened in Los Angeles.)[30] In addition, though women's liberation and gay male liberation have often been historicized as parallel, yet somewhat separate movements in which gay men and feminists are frequently pitted against each other, the Angels of Light provide a crucial, different narrative.[31] Openly feminist participants like Bauer and Copen advocated for strong female roles in the performances and for gender parity in terms of the labor of the communal house.[32] As Bauer states, "We didn't want to be fan-carriers for drag queens making a grand entrance." Perhaps because fashion design is equally gendered female and coded homosexual, one place where equality was relatively easily established within the Angels was in the creation of costumes—in other words, handmaking was the sphere where feminist and gay male labors were most equally valued.

DECADENT DÉCOR

In the 1960s and 1970s, California in particular was a space where the revitalization of craft fed off of and into gay liberation, feminism, and communal living. An awareness of geography factors heavily in the literature on the decade's craft revival as it details the regional blossoming of local artisan communities.[33] The fact that the Cockettes and the Angels surfaced in the Bay Area is significant and is related to certain economic and architectural circumstances, for instance, the availability of rambling, low-rent Victorian houses that were well suited to large groups.[34] The formation of the Cockettes in late 1969 demonstrates that, despite the insistence on the June 1969 Stonewall rebellion (just six months earlier) as the singular origin point of gay liberation in the United States, the genderfuck movement had a unique formation in the hippie counterculture of California.[35]

Furthermore, the turn to handmade fashion, redolent with sequins and beads, also resonates with the negative stereotype of California as a place obsessed with "the superficial" and appearance—politics as style, rebellion reduced to aesthetics. One of the signature features of these groups and their costumes is decorative flourish. *Decoration,* of course, is a charged word within the history of art and design. In the 1950s, Clement Greenberg warned that it was the "specter that haunts mod-

ernist painting," as it threatens to devolve art into kitsch.[36] Earlier in the
century, Adolf Loos in his 1908 essay "Ornament and Crime" cast self-
decoration as "criminal" and "degenerate," writing that "the evolution
of culture marches with the elimination of ornament from useful objects."[37]
Loos was especially disgusted with the art nouveau style that so enchanted
the Cockettes and the Angels of Light—its hyperbole, its disregard for
the categories of high and low, and its mixing of art, design, and craft. In
his important reconsideration of Loos, Hal Foster notes that Loos's
terror of art nouveau is related to his disgust for how it "commingles subject
and object"—just the sort of fantasy of the ecstatic, hybridized merging
the Cockettes and Angels celebrated.[38] What Loos saw as degradation
and decadence, they understood as a psychically charged remaking of both
self and society as they draped their bodies and their sets in swooping
designs using boas in every color and shining lamé.

Though decoration is never explicitly queered in either Loos or Greenberg, Richard Dyer in his book *The Culture of Queers* discusses the negative
association of homosexuality with the decorative and the superficial.[39]
The Cockettes and the Angels of Light reveled in extending the self with
florid, oversized headdresses and trailing garments, pleasuring in artifice, and showing little concern for the difference between surface and
depth. Or, better, they demonstrated what it might look like when those
terms converge to become, to quote a phrase sometimes attributed to
Andy Warhol, "deeply superficial."[40]

WHEN MEMORY SURFACES

In the late 1960s, not everyone saw utopian potential beneath the
sparkles and the makeup in San Francisco. Joan Didion's famous 1967
account of Haight-Ashbury, "Slouching Towards Bethlehem," instead
registers a numbed discomfort with drug culture and a freewheeling,
hippie approach to living: "We were seeing the desperate attempt of a
handful of pathetically unequipped children to create a community in
a social vacuum."[41] Didion, taking off from a poem by William Butler
Yeats, bleakly notes that all these art-into-life experiments were proof
that American society was rotting from within: "The center was not
holding."[42] And it is important not to wax overly nostalgic or romanti-
cize these groups, which had their share of jealousies, infighting, over-
doses, and so forth. Yet for the Angels, the center did hold together for
almost a decade; they lived and worked together until the early 1980s,
until they, too, unraveled. That decade saw a further devastation: Hibiscus—inspiration and figurehead—became an early casualty of AIDS in
the United States when he died in 1982. Despite these groups' idealistic
attempts to transcend gender, sexuality proved vitally significant when
gay men began to contract HIV in the 1980s; many of the men involved
in the Cockettes and the Angels have died of AIDS-related illnesses,
including Sylvester, Martin Wong, Wally, and Prissy.

Art and design historian Christopher Reed has declared: "There is something queer about archives."[43] That statement has been borne out in this research project in unexpected, and unsettling, ways. When interviewing Bauer, for example, I asked to see some of her photographs of her time with the Angels. "I'll need to think about that," she responded. "To be honest, dredging up that past is very painful for me. When I look at those pictures, I am reminded of tremendous loss and death." Talking with former members constantly reminded me of the fragmented, piecemeal nature of history itself, the tattered skein of time. Some of their stories were detailed and precise; other times they confessed to large gaps in their recollections. Pam Tent's memoir emphasizes the communally crafted nature of trying to recall this heady era; its first sentence describes the book as a "collective memoir, and much like a Cockettes show, was pasted together from scraps in our closets and our shared experiences."[44] She is quick to acknowledge holes in the narrative. Likewise, Brooks interrupts his memoir with the phrase "memory fails."[45] Lost films, missing photographs, vanished costumes: it is easy to lose the thread.

In the wake of the Cockettes documentary and the publication of memoirs by former members, this history (and, to a lesser extent, that of the Angels of Light) is being rediscovered for a new generation.[46] Unfortunately, the majority of the costumes made by the Cockettes and the Angels did not survive. Though they made spectacular first impressions, many of their outfits were in constant states of disrepair (and some of them were disassembled at the time and reused to make other garments). The performers shed sequins as they staggered offstage. As Tent states, "We ate and even pooped glitter."[47] This statement crystallizes how, with these handmade costumes, outside decoration was incorporated inside, ingested and excreted, traversing the porous membrane between exterior surface and what lies beneath. In a time and place that seemed ripe for social revolution, these groups dreamed of a queer and feminist politics of handmaking, world-making, and self-making that would eradicate the lines between performing theatrical numbers and performing a new way to live. They were crafting their own skin.

Handmade costumes—not to mention radical queer culture—are still considered somewhat marginal within art history, perhaps rightly so. (There are, however, some striking exceptions: for example, Wong is represented in a new textbook on Asian American art history for his Angels of Light stage designs, in an important recognition of the cross-racial nature of this group.)[48] Yet despite this marginalization, and despite of the destruction of many of these outfits and stage sets (and the deaths of many former members), the residue of this craft stubbornly lingers. To conclude with one last anecdote, in the early 1970s, Allen Ginsberg had a sexual liaison with Hibiscus. Ginsberg later commented that the erotic encounter was less than comfortable: "His bed was a little gritty because he had a lot of sequins in it. And it was difficult to sleep on the sheets because there was sort of like difficult glitter stuff there."[49] It is a peculiar conjunction—glamour so excessive that it can admit and embrace its own decrepitude. This is one lesson of the queer handmade aesthetic: it exists where grit and glitter meet, ostensibly right on the surface of things, and yet profound.

NOTES

A previous version of this essay appeared in *Octopus*, the graduate journal of the Ph.D. program in visual studies at University of California, Irvine. Thanks to audiences at the School of the Art Institute of Chicago and the California College of the Arts for their comments, to Amber Straus for her support and wisdom, and to Mel Y. Chen for being endlessly inspiring.

1. Alexandra Jacopetti, *Native Funk & Flash: An Emerging Folk Art* (San Francisco: Scrimshaw Press, 1974).

2. Ibid., 47.

3. These are just a few of the most influential writings on this topic. See Susan Sontag, "Notes on 'Camp,'" *Partisan Review* 31, no. 4 (Fall 1964): 515–30; reprinted in *Against Interpretation and Other Essays* (New York: Farrar, Strauss, and Giroux, 1966), 275–92; Esther Newton, *Mother Camp: Female Impersonators in America* (Chicago: University of Chicago Press, 1979); Judith Butler, *Gender Trouble: Feminism and the Subversion of Identity* (New York: Routledge, 1990). The literature on both drag and camp is vast and includes important recent work by Judith Halberstam, José Esteban Muñoz, and Ann Pellegrini.

4. Lauren Berlant and Michael Warner, among others, have theorized queer world-making; see "Sex in Public," *Critical Inquiry* 24, no. 2 (Fall 1998): 547–66.

5. The David Weissman and Bill Weber documentary *The Cockettes* (2002) is to date the most comprehensive overview of the founding of the group and its demise. Photographic documentation, films, and other ephemera have been the subject of several recent exhibitions, including at San Francisco's Yerba Buena Center for the Arts (2002), and *Dear Cockettes* (2007), curated by Ida Ekblad and Anders Nordby at UKS Gallery in Oslo, Norway. Though former members are attempting to put images and information online, many of the primary sources exist in boxes in their basements (or in the homes of the dead members' families). Some archival material can be found in the Martin Worman papers in the New York Public Library. I am grateful to the following former members of the Cockettes and the Angels of Light, each of whom generously discussed with me this subject at length: Beaver Bauer, Jessica Copen, and Fayette Hauser.

6. Quoted in Mark Thompson, "Children of Paradise: A Brief History of Queens," in *Out in Culture: Gay, Lesbian, and Queer Essays on Popular Culture*, ed. Corey K. Creekmur and Alexander Doty (Durham, N.C.: Duke University Press), 452.

7. See Christopher Lonc, "Genderfuck and Its Delights," *Gay Sunshine* 21 (Spring 1974), reprinted in *Gay Roots: Twenty Years of Gay Sunshine*, ed. Winston Leyland (San Francisco: Gay Sunshine Press, 1991), 223–26.

8. Other histories on alternative communities in the United States include Peter Braunstein and Michael William Doyle, eds., *Imagine Nation: The American Counterculture of the 1960s and 1970s* (New York: Routledge, 2002).

9. Author interview with Beaver Bauer, San Francisco, October 2008.

10. Quoted in Thompson, "Children of Paradise," 459.

11. John Flowers, quoted in Pam Tent, *Midnight at the Palace: My Life as a Fabulous Cockette* (Los Angeles: Alyson Books, 2004), 37.

12. Author phone interview with Jessica Copen, October 2008.

13. However, as the Angels became more confident in their movement and dance skills over the years, their outfits became more body-conscious and formfitting, though no less extravagant. There was still an emphasis on unexpected prostheses or attachments, like Hibiscus's peacock feathers, to project the figure farther out into space.

14. Tent, *Midnight at the Palace,* 34.

15. Adrian Brooks, *Flights of Angels: My Life with the Angels of Light* (Vancouver: Arsenal Pulp Press, 2008), 46.

16. Interview with Bauer.

17. Such skills in crafting and design proved useful even after these groups stopped performing; Bauer now makes her living as a professional costume designer. Former Cockette Fayette Hauser is also a noted costume and textile designer.

18. For an excellent discussion of theatricality and its relationship to performativity and gender theory, see Shannon Jackson, "Theatricality's Proper Objects: Genealogies of Performance and Gender Theory," in *Theatricality*, ed. Tracy C. Davis and Thomas Postlewait (Cambridge: Cambridge University Press, 2004), 186–214.

19. Tent, *Midnight at the Palace,* 28.

20. Thompson, "Children of Paradise," 454.

21. Sontag, "Notes on 'Camp,'" 275

22. Interview with Bauer.

23. Author interview with Fayette Hauser, Los Angeles, October 2008.

24. Tent, *Midnight at the Palace,* 30.

25. For more on the shifting definitions of craftsmanship, see Howard Risatti, *A Theory of Craft: Function and Aesthetic Expression* (Chapel Hill, N.C.: University of North Carolina Press, 2007).

26. Jacopetti, *Native Funk and Flash,* 46.

27. See, for example, Eudorah Moore, *Craftsman Lifestyle: The Gentle Revolution* (Pasadena: California Design Publications, 1976); this publication was brought to my attention by Glenn Adamson's "Craft and the Romance of the Studio," *American Art Journal* 21, no. 1 (Spring 2007): 14–18. Adamson also helpfully provides a framework for reconsidering craft as a form of production in his *Thinking through Craft* (Oxford and New York: Berg, 2007).

28. The term *counter culture* was put into wide circulation by Theodore Roszak in 1969; he theorized that the turn to "cultural" modes of protest such as hippie living was a response to the imperious face of industrialization, mass production, and the destruction from the Vietnam War: Roszak, *The Making of a Counter Culture: Reflections on the Technocratic Society and Its Youthful Opposition* (New York: Doubleday, 1969). For more on this term, see the introduction to this volume.

29. The feminist literature here is vast; one important, widely cited text is Rozsika Parker and Griselda Pollock's chapter "Crafty Women and the Hierarchy of the Arts," in their *Old Mistresses: Women, Art and Ideology* (London: Routledge and Kegan Paul, 1981). A recent reconsideration of the relationship between fiber arts and feminism is found in Elissa Auther, "Fiber Art and the Hierarchy of Art and Craft, 1960–1980," *Journal of Modern Craft* 1, no. 1 (March 2007): 13–34.

30. For more on *Womanhouse,* see Arlene Raven, "Womanhouse," in *The Power of Feminist Art: The American Movement of the 1970s, History and Impact*, ed. Norma Broude and Mary D. Garrard (New York: Harry N. Abrams, 1994), 48–65.

31. Art historian Richard Meyer has also documented another movement that sought to mend this rift, in "Back to the Effeminist Future," presented at the Museum of Modern Art's the Feminist Future Conference, January 2007.

32. They even made an all-female film (sadly now lost) to showcase their talents and to emphasize that they were sick of "playing second fiddle to the men," according to Copen.

33. Jo Lauria and Suzanne Baizerman, *California Design: The Legacy of West Coast Craft and Style* (San Francisco: Chronicle Books, 2005).

34. See Charles Perry, *The Haight-Ashbury: A History* (New York: Vintage, 1984).

35. The history of 1960s and 1970s San Francisco–area gay and

lesbian history is documented in numerous books and articles, including Elizabeth A. Armstrong, *Forging Gay Identities: Organizing Sexuality in San Francisco, 1950–1994* (Chicago: University of Chicago, 2002); and Susan Stryker and Jim van Buskirk, *Gay by the Bay: A History of Queer Culture in the San Francisco Bay Area* (San Francisco: Chronicle Books, 1996). For more general histories that touch on the regional differences in the gay rights movement, see John D'Emilio, *Sexual Politics, Sexual Communities: The Making of a Homosexual Minority in the United States, 1940–1970* (Chicago: University of Chicago, 1983); and David Eisenbach, *Gay Power: An American Revolution* (New York: Carroll and Graf, 2006).

36. Clement Greenberg, "Milton Avery," in Greenberg, *Art and Culture: Critical Essays* (Boston: Beacon Press, 1961), 200. David Joselit's essay "Notes on Surface" has been formative to my thoughts on this topic: see Joselit, "Notes on Surface toward a Genealogy of Flatness," *Art History* 23, no. 1 (March 2000): 19–34.

37. Adolf Loos, "Ornament and Crime" (1908), reprinted in Bernie Miller and Melony Ward, *Crime and Ornament: The Arts and Popular Culture in the Shadow of Adolf Loos* (Toronto: YYZ Books, 2002), 29–36.

38. Hal Foster, *Design and Crime (and Other Diatribes)* (London and New York: Verso, 2002), 15.

39. Richard Dyer, *The Culture of Queers* (London: Routledge, 2002), 6.

40. See the exhibition *Deeply Superficial: Andy Warhol's "Voyeurism,"* Muscarelle Museum of Art, the College of William and Mary, Williamsburg, Va., 2009–2010.

41. Joan Didion, "Slouching Towards Bethlehem," first published in *The Saturday Evening Post* (1967), reprinted in *Slouching Towards Bethlehem* (New York: Farrar, Straus, and Giroux, 1968), 122.

42. Ibid., 84.

43. Christopher Reed, "Design for (Queer) Living: Sexual Identity, Performance, and Decor in British Vogue, 1922–1926," *GLQ: A Journal of Lesbian and Gay Studies* 12, no. 3 (2006): 377.

44. Tent, *Midnight at the Palace.*

45. Brooks, *Flights of Angels,* 63.

46. This includes revivals of the play *Pearls over Shanghai,* screenings of the Cockette's film *Tricia's Wedding,* and various reunions of former members. Coinciding with the contemporary renaissance in hipster crafting, *Native Funk and Flash* has become something of a sensation as well in recent years, with many do-it-yourself crafters acknowledging it as a major influence. Furthermore, Balenciaga designer Nicolas Ghesquiere admitted to copying outright a vest he saw in the book for his 2002 spring collection; Cathy Horyn, "Is Copying Really a Part of the Creative Process?" *New York Times,* 9 April 2002, B10. See also Allison Smith's writing about this book on the blog for the *Journal for Modern Craft,* journalofmoderncraft.com/responses/native-funk-and-flash-part-one.

47. Tent, *Midnight at the Palace,* 37.

48. Gordon H. Chang, Mark Johnson, and Paul Karlstrom, *Asian American Art: A History, 1850–1970* (Stanford, Calif.: Stanford University Press, 2008), 260.

49. Quoted in Tent, *Midnight in the Palace,* 37.

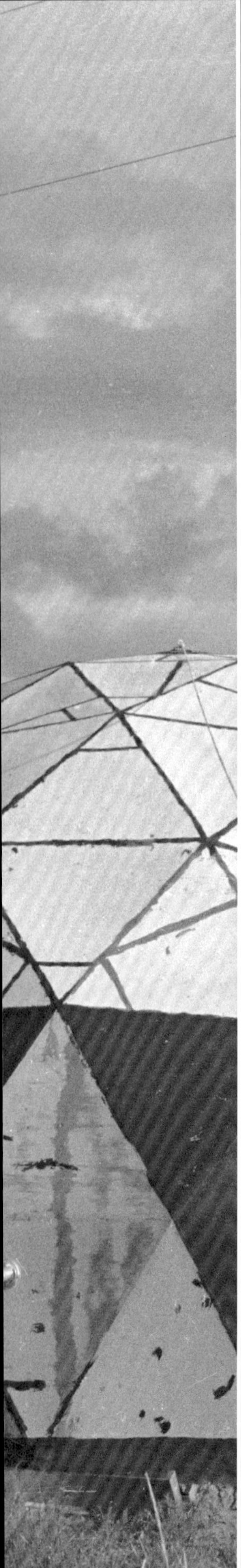

CHAPTER 6
LIBRE, COLORADO, AND THE HAND-BUILT HOME

Amy Azzarito

From Bronson Alcott's Fruitlands in Massachusetts to Oneida in upstate New York, communal settlements have long been a fixture of American culture. As Emerson wrote to Thomas Carlyle in 1840, every man had a draft of a new community in his pocket, a sensibility that has fostered many subsequent generations of utopian thinkers.[1] The most recent peak in the history of American communal settlements was the explosion of countercultural communes in the 1960s and 1970s. Although estimates of the number of communal participants vary widely, the movement's most thorough surveyor, Judson Jerome, estimated that by the early 1970s, 750,000 people lived in tens of thousands of communes in areas all over the country.[2] This would be the largest communal movement in history, as alienated youth dissatisfied with mainstream society explored alternative forms of living. Like their nineteenth-century forebears, the architectural structures they built and the lifestyles supported therein were as unique as the beliefs behind their conception.

The focus of this essay, the community known as Libre founded in 1968 in southeastern Colorado, was integral to the development of a countercultural design aesthetic on two fronts. First, Libre residents were early adopters of styles and forms considered quintessential to countercultural ideology. At nearly every juncture, Libre residents were in step with or ahead of their countercultural peers and were lauded as a shining example by influential counterculture publications such as the *Whole Earth Catalog* and Lloyd Kahn's trio of how-to surveys of hand-built structures, *Domebook 1, Domebook 2,* and *Shelter.*[3] Second, the Libre community was willing to experiment with and respond to evolving counterculture styles of building. After a period of dome building, inspired by the neighboring commune Drop City outside Trinidad, Colorado, residents of Libre began to focus on traditional building and handicraft, with an emphasis on using recycled materials and elementary building practices. This switch presaged the general turn away from domes within the counterculture by early the 1970s.[4] Libre residents' early adoption of these countercultural building styles and practices, whether dome building or a looser style with a focus on construction materials, ensured that they received visits from a constant stream of journalists, authors, and artists, who reported on the progress of the Libre community in print publications.

The possibility of creating a new society with its own rules, beliefs, and values, in direct contrast to the mainstream, was intoxicating to the founders of Libre, as it was for all those who participated in communal living in the period. And the communards of the 1960s and 1970s were intent on developing an aesthetic vocabulary that was reflective of their social beliefs. Not only did they reject the values of mainstream America, but also they strove to reject the look of mainstream America. While that aesthetic vocabulary was apparent in all aspects of the communal lifestyle, it was through the communal building process that a clear vision for the future was articulated.

paper and constant maintenance. A dome's tendency to leak along with a variety of suggested solutions became a major discussion point in dome building handbooks and eventually led to its dismissal by gurus of countercultural architecture like Lloyd Kahn.[12]

The residents of Libre were interested in spreading the word about their experiment beyond the mountains of Colorado. In 1969, six members of Libre—the Flemings, the Rabbit-Douthits, and two new members, Tony and Marilyn Magar—embarked on a twenty-stop lecture tour in an effort to raise money for building materials (Figure 6.1). The academic community was intrigued by the communal experiments throughout the United States, and a contact at Washington University in Saint Louis assisted Libre residents in arranging the tour. Neighbor Michael Duncan loaned the group his stainless steel step van, which they outfitted for their six-week trip by placing a fifty-five-gallon drum on the roof for diesel fuel and equipping the inside of the van with places to eat and sleep.[13] Their first stop, in March, was near Alamogordo, New Mexico, to attend ALLOY, a conference organized by Stewart Brand, Stephen Durkee, and Steve Baer and reported on by *Whole Earth* publications. The conference was an attempt to articulate the environmental design thrust of the counterculture, and to Brand, ALLOY was the physical manifestation of the *Whole Earth Catalog*. "If I had to point at one thing that contains what the catalog is about, I'd have to say it was ALLOY," he wrote soon

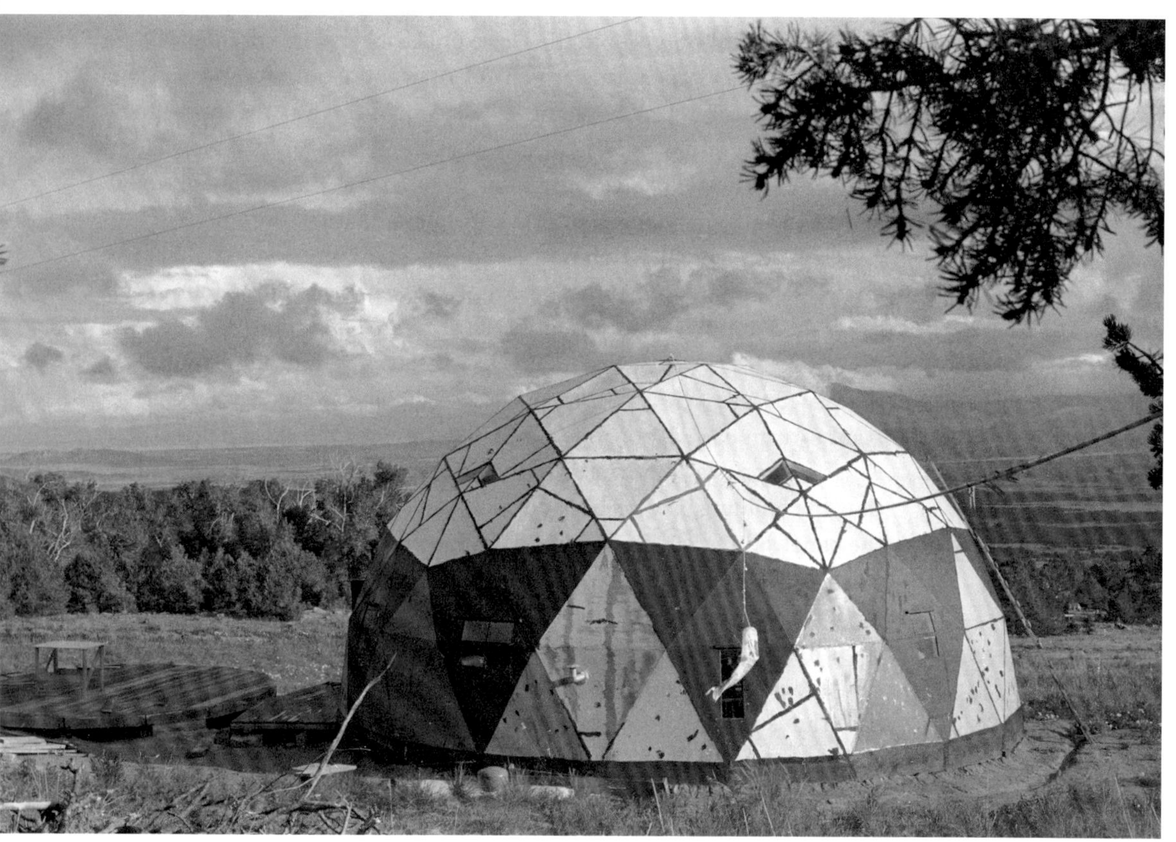

LIBRE, COLORADO, AND THE HAND-BUILT HOME

Magar Dome, Libre, Colorado,
1969. Copyright Roberta Price.

after the March 1969 conference.[14] It is significant that the conference was held in the Southwest, which rivaled the San Francisco Bay Area in terms of experimental building and forms of living. One hundred and fifty people came from as far as New York, Washington State, and Canada to attend the conference, which ranged in content from discussion on the constraints of materials and structures to energy and consciousness.[15] After ALLOY, the Libre residents visited universities around the country including Washington University, Cranbrook Academy of Art in Michigan, the Corcoran School of Art in Washington, D.C, Columbia University, the School of Visual Arts, SUNY Purchase, Wagner College in Staten Island, and Rochdale Free University in Toronto. Not only did the trip provide the Libre residents an opportunity to articulate their vision for communal living and raise funds to continue their project, but the tour also resulted in a flood of would-be communards to the Huerfano Valley.

The flurry of countercultural dome building, which began at Drop City in 1965 and spread to communes around the country, would peak in the late 1960s. By the early 1970s, domes had become a decidedly un-popular building choice. Just as quickly as they had become the counter-cultural emblem, they suddenly seemed clichéd, dated, and impractical. This was partially because it remained difficult to adapt rectangular materials intended for balloon-frame construction to a structure that depended on triangles. Even Kahn, who had championed dome building with his two *Domebooks,* was beginning to grow tired of dome living: "After four years of living in domes, the excitement of moonlight through overhead windows has worn off."[16] In a third publication, *Shelter,* Kahn looked back on his part in the dome movement: "*Domebook 2* made domes look too easy, too much like a breakthrough solution, too exciting."[17] For other countercultural builders, the issue was the rigidity of the dome mathematics, which required working out the complex geometry that dome building required. Instead, they preferred a looser, more adaptable style of building, which would allow for improvisation.

Although dome homes could be built quickly in the short burst of warm weather in the Huerfano Valley, the transition from domes to more free-form buildings in the larger countercultural community was echoed at Libre. New residents, settling at Libre from 1970 on, found ways to express themselves and their individuality through a building process that was far more improvisational and involved as much attention to selecting materials as to a building's form. The families and individuals who moved to Libre in the early 1970s wanted their homes to reflect their personalities, in a way that seemed impossible using rigid dome formulas.

Richard and Vicki Wehrman were one such couple. The pair, with their two children, came to Libre in 1970 after meeting the founders and hearing about the community at the Washington University stop on the Libre tour. Interested in designing and building a home that would be self-expressive, the couple built a star-shaped structure, intended to echo the mountain's peak (Figure 6.2). It was a true owner-built home

   LIBRE, COLORADO, AND THE HAND-BUILT HOME

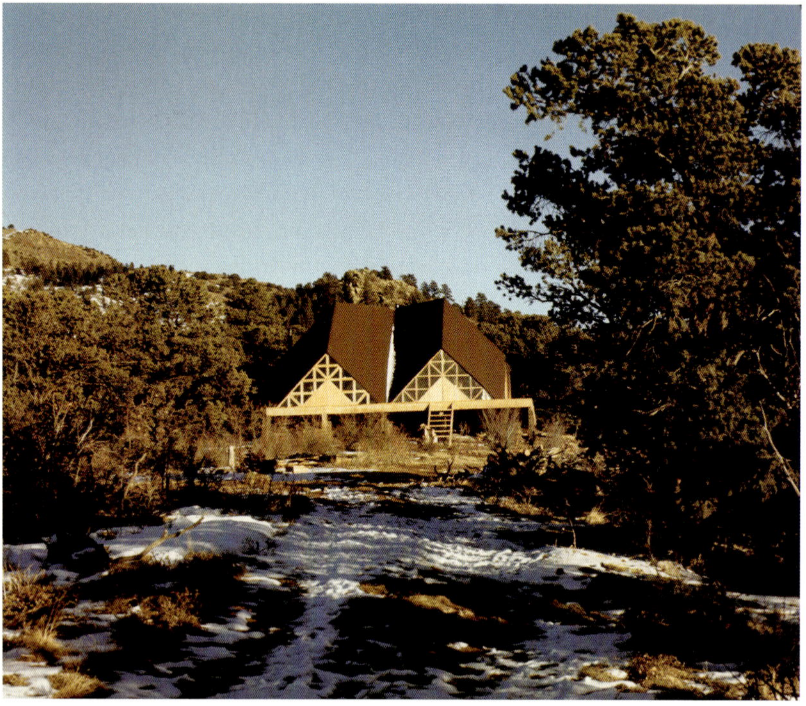

designed to articulate the personality of the builder. Richard, a trained jeweler, who designed the structure, also intended the structure to appear faceted like a gem. The house was a thirty-two-foot square that was divided equally into four living areas—living room, kitchen, workshop, a children's room—and two sleeping lofts overhead. The home was built in four months with inexpensive lumber at the total cost of twelve hundred dollars.[18] The walls were wood paneled and the floor was finished with long wood planks that were placed at a diagonal in a modified chevron pattern. The serene, spare interior was furnished with handmade furniture built low to the ground. Like most Libre residents, home building was only one facet of art production, and Richard continued to earn a living by making jewelry at Libre.

After spending the summer of 1969 traveling around the Southwest on a grant-funded project to study communes, Roberta Price and David Perkins also joined Libre. During the year between visiting Libre and returning to build their own home, the population at Libre had grown significantly. This was partially a result of the Libre spring tour, but also a result of the press that Libre received in the late 1960s and early 1970s. During that time, approximately half a dozen journalists went on tours moving from commune to commune, relaying stories of the countercultural lifestyle back to the mainstream through articles and books. These stories, which were often embellished by their authors, became virtual advertisements for the countercultural communes. However much communards detested the interruption, media attention was a necessary component of staying relevant and legitimizing the Libre experience.

By the time Price and Perkins returned to Libre in the summer of 1970, all the lots in the lower valley were occupied, and the couple turned to a building site beyond the reach of water and electricity lines. The main attraction of the site was an immense boulder in a small meadow directly above the homes in the lower valley, which Price and Perkins decided to use as the central support for their house.[19] Only a few years prior, technology had been the cornerstone of the Libre community; now new residents were open to forms of living less technically advanced but unique in terms of design. It was partially this mix of countercultural living styles that made Libre interesting to the larger communal network.

After receiving permission from the Libre council to build, the couple erected a temporary structure on site. Like the Comanche and other Plains Indians who had been on the land before, the housing of choice for a Libre member without a permanent home was the tepee, which was constructed according to a how-to handbook frequently consulted in the community. The plan for the permanent home was octagon shaped with the twenty-nine-ton bolder as the central support (Figure 6.3). A wagon wheel was placed on the crown of the boulder to act as the hub for eight spokes that would project outward from the rock to meet the upright, log supports of the structure.[20] Too heavy for the couple to position on their own, the logs were slowly put into place as help from other Libre residents or friends passing through the community became available (Figure 6.4).

The couple was unable to finish construction before winter, so they moved in when only two out of the eight walls were completed. Writing about the experience, they remarked: "Although living in a construction site can be both chaotic and hazardous, we found this was the only way the house could grow organically to fulfill our living needs. There are no blueprints and very little conception of what the end product will be. The house builds itself."[21] Price and Perkins's desire for their home to evolve rather than to be precisely constructed encapsulates the sentiment of the owner-built home in the 1970s. While dome homes needed precise construction plans as well as models and the understanding of dome mathematics to be successful, the more individualized homes of the 1970s were free-form. It was all trial and error, and new builders embraced learning on the job.[22]

As this essay suggests, Libre was different from many intentional communities of the period in that the building process was more individual than communal. While Libre residents occasionally pitched in, the individual resident was responsible for providing his or her own living structure. The process could be lonely and demanding. Linda Fleming described how the intensity of building could impact relationships: "It took so much focus and back-breaking labor, that many couples who finally made it through the building process broke up afterward because the focus of building was gone and it had supplanted other meanings in the relationship."[23] After eight years of struggling to build her home

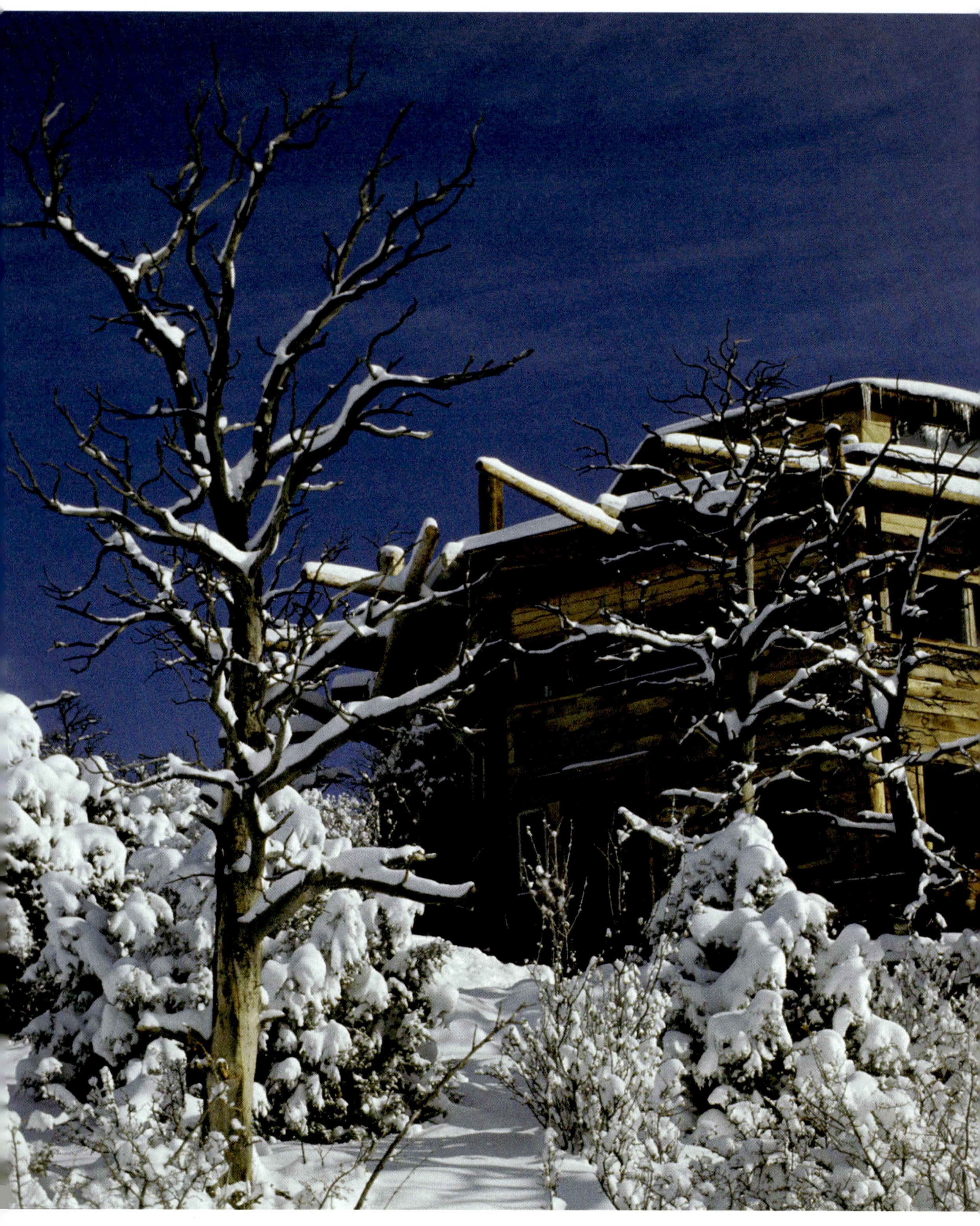

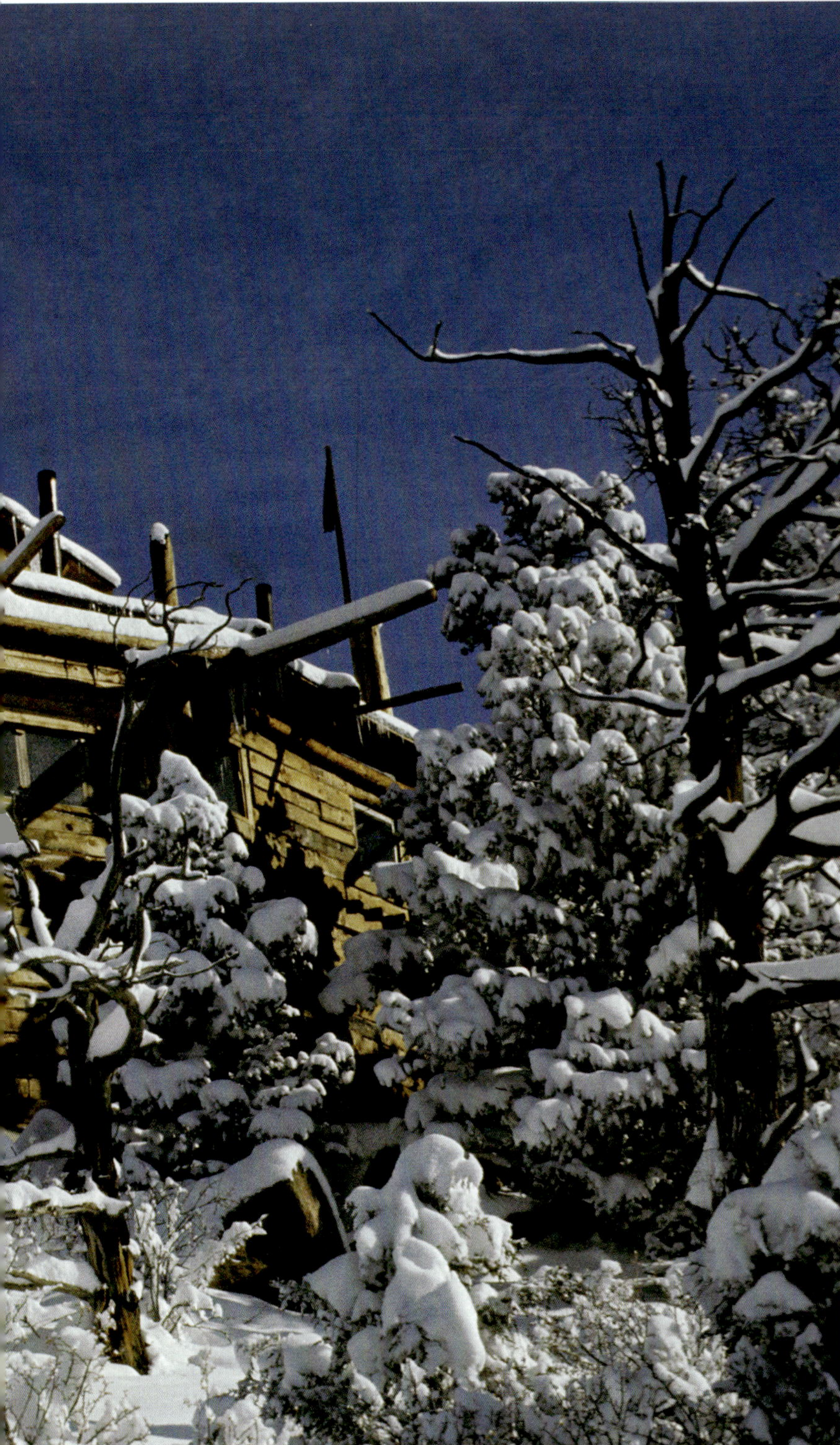

Figure 6.3
Price–Perkins Home, Libre, Colorado, 1971. Copyright Roberta Price.

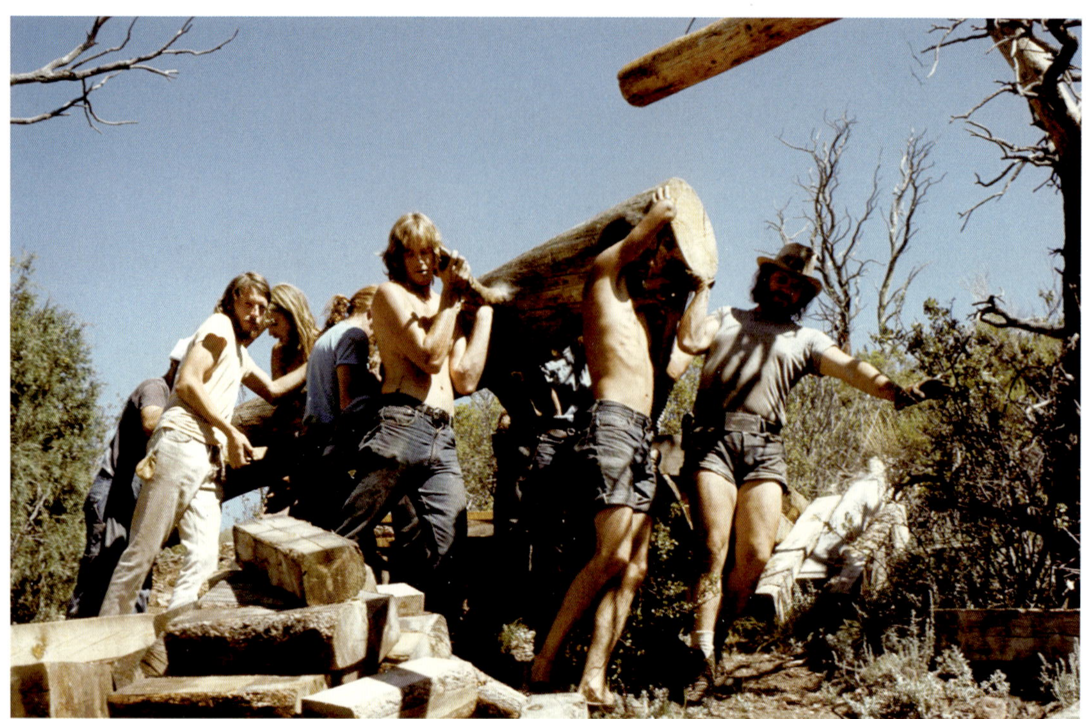

and living in virtual poverty, Price left the community in 1978. Perkins moved into resident Richard Wehrman's house two years later. Fundamental to the countercultural ethos was a willingness to embrace experimentation, even if the experiment was not ultimately sustainable.

Just as books and pamphlets had been produced quickly to capture the spirit of dome building, there was an interest in writing about the new, freestyle, self-expressive method of construction. After publishing two books on dome building, Kahn moved to capture the movement of owner-built construction that was happening all over the country. Even as Kahn was reporting on domes, he was thinking past them toward this new frontier of building. The first edition of *Domebook 2* was published in May 1971; by August the same year Kahn concluded a revised edition of the publication with a solicitation for information about new building projects for what would be *Shelter.* He wrote:

Although the structures described in this book are domes, we are continuing our experimentation; we are looking for new methods, materials and shapes to share in another book in 1973. It will be a book on homes, domes, barns, houseboats, trailers and campers with soul. . . . Our parameters this time will be what is beautiful, inventive and what can be done by hand. . . . Our third book will be called *Shelter.*[24]

Shelter contained more than one thousand photographs, which were collected over a two-year period from 1971 to 1973. The publication sold more than 185,000 copies.[25] However, for all his interest in the more free-form buildings, Kahn was unable to leave domes completely in the past. In *Shelter* there is a small section titled "Domebook 3," in which dome building is presented as one building option among the many others presented in the rest of the volume. The tone of the section is mostly discouraging to any potential dome builder. Kahn offers caveats for would-be dome builders, warning them that dome construction was not as easy as it might have seemed to earlier enthusiasts. Where he once assumed that technology would be the answer to all problems, Kahn had begun to develop a distrust of technology, and part of that distrust seems to have stemmed from the practical difficulties of dome living, from leaks to broken plastic hubs, contributing to an overall dismissal of domes as a worn-out aesthetic.

By the early 1970s, other communes in the Huerfano Valley had also moved on from dome building. One such group was the Red Rockers, a group of young artists from Beverly Hills, California, who had met the Libre founders on their 1969 tour and were inspired to establish their own community.[26] This group—consisting of eleven individuals—visited Libre in the spring of 1969 and collectively purchased land nearby in an area named Red Rock Canyon. Calling themselves the Red Rockers, they all took the last name *Red Rock* as an expression of the political commitment to communal living.[27]

Initially, the group erected a sixty-foot dome on their property with the help of Libre members.[28] Although the largest of all domes built in a countercultural commune, it was also the last to appear in Huerfano County.[29] The Red Rockers had been living in their dome for only a few months when they shared their experiences with *Domebook 2* readers. They seemed pleased with the result of their project: "We like living together in a heap with one kitchen and lots of shared space."[30] Kahn revisited the Red Rockers in *Shelter* and included the community in the "Domebook 3" section. After a couple of years, however, the building had to be adapted as the group grew and began having more children, and each summer most of the Red Rockers would move out of the dome and live in tepees. In a collectively written article for *Shelter,* the Red Rockers drew a cartoon to illustrate what they liked and what they disliked about the dome. The dislikes—leaking windows, excessive heat in the summer, and a lack of privacy—outnumber the likes, which are primarily that the space is large and children like it. Although the sixty-foot dome had been built for only twenty-five hundred dollars, when contemplating their new building projects, the Red Rockers wanted to build even less expensively with only found materials. Like many communal builders, the Red Rockers' interest in the new technology of dome building had shifted in favor of experimentation with building forms and materials. After three years of dome living, the Red Rockers began building small satellite shelters and using the dome as a community center. They were still interested in living in close proximity to others, but a desire for individuality had outweighed the passion for the initial communal living experiment centered on the dome.

Whether the home was a dome or star shaped, Libre, like the majority of other countercultural communes, was built using salvaged or scavenged materials, not only as an economic imperative but also as an ideological stance against the trappings of the middle-class consumer culture in which residents had been raised. There was a great sense of pride in being able to build a home for little money with recycled materials that equaled the earlier enthusiasm for the dome's rejection of the "straight" right angle and the subdivisions it spawned.

Using salvaged materials was also a way of ensuring that the structure was as unique as the community. In her study *Seven American Utopias,* Dolores Hayden noted that for the communards "salvage encouraged adaptation and perfectionism, the creation of a richer, more developed environment over time."[31] The Libre founders had witnessed the Drop City model where car tops, purchased for twenty-five cents apiece from a junkyard, were chopped into triangles to construct the domes. Like the individuals at Drop City, the communards at Libre and Red Rock were artists, and likewise the construction of their homes became an extension of their artistic practices. As their building styles changed from dome construction to more personal structures, the commonality between them resided in the use of salvaged materials. The Red Rockers used tongue-and-groove oak, salvaged from an old dance hall, to build their kitchen counters and cabinets.[32] Libre residents would also make group trips to the lumber mill to purchase reject lumber or untreated railroad ties.[33] If one local communard found a cache of materials, he or she would share with the others. By using similar materials and sharing building knowledge, residents developed a "Libre style" of architecture despite the unique design of each structure.

The idea of using salvaged building materials was spread through publications such as the *Whole Earth Catalog,* Ken Kern's *The Owner-Built Home,* and Art Boericke and Barry Shapiro's *Handmade Houses: A Guide to the Woodbutcher's Art.*[34] These books provided inspiration and encouragement for hand-built homes through photographs and first-person accounts of building. *Handmade Houses,* for example, a small book filled with color photographs and anecdotes about the building process, extols the virtues of building with salvaged materials and encourages builders to allow their homes to evolve slowly. In the preface, Boericke advises builders to "just get a start and let it grow."[35] Each home showcased in the book is completely unique and individual, ranging from a little woodland cabin built by a retired engineer who worked the logs in place himself using a block and tackle, to the fishing shack built with scraps of material extracted from the river. Because the homes are built from locally sourced, salvaged, or found materials, the aesthetic of these buildings stems not only from the individual builder and homeowner but also from the local landscape.

Today, Libre is one of the small percentage of countercultural living experiments from the 1960s that remain viable. Out of the tens of thousands of inclusive, open-door communities, many collapsed under quick population expansion. For other communities, the sensationalized press coverage contributed to a quick decline. "The powers of the media won out," said Gene Bernofsky of Drop City. "Too much, too early, and that was the end."[36] Those few communities that survived balanced adaptability with a concerted effort to remain out of the spotlight. Many of those hundreds of thousands of young communards dropped back into the mainstream just as quickly as they had dropped out.

Following a marijuana bust in the early 1980s, some Libre members dismantled Rabbit-Douthit's zome while he served time in prison, reusing the lumber and appliances in other projects.[37] Otherwise, the architecture of the site has remained relatively stable. The population at Libre shrinks in the winter, but many residents continue to return in the summer. Part of Libre's longevity may be the result of the community's built-in acceptance of the need for some privacy. Although they did own the land in common, the Libre rule requiring each member to construct his or her own home also seems to have given many residents a stake in the continuing stability of the community. Even those who have left the community remain connected, often returning to celebrate Libre birthdays.

Like their communal predecessors in the nineteenth century, the countercultural communards were able to use design to articulate their vision for the future. Whether it was a belief in the future of technology, expressed through domes and zomes, or the desire to live more sustainably, expressed through the incorporation of reused and scavenged materials in design, countercultural communards were determined to broadcast their value system through design that radically departed from mainstream building and architectural practices.

From a design perspective, Libre is an intriguing case study because its longevity ensured that a variety of building forms, from domes and zomes to more free-form structures built out of reused railroad ties, existed on the same site. The community evolved out of the experimentation begun at Drop City, and the residents continually refined and adapted their buildings. That it still exists is probably due to the success of the community in melding both the communal spirit and individual aesthetic.

NOTES

1. Emerson to Thomas Carlyle (Concord, 30 October 1840), in *The Correspondence of Thomas Carlyle and Ralph Waldo Emerson, 1834-1872, Vol. 1*, ed. Charles Eliot Norton (Boston: Houghton Mifflin, 1884). Accessed through Project Gutenberg, www.gutenberg.org/files/13583/13583.txt.

2. Timothy Miller, *The 60s Communes: Hippies and Beyond* (Syracuse, N.Y.: Syracuse University Press, 1999), xix–xx.

3. *Last Whole Earth Catalog: Access to Tools,* ed. Stewart Brand (Menlo Park, Calif.: Portola Institute, 1971); Lloyd Kahn, *Domebook 1* (Los Gatos, Calif.: Pacific Domes, 1970-71); Kahn, *Domebook 2* (Bolinas, Calif.: Pacific Domes, 1970); Lloyd Kahn, *Shelter* (1973) (Bolinas, Calif.: Shelter Publications, 1990).

4. On this switch, also see Margaret Crawford, "Alternative Shelter: Counterculture Architecture in Northern California," *Reading California: Art, Image, and Identity, 1900-2000* (Berkeley: University of California Press and Los Angeles County Museum of Art, 2000), 248-70.

5. By 1967, Dean Fleming was already an established New York City artist and had helped to found the Park Place Gallery in New York's SoHo.

6. Most Droppers adopted a humorous pseudonym upon arrival to the community. For more about Dropper culture, see Mark Matthews, *Droppers: America's First Hippie Commune, Drop City* (Norman: University of Oklahoma Press, 2010).

7. The purchase price for the land in 1968 was $12,600.

8. Linda Fleming, interview with author, New York, 25 October 2008. Further quotations from Linda and these details of the inner workings of Libre's building policies were also shared in this interview.

9. Steve Baer, *The Dome Cookbook* (Corrales, N.M.: Lama Foundation, 1968), 39. On the Lama Foundation, see Ahad Cobb, *Early Lama Foundation* (San Cristobal, N.M.: Lama Foundation, 2008).

10. "Libre," *Architectural Design* 44 (December 1971): 729.

11. Linda Fleming interview. Di Suvero knew Dean Fleming from New York, where the two were active at the Park Place Gallery.

12. Forty years later, the prevailing wisdom is to treat the entire structure like a roof. Dean Fleming, who still lives in his dome, covered the entire structure with roofing paper and applies tar every summer. More recently, he has shingled the dome.

13. Linda Fleming, e-mail message to author, 30 December 2008.

14. Stewart Brand, "Alloy," in *Last Whole Earth Catalog,* 111.

15. Andrew G. Kirk, *Counterculture Green: The Whole Earth Catalog and American Environmentalism* (Lawrence: University Press of Kansas, 2007), 74.

16. Kahn, *Domebook 2,* 61.

17. Kahn, *Shelter,* 109.

18. Ibid., 106.

19. Roberta Price, *Huerfano* (Amherst: University of Massachusetts Press, 2004), 44–46.

20. "Libre," *Architectural Design,* 731.

21. Ibid.

22. Price, *Huerfano,* 150. In the case of the Price and Perkins's building, a miscalculation about the amount of heat that could be generated from the boulder during the winter meant making adjustments to the interior and eventually hitchhiking to Florida to avoid the cold.

23. Linda Fleming, e-mail message to author, 12 December 2007.

24. Kahn, *Domebook 2,* n.p.

25. Kahn, *Shelter,* 174.

26. Price, *Huerfano,* 60.

27. Miller, *The 60s Communes,* 83.

28. Ibid., 139.

29. Ibid., 83.

30. Kahn, *Domebook 2,* 61.

31. Quoted in ibid., 339.

32. Kahn, *Shelter,* 138.

33. Price, *Huerfano,* 78.

34. Ken Kern, *The Owner-Built Home* (New York: Scribner, 1975); Art Boericke and Barry Shapiro, *Handmade Houses: A Guide to the Woodbutcher's Art* (San Francisco: Scrimshaw Press, 1973).

35. Boericke and Shapiro, *Handmade Houses,* 2.

36. Quoted in Alastair Gordon, *Spaced Out: Radical Environments of the Psychedelic Sixties* (New York: Rizzoli, 2008), 285.

37. Price, *Huerfano,* 350.

CHAPTER 7
CRAFT AND THE HANDMADE AT PAOLO SOLERI'S COMMUNAL SETTLEMENTS

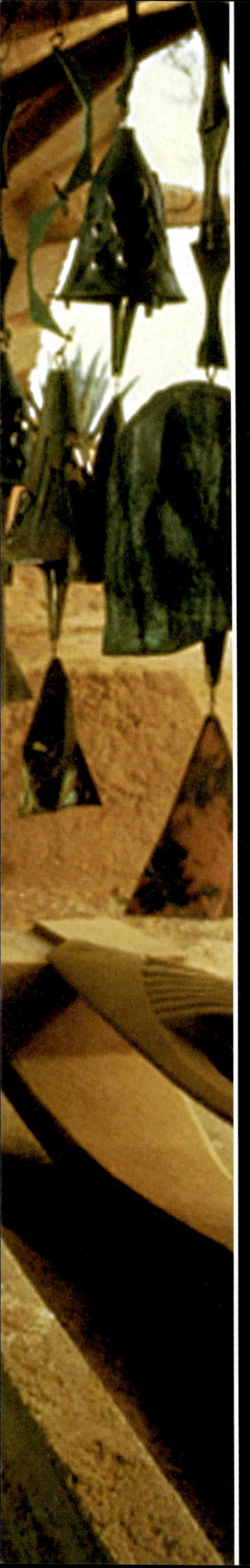

Elissa Auther

In 1970, atop a low mesa in the central desert of Arizona, the visionary, Italian-born architect Paolo Soleri broke ground on Arcosanti, his radical plan for the city of the future (Figure 7.1). On paper, Arcosanti comprises multiuse megastructures designed to meet all the economic, social, and physical needs of a projected three thousand to four thousand occupants on a mere fourteen square miles of land. It is one example—to date, the only to move beyond the design phase—of what Soleri refers to as an "arcology," a gigantic, self-contained, collectively organized and governed community.

Soleri is one of the best-known utopian thinkers and architects of the twentieth century. His elaborate philosophies, eccentric artistic practices, and visionary city plans—all of which I discuss in this essay—represent an intersection of influences ranging from the history of architecture, especially utopian design and city planning that emerged in the late 1960s and 1970s; countercultural forms of lifestyle of the same period that revolved around consciousness raising, environmentalism, and communal encounter; and the rise of craft as a legitimate aesthetic practice after centuries of being subordinated as a lesser artistic form in the hierarchy of the arts (a phenomenon that also dates to the '60s and '70s).[1]

While Soleri emerged as a major cultural force in the 1960s and 1970s in the United States, he was born in 1919 in Turin, Italy, where he completed his architectural training. In 1946, he joined Frank Lloyd Wright's Taliesin West in Scottsdale, Arizona. During his tenure at Taliesin, Soleri gained international recognition for a bridge design that was exhibited at the Museum of Modern Art in New York, a success that also led to him being cast out of Wright's fellowship. After a working sojourn in Italy and a short residency in Santa Fe, New Mexico, Soleri returned to

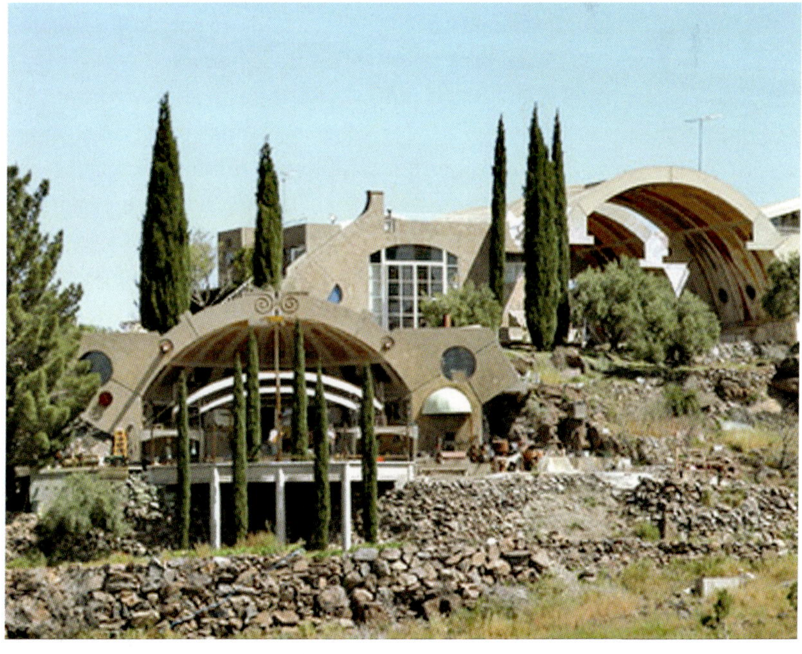

     CRAFT AND THE HANDMADE

Arizona, settling in 1956 on his own land in Scottsdale with a Wright-inspired plan to establish a fellowship or community committed to the exploration of alternative ways of living in harmony with nature. Regarded as test sites for his vision of the cities of the future, Cosanti—as the site where he settled in Scottsdale is called—and Arcosanti reflect contradictions typical of any visionary project that moves beyond the design stage.[2] Even so, from the early years of their construction through the present period, Soleri's settlements Cosanti and Arcosanti have offered a compelling experience to visitors and residents interested in the possibility of rebuilding civilization from the ground up.

Although in 1976 *Newsweek* declared Arcosanti to be "probably the most important experiment [in urban architecture] in our lifetime," the project currently exists in an early stage of realization, with no more than sixty long-term residents having ever resided on the site.[3] Short-term visitors and workshop participants, numbering in the thousands at this point, have provided the bulk of the volunteer labor at Arcosanti, resulting, to date, in the construction of eight structures, including living quarters, offices, a ceramics studio, a bronze foundry, and a music center. Work continues at Arcosanti, largely funded (as it has been since its inception) through seminars and workshops, as well as tours to the general public and the sale of Soleri's popular ceramic and bronze bells (Figure 7.2). It is this latter practice—bronze and ceramic casting—to which I turn my attention first in this essay. In writings about Arcosanti, largely confined to Soleri's own publications and architectural journalism from the 1960s and 1970s, the production and sale of the Cosanti Bells, as they are called, are viewed as incidental at best.[4] By contrast, in this essay I discuss the production of the ceramic and bronze bells as central to Soleri's conception of Arcosanti's distinctive architectural style and emblematic of the place of craft within the arcological utopia specifically and the counterculture generally.

Soleri published the design for Arcosanti, along with thirty additional designs for arcologies—some conceived to support anywhere from nine hundred thousand to two million occupants—in 1969 in a manifesto-like portfolio titled *Arcology: The City in the Image of Man.* Alongside Soleri's designs, the book graphically illustrates the architect's theory of evolution, in which an inner compulsion toward perfection drives increasing complexity and efficiency in organisms.[5]

The term *arcology*—a fusion of the words *architecture* and *ecology*—reflects the nascent counterculture environmental movement of the 1960s in the United States and the anxious debate over the status and survival of cities at a time when congestion, pollution, decaying infrastructures, municipal bankruptcy, political corruption, and urban rioting were viewed as clear evidence of their decline and ultimate uninhabitability.[6] In opposition to calls in this period for suburbanization, urban renewal, or the occasional plan to spread out across the galaxy, Soleri's philosophy affirmed rather than dismissed the centralization of people

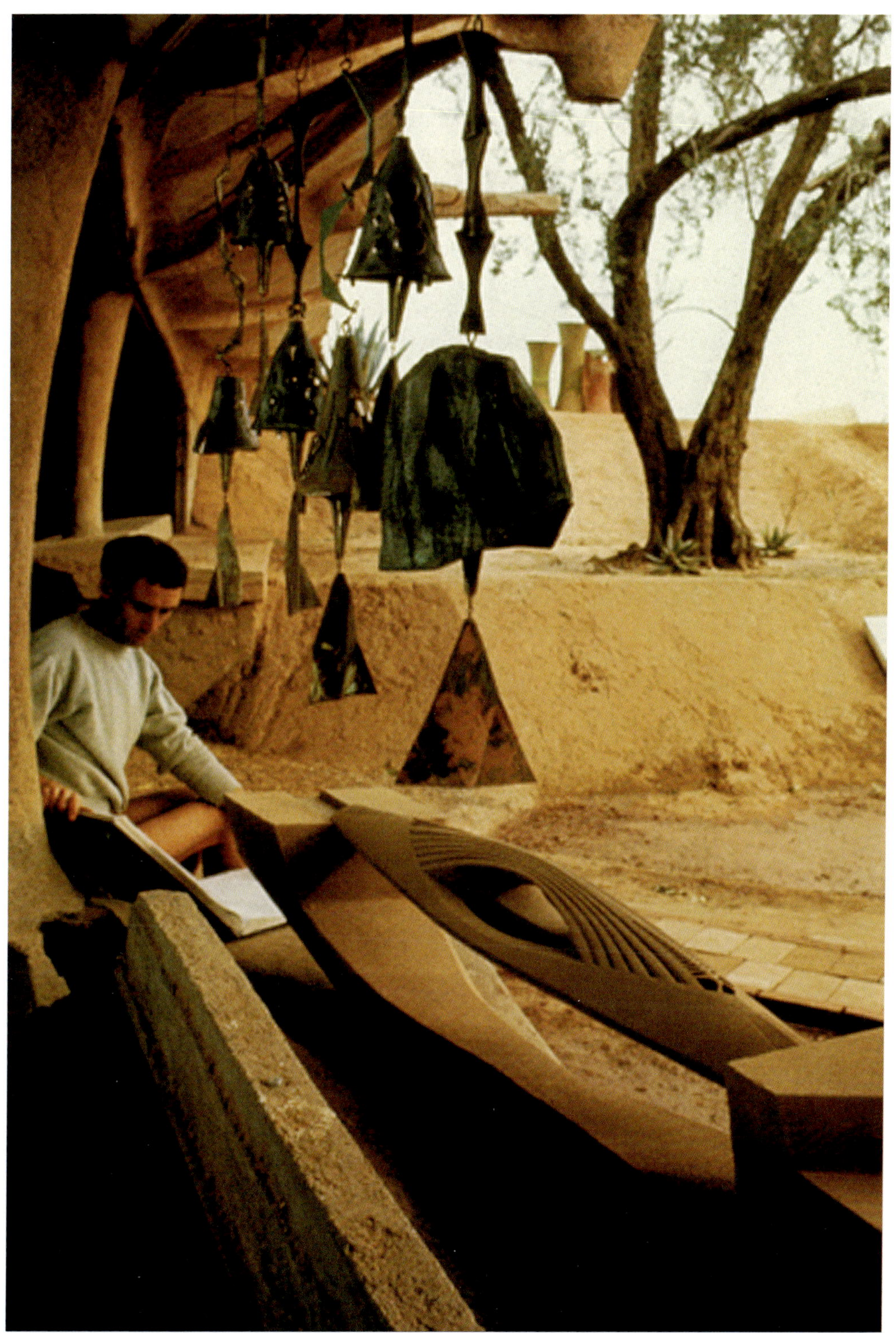

and resources as essential to the survival of the planet and humankind. His embrace of centralization was dictated by his theory of evolution: "Dispersal," he has argued since 1969, "is antagonistic to life. Density is ... the only morphology that can give us a lively existence."[7]

In concert with countercultural sentiments, Soleri blamed the dysfunction and pathology of the city on individualism, materialism, and the car and embraced a model of collective, ecologically sustainable living. About the car he complained in 1970, "It is 5,000 pounds of metal using 6 gallons of poisonous fumes to transport 150 pounds of flesh who wants to buy one pack of cigarettes. That is absurd."[8] He rejected, however, the antitechnology strain of the counterculture embodied by the back-to-the-land ethos and the establishment of rural communes as nostalgic and contributing to the destruction of nature through further development, however ecologically progressive. For Soleri, the arcology, a self-sustaining unit conceived to eliminate the car and human impact on nature through extreme high-density living, was the only option for the future.

But it wasn't just the survival of the human race or nature that interested Soleri, for the fully realized arcology was also conceived to be a driver of human evolution toward a utopian state of perfect consciousness. "The city is the necessary instrument for the evolution of man," Soleri proclaims in his manifesto. Significantly, it was "aesthetic man" and his creative acts, rather than the leader of science, politics, or religion, who was to spearhead this realization.

Predating the first structures at Arcosanti by almost fifteen years is Soleri's complex called Cosanti (Figure 7.3) erected in the (once) pristine desert of Paradise Valley, Arizona, a community located approximately fifteen miles southwest of Frank Lloyd Wright's Taliesin West, where Soleri had lived, studied, and labored as a fellow between 1947 and 1949.[9] On his land beginning in 1962, Soleri designed and erected with the help of students and volunteers a group of hand-built structures, including his residence, architectural office and drafting rooms, and open-air craft studios, where Soleri and his students carried out castings of ceramic bells sold to the occasional visitor.[10] Called Cosanti, from the Italian words *cosa* for thing and *anti* meaning before or against, the complex is the earliest example of Soleri's abiding interest in the idea of the antimaterialistic "creative life close to nature."[11]

Cosanti is composed of a cluster of free-form Earth Houses and other hollowed-out structures. *Earth or silt casting* was the term Soleri used to describe the elementary construction method used at the complex, which consisted of pouring concrete over hand-tamped, reinforced mounds of desert soil or silt. Once the concrete dried, the earth was excavated from under the concrete shells and distributed around the perimeter of the structure, providing insulation and turning the casting process "inside out."[12] Floors, fireplaces, built-in furniture, and interior partitions were also formed by hand directly in concrete. All of the forms were

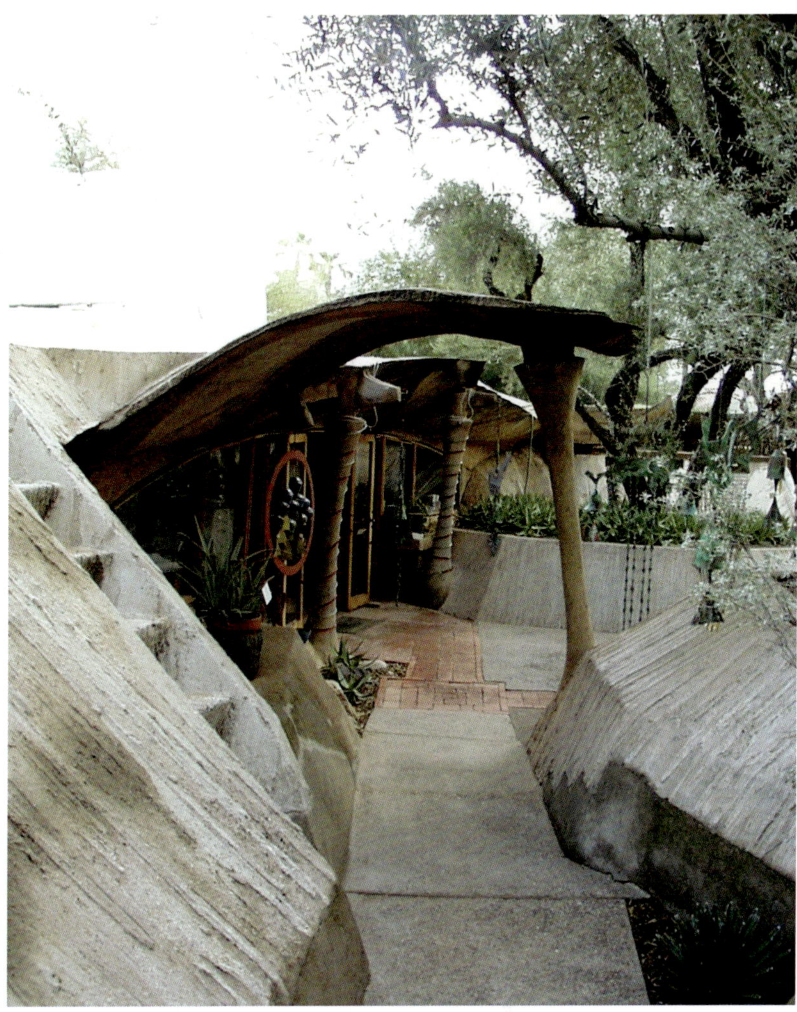

designed and oriented to allow for the moderation of intense summer heat and the passive capture of solar energy in the winter.

Largely overlooked in writing about Soleri's architecture is the connection between his unusual construction method, which he characterized as a "new variation" on "ancient craft techniques," and his early experiments casting ceramic objects directly into the desert ground.[13] "My original approach to earth-casting ceramics involved simply digging variously shaped holes into the desert soil," he explains. "We then poured liquefied clay into these molds, and, when the castings had dried, pulled them out of the ground" (Figure 7.4).[14] At Cosanti (and later Arcosanti) the directness of this approach is preserved in a slip-cast production method using simple one- and two-piece molds.[15] About the connection between this method and his adoption of earth casting, he elaborates:

Moving from fractions of a square foot to many square feet and from liquid clay to concrete (a plastic material, too) was simply an extrapolation. What had been a pot became a roof. In both cases, the soil was very instrumental, not only as the

    CRAFT AND THE HANDMADE

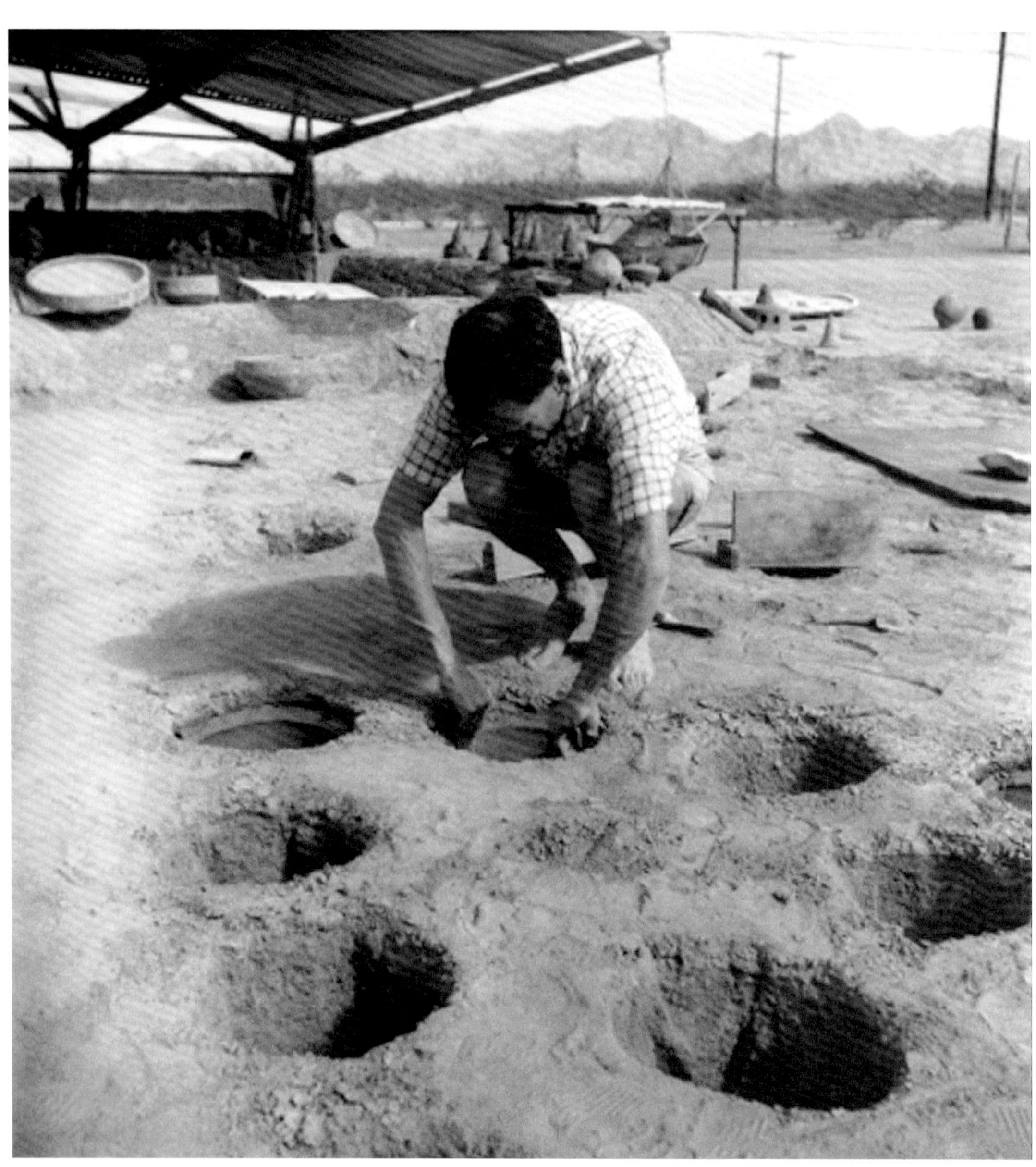

shaping material, a negative mold, but also in characterizing the texture, color, and feeling of the final product.[16]

Solidifying the connection to the handmade is Soleri's characterization of the Cosanti complex as a kind of "handicrafts" rather than "real construction," a view borne out by the American Institute of Architecture's award of the Craftmanship Medal to Soleri in 1963 for the development and implementation of the silt-casting technique at Cosanti.

With few exceptions, the structures at Arcosanti are also variations on earth casting. Its dominant architectural form, the half-dome or apse, which seasonally captures or shields individuals from the strong desert sun, is a continuation of Soleri's interest in building in harmony with nature, as seen at Cosanti.[17] On-site production of cast ceramic bells was also transferred to Arcosanti, where one of the first structures to be raised was the Ceramics Apse in 1972, followed by the Foundry Apse in 1973 for the casting of bronze bells. Both sites were conceived to allow public viewing of ceramic and bronze casting on a daily basis, a practice that was, and remains, a group activity carried out by residents and workshop participants.

To understand the incorporation and pronounced visibility of craft production at Arcosanti beyond its ostensible function as an income-generating practice, one must turn to the cluster of ideas regarding evolution that informed Soleri's concept of the arcology. As Soleri has confirmed, the arcologies are an expression of eschatological thinking based on the writings of the renegade Jesuit priest Pierre Teilhard de Chardin. In his eccentric theoretical model, set out in the 1930s and 1940s, Teilhard argued for the existence of a spiritual reality animating all things (people, animals, and nature in general) and directing the evolution of human consciousness toward spiritual perfection.[18] As this evolution progressed, with Catholicism functioning as its vehicle, "man" would transcend his individualism, reconcile as one, and converge at the "Omega Point" with the Omega—Christ.

In Soleri's adaptation of Teilhard's evolutionary model, architecture and the aesthetic act replace religion. For Soleri, it is the arcology rather than the Catholic Church that plays the role of directing the future development of human consciousness toward the convergence that Teilhard called the Omega Point. By contrast, in Soleri's scheme a collective humanity seeks its cosmic center, not union with Christ. While for Teilhard the concept that humanity was moving toward a collective, spiritual future required faith in God, Soleri's emphasis was different. Alongside his claim that "the city is the necessary instrument for the evolution of man," Soleri posited architecture and aesthetic practice as the thrust behind humanity's evolution to the point of collectivity, perfect consciousness, even divinity.

Soleri's conception of the arcology precluded the institution of art, based, as it is, on individualism, distinction, and aesthetic autonomy—

   CRAFT AND THE HANDMADE

values with no place in a future organized around an advanced form of collectivism. On the opposite end of the creative spectrum from art was what Soleri called "standard production" or "the computed," which would fulfill all human needs for functional objects such as utensils, clothing, and furniture. What was left—and what mattered to Soleri— was an in-between state that he identified as craft and that he envisioned as bringing the creative and the computed into harmony within the arcology. If such an in-between practice could be realized, craft "would be in an eminent position in the structure of society," he has argued.[19] "What makes the craftsman necessary to society is a particularly qualitative element to be found in the esthetic world, not in the field of the functional,"[20] which, in his view, is the domain of standardized production. "In very general terms," he writes,

I would venture to say that the most promising field for a craft is not the instrumentation of those activities that are at the micro- [or macro] end[s] of the physical scale. . . . That is to say, not the spoon or the shoe, . . . the table or the chair, nor certainly the mega-structure defining the environment. . . . I would find the most rewarding action of the crafts in the "in-between" of the two; the homemaking, the landscaping, the special characterization in some public facilities, schools, restaurants, shops, temples.[21]

Bells do not exactly satisfy Soleri's definition of an "in-between" practice, but as a class of objects they do mark various kinds of thresholds or moments of transformation that are related to in-between sites or movement from one state of being to another. The hanging of bells on architectural features that mark the transition from outside to inside such as the domestic porch, or the ringing of bells at the moment of transubstantiation in the Catholic mass, among many other religious rituals, are good examples.

The iconography of the Cosanti bells (Figures 7.5 and 7.6), which is dominated by vectors or lines of force, connects them to Soleri's evolutionary model of progress (as well as its graphic expression in his book *Arcology: The City in the Image of Man*) toward perfection and the bell's function as a signifier of transitional sites or moments. Regarding the vector, Soleri has stated, "I have little doubt that life in general and human life in particular can be symbolized by a vector. . . . Vectorality is the character of living reality, and the case of man is basically a willful or unconscious action with or against it."[22] The application of this iconography to the elementarily cast clay and bronze bells neatly encapsulates the transition from one state to another represented in Soleri's evolutionary model in which the brute physicality of matter moves toward pure mind and spirit.

The collectivism of the arcology—a feature that inherently privileges craft, given the field's connection to the multiple and collaborative workshop production—accounts for much of the way the casting process

     CRAFT AND THE HANDMADE

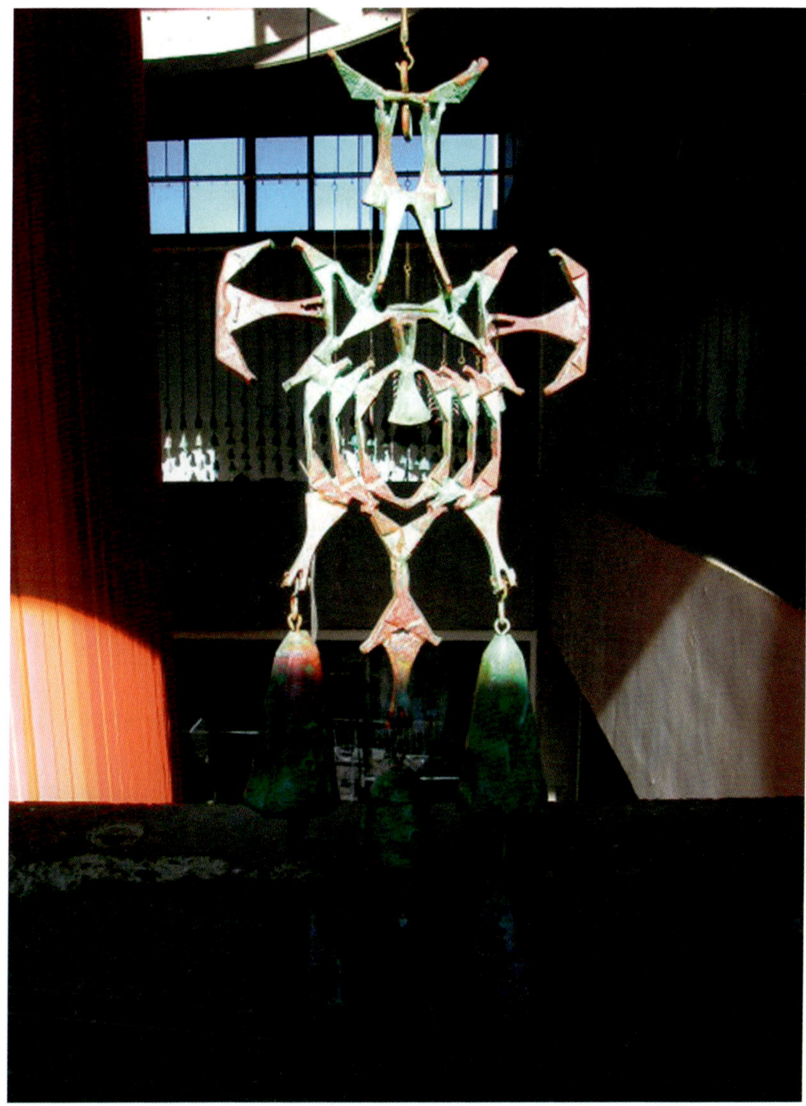

is incorporated into Arcosanti. For instance, Soleri's decision to create open-air studios to house ceramics and bronze casting at Arcosanti is plausibly explained by his desire to illustrate collective, cooperative work in the arcology. In the daily demonstration of the casting process—a form of "showing doing," to borrow a phrase from the performance theorist Richard Schechner—what at first glance looks like a living history exhibit is more accurately described as a visual equation between the craftsperson's shaping of raw material and a future community's shaping of the arcology.[23] Given the fact that Soleri has sometimes referred to Arcosanti as a test or demonstration site, the public character of craft production has a didactic purpose beyond that of simply keeping ceramics or bronze casting alive. Furthermore, Soleri consciously chose the simplicity of the casting process, which allows for participation on the part of resident amateurs, to facilitate the goal of illustrating collective

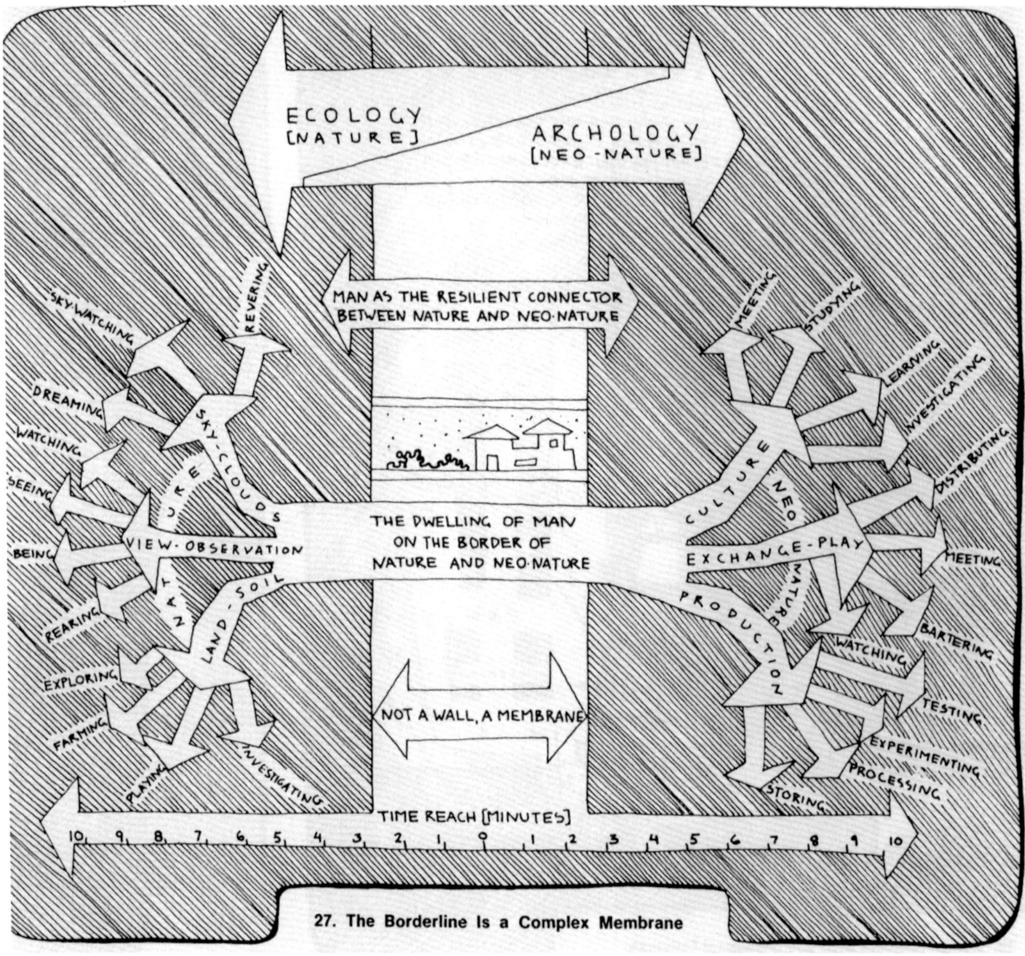

27. The Borderline Is a Complex Membrane

aesthetic practice. As one visitor to Cosanti observed in 1975, the ceramics studio was an example of a "people-oriented utilization of resources."[24] As Elena Karina-Canavier explains in a 1975 article on the bells:

For forming ware, the slip is directed via paddle pump into the rows of molds arranged on a low troughlike wall encircling the island. . . . the clay bells and the conelike clappers have no undercuts, thus facilitating slip casting in simple 1 and 2 piece molds. . . . this design . . . eliminates trimming and fettling, and permits bells to be removed from molds at the convenience of the ceramist.[25]

Like most utopian thinkers of the period Soleri envisioned a sharp increase in leisure time within the arcology, time that he viewed as properly put to use in sustaining the structure of the arcology.[26] In this sense, the way of life within the arcology is essentially a work of art, augmenting aesthetic activity's organic connection to the whole. Soleri surmised that

the ever-increasing pool of leisure-energy would offer to the craftsman-environmentalist abundant and cooperative working forces. Then the man-made environment

"The Borderline Is a Complex
Membrane," Figure 27
from Paolo Soleri, *Arcology:
The City in the Image of
Man*, 1969. Courtesy of the
Cosanti Foundation.

would become an integrated combination of fine technological skill carrying on the definition of the mega-elements . . . the ecological planning, public architecture, utilities, facilities.[27]

Soleri's self-contained, total system—encompassing the intellectual, physical, and cosmic realms—prohibits a treatment of the Cosanti bell as an autonomous object. Craft production in the arcology was not conceived as an outlet of self-expression for residents. Rather, the Cosanti bell is an iconographical emblem and keyhole through which one may view Soleri's entire ecology, the only context that allows us to make sense of their production. As an object that embodies a complete cosmology, the bell is categorically different from other objects linked to utopian thought such as neo-plastic or suprematist painting, where the intellectual aspirations intervene in the material world only through the surface of the canvas, not the walls that they hang on, and the systems of production, consumption, and settlement in which they exist. Although the Cosanti bell shares with such objects a connection to the intellectual and spiritual realms, it is, distinctively, part of the material effort—the actual building—of a new civilization that includes the redefinition of social relations, the collection and use of natural resources, and alternative modes of production.

Soleri's philosophy of the arcology and the place of craft within it as a way of life connects Cosanti and Arcosanti to the broader American counterculture of the late 1960s and 1970s in other ways as well. While Soleri derisively referred to hippies or flower children as "butterfly brains" and was critical of the back-to-the-land ethos, he also accepted that his settlements were recognized and essentially functioned as hubs of countercultural activity in the Southwest for their commitment to communal encounter, ecological sustainability, and craft production.[28] And despite his limited patience with the butterfly brains, Soleri located the "first coagulations" of the rebirth of society in the form of a progressive collectivism manifested in countercultural communes.[29] The conflation of work and leisure, a noted aspect of life within the arcology, further linked Cosanti and Arcosanti to a broader set of countercultural ideals surrounding the reform of the relationship of work to everyday life.

Cosanti and Arcosanti participated in this critique through not only the craft production of Cosanti bells but also the communal construction of the sites themselves through workshops open to the public. In their earliest days, from 1962 to 1969, these events were referred to as Silt Pile Workshops, and they were organized around the erection of the Cosanti complex through instruction in Soleri's unique earth-casting method of construction. These workshops—nine in total—put to work Soleri's students living on-site at Cosanti and students of architecture from Arizona State University, among other institutions. Upon the groundbreaking of Arcosanti in 1970, the workshop model of construction was implemented there as well.[30]

     CRAFT AND THE HANDMADE

As Robert Jensen, a 1973 workshopper at Arcosanti reported, the "daily framework of activity . . . is the antithesis of the way large buildings are built today," and the differences he experienced and subsequently articulated in an essay published in *Architectural Record* in 1974 illuminate the connections between Soleri's settlements and the countercultural critique of work. This critique, in which craft played a key role, revolved around the rejection of hierarchies and expertise, alienating forms of labor, and the blurring of work and leisure.

"Among the workshoppers," Jensen reported, "there is an inarticulate but real feeling that larger society offers few patterns in daily life that allow significant choice, expansion or a beginning of a vision of self-worth."[31] In his view, Soleri's intention at Arcosanti was to create a framework to "make it possible for individuals to discover, or even invent" (125) a kind of work for themselves that was fulfilling because it was self-driven, acting as an avenue for self-discovery and personal transformation. Arcosanti modeled this nonalienating form of labor for workshop partici-pants in unique ways. As Jensen noted, at Arcosanti "categories such as lender, contractor, [and] client all disappear," and hierarchies of expertise were also eliminated, resulting in everyone working on "equal footing with others" (122). Jensen also surmised that, in addition to leaving behind "technical knowledge" and "intellectual credentials," "work-shoppers might leave behind *subsidiary* experts—friends, parents, the moral codes of a town or university, the boss, the professor. With geographical distance between them and these experts, the workshop-pers can perhaps escape some habitual power these experts hold over their lives" (122). Jensen also observed that for many workshoppers, Arcosanti offered "some other reward for working there than money, or the pleasure achieved after work in the time society usually calls 'free'" (122). He continues: "To more than a few workshoppers—like Mike, a painter from Ohio—there was little difference between 'work' and 'after work,' little change in attitude towards the different parts of the day, no internal or idealized separation. Arcosanti seems to attract people with this spirit, and it can generate it in others" (122).

As described earlier, construction work at Cosanti and Arcosanti was conceived by Soleri as a kind of handicraft that was connected to his earliest practice of casting ceramic bells directly into the desert ground. The earth-casting technique used at Cosanti was transferred to Arco-santi and supplemented with the erection of precast concrete elements. The work of earth casting and that surrounding the casting of concrete elements—from the building of frames, to the pouring, coloring, and finishing of the concrete—were in method and intention simple processes, allowing for individuals with varying skills the opportunity to partici-pate in a creative endeavor. Jensen's observations about his experience and those of others at Arcosanti, whose daily existence revolved around these tasks in addition to bronze and silt casting, characterize Arcosanti as a lifestyle with craft at its center. Earlier in this essay, I expressed this by explaining life in the arcology as essentially a work of art, and both conceptualizations connect Cosanti and Arcosanti to one of the most prominent ideologies of the counterculture, that defining lifestyle as a creative act.

Lifestyle conceived as such is the subject of sociologist Sam Binkley's study *Getting Loose,* which examines the rise of countercultural lifestyle publications of the late 1960s and 1970s from *Whole Earth Catalog* to the *Tassajara Bread Book.*[32] In these publications and others like them, lifestyle is conceived and promoted as a "reflexive project of identity" with the attending demand that one "take responsibility for one's life as the product of one's own artistry, and . . . work on oneself to enhance one's authenticity through daily lifestyle choices."[33] As opposed to a form of selfhood premised on "fixed cultural and institutional authorities" from class membership to religious affiliation, the creation of a social identity called lifestyle in the 1960s and 1970s was individualistic and embraced as an active, inventive mode of self-expression.[34] Craft—like the other practices examined by Binkley ranging from home building to massage to organic farming—was a locus of lifestyle in the late 1960s and 1970s, a period in which it enjoyed a popular upswing of interest. Coincident with this upswing was the revival of belief in craft's restorative power, particularly as it related to the integration of work and life, a central feature of Soleri's arcologies, Cosanti and Arcosanti.

With the rise of the Arts and Crafts movement in the nineteenth century, craft as a way of life was often expressed in the phrase *craftsman ideal.* The craftsman ideal encapsulated a return to a precapitalist context in which work, creative practice, and everyday life had not yet been divided from each other or compartmentalized through industrialization. For John Ruskin and William Morris, the movement's leading spokesmen, craft represented a meaningful form of work capable of restoring, among other positive benefits, the integrity and moral health of workers destroyed in the Industrial Revolution: "It is only by labor that thought can be made healthy, and only by thought that labor can be made happy. . . . It would be well if all of us were good handicraftmen in some kind, and the dishonour of manual labor done away with altogether," declared Ruskin.[35] Morris too viewed craft as capable of restoring the dignity of labor, and his writings further established the equation of craft or creative labor and the well-being of the laborer or maker central to craft culture.

The surge of interest in craft in the 1960s and 1970s was also fueled, in part, by the counterculture's rejection of work and patterns of consumption under capitalism, a critique that reiterated the nineteenth-century conceptualization of craft as a conscious life choice that restored honesty, integrity, and self-sufficiency in work and fostered the creative development of the whole person through process and self-discovery. Furthermore, craft played an important role in the search for a way of living in which one's work life and everyday life become one, indivisible,

organic whole, an ideal that underscored a number of countercultural
projects, including Cosanti and Arcosanti. Tom D'Onofrio, woodworker
and founder of the Baulines Craftsman's Guild in 1970, a countercultural
organization of craftspeople in and around Bolinas, California, was guided
by this principle, and it was reflected in many additional countercultural
projects. "To be a master craftsman," D'Onofrio explains, "is really to become an enlightened being whereby all of life is an artistic expression."[36]
Members of the guild (as the name implies) reached back further than
the nineteenth century, to the medieval period, in which craft work was
centered in the individually owned workshop and organized around the
apprenticeship system.[37]

Besides the Baulines Craftsman's Guild and Soleri's settlements, the
idealized integration of work and life through craft was a guiding principle
of the Pilchuck Glass School, established in rural Washington State by
glass blower Dale Chihuly in 1971. In the early days of the school, students
were required to build their own personal shelters on the Pilchuck property before gaining access to the makeshift hot shop. In a letter from
Chihuly and coorganizer Lewis (Buster) Simpson to registered participants
of the 1972 summer workshop detailing this requirement, they encouraged students to "develop . . . your own ideas for the type of shelter you
might want to live in." Furthermore, they wrote, "it is hoped that the
same considerations given your art will also apply to the way you live,
the shelter you construct, your food and the way it's prepared."[38]

One of the most interesting illustrations of the craft lifestyle and its
intersection with the countercultural desire to live an integrated life
in opposition to the expectations and constraints of "straight" society
and the mainstream economy appeared in book form. Titled *Craftsman
Lifestyle: The Gentle Revolution,* this publication appeared in 1976 in
conjunction with the last of a series of exhibitions called California Design
organized by Eudorah M. Moore.[39] *Craftsman Lifestyle* brought together
individual profiles of eighty California-based craftspeople with the goal
of capturing their distinctive values, work environments, and ways of
life. Highlighted throughout the book is the achievement of an integrated
life with craft functioning as the linchpin holding its parts together.
Craftsman Lifestyle is profusely illustrated, and the photos, shot by Tim
Anderson, are captionless arrangements of images of living rooms,
workspaces, windowsill arrangements of objects and artifacts, hand-built
architecture, boats, outdoor showers, kitchens, gardens, children, and
pets. Within the individual profiles, the photographs provide a record of
daily activity consciously composed to visually dissolve the boundaries
between work, craft practice, and everyday life. In addition to the book's
text and photographic layout, its cover of unbleached cardstock complemented the contributors' stories of the rejection of materialism and
alienating work for a holistic, creative life through craft.

Likewise, Soleri's settlements, Cosanti and Arcosanti, were organized
around craft-based forms of work that were theoretically conceived and

practically carried out as a key signifier of a new form of integrated lifestyle intimately tied to the counterculture by virtue of its emphasis on living in harmony with nature, organization around communal encounter, and commitment to meaningful work inextricable from everyday life.

NOTES

I would like to thank Hanne Sue Kirsch, Soleri Archives manager, for her help in locating documents, articles, and photographs essential to my research on the history of silt casting at Cosanti and Arcosanti. I am deeply appreciative of her support of my project.

1. On the subject, see Auther, *String, Felt, Thread: The Hierarchy of Art and Craft in American Art* (Minneapolis: University of Minnesota Press, 2010).

2. In the words of Robert Jensen, an Arcosanti resident in the early 1970s, "While the forms of Arcosanti are visionary, *life* there today is in the present; it is temporary, confusing, boring, permeated with curiosity and hope—but not Utopian." See Jensen, "The Arcosanti Antithesis: Paolo Soleri and the Counter Culture," *Architectural Record* 156 (August 1974): 121.

3. As quoted by Mija Riedel, "Time in Utopia: Idealistic Arcosanti in Arizona Desert Is a Glimpse of the Future from the Past," *San Diego Union-Tribune*, 20 August 2006.

4. Currently, about twenty-five thousand bells a year are sold at Cosanti, Arcosanti, and online through Cosanti Originals.

5. This was referred to as "complexity-miniaturization" in Soleri's scheme. In his own words, "In its evolution from matter to mind the real has been submitted to numerous phases of miniaturization so as to fit more things into smaller spaces in shorter times. This process, from haphazardness and dislocation to co-ordination and fitness, has been mandatory because each successive form of reality carried in itself a greater degree of complexity. Any higher organism contains more performances than a chunk of the unlimited universe light years thick, and it ticks on a time clock immensely swifter. This miniaturization process may well be one of the rules of evolution." Soleri, *Arcology: The City in the Image of Man* (Cambridge, Mass.: MIT Press, 1970), 31.

6. On the subject, see Simon Sadler, *Archigram: Architecture without Architecture* (Cambridge, Mass.: MIT Press, 2005); *Archigram*, ed. Peter Cook (New York: Princeton Architectural Press, 1999); Yona Friedman, *Comment habiter la terre = How to Settle on Earth* (Paris and Vancouver, 1976); Yona Friedman, *Toward a Scientific Architecture*, trans. Cynthia Lang (Cambridge, Mass.: MIT Press, 1975); *Kenzo Tange, 1946–1996: Architecture and Urban Design*, ed. Ugo Kultermann (New York: Praeger, 1970); and Jane Jacobs, *The Death and Life of Great American Cities* (New York: Random House, 1961). On the counterculture environmental movement and its disagreements with preservationists of an earlier generation, see Andrew G. Kirk, *Counterculture Green: The Whole Earth Catalog and American Environmentalism* (Lawrence: University Press of Kansas, 2007).

7. As quoted by John Morris Dixon, "Job Site for Utopia," *Progressive Architecture* 54 (April 1973): 79.

8. As quoted by Don Ramey and Chet Mantolesky, "The World: Love It or Leave It," *Progressive Architecture* 51 (June 1970): 180.

9. In 1956, Soleri also established the Cosanti Foundation in order to start a school based on the model of Wright's Taliesin Fellowship.

10. The first workshops, called Siltpile Workshops, began at Cosanti in 1962. Three concrete structures on the Cosanti premises—the Earth House, the Ceramics Studio, and the North Studio—were completed before this time. From 1964 to 1974, six additional structures were completed.

11. Two commissioned structures—the 1949 Dome House in Cave Creek, Arizona, codesigned and built by hand by Soleri and fellow Taliesinite Mark Mills, and Soleri's 1950 ceramics factory, Ceramica Artistica Solimene in Vietri, Italy—predate the Cosanti compound.

12. Soleri, *The Sketchbooks of Paolo Soleri* (Cambridge, Mass.: MIT Press, 1971), 12.

13. Soleri, *Paolo Soleri's Earth Casting for Sculpture, Models and Construction* (Salt Lake City: Peregrine Smith Books, 1984), 4.

See also Tim Luke's "The Politics of Arcological Utopia: Soleri on Ecology, Architecture and Society," *Telos* 101 (Fall 1994): 55.

14. Soleri, *Earth Casting*, 29.

15. See Elena Karina-Canavier, "The Ceramic Bells of Paolo Soleri," *Ceramics Monthly* (October 1975): 24–27.

16. Soleri, *Sketchbooks*, 217.

17. A significant amount of construction is in precast silt panels that are moved into place by a crane.

18. Teilhard de Chardin's best-known work, *The Phenomenon of Man*, was published posthumously (New York: Harper, 1959). His teaching and public appearances were curtailed and writings suppressed by the Jesuit order and the Vatican throughout the 1930s and 1940s.

19. Paolo Soleri, *The Bridge between Matter and Spirit Is Matter Becoming Spirit: The Arcology of Paolo Soleri* (New York: Anchor Books, 1973), 76.

20. Ibid., 77.

21. Ibid., 78.

22. As quoted by Edward Higbee, "Soleri: Plumber with the Mind of St. Augustine," *AIA Journal* 55 (February 1971): 20.

23. Richard Schechner, *Performance Studies: An Introduction* (London: Routledge, 2002), 22. Regarding the counterculture's relationship to forms of "doing," see Philip Auslander, *Performing Glam Rock: Gender and Theatricality in Popular Music* (Ann Arbor: University of Michigan, 2006).

24. Karina-Canavier, "The Ceramic Bells," 26.

25. Ibid., 24.

26. On the subject of increased leisure time, a view shared by Soleri and numerous public intellectuals who embraced the idea that the United States was entering a permanent period of post-scarcity, see Theodore Roszak, *The Making of a Counter Culture: Reflections on the Technocratic Society and Its Youthful Opposition* (New York: Doubleday, 1969).

27. Paolo Soleri, "The Craftsman and Obsolescence," unpublished paper delivered to the Milwaukee Art Center, 10 November 1966, retained by the Soleri Archives. A revised version of this paper appears as chapter 6 in Soleri, *Bridge between Matter and Spirit*, 70–80.

28. Soleri is quoted by Robert Jensen, "The Arcosanti Antithesis," 124.

29. On the subject, see ibid.

30. Arcosanti workshops during the 1970s were six weeks in length and consisted of fifteen to forty individuals. In 1971, tuition was $250; in 1973, $320; and by 1975, $380 per attendee. In the summer months, overlapping workshops were held, which could result in more than a hundred individuals residing on-site for several months at a time. In this period and beyond, workshoppers received free room and board. In 1973, a total of 375 workshoppers, bringing in approximately $120,000 to the project, participated in the construction of Arcosanti. See Jensen, "The Arcosanti Antithesis," 121. Today Arcosanti workshops are two to five weeks in length and consist of a similar mix of seminars with Soleri and his staff on the theory of the arcology and the history of Cosanti and Arcosanti, and hands-on work ranging from construction to agriculture to facilities maintenance.

31. Jensen, "The Arcosanti Antithesis," 123. Further page references to this article will appear parenthetically in the text.

32. Sam Binkley, *Getting Loose: Lifestyle Consumption in the 1970s* (Durham, N.C.: Duke University Press, 2007). Additional titles include but are not limited to Alicia Bay Laurel, *Living on the Earth* (New York: Random House, 1971); Lloyd Kahn's *Shelter I* and *Shelter II* (Bolinas, Calif.: Shelter Publications, 1973); the Boston Women's Health Book Collective, *Our Bodies, Ourselves* (New York: Simon and Schuster, 1974); and George Downing, *The Massage Book* (San Francisco: Bookworks and Random House, 1972).

33. Binkley, *Getting Loose,* 61, 14.

34. Ibid., 7.

35. As quoted by Eileen Boris, *Art and Labor: Ruskin, Morris, and the Craftsman Ideal in America* (Philadelphia: Temple University Press, 1986), 5.

36. Tom D'Onofrio, "Craftsmanship and Quest for Self-Discovery" (master's thesis, University of California, Berkeley, 1976), i.

37. The Baulines Craftsman's Guild was composed of master craftspeople representing a wide range of disciplines who agreed to train others in their respective craft practice through an apprenticeship program. See ibid. for a description of the structure of the program. Applicants to the apprentice system were required to secure their own housing and health insurance.

38. Letter from Chihuly and Simpson to Pilchuck participants, 1972, John H. Hauberg Papers, Special Collections, University of Washington Libraries (acc. no. 2850-7), Seattle, Washington. Reprinted in Vicki Halper and Diane Douglas, eds., *Choosing Craft* (Durham, N.C.: University of North Carolina Press, 2009), 110.

39. Olivia Emery, *The Craftsman Lifestyle: The Gentle Revolution* (Pasadena: California Design Publications, 1976).

CHAPTER 8
POND FARM AND THE SUMMER CRAFT EXPERIENCE

Jenni Sorkin

During the mid-twentieth century, studio craft provided a vital arena for women as teachers, thinkers, and makers. Ceramics in particular, with its emphasis on self-sufficient rural living, offered women unprecedented social freedoms, with the opportunity to live and teach in nontraditional settings, such as cooperative, experimental, or self-initiated communities. Able to barter their unique wares and skill sets, women, too, found varying degrees of financial autonomy through the informal economies of exchange that existed in midcentury ceramics.

Certainly this was the case of Bauhaus-trained potter Marguerite Wildenhain (1896–1985). From 1952 until 1980, she presided over Pond Farm, a community entirely of her own making: a summer program devoted to the discipline of pottery, which ran twenty-eight consecutive summers. Pond Farm's setting was a redwood forest seventy miles north of San Francisco, outside of Guerneville, California, along the banks of the Russian River. Each summer, around twenty-five students would come to study ceramics with her for nine weeks at a time. Wildenhain did not accept beginners; students were routinely turned away or sent elsewhere, to gain basic skills. But Pond Farm willfully lacked institutional status. Without any kind of accreditation or degree structure, it had no credibility within the larger American educational system. As Wildenhain wrote, "Pond Farm is not a 'school'; it is actually a way of life."[1]

Born Marguerite Friedlaender in Lyon, France, in 1896 to Jewish parents of English and German origin, Wildenhain was a student in the Weimar Bauhaus ceramics workshop until its closure in 1925. Owing to the school's pervasive institutional sexism, Wildenhain, like other Bauhaüsler women, was offered enrollment in only one of three workshops: textiles, ceramics, or bookbinding.[2] She was the first woman to be named a master potter in Germany, earning her certification in 1925, amid severe deprivations as Germany's economic situation rapidly deteriorated, resulting in severe inflation and an insecure food supply. Based in Dornburg, a provincial village eighteen miles from the main Weimar campus, the ceramics students lived through near-starvation, eating oatmeal, supplemented with homegrown Swiss chard, three times a day.[3]

The isolation and solidarity of the Dornburg workshop was a formative experience for Wildenhain. The sheer will of the group fostered a climate of high standards, where artistic productivity and endless inventiveness were expected despite poverty and political upheaval. The Dornburg workshop became the artist's bedrock, a strong foundation from which to begin, again and again, during the years of turmoil that would mark her plight as a Jew in the years leading up to the Third Reich.

Upon the Bauhaus's move to Dessau in 1926, the ceramics workshop was canceled, and Wildenhain took a position as head of ceramics at the School of Fine and Applied Art in Halle, Germany. There, she established a productive and well-regarded workshop, as well as a solid reputation as a designer for industry, developing an extensive collection of tableware for porcelain manufacturer Royal Berlin. Because Royal Berlin's factory was destroyed during an Allied bombing raid, her wares never went into mass production.

Owing to her Jewish heritage, in 1933, she was asked to resign and fled to Holland where she and her husband Frans Wildenhain founded a pottery workshop in the rural southern town of Putten. After the Nazis invaded Holland, Wildenhain took refuge in the United States in 1940, gaining entry as a French citizen.[4] She taught for two years at the California College of Arts and Crafts before settling at Pond Farm. An important figurehead in modern ceramics, Wildenhain published several books, including a memoir, and continued to teach both nationally and internationally until her death in 1985.[5]

This essay examines the extreme lifestyle, somewhere between summer camp and boot camp, surrounding Marguerite Wildenhain's teaching methodology at Pond Farm. Students threw forms eight hours a day, according the Wildenhains' rigorous European-workshop style instruction but took nothing with them when they left. By purging her students of the desire to produce finished pots, Wildenhain set her students on a course of nonobject production. This is a radical reformulation of pottery, redirecting it away from its traditional object-based orientation in favor of process. Thus, at Pond Farm, craft became valued not as a commodity but as an experience.

The disappearance of the potted object, and its subsequent passage into immateriality, runs parallel to the greater avant-garde ethos of the 1960s. The antiobject stance of performance, video, and land art, and to a lesser degree, minimalism, which rejected the hand-produced or individually wrought object, challenged the hegemony of the materialist tradition in artistic production. It also functioned as a critique of the market and its easy commodification of the art object. In doing so, artists were able to propose new relationships between objects and viewers, artists and audiences, and artists and institutions. Ceramics has been left out of this history. However, Pond Farm's antiobject stance troubles the dominant narrative, marking an important and overlooked moment in modern craft.

POND FARM

Pond Farm began its life as an artist's colony and school, founded by Gordon and Jane Herr, an urban couple who had purchased 160 acres of previously farmed land in Sonoma County, California.[6] A sometime-jeweler and architect, Gordon Herr was influenced by the seductive combination of the Arts and Crafts movement and D. H. Lawrence's writings, which championed passion and instinct. Fortunately, for him, Jane Brandenstein Herr was an heiress from a prominent Jewish family in San Francisco, willing to support his vision. Known as the Pond Farm Workshops, the program, however, was short-lived, running only from 1949 to 1952. Gordon Herr (architecture), Marguerite Wildenhain (pottery), and Frans Wildenhain (ceramic sculpture) were joined by two other German Jewish refugees: Trude Guermonprez (weaving) and Victor Ries (metals). Additionally, the Greek collage artist Jean Varda (who had previously taught at Black Mountain) came from nearby Sausalito to teach once a week, as did the San Francisco–based sculptor Clare Falkenstein. Like Varda, Guermonprez had also already taught at Black Mountain between 1947 and 1948, filling in for Anni Albers, who was on sabbatical until the winter of 1948, and then teaching alongside her. Friends and colleagues since their time together in Holland, the two women visited each other in their respective locations in the United States. So Marguerite had experienced Black Mountain firsthand, in 1947, likewise Guermonprez, whose parents (the composer Heinrich Jalowetz, and his wife, Jalena, who taught voice and bookbinding) had been music professors at the college since 1939. Guermonprez must have seen something promising at Pond Farm, since she opted to leave Black Mountain for the fledgling artist's colony. As she recounted:

[Black Mountain] was such an intense place that it . . . wasn't good to stay there very long for faculty. My parents stayed there because I suppose it was a matter of need, and they were the older ones. . . . My father apparently from what I hear and read suffered greatly from the personal, you know, sort of currents and anti-currents that constantly are present in such a situation.[7]

Concurrent to Black Mountain College, Pond Farm is best interpreted as a site somewhere in between: neither a college with a traditional humanities curriculum nor a purely communal utopian venture. Like Black Mountain, too, Pond Farm was routinely misconstrued as a haven for "communists, nudists, and anarchists," as the local mantra went.[8]

As at Black Mountain, Pond Farm had struggled to build during the war years, using scrap and salvaged materials. Gordon raised chickens to avoid the draft, and the poultry buildings eventually were turned into artist's studios. Here, too, the planned vision exceeded the reality of the situation, where very little actually came to fruition. Black Mountain's odd corrugated metal structure, known as the Studies Building, became a central gathering point, with mixed usage over the years, accommodating both academic and living spaces. Similarly, Gordon designed and built Hexagon House in 1949, an eclectic hexagon-shaped wooden structure with a gallery space, a three-story atrium, and a peaked roof held aloft with gigantic Douglas fir poles. Hexagon House was to be the central building for classes, flanked by cabins that would house students. In actuality, these primitive structures, wooden cabins built on concrete slabs, without running water, housed Guermonprez and Ries.

The school's demise can be attributed to various reasons, first and foremost, Gordon Herr's poor leadership, which asserted itself as top-down dominance rather than the cultivation of a collective vision. The artists' insistence on communal ownership of the school, and with it, some sort of long-term deed or lease, went unheeded. Additionally, Marguerite

Wildenhain had financed the construction of her own house on the property but was not offered a mortgage in return. In contrast, Victor Ries attributed many of Pond Farm's issues to Marguerite's gender "problem":

[Frans] was teaching painting, pottery, sculpture together with his wife. But he couldn't make it with his wife. He was a real man, but she was a "man" too. And this didn't work. And she gave the whole tone on Pond Farm, since Gordon was not able to handle the situation. In meetings, which were mostly evenings, there was a terrible situation between Gordon Herr and Marguerite Wildenhain. They hated each other! They fought each other. He sometimes took his hunting knife, which he always had here, and threw it in front of her into the floor. And things were going on that way all the time. Unbelievable. Anyway, Marguerite actually dictated what has to be done and what has not to be done on Pond Farm, and he had no word whatsoever. But we had nothing to say, too. Marguerite was the one who dictated about everything.[9]

Unwilling to defer or acquiesce, either to her husband or Gordon Herr, Marguerite's "manhood," then, was a source of disgust to the men in the community, who equated leadership with masculinity. Frans is pitied, cast in the role of the cuckolded husband.

However, it is questionable if female authority would ever have been possible for this particular generation of men, who could not envision true parity for women artists. Even her Bauhaus-era teacher, the sculptor Gerhard Marcks, had praised her for her masculinity, concluding that "she really had the mental and physical strength of three men."[10] Thus, Marguerite's ambition and strength were considered male virtues, since it was inconceivable for a woman to embody such character traits. Similarly, assigning Marguerite a male persona made her easier to dislike, or discredit, as Ries's statements express, portraying her as a severe and unwelcome authoritarian.

But Ed Rossbach, the Bay Area fiber artist, who visited Pond Farm as a student on a class trip during the late 1940s, described being differently affected by her pedagogy, awestruck by her absolute power, which he identified as distinctly feminine:

[Her] approach, which is the antithesis of what I believe in now. The absolute antithesis. Very rigid and authoritarian. I hate authoritarian approaches to things. This woman knew, she knew. It's marvelous that people know anything. And she had these ideas that you threw, and I don't know how many years or months or whatever, you threw, and you threw, learning to throw these certain [forms] well, they're really traditional forms, although they've become identified with the Bauhaus as Bauhaus forms. She was there [at Pond Farm], a very vigorous sort of earthmother type of woman. You probably think I'm pushing this too much, but I just felt like an innocent moving through this scene of sophistication and what? It's more than sophistication. It's different moral standards. . . . I was just agog, you know, at everything I was seeing.[11]

In the end, Pond Farm proved vulnerable to the same in-fighting from which Black Mountain had also suffered. Yet its key players were not embroiled in intergenerational conflict. Pond Farm is markedly different, in that it offers a snapshot of the collective aftermath of the Holocaust. Marguerite, Guermonprez, and Ries were all Jewish refugees with disparate wartime experiences: Wildenhain had fled Holland in 1940 on the last boat; Guermonprez had spent the war years in Holland, hidden by righteous gentiles; Ries had left Germany in 1933 and spent twelve years abroad in Palestine before arriving in California. As exiles sequestered in near-isolation, struggling with the burden of their own experiences, their situation can only be described as charged, with the potential for either collective estrangement or catharsis. Indeed, by 1950, Frans had moved apart from the others, to a remote cabin on the edge of the property. Yet the war was never discussed. As Ries affirms: "We did not talk about it [the war]. What for? We were not Jews at Pond Farm, we were artists."[12] His point is key: marked as Jews, and persecuted as Jews, in Europe, they had been one thing only. In being forced to be Jews, they had ceased to be artists. At stake was the ability to reclaim selfhood and individual identity. However, as German modernists, trained to simplify centuries of decorative excess, any narrative strain of artistic production would have been excess. To make work steeped in form, then, was to self-actualize. Perhaps this is why Pond Farm Workshops failed to cohere, the fierce quest for individuality exceeding the collective enterprise.

Things did not go as planned: just three years after their reunion, Frans left Marguerite for a local woman and resettled permanently in upstate New York, teaching at the School for American Craftsmen, a division of the Rochester Institute of Technology, for the remainder of his career. Finally, Jane Herr's death from cancer in 1952, at age forty, was a tragic blow to the already-fragmented community. Both Guermonprez and Ries departed soon after, and Gordon Herr, grief-stricken, quickly lost interest, preoccupied with the immediate needs of his two small children.

Only Marguerite remained. Released from the burdens of both male authority and collectivity, Pond Farm took a drastic turn, toward the camp. From 1952 until 1980, Marguerite Wildenhain presided over a community entirely of her own making: a summer program devoted to the discipline of craft.

FORMS OF LIFE

As an extreme form of living, Pond Farm exceeded any previous limits of labor and discomfort in relation to the production of studio pottery in midcentury America. In its initial years, Wildenhain provided basic barracks-type lodgings on her property, nearly replicating her experience at Dornburg: students were to learn to fend for themselves without a modern kitchen, pooling cookware and food to prepare common meals cooked in a fire pit. For most of Pond Farm's existence, however, students rented rooms in Guerneville, an affluent summer resort town, or camped outside the town, which sat on the edge of a redwood forest. Roy Behrens, a former student, recalled the rudimentary nature of camp living:

By way of Marguerite's fine map, we not only found the Ridenours [a local couple] that day, they also readily agreed that we could set up our two-person campsite (at no cost, I recall) in a deep ravine of redwood trees, adjacent to their hilltop house. What an exotic way to spend the summer, in a grove of these towering giants— one of which (thank goodness in terms of our bathroom needs) was wide and dead and hollowed out. It truly was primitive living: our only refrigerator was an ice-filled Styrofoam cooler, which was constantly coated with moisture. Among the most repugnant sights of the day (every morning) was to wake up to find the outside of the cooler crawling with dozens of huge green slimy slugs.[13]

Such conditions would not have impressed Wildenhain—who did not own a refrigerator until the mid-1960s—but this was in keeping with her distaste for convenience, which led to the laziness and shortcutting she found to be so pronounced in American students. Those who came to Pond Farm, however, were broken of these and other poor habits.

The distance between Guerneville and Pond Farm was a daily four-mile hike uphill on unpaved roads. Upon arrival, students gathered under the peach tree before 8:00 a.m. to observe a ritual silence. Afterward, students were expected to spend seven to eight hours per day at the pottery wheel, throwing forms dictated by Wildenhain. While she herself was a studio potter, making singular objects for the art market, her teaching methodology, like the Bauhaus, was geared toward industry, or what is known as production pottery, making dozens of wares to be sold as complete, handmade sets:

Students were thoroughly instructed on wheel techniques and on how to develop a critical eye. The workshop was as demanding as one could find. Beginning students started with the infamous "doggie dish"—a shape that is somewhat troublesome for beginners. After making ten or twenty of these, permission was given to move on, and the students worked through about fifteen basic forms such as flower pots, bowls, bellied coffee pots, spouted pitchers, footed bowls, cups, plates, and eventually teapots.[14]

Students brought their lunch and ate together at long wooden picnic tables behind the work barn. Monday through Friday the workday ended at 4 p.m., and each Wednesday afternoon was devoted to drawing from nature. Wildenhain would frequently hold outdoor seminars and discussions, lecturing on various topics, showing her own work or that of other artists, and often reading literature aloud, poetry or the journals of Van Gogh, Rodin, and Delacroix.[15] At the end of the day, students trudged back down the hill into town, unless invited to drink sherry with Wildenhain in her garden. Three or four times a session, evening parties would be held at the beach.

Perhaps the most startling fact was that students had nothing to show for their labor at the end of the summer. In the earliest years, Wildenhain taught glazing and firing techniques, where students, after throwing five or six hundred pots, would leave with five or six glazed pieces.[16] However, for most of Pond Farm's nearly thirty-year history, students threw hundreds of pots and left with nothing. This is described by Nancy Neumann Press, the curator of Wildenhain's 1980 retrospective:

As we stood in front of the kiln, Marguerite told us how she conducts her summer workshops. Students learn how to use the wheel and how to make pots. They are taught no glazing, nor are their pots fired. They learn how to throw pots, and they learn how to look at things, how to see. One day a week is devoted to looking at, and drawing from, nature. At the end of the workshop the students' pots are re-ground into clay. They take no pots with them when they leave.[17]

Nathan McMahon, a student who first came to Pond Farm in 1954, described the destruction of the pots as an act of submission, in which the objects and their makers were broken down—only to be rebuilt more robustly:

More often the pots were destroyed while the clay was yet plastic, cut through with a wire to gauge the thickness of the walls and to evaluate the quality of our throwing technique. It was a sound practice, offering lessons that would otherwise have been impossible to learn, and they helped separate us from the tendency toward regarding every standing pot as worthy or precious. It helped to speed up the learning process by undermining the persistent ego.[18]

This ritualized destruction contained within it an exchange of power: students giving themselves over to the master, allowing themselves to be trained according to her will. Summer workshop participants, then, came as seekers, looking for an encounter with craftsmanship through subordination rather than a mastery of technical knowledge.

At times, Marguerite's power asserted itself physically as well. Several students, in their written testimonies gathered by Dean Schwarz, a former student himself, recounted that Marguerite, even into her sixties, would occasionally wrestle her students, pinning them before an excited group of their peers.[19] This thirst for total domination, intellectual and physical, makes her seem something of a brute, intent on enforcing the supremacy of her position.

In his 1973 treatise on pedagogy, *Fellow Teachers,* the cultural sociologist Philip Rieff asks, "Would you like to know how to recreate authority? You would have to again begin outside yourself. A true interdictory authority must be taught to us; it cannot be thought up by us."[20] The specter haunting Wildenhain's camp was, of course, the concentration camp: the personal truth of Wildenhain's life was the narrowness of her escape— twice—from the jaws of Hilter's Final Solution. Yet this survival was overdetermined, as she was not subject to the most distinctive and disturbing aspects of the Holocaust, camp life. As a Jewish refugee whose hardscrabble endurance had empowered her to flee, Marguerite Wildenhain arrived in the United States relatively unscathed, one of the lucky ones.

Those who survived—and flourished—confronted a different sort of burden, often known as survivor's guilt. As Holocaust scholar Lawrence Langer has written, "the postmodern replacement of the death sentence that dominated Western thought from Freud to Camus is the life sentence."[21] Though she wrote three books in her lifetime, like many survivors of her generation, Wildenhain never wrote of the Holocaust. She never spoke of it. She never mentioned it by name. Like so many others, Marguerite did not even consider herself to be Jewish. After her divorce from Frans, she did not reinstate her Jewish maiden name; years later, when Marcks refers to her as a "Jewess," she retorts:

Whatever you think of me as a "Jew" is completely wrong, I believe. . . . We never celebrated any "Jewish" festivals or anything else. Father wanted us to belong to the "whole world." He was well traveled, so were we children for that time. I have been in a Catholic church much more often than in a synagogue (in my whole life hardly six or eight times, if even that often).[22]

CAMP LIFE

In his book *Homo Sacer: Sovereign Power and Bare Life,* Giorgio Agamben theorizes the concentration camp as the paradigm of modern nonjuridical, or sovereign, power in the twentieth century.[23] In its convergence of the body and the law, it is a site of exceptionalism and crisis, imposing the threshold of existence, or what he terms "bare life": the abandoned body stripped of all its identities, without recourse to life, death, or autonomy. Pond Farm, then, reinstated the logic of the death camp, where the intensity of bare life was experienced symbolically, with personal freedom suspended for a temporary period of time. Thus, as a nonschool and a noninstitution, Pond Farm reflected the camp paradigm of a structured existence, through the adversity of exceptionalism and crisis.

Its site was both a *campus,* a topography of learning, the grounds that comprised the buildings of an educational facility, and an *encampment,* a series of provisional, makeshift structures, utilized seasonally, for a temporary amount of time, where most of life is lived outdoors. It also approximated the traditional notion of summer camp, which would constitute the *enchantment* of encampment, where leisure is achieved through fellowship and collective skill building.

Camp life is intimate and always public: at Pond Farm, Wildenhain's allegiance to Dornburg's workshop-based training established a situation of dominance predicated on "discipline, restraint, orderliness, and control," to use Agamben's words.[24] These values were reinforced publicly as well: each day in the studio, Marguerite would begin by "tearing apart" the work of the previous day. For each student, labor was a crucial act of self-formation, performed and reperformed, as an intricate exercise of power and compliance. Michel Foucault writes that "discipline produces subjected and practised bodies, 'docile bodies.'"[25] Rather than seeking freedom from Wildenhain's self-styled cultural imperialism, American potters were eager to partake in the perceived supremacy of the Bauhaus workshop tradition, becoming docile subjects obedient to Wildenhain's sovereign power, molded, in effect, by her forming.

This self-formation is consistent with the *clay body,* a ceramics term that refers to the material composition of the vessel, the mixture of clays combined for specific properties, such as translucence or durability. If the clay body is a body both predicated on and commensurate with form, then the craftsman's form-of-life is an indivisibility between the format of production and the production of form. That is, the craftsman is an intensely productive subject of his or her own labor, reinscribing the body within the replication of hundreds and hundreds, and over a lifetime, thousands and thousands, of clay bodies. An army of clay bodies. This energy of near-constant production manifests what Gilles Deleuze and Félix Guattari call "the process of self-cure that brings . . . the production of a new humanity."[26] In teaching craft as an ethical imperative, Wildenhain endowed her students with a new humanity, forcing them to accept the "different moral standards" that Rossbach had glimpsed during his brief visit.

The experience of the camp, in any of its forms, from Auschwitz to government internment, to basic military training, to eight weeks of overnight camp at the age of twelve, is marked by two conditions: transformation and trauma. Despite time and distance, the residue of the camp persists as a powerful mark of lived experience, and as a divider of the self into the person before and the person after. Such splitting is what constitutes the traumatic experience, the unseen evidence of exposure and endurance: "Pond Farm is so much a part of me that it is hard to see where I stop and it begins."[27] Deeply altered, the self is a dislocated entity, set apart from others, but intimately joined to those who lived through the same experience. "For me, Marguerite and Pond Farm were everything. I learned my craft there, proposed to my wife there, and was married there. I met most of my dearest friends there and learned the meaning of life there. In my heart I will always be there."[28] "There" is the site of Pond Farm itself, enveloped and embodied by the student, the wound seared upon the heart, a happy wound, but a wound nonetheless, pleasurably burdened by its difference. This wounding represents the process of mental and emotional scarification, the violence inflicted on the body, and the permanent reformulation of the soul. "I feel very strongly about the absence of Marguerite from my art life. She left a void in all our lives that is next to impossible to fill and that is not readily understandable by those who were not there."[29] The suppression of individual identity in favor of a collective identity ("those who were there") is to pay tribute to insularity, reenacting the Pond Farm community as a site of exception, so as to achieve an afterlife that functions as an afterglow, its purpose and its achievement conferred on a special group of people. This is similar to any survivor or veteran communities, who gather to commemorate and honor their wartime experiences.

What Wildenhain offered her students was a format for living, or what Agamben calls a "form-of-life": "If we give the name 'form-of-life' to this being that is only its own bare existence and to this life that, being its own form, remains inseparable from it."[30] If we take Wildenhain at her word, where form is taught as a life skill rather than as a lesson, as a survival mechanism rather than a novel experience—then Pond Farm, as a site of unproductive labor, was indeed a site of exceptionalism, making and remaking exile as a form-of-life. In her work regarding the teaching of Holocaust survivor narratives, literary theorist Shoshana Felman notes that "if teaching does not hit upon some sort of crisis, if it does not encounter either the vulnerability or the explosiveness of an (explicit or implicit) critical and unpredictable dimension, it has perhaps not truly taught."[31] For Marguerite Wildenhain, this crisis was the crisis of freedom. To be without discipline was to be without a form-of-life and, therefore, without a framework on which to structure artistic practice. But her militant and transformative pedagogy was more than just a cathartic response to the trauma of exile, or a solution to the inadequacies of the American situation. It was also a reenactment of Dornburg, the Bauhaus original site of exception and crisis.

But what, then, is the relationship between exceptionalism and exclusion? Marguerite Wildenhain herself represents a series of exclusions: a Bauhaus-trained Jew, a French refugee/German émigré, a woman in the elite reaches of her male-dominated profession, and, moreover, a pedagogical demagogue—a proclaimed and self-proclaimed Master. But as a woman, Wildenhain was without access to the same system of rewards: she was neither a Master at the Bauhaus nor Rector of an American college. Rather, she was an independent potter whose successes were modest, whose triumphs were incremental, and whose freedoms were hard-won.

NOTES

The author wishes to acknowledge Jane Kemp, professor of Library and information services and head librarian, circulation and special collections at Luther College, for all her help and hospitality in Decorah, Iowa.

1. Wildenhain, *The Invisible Core: A Potter's Life and Thoughts* (Tokyo and New York: Kondansha International, 1973), 145.
2. I am indebted to Sigrid Wetge-Wortmann's volume *Bauhaus Textiles: Women Artists and the Weaving Workshop* (London: Thames and Hudson, 1993), which details this phenomenon. See also Magdalena Droste's account, *Bauhaus, 1919-1933* (Berlin: Taschen Verlag, 1990), 38–40.
3. Droste, *Bauhaus,* 28–29.
4. As a German citizen, Frans was denied entry. He remained behind and was conscripted involuntarily into the Nazi army. He was unable to join Marguerite at Pond Farm until 1947. While the couple divorced soon after, in 1951, Marguerite Wildenhain chose to keep her married name and continued to use it professionally. To avoid confusion, I will refer to Marguerite Wildenhain as *Wildenhain,* and her husband by his full name. Also a potter, Frans entered the Bauhaus ceramics workshop in 1925 and trained under Marguerite in Halle, who supervised his master's credential, a most unusual arrangement for the era. The couple married in 1930. See Billie Sessions, *Ripples: Marguerite Wildenhain and Her Pond Farm Students* (San Bernardino: California State University Fullerton Art Museum, 2002), 15. Exhibition catalog.
5. Wildenhain's books include *Pottery: Form and Expression* (New York: American Craftsmen's Council, 1959); *The Invisible Core;* and *. . . That We Look and See: An Admirer Looks at the Indians* (Decorah, Iowa: South Bear Press, 1979). Dean (her last studio assistant) and Geraldine Schwarz have been instrumental in preserving Wildenhain's legacy within the United States. The placement of her secondary archive (and in my opinion, the better one), at Luther College, in Decorah, Iowa, is the result of their work.
6. See Jonathan Guthrie Herr's memoir, "Love, Because Nothing Else Matters," in *Marguerite Wildenhain and the Bauhaus: An Eyewitness Anthology,* ed. Dean and Geraldine Schwarz (Decorah, Iowa: South Bear Press, 2007), 314–36.
7. Trude Guermonprez, interview by Mary Emma Harris, 8 December 1971. Black Mountain College Research Project, North Carolina State Archives, Raleigh (spool 83A), 14.
8. Nathan McMahon, "Madam Was Indisputably French," in *Marguerite Wildenhain and the Bauhaus,* 476.
9. Victor Ries, "Religious Artistic Expression in Metal Sculpture," in *Renaissance of Religious Art and Architecture in the San Francisco Bay Area, 1946–1968, Vol. II,* an oral history conducted 1983 by Suzanne B. Riess (Regional Oral History Office, Bancroft Library, University of California, Berkeley, 1985). In a 2009 interview I conducted with Ries, at the advanced age of 101, he was much less articulate about Pond Farm but emphatically affirmed this remark about Wildenhain, unprompted: "She was a man. Marguerite was a man." Victor Ries, interview by author, Reutlinger Center for Jewish Living, Danville, Calif., 27 May 2009.
10. Gerhard Marcks, "A Biography of Marguerite Friedlaender Wildenhain," Luther College Archives, Decorah, Iowa, box 8.
11. Charles Edward Rossbach, "Fiber Arts Series," an oral history conducted 1983 by Ann Nathan (Regional Oral History Office, Bancroft Library, University of California, Berkeley, 1987).
12. Ries interview by author.
13. Roy R. Behrens, *Recalling Pond Farm: My Memory Shards of a Summer with Bauhaus Potter Marguerite Wildenhain* (Dysart, Iowa: Bobolink Books, 2005), 5.
14. Sessions, *Ripples,* 84.
15. Wildenhain, *The Invisible Core,* 143.
16. Sessions, *Ripples,* 84.
17. Nancy Neumann Press, "Preface," in *Marguerite: A Retrospective Exhibition of the Work of Master Potter Marguerite Wildenhain* (Ithaca, N.Y.: Herbert F. Johnson Museum, 1980), 7.
18. Nathan McMahon, "Madam Was Indisputably French," in *Marguerite Wildenhain and the Bauhaus,* 483.
19. Ibid., 467.
20. Philip Rieff, *Fellow Teachers* (New York: Harper and Row, 1973), 137. Rieff was something of a celebrity scholar, best know for his brief and scandalous marriage to his former student, Susan Sontag, while teaching in the sociology department at the University of Chicago.
21. Lawrence Langer, *Admitting the Holocaust: Collected Essays* (London: Oxford University Press 1995), 38.
22. Letter from Marguerite Wildenhain to Gerhard Marcks, 29 September 1980, in *The Letters of Gerhard Marcks and Marguerite Wildenhain, 1970-1981: A Mingling of Souls,* ed. Ruth Kath and Lawrence J. Thornton (Ames: Iowa State University Press, 1991), 189.
23. Giorgio Agamben, *Homo Sacer: Sovereign Power and Bare Life,* trans. Daniel Heller-Roazen (Stanford, Calif.: Stanford University Press, 1998).
24. Ibid., 103.
25. Michel Foucault, *Discipline and Punish: The Birth of the Prison,* trans. Alan Sheridan (New York: Vintage, 1977), 138.
26. Gilles Deleuze and Félix Guattari, *Anti-Oedipus,* trans. Robert Hurley, Mark Seem, and Helen R. Lane (Minneapolis: University of Minnesota Press, 1983), 17.
27. The following quotes are taken from student memoirs collected by curator Billie Sessions, in Sessions, *Ripples,* 111. This first is from Gail Stewart, in attendance 1973-80.
28. Wayne Reynolds, in attendance seven summers between 1963 and 1979, quoted in ibid., 109.
29. John Conners, quoted in ibid., 91.
30. Agamben, *Homo Sacer,* 188.
31. Shoshana Felman, *Testimony: Crises of Witnessing in Literature, Psychoanalysis, and History* (New York: Routledge, 1991), 55. Interestingly, in his memoir, David Stewart, Wildenhain's studio assistant for sixteen summers, pointedly recalls a young woman once asking, "How come everything at Pond Farm is a crisis?" Quoted in *Marguerite Wildenhain and the Bauhaus,* 450.

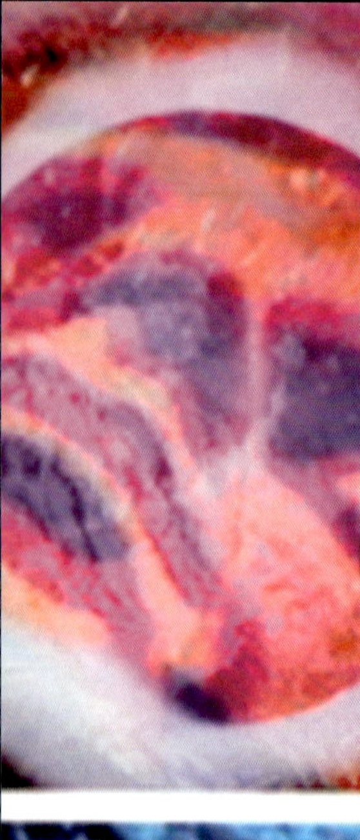

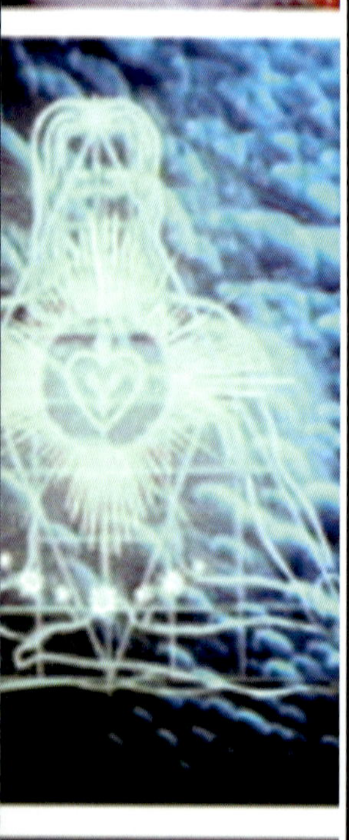

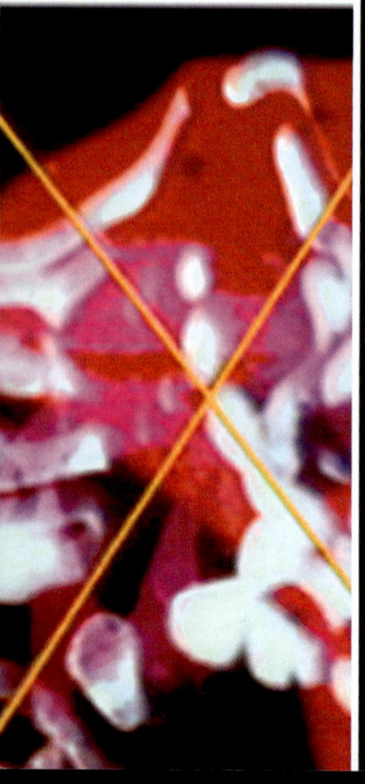

CHAPTER 9
EXPANDED CINEMA IN LOS ANGELES: THE SINGLE WING TURQUOISE BIRD

David E. James

During the last years of the 1960s and the first of the 1970s—the heyday of the psychedelic era—the premier light show in Los Angeles, and one of the best in the world, was the Single Wing Turquoise Bird.

Long before this period, the city had seen several projects involving the projection of abstract light, "color organs," and similar apparatuses, versions of which date back at least to the 1720s when Louis-Bertrand Castel proposed that color transparencies could be linked to the keys of a harpsichord. In the early 1920s, Stanton MacDonald-Wright, a painter and self-styled Color Motion Picturist, began to research abstract color projection and eventually made several kinetic light projectors, one of which was used in several theatrical productions in Santa Monica in 1927. Probably the most sophisticated of such light machines was Thomas Wilfred's Clavilux, built in the early 1920s; it consisted of a cabinet in which revolving discs and mirrors could be "played" so as to rear-project light onto a two-foot square screen. Wilfred wrote compositions for it that he called *lumia* and performed them publicly. Seeing a performance when he was recovering from a syphilitic eye infection, Los Angeles avant-garde filmmaker Dudley Murphy found it "one of the most ecstatic experiences of [his] life," and when artist, Sara Kathryn Arledge saw Wilfred perform in Pasadena in 1928, she was inspired to become involved in time-based visual art and eventually to make important avant-garde films. Oskar Fischinger, who shared Wilfred's mystical bent, worked in a similar vein. In 1950, he built his "lumigraph," an upright wooden frame, about five feet high containing light sources that project inward onto an open area three to four feet square holding an elastic white screen just behind the light sources. In a darkened room, the screen is invisible, but any area of it lightly pushed forward by the player catches the light, so that the player may spontaneously shape light in space.[1]

Inspired by both the technological and sociocultural possibilities of its own time, the Single Wing Turquoise Bird expanded and elaborated such intersections between avant-garde film and visual music. First formed in the spring of 1968 to accompany rock concerts at the Shrine Auditorium and Exposition Hall in Los Angeles, the light show several times reconfigured its membership and its performance modes, freeing itself from supplementarity to the rock events. Developing many different technologies and sources of both imagery and abstract light, it evolved into an autonomous multimedia unit that innovated the collectively improvised, real-time composition of projected light. The group was able to maintain itself for more than five years, but eventually several of its members became involved with cinematic projects of a more traditional kind, and though they still did occasional performances for several years after, the Single Wing effectively dissolved into a theatrical film exhibition company in 1973.

In the fall of 1967, John Van Hamersveld, an artist who had trained at Chouinard Art Institute and who had designed the iconic poster for Bruce Brown's surfing epic, *The Endless Summer* (1966) and, very recently,

EXPANDED CINEMA IN LOS ANGELES

the cover for the Beatles' *Magical Mystery Tour* album (1967), received a
grant to organize a Happening. With a businessman and a journalism student
from the University of Southern California (USC), he formed Pinnacle
Productions, and on November 10 and 15 they staged the Electric Wonder,
a rock concert at the Shrine, featuring the Grateful Dead, Buffalo Spring-
field, and Blue Cheer, accompanied by various lighting effects. The event
was so successful that they decided to sponsor more concerts, and for
them they hired a local light show, the Thomas Edison Lighting Company,
who projected on several screens at different points in the Shrine's
cavernous interior, a space large enough to accommodate some five thousand spectators. Dissatisfied with the light show, Pinnacle invited several
young filmmakers, most of whom were either enrolled in or had recently
graduated from University of California at Los Angeles (UCLA), to form
a new one.

This group included Burton Gershfield, Jon Greene,[2] Bruce Lane, David
Lebrun, Peter Mays, and Jeff Perkins.[3] Motivated by developments in
the New York and San Francisco undergrounds and by the Los Angeles
heritage of abstract animation, especially the work of Fischinger and
John and James Whitney, the group was trying to expand the visual language
of cinema with effects inspired by psychedelic drugs. Gershfield's ecstatic film *Now That the Buffalo's Gone* (1965, edited by Lebrun), in which
ethnographic imagery of the Plains Indians is transformed into solarized red or amber monochrome and reanimated by interruptive blank
and negative frames, was in many ways the exemplary production of
the group, with Pat O'Neill's *7362* also influential (and in fact several of
the group were experimenting with a contact printer that O'Neill, then
a UCLA photography instructor, had set up in the basement of the art
department). Several of them were living at a house on Cresthill Road
just above the Sunset Strip, then the focal point for the city's hippie subcultures, of which the Doors (of whom Ray Manzarek and Jim Morrison
were both former UCLA film students) were one of the leading bands. Mays
had in fact first met Perkins in 1966 when the latter was the projectionist
at the Cinematheque 16 on the Strip, the first theater in Los Angeles to
specialize in underground films; Perkins had appeared in Mays's experimental films, one of which had been booked into the theater. Since then,
they had been experimenting with light shows at UCLA and also sometimes at USC, using eight small projectors and outtakes from *Buffalo,*
and working with others, including Scott Hardy, a liquid projectionist
from San Francisco, whom they had met through an advertisement
in the *Los Angeles Free Press.* As was common in San Francisco, Hardy
worked with liquid projection: two overhead projectors, each with a clear
dish (typically a large clock glass) in which he manipulated mixtures
of oil and water with different-colored dyes, dimmers on each allowing
him to dissolve from one to the other. He had also experimented with
spraying Crystal Craze (a lacquer that formed crystalline patterns) on the
water surface.[4]

Lebrun was a bridge between this UCLA group and another whose home was the Hog Farm, a commune in Sunland, a township just north of Los Angeles.[5] Formed around Christmas 1966, the commune also included Helena Hartshorn, who had met Lebrun in Mexico, where he had been shooting his film *Sanctus* and she had been traveling, performing liquid projection light shows in bars and schools, and they married soon after. Hartshorn had learned liquid projection in San Francisco from Bill Ham and Elias Romero, who had pioneered its use in countercultural events and who had projected for Ken Kesey's San Francisco Trips Festival in January 1966 and other Acid Tests.[6] Hartshorn taught the dye chemistries and technical procedures she had learned in San Francisco to Lebrun and others at the commune, including Jon Greene, a friend of Gershfield's who had lived at the Cresthill house, and Michael Scroggins, a surfer who had been living on a commune in Topanga Canyon that joined with the Hog Farm. Apart from high school classes and a brief period working as an apprentice in the studio of sculptor Miguel Miramontes, Scroggins had no formal art background; he had been fascinated with light shows since childhood, and inspired by the planetarium sequence in *Rebel without a Cause* and by seeing the films of Len Lye, Fischinger, Jordan Belson, and others at the Movies 'Round Midnight series at the Cinema Theatre in Hollywood, he had maintained his interest in abstract animation.

The Single Wing Turquoise Bird came together as a group of the Hog Farm liquid projectionists, including Hartshorn, Scroggins, Evan Engber, Bonnie Zee, and Rick and Erin Sullivan, began working with the filmmakers, primarily Gershfield (who soon dropped out of the group), Lebrun, Mays, and Perkins from UCLA and Charles Lippincott from USC. Other friends occasionally participated, working the projectors, washing the liquid plates, or doing other odd jobs. As well as projecting films, Lebrun acted as the group's business manager while Lippincott became the general manager. Alan Keesling, who specialized in hand-painted slides and owned a set of six projectors with dimmers and strobe wheels, and Rol Murrow also became associated with the group. The name was supposedly found by Perkins by stabbing his finger blindly into a book of Vedic hymns,[7] while he and Lebrun were driving to meet with John Van Hamersveld at the White House near Hoover and Third Street (where the members of Pinnacle lived) to discuss their first show at the Shrine.

The first Single Wing Shrine performance on March 15–16 accompanied Cream, James Cotton, and Mint Tattoo. For the next few months they performed approximately every second weekend on Friday and Saturday nights for all the big groups of the period that Pinnacle booked, including Traffic, Quicksilver Messenger Service, Big Brother and the Holding Company with Janis Joplin, Pink Floyd, the Grateful Dead, and the Velvet Underground.[8] Pinnacle paid them $1,200 for each weekend, half of which was split evenly among the dozen regulars with the other half invested in new material and equipment and the occasional guest artist.

the group continued to perform at the Shrine; now all of them worked together on the platform in front of the stage, which allowed them to communicate more directly with each other. But in early fall 1968, after an extremely ambitious all-day American Music Show at the Pasadena Rose Bowl on September 15 featuring a dozen major groups drew only a small audience, Pinnacle failed financially and the Shrine concerts ended. By this point, however, the Single Wing had already begun to shift their aesthetic orientation and ambitions.

They found a rehearsal space at Joe Funk's litho shop (which had been featured in Murrow's 1967 UCLA student film *The Tin Shack*), adjacent to the Pot Shop ceramic studio at 334 Sunset Avenue in Venice. The painter Sam Francis, who had been introduced to the group's Shrine performances by Greene, was then making lithographs there.[11] Well known for his support of younger artists, Francis became the group's patron, providing more equipment and eventually allowing them to use his studio on Ashland Street in the Ocean Park distinct of Santa Monica. There they both rehearsed, projecting onto his canvases, which were at that time very large, and performed publicly on two or three occasions, though for smaller audiences of thirty to forty people. At this time, Single Wing had consolidated itself around six members, Keesling, Lippincott, Mays, Perkins, Scroggins, and Greene, and in their ongoing rehearsals this group augmented and then transformed the on-the-spot improvisation of their initial period and created a wholly unique artistic identity.

Where previously their projection had been supplementary to the rock concerts, now they became an autonomous performing entity. The performances were still collaborative and fundamentally spontaneous, but the discipline of the practice sessions and the discoveries they produced allowed their work new refinement, control, and complexity. They still composed in real time in coordination to music, but since it was chosen from records and tapes (sometimes spliced and extended into hypnotic lengths), they were able to practice repeatedly to the same piece. The Velvet Underground's "Sister Ray" was a favorite among the rock songs, but they also used works by Steve Reich and other contemporary composers, especially Terry Riley's then-recent "In C." Artists including James Turrell, Wallace Berman, Ed Moses, and Dewaine Valentine visited; Francis introduced the group to his patrons; and these entrées reoriented the group toward more formal institutions, especially those of the art world. As well as performing in Francis's Ashland Street studio, the group appeared at Occidental College (where William Moritz was then teaching), UCLA, the Santa Barbara Museum of Art (where on the same occasion Judy Chicago did a piece using colored smoke), the Venice public library, Hollywood High School (for a celebration of Huey Newton's birthday), Loyola/Marymount University, and the Cinematheque 16. Many members regard the approximately six months from late 1968 to mid-1969 as the period of their best and most distinctive work. We are fortunate in having several first-person accounts of it.

One evening in late summer 1968, Anaïs Nin attended one of the litho shop performances, along with Henry Miller, P. Adams Sitney, and Gene Youngblood. In her dairy, Nin notes, "Like a thousand modern paintings flowing and sparkling, alive and dynamic, of incredible richness, a death blow to painting in frames, stills."[12] Youngblood, at that time film critic for the Los Angeles Free Press, also described the performance in his Expanded Cinema column:

It's a combination of Jackson Pollock and *2001*. Of Hieronymus Bosch and Victor Vasarely. Of Dali and Buckminster Fuller. Time-lapse clouds run across magenta bull's-eyes. Horses charge in slow motion through solar fires. The hands of a clock run backward. The moon revolves around the earth in a galaxy of Op Art polka dots. Flashing trapezoids and rhomboids whirl out of Buddha's eye. Pristine polygraphic forms are suspended in a phosphate void. Exploding isometrics give birth to insects. A praying mantis dances across an Oriental garden. Spiraling cellular cubes crash into electric-green fossil molds. The organic symbiosis of universal man. A huge magnified centipede creeps across a glowing sun. Sound: Tod Dockstader's Quatermass. Cascading phosphorescent sparks. Waffle grid-patterns strobe-flash over Roy Lichtenstein's 1930 Ultramoderne architecture. A butterfly emerges from its cocoon. New dimensions of space and time. Bodies become plants. Acid-Oracle visions of universal unity. White translucent squids wrestle with geometric clusters.[13]

Where both Nin and Youngblood referenced painting in their descriptions, in William Moritz's account of the Cinematheque 16 performance, published in January 1969 in a local underground paper and the fullest verbal record of a Single Wing performance we have, he emphasized the film component, though also invoking the sense of a continuous present he associated with Gertrude Stein's writing:

Friday and Saturday, January 17 and 18, at midnight in the Cinematheque 16 on Sunset Strip, Single Wing Turquoise Bird presented a two-and-a-half hour light show, EIDOLA, as an artwork in its own right separate from the context of a rock dance or a happening, proving that a "living" art work of organic complexity was (in addition to commercially feasible) considerably more interesting, challenging, and satisfying than any of the flat, static art styles of the past, including painting and the traditional fictional cinema.

EIDOLA demonstrated in five half-hour segments five different styles or formats that the Single Wing Turquoise Bird have mastered. . . .

First the 180-degree screens light up with scenes of the street outside, across from the door of the theater, and the noises of traffic and pedestrian cackles seem to be leaking in as well. Vertical shadow bars whiz by to the sound of passing cars faster and faster until the street is a flickering strobe and the neon signs leap out and flash a hundred times too large or maybe that's the way they always were DON'T WALK DON'T WALK Don't Walk don't walk don't don't. The voices of the idle passerby become mixed with the voices of the idle newscaster straight muffled electronically altered fragmented but telling us just by inflections that

they're saying these same things again just like WALK WALK WALK WALK and
MUNTZ MUNTZ MUNTZ and the smooth electronic music gliding beautifully in
between the noise-music of the city pulsing. And then suddenly, as if all that could
be erased, as it can, the revolving neon becomes also revolving wings of a mandala,
a garuda, a bodhisattva choir, faces now of people instead of faces then of media
and once it's started the other lost faces come too—the bleeding twisted Christ
of a Reformation nightmare and the phosphorescent faces of an Indian tribe in the
dancing and smoking rituals seen by Bert Gershfield's *Now That the Buffalo's
Gone* with its sounds of chanting drumming inside the other sounds and the other
Indians appear again in the piercing gaze of the Lord Shiva which the more it flashes
the more you know the face is really made up of people like that rishi whose
lotused legs are lips and mustache and his folded hands nostrils and so on until
flames begin erasing everything except the electronic sounds and the sun blazes
up and then fades out as the tones of the music cool, metallic, pale and paler. . . .

One measure of the genius of this first movement is perhaps that we have no
language to describe it—no way of telling simultaneity, no precise words for the
electronic-musical sounds and modulations, no terms for so many of those hues
and tones and motions that the light show had revealed to us as an essential part
of our daily lives. . . .

The first movement performed the continually nowness of the present. The second movement took as its point of departure a short film of considerable artistic
integrity and force, *Dream of Wild Horses,* which was subtly altered, expanded with
additional material, extended with flumes of its color and echoes of its shapes, the
nuances looped in mirror cadences bathing a space and time much grander than
the little square of the original. The sound as well extrapolated the lush organ-like
tones of Jacques Lasry's sounding sculptures from the film's soundtrack into a
more symphonic development.

The third movement similarly presented a fantasia on the theme of Pat O'Neill's
film *7362,* which offered a mood and subject-matter radically different from the
slow-motion romance of fleeing stallions. *7362* juxtaposes hard, fast imagery of
naked women and escalating oil-pumping machinery, rendered abstract by close-
ups and layering, solarized textures and iridescent colors. Once more the light
show filled out the complex universe where those images could live, letting cadences
echo, taking a flickering abstraction to its limits and back again, mirroring O'Neill's
images with considerable new film footage shot especially for this piece by Peter
Mays (an old school chum of O'Neill's).

The fourth movement, using Pink Floyd's "Interstellar Overdrive" as a soundtrack, evoked sensations of travel in time and space using only non-objective, non-
representational abstractions: boiling corduroy bubbles, enamel soapsuds breaking
like surf, fluorescent crystals branching out, pulsating circles, pure geometrical
shapes greased slipping away from you, spurts of chalky white exploding and re-
exploding out of itself like a cauliflower periscope or high-rise mushroom clouds.

The final movement, almost entirely black-and-white, generated a wide spectrum
of forms and iridescent colors that were not directly projected by the light machines
but rather induced either by the Grateful Dead's "Alligator" or as carefully calculated
after-images of the projections with your mind's eye as the ultimate screen this time. . . .

These words are not telling it all because it is a 1960s thing and most English words are a 14th or 16th century thing and if Single Wing Turquoise Bird could be writing it they would be writing it, but they are showing it and always only once because Friday January 17, 1969 was not like Saturday January 18, 1969, even though many things about them seemed to be being the same and if you did not see Friday January 17, 1969 when it happened you will not have a chance now because it was living not writing and this is just writing you are doing now.[14]

Ever ambitious for the group, in summer 1969 Francis rented the ballroom of the Santa Monica Hotel, where they gessoed seven of his huge canvases for use as screens. But though they held numerous rehearsals in the large space, the hotel management expelled them at the end of September 1969 because of their hippie appearance and the fact that several of them were living in the ballroom. After a short period without a regular rehearsal space, the group entered into its third major phase when they found a home from the end of 1969 until 1975 in a studio and business space in a large loft above the Fox Venice Theatre at 620 Lincoln Boulevard in Venice, which Murrow had leased to house the Cumberland Mountain Film Company, his production group.[15] They continued to allow guest artists to perform with them, and Larry Janss, who had worked with them occasionally at Sam Francis's studio, joined to perform slides. In this period the regular group consisted of Greene, Janss, Keesling, Mays, Murrow, Perkins, and Scroggins. As during their previous phase, their projection platform was multilevel, with film and slide projectors on risers at the rear, and overhead projectors at the front, with an additional high-powered film projector located high up in the rafters effectively adding a third tier. They rehearsed regularly in Murrow's space and also performed there for small public groups, as they had in Francis's studio, and made innovations in their use of sound, sometimes drawing in the sound of the traffic outside and people talking on the sidewalk by means of outside microphones fixed to the theater marquee (Figure 9.1).[16] And here the rapprochement with Hollywood, virtually inevitable for any counter-cultural art practice in Los Angeles not specifically identified with the working class, occurred.

Francis had introduced the group to his friend Jim Bridges as he was planning to direct his first feature, *The Baby Maker*. Bridges persuaded his production company to give the group $10,000 to produce a 35 mm film to be used to simulate a light show performance in a rock 'n' roll nightclub scene in his movie (Figure 9.2). Since the light levels and film sensitivity made it impossible to photograph an actual performance adequately for theatrical film projection, coordinated sequences of the various components—the liquids, the movies, and the slides—were made separately on 35 mm, and then these were edited together by Peter Mays with Butler-Glowner, an optical house, providing dissolves and superimpositions. In *The Baby Maker,* the Single Wing material is featured in a four-minute sequence in which a hippie couple visit a rock 'n' roll

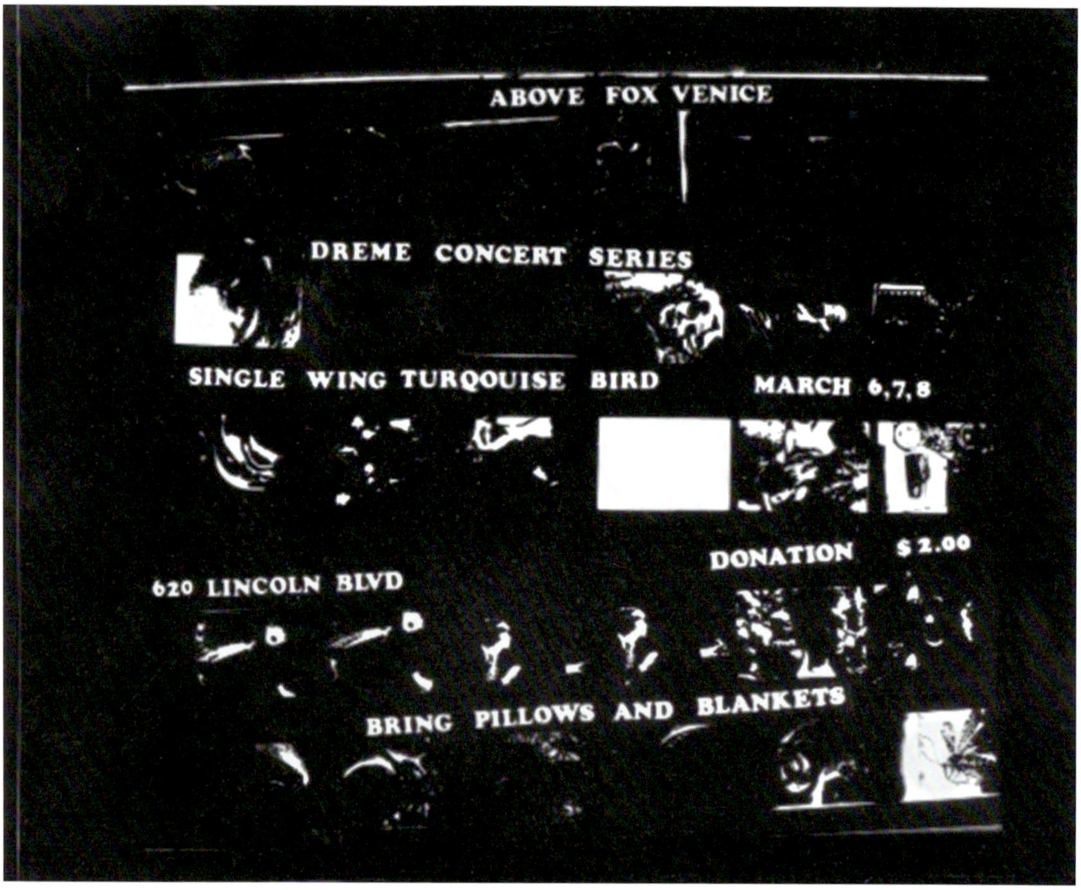

ABOVE FOX VENICE
DREME CONCERT SERIES
SINGLE WING TURQOUISE BIRD   MARCH 6, 7, 8
DONATION $2.00
620 LINCOLN BLVD
BRING PILLOWS AND BLANKETS

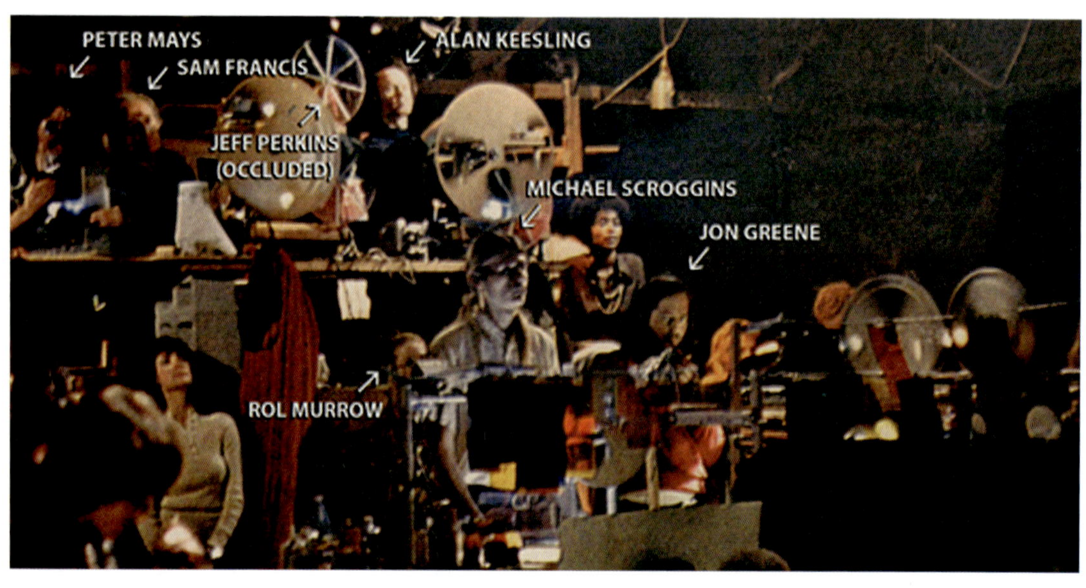

PETER MAYS
SAM FRANCIS
ALAN KEESLING
JEFF PERKINS (OCCLUDED)
MICHAEL SCROGGINS
JON GREENE
ROL MURROW

Figure 9.1
Single Wing Turquoise Bird,
Dreme Concert Series Flyer,
1969.

Figure 9.2
Still from *The Baby Maker*,
released 1971, showing Single
Wing Turquoise Bird at work.

nightclub; the girl is pregnant as a surrogate mother for a bourgeois family, and they quarrel just before a police raid ends the performance.

Composed from the superimposition of three separately edited films, the light show is somewhat denser than a typical Single Wing performance, but on the other hand, the twenty-four frames per second of film photography and projection fail to capture the much faster effects of the strobes. Since the sequence may be seen in the video of *The Baby Maker*, only a simplified description of it will be given here (Figure 9.3). It begins with swirling nebulous organic forms in red and blue made by liquid projection over which a movie of a solar eclipse enters in the center with rapidly strobed slides from Gustave Doré's illustrations for Dante's *Inferno* in the bottom half of the frame. Two alternating but slightly offset slides, one with a blue and the other with a red filter and featuring a close-up of Jim Morrison's face, enter in the black center of the eclipse. As the liquids fade out, a different movie of galaxies of stars seen through alternating green and blue color wheels covers the transition from Morrison's face to several rapidly alternating anthropological high-contrast slides of the face of an Amazonian man; this is strobically intercut with a home movie of a man emerging from the sea seen though a yellow and red color wheel, while several slides of Egyptian figures come to dominate the center. By this point Morrison's face has been thrown out of focus and disappears under Lebrun loops of the thin white lines of multiple geometric drawings, but then Morrison reappears again strobically alternating with the Egyptian figures. An effect made by projecting out of focus a black slide with a hole in the center creates a fuzzy sphere in the center for a few seconds, alternating with a slide of a yogi, before the Lebrun loops change to outlines first of mythical animals and then of mystical symbols. These occupy the center, as the bipacked images of outtakes from Pat O'Neill's movie *7362* appear behind them, until the bubble-like forms of a silvery clear oil slowly churn behind them. A red liquid projection takes over the foreground, and the two plates intermingle as the golden-green lines of outtakes from John Stehura's *Cybernetik 5.3* make their appearance, and, as yet another liquid projection enters, the sequence ends.

The group continued to work in the studio space above the Fox Venice for several years. Every spring they held a series of five to ten public shows, accompanying either records (still typically the Grateful Dead's "Dark Star," Velvet Underground's "Sister Ray," Henri Posseur's "Trois Visages à Liège," and Steve Reich's "Come Out") or live music, to audiences of around forty to sixty people drawn by mailings or word of mouth. But by 1973, the public culture that had sustained them was in decline, and the financial support obtained through admission charges was insufficient. Though he occasionally returned for special events, Scroggins left the group to attend the recently opened California Institute of the Arts, where he worked in real-time videographic animation and eventually in interactive computer virtual reality animation. At the same time, Murrow

   EXPANDED CINEMA IN LOS ANGELES

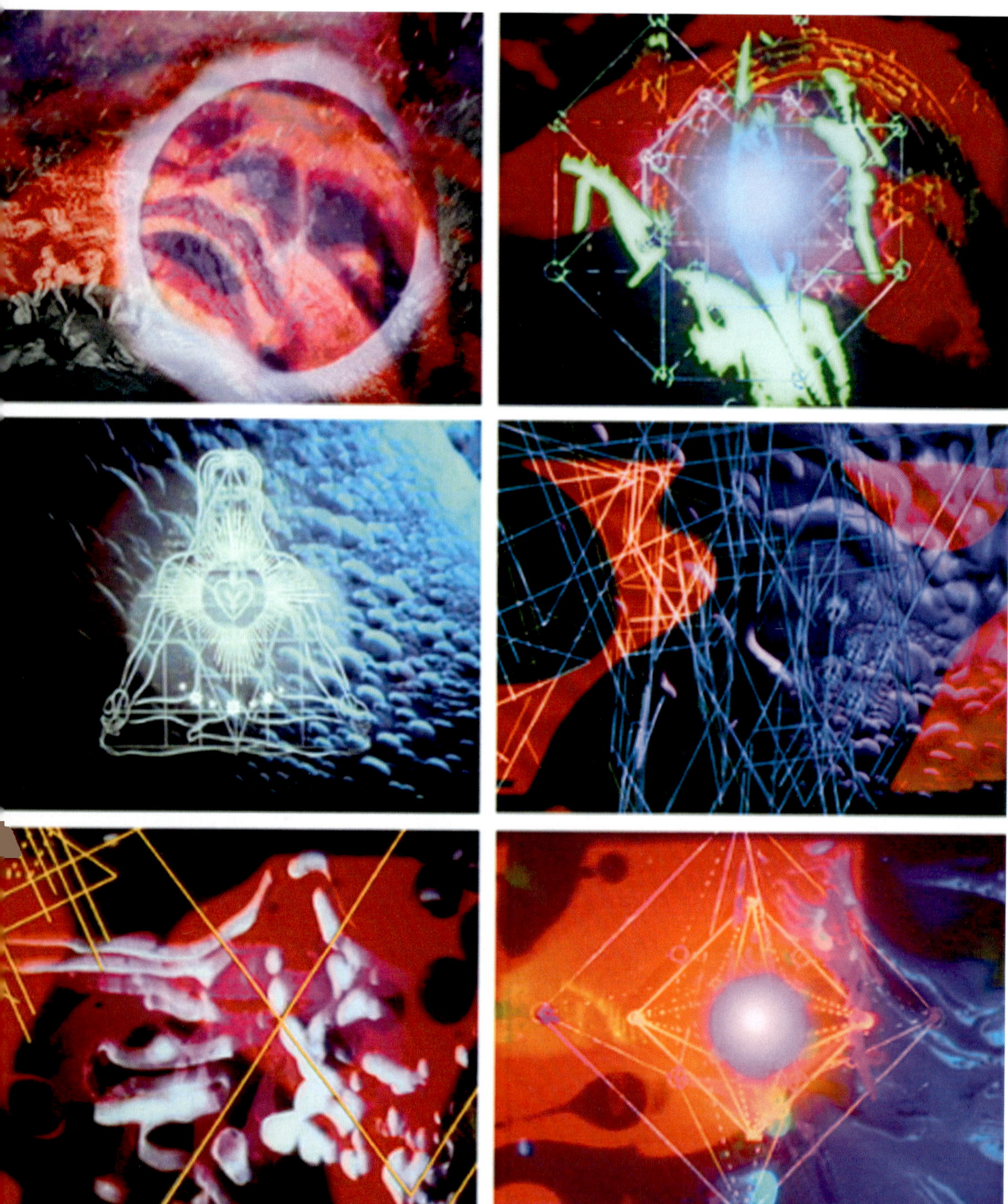

(who had meanwhile worked on the editing of Dennis Hopper's epic *The Last Movie*), Janss, Bob Maestri, and theater manager Kim Jorgensen formed Cumberland Mountain Theaters. The company took over the Fox cinema space and turned it into the premier repertory revival theater in Los Angeles, with a new double bill every night. With several Single Wing Turquoise Bird members working for them—Perkins as a graphic designer, Scroggins as a calendar distributor, and Mays as projectionist— the Fox Venice prospered, its screenings including *Performance, Walkabout, Night of the Living Dead, The Last Movie, Underground,* John Waters's films, and similar countercultural classics, as well as Mays's own underground feature *Sister Midnight. The Rocky Horror Picture Show* had its first public screening there, at a sneak preview at midnight just before it officially opened, foreshadowing decades of Friday night midnight screenings held of it since.

The light show waned as the group members threw their energies into operating the theater, but they still did occasional performances. As late as 1976, at the Fox they staged a Freak Night, a '60s revival show when the group projected its signature imagery from both the theater projection booth and a large platform constructed on top of the seats at the rear of the theater. The event included a snake dance led by Hugh Romney (aka Wavy Gravy), and Alejandro Jodorowsky danced around the projection platform in excited delight. This was the Single Wing Turquoise Bird's final performance, but Perkins and Mays regrouped for a handful of revival concerts in a different cultural era. On New Year's Eve 1980, briefly assisted by Lebrun, they projected films and slides for a concert featuring X, DOA, and other Los Angeles punk bands at the Stardust Ballroom that concluded with Exene Cervenka, lead singer of X, tearing down a paper screen on which was being projected a fragment of *Un chien Andalou.*

As a collaboration among its members and their audiences, the art of the Single Wing Turquoise Bird was, as William Moritz emphasized, fundamentally a new medium, the cultural creation and self-articulation of a social group in a historical moment that are both gone forever, "always only once," as Moritz's Steinian syntax had it. Such a *past,* as Thoreau remarked, cannot be *presented,* and no one who didn't participate in it then will ever experience the light show. Nor has history been attentive. Few traces of the group remain, and their memory has not been preserved in either the scholarly records or television commercials where other shades of the sixties linger. But we are fortunate in that Moritz and Youngblood, two of the most perceptive commentators, both described it in the accounts already quoted and made summary evaluations. Moritz, the foremost American scholar of visual music who saw many of the most prominent light shows of the late twentieth century in the United States and Europe, testified that the Single Wing Turquoise Bird "stood head-and-shoulders above all the rest."[17] And Youngblood concluded, some two years after he first saw them: "In almost total obscurity the group perfected an art of light manipulation virtually unequalled by any mixed-media organization with the possible exception of USCO."[18] As for other twentieth-century vanguard cultural movements in Los Angeles, and especially all forms of experimental cinema, that combination of achievement and obscurity is part of the Single Wing's social meaning, specifically in marking a historical possibility in the ongoing struggle for liberation from the capitalist media industry that exists there in an overwhelmingly proximate form.

Youngblood's celebration of the group as the apotheosis of multiple-projection environments reflected his reiteration of Jonas Mekas's expectations for "expanded cinema" generally in the mid-1960s. Mekas envisaged that, on the one hand, the narrative syntax associated with underground film and the expansion of film's visual languages beyond the restrictions of the commercial cinema's illusionism and, on the other, the expansion of the projection situation out from the flat theatrical screen into three-dimensional environments associated with developments in the art world, both prefigured the eventual transcendence of the materiality of cinema *tout court* into the actualization of the dreams and visions of the human mind: "We give up all movies and become movies."[19] Mekas was writing in a context in which expanded cinema was only one, though certainly a privileged one, of cognate "expanded arts," all of which were supposed to be similarly auspicious. Their cultural impetus was such that in 1966 *Film Culture* published a special edition on that very topic—one in a special expanded format—that prominently featured Stan Vanderbeek's experiments in multimedia environments at his Movie Drome in Stony Point, New York.[20] Earlier that year, *Film Culture* had already published Vanderbeek's "Culture: Intercom and Expanded Cinema: A Proposal and Manifesto" that, as well as glossing his own work, summarized the urgent need for massively enlarged modes of cognition, the centrality in them of new forms in cinema, and the utopian expectations associated with them:

> . . . a rapid panoply of graphics and light calling upon thousands of images, both still and in motion [. . . .] if an individual is exposed to an overwhelming information experience. . . . It might be possible to re-order the levels of awareness of any person . . . it certainly will re-order the structure of motion pictures as we know them . . . Cinema will become a "performing" art . . . and image-library.[21]

Made both more concrete and apocalyptic by his assiduous attention to contemporary developments in cybernetics, Youngblood's parallel projections for expanded cinema inflated it into a universal metaphor within which developments in the inner world of the human spirit were reciprocated in the spirit's actualization in the outer world of scientific advancement: "When we say expanded cinema we actually mean expanded consciousness. Expanded cinema does not mean computer films, video phosphors, atomic light, or spherical projections. Expanded cinema isn't a movie at all: like life, it's a process of becoming, man's ongoing historical drive to manifest his consciousness outside his mind, in front of his eyes."[22] Even though, in Youngblood's 1968 *Free Press* account, the Single Wing performance depended on movies and other forms of projected light, in fact its greatest achievement was the artists' success in subordinating their individual egos to the group that enabled them to combine the diverse constituent projection elements so integrally that the result appeared to have the organic coherence of a movie; this was for him only the form of appearance of a more radical achievement. Dismissive of the group's initial activities in the Shrine, when he thought it merely a light show for rock 'n' roll bands, Youngblood believed that it had subsequently developed as a performance unit of revolutionary promise, albeit "more occult than psychedelic; mystic rather than Maoist." A new consciousness was being born, he argued, internationally but initially and most dramatically in California, and "in an artists' cooperative in Venice, a group of six visionaries are defining the first words of an entirely different kind of vocabulary, a tribal language which expresses not ideas but states of consciousness—not of individuals but of groups." And the possibilities for this kind of "social interaction on a global scale are limitless: one imagines entire nations cooperating through computers and satellites to produce an intercultural 'light show' which would never end."[23]

We now know that the global cultural revolution of which Youngblood, Vanderbeek, and other visionaries of the time dreamed in fact produced, not utopia, but the imperial expanded cinemas of electronic advertising, Fox News, CNN, and so on—the consciousness industries that frame the invasion of Iraq, the manufacture of global misery, and the rape of the Earth. Sublated into this dystopian actualization of spirit, the historical moment of the Single Wing and other expanded arts is not yet sufficiently far from us that a definitive reckoning of its function can be expected. Beginnings in the reconstruction of the lost connections between the cultural possibilities engendered in that moment and other forms of resistance to the corporate state are being made by, for example, reconsiderations of the cognitive and psychic implications of the perceptual reorganizations that events like light shows entailed.[24] But in cases of expanded cinema in Los Angeles, the imminence of Hollywood—their socially and psychically "contracted" other—that historically overshadowed them also ensured that the fault lines between them and corporate culture are especially revelatory. The connections and disconnections among different forms of expanded cinema in Los Angeles, and the connections and disconnections between them and the film industry itself, illustrate the way local developments in the city anticipate cultural movements in the United States generally.

During the period of the Single Wing, Los Angeles was home to an unequaled efflorescence of attempts to extend the boundaries of cinema. The late-sixties Ethno-Communications Program at UCLA, for example, introduced African, Asian, and Mexican American students into the film school and so inaugurated the minority filmmaking of the 1970s that allowed large sectors of the working class to contest their previous objectification and to become producers rather than merely consumers of cinema. Another venture, one that was precisely Maoist rather than mystic, was the Los Angeles Newsreel. Founded also in Venice and also by a group of mainly UCLA film students (some of whom were also involved in the Single Wing) and also in October 1968 (when Single Wing was beginning its unique self-creation in the rehearsals during its second phase at Joe Funk's Litho Shop), the Los Angeles Newsreel dedicated itself to a global working-class revolution.[25] Believing the Black Panther Party to be the domestic arm of a political avant-garde led globally by the Vietnamese struggle against neocolonial U.S. imperialism, they screened films made by other Newsreel branches and by Third World revolutionaries in factories, union halls, and colleges, meanwhile working on their own film about the Los Angeles Panthers. Their project, called *Repression,* was interrupted when the Los Angeles Police Department collaborated with the FBI and destroyed the Los Angeles Panther headquarters on December 8, 1969, two days after the Illinois police murdered Black Panther Party Deputy Chairman Fred Hampton, and a month or so before the Single Wing moved to the Fox Venice to begin their third phase. The Newsreel reconstructed their film, adding footage of the police occupying the black community and the burnt-out building, and completed the editing of both sound and visual tracks. But then, unable to raise funds to finish it, they abandoned it.

The repression of Newsreel was, of course, more crucial than the gradual depletion of the Single Wing, but neither this nor their different value systems—Maoist or mystic—should obscure the fact that they lived in immediate proximity to their common adversary, corporate culture, which was already mobilizing a counteroffensive. In summer 1969, Columbia Pictures released *Easy Rider,* the studio's first successful attempt to exploit and assimilate the counterculture of which, in their different ways, both Single Wing and Newsreel were the dialectically complementary halves. In other films, Hollywood continued to ridicule or neutralize oppositional cultural movements, before reasserting industrial control by appropriating expanded visuality itself in *Star Wars* and the subsequent renewed blockbuster production. Light shows from other parts of the country are preserved in independent films where they unironically occupy the entire diegesis—USCO in Jud Yalkut's *Diffraction Film* (1965) and *Us* (1966), the Trips Festival in Ben Van Meter's film, and the *Exploding Plastic Inevitable* in Ronald Nameth's eponymous film of 1966. But it is symptomatic of the capitalist entertainment industry's framing of all countercultural activity in Los Angeles that the only visual record of the Single Wing—which never used fragments of Hollywood films in their otherwise limitless image library—should be a brief, thematically over-determined interlude in a commercial film. Its position there limns the contradictory threat it posed to the cultural establishment.

The Baby Maker's plot revolves around an affluent upper-middle-class couple, Suzanne and Jay Wilcox, who live in Brentwood, and a working-class bohemian couple, Tish and her boyfriend, Tad, who live in a shack in Venice (where most of the Single Wing members lived). Since Suzanne cannot bear children, the Wilcoxes make a financial arrangement with clearly stipulated rules for Tish to be a surrogate mother for Jay's child. But as the pregnancy proceeds, all become personally involved. Suzanne begins to resemble her husband, an "efficiency expert" or "management engineer," and insists on monitoring and regulating Tish's pregnancy; Tish and Jay become emotionally entangled; and Tad grows frustrated and angry at being sexually deprived of Tish. The crisis comes when Tad takes Tish, by this time well into her pregnancy, to a rock 'n' roll nightclub up the Pacific Coast Highway toward Malibu, where the Single Wing are performing. Dominated by the light show, the sequence in the club places the dramatic action against a background of the screen on which the group is projecting; scenes of the performers creating the light show, including wide-angle shots of them and their equipment, close-ups on Scroggins's manipulation of the liquids, and extended footage of the show itself, including several minutes where it occupies the full screen. Angry with Tish, Tad openly flirts with an African American woman, sharing his joint with her, and causing Tish, who has previously boasted of their "open" relationship, to demand to be taken home. But before they can leave, the club (like the Panther headquarters in *Repression*) is invaded by the police and in the ensuing fracas Tad is arrested for disturbing the peace. Tish goes to live with the Wilcoxes where she becomes deeply attached to Jay as his surrogate wife, but the film ends with her sadly watching the Wilcoxes drive away with her newborn baby (Figure 9.4).

Though *The Baby Maker*'s overall insubstantiality resists its being taken too seriously, it also allows its political unconsciousness relatively uncensored expression. Based on the common fantasy of a relationship between a bourgeois man and a working-class girl that dates back to the earliest days of bourgeois society, the film is a clear allegory of class society, however sugared over with humanist pathos. Class relations are dramatized in generational and lifestyle terms, and general relations of production are recast in terms of sexual reproduction. Itself nonproductive, the bourgeoisie hires the working class to produce for it (in this case, Jay actually fucks Trish), imposes its own standards of efficiency on it, and temporarily draws its productive members into its own ideological and social orbit before abandoning them when their productivity is exhausted, while excluding recalcitrant, nonproductive lumpen elements. The Single Wing sequence occurs at a pivotal moment in this process. Resentful of the bourgeoisie's appropriation of his partner's sexuality, her (re)productive power, Tad follows the various sixties radicals who understood the civil rights struggles in class rather than nationalist terms and attempts to affiliate with the black working class—like, most notably, the Los Angeles Newsreel. He is interrupted from doing so by

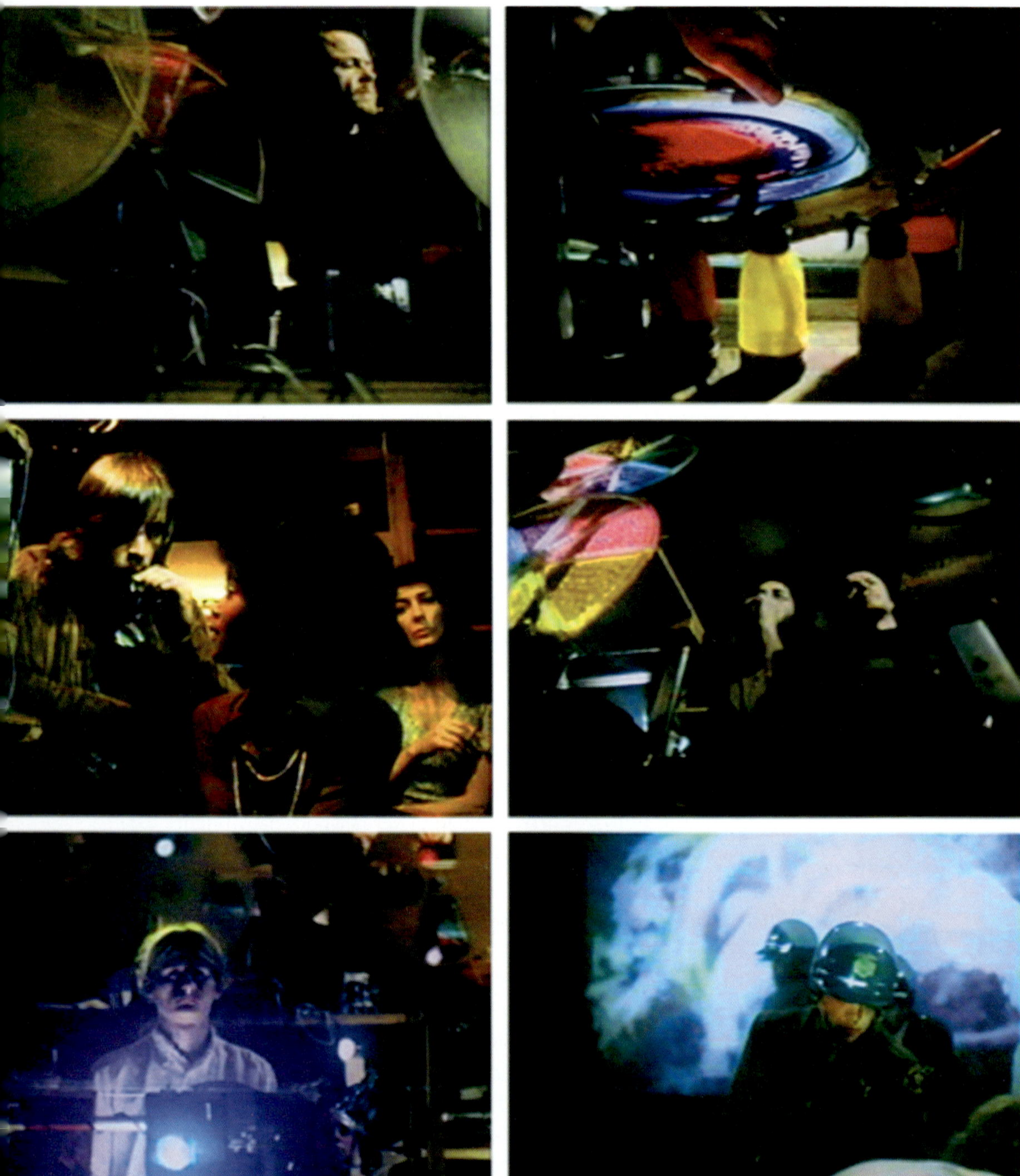

Tish, the faction of the working class who has sold her labor power to the bourgeoisie and become effectively co-opted, and by the police, the Repressive State Apparatus in the period's idiom.

The Baby Maker, then, schematically envisions the Single Wing as organizing a Dionysian cultural space where unruly energies are released and subversive interracial class affiliations explored, and also a catalytic space where social realignments are organized. Occupying the habitat and habitus of the Single Wing members themselves, Tish and Tad are both a resource to be plundered and a threat to be contained, a counterculture that must be divided and its separate factions appropriately assigned. As the filmic form of this counterculture, the Single Wing is similarly a productive resource: hired like Tish for a few thousand dollars, it increases the Hollywood film's value by supplying youth appeal that will expand the capital invested in it and participate in the renewal of the industry and the production of the "New Hollywood." But as an expanded visual language and as an expanded mode of film production, it is a cultural threat that must be denigrated and policed, for if—as Vanderbeek and the underground anticipated—cinema were to become a performing art and the masses became performers rather than merely consumers, then "the structure of motion pictures as we know them" would be re-constructed and their commodity function and their economic and ideological roles in the late capital era would be jeopardized. Hence the sequence is terminated by the police, and the group disappears entirely from the film, remaining only as a brief glimpse, a framed memory of a cultural form that can be exploited but not endorsed.

The Baby Maker's use of the Single Wing Turquoise Bird does not pro-vide a definitive analysis of the light show's historical meaning—only of what the dominant culture desired and feared in it. In fact, para-Holly-wood modes of production had begun to appropriate parallel counter-cultural initiatives, even before they had been fully formed, and as these proved profitable, commercial media's exploitation of the counterculture rapidly escalated.[26] But in this case what remains outside the attempted industrial assimilation is the promise of a form of film practice in which expanded visual and sensual experience was reciprocated in the liberation of similarly expanded social energies, the cynosure of a cultural revolution.

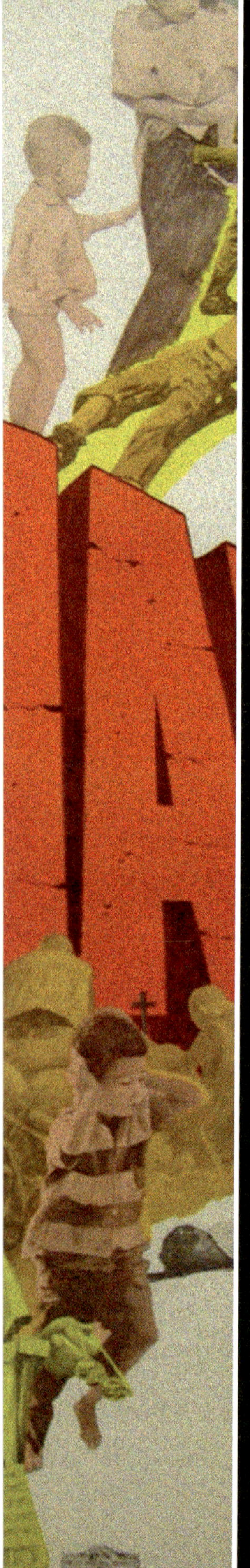

CHAPTER 10
PAPER WALLS: POLITICAL POSTERS IN AN AGE OF MASS MEDIA

Tom Wilson

In 1970, a Californian resident recalled walking down Berkeley's Telegraph Avenue "on a warm August night . . . past the endless collection of posters stuck up on walls and poles on the Avenue—the Young Socialists protest this, rally next week against that, free all political prisoners. Saw some people putting up hand-scrawled posters."[1] Printed in the thousands and representing the divergent concerns of various social movements—all united in bitter opposition to military intervention in Southeast Asia—the posters presented a dramatic and eye-catching sight across U.S. West Coast cities during the late 1960s and the following decade. Calling for a new social order and imposing themselves over the consumer advertising of the old order, political posters of the time are particularly intriguing because they encapsulated concerns about the growing influence of the mass media at home as well as protesting America's political actions abroad. The debate about the role and structure of the mainstream media was recognized by a poster-making student at Stanford University, who claimed that "the traditional graphic arts can no longer compete with television and films as propaganda media and . . . the artist who wishes to make a political or social statement must move into these forms."[2]

The student was correct in one crucial respect, in that the mass media at the time was unlikely to transmit dissenting ideas or images. There had long been a sense among the counterculture that the national media, heavily controlled by corporate and government interests, were guilty of censorship by omission in their unequivocal support for the war. In such a proscribed environment, the underground media were the first to openly oppose the war, and posters quickly became an alternative and experimental means of communication for dissenters. Times of instability are often an impetus for powerful graphic propaganda, but the political poster is notable for its resurgence as a medium of protest in an age of ascendant mass media. The Berkeley Free Speech Movement of 1964 lasted three months and involved ten thousand students, but according to participant Michael Rossman, it produced very few posters.[3] By 1970, the political poster had experienced a sustained revival to the extent that a poster workshop at the California College of Arts and Crafts in Oakland was reported to have produced some eighty thousand posters in the space of a year. Rossman's observation parallels a wider paradox, in that posters occupy a blind spot for media theorists of the time. In his 1964 book *Understanding Media,* the Canadian communications theorist Marshall McLuhan articulated a change in the world's communications media, showing how different forms of technologies such as television, newspapers, and movies mediated human communication and offered alternative ways of looking at the world.[4] In his otherwise comprehensive study, McLuhan completely overlooks the poster, a surprising omission considering its long and varied history as a means of communication.

McLuhan's oversight can, perhaps, be forgiven. Posters have long been appreciated for their illustrative value, and the guardians of poster histories tend to focus exclusively on their composition and style. While this art historical approach is valid, the emphasis on their formal qualities has the effect of treating posters as autonomous objects, and somehow distinct from the events that provoked them. This process of transforming objects into reified "radical chic" was noted by Susan Sontag in her introduction to *The Art of Revolution,* a book about Cuban revolutionary posters. Sontag succinctly describes how recasting posters in the privileged role of art objects, viewed in museums or in the pages of coffee table books, robs them of their transient nature and converts them "into something other than what they are—or were ever meant to be. They are now cultural objects, offered up for our delectation."[5] The survival of posters goes against their intended purpose and raises interesting questions. Does the co-option of protest posters light a mnemonic flame that continues to burn over decades, or does it mean their political fervor has been defused for good?

Printed in mass quantities, the poster is one of the earliest mediums of the modern age, and they allow for far more than just the simple transmission of messages. When identifying posters as a form of media, it is tempting to identify the medium as simply the material support—in other words, the paper on which the image appears. This definition is too limited. As Raymond Williams insists, the media are more than just the materials of which they are composed—they are a material *social practice,* a set of skills, habits, techniques, tools, codes, and conventions.[6] The natural habitats of the political poster are the walls and lampposts of the streets, not libraries or art galleries, and this affects the ways in which we read them. Posters are never seen alone or independently of each other. (Scott B. Montgomery's essay "Signifying the Ineffable" in this volume makes a similar claim.) Like all media, we view posters in conjunction with other media. As such, it is important to consider how posters operate alongside other media of the time, whether they take the form of the national press, television, or commercial advertising, and not as a separate entity.

It is tempting at this point to draw a neat distinction between activist political posters and their psychedelic counterparts, such as those produced by Victor Moscoso and Wes Wilson in the late 1960s.[7] With their emphasis on form, color, and style, psychedelic posters constitute an indirect challenge to the materialistic values of society, whereas posters by the more politicized wing of the counterculture are more explicit in attacking the government's role in Vietnam as well as representing the myriad concerns of numerous social movements. However, as Julie Stephens suggests, the relationship between the countercultural and activist wings of the New Left is more complicated than a simple division based on political issues. In contrast to the supposedly organized politics of the New Left, Stephens views the counterculture as a form of antidisciplinary protest, "which rejected a politics of bureaucratic organization, hierarchy and leadership, strategy and planning, and the notion that political commitment required grim seriousness and sacrifice to be effective."[8] While political posters are involved in decidedly disciplinary practices (such as antiwar protests), they are also intricately linked with the creative practice that defines the anti-disciplinary counterculture.

This is particularly evident when investigating political posters in the context of the mass media. Such posters do not only concern themselves with political issues; they also constitute a creative critique of mass-media distortion. This essay begins by investigating how designers used techniques of remediation in order to practice a rhetoric of exposé. According to protesters, the everyday public is rendered passive to the war in Southeast Asia by capitalist desires at home. By remediating the graphic conventions of consumer advertising, branding, and news imagery through inventive means, poster designers aimed to draw attention to media techniques of manipulation and desire, as well as condemning the Vietnam War and materialistic appetites in general. The second section shows how other posters highlight biased or unequal representations of social movements in the mainstream media and challenge the dichotomy between active creator and passive spectator by engendering dialogue between social movements. This is particularly evident in a rich cross-cultural exchange between the Black Panther movement in the United States and revolutionary organizations in Cuba. Lastly, this essay considers how, when pasted up on the walls of the street, posters demonstrated the potential to become makeshift forums for the distribution of ideas, ripostes, and alternative readings. This is an area of study that warrants greater investigation, but it contributes to a wider reevaluation of political posters and their use by the counterculture. When studied in the context of the mass media, such posters are revealed to be an important area of cultural production for both the disciplinary and anti-disciplinary wings of the counterculture, and instead of being divided, the two actually co-mingled their interests and values.

INTERRUPTING THE SPECTACLE

In 1970, a San Francisco Bay Area group calling themselves 1044 started pasting speech bubbles directly onto advertisements featuring female models selling products aimed at men. The models now appeared to say:

Hello Men! I'm a picture of a woman that doesn't exist, but my body corresponds to a stereotype that you have been conditioned to desire. . . . The people who put me up here have got you just where they want you—by the balls. With your "manhood" challenged, you're putty in their hands. They can convince you to buy the objects they've made you think you need, instead of taking what you really want. . . . If you continue to "live" like this, you won't be satisfied till the day of your death. Sucker.[9]

As well as drawing covert attention to the use of the female body as a sales tool, 1044s were attacking what they saw as the stultifying effects of advertising. The perpetrators, Isaac Cronin and Ken Knabb, explained their reasoning behind their act: "If a pretty woman on an advertising poster is altered so that 'she' talks about her manipulative *raison-d'être* in the commodity system, the purpose is to make things *clear*. The fragment is made to expose itself."[10]

From one of three early situationist groups based in the San Francisco Bay Area, 1044's act of vandalism drew its cue from the Situationist International's tactic of *détournement*. Largely inspired by Guy Debord's *The Society of the Spectacle,* the Situationist International sought to challenge the increasing ubiquity of the mass media, which they claimed had the power to render the public indefinitely passive and distracted.[11] Debord was not alone in expressing concern about the ubiquity of the spectacle during the 1960s. The American historian Daniel Boorstin propounded a similar theory in his 1962 book *The Image,* in which he argued that America was living in a similar "age of contrivance," in which illusions and fabrications had become a dominant force in society. "A new kind of synthetic novelty," he announces, "has flooded our experience."[12] He laments the fact that the public appears to be a willing participant in the fabrication and enjoyment of the illusionary image and asks, "How can we immunize ourselves against [the image's] bewitching allusive power?"[13] Boorstin gives no strategy for counteracting this malaise, but 1044's act of *détournement* demonstrates how designers sought to interrupt sites of the spectacle through creative and experimental means.

Boorstin's concerns about the immersive powers of the image were given credence by Marshall McLuhan, who described the Vietnam War as America's "first television war": "We are now in the midst of our first television war . . . [which] has meant the end of the dichotomy between civilian and military. The public is now a participant in every phase of the war, and the main actions of the war are now being fought in the American home itself."[14] While the Vietnam War was not, strictly speaking, the first war to be televised, it was certainly the first to be popularly consumed through the pages of pictorial magazines such as *Time* and *Life,* daily news bulletins on television, and Hollywood movies (one notable example being the 1968 John Wayne film *The Green Berets,* in which the actor reprised his role as an all-American hero, substituting the Wild West with the jungles of Asia). Such interests were held to be heavily one-sided, in that they expressed broad support for the war. If there was any criticism in the media, it tended to focus on the effectiveness of tactics used by the American military and not of the intervention itself. The counterculture sought to respond to what they saw as techniques of persuasion by the media through remediating images from popular culture with antiwar sentiment. David Nordahl's poster for Gross National Product, for example, imagines the Vietnam War as an epic Hollywood spectacular (Figure 10.1). President Lyndon B. Johnson is shown reclining on a deck chair, ostensibly enjoying the sight of U.S. soldiers dragging away the bodies of dead Vietnamese. Ironic quotes heap praise on the

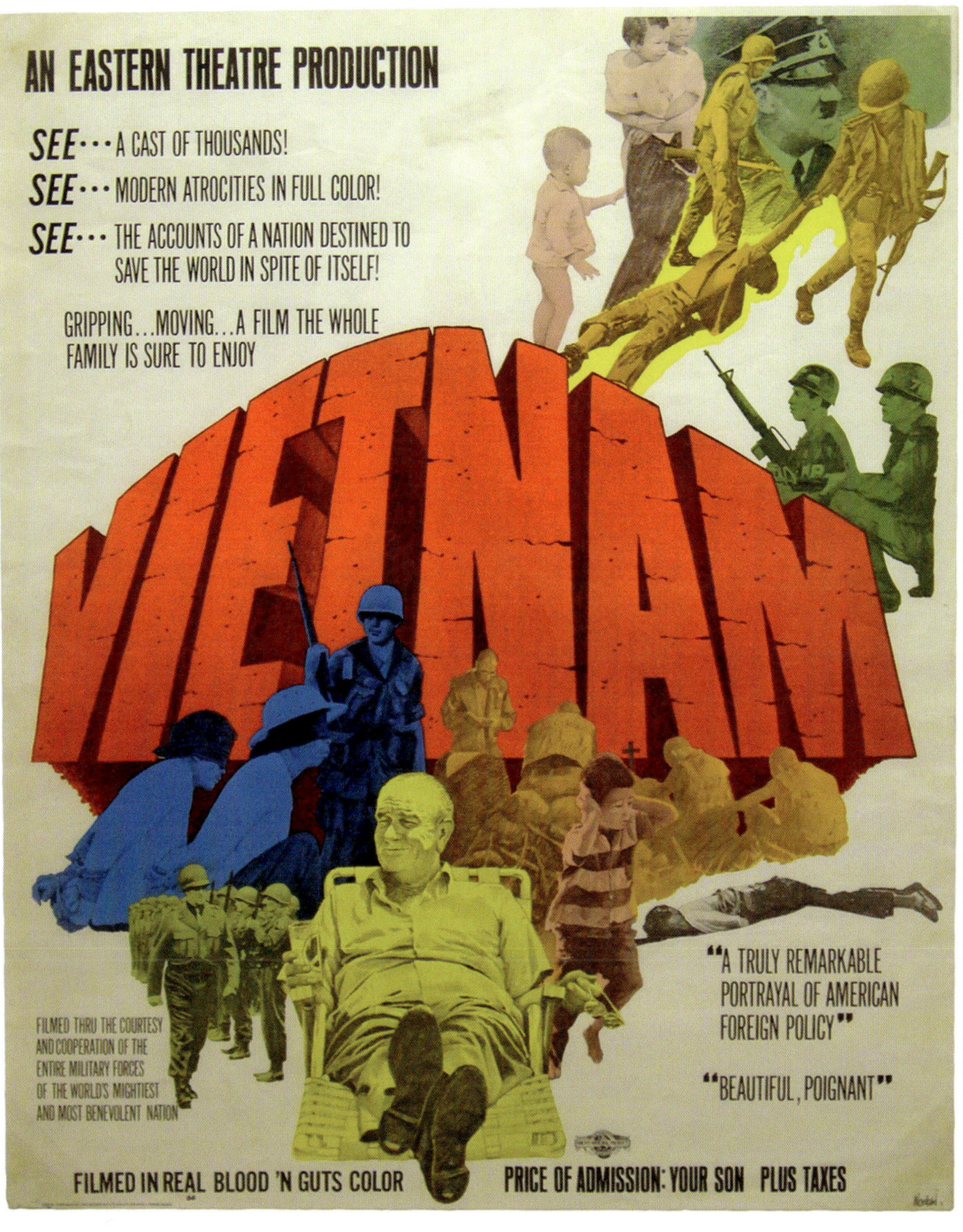

AN EASTERN THEATRE PRODUCTION
SEE··· A CAST OF THOUSANDS!
SEE··· MODERN ATROCITIES IN FULL COLOR!
SEE··· THE ACCOUNTS OF A NATION DESTINED TO SAVE THE WORLD IN SPITE OF ITSELF!
GRIPPING...MOVING...A FILM THE WHOLE FAMILY IS SURE TO ENJOY
VIETNAM
FILMED THRU THE COURTESY AND COOPERATION OF THE ENTIRE MILITARY FORCES OF THE WORLD'S MIGHTIEST AND MOST BENEVOLENT NATION
"A TRULY REMARKABLE PORTRAYAL OF AMERICAN FOREIGN POLICY"
"BEAUTIFUL, POIGNANT"
FILMED IN REAL BLOOD 'N GUTS COLOR
PRICE OF ADMISSION: YOUR SON   PLUS TAXES

Figure 10.2

Gary Brown, graphic artist, and
Felix Greene, photographer,
Johnson's Baby Powder, 1968.
Silkscreen on sheet metal, 33
x 23 inches. Courtesy of the
Center for the Study of Political
Graphics.

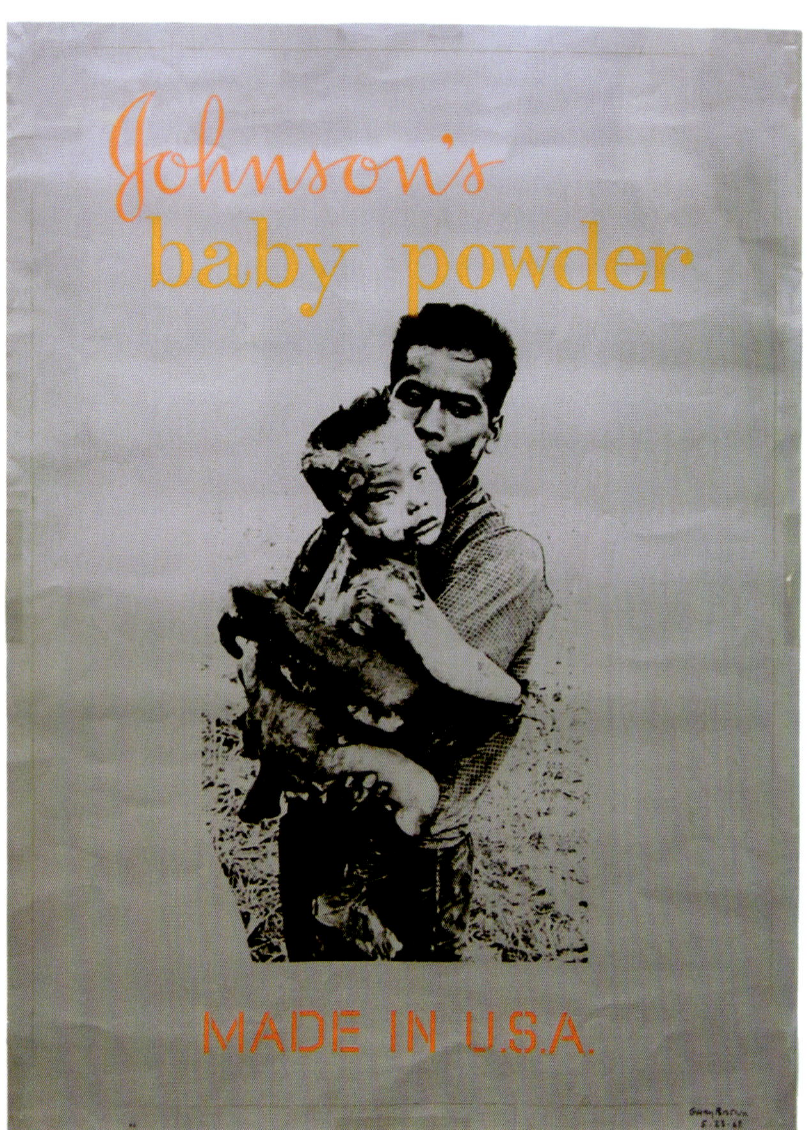

Johnson's
baby powder
MADE IN U.S.A.

"movie," suggesting it represents "a truly remarkable portrayal of American foreign policy." As well as attacking America's political and military intervention in Vietnam, Nordahl's poster is a savage critique of the way that American mass culture tended to repackage the war in Vietnam as entertainment, with the effect of fostering popular support.

The film industry was not the only target for poster designers; cartoon and toy industries were equally condemned. One anonymous poster depicts a panel from an imaginary comic, featuring a chisel-jawed, cigar-chomping U.S. soldier firing a machine gun. A cartoon bubble above his head declares, "G.I. Joe is an imperialist tool!," a reference to the popular boy's toy of the same name. Not only is this a criticism of how cartoons trivialize the horrors of war, but it also suggests at how comics and toys can be seen as potentially powerful carriers of imperialist values, masquerading as harmless fun. This was the view put forward by Chilean novelist Ariel Dorfman and Belgian sociologist Armand Mattelart in their study of Disney cartoons, *How to Read Donald Duck*.[15] Writing at a time when Chile was attempting to extricate itself from economic dependence on the United States, the authors contended that Disney cartoons contained embedded pro-capitalist messages that indoctrinated Chilean children not to rebel against their country's subordinate position in the international economy.

Boorstin recognized the link between branding and the seductive quality of the image, noting "the graphic revolution has made the hypnotic appeal of the image take the place of the persuasive appeal of the argument. . . . in a flash the entire corporate image is etched into the mind."[16] A poster by Gary Brown seeks to capitalize on the "hypnotic appeal" of instantly recognizable brand imagery to promote unintended connections and to suggest alternative meanings (Figure 10.2). Featuring a photograph of a Vietnamese man holding a badly napalmed child underneath the logo for the popular brand Johnson's Baby Powder, a damning correlation is made between the burnt child and President Lyndon B. Johnson's sanction of napalm bombing in Vietnam. The destabilizing effect occurs in the mind of the viewer, as they are forced to ask what the connection is between the Johnson's logo, the talcum powder product, the photograph of the napalmed baby, and President Johnson. Like other posters of the period that attempt to subvert the meanings of individual brands (including a memorable silkscreen poster from Berkeley that adapts the idiosyncratic contours and distinctive script lettering of the Coca-Cola bottle to read "Napalm: It's the real thing for S.E. Asia"), it aims to reveal the "hidden" infrastructure—that of capitalism—on which the brand is founded, as well as raising questions about the nature of branding. The presence of the words "MADE IN USA (the stencil lettering of which references those on munitions crates) has a double relevance; not only did the United States manufacture and export napalm, but it also produced and exported consumer goods. In this sense, such posters attempt to draw attention to the very conditions that gave rise to both Johnson's Baby Powder and napalm bombing.

Some of the more provocative posters of the time were produced by the Eyemakers collective, led by artist and designer Violet Ray. Juxtaposing disturbing imagery of injured Vietnamese or U.S. troops bearing tear gas with advertising images, the collages aimed at attacking "the subtleties which pacify housewives and enslave countries."[17] One poster appears, at first glance, to be a conventional advertisement for Chanel bath oil, featuring a naked Ali McGraw alongside the heading "This is the spell of Chanel for the bath" (Figure 10.3). On closer inspection, a half-drowned Vietnamese family can be seen struggling to escape the same waters as the model. The image—of a mother and her four children wading across a river to escape U.S. bombs, taken by the Japanese photographer Kyoichi Sawada—has been added directly to the Chanel advertisement, taking up the space normally occupied by the product shot. Without the qualifying image of the product, the direct gaze of the siren becomes a direct challenge to the viewer, accusing him or her of being complicit in the atrocities.

The Eyemakers made a connection between the war in Vietnam and consumerism at home, declaring: "For it's the products that make the war, we've finally learned. It's the products that make the ghettos; it's the products that have made our media-massaged heads take so long to figure out the message. And from the depths of the consumer shit is borne these advertisements—ominous, anonymous." The collective's aim was to shock their viewers to the extent that they would "remember the message each time they reach for a cold cream jar, a pop bottle or a razor blade," and they hoped that their form of "super-graffiti" had the potential to bring down the entire advertising industry: "For a couple of cents invested in some old magazines, you have available to you all the resources which cost Madison Avenue millions of dollars and years of research to produce. . . . They'd have to stop producing ads, they'd have to stop printing magazines; there'd have to be no scissors left in the land to stop collages."

While the Eyemakers' dream was never truly realized, their collages invite comparison with the works of artist Martha Rosler, whose photomontages from the late 1960s contributed a many-sided critique of the Vietnam War through an examination of suburban life, consumerism, and the mass media's representation of women. In a series titled *Bringing the War Home: House Beautiful* (1967–72), Rosler juxtaposes war images taken from Life magazine with interiors from *House Beautiful* magazine. This series comprised twenty or more images and were reprinted in the underground press or on flyers that were handed out in the street. In *Cleaning the Drapes* (1966–72), an elegantly attired housewife vacuums the curtains in her well-kept home. Through the window Rosler inserted an image of soldiers embedded in a trench, but the woman shows no sign of being aware of the troops, absorbed as she is in her role as a domestic goddess. By removing the war from the television screen and placing it on the other side of the window of a desirable suburban home, Rosler's

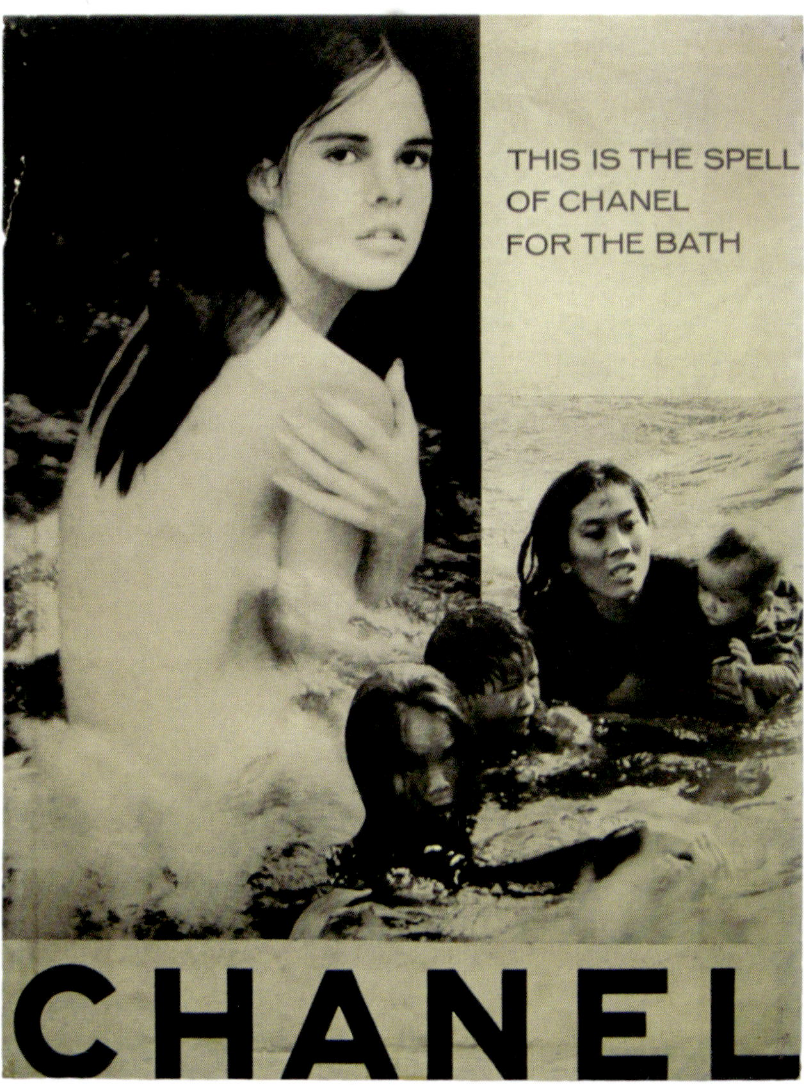
THIS IS THE SPELL
OF CHANEL
FOR THE BATH
CHANEL

collage joins together two images typically and falsely separated in the mass media. As she suggests, "I was trying to show that the 'here' and the 'there' of our world picture, defined by our naturalized accounts as separate or even opposite, were one."[18] Both Rosler and the Eyemakers appear to hold the mass media's construction of this "illusionary distance" responsible for the public's apparent indifference to events in Southeast Asia. By juxtaposing imagery from consumer advertising with war photography, they aimed to achieve the opposite effect, bringing atrocities of the Vietnam War closer to the public's attention.

Remediation practices a rhetoric of exposé. It uncovers not an opposite meaning but a deeper truth, alleging that the distractions of the news media and advertising at home have the effect of numbing the public to moral outrages abroad. However, it is important to note that the war in Vietnam is somewhat paradoxically incidental to the poster designers' denouncement of the mass media. In this sense, these posters masquerade as criticism of the war abroad, while their real target is the culture created by consumer advertising at home. In their attack on the mass media's hegemonic dominance, such posters can be seen as ironically perpetuating the same myths as the media they so roundly denounce, in particular the way in which the Vietnamese are presented as victims and consequently unable to help themselves. Designers belonging to the Black Panther Party shared similar concerns about the hegemony of Western media but went a step further in their strategy by seeking to redress the issue of biased representation. The Panthers are also particularly intriguing for their use of graphic design in fostering cross-cultural dialogues, particularly with Cuban designers.

INTERTEXTUAL DIALOGUES

Concerns about media representation during this time were not new. The civil rights movement of the early 1960s recognized the importance of positive representation in the press and used posters not only as a political weapon but also as a signifier of broader values. When John Lewis, a civil rights leader, was asked about media coverage of the movement, he replied: "Any time there was some violence, we would get a story on television. But when we were involved in in-depth experiences, when people gathered to express feeling, spirit, like in the non-violent workshops, there was no press. There was seldom an in-depth story on things like when white people really did change."[19] The movement attempted to correct this skewed view, in part, by recruiting photographers to document their activities. Danny Lyon's photographs for the Student Nonviolent Coordinating Committee (SNCC) sought to capture the quiet dignity and determination of the movement workers. Lyon's photographs were reproduced as posters, one of which features the rapt expressions of two peaceful protesters captioned with the stark call "Now." Not only does this convey a powerful demand for immediate integration, but it also presents a different side of the movement from that normally encountered in the press.

While the civil rights movement promised peaceful integration, the Black Panther Party threatened revolutionary violence. Founded in Oakland in 1966, the party was seen as both a continuation of and departure from the civil rights movement, initially espousing a doctrine of militant self-defense of African American neighborhoods. The Panthers were adept in their criticism of the mass media through the pages of the *Black Panther* newspaper, which claimed to be "free from the . . . lies of the oppressor controlled mass media."[20] The accusation of distortion and bias in the mainstream press was continued through their posters. Emory Douglas, the Panther's primary designer and Minster of Culture, created hundreds of fierce posters depicting proud black militants defending their neighborhoods against grotesque pig-policemen and insalubrious landlords, which were "plastered on the walls, in store front windows, on fences, doorways, telephone poles and booths, passing buses, alleyways, gas stations, barber shops, beauty parlors, laundry mats, liquor stores, as well as the huts of the ghetto."[21] Douglas's inflammatory images of inner-city poverty are undeniably sentimental, but such posters nonetheless aimed at recuperating media constructions of black people as a subordinated race. Similarly, after six African Americans were killed in Augusta, Georgia, on May 11, 1970, the result of police firing on a protest against the death of a black man in prison, the Panthers released a poster of one of the victims with the simple, stark headline "Augusta." The outraged subheading, "He Only Made Page 5," is a clear indication of how the Panthers felt black issues were being consistently underrepresented in the mass media.

The Black Panther Party saw the revolutionary government in Cuba as a natural ally in their struggle. Not only did Cuba offer sanctuary to both civil rights and Black Panther activists after the Watts riot of 1965, but the revolution also exemplified a successful liberation from imperialist rule and was involved in anticolonial struggle in Africa. The shared ideological similarities between the Cuban revolution and the Black Panther Party (and the Party's sympathizers) can be seen through their use and appropriation of posters. Fidel Castro may have attacked the American notion that Cuba exported its revolution like a commodity in the world market, saying "in their sleepless merchants' and usurers' minds there is the idea that revolutions can be bought, sold, rented, loaned, exported and imported like some piece of merchandise," but through its posters, Cuba certainly encouraged the idea that it constituted a model revolution.[22] In *The Art of Revolution,* Susan Sontag suggested, perhaps naively, that Cuban posters "are evidence of a revolutionary society that is not repressive and philistine . . . a culture which is alive, international in orientation and relatively free of the kind of bureaucratic interference that has blighted the arts in practically every other country where a communist revolution has come to power."[23] Sontag suffers from a certain kind of myopia (along with several other Western intellectuals including the French philosopher Jean-Paul Sartre) in that she admired the revolution to such an extent that she turns a blind eye to the reality of violence

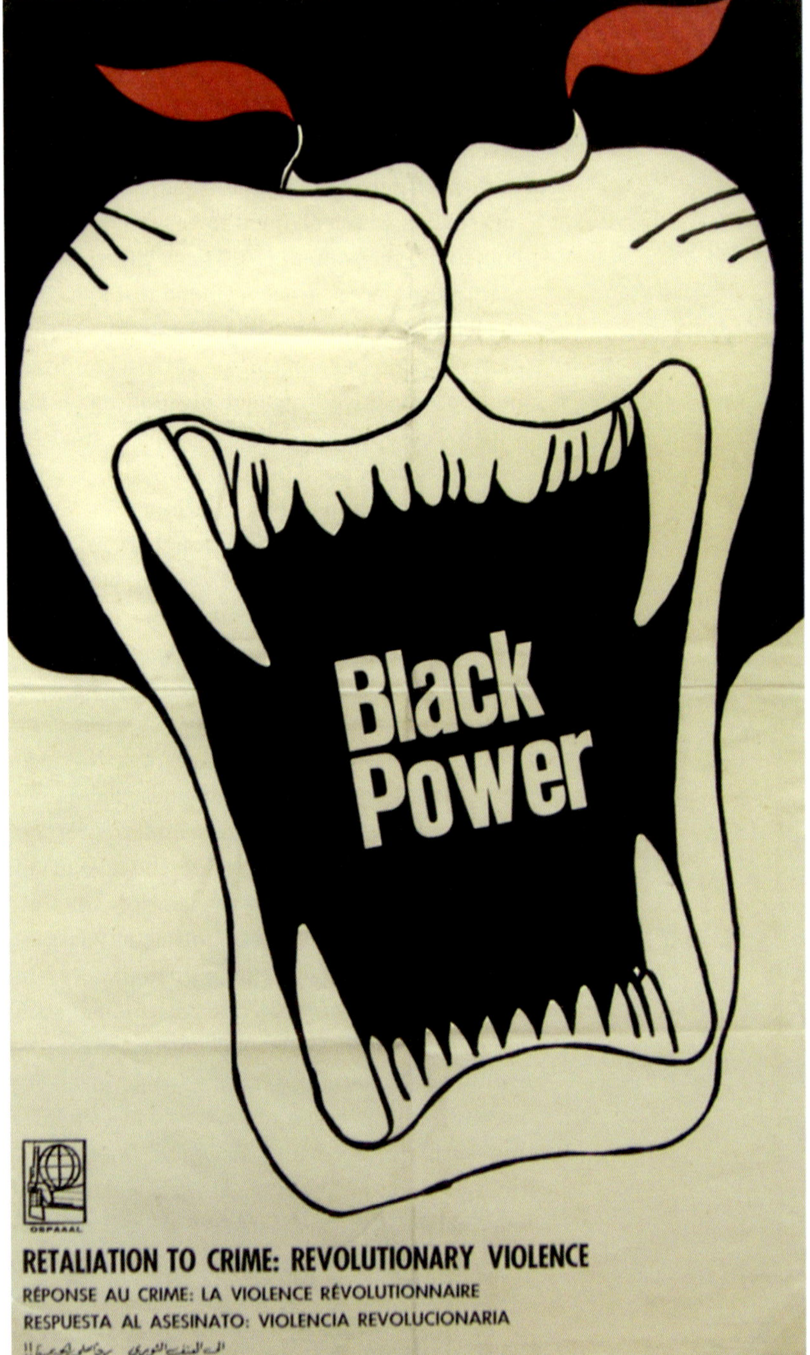

Figure 10.4
Alfredo Rostgaard, *Black Power,* 1968. Offset litho print, 21 x 13 inches. Organization of Solidarity of the Peoples of Asia, Africa and Latin America (OSPAAAL), Havana, Cuba. Courtesy of the Center for the Study of Political Graphics.

and appears to confuse freedom of stylistic expression with freedom from repression. Nonetheless, Cuban posters were widely appreciated for their colorful style and made their way to the United States through a variety of means. The publication of *The Art of Revolution* preceded several features about Cuban posters in the pages of the U.S. West Coast magazine *Ramparts,* founded in 1962 as a counterpoint to the mass-circular magazines of the mainstream. American organizations in solidarity with Cuba, such as the Venceremos Brigade, brought posters back to the United States, and posters produced by the Cuban organization OSPAAAL (Organization of Solidarity of the Peoples of Asia, Africa and Latin America) were included in the pages of the magazine *Tricontinental,* which was sold in progressive bookstores along the West Coast. One such poster by the Cuban designer Alfredo Rostgaard featured a fierce, red-eyed panther with the words "Black Power" inset between its fangs (Figure 10.4). Accompanying the poster was a mimeographed message signed by the executive secretariat of OSPAAAL that read: "On the occasion of Dr Martin Luther King's assassination, we have published a poster that is now being circulated all over the world. We are sending you herewith a certain amount of these posters, which may be used in your country for the activities to be carried out in this regard."[24] Rostgaard's powerful image quickly gained extra currency beyond the original poster run. The Black Panther Party took the image of the panther and inserted a photograph of Huey Newton (the Party's cofounder who was imprisoned in September 1968 for alleged manslaughter) in its jaws (Figure 10.5). The resulting image was used as a poster and a postcard demanding Newton's release. The copy declared, in the Panther's typically confrontational rhetoric, the Party's alliance with OSPAAAL and the struggle with the oppressed peoples of the world. This was not necessarily a one-way appropriation of imagery. OSPAAAL repaid the compliment; Emory Douglas's illustrations were featured regularly in the pages of *Tricontinental,*[25] and a poster depicting three armed black guerrillas was used in an OSPAAAL poster designed by the Cuban designer Lazaro Abreu, in "Solidarity with the African American People" (Figure 10.6).

The Black Panthers' act of reworking of OSPAAAL posters to meet their own purposes (and vice versa) not only implies identification with each other's politics; it also provided a basis for a dialogic exchange of cultural and political ideals. It should be noted that this was not considered to be theft or the unauthorized appropriation of another's work or culture, as Sontag mistakenly suggests in her introduction to *The Art of Revolution*. When describing the close relationship between poster design and "visual fashion," she suggests that "plagiarism is one main feature of the history of poster aesthetics."[26] To suggest that this practice is akin to plagiarism is to misunderstand the ethos of the production of countercultural media. Many authors and publishers explicitly encouraged the copying of their work through the inclusion of anticopyright or open-copyright statements, which indicated that the reader was free to copy

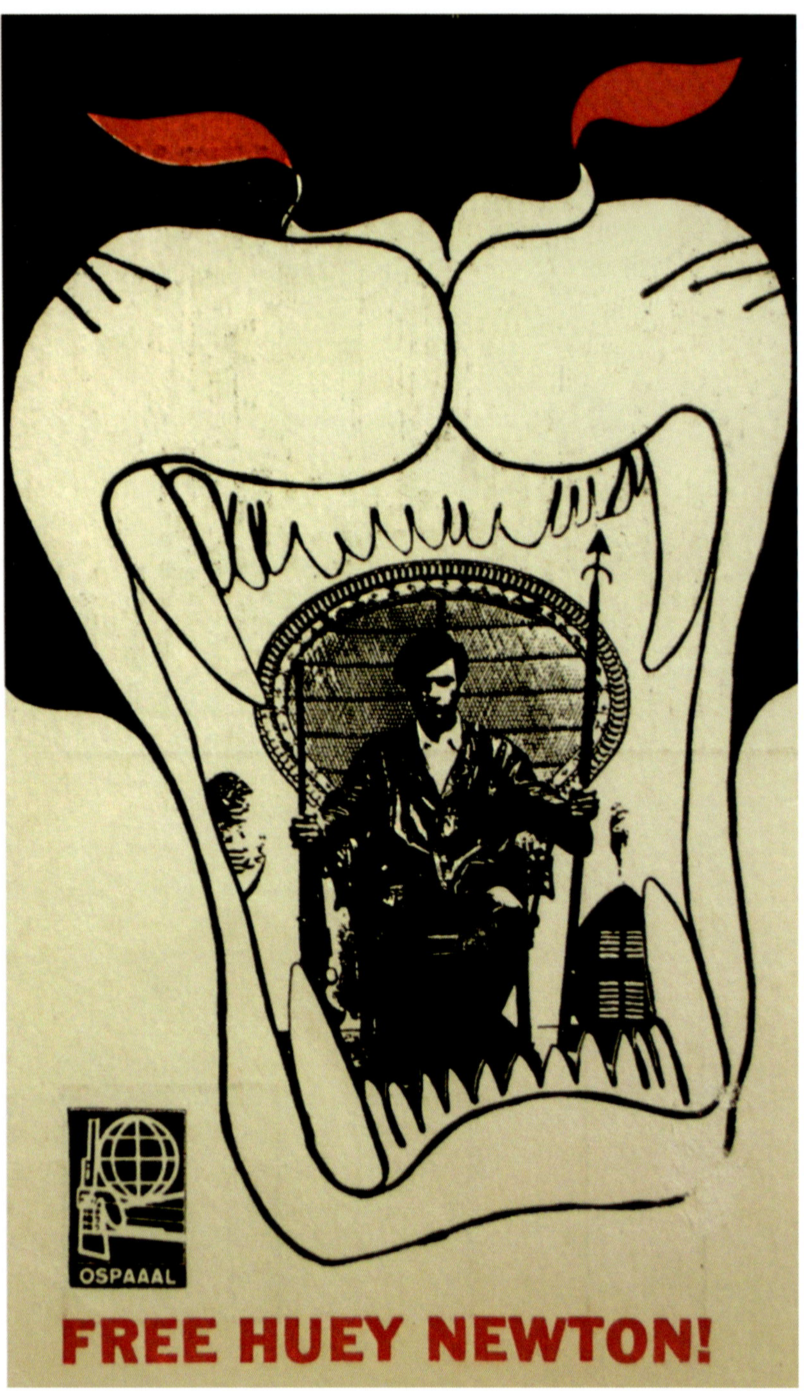

Figure 10.5
Free Huey Newton! c. 1968. Offset litho print, 6.1 x 3.7 inches. Artist unknown. Private collection.

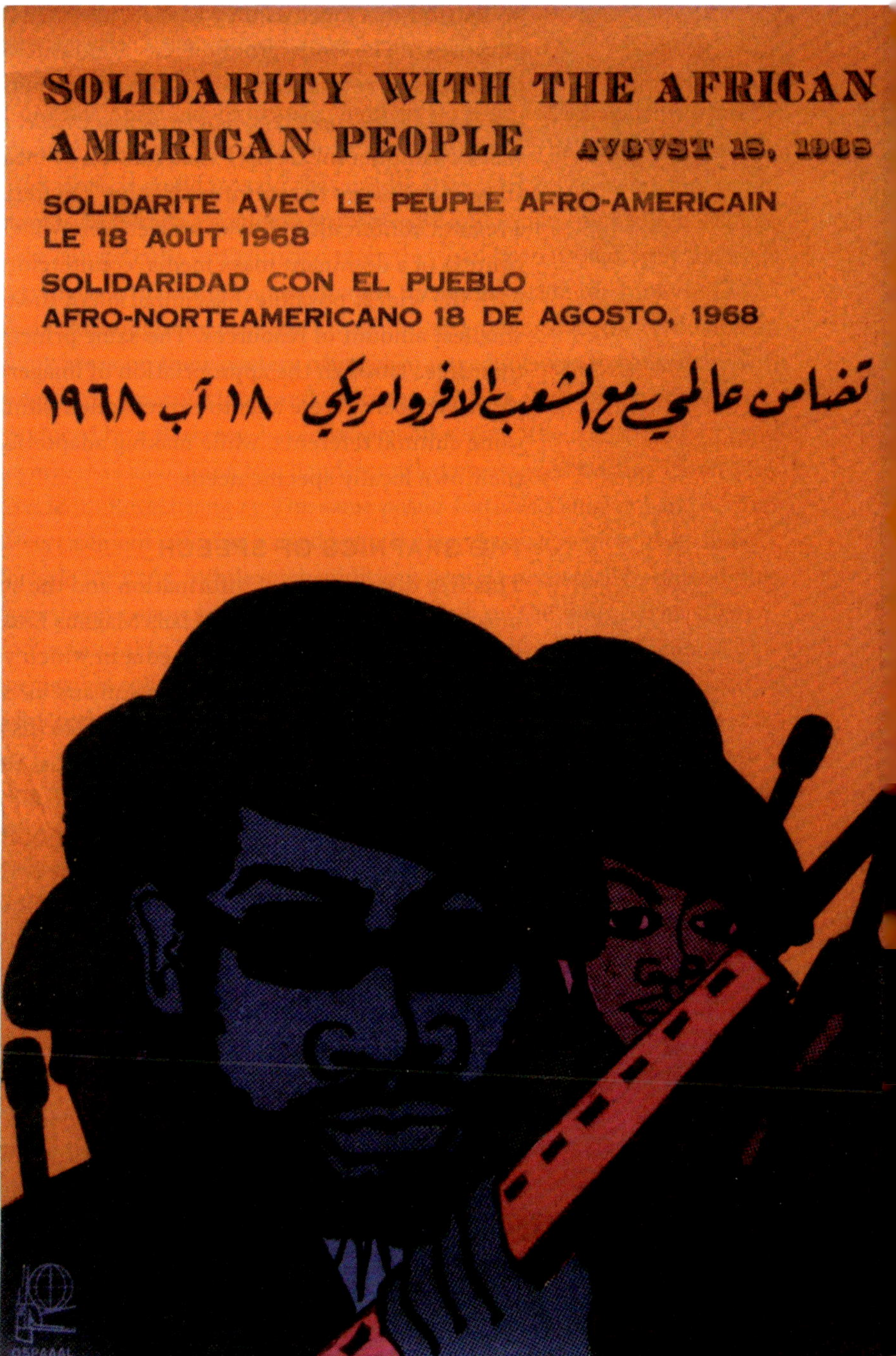

Figure 10.6

Lazaro Abreu, *Solidarity with the African American People,* 1968. Offset litho print, 21 x 14 inches. Organization of Solidarity of the Peoples of Asia, Africa and Latin America (OSPAAAL), Havana, Cuba. Courtesy of the Center for the Study of Political Graphics. Original illustration by Emory Douglas.

NOTES

This essay is based in part on my unpublished dissertation, "An Interruption on the Wall: Political Posters from France, the United States and Cuba, 1965–1975," produced for the history of design master's at the Royal College of Art and the Victoria and Albert Museum, London (2008). I would like to thank my supervisors, Jeremy Aynsley and David Crowley, for their critical and constructive support. I would also like to thank Elissa Auther and Adam Lerner for including the essay in this volume.

1. Eric Mann, *Comrade George: An Investigation into the Life, Political Thought and Assassination of George Jackson* (New York: Harper & Row, 1972), 19.

2. Paula Hays Harper, "California Art for Peace: May 1970," *Arts Journal* 30, no. 2 (Winter 1970–71): 163. The student was one of many participants who created posters at one of the spontaneous silkscreen poster workshops that emerged across university campuses in response to President Richard Nixon's sanction of the invasion of Cambodia and the riots that subsequently followed. The largest poster workshop was at the College of Environmental Design in Berkeley, where an estimated fifty thousand copies of some 450 designs were produced in a month.

3. Michael Rossman, interview with author, 10 December 2007.

4. Marshall McLuhan, *Understanding Media: The Extensions of Man* (New York: McGraw-Hill, 1964).

5. Susan Sontag, "Posters: Advertisement, Art, Political Artifact, Commodity," in *The Art of Revolution: 96 Posters from Cuba*, ed. Dugald Stermer (New York: McGraw-Hill, 1970), 218.

6. Raymond Williams, *Marxism and Literature* (Oxford: Oxford University Press, 1977), 158–64.

7. Again, see Montgomery's essay in this volume for a closer investigation of the rock poster and the psychedelic counterculture. Montgomery makes a convincing argument about the way in which psychedelic posters deliberately sought to merge boundaries and to draw on intertextual allusions in order to defy categorization.

8. Julie Stephens, *Anti-Disciplinary Protest: Sixties Radicalism and Postmodernism* (Cambridge: Cambridge University Press, 1998), 22–23.

9. This was a drawn and typed cartoon speech bubble printed onto sticky-backed paper, designed to be cut out and pasted onto advertisement posters. See Ken Knabb, *Public Secrets: Collected Skirmishes of Ken Knabb* (Berkeley, Calif.: Bureau of Public Secrets, 1997), 117–18.

10. From a pamphlet by Isaac Cronin and Ken Knabb, "What Subversion Really Is" (November 1970).

11. Guy Debord, *The Society of the Spectacle* (Detroit: Red and Black, 1970).

12. Daniel Boorstin, *The Image; or, What Happened to the American Dream* (London: Pelican, 1962), 21.

13. Ibid., 258.

14. Marshall McLuhan, *War and Peace in the Global Village* (Corte Madera: Gingko, 2001), 134.

15. Ariel Dorfman and Armand Mattelart, *Para leer al Pato Donald* (Chile: Ediciones Universitarias de Valparaíso, 1971). The English edition, *How to Read Donald Duck* (New York: IG Editions, 1975), carries the subtitle "Imperialist Ideology in the Disney Comic."

16. Boorstin, *The Image*, 197.

17. "Bananas Are Dead This Year," *Rat* 1, no. 2 (March–April 1968): 8. Quoted passages about the Eyemakers posters discussed in this and the next paragraph come from this article.

18. Martha Rosler, "Place, Position, Power, Politics," in her *Decoys and Disruptions: Selected Writings, 1975–2001* (Cambridge, Mass.: MIT Press, 2004), 355.

19. John Lewis, quoted in Pat Watters, *Down to Now: Reflections on the Southern Civil Rights Movement* (New York: Pantheon, 1971), 70.

20. "The Black Panther: Mirror of the People," *Black Panther Community News Service*, 17 January 1970, 1.

21. Emory Douglas, quoted in Erika Doss, "Revolutionary Art Is a Tool for Liberation," in *Liberation, Imagination and the Black Panther Party: A New Look at the Panthers and Their Legacy*, ed. Kathleen Cleaver and George Katsiafiacs (New York: Routledge, 2001), 184.

22. Fidel Castro, "Second Declaration of Havana" (1962), in *Fidel Castro Speaks*, ed. M. Kenner and J. Petras (London: Harmondsworth, 1972), 144.

23. Sontag, "Posters," 210.

24. "Cuban Poster Urges U.S. Negro Revolt," *Charleston Daily Mail*, 13 April 1968, 10.

25. See, for example, the back cover of *Tricontinental* 10 (1969). Similarly, Cuban posters were often reprinted in the pages of the *Black Panther Newspaper*. See Sam Durant, ed., *Black Panther: The Revolutionary Art of Emory Douglas* (New York: Rizzoli, 2007), 135.

26. Sontag, "Posters," 200.

27. One such example is *Unite Against the War* (Kentfield, Calif.: Western Star Press, 1970), a portfolio of posters selected from an exhibition of posters that opened in Berkeley on May 15, 1970. This carried an open-copyright statement that read, "Permission is granted to copy these posters, or to reproduce them in any way that will assist in the cause of peace."

28. Hans Magnus Enzensberger, "Constituents of a Theory of the Media," *New Left Review* 64 (December 1970): 18, 17.

29. Ibid., 16.

30. Jean Baudrillard, "Requiem for the Media" (1972), in *For a Critique of the Political Economy of the Sign* (St. Louis: Telos Press, 1981), 170.

31. Ibid., 176.

32. Enzensberger, "Constitutents," 19.

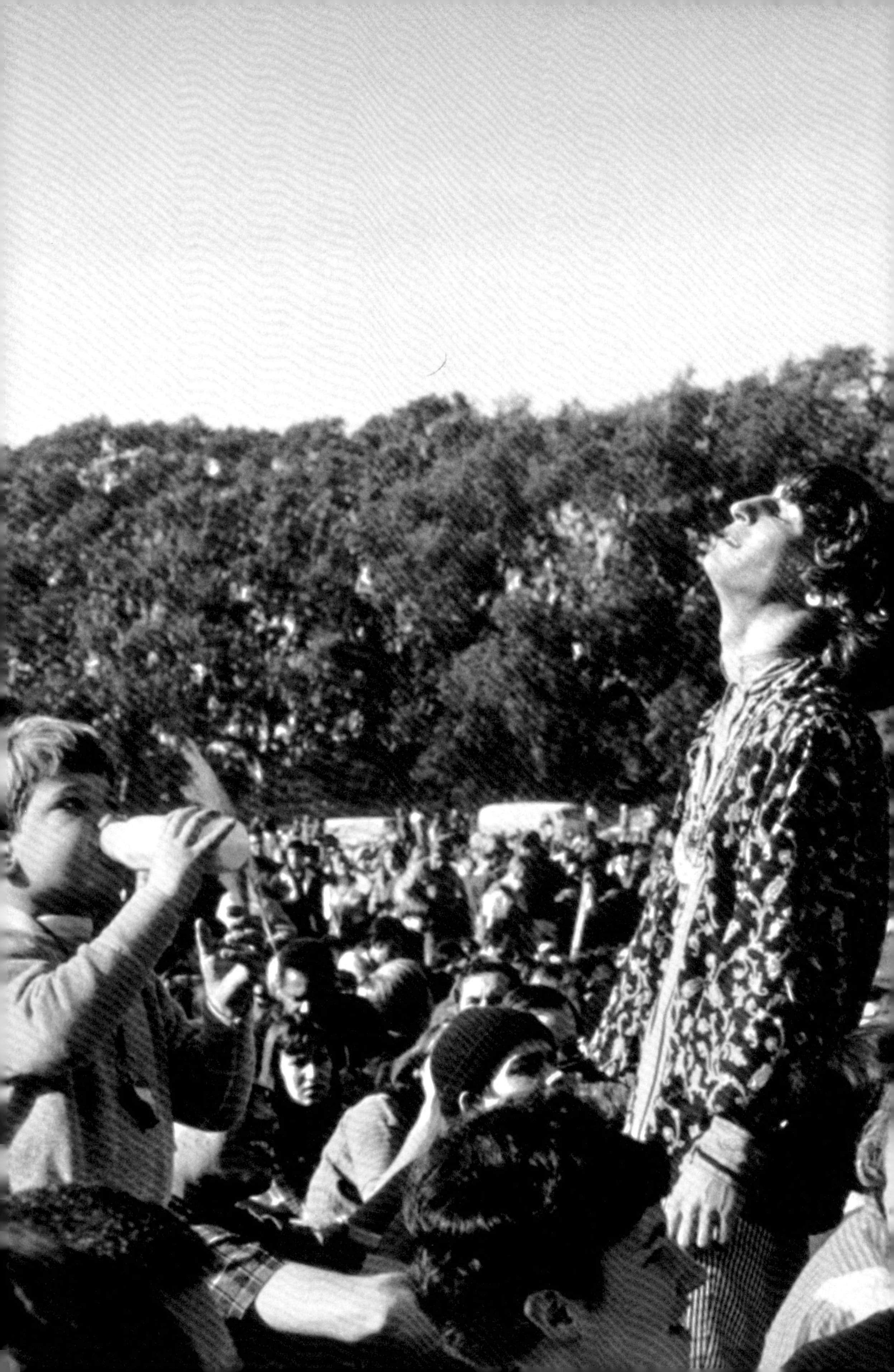

PART III
CULTURAL POLITICS

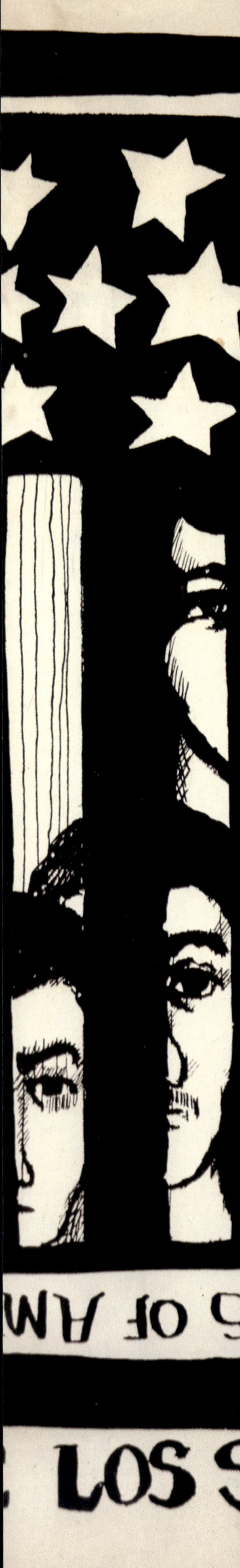

Karen Mary Davalos

An open hand holding a broken chain signals the readership from the masthead of the earliest editions of *¡Basta Ya!,* the newspaper of the defense committee Los Siete de la Raza (Figure 11.1). Produced to mobilize the San Francisco Mission District residents for crusades for justice, notably a call to support seven Latino youth accused of killing a police officer in the summer of 1969, *¡Basta Ya!* graphically announces its title, which translates as "Enough already!"[1] The exclamation and the vernacular Spanish phrase proclaim the Latin@ community's impatience with and demand to stop police brutality, gentrification and housing displacement, slumlords, poor education, labor exploitation, and lack

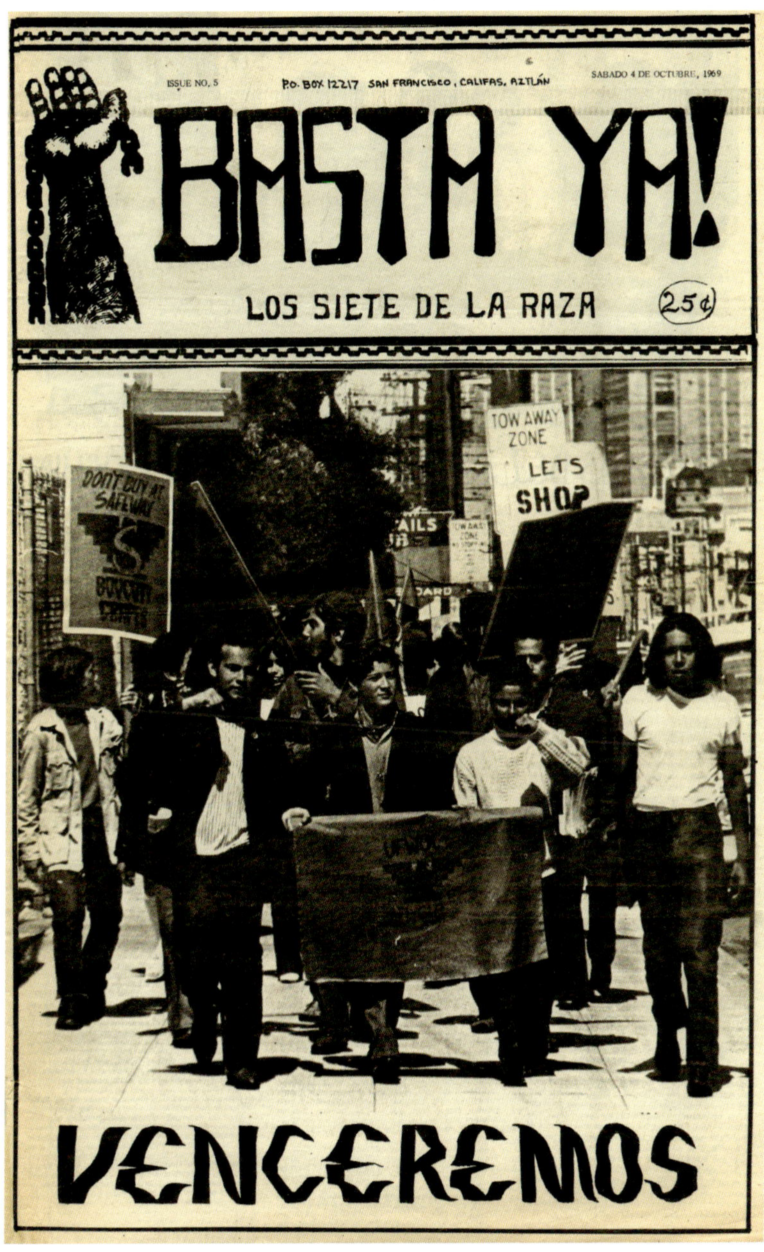

PRINT CULTURE OF YOLANDA M. LÓPEZ

of political representation in their neighborhood. This drawing by one of the most visible and influential Chicana artists, Yolanda M. López, is located in the top left corner of the newspaper, the conventional spot for print media's visual identity, and it signifies the vision of the San Francisco Mission District advocacy organization Los Siete de la Raza.

The palm gestures up to the sky as if to signify the hope and future of Chican@s and Latin@s.[2] Because it is raised above the head and shoulders of the unknown figure, the image conveys energy and exuberance, an important attitude for López that resurfaces in her later and most recognized works, especially *Portrait of the Artist as the Virgin of Guadalupe* (1978). The newspaper image is a "visual quotation" that recognizes through compositional similarity the black power salute, a straight-armed, clenched fist raised to signify solidarity against the struggle.[3] *¡Basta Ya!* was sponsored by and appeared on the back pages of the Black Panther Party newspaper, further charging the cry and the image as a signal of recognition of and solidarity with the Black Power movement. But unlike the Black Power salute, the open hand and solid forearm by López present an empowerment already achieved. Hers is a gesture toward the future in which the battle is won, the struggle is over, and the inequalities have ended. The chains of institutionalized racism, capitalist exploitation, and sexist exclusion are literally broken. Hanging to the left of the forearm, the metal chain with its visibly broken link rests on the open palm. The hand appears to offer; with the fingers relaxed, unfurled from the clenched fist, it is a gesture of praise, homage, or freedom. It is an image that signals new possibilities as well as the artist's strategy to employ art as a tool for social transformation.

Using this and other images, López offered radically new representations of Chican@s and Latin@s during her earliest venture into grassroots organizing and advocacy. Through print culture produced between 1969 and 1970, the first period of her professional artistic career, López aimed to alter consciousness among Latin@s living in the San Francisco–Oakland Bay Area. Emblematic of the counterculture of the 1960s and 1970s, her activism with Los Siete de la Raza illustrates a rejection of the status quo, the desire to build consciousness—both cultural and political—and the embrace of self-determination as a means toward enfranchisement. Equally important was the collective as the means to achieve these goals. Supporting new domestic relations for activists and constituents, Los Siete even promoted the countercultural practice of cooperative living, and as one of the residents in this communal house in the Mission District, López came to negotiate her own vision of artist for "the people."

Even as López offered a hemispheric vision, it was influenced by the coalitional politics of the Bay Area counterculture. She learned the techniques of newspaper layout from Emory Douglas, Minister of Culture for the Black Panther Party, and he also inspired her aesthetic approach in print culture. Using a combination of collage, photomontage, line drawings, and text, she created images for posters, buttons, and placards as well as the community newspaper, *¡Basta Ya!* As such, López's work for Los Siete provides an ideal example of the ways in which artist-activists—consciously or not—blurred the presumed divide between the political and the cultural.

As important as it was, López's early body of work with Los Siete is very understudied. Its content, style, and political orientation place it largely beyond the purview of art history. Like other forms of countercultural visual expression that stressed direct action or empowerment or borrowed the language of mass media, it has been dismissed as lowbrow or simply nonaesthetic. Yet López was creating art that she believed was transformative, and she hoped to generate new representations of and reformulate ideas about Latin@s. Living among and working in solidarity with Los Siete activists, López intended to alter the position of Latin@s in society with her graphic imagery.

López's contributions to print culture are not considered as important as her conceptual engagement with Guadalupan iconography, which receives the most attention from scholars and art critics, albeit misunderstood as figurative or representational art.[4] The Guadalupe series, particularly *Portrait of the Artist as the Virgin of Guadalupe* and the other works in the Guadalupe triptych, is widely recognized in feminist studies, art history, theology, and Chican@ scholarship, and the self-portrait is one of the most circulated images of Chican@ visual arts.[5] In contrast, her contributions in print culture are relatively undocumented, even though the images are graphically compelling articulations of a complex political consciousness. The print culture of the social and civil rights movements of the 1960s and 1970s as well as the visual modes distinctive to countercultural movements—the button, the placard, the poster, the mimeographed flyer, and the alternative newspaper—became her venues for exhibition.

There are other reasons for the lack of acknowledgment of López's early print work. In part, its dismissal is due to its relation to the counterculture, which is generally understudied in art history. In addition, like many artist-activists in the San Francisco Bay Area, including Emory Douglas, she rarely signed her work, and it circulated widely but anonymously in the community. By using public space rather than the art gallery for display, López reinforced a political consciousness that intermingled ideological orientations from the global Left, the civil rights movement, the Chicano movement, and the women's movement that intersected with a general countercultural emphasis on liberation. While López's goal was to produce art for "the people" necessitating, in her mind, her anonymity, her strategy reflects the decisions of other countercultural artists such as the members of the radical theater group the Diggers, all of whom assumed the same pseudonym in their published broadsides in order to disable the hierarchical relations between leaders and followers.

López's anonymity often resulted in residents of the Mission District assuming that a man created her posters, placards, and buttons for Los Siete, an assumption informed by Chicano nationalist discourse, which categorized women artists differently from men. Scholars such as Norma Alarcón, Chela Sandoval, Angie Chabram Denersesian, and others convincingly argue that Chicano nationalism equated cultural loyalty, pride, and identity with masculinity, erasing Chicana subjectivity, activism, and experience. This patriarchal privileging not only constructed a singular male identity for Mexican Americans, but it flattened all differences within the population—race, class, sexual orientation, and language differences were unrecognized. Within the visual arts, patriarchal privileging became the major debate for several decades and continues to shape Chican@ art criticism.

Chicano nationalists accused female artists of creating personal images rather than "relevant" or "political" works of art.[6] When Shifra M. Goldman, who at the time was the most prolific art historian of Chican@ art, declared that Chicana art is "personal," she was attempting to rescue it from a nationalist erasure that would not consider women's reproductive rights, child care, domestic violence, or household divisions of labor as politically relevant for Mexican American liberation.[7] Her revisionist art criticism, however, has had the unfortunate effect of replicating the divide between conventional forms of political organizing and artistic and cultural radicalism associated with the counterculture. Similar to other women artists, López fuses politics (due to the form of the work and its use in protests) and an emancipatory vision that is imaginative and utopian, and thus moves beyond mainstream political conventions into the realm of the cultural. Its hybrid quality is the basis of its success and, ironically, its erasure. That is, even when art historians, Chicano nationalists, or feminist scholars consider the countercultural engagements of Chican@ visual arts, they rarely look to a Chicana artist for political commentary or activism because they operate with this divide between political tools for social change and cultural expression. Nevertheless, López's exploration of socially transformative messages in print culture locates her within the larger countercultural movement of the 1960s and 1970s, and more critically, it also challenges the common view that her work is merely an expression of identity politics or cultural nationalism.

In what follows I provide a developmental analysis of López's countercultural art and politics. Scholars typically discuss how countercultural practices involve the rejection of one's upbringing and parents' values, a personal struggle unknown to López who learned from her family to value difference, autonomy, and justice. These lessons were strengthened during her college years in northern California. Finally, the article explores López's joining of art and politics through her work with Los Siete de la Raza.

FAMILY AND POLITICAL CONSCIOUSNESS

The formation of Yolanda M. López's countercultural orientation began at home. From her multigenerational family living in San Diego, California, López developed a political consciousness about labor and worker's rights, the democratic process and its weaknesses, and gender norms. Born in 1942, López grew up at a time when the town was developing a military-industrial complex to support U.S. involvement in World War II.[8] Her grandparents, Senobio and Victoria Franco, who had migrated from Mexico in 1918, informed her agentive and feminist sensibility; her mother, Margaret, taught her to respect laborers and the value of political participation; and several uncles taught her to use her hands. They also modeled patriarchal gender norms that López would later reject. López observed that although Senobio treated his unschooled wife with respect and dignity, her uncles largely took Victoria's labor for granted and expected her to clean up after them. This emergent feminist analysis of gender relations was reinforced by her mother's independence and self-assuredness. Margaret divorced twice and modeled a feminist orientation that women need not depend on men's wages or decision making. Working first at the Grant Hotel and later at the Naval Training Center, Margaret was employed as a seamstress and presser, and she taught her daughter to respect labor, to support unions, and to "never cross a picket line."[9]

Margaret was the secretary in the labor union but also reinforced participatory democracy in other ways. López remembers excitement in the family as they watched several Democratic conventions. She recalls that her mother took all three sisters to "stuff envelopes for Jack Kennedy's [presidential] campaign" in 1960.[10] In addition, her mother's union membership signaled the importance of collective action, and López understood at a young age the importance of solidarity across multiple constituents. After she left home, all of these experiences, values, and critical perspectives informed her decision to join the picket lines of the Third World Liberation Front movement at San Francisco State College. As a young woman, López had a firm sense of racial and material inequality and sexism as well as the country's inability to deliver on its promise of democracy and liberty for all.

POWER AND IMAGE

In 1966, two years after completing her associate's degree at the College of Marin, López transferred to San Francisco State College where she continued her involvement in the cultural revolution in full swing in northern California. Her participation extended from personal self-fashioning and choice of friends (a personal liberation from the conventions of femininity and mainstream taste) to political activism. She experimented with style and comportment, dressing in men's and army surplus clothes and avoiding makeup and feminine hairstyles. Explaining the countercultural fashion aesthetic, she notes:

    PRINT CULTURE OF YOLANDA M. LÓPEZ

It was experimentation; [but] I wasn't the only one. We tried to dress very non-gender-specific, to see how [people would react]. It's almost like a cleansing exercise to be as neutral and as androgynous as a woman, to see how other people, and specifically men, react to you when you wear no makeup, you don't shave your hair [on your legs or under your arms], you don't pluck your eyebrows, you wear big denim shirts, and you wear bellbottom pants.[11]

López enjoyed the freedom of this look and felt more authentic when she did not emphasize feminine styles and the body, and the androgynous aesthetic she crafted provided a sense of liberation from the sexualized gaze. In addition, she sought out intellectual circles that supported radical consciousness. Along with her peers, she was reading Mao's *Little Red Book* and developing solidarity with laborers and political prisoners. López also frequented the local alternative bookstore, Tides, in Sausalito, a small hippie community north of San Francisco. She was fascinated by a range of creative sources, reading German writers Hermann Hesse and Rainer Maria Rilke, listening to various music genres including Mahler's *Das Lied von der Erde* and black opera singer Leontyne Price, and going to the movies and seeing independent films, such as Fellini's *8½*. Her eclectic cultural taste may have a common thread, which is best identified in her explanation for her love for Maurice Sendak's book *Where the Wild Things Are*. It indicates she was excited by an alternative stance and way of living: "*Where the Wild Things Are* was published at that time, and I bought the book, and I carried it around for years and years because it was such an amazing book. . . . It was an intelligent, beautifully drawn, and sort of not overly explain[ed], *and there was a kind of audacity in Max. . . .* That was wonderful."[12] López seems to have been exploring the extraordinary, the defiant, the struggle and grit as well as the engagement of the journey that are found in these works.

Arriving during a time of intensive student activism, particularly against the Vietnam War, López joined her campus Student Nonviolent Coordinating Committee (SNCC), her first effort to mobilize and enfranchise students, people of color, and the poor. It also indicates her support for multiracial coalitions and interracial solidarity, a feature of northern California counterculture. By May 1968, López was working with the Third World Liberation Front (TWLF)—a multiracial and multiethnic student coalition at San Francisco State College—an experience that forms the backdrop to her understanding of the role of the artist and the formulation of her aesthetic approach.[13] In March 1968, TWLF mobilized to demand courses in ethnic studies, a voice in faculty hiring, and admissions and financial aid policies that would create a student body more reflective of the demographic profile of San Francisco. A coalition of African American, Latin@, Native American, and Asian American students led a five-month strike using radical tactics that included building occupations, chanting, trash can fires, amplified speeches, picket lines, and sit-ins. Her mother's instructions about solidarity proved invaluable, and López joined the picket lines nearly every day, failing most of her classes during that academic year.[14] However, it was these activities that taught her important lessons about herself, society, and the role of the artist working for social and political change from which she would draw to create her own distinctive political aesthetic.

The coalition of ethnic minority students also taught López that inclusive political action and self-determination could coexist. This inclusive consciousness emerged from an analysis of the shared structural inequalities that people of color experience, but the demand for self-determination affirmed that Chicanas and Chicanos become the producers of their own history, visual library, and futures. Questioning the biased approaches that Euro-American discourse had produced about people of color, TWLF demanded the hiring of faculty of color who would challenge a Eurocentric curriculum. According to López, it was her action on the picket lines that taught her to appreciate the production of knowledge:

We were being photographed [by police], all the way up and down the line. . . . So we were told to bring our own cameras . . . whether they had film or not, just bring it out there and start shooting back because . . . if you're going to take a photograph of me, I'm going to take a photograph of you. . . . There was a real recognition that the power of the image was really important.[15]

These encounters with surveillance and state power made explicit the struggle over self-definition and self-representation. While the producer of the image—in this case, the police—controlled and defined its subject by aiming a camera at the students, López saw that the camera could also empower. Through direct action with TWLF, López learned to question the production and function of images, and this critical orientation sharpened during her work in the Mission District.

PRINT CULTURE AND LOS SIETE DE LA RAZA

López's interwoven aesthetic and political orientations brought her to the organizing effort that she launched with her fellow students and collaborators from San Francisco State College. In March 1969, López along with other Latin@ activists formed America Latina Unida, a community-based organization for Mission District youth. One of the most thorough chroniclers of Los Siete de la Raza, Jason Ferreira documents that early members included Roger Alvarado, Donna James (Amador), Roberto Vargas, Al Martinet, Yolanda López, Ralph Ruiz, Jimmy Queens, Jose Delgado, Tony Martinez, and Mario Martinez. The latter two brothers would become defendants in the 1969 homicide case. Originally, the group's goal was to address education, recreation, and police brutality, but "within two months of its inception" the members turned their organizing efforts to support the youths, including Tony and Mario,

     PRINT CULTURE OF YOLANDA M. LÓPEZ

Yolanda M. López, cover of *¡Basta Ya!* no. 12, October 1970, collage.

who were accused of killing police officer Brodnick in the May 1 incident.[16] Activism within Los Siete provided the first platform for López to "function as an artist."[17]

Los Siete de la Raza was primarily a defense committee for the Martinezes and the others accused of homicide, but it followed the Black Panther Party's organizing methods by also addressing the basic needs of its constituents.[18] Thus Los Siete offered a breakfast program for school-age children, health services for low-income residents, legal counsel to immigrants, and political education classes. This strategy for mobilization was designed to reach through services the poor, people of color, and recent immigrants. Indeed, "serve the people" was the popular Maoist refrain adopted and declared by Los Siete in their newspaper. Like other activists of the period who believed that the education and consciousness raising of an oppressed people would foster collective political consciousness and mobilization, Los Siete used not only the language of international revolutionaries, but also they grounded this framework in the realities of the Mission District, such as lack of political representation, insufficient health care services, poverty, unemployment, and substandard education and housing. For López, the contribution of the artist within this organizing strategy was to provide alternative representations of Latin@s in order to gain the support of the community, develop their individual awareness about the sources of structural inequalities, and thus foster solidarity among residents.

Another goal was to reinforce the inclusive and generative political consciousness within the Mission District. Because the accused seven youth were of Mexican, Salvadoran, Honduran, and Nicaraguan heritage, the group required an inclusive rather than a nationalist orientation for developing solidarity. Published two to four times per month on the back section of *Black Panther*, *¡Basta Ya!* articulated this inclusive and interstitial consciousness against racism, material inequality, and U.S. imperialism.[19] According to art critic Tomás Ybarra-Frausto, Bay Area Latin@s drew on Mexican scholar José Vasconcelos for his "utopian vision of cultural coherence" to "solidify group consciousness." The vernacular affinity of *la raza* (the race, or our people) was an ideal foundation for generating unity among Latin Americans in the Mission District.[20] This vernacular expression informed and influenced López's aesthetic that emphasized collage and photomontage.

Within *¡Basta Ya!,* López used a variety of styles and techniques, but the most common were drawings that combined photographs and photomontage and incorporated contrasting scale for dramatic effect, a technique also favored by Emory Douglas (Figure 11.2).[21] The photomontage format served several aesthetic and political purposes. By overlapping a variety of images, López could document the diversity within the Latin@ community. Ideally, a range of faces and figures demonstrated the racial, gendered, and age complexity within the movement and the Mission District. In addition, a collection of photos graphically linked

PRINT CULTURE OF YOLANDA M. LÓPEZ

NUMBER 12
October

¡BASTA YA!

NUMERO 12
octubre

MISSION COMMUNITY NEWSPAPER

PERIODICO DE LA MISSION

LOS SIETE DE LA RAZA — P. O. BOX 12217 — SAN FRANCISCO, CALIFORNIA — 25¢

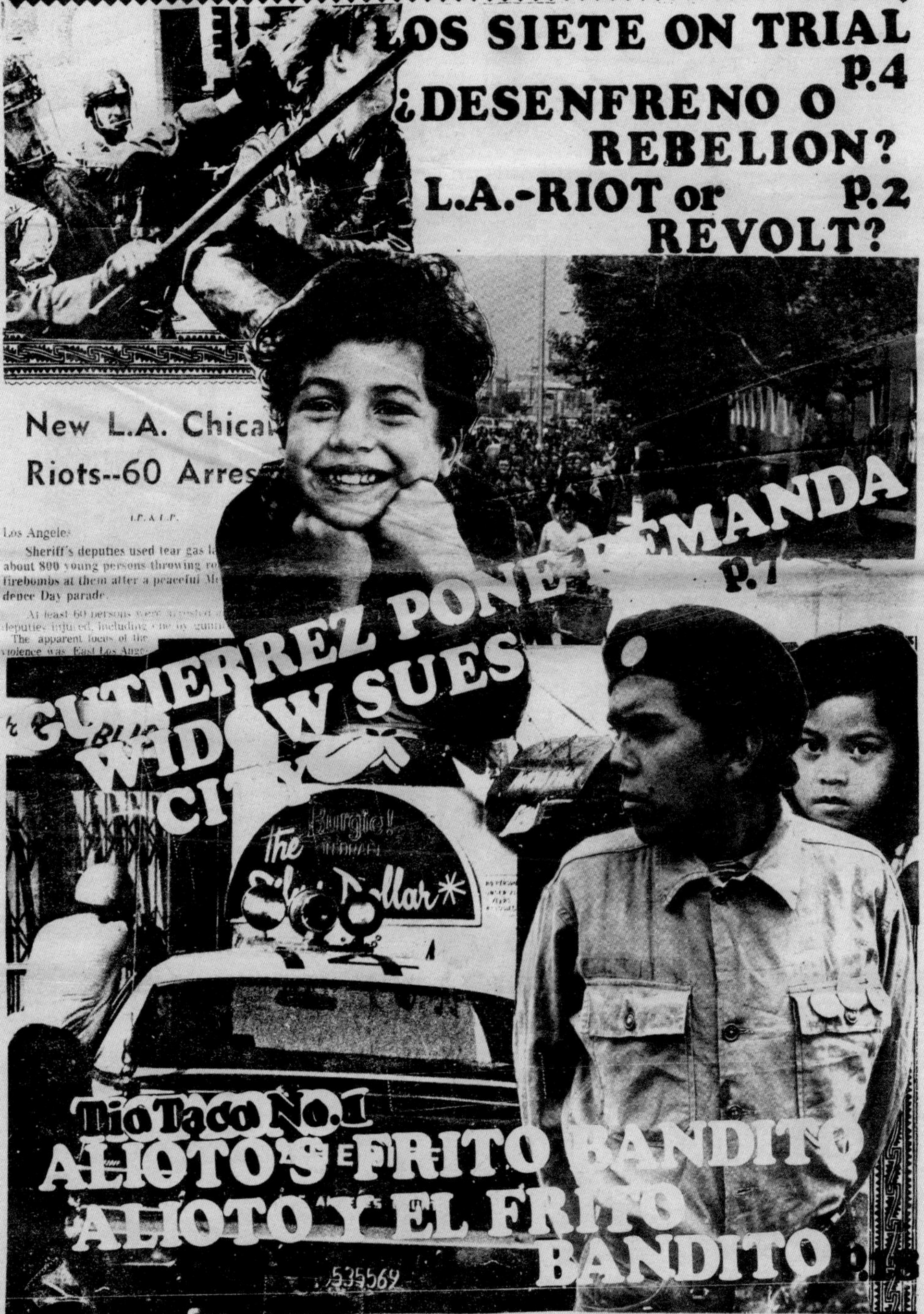

LOS SIETE ON TRIAL

¿DESENFRENO O REBELION? — P. 4

L.A.-RIOT or REVOLT? — P. 2

GUTIERREZ PONE DEMANDA — P. 7

WIDOW SUES CITY

New L.A. Chica... Riots--60 Arres...

Los Angeles

Sheriff's deputies used tear gas l... about 800 young persons throwing ro... firebombs at them after a peaceful M... dence Day parade.

At least 60 persons were arrested... deputies injured, including one by gun... The apparent locus of the... violence was East Los Ange...

Tio Taco No. 1

ALIOTO'S FRITO BANDITO

ALIOTO Y EL FRITO BANDITO

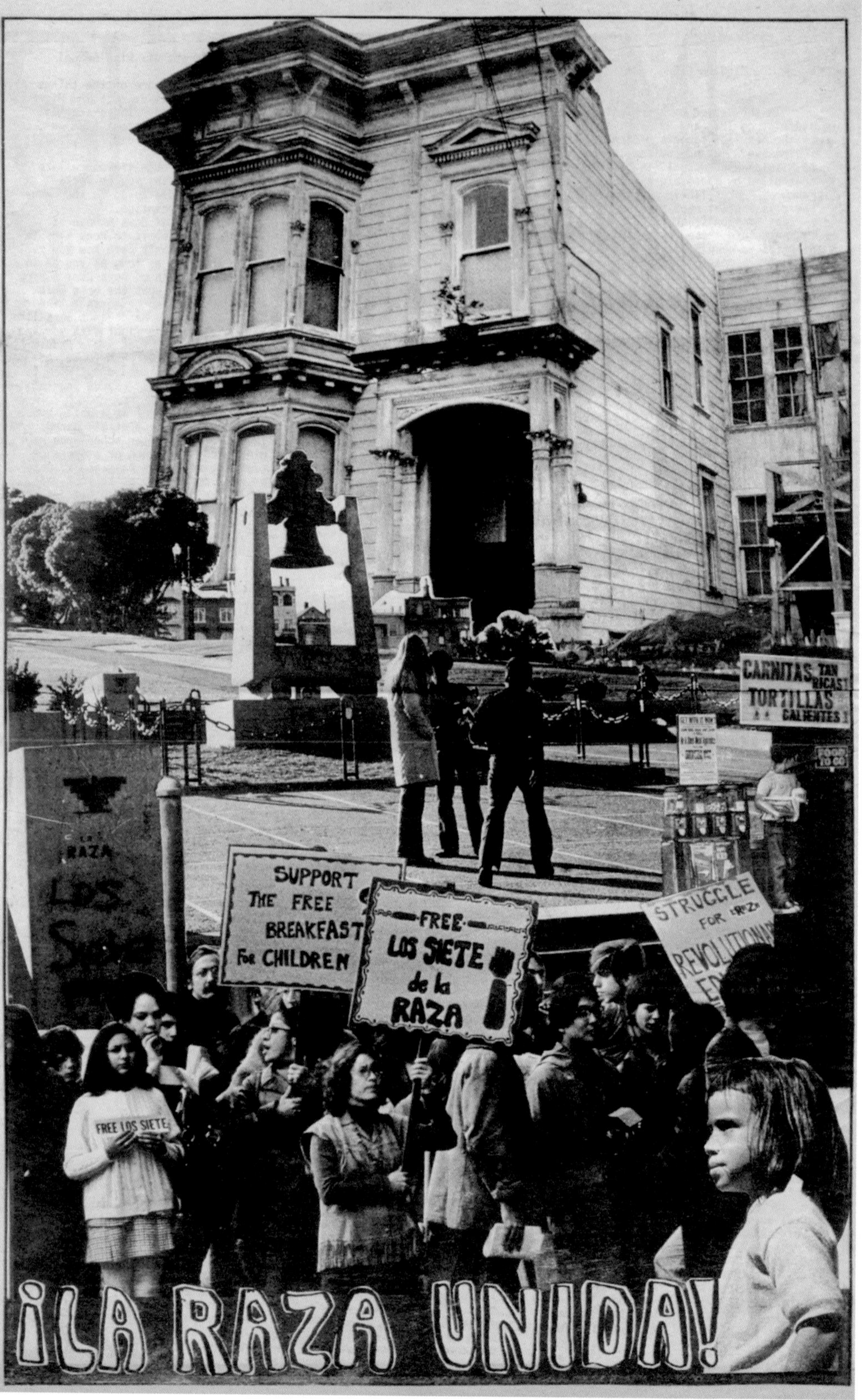
LA RAZA
LOS SIETE
CARNITAS TAN RICAS!
TORTILLAS CALIENTES!
SUPPORT THE FREE BREAKFAST FOR CHILDREN
FREE LOS SIETE de la RAZA
STRUGGLE FOR LA RAZA REVOLUTIONARY
FREE LOS SIETE
¡LA RAZA UNIDA!

Yolanda M. López, page 16 of
¡Basta Ya! no. 9, April 1970,
collage.

experiences and struggles to imply structural or historical connections. The collage of images documenting social injustices across racial groups, national borders, and political causes helped to visualize the common position of the poor, people of color, and workers. Photomontage was thus a powerful way to illustrate shared oppression and resistance. But the collage and retouched photographs also reminded readers of the construction of the image, and in López's work it is obvious that each photo has been cut from its original context before being recombined with the others for the newspaper layout. This approach to the construction of images, which encourages the viewer to acknowledge the fabrication of the work while also demystifying the artist as the "autonomous auteur with a capacity for genius," allowed López to articulate her developing conceptual critique of the construction of the image.[22] This conceptual and critical attention to representational practice is an essential message for a community bombarded with media images of Latinos as hoodlums, drug addicts, and criminals.

A notable example of López's visual narrative of inclusion and shared experience appears on page sixteen of the April 1970 issue of *¡Basta Ya!* (Figure 11.3). In this case, the collage covered the entire page and conveyed a complex message about the struggle for freedom across space and time. The composition is dominated by a photograph of Casa de la Raza (the People's House), the three-bedroom home at 960 Guerrero Street that served as the headquarters and communal housing for individual members of Los Siete, including López.[23] Occupying the entire top register of the collage, the early twentieth-century Victorian-style house looms over the images in the bottom register, occupied by dozens of people at a rally, the replica of Mexico's liberty bell in the Mission District's Dolores Park next to three people standing nearby, a small image of a child handing out free copies of *¡Basta Ya!*, and a girl in the right corner who is proportionately larger than all of the figures in the collage. The humble condition of the house does not detract from it as a symbol of power and possibility, and the effect created through the low angle of the camera lens and the expansive empty space behind the house is that it appears to rise from the horizon.

At the midline of the collage, a series of landscape photographs of houses and trees in the Mission District unite the upper and lower registers. The purpose of this element of the collage is revealed through its relationship to the other components. At the center of the collage is a photo of three young people standing in a circle near the replica of the bell that Father Miguel Hidalgo rang to alert the people to the call to arms at the start of the Mexican Revolution. A young woman with long hair and wearing a coat, a figure with an Afro who is carrying books, and a male with his back to the camera are engaged in a conversation. This contemporary meeting signifies the interracial network and political solidarity of the Mission District, but it also changes the meaning of the bell, which now rings to mobilize local residents in San Francisco.

PRINT CULTURE OF YOLANDA M. LÓPEZ

Several visual gestures link the Mexican Revolution to the Mission District's political campaigns, signaling a spatial-temporal unity across the Americas. First, graffiti charges the bell with new associations. The word *viva* (long live) is visible on the base of the structure that holds the bell, and like the column at the left side of the collage, it is written in the language of the Mission District, announcing in Spanish *la raza* and *Los Siete*. The symbol of the United Farm Workers, an eagle that also resembles an inverted pyramid, reinforces connections between the contemporary struggle for justice and the historical one. Second, the placement of the three bodies in the middle space of the collage visually unites past and present actions for liberty. The three figures converge before the monument for liberty. The compositional difference between the three figures, who stand in an open space (on a sidewalk?), and the crowd of people located at the bottom of the collage, who stand shoulder to shoulder, suggests that the occupation of public space is one of the messages of the image. Third, the landscape of the Mission District peeks through the structure that holds the bell, signifying the ideological connection between the revolution of the past and the present struggle for liberation indicated by the rally located in the bottom portion of the collage.

In this photograph, it is mostly women who are at the front of the crowd and who hold placards—created in the same style of lettering that López uses elsewhere and at the bottom of the collage—that read "Free Los Siete de Raza" and "Support the Free Breakfast for Children." The visible text of the third placard adds to the spatial-temporal gesture of the collage because it uses the words *struggle* and *revolutionary,* evoking yet again the Mexican Revolution and the one emerging within the Mission District community. This complex narrative joins political struggles to suggest a solidarity that extends beyond racial, class, gender, and ethnic boundaries as well as nation-states. The handwritten words at the bottom of the collage, *"¡La Raza Unida!"* (the People United), openly declare this solidarity.

However, there is more to López's countercultural melding of the aesthetic and politics. The composition is striking because of the disproportion of the house, and it signals at least two meanings to the readership. For those familiar with Los Siete and their services, the building indicates the physical site of organizing and leadership for the community. It is the people's house in name and action. It helps the community identify Los Siete as a source of service, mobilization, and political empowerment. For those unfamiliar with Los Siete, the house is still symbolic of the place from which revolutionary struggle emerges. Both gestures complement the overall narrative of the collage, but two additional elements in the collage convey the significance of identifying the home as the site or source for political consciousness and action. Spatially near the house are two children, figures also connected to household and family life. Each reinforces López's hopeful proposal found in the masthead of the newspaper. Appearing in the bottom right corner of the collage, the girl in profile gazes over the words *La Raza Unida,* which literally emerge from her torso. The boy stands on the street in front of a taco shop and hands out free copies of *¡Basta Ya!* Their age and activism are bold and positive claims about the future of solidarity, activism within La Raza, and the legacy of struggle. The building is their home, their space of sanctification and rejuvenation.

The rough collages, often separated by the black lines that Douglas taught her to use, were precursors to López's color Xerox studies for the Guadalupe series. Similar to her later works, López used collage and photomontage in the pages of *¡Basta Ya!* to decenter the artist and "dissolve the work of art into a tool of communication."[24] Her work for the newspaper required a blurring of the boundaries between artwork, text, and viewer. She developed a narrative style in order to convey messages about the struggle to liberate the accused youths and create solidarity within the community, and she rejected the signature to avoid any elevation of the artist over other members of the community. Moreover, López was dedicated to an aesthetic approach that would be accessible to a Latin@ audience. Even when the collage was complex and polyvalent, she used vernacular Spanish and everyday symbols to achieve her goal of communication.

More important, her direct style depicted ordinary people, an aesthetic approach that would crystallize in the decade that she created the Guadalupe series. Because the mass media portrayed the Latino defendants as "hoodlums" and "militants," López was determined to examine the role and function of these images by offering new ones.[25] But rather than offering positive archetypes, she used actual people. As noted above, the newspaper included coverage of revolutionary struggles throughout the world including those in El Salvador, Nicaragua, Chile, Brazil, Puerto Rico, Mexico, Cuba, Vietnam, China, and Palestine. It was explicit in reclaiming the term *Third World* from the discourse of economic development that subordinated it to the First World. Although the international coverage was significant, the bulk of the articles emphasized the defense of the seven youth and linked their case to the imprisonment of Huey Newton and Bobby Seale, Luis Talamantez, and other activists of color. Here is where López made her second visual and political contribution.[26]

In the first issue of *¡Basta Ya!,* published on June 17, 1969, the lead story told the tale of police harassment that resulted in the death of officer Brodnick, the arrests, and the murder charges. Another lead article challenged the mayor's portrayal of the accused youths as hoodlums, punks, and vandals by describing the community-based advocacy of Tony and Mario Martinez, who recruited and prepared Latin@s for college.[27] Aiming to construct a humanizing profile of the brothers, the newspaper also published poems and letters written by or about the youths on trial, ran stories about their families, and illustrated each

with portraits of the young men. This strategy was continued throughout the trial, and each issue contained a combination of stories about
the rallies, court actions, biographies, creative writing about the accused, and visual images to counter the mass-media portrayal of the
defendants as common criminals.

López's contribution to this oppositional-media strategy included
simple portraits that accompanied the lead story about the evidence,
the mistreatment of the six imprisoned youth, and poems and letters
to the accused. In the October 4, 1969, issue of *¡Basta Ya!*, López also
created line drawings of the defendants, in which each was conveyed as
quiet and reflective. Below each portrait, written in a calligraphic style
that evokes the favored Old English font of West Coast graffiti writers,
were the birth names and nicknames of the young men. This compositional element once again locates the artist and her subjects within
the Mission District community. Although the portraits may resemble
police sketches because of their simplicity, they are representations of
dignified and largely unassuming youth. In López's portraits none of the
defendants aggressively confronts the viewer. On the contrary, these are
portraits of gentle men, whose gazes are soft, innocent, or introspective.[28]

López also merged the real with imaginary images in her representations of Los Siete. For example, her collage *Libertad para Los Siete*
(Liberty for the Seven) transforms a vacant lot and the old, decaying
housing of the Mission District into a place of comfort and sanctuary
(Figure 11.4). The new vision of dilapidated housing as a site of belonging, safety, and refuge is embodied in the slogan "Bring the brothers
back home to the Mission!," which appears in the middle register of the
poster. At bottom left is a drawing of a small child, an appropriation
from a painting by Diego Rivera. Sitting barefoot on the ground, the boy
is holding on his lap a piece of paper and a pencil in his hand, and he has
written "Free Los Siete." It is as if the child is creating a placard for the
coming rally, and this form of mobilization signals the future and the
role of children in the Mission's collective consciousness. Slogan-like
headlines were frequently used in *¡Basta Ya!,* but in this case the call
for liberty and the imaginary home present a double message that also
invokes local residential control of the Mission District.

The leaflet was meant to illustrate a future community and encourage Mission residents to see their neighborhood through their own
eyes, rejecting the media portrayal of the area as dangerous, dilapidated,
and dirty. Freedom for the brothers meant freedom for the residents of
the Mission to create the community they desired, particularly in their
struggle for control within the Model Cities Program and for a voice
in the design of BART, the Bay Area transportation system intended to
serve the middle class and predominantly white residents of the San
Francisco suburbs by cutting through the Mission District without
directly serving the neighborhood.[29]

Figure 11.4

Yolanda M. López, *Libertad para Los Siete: Bring the Brothers Back Home to the Mission!* Printed in *¡Basta Ya!* no. 8, March 1970.

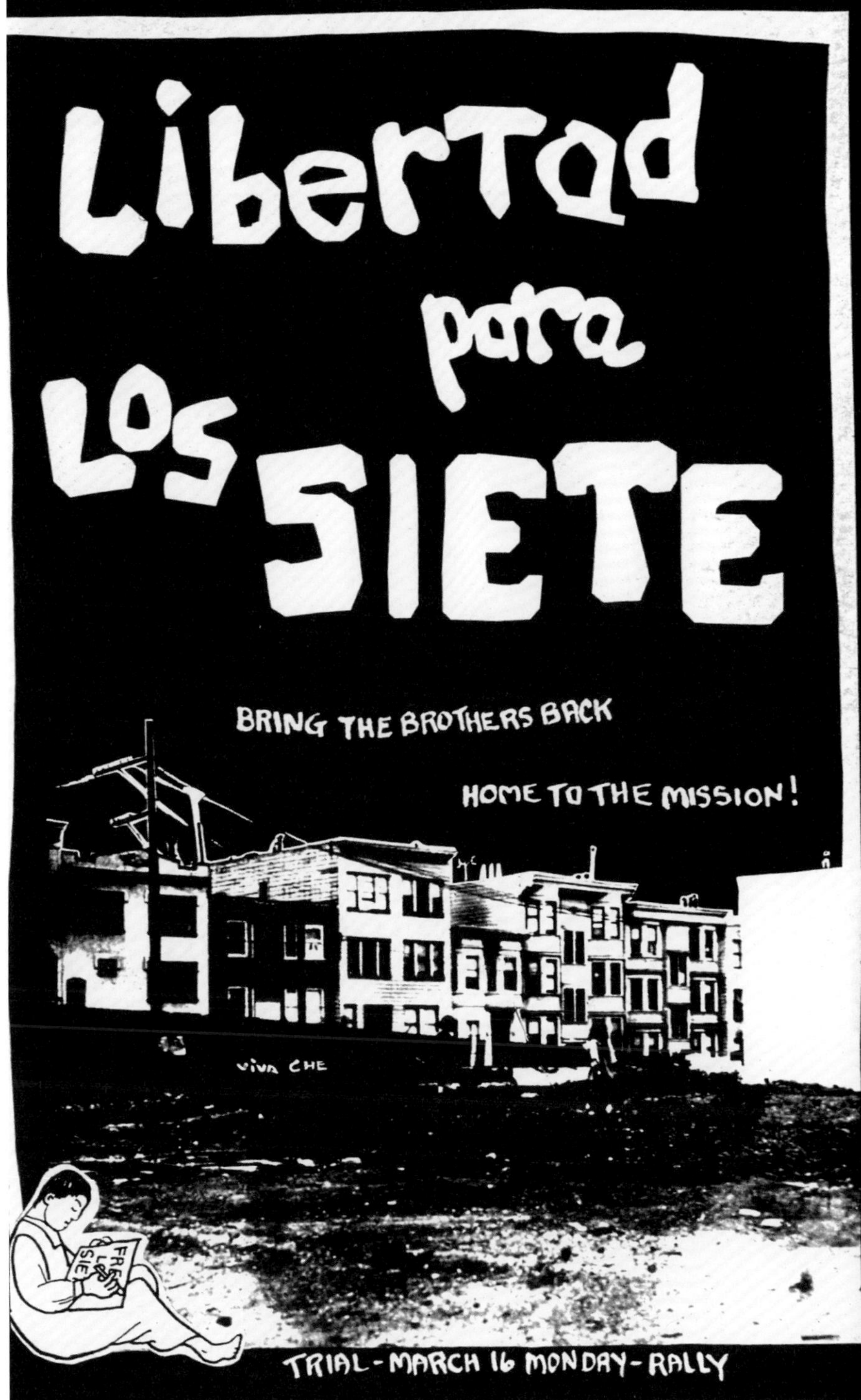

Libertad
para
Los SIETE
BRING THE BROTHERS BACK
HOME TO THE MISSION!
viva CHE
FREE LOS SIE
TRIAL - MARCH 16 MONDAY - RALLY

NUMBER 9
APRIL

¡ BASTA YA !

NUMERO 9
ABRIL

MISSION COMMUNITY NEWSPAPER   PERIODICO DE LA MISSION

LOS SIETE DE LA RAZA   P. O. BOX 12217   SAN FRANCISCO, CALIFORNIA   25¢

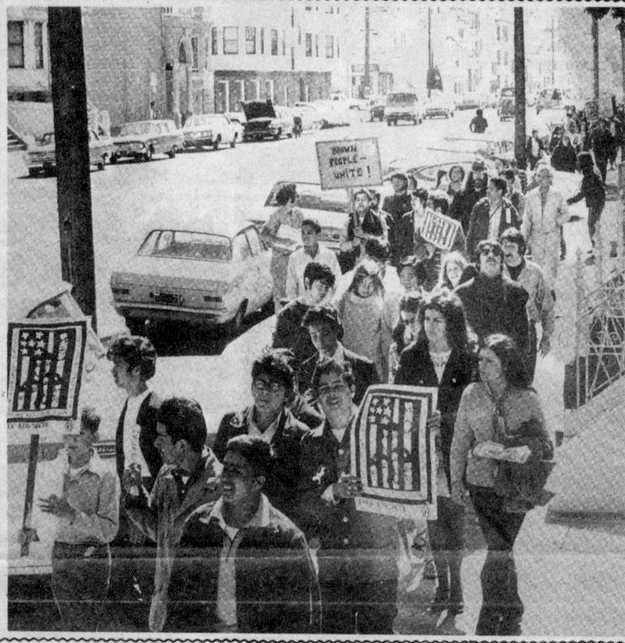

IN THIS ISSUE:

LOS SIETE   2

BART CHANGES THE MISSION   6

HOSPITAL NEWS   4

WELFARE RIGHTS   8

HIGH SCHOOL STUDENT UNION   14

MISSION NEWS SPECIAL: LEVIS   9

EN ESTA EDICION:

LOS SIETE   2

BART CAMBIA LA MISSION   66

NOTICIAS DEL HOSPITAL   4

LOS DERECHOS DEL WELFARE   8

UNION DE LOS ESTUDIANTES   14

NOTICIA ESPECIAL DE LA MISSION: 9
LEVIS   9

MISSION UNITES FOR JUSTICE

MISSION UNIDA POR LA JUSTICIA

'Viva Los Siete' rang through the streets of the Mission District on Monday, March 16th as supporters of Los Siete marched through the Mission to tell all our brothers and sisters what was happening in their trial and in the community.

A rally at Garfield Park started the march. Speakers were Ramon Pena of the United Farm Workers Organizing Committee, Manuel Lares of LULAC, Cleveland Brooks of the Hospital Workers Union and members of Los Siete.

The march went up 24th Street to Mission, along Mission, with everyone leafletting and talking to the shoppers and workers and getting them to join in the line. Then it turned down 17th Street to the carbarn where we joined the striking MUNI Railway workers in solidarity. The police, who had been following the march, blocked off the streets and tried to keep the marchers from talking with the MUNI workers.

The March went on from there to the General Hospital on Potrero. The police, knowing the solidarity between the workers and community people, ran down the street with clubs and guns to keep the two groups from getting together. They formed a line down Potrero and no one was allowed to cross it. The workers asked that their supporters be allowed to join them in protesting the treatment of patients and workers at San Francisco General Hospital but were rudely treated and shoved by the police.

The marchers formed a picket line across the street from General and shouted 'On strike, shut it down,' to their brothers and sisters in the union picket line across the street.

The people then decided to go on to the Safeway at 24th and Potrero, another known oppressor of brown people. Safeway has refused to take grapes off its shelves for the last two years and will not meet with the Farmworkers to insure our brothers and sisters who work in the fields a living wage. The Huelga has been going on for 5 years now. How many years must hungry people wait for their rights before the rich corporations will recognize them?

The march then went to Bank of America which owns the land in the Central Valley as well as much land in Latin America where our brothers and sisters are treated like slaves in their own lands. The Bank is an enemy of the people, wherever we are, and the people are aware of it.

The march returned to Garfield Park where the people gathered to talk about the day's events and have a fiesta. The police escort watched from the street.

"Viva Los Siete" sonaban por las calles del distrito de la Mission el lunes 16 de Marzo, cuando los defensores (gente que respalda a Los Siete) marchaban por las calles de la MIssion para decirles a todos los hermanos y hermanas lo que estaba pasando en el juicio y en la comunidad.

Una demonstracion en el parque Garfield empezo la marcha. Oradores fueron Ramon Pena de United Farmworkers (Huelga), Manuel Lares de LULAC, Cleveland Brooks de la Union de Trabajadores del hospital y miembros de Los Siete.

La marcha subio a la calle 24th, hasta la Mission, sobre la Mission, con todos papeliando y hablando con los compradores y trabajadores convenciendolos a que se juntaran en la fila. Despues doblo bajo sobre la calle 17th, al garage de buses donde nos juntamos con los trabajadores de Muni que estaban en huelga en solidaridad. La policia que habia estado siguiendo la marcha, cerro las calles y trato de evitar que los marchadores hablaran con los trabajadores de Muni.

La marcha siguio de alli al hospital general situado en Potrero. La policia sabiendo la solidaridad entre la gente de la comunidad y los trabajadores, corrieron sobre la calle con palos y pistolas para mantener a los dos grupos separados. Ellos formaron una linea sobre Potrero y nadie fue permitido a cruzarla. Los trabajadores pedieron que sus aliados fueran permitidos de juntarse con ellos en quejarse del tratamiento recibida por pacientes y trabajadores de S.F.G.H. pero fueron vulgarmente tratados y empujados por la policia.

Los marchadores formaron una linea de huelgistas al otro lado de la calle (enfrente del hospital), gritando "En huelga, cierrenlo", a los hermanos y hermanas en la huelga de la union al otro lado de la calle.

La gente entonces decidio ir a Safeway en la 24th y Potrero, otro opresor conocido por la gente latina. Safeway ha negado quitar las uvas desde hace dos anos, y no se encontrara con nuestros hermanos y hermanas para hablar referente a sueldos suficiente para sobrevivir. La huelga ha estado ya por 5 anos. Cuantos anos tendra que esperar la gente con hambre por sus derechos hasta que las corporaciones las reconosca?

La marcha entonces se fue al Bank of America, que es dueno de tierras en Central Valley y en America Latina donde tratan a nuestros hermanos y hermanas como esclavos en sus propias tierras. El banco es enemigo de la gente donde quiera que estemos. La gente esta sabedora de esto.

La marcha regreso al Parque Garfield, donde la gente se junto para hablar de los hechos del dia y tener una fiesta. La policia vigilaba de la calle.

Figure 11.5

Yolanda M. López, cover of
¡Basta Ya! no. 9, April 1970.

Figure 11.6

Yolanda M. López, *Free
Los Siete,* 1969. Printed in
¡Basta Ya! no. 3.

DEMANDING AND DELIVERING THE PROMISE: FREE LOS SIETE

López's success as a countercultural artist-activist is found in the repeated use of *Free Los Siete* (1969), a drawing she created for the newspaper, which was reproduced for rallies and demonstrations (Figures 11.5 and 11.6). Similar to her other work with Los Siete, the image merges new visual representations of Latin@s, a graphic realism, and the previously unimagined. *Free Los Siete,* a black-and-white poster of 4 × 5 feet, is a startling commentary by López. The poster depicts an American flag hanging vertically, the stripes converted into prison bars that partially

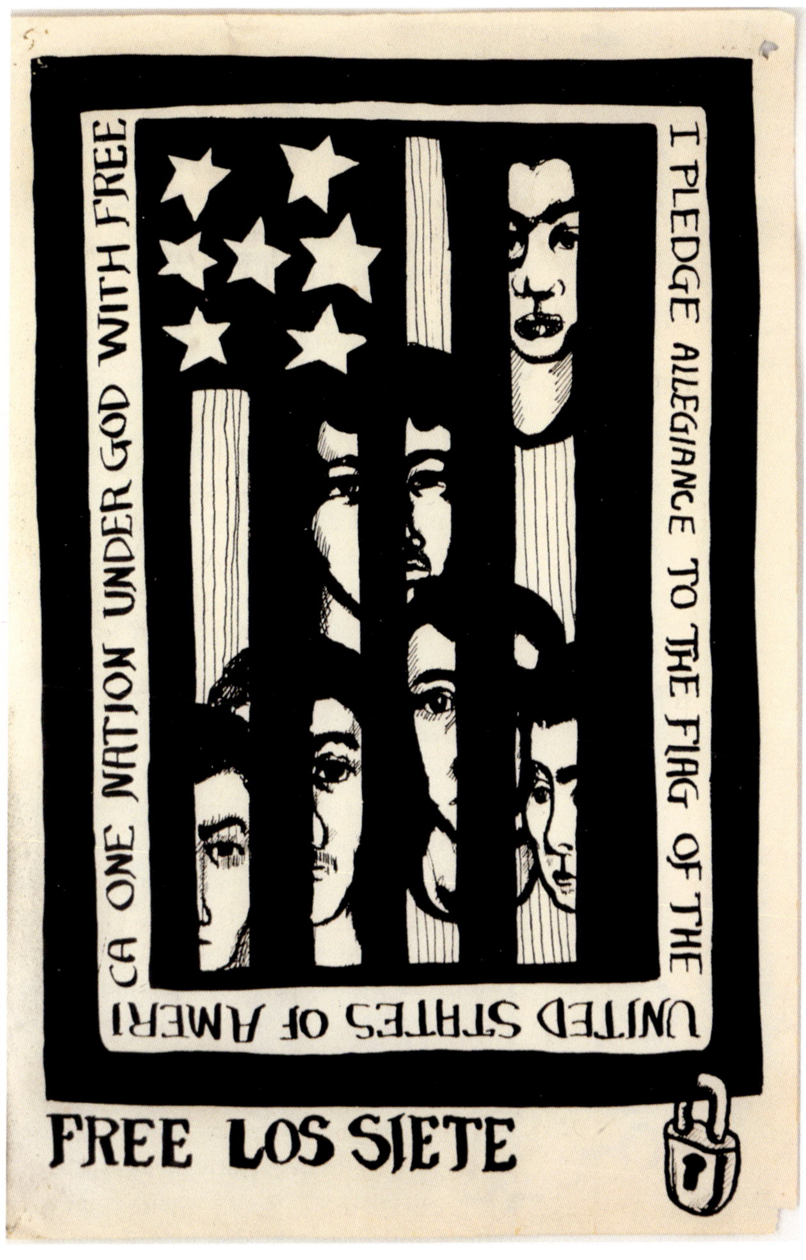

obscure six faces. (The seventh figure is omitted from the poster because he was never apprehended.) The faces cluster near the bottom portion of the image, except for one figure whose face is located in the top register, unobstructed by the prison bars. His unflinching gaze looks directly at the viewer. Only one figure looks away from the viewer, but his gaze draws the eye to the words that wrap around the flag. The heavy black lines of the flag stripes/jail bars are framed by part of the text from of the Pledge of Allegiance.

The blending of text and image is a technique that López would use again in one of her most celebrated posters, *Who's the Illegal Alien, Pilgrim?* In the case of *Free Los Siete,* omitted text creates a powerful dialogue between word, image, and viewer. Bordering the poster, reading from the top right, are the words "I pledge allegiance to the flag of the United States of America." But the next line, "And to the Republic for which it stands," is absent, as if the flag does not signify the nation, a formal comment on the hollowness of the symbol. The final lines of the pledge are truncated. Reading from bottom left are the words "One nation under God with free." The viewer expects "with freedom" or the complete phrase, "indivisible, with liberty and justice for all," which is missing. It is only the internal script of the viewer that can complete the phrase of the pledge. Tellingly, López has located these words inside the padlocked cage. A thick black frame surrounds the entire image, and at the bottom outermost edge of the frame is a padlock, which holds the cage shut. The poster questions if the accused youth will benefit from the promise of the pledge, since the missing words "indivisible, with liberty and justice for all" signal the figures' captivity within the U.S. justice system that cannot produce freedom and fairness.[30] The bilingual demand "Free Los Siete," which appears outside the cage at the bottom of the poster, reminds the viewer that only community action can protect the rights of the Latino youth and guarantee freedom.

The work's composition and message also reinforce the radical politics operating in northern California. As Chon A. Noriega notes, López "actively withholds her authorship in order to have the poster circulate as an expression of the community itself."[31] López's own retelling of her work with Los Siete reveals this countercultural strategy that rejected the individual identity and genius of the artist: "But they found out that I was the artist for Los Siete. I [don't know] how they found out, because none of the work was signed, and a lot of us did not sign our work. . . . Number one, it was dangerous, and number two, it was the people's work, literally; this is for 'the people' and I was one of 'the people' and I didn't want singular credit."[32] The anonymous but widely circulated poster demonstrates how López was an effective countercultural artist-activist: "The streets were my gallery . . . posters, leaflets, lapel buttons, and graphic art for neighborhood newspapers. I saw my work everywhere, and unsigned."[33] Participants at rallies and demonstrations waved banners made from reproductions of *Free Los Siete,* and the image appeared repeatedly in photographs of public events by local newspapers. López's work found a venue as large as the Latin@ community.

Inspired in part by Maoist principles, López believed that art should serve the people. This socially motivated artistic commitment rejected the codes of the capitalist market and Western individuality. Like Betty Kano, who contributed to the Third World Liberation Front in Berkeley in 1968, and Jean LaMarr, whose poster of Wounded Knee was widely distributed, López did not sign the broadsides, buttons, and flyers she created for Los Siete de la Raza.[34] The impassioned sensibility of revolutionary excitement infused her style and the tone of her artistic endeavors. This blending of life and art crystallized her identity as an artist: "It was only within Los Siete that I understood what I was about. And that was because it combined my interest in politics and art, and it was a very comfortable fit for me."[35] Through print culture, López "encompassed both a political position and an aesthetic one."[36]

This "comfortable fit" reflects her complex political consciousness that embraced the Chicano movement, the Left, the Black Power movement, the Third World movement, and, by 1971, women of color feminism. Her countercultural position drew from multiple orientations and strategies, and the shared vision of art as a tool of the Cultural Revolution allowed for this complexity. In addition, López's understanding of the Cultural Revolution did not assume that social institutions would remain intact. She pushed against ideas, images, and systems. Her work with Los Siete aimed to discredit American values and perceptions of Latin@s, and this strategy has had lasting results.[37] Breakfast programs for impoverished school children are now provided by the nation-state. The 1970s and 1980s witnessed the flourishing of alternative media sources for and by Latin@s.[38] Today, media outlets are expected to employ a diverse range of journalists. Even after 9-11, the misguided tactic of racial profiling has come under attack from multiple fronts. As a participant in the countercultural revolution in the San Francisco Bay Area, López assisted in changing ideas and practices.

POLITICAL ART AND THE ART OF POLITICS

López returned to San Diego in 1971, and she again sought work within community-based advocacy organizations. After a brief time with a settlement organization, she took a job with the Chicano Park Steering Committee, the group responsible for coordinating efforts to create one of the most important urban land-use claims by a disenfranchised neighborhood. Although the activists in San Diego were employing nationalist tactics in Southern California, her countercultural stance did not waiver. She continued to produce images to change perceptions, raise political consciousness, question the status quo, and mobilize a range of people—women and men, young and old, monolingual Spanish or English speakers. It was during her work with the steering committee that Herman Baca of the Committee on Chicano Rights approached

López to create what became one of her most recognizable images, *Who's the Illegal Alien, Pilgrim?*, a poster for the campaign against President Carter's immigration plans.

Although the Committee on Chicano Rights was "somewhat reluctant" to use the pen-and-ink drawing for a poster because they could not get past its forceful composition and appreciate López's wit and sarcasm, the offset print first circulated in the early 1980s.[39] Since then, it has been reproduced in a variety of print media to mobilize against other immigration policies, activities on the United States–Mexico border, or anti-Latin@ measures, such as California's Proposition 187. In short, the image has continued to circulate because it proclaims an oppositional consciousness that talks back to power by subverting conventional wisdom and challenging American historical amnesia. Moreover, it mobilizes for both ideological and political change: we are implored to think differently about Mexicans and Europeans, and we are encouraged to revise existing immigration law to account for this new historically based political vision. The 1978 print functions as a coda to her intensive countercultural activism with Los Siete de la Raza; it is not the closing remark but a visual summation of her political aesthetic. It signals the basic structure, form, and approach of her countercultural artistic practice.

As Lucy Lippard argues, the politicization of art and the creation of political art are two different strategies, with the former making no argument about content or form and the latter more interested in ethics.[40] That is, the politicization of art is a strategy that calls attention to the role of power in the art world, an approach frequently associated with the institutional critique proposed by conceptual art. Political art emphasizes the role of power in society, which includes the politics of the art world, but it aims its focus on larger arenas.

Countercultural artistic practices blur these distinctions by investing in both strategies, although the gallery and the museum were less frequently targets of institutional critique as countercultural artists, such as López, advocated more consistently for institutional equality outside of the arts scene. Given the lessons from home and her experimentation in northern California, she was initially drawn to community and national issues such as the antiwar campaigns, education, civil rights, international women's rights, and the death penalty, but her interests expanded with a political consciousness that encompassed all laborers, racially disenfranchised populations, women, and young people. Since her childhood, López imagined that artistic talent must be useful to society, although her adolescent dreams could only imagine careers in costume or set design and film animation. Working with a counterculture group allowed López to join a larger ideological and practical movement in which art functioned to "nurture and sustain an insurgent consciousness."[41] She found a function for her artwork, and it served a larger social good, rather than her own reputation and identity. In this

   PRINT CULTURE OF YOLANDA M. LÓPEZ

way, her work pushed against the conceptual strategy that emerged in the 1960s because she was openly rejecting the established art-market system. Not only was the art-market system another facet of capitalism, it was not accessible to the audience she preferred. Moreover, López's refusal to sign her work deflated the notion of the artist-genius. She also encouraged the political agency of the audience by openly dialoguing with the viewer. Indeed, the viewer determines the meaning of the image, and its success is measured by direct action or mobilization of the viewer. In her approach to art, the passive spectator could not exist. López's overall practice amounts to a new way of thinking about political art, political artists, and the politicization of the arts. Her oppositional consciousness supported a broad understanding of politics that would make good on the errors of art history, particularly the assumption that art is separate from life.

1. The incident occurred on May 1, 1969, when two undercover police officers, Joseph Brodnick and Paul McGoran, stopped a group of Latino youth who were removing a television set from a parked car to the apartment of José Rios, one of the young men. The white San Francisco police officers suspected a burglary in progress, although trial records indicate that one of the group was actually moving his personal property. A heated verbal exchange, during which McGoran called the youths "wetbacks," led to a physical altercation that left Brodnick dead from his partner's gun. Seven youth fled the scene, including two who had been inside the apartment when the gun was fired, and after an intensive hunt, reinforced by the declaration of martial law, six Latinos were apprehended near Santa Cruz, California. In November 1970, the trial ended in their acquittal. See Jason Ferreira, "All Power to the People: A Comparative History of Third World Radicalism in San Francisco, 1968–1977" (Ph.D. diss., University of California, Berkeley, 2003); Marjorie Heins, *Strictly Ghetto Property: The Story of Los Siete de la Raza* (Berkeley, Calif.: Ramparts Press, 1972).

2. Note: academic conventions require use of *Chicana/o* and *Latina/o* as well as their plural forms *Chicanas/os* and *Latinas/os* to indicate gender inclusion for Spanish-language heritage speakers and feminists attentive to the ways the terms code-switch into English and can hide all gender diversity. Angie Chabram Denersesian was the first scholar to describe this splitting in "And, Yes . . . the Earth Did Part: On the Splitting of Chicana/o Subjectivity," in *Building with Our Hands: New Directions in Chicana Studies,* ed. Adela de la Torre and Beatríz M. Pesquera (Berkeley: University of California, 1993), 34–56. As Chela Sandoval notes, technology allowed for the shorthand with the ampersand. The terms *Chican@* and *Chican@s* combine the a and o and signal both feminine and masculine subjects and the potential for a third subjectivity. See Karen Mary Davalos, Eric R. Avila, Rafael Pérez-Torres, and Chela Sandoval, "Roundtable on the State of Chicana/o Studies," *Aztlán: A Journal of Chicano Studies* 27, no. 2 (2002): 139–52. The @ sign also eliminates the awkward placement of s before and after the virgule.

3. Guisela Latorre, *Walls of Empowerment: Chicana/o Indigenist Murals of California* (Austin: University of Texas Press, 2008), 37. The open palm is unlike the clenched fist that appeared on the very first issue of the newspaper. The original masthead included a masculine icon—the gesture of American popular expression "to make a muscle" that demonstrates the muscular, upper bicep and the clenched fist—that could not suit the actual female leadership of Los Siete de la Raza. Given this other imagery, López's masthead conveys a nongendered and inclusive subjectivity.

4. Karen Mary Davalos, *Yolanda M. López* (Los Angeles: UCLA Chicano Studies Research Center Press, with distribution by the University of Minnesota Press, 2008).

5. Elsewhere, I have argued that López's self-portrait, *Portrait of the Artist as the Virgin of Guadalupe* (1978; oil pastel on rag paper, 22 x 30 inches), from the Guadalupe series, is the most circulated work of Chican@ art between 1978 and 2006, appearing as the only or the main illustration for exhibition reviews, announcements, as well as catalogs, brochures, and flyers for group shows. It is also selected in textbooks of American art as the representative work of Chican@ or contemporary art. See Davalos, *Yolanda M. López,* 89, 124.

6. For book-length feminist critiques of Chican@ art history, see Davalos, *Yolanda M. López;* Alicia Gaspar de Alba, *Chicano Art Inside/Outside the Master's House: Cultural Politics and the CARA Exhibition* (Austin: University of Texas Press, 1998); María Ochoa, *Creative Collectives: Chicana Painters Working in Community* (Albuquerque: University of New Mexico Press, 2003); and Laura E. Pérez, *Chicana Art: The Politics of Spiritual and Aesthetic Altarities* (Durham, N.C.: Duke University Press, 2007).

7. Shifra M. Goldman, "'Portraying Ourselves': Contemporary Chicana Artists," in *Feminist Art Criticism,* ed. Arlene Raven, Cassandra L. Langer, and Joanna Frueh (Ann Arbor, Mich.: UMI Research Press, 1988), 193–95.

8. For an analysis of San Diego development, see Raúl Homero Villa, *Barrio-Logos: Space and Place in Urban Chicano Literature and Culture* (Austin: University of Texas Press, 2000).

9. Yolanda M. López, interview by author, 22–23 March 2007. My two-day interview with López was conducted in Los Angeles, California, and the transcript is housed at the UCLA Chicano Studies Research Center Library and Archive. Unless otherwise noted, biographical information about López is from this interview.

10. Cary Cordova, "The Heart of the Mission: Latino Art and Identity in San Francisco (California)" (Ph.D. diss., University of Texas, Austin, 2005), 15.

11. López, interview by author.

12. Ibid., emphasis added.

13. Growing out of several years of frustrating negotiations with the administration at State College over free speech, the draft, admissions policy, and faculty, TWLF mobilized by using Frantz Fanon's call for revolutionary consciousness among Asians, Africans, and Latin Americans as the only viable strategy against imperialism. Their use of the term *Third World* reconceptualized its original Cold War designation for nations not aligned with either the Western (U.S.) or Eastern (Soviet) bloc. The students from the Black Students' Union, the Mexican-American Student Confederation, the Philippine-American College Endeavor, the Intercollegiate Chinese for Social Action, and the Latin American Student Organization, as well as black and Latino faculty and staff, such as Juan Martinez, Nathan Hare, and Roger Alvarado, developed this ideological reframing of the term to create solidarity across lines of race, ethnicity, social class, national heritage, color, and immigration status but also maintained autonomy within their own organizations. Although several concessions were made in the final negotiations with administrators, TWLF was successful in its creation of the School of Ethnic Studies. See William Barlow and Peter Shapiro, *An End to Silence: The San Francisco State College Student Movement in the '60s* (New York: Pegasus, 1971).

14. Cordova, "Heart of the Mission," 17.

15. Quoted in ibid., 208.

16. Ferreira, "All Power to the People," 265–66.

17. López, interview by author.

18. This strategy was part of the Ten-Point Program, which emphasized a comprehensive approach to liberation and autonomy.

19. According to Carol Wells, *¡Basta Ya!* appeared four times per month, while Jason Ferreira claims it was published twice per month. See Wells, "La Lucha Sigue: From East Los Angeles to the Middle East," in *Just Another Poster? Chicano Graphic Art in California,* ed. Chon A. Noriega (Santa Barbara: University Art Museum, 2001), 193; Ferreira, "All Power to the People," 301.

20. Tomás Ybarra-Frausto, "The Legacy of La Galería de la Raza/ Studio 24," unpublished paper presented at Galería de la Raza for the (Re)Generation Project, San Francisco, 5 March 1996, 2, 7.

21. Colette Gaiter, "What Revolution Looks Like: The Work of Black Panther Artist Emory Douglas," in *Black Panther: The Revolutionary Art of Emory Douglas,* ed. Sam Durant (New York: Rizzoli, 2007), 106.

22. Allan Sekula, "Dismantling Modernism, Reinventing Documentary (Notes on the Politics of Representation)," in *Photography against*

the Grain: Essays and Photo Works, 1973–1983 (Halifax: Press of the Nova Scotia College of Art and Design, 1984), 54.

23. In 1970, Los Siete de la Raza lost its lease to the original storefront office at 2680 York Street, but a benefactor provided them with an alternative space at 960 Guerrero Street. See López, interview by author; Ferreira, "All Power to the People," 354.

24. Alexander Alberro, "Reconsidering Conceptual Art: 1966–1977," in *Conceptual Art: A Critical Anthology,* ed. Alexander Alberro and Blake Stimson (Cambridge, Mass.: MIT Press, 2000), xxvi–xxvii.

25. López, interview by author.

26. In addition to offering Los Siete one side of its weekly newspaper in 1969, the Black Panthers also provided the services of Charles Gary, the lead attorney for Huey Newton and Bobby Seale, and $25,000 for the legal defense of the six Latino youths facing prosecution (only six were apprehended, and the seventh youth was never arrested).

27. The media stereotypes were a significant hurdle that Los Siete had to overcome in order to not only mobilize community support for the youths on trial, but also to create trust so that residents would send their children to the breakfast program or the health clinic.

28. López notes that Douglas influenced her strategy to create new images for Latin@s, just as he did for African Americans. See López, interview by author..

29. Eventually, residents successfully battled for two underground stations in the Mission District.

30. Cordova, "The Heart of the Mission," 220.

31. Chon A. Noriega, "Forward," in Davalos, *Yolanda M. López,* xi.

32. López, interview by author.

33. Betty LaDuke, "Yolanda López: Breaking Chicana Stereotypes," *Feminist Studies* 20, no. 1 (Spring 1994): 119. When *Free Los Siete* was exhibited at the Mission District's Galería de la Raza in 1970 as part of the First Annual Women's Show, the poster surprised the audience because they had assumed it was the work of a male artist. See ibid., 104. See also López, interview by author.

34. Yolanda López and Moira Roth, "Social Protest: Racism and Sexism," in *The Power of Feminist Art: The American Movement of the 1970s, History and Impact,* ed. Norma Broude and Mary D. Garrard (New York: Harry N. Abrams, 1994), 146. For this article, López interviewed Betty Kano and Jean LaMarr about their activism in California. Reflecting on the strategy of being an "artist for the people" or a "facilitator" of the revolution, López and Roth note that in the 1970s it produced relative anonymity for women artists such as Linda Lucero at La Raza Silkscreen, which was later named La Raza Graphics; Gail Arantani, Nancy Hom, Stephanie Lowe, and Wendy Yoshimura in the Kearny Street Workshop and Japantown: Art and Media; and Rachel Romero, who cofounded with Leon Klayman the San Francisco Poster Brigade, which was previously called the Wilfred Owen Brigade (see ibid., 293, note 22).

35. López, interview by author.

36. Tomás Ybarra-Frausto, "Chicano Movement/the Movement of Chicano Art," in *Exhibiting Cultures: The Poetics and Politics of Museum Display,* ed. Ivan Karp and Steven D. Lavine (Washington and London: Smithsonian Institution Press, 1991), 140. I am intentionally quoting Ybarra-Frausto out of context in order to demonstrate that López's work does not conform to Chicano art historiography.

37. For a similar countercultural political strategy, see Michael William Doyle, "Staging the Revolution: Guerrilla Theater as a Countercultural Practice, 1965–1968," in *Imagine Nation: The American Counterculture of the 1960s and '70s,* ed. Peter Braunstein and Michael William Doyle (New York and London: Routledge, 2002), 71–97.

38. According to assessments by librarians in the 1970s, the proliferation of Latin@ serial publications in that decade was impressive. Hundreds of newspapers, magazines, academic journals, and newsletters were produced to answer the need for publication venues that would support the critical orientations that emerged from the civil rights movements. See "Alternative Periodicals: Chicanos," *Wilson Library Bulletin* 50, no. 8 (April 1976): 628–33; Roberto Cabello-Argandoña, Juan Gómez-Quiñones, and William Tamayo, "Library Services and Chicano Periodicals: A Critical Look at Librarianship," *Aztlán: A Journal of Chicano Studies* 2, no. 2 (1971): 151–72; Guillermo Rojas, "Chicano/Raza Newspaper and Periodical Serials Listing," *Hispania* 58, no. 4 (December 1975): 851–63; and Richard D. Woods and Ann Hartness Graham, "Hispanic American Periodicals for Libraries," *Serials Librarian* 1 (November 1979): 85–98.

39. López, interview by author.

40. Lucy R. Lippard, *Get the Message? A Decade of Art for Social Change* (New York: E. P. Dutton, 1984).

41. George Lipsitz, "Not Just Another Social Movement: Poster Art and *El Movimiento Chicano,*" in *Just Another Poster?,* 73.

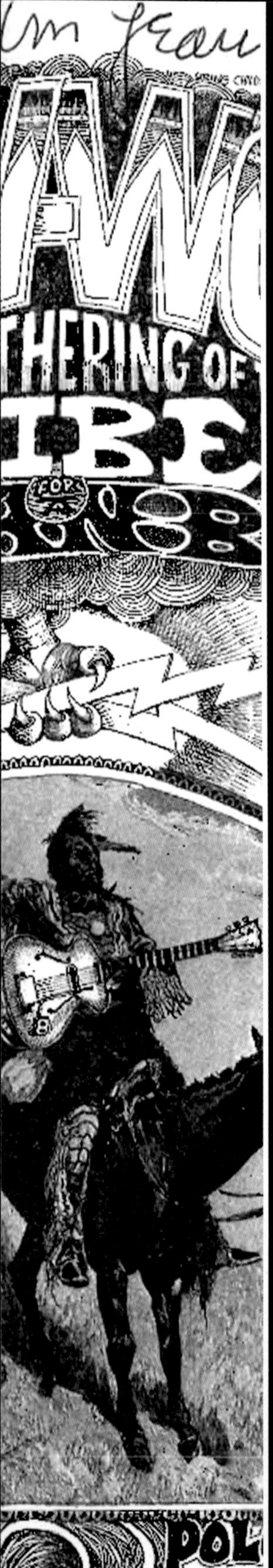
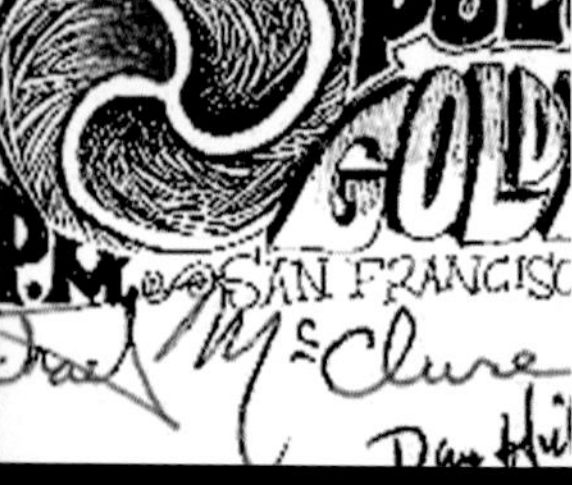

CHAPTER 12
THE COUNTERCULTURAL "INDIAN": VISUALIZING RETRIBALIZATION AT THE HUMAN BE-IN

Mark Watson

At Be-Ins and other communal Happenings, the 1960s counterculture employed politics and performance art to fashion what they called a "community of the tribe."[1] This alternative political community was expressed through citations of "Indian-ness," in which appropriated fragments of Native American cultural tradition were deployed as expressions of the counterculture's own "tribes" (Figure 12.1). This fundamental aspect of the counterculture's political aesthetics was not a repetitive rehearsing of the primitivism that had existed as a countercurrent in Western art since Paul Gauguin's flight to Tahiti. Nor was it only a reconstruction of American identity, in the tradition of the Boston Tea Party, as the counterculture consistently appealed to a postnational identity and, in practice, the "politics of the tribe" extended outside North America.[2] Rather, the 1960s conception of the *tribe* as an emergent political alternative was historically specific, drawing from a number of idiosyncratic 1960s sources, most important the then-fashionable media theory of Marshall McLuhan.[3] This 1960s tribe tied small-scale collectivity together with high technology and aesthetic experimentation in order to reinvent the relationship among art, technology, and politics. As the United States became increasingly dominated by high technology and the information economy—a "technocracy," in Theodore Roszak's 1969 coinage—this "techno-primitivist" political aesthetics grew in urgency and became a long-lasting part of late-twentieth-century underground aesthetic politics.[4]

Easily the most influential event to articulate the political aesthetics of the tribe was the Human Be-In, held January 14, 1967, at San Francisco's Golden Gate Park (Figure 12.2).[5] Organized in late 1966 by two underground artists, Allen Cohen and Michael Bowen, the event was conceived as a political alternative to the period's sit-ins, demonstrations, and marches.[6] Writing in the San Francisco *Oracle,* the primary print organ of the San Francisco counterculture, they proclaimed the Be-In a "union of love and activism previously separated by categorical dogma."[7] Here "the humanization of the American man and woman can begin" and the "new concert of human relations developed within the youthful underground . . . [can] emerge, become conscious, and be shared." Indeed, the *Oracle* promised that the event would be nothing less than "the joyful, face-to-face beginning of the new epoch." On the appointed winter afternoon, at least twenty-five thousand people descended on Golden Gate Park for what was called a "Pow-Wow" and "Gathering of the Tribes." For four hours, the so-called tribes were addressed by what the Be-In organizers referred to as the "leaders, guides, and heroes of our generation." These included the Beat poets Allen Ginsberg and Gary Snyder, East Coast LSD guru Timothy Leary, political activist/provocateur Jerry Rubin, and a large number of local rock bands, including Jefferson Airplane and the Grateful Dead. It was announced that the comedian Dick Gregory would be unable to perform after being detained in Washington State for "attempting to aid the Puget Sound Indians with

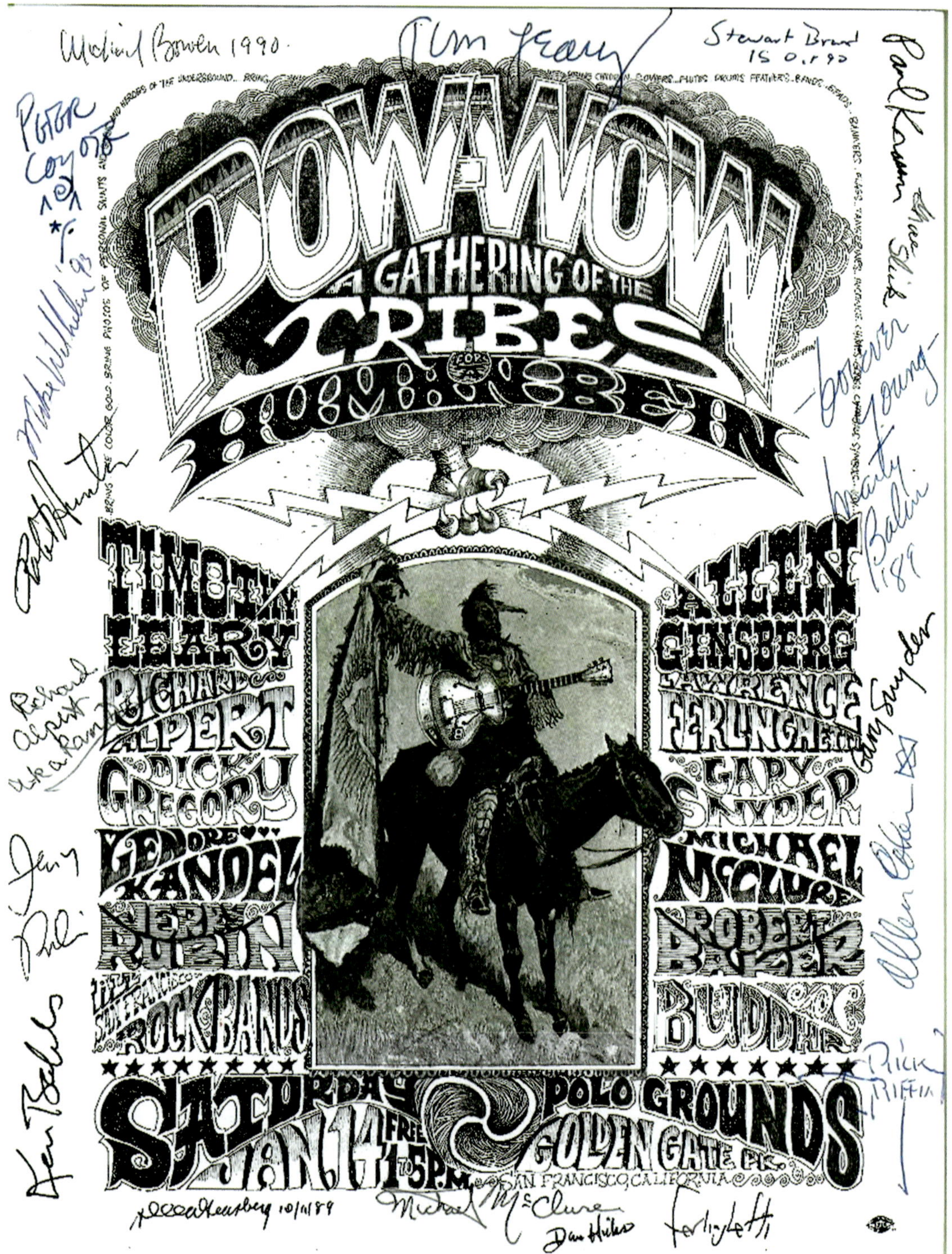
POW-WOW
A GATHERING OF THE TRIBES
HUMAN BE-IN
TIMOTHY LEARY
RICHARD ALPERT
DICK GREGORY
LENORE KANDEL
JERRY RUBIN
SAN FRANCISCO ROCK BANDS
ALLEN GINSBERG
LAWRENCE FERLINGHETTI
GARY SNYDER
MICHAEL McCLURE
ROBERT BAKER
BUDDHA
SATURDAY JAN 14 1 TO 5 P.M. FREE
POLO GROUNDS
GOLDEN GATE PK.
SAN FRANCISCO, CALIFORNIA

a 'fish-in.'"[8] Underground veterans Snyder and Ginsberg, serving both as "priests and poets," in the words of an *Oracle* review, chanted Hindu and Buddhist mantras calling for a restoration of "this once voluptuous country," a "regaining of the forests and the great herds."[9] The mantras, speeches, and poetry were interspersed with rock music, making clear the connection between the aesthetics of the new music and the "new epoch" of tribes the event was to usher in. After four hours and the fiery "mandala" of the Pacific sunset, the tribes scattered across the West Coast, visions of what Snyder and Ginsberg called "the new and better age that has already begun" dancing in their heads.

The counterculture's politics of the tribe was persuasively visualized in Rick Griffin's poster for the event (see Figure 12.1). The poster combines appropriated photographs with additional pictorial elements added in a lyrical hand-drawn style. At top, it conveys the name of the event in the hand-drawn lettering of the underground, echoing the concert posters and other visual culture through which countercultural sociality was maintained. Highlighting what Theodore Roszak described as the counterculture's belief that "real politics can only take place in the deeply personal confrontations" available in a "tribe," the poster records how the organizers coded the seemingly open-ended concept of a Human Be-In with "Indian-ness" through the appellations *Pow-Wow* and *Gathering of the Tribes*.[10] The Be-In's reference to Native America is reinforced at the bottom center of the poster, where the artist appropriates and manipulates a historical photograph of a late-nineteenth-century Plains Indian man holding a painted buffalo robe. While in the historical photograph the warrior carried a carbine in his left hand, Griffin replaces the gun with a hand-drawn electric guitar, symbolizing the way rock

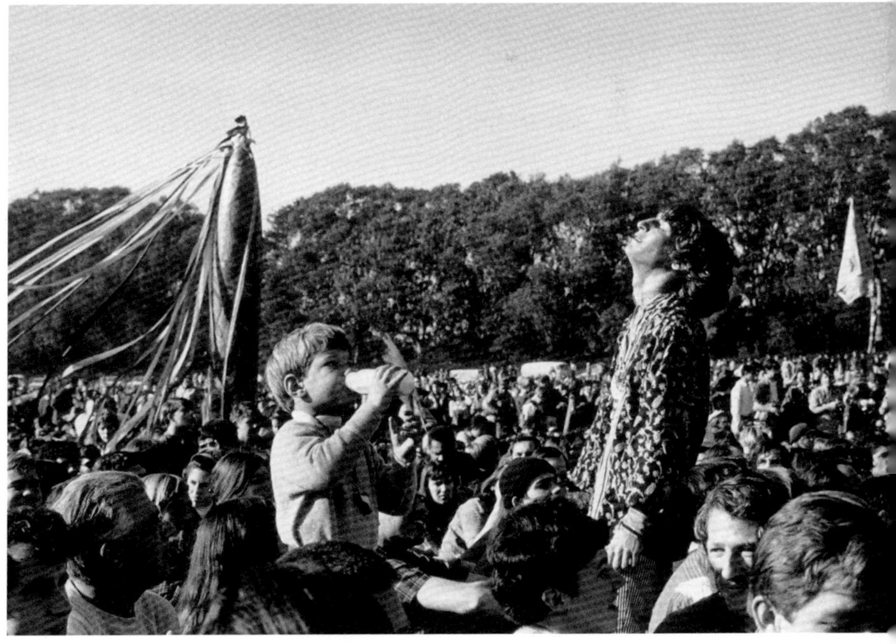

THE COUNTERCULTURAL "INDIAN"

and roll music—rather than violent confrontation—defined countercultural opposition, particularly in San Francisco.[11] Finally, the typographic top and pictorial bottom are visually united with two crossed lightning bolts, clutched by an eagle's talon shooting down from a cloud. These lightning bolts are code for *White Lightning,* a Prohibition-era term for bootleg whiskey applied to LSD after its criminalization in November 1966. The artist, then, underscores the counterculture's emphasis on both subjective and collective revolution, visually combining both the tribal social structure and the shift in individual consciousness believed available through an LSD trip.

Both the political aesthetics of Griffin's poster and the emancipatory project of the Human Be-In are seminal examples of what historians Peter Braunstein and Michael William Doyle have dubbed the 1964–68 pre-Nixon first phase of the counterculture.[12] They are structured by three of the key discourses of the first phase counterculture: the expression of radical cultural politics through the appropriation of Native American culture and imagery; the belief that "real politics" can only happen at the face-to-face level of a tribe; and the belief that rock music and psychedelic drugs were tools to bring about the emancipatory turn that lay in the immediate future of the world. In terms of the period's often misunderstood appropriation of Native American imagery, the poster shows the way in which Indians expressed the counterculture's vision of the emergent new epoch and its tribal social form. Griffin's work was an expression of a collective—if racially naive—political imagination that was portrayed throughout both the visual and written discourses of the counterculture, most notably in the press, activism, and creative output of the San Francisco underground. As Timothy Gray notes, while mass-media accounts portrayed the event as a superficial party, "people in the Haight believed that the Be-In had served notice of a new tribal collectivity" about to emerge globally.[13] This article unpacks how Griffin's poster and the Human Be-In are concrete examples of the counterculture's deployment of Indians to express a new form of tribal emancipatory politics that bridged the divide between cultural experimentation and forms of political protest.[14] Indian visual culture and tribal politics did not disappear after 1968 but, like other aspects of the early counterculture, came to "designate a look, a fashion, an attitude, or a lifestyle" within an increasingly commercialized sphere of youth, popular culture, and New Age spirituality devoid of the counterculture's emancipatory project of "total freedom."[15] However, a more generalized tribal political aesthetics continued as part of the late-twentieth-century underground, manifesting itself in do-it-yourself, rave, and other experiments in alternative political and artistic communalism.

Importantly, Griffin's poster makes central the combination of the Indian and the electric guitar, a juxtaposition that is key to deciphering both the poster and the Be-In itself. Together, the Indian and the guitar—a metonym for rock music—put forth the distinctive version of "techno-primitivism" that structured countercultural political aesthetics. As A. J. Miller writes, the electric guitar was a potent signifier in postwar America, functioning as a "symbol of progress . . . [evoking] . . . modernity and high technology . . . a symbol of humankind's technological dominance over the environment. Virtually all new forms of American vernacular music after 1940 incorporated it, and by the 1950s it was a mainstay of the entertainment industry."[16] It was broadly perceived as a "democratic instrument," according to Daniel Boorstin, modern, mass-produced, and affordable by the 1960s.[17] This optimistic rhetoric about guitar-based music, especially rock, saturates the *Oracle* and other countercultural publications. Griffin himself was immersed in the electric music of the period—designing concert posters and album art for bands—and, prior to coming to San Francisco, he was a surfer and staff artist for *Surfer* magazine, the first magazine of the postwar Southern California surf community.[18] Electric guitar–based music was central to the surf community, including the early 1960s surf genre of rock music that had developed as a way of conveying the values of the surf community.[19] As an artist, then, Griffin was highly aware of the broader associations the electric guitar carried as a symbol of new forms of creative expression as well as emergent forms of community. In mid-1960s San Francisco this was underscored by the omnipresence of rock and roll, including at the Be-In, which purported to include "all San Francisco rock bands." The electric guitar by this point was a symbol not only of progress but of new forms of youth-based community, increasingly dubbed *tribal* in the underground.

By 1967, the Indians and tribes were political symbols, as Roszak has noted. In an article in the February 1967 *Oracle,* "The Community of the Tribe" (published adjacent to an outline of a do-it-yourself "Omaha ritual"), the author defined the *tribe* as a creation of "our own communities" apart from the "profit" motive of "those people led and fed by the machine" and the "hate" of our "brothers, neighbors, and childhood friends" who were "killing innocent human beings around the world." This anticapitalist and pacifist tribe was a place of "organic growth" through which a change in consciousness could eventually "extend . . . beyond the tribe to our entire planet."[20] Elaborating on this retribalization, Gary Snyder wrote in Mitchell Goodman's encyclopedic "guide" to the counterculture that "we use the term tribe because it suggests the new type of society now emerging within the industrialized nations. In America of course the term has associations with the American Indians, which we like. This new subculture is in fact more similar to the European gypsies—a group without nation or territory that maintains its own values."[21] Snyder's postnational interpretation of the tribal ideal helps us distinguish it from many other appropriations of tribal identity in American cultural history.[22] While earlier examples were typically revitalizations of a specifically white male American identity and/or searches for "authentic" premodern experience, for the counterculture tribalism was not American, masculine, or antimodern.[23] It also makes clear that the counterculture's primitivism was significantly different from the cultural radicalism of earlier modernist avant-garde artists. While Paul Gauguin and other modern primitivists sought escape from technological society in favor of an Arcadian "primitive" social order at the core of humanity, the counterculture believed high technology and historical progress were the means to such a tribal social order.

The counterculture's seemingly contradictory embrace of technology and primitivism found firm support in mainstream 1960s intellectual culture. Easily the two most important books in this regard were Marshall McLuhan's best-selling *The Gutenberg Galaxy* (1962) and *Understanding Media: The Extensions of Man* (1964). As Fred Turner has written in his groundbreaking work on the "digital utopianism" that emerged from the counterculture, "hippies from Manhattan to Haight-Ashbury read . . . Marshall McLuhan. . . . [His] notion of the globe as a single, interlinked pattern of information was deeply comforting . . . [and] many thought they could see the possibility of global harmony."[24] The importance of McLuhan to the San Francisco counterculture, in particular, led to the creation of a McLuhan Festival in the city during August 1965, an event that included a visit from the author himself.[25] The lead article in the February 1967 *Oracle* proclaimed that McLuhan "somehow . . . manages to explain to perfection . . . the psychedelic revolution . . . the Haight-Ashbury community, and especially . . . Rock & Roll."[26] To the *Oracle,* McLuhan showed that rock was a "tribal phenomenon," a fundamentally "synthetic" social form that exceeded the boundaries of music to create a sociopolitical epoch of "total freedom, total experience, total love, peace & mutual affection" that was "international & verging in this decade on the universal." Drawing on McLuhan's thesis that a culture's communication media determine both its social structures and its style of cognition, the creation of electric rock music was interpreted as producing a neotribal culture of "synthesis & synaesthesia; nontypographic, non-linear, basically mosaic and mythic modes of perception . . . participation in depth . . . [and] extended awareness." "Put 'em all together," as the *Oracle* writer summed up McLuhan's descriptions of electronic tribal perception, and "you have a weekend on Haight Street."

Although he did not write about rock music or Haight Street, McLuhan underscored the shift from nation-states to tribes that would emerge from new media. In *The Gutenberg Galaxy,* he coined the term *retribalization* to describe the way technology made possible an "organic" overcoming of the alienation, hierarchy, and individualism of the modern era. He analyzed human history in four epochs, each based on a different communication medium: oral tribal culture, medieval manuscript culture, the modern Gutenberg galaxy, and the emergent electronic age of the 1960s. While oral tribal culture and the medieval manuscript culture encouraged multisensory cognition, collective reception, and flexible social roles, the creation of movable type and the printing press led to "the visual homogenizing of experience" that isolated and emphasized the visual sense in the individualistic activity of reading.[27] For McLuhan virtually all the modern world was produced by the printing press and its individualistic visual culture of reading: Protestantism, representative democracy, capitalism, and the nation-state (11–265). Yet this modern historical galaxy was already being superseded by the rise of electronic communications media of the twentieth century, according to McLuhan, which necessitated oral and aural participation, collective reception, and the compression of time and space, with a restoration of organic social relations and tribal consciousness (265–80).

In 1962, the year of the Cuban Missile Crisis, the neotribal era had obviously not fully emerged. Instead, according to McLuhan in the last section of his book, there was a pointed "clash" between print and electronic cultures—effectively a "generation gap" between Baby Boomers raised with television, movies, private phones, and other dominant media, and those raised in an earlier print culture. McLuhan emphasized that the "electronic and organic age" and its rising generation would create a whole new world from that of the "modern" period of individualism and nationalism (275). What would arise was nothing less than a "global village," McLuhan's term for the postnational collectivity and multisensory modes of perception and communication that would effectively replace printed culture and the artificial borders of nation-states. For the older members of society this "retribalization" would create "trauma and tension" as suddenly "our most ordinary and conventional attitudes seem twisted . . . [and] familiar institutions and associations seem at times menacing and malignant" (279). The future, in short, belonged to the youth and its electronic tribal culture.[28]

Reasserted and further developed in his 1964 follow-up *Understanding Media,* McLuhan's theory of electronic retribalization provided the counterculture a meaningful and comforting vision of an organic, intimate, and historically determined epochal shift. Like Griffin's poster, it linked together the counterculture's embrace of electric rock music, the synesthetic tribal experience of LSD, and its conception of real politics as what *The Oracle* called the "community of the tribe." It also provided an up-to-date yet futuristic form of primitivism for the counterculture, in which an embrace of premodern tribal (especially Native American) fashion, communalism, drumming, peyote and magic mushrooms, rituals, and other cultural fragments could—when taken up by the primarily white youth underground—express the technology-driven new epoch prophesied at the Human Be-In, in print organs like *The Oracle,* and in the art, music, and expanded visual culture of the period. Phil Deloria has suggested that this combination of the Indian and the technological reveals the "dissipation of meaning" supposedly characteristic of late-twentieth-century postmodern culture. For Deloria, the Be-In poster suggests the way the counterculture helped produce a postmodern culture of "pastiche" in which "meaning itself was often up for grabs," and the "world is like Strawberry Fields, a mystical, drug-hazy place where 'nothing is real.'"[29] Yet this reading assumes postmodern strategies of irony and random juxtaposition in countercultural visual culture (to say nothing of Beatles lyrics), which fails to see the stable and consistent set of meanings ascribed Indians and technology by the counterculture. Far from vague pastiche, this techno-primitivist discourse employed and updated long-standing primitivist narratives in Western culture, dating at least to Enlightenment visions of the noble savage, in which Native Americans and other so-called tribal people were seen as living in a harmonious, nonalienated, and more authentic state of nature. Now, paradoxically but not randomly, this countercultural vision of a "natural" tribal utopia included electric guitars, amplified rock music, and laboratory-synthesized drugs like LSD. It was an emancipatory primitivism fit for technological second nature, in which the human environment was more significantly structured by electricity, machines, and planned suburban subdivisions than the natural environment. The nihilism suggested by Deloria's reading of the counterculture as "postmodern" completely suppresses the counterculture's characteristic optimism about the world-changing possibilities of postindustrial technology.

The remarkable ability of the Indian and tribal to convey the counterculture's emancipatory cultural politics led to Indian-ness becoming a kind of visual and conceptual lingua franca for the counterculture. Writing that the baby boomers were "considered by many to be the reincarnation of the American Indians," the *Oracle* proclaimed that the Human Be-In was nothing less than a restoration of a wrongly conquered Native America.[30] Those gathered in the peaceful tribal "Pow-Wow," listening to Gary Snyder and rock music, were a "culture reincarnated" after centuries of genocide. Now reborn, these tribes had a specific epochal role: to prevent cold war nuclear catastrophe brought about in the new electronic age. In the words of a writer for the *Oracle,* the "'White-eye' who annihilated the buffalo must now . . . be 'saved' from slaughtering himself by the Indian incarnate" in the tribes of the counterculture.[31]

This sense of "inherited" generational responsibility was evident elsewhere in the counterculture and activist scene, perhaps most famously in Frank Bardacke's *People's Park Manifesto* (Figure 12.3). This leaflet, created "in the spirit of the Costanoan Indians" who are indigenous to Berkeley, equated the counterculture's struggle against the domination of public space by the University of California with the historic theft and land fraud that put the land in white hands in the first place. With its iconic photograph of the rifle-wielding Apache resistance fighter Geronimo as a background to the manifesto, it strongly connected the counterculture's antiproperty struggle for freedom with that of indigenous peoples' defense of their homelands. The shift to a more militaristic image of Native Americans suggests the way the early

WHO OWNS THE PARK?

Someday a petty official will appear with a piece of paper, called a land title, which states that the University of California owns the land of the People's Park. Where did that piece of paper come from? What is it worth?

A long time ago the Costanoan Indians lived in the area now called Berkeley. They had no concept of land ownership. They believed that the land was under the care and guardianship of the people who used it and lived on it.

Catholic missionaries took the land away from the Indians. No agreements were made. No papers were signed. They ripped it off in the name of God.

The Mexican Government took the land away from the Church. The Mexican Government had guns and an army. God's word was not as strong.

The Mexican Government wanted to pretend that it was not the army that guaranteed them the land. They drew up some papers which said they legally owned it. No Indians signed those papers.

The Americans were not fooled by the papers. They had a stronger army than the Mexicans. They beat them in a war and took the land. Then they wrote some papers of their own and forced the Mexicans to sign them.

The American Government sold the land to some white settlers. The Government gave the settlers a piece of paper called a land title in exchange for some money. All this time there were still some Indians around who claimed the land. The American army killed most of them.

The piece of paper saying who owned the land was passed around among rich white men. Sometimes the white men were interested in taking care of the land. Usually they were just interested in making money. Finally some very rich men, who run the University of California, bought the land.

Immediately these men destroyed the houses that had been built on the land. The land went the way of so much other land in America—it became a parking lot.

We are building a park on the land. We will take care of it and guard it, in the spirit of the Costanoan Indians. When the University comes with its land title we will tell them: "Your land title is covered with blood. We won't touch it. Your people ripped off the land from the Indians a long time ago. If you want it back now, you will have to fight for it again."

utopian techno-primitivism of the Be-In would become increasingly pulled into open conflict and political struggle in the last years of the 1960s and early 1970s.

As the contrast between Griffin's poster and Bardacke's leaflet shows, the Human Be-In's version of techno-primitivism was historically conditioned, born and articulated in the cultural and historical peculiarities of mid-1960s America. Its attempt to avoid conflict and emphasize peaceful universality put McLuhan's theory that "the spiritual form of information . . . [unites] the entire globe [with] a single

   THE COUNTERCULTURAL "INDIAN"

consciousness" into practice.[32] The stunning optimism of both McLuhan and the counterculture is an artifact of the economic prosperity, relative peacefulness, and sense of confidence that defined the United States in the early and mid-1960s.[33] The counterculture emerged in this context and sought to radicalize the rhetoric of postscarcity progress employed in the mainstream political and intellectual culture. As Braunstein and Doyle have noted, "the sustained peacetime boom . . . prompted expectations of an immanent postscarcity society . . . in which the need to work for a living might soon be . . . eliminated altogether." Within this coming "leisure society," they continue, "human pursuits . . . might be redirected to self-actualization involving the cultivation of each individual's creative talents." In 1964, Lyndon Johnson institutionalized these beliefs, proclaiming that "in the past we fought to eliminate scarcity. In the future we will also have to learn the wise use of abundance."[34]

With presidents and intellectuals predicting a future overflowing with milk and honey, the counterculture focused on accelerating the epochal shift. Braunstein and Doyle write that it seemed "easier to transcend capitalism than destroy it," using older left-wing models developed in a different economic context.[35] The counterculture's struggle became one of radicalizing the cultural practices of American society, creating social forms and modes of consciousness that could neutralize cold war militarism while speeding up the human liberation assumed in the postscarcity discourse of the period. For this reason, the cultural radicalism of the counterculture was defined by a politics of relationality, creating spaces—communal, musical, artistic—in which personal and small-scale collective liberation could be achieved. Employing an avant-garde rhetoric associated with modern countercultures since at least the nineteenth century, they conceived of such liberatory spaces as representing the forefront of history, ushering in the new epoch celebrated at the Human Be-In and dubbed the Aquarian Age in much of the discourse of the time.[36]

The emancipatory thrust of the counterculture's "tribe" distinguishes it from later postmodern inheritors of the politics of group encounter. Consider Hakim Bey's postmodern concept of "temporary autonomous zones," his counterculture-influenced politics of immanent, temporary liberation developed in the context of digital and Web technology. For Bey, much like the counterculture of the 1960s, political struggle must be based in concrete experiences of liberation, which he argues are available on a temporary, nomadic basis in various countercultural spaces at the margins of mainstream society. Combining discourses of politics and performance art, he writes that the "temporary autonomous zone," is a "guerilla operation which liberates an area (of land, of time, of imagination) and then dissolves itself to re-form elsewhere/elsewhen, *before* the State can crush it."[37] Contemporary counterculture-inspired events like the Burning Man Festival are examples of such a politics of the ephemeral, nomadic event or situation, and they obviously share much with the Be-In and its late 1960s offshoots. The crucial difference, however, is that the 1960s counterculture imagined its neotribal communalism as the beginning of a coming epochal emancipation, while later countercultures would define their tribalism in terms of a "guerrilla" freedom available only as a brief alternative to an otherwise repressive society.

Just as the optimism of the Be-In was a product of the postwar era, the countercultural appropriation of Indian-ness was a critical response to postwar visual culture. Helen Swick Perry, a researcher funded by the National Institute of Mental Health Research to study countercultural deviance, remarked on the importance of Indians to the self-image of Haight-Ashbury: "On almost any given day on Haight Street one could find the beautiful and colorful trappings of an Indian girl or brave; the other costumes . . . were much more difficult to identify." She suggested that the counterculture's identification with Indians was driven by the unique generational experience of the baby boomers. "I always felt the strong influence of the American Indian on the dress and thinking of the hippies was related to their first contact with the credibility gap in the values of American society . . . in the legends about the 'bad' American Indians," she wrote. Baby boomers had grown up immersed in the Wild West films and television programs of the 1940s, '50s, and '60s, in which Indians were typically the enemy of white protagonists. As children they had played "Indian," wearing costumes and acting out the violent cowboys-and-Indians dramas of popular culture. Yet as they grew older, television exposed them to increasing amounts of "news stories, more serious drama, and particularly . . . educational channels," Perry suggested, and through these they learned that American "legends" about "bad Indians" obscured the historical fact that white settlers were the "bad guys." This was, as Perry suggested, a powerful subversion of the triumphant rhetoric of cold war America, in which the nuclear-bomb-stockpiling "American way" was presented as a moral high ground in international geopolitics.[38]

The baby boomers' televisual consciousness raising led to the paradoxical embrace of Indian-ness by the 1960s counterculture.[39] While *Indians* could become a kind of shorthand for a new kind of cultural politics, as in the case of Griffin's poster, they also inevitably reinscribed the very structures of colonial domination that the counterculture wished to escape. This was not apparent to activists of the counterculture, whose utopian optimism precluded questions of the politics of race and indigenousness: the general assumption of an immanent universal human consciousness and emergent global village made fading structures of colonial domination moot. However, the dialectical structure and political ambivalence of the counterculture were clearly observed by 1960s Native American cultural leaders and are key to understanding the counterculture's implications. The Cree singer-songwriter and activist Buffy Sainte-Marie told the *Berkeley Barb* in July 1967 that the

counterculture's embrace of Indians was "the weirdest vampire idea."
It "has something to do with the idea that people are always trying to
identify with the race they've conquered. . . . they won't even let the
Indians have a soul," she said.[40] This vampire practice of cultural appropriation, then, was for Sainte-Marie a kind of "imperialist nostalgia" in
which, according to Renato Rosaldo, settlers "mourn the passing of what
they themselves have transformed."[41] While perhaps a bit sweeping,
Sainte-Marie's assessment is not inaccurate. It rightfully points out the
almost painful naïveté of the overwhelmingly white and middle-class
counterculture, most of them products of racially segregated suburbs in
which encounters with different cultures and races were primarily sec-
ondhand. While older leaders of the counterculture, most notably Gary
Snyder, had studied and spent time with indigenous nations and other
cultures in both North America and Asia, most of the youth on the
Haight or in Berkeley had learned about Native people through the lens
of the camera or through white-authored popular books and magazines.
Indeed, Sainte-Marie's assertion that the counterculture would not "let
Indians have a soul" was almost literally found in the *Oracle*'s review
of the Be-In, which presented Native Americans as a vanished people
whose souls were "reincarnated" as the white baby boomers.[42]

Other Native leaders overlooked the naive rhetoric of the counterculture and emphasized its capacity for positive social transformation.
Vine Deloria Jr., the leading intellectual of the 1960s and 1970s Native
rights movement, emphasized this radical substance, which he believed
was capable of building a "new cosmopolitan society." Like many in the
period, Deloria approached the Be-In and the counterculture through
McLuhan's theory of retribalization. He wrote that "the be-in and rock
festival have become the important events of our time," constituting
"a whole new way of adjusting to the technology which dominates life."
For Deloria, this electronic retribalization was a positive step toward
Native empowerment: "Indian people are just as subject to the deluge
of information as are other people," and contrary to "vanishing Indian"
stereotypes, "[Indians] are best able to cope with the modern situation"
because electronic communication has again "become oral and experiential" in the fashion of Native tradition. For Native people, in short,
this new era of electronic information would reinforce the existing tribal
structures of Native communities, while eliminating the state-based
structure of domination imposed on Native people. The counterculture's
Be-Ins, rock music, and communes were, in Deloria's analysis, part of
the transition to a new historical epoch of tribal "sovereign groups" that
would empower Native Americans, a view no less grand and utopian
than the counterculture's own techno-primitivist prognostications.[43]

Considered together, Sainte-Marie and Deloria point out the
simultaneously reactionary and progressive aspects of the techno-
primitivism expressed in Griffin's poster and the Human Be-In structure. Although this dialectic of tribal radicalism arose in the context

of the postwar boom, it was not confined to the first phase of the counterculture. It had compelling power to envision the emancipatory potential that resided in the transition to an information economy and thus mutated so as to fit the needs of various future-oriented forms of cultural radicalism in later years. It found an apotheosis in Gene Youngblood's landmark book on 1960s "expanded cinema," which christened this emancipated epoch the Paleocybernetic Age. Combining the counterculture's techno-primitivism with the "intermedia" art and technology experiments of the 1960s, Youngblood argued that 1960s humans had transcended the industrial age and suddenly found themselves with the unlimited possibilities of a technological "second nature." He prophesied: "So I call it the Paleocybernetic Age: an image of a hairy, buckskinned, barefooted atomic physicist with a brain full of mescaline and logarithms. . . . [It is] the dawn of man: for the first time in history we'll soon be free enough to discover who we are."[44] This paradoxical combination of the signifiers of high technology and the primitive—with a residual Indian coding ("buckskinned" and "mescaline," the psychedelic drug synthesized from peyote and associated with the religions of Native America)—also was systematically deployed in the later guerrilla manifestations of the rave underground, one of the postmodern inheritors of the counterculture's politics of the tribe.[45] Yet as Native Americans became visible contemporary political agents in the early 1970s, the ability of white-appropriated Indian-ness to stand in for radical politics diminished, with a much more open-ended tribalism and discourse of the primitive structuring later undergrounds.

Forty years hence, the counterculture's synthesis of the Indian and the electric guitar to visualize an age of total freedom is an artifact of a bygone era. The hermeneutics of cultural radicalism have moved on. Today, electronic age technology is thought of as a "normal" way of reinforcing existing social or business networks, rather than a means of building fundamentally new social structures. Rock music—now a cultural source for political campaign songs and corporate advertising—has no utopian imagination and certainly no longer symbolizes progress or high technology. Native Americans have gained increasing amounts of political and economic power as players in contemporary society, and the decline of Wild West visual culture has diminished our ability to appreciate the power of Indian symbolism in the 1960s. Moreover, Marshall McLuhan is less a cutting-edge utopian thinker than an old ideologue of information capitalism, symbolized by *Wired* magazine's adoption of McLuhan as a "patron saint." Yet faint echoes of the period's emancipatory techno-primitivism persist today, in the guerrilla spaces of contemporary undergrounds, where new technologies, art, music, and neotribalism—as well as psychedelic drugs—may offer a fleeting glimpse of a radically redeemed future. Yet, even in the underground, few mistake this hopeful vision for a "new and better age that has already begun."

NOTES

1. Tom Law, "The Community of the Tribe," *The San Francisco Oracle: Facsimile Edition*, ed. Allen Cohen (Berkeley, Calif.: Regent Press, 1991), 129.

2. For a discussion of the counterculture in relation to American identity, see Phil Deloria, *Playing Indian* (New Haven, Conn.: Yale University Press, 1998), 154–80. For an example of the tribe outside the United States, see the Japanese countercultural group Buzoku (the Tribe) of which Gary Snyder, Nanao Sakaki, and other poets were a part. Buzoku is discussed in *Gary Snyder: Dimensions of a Life*, ed. Jon Halper (San Francisco: Sierra Club Books, 1991).

3. See Marshall McLuhan, *The Gutenberg Galaxy: The Making of Typographic Man* (Toronto: University of Toronto Press, 1962); and *Understanding Media: The Extensions of Man*, critical ed. (Corte Madera, Calif.: Ginkgo Press, 2003). Originally published in 1964.

4. Theodore Roszak, *The Making of a Counter Culture: Reflections on the Technocratic Society and Its Youthful Opposition* (Garden City, N.Y.: Doubleday, 1969).

5. The event spawned both a second Human Be-In in New York's Central Park two months later, as well as innumerable spontaneous Human Be-Ins around the United States and Europe over the next several years. The events spread an ideology of love and face-to-face community (the tribe) that became synonymous with the counterculture's politics.

6. Neville Powis, "The Human Be-in and the Hippy Revolution," *Radio Netherlands Worldwide*, 22 January 2003.

7. Allen Cohen, "The Gathering of the Tribes," in *San Francisco Oracle: Facsimile Edition*, 90. (Quoted passages that appear in the next four sentences of the text also come from this source.) The famous distinction between the San Francisco counterculture and the Berkeley activists was already part of the discourse of the Be-In. In part, the Be-In sought to unite these two groups and their different tactics of dissent, hence the "union of love and activism" mentioned in announcements for the event.

8. Steve Levine, "A Gathering of the Tribes: The First American Mehla: A Baptism," *San Francisco Oracle: Facsimile Edition*, 123.

9. Ibid.

10. Roszak, *Making of a Counter Culture*, 54. Note that *Pow-Wow* and *Gathering of the Tribes* were parts of the official name of the Be-In, not Griffin's invention.

11. I have been unable to locate this photograph, but Gary Snyder recalled the change Griffin made for the Be-In poster. See Gary Snyder, quoted in Timothy Gray, *Gary Snyder and the Pacific Rim: Creating Countercultural Community* (Iowa City: University of Iowa Press, 2006), 230.

12. Peter Braunstein and Michael William Doyle, "Introduction: Historicizing the American Counterculture of the 1960s and '70s," in *Imagine Nation: The American Counterculture of the 1960s and '70s*, ed. Braunstein and Doyle (New York: Routledge, 2002), 11.

13. Gray, *Gary Snyder and the Pacific Rim*, 229.

14. Julie Stephens has shown a similar relationship between the counterculture's embrace of India and its "personalization of politics" in which "'you' were the revolution." In contrast, Native America typically symbolized the collective or tribal dimension of countercultural politics. See Stephens, *Anti-Disciplinary Protest: Sixties Radicalism and Postmodernism* (Cambridge: Cambridge University Press, 1998), 48–72.

15. Braunstein and Doyle, "Introduction," 11.

16. A. J. Miller, *The Electric Guitar: A History of an American Icon* (Baltimore: Johns Hopkins University Press, 2004), 5, 6.

17. Quoted in ibid.

18. Gordon McLelland, *Rick Griffin* (San Francisco: Last Gasp, 2002), 6.

19. Roy Shuker writes that "surf music was the most guitar-oriented style of early rock'n'roll." See Shuker, *Popular Music: The Key Concepts* (New York: Routledge, 2005), 262.

20. Law, "Community of the Tribe," 129.

21. Snyder, quoted in Mitchell Goodman, *The Movement Toward a New America: The Beginning of a Long Revolution* (Philadelphia: Pilgrim Press, 1970), 662.

22. As Snyder implies, the concept of "the tribe" as a paradigm of countercultural cultural radicalism extended beyond the borders of North America during the 1960s. See note 2 above, regarding Buzoko, a Japanese countercultural community devoted to anticapitalist and pacifist principles similar to those in the American West Coast counterculture.

23. See Deloria, *Playing Indian*.

24. McLuhan, *Gutenberg Galaxy* and *Understanding Media*; Fred Turner, *From Counterculture to Cyberculture: Stewart Brand, the Whole Earth Network, and the Rise of Digital Utopianism* (Chicago: University of Chicago Press, 2006).

25. Tom Wolfe mentions this festival in his 1965 essay "What If He's Right?," which addresses McLuhan's theory and celebrity. The essay, originally published in the *New York Herald Tribune*, is collected in Wolfe's essays on the counterculture, *The Pump House Gang* (New York: Bantam, 1968).

26. Chester Anderson, "Notes for the New Geology," in *The San Francisco Oracle: Facsimile Edition*, 116, 136–37. The rest of the quoted material in this paragraph comes from this source.

27. McLuhan, *Gutenberg Galaxy*, 125. Further page references to this source appear parenthetically in the text.

28. In a 1969 interview with *Playboy* magazine, McLuhan emphasized that the counterculture was produced by electronic media. He asserted that "print gave man private habits and a public role of absolute conformity. That is why the young today welcome their retribalization . . . as a release from the uniformity, alienation, and dehumanization of literate society. . . . electric media brings man together in a tribal village that is a rich and creative mix, where there is actually more room for creative diversity than within the homogenized mass urban society of Western man." Reprinted in *Essential McLuhan*, ed. Eric McLuhan and Frank Zingrone (Toronto: House of Anansi, 1995), 259–60.

29. Deloria, *Playing Indian*, 156–66.

30. Levine, "A Gathering of the Tribes," 123. The *reincarnated Indian* counterculture seems to have been one of the stock phrases of this period. Recently, guitarist Carlos Santana has remembered that "the hippies I hung out with . . . represented the highest good for people on the planet—not for blacks, or whites, but for the whole thing. The real hippies, I feel, are like reincarnated American Indians that we call Rainbow Warriors." See Dann Dulin, "Rainbow Warriors," *Arts and Understanding: America's AIDS Magazine* (May 2004), aumag.org/coverstory/May04cover.html. Accessed June 2011.

31. Levine, "A Gathering of the Tribes," 123.

32. McLuhan, *Understanding Media*, 90.

33. Canada, McLuhan's place of birth, experienced a comparable economic boom after the war.

34. Braunstein and Doyle, "Introduction," 11.

35. Ibid., 12.

36. For example, the first theme issue of the *Oracle* was on "The Aquarian Age" and ran in February 1967.

37. Hakim Bey, *T.A.Z.: The Temporary Autonomous Zone, Ontological Anarchy, Poetic Terrorism* (New York: Autonomedia, 1991), 101.

38. Helen Swick Perry, *The Human Be-In* (New York: Allen Lane-Penguin Press, 1970), 50.

39. Television and cinema Westerns also fostered the gunslinger and outlaw poses of many musicians and others during the period. While they did not occupy the central role of the Indian, these visual culture–based identities helped express the new personal-

ized politics at stake in countercultural aesthetics and lifestyles.

40. Buffy Sainte-Marie, quoted in Timothy Gray, *Gary Snyder and the Pacific Rim,* 235.

41. Renato Rosaldo, "Imperialist Nostalgia," *Representations* 26 (Spring 1989): 107.

42. Levine, "A Gathering of the Tribes," 123.

43. Vine Deloria Jr., *We Talk, You Listen: New Tribes, New Turf* (New York: MacMillian, 1970), 31.

44. Gene Youngblood, *Expanded Cinema* (New York: Dutton, 1970), 41.

45. See, for example, Gina Andrea Fatone, "*Gamelan,* Techno-Primitivism, and the San Francisco Rave Scene," in *Rave Culture and Religion,* ed. Graham St. John (London: Routledge, 2004), 197–210.

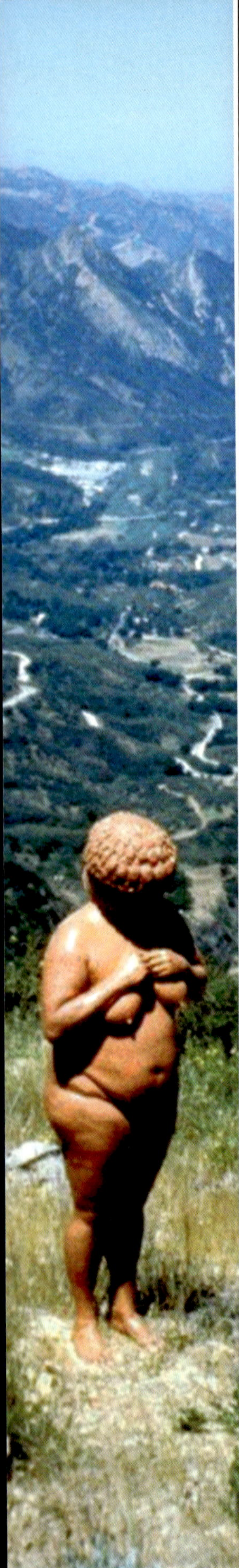

CHAPTER 13
GODDESS: FEMINIST ART AND SPIRITUALITY IN THE 1970S

Jennie Klein

In 1977, Mary Beth Edelson, an artist and feminist activist, set out with her traveling companion, Anne Healy, to visit the Neolithic Goddess Cave on Grapceva in Hvar Island, part of the former Yugoslavia. Edelson was armed with the archeological maps in Marija Gimbutas's *The Gods and Goddesses of Old Europe, 7000–3500 BC: Myths, Legends, and Cult Images* as a reference source. Edelson managed to find an elderly tourist guide in the nearby town of Jelsa, who arranged for his son to take them up the mountain to the Neolithic site. The following day, carrying two Yugoslav flashlights and a number of candles, Edelson returned to the cave, where she engaged in a ritual designed to connect her to the power and female energy of the Neolithic Goddess worshippers. In an article about the experience that she later published in the Great Goddess issue of the journal *Heresies,* Edelson documented both her journey and the indescribable feelings that she encountered while practicing her rituals in such an ancient and sacred setting: "I felt one long hand extending across time, sending a jolt of energy into my body. I began my rituals—the energy from the rituals seemed to pulsate from the vaulted ceiling to me and back again."[1] The photo documentation of Edelson's ritual, enacted with no artificial light other than the candles that Edelson had brought with them, show a nude figure that seems to glow from a spiritual fire that burns from within, seated in the midst of a fire circle (Figure 13.1). At the uppermost edge of the photograph the ceiling of the cave is just visible, as though the ritual took place in a womb-like structure.

Edelson's journey to Grapceva cave was taken long before Goddess tourism had turned into a thriving capitalist enterprise complete with tour guides, cruise ships, and well-marked, easy-to-locate archaeological sites.[2] In order to journey to Grapceva, Edelson had unsuccessfully applied for a number of grants. She finally sold her car in order to finance her pilgrimage/performance/artwork. When she went to the Balkans, Edelson had been doing ritualistic performances such as *See for Yourself* at various sites in the United States, particularly in Los Angeles and New York, where cultural feminism was strongest. Deeply committed to feminist spirituality and radical leftist politics, Edelson viewed her embrace of feminist spirituality—albeit a feminist spirituality that was grounded in an overarching, universal worldview—as a catalyst for her political activism.

Unlike other gender radical movements such as gay rights or even radical feminism, feminist spirituality has always remained on the margins of mainstream culture and academic acceptability. To this day, the nature Goddess/witch figure is depicted as monstrous, abject, and horrific. In this paper, I return to feminist artwork that references the Goddess in order to answer the following questions. First, what is feminist spirituality? Second, why was feminist spirituality so appealing to artists, particularly artists based on the West Coast? Third, what is the relationship between feminist spirituality and the counterculture movements? Fourth, why has feminist art that references spirituality and/

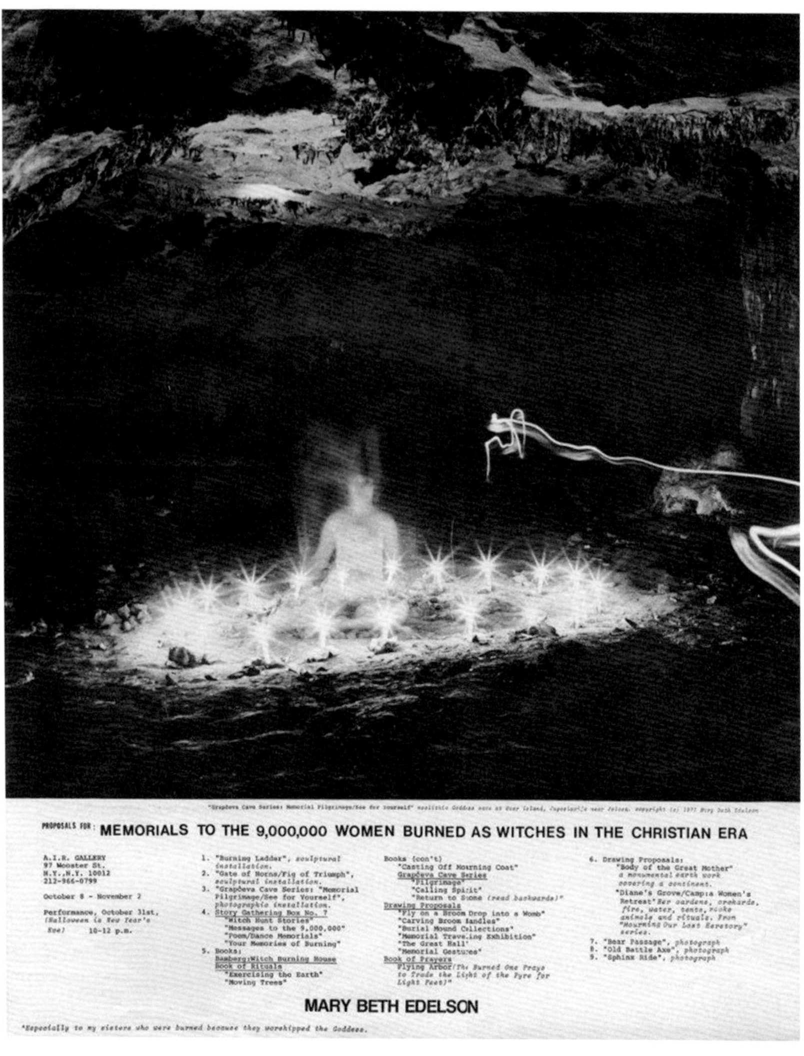

PROPOSALS FOR: **MEMORIALS TO THE 9,000,000 WOMEN BURNED AS WITCHES IN THE CHRISTIAN ERA**

A.I.R. GALLERY
97 Wooster St.
N.Y.,N.Y. 10012
212-966-0799

October 8 - November 2

Performance, October 31st,
(Halloween is New Year's
Eve)   10-12 p.m.

1. "Burning Ladder", *sculptural installation.*
2. "Gate of Horns/Fig of Triumph", *sculptural installation.*
3. "Grapčeva Cave Series: "Memorial Pilgrimage/See for Yourself", *photographic installation.*
4. Story Gathering Box No. 7
   "Witch Hunt Stories"
   "Messages to the 9,000,000"
   "Poem/Dance Memorials"
   "Your Memories of Burning"
5. Books:
   Bamberg:Witch Burning House
   Book of Rituals
   "Exercising the Earth"
   "Moving Trees"

Books (con't)
   "Casting Off Mourning Coat"
   Grapčeva Cave Series
   "Pilgrimage"
   "Calling Spirit"
   "Return to Stone (read backwards)"
Drawing Proposals
   "Fly on a Broom Drop into a Womb"
   "Carving Broom Handles"
   "Burial Mound Collections"
   "Memorial Traveling Exhibition"
   "The Great Hall"
   "Memorial Gestures"
Book of Prayers
   Flying Arbor/The Burned One Prays
   to Trade the Light of the Pyre for
   Light Feet)"

6. Drawing Proposals:
   "Body of the Great Mother"
   a monumental earth work
   covering a continent.
   "Diane's Grove/Camp:a Women's
   Retreat" Her gardens, orchards,
   fire, water, tents, smoke
   animals and rituals. From
   "Mourning Our Lost Herstory"
   series.
7. "Bear Passage", *photograph*
8. "Old Battle Axe", *photograph*
9. "Sphinx Ride", *photograph*

MARY BETH EDELSON

Especially to my sisters who were burned because they worshipped the Goddess.

or the Goddess continued to be marginalized in discussions of that art, even by scholars who are very sympathetic to the artwork?

When I first began researching this topic, it struck me that a lacuna existed in this particular area of feminist art scholarship. Much of the feminist artwork made in the mid-1970s to late 1980s was informed by cultural feminism, which emphasized feminist separatism, the value of female connections, and feminist spirituality/embrace of the Goddess. Sympathetic art critics such as Lucy R. Lippard, Gloria Orenstein, and Arlene Raven readily acknowledged this influence on feminist art, documenting it in their published criticism.[3] Even though there was a renewed critical interest in the mid- to late '90s in this artwork, documented in important exhibitions such as *Sexual Politics* curated by Amelia Jones in 1996, there has been very little mention of the role played by feminist spirituality and belief in the Goddess for these artists. Nor has feminist spirituality been addressed in any systematic manner today, in spite of a recently published biography on Judy Chicago, a number of panels and events celebrating the thirtieth anniversary of the founding of the Woman's Building, and two major exhibitions of feminist art in 2007, *Wack! Art of the Feminist Revolution* (Los Angeles) and *Global Feminisms: New Directions in Feminist Art* (New York).[4] Feminist art historians and critics have shied away from mentioning the invocation of feminist spirituality and the Goddess in this art, preferring instead to engage it in terms of contemporary theory, such as the use and meaning of the body, the performative articulation of identities, and its relationship to contemporary feminist activist art. For feminist critics writing sympathetically about '70s feminist art in the postmodern '90s the Goddess—and the counterculture's liberation of the self and body in the name of an alternative politic—was the unacknowledged white elephant in the room of the feminist body of art. I propose to revisit feminist theology as it was constructed and articulated at the time, in order to understand what it meant to feminist artists in the '70s and what it might mean to artists and critics working today.

ARTISTS AND CULTURAL FEMINISM

In the early to late '70s, cultural feminism, with its emphasis on feminist spiritualities including Goddess worship, was in its ascendancy. In 1973, Mary Daly published *Beyond God the Father,* which called for the complete disavowal of all patriarchal systems, including religious systems, and the creation of a cosmic covenant of sisterhood through the raising of female consciousness.[5] *Beyond God the Father* was quickly joined by a number of nonacademic publications on feminist spirituality, ecofeminism, and the Goddess such as Merlin Stone, *When God Was a Woman,* Adrienne Rich, *Of Woman Born,* Susan Griffin, *Woman and Nature: The Roaring Inside Her,* and Daly's follow-up to *Beyond God, Gyn/Ecology: The Metaethics of Radical Feminism.*[6] It did not take long for feminist artists on both the East and West Coasts to embrace the philosophical and cultural approach of the writers listed above and to in turn engage in a practice that engendered more debate.

Women's spirituality was very appealing to visual artists for several reasons. First, "proof" of the existence of ancient matrifocal cultures existed in the form of small, anthropomorphic sculptures, ephemeral cave paintings, and monumental stone structures from the prehistoric era that appeared to be female and that cultural feminists assumed were priestesses and Goddess figures, giving many artists an already existing bank of nonpatriarchal images to tap into. Betsy Damon's *The 7,000 Year Old Woman* (1977) referenced the many-breasted Diana of Ephesus, associated with a Neolithic Goddess site in Turkey where she had lived as a child. Covered in small bags of colored flour that she ritualistically punctured in a public ceremony on Wall Street, Damon eventually formed a spiral/labyrinthine pattern on the ground (Figure 13.2). Damon based *The 7,000 Year Old Woman* on a dream that she had had years before. She resolved to realize the images in her dream. Cheri

GODDESS

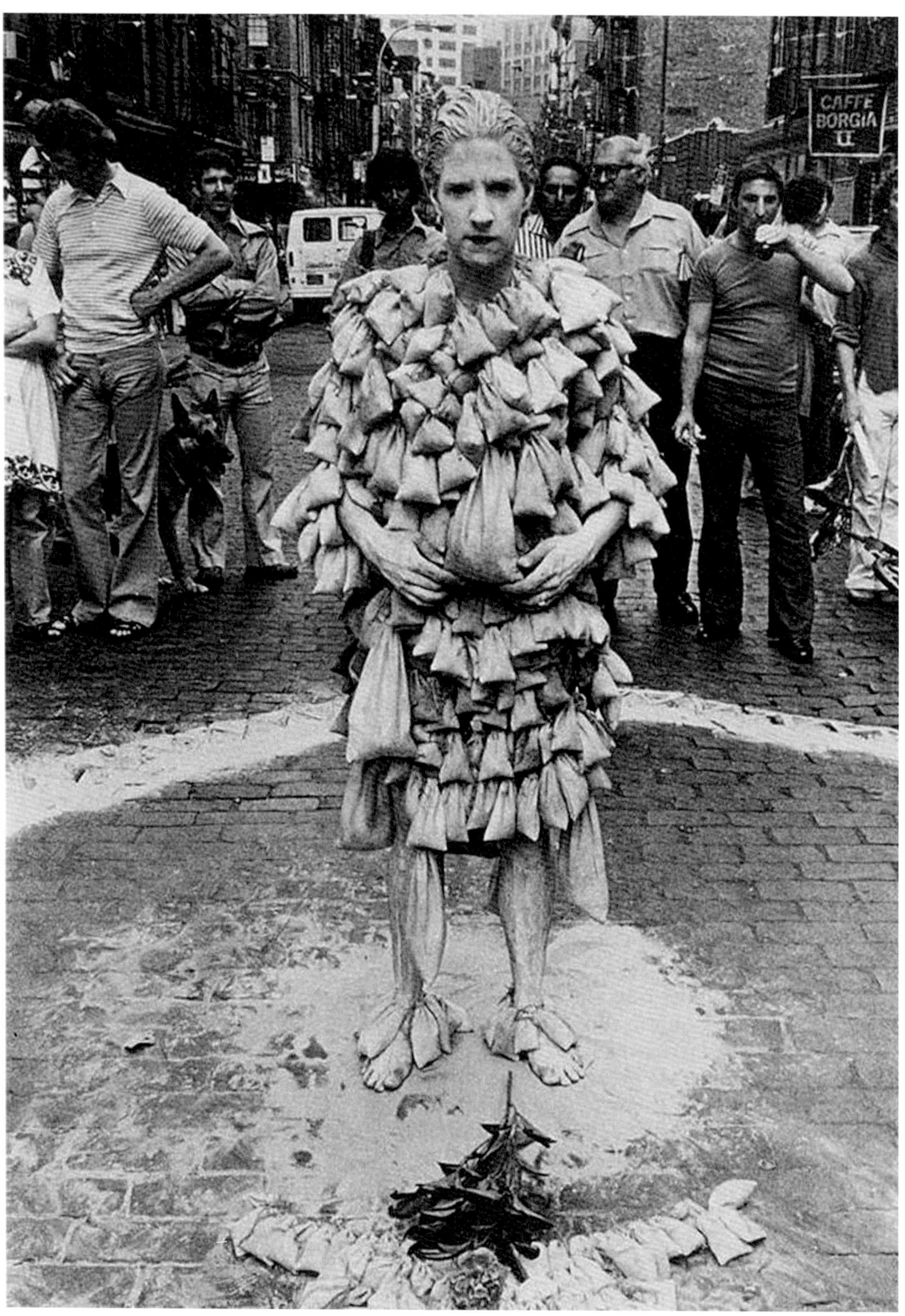

Gaulke employed a video image of the Woman from Willendorf for her 1985 performance *Revelations of the Flesh* at Wilshire United Methodist Church in Los Angeles (Figure 13.3). Second, the belief in immanence, or the recognition of the divine in all life forms associated with the feminist spirituality movement, meant that nature and the body were honored. Ana Mendieta connected nature and the female body in her *Serie Arbol de la Vida* (1976), an earth-body work in which a mud-covered Mendieta pressed her body against a tree. Many artists used nudity to suggest divinity, as did Gaulke in *This Is My Body,* a performance done to counter the patriarchal suppression of women's spirituality.

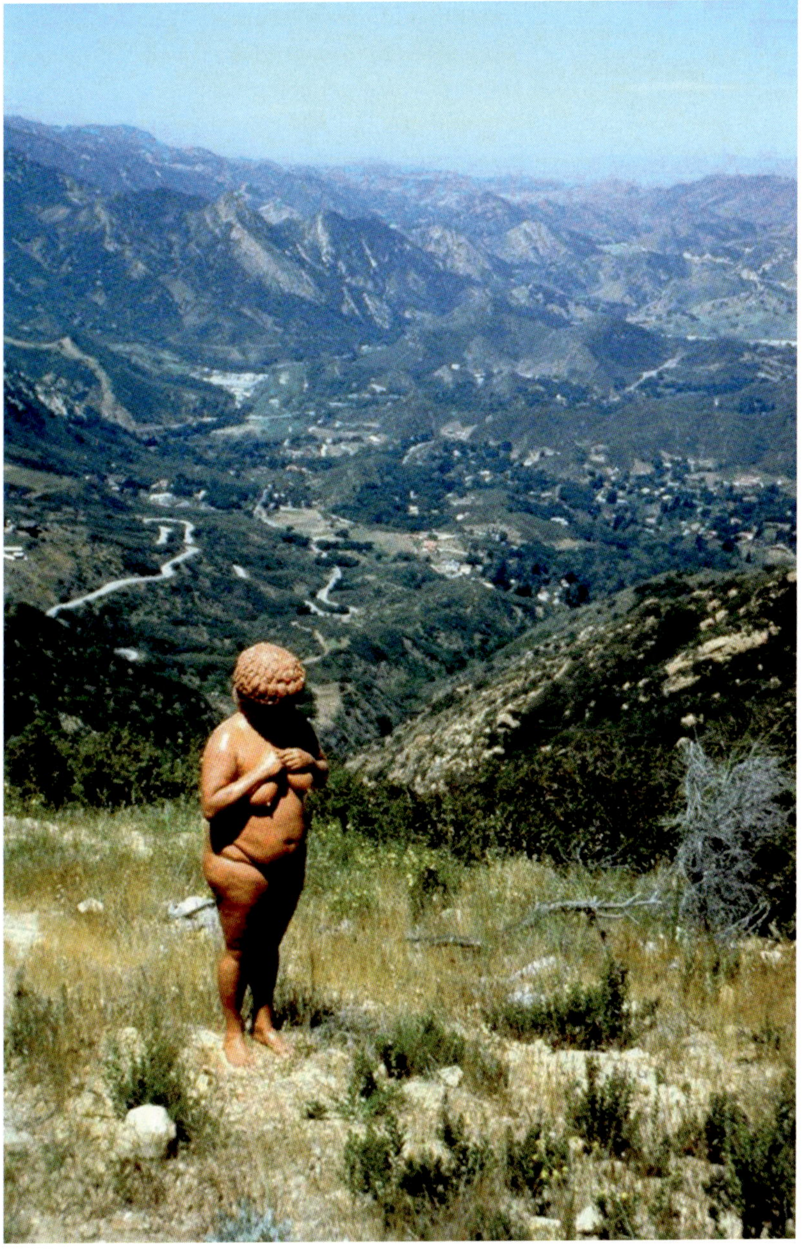

GODDESS

Third, cultural feminists, with their embrace of ritual and performance, were particularly appealing to feminist artists such as Edelson who were interested in reconfiguring avant-garde performance so that it had meaning and significance beyond the narrow concerns of the avant-garde art world. Edelson's ritualistic treatment of ordinary life had much in common with Allan Kaprow's dissolution of the line between art and life in his Happenings. But unlike Kaprow's events, Edelson's rituals were meant to be personal and sacred. Of the early rituals that she did with her children, Edelson has written, "I was trying to tie them to the Earth, to help them feel in a direct way that nature is not outside, but a part of them. We merged—mother, child, and nature—becoming one again for a moment."[7] Barbara T. Smith, performing as a living sculpture in *Feed Me* (1973), also viewed herself as a temple priestess, asking visitors, who entered her space one at a time, to "feed" her in some way (Figure 13.4). In 1979, Donna Henes made process environmental sculptures that looked like macramé webs based on Spider Woman from the Navajo Emergence Myth.

Although performers influenced by cultural feminism worked on both coasts, Southern California was the mecca for artists interested in feminist spirituality and/or the Goddess, which was loosely interpreted to include just about everything that wasn't patriarchal. As Jenni Sorkin puts it, Los Angeles in the '70s was "a beacon of the counterculture set in the shadows of Hollywood" that "witnessed the sexual revolution, the birth of the aerospace industry, bodybuilding, roller-skating, surfing, and vegetarianism, as well as a myriad of alternative religion, lifestyle, and spiritual practices."[8] The anything-goes attitude of the hippie culture in Southern California was much more conducive to the development of an alternative feminist spirituality than the considerably more regimented East Coast culture of New York City. The art scene in Los Angeles was newer and less established than the scene in New York. It was considerably less organized, making it possible for a geographically diverse group of artists to come together as a community based on affinity rather than address. Los Angeles also had three things that New York did not: the archaeologist Marija Gimbutas, the Woman's Building, and *Chrysalis: A Magazine of Women's Culture*.

MARIJA GIMBUTAS

The "high priestess" of the women's spirituality movement in Southern California was not a theologian, an artist, a philosopher, or a psychologist. In fact, for most of her career, Marija Gimbutas was best known as a Bronze Age archaeologist. The 1974 publication of her book *The Gods and Goddesses of Old Europe* (reissued in 1982 as *The Goddesses and Gods of Old Europe*) changed all that.[9] *Gods and Goddesses of Old Europe* was based on her experiences as the director of several major Neolithic excavations in Eastern Europe after she had taken a faculty position at the University of California, Los Angeles (UCLA). Along with other

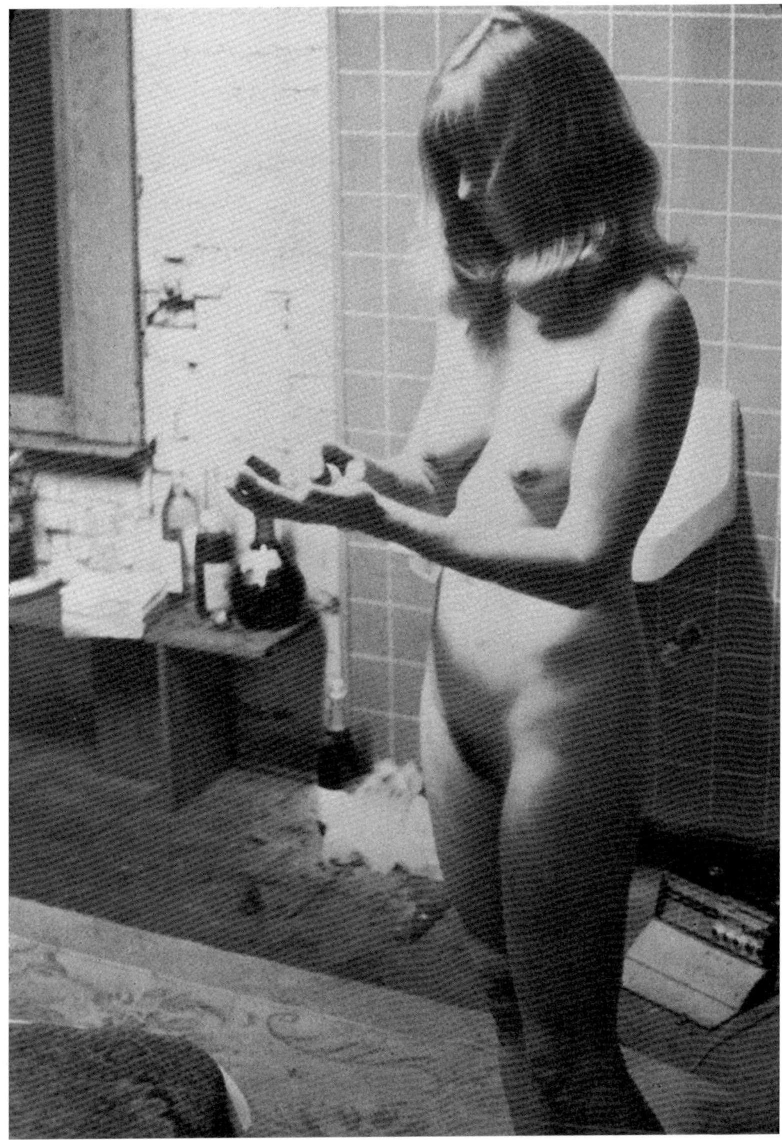

archaeologists who were trained in the first part of the twentieth century such as James Mellaart (best known for excavating Çatal Hüyük), Gimbutas turned to Greek and Roman mythology, which she believed contained the vestiges of the beliefs of the Neolithic past. The Goddess society that Gimbutas reconstructed—based on her belief that all the Neolithic figurines were female and most structures were temples—was extrapolated from her extensive knowledge of Eastern European folklore and religious beliefs. Gimbutas, who invented a methodology that she called archaeomythology, believed that the remnants of this ancient civilization continued to exist—albeit in a very different form—in Eastern European folklore. Goddesses such as Athena or Artemis, for example, were carried over from Old European beliefs and incorporated into Indo-European mythology.

GODDESS

Gimbutas's myth-inflected theories, based on visual rather than historical evidence and deeply imbued with a Eurocentric point of view, found little support among her archaeological colleagues, who were deeply suspicious of her big-picture generalizations regarding religion, myth, and prehistoric cultures.[10] Support for Gimbutas's theories came not from her colleagues but from feminists who were intrigued by the idea that a matriarchy might have existed in prehistoric Europe. Carol Christ has observed that had Gimbutas published *Gods and Goddesses of Old Europe* twenty years earlier it probably would have been ignored.[11] *Gods and Goddesses of Old Europe* was published one year after Daly's *Beyond God the Father* and the same year that *WomanSpirit* magazine was launched. It was quickly followed by Merlin Stone's *When God Was a Woman,* which also looked to Paleolithic and Neolithic artifacts for proof of an ancient, Goddess-centered culture. Stone was an artist and art historian, and not an archaeologist. It was Gimbutas who gave Goddess civilization legitimacy. Her ideas about the peaceful and artistic Neolithic culture were eagerly received by artists, writers, linguists, and anthropologists. Gimbutas, who went on to publish *The Language of the Goddess* and *The Civilization of the Goddess,* responded graciously to this new audience, taking time to give lectures and interviews to artists, writers, and filmmakers interested in Goddess civilization.[12] She became a hagiographic figure for these women, who wrote essays and poems about her and made a documentary of her life.

THE LOS ANGELES WOMAN'S BUILDING (1973-1991)

It was more than a serendipitous coincidence that the city in which Gimbutas taught and lectured for the latter part of her academic career was also the home of the Woman's Building, the only institution in the United States dedicated to providing a feminist art education. The Los Angeles Woman's Building, which opened on November 28, 1973, was founded by Judy Chicago, Arlene Raven, and Sheila Levrant de Bretteville. The Woman's Building housed bookstores, art galleries, a thrift store, and the Feminist Studio Workshop (FSW), the first ever art school devoted to a feminist education.[13] By 1981, the FSW was dissolved, and the administrators of the building, composed of women who had begun their career at the building as students, turned their attention to promoting cultural events and activities, broadening the constituency to include minorities, working women, and single mothers. In 1991, just three years before Gimbutas lost her battle with cancer, the building finally closed.

Feminist/Goddess spirituality was extremely important at the Woman's Building, at least during its first decade. During its heyday, the Woman's Building hosted two major conferences concerned with feminist spirituality, Public and Private Rituals: Women in Performance Art (1975) and Lady Fingers/Mother Earth (1975). The curriculum of the FWS, modeled on Chicago's earlier experiments with the Feminist Art

Project at Fresno State and CalArts, was geared toward an exploration of female identity, corporeality, and spirituality. Consciousness raising, in which women gathered in groups in order to speak collectively about their experience of oppression, along with collaboration and construction work, was the linchpin of the educational program.[14] One theme that came up frequently in the consciousness-raising sessions was the pervasiveness of violence and sexual exploitation experienced by the young women students in the FSW. Feminist/Goddess spirituality, with its emphasis on the sacredness and beauty of the female body, was taught as one way of countering the unrelenting misogyny experienced by faculty and students alike. Arlene Raven, for example, had changed her last name after her first encounter with Judy Chicago, who urged her to re-create herself after the devastating experience of being raped.[15] Along with Terry Wolverton, Raven later proposed a radical lesbian pedagogical practice: the Sapphic Model of Education. Based on the community and school of Sappho on the island of Myteline, the Sapphic Model of Education stressed a seasonal approach to learning and knowledge with spring as the season for bursting forth. The Sapphic Model of Education, which was never realized, proposed to resurrect a community much like that described by Gimbutas. According to Wolverton, "education included living within a community of women, having love affairs, worshipping the Goddess, developing creativity and self-awareness, and celebrating the seasons."[16] Edelson did her first public ritual performance *Mourning Our Lost Herstory* for the Mandeville Gallery at University of California, San Diego in 1977 using students from the FSW whom Raven had brought with her. Raven has also curated Edelson's exhibition *Your 5,000 Years Are Up* for the gallery.[17]

CHRYSALIS: A MAGAZINE OF WOMEN'S CULTURE

Probably the most important contribution made by the Woman's Building to feminist spirituality was *Chrysalis: A Magazine of Women's Culture* (1977–1980), whose readership numbered thirteen thousand at its high point. Funded by reader contributions and a small grant from Adrienne Rich that came from the proceeds of her book *Of Woman Born* (a history of motherhood that begins in the Neolithic Goddess worshipping period), the editorial staff managed to produce ten issues before being forced to cease publication due to lack of funds. *Chrysalis* appeared at around the same time as a number of other important feminist periodicals including *Signs* (1975), *Frontiers* (1975), *Heresies* (1977), *Feminist Studies* (1972), and *Woman's Art Journal* (1980). From the beginning, *Chrysalis* was devoted to all aspects of women's culture, particularly the intersection of feminist spirituality and the visual arts. The list of contributing editors reads like a who's who in feminist spirituality and feminist art criticism. The five-member editorial board that founded the magazine included Raven, Ruth Iskin (the editor of the important but brief *Womanspace Journal*), and Levrant de Bretteville.[18] Managing editor

Kirstin Grimstad had previously traveled around the United States interviewing women in alternative communities about their beliefs in spirituality.[19] Audre Lorde served as the poetry editor for the first seven issues. Contributing editors included Judy Chicago, Mary Daly, Carol Duncan, Susan Griffin, Lucy Lippard, Linda Nochlin, Deena Metzger, Gloria Orenstein, Adrienne Rich, and Michelle Wallace.

During its two-year run *Chrysalis* confirmed its commitment to cultural feminist values and writers by publishing material that supported an alternative feminist spirituality that by and large was organized around a Goddess or Goddesses. Every one of the ten issues included an article, poem, or original work of art that embraced feminist spirituality or the Goddess in a positive light, and issue 6 included a resource catalog on women's spirituality compiled by Linda Palumbo, Maurine Renville, Terry Wolverton, and Charlene Spretnak.[20] Excerpts from books by key players in the feminist spirituality movement such as Lucy Lippard, Mary Daly, and Adrienne Rich appeared in *Chrysalis* prior to publication.[21] Of these writers, only Daly was an academic. The other two writers were primarily critics, novelists, and poets. Lucy Lippard, like Arlene Raven, was an art critic who was sympathetic to feminism and feminist spirituality. The editorial staff at *Chrysalis* continued their support for these authors after their books were published by commissioning extended—and extremely sympathetic—reviews. In issue 7, for example, Susan Griffin and Mary Daly sympathetically reviewed their respective new books, *Gyn/Ecology: The Metaethics of Radical Feminism* (Griffin on Daly) and *Woman and Nature: The Roaring Inside Her* (Daly on Griffin).[22]

Chrysalis has undeservedly been characterized as a cultural—as opposed to socialist—feminist magazine, with the implication that its approach was apolitical.[23] In fact, the articles in *Chrysalis* addressed topical issues such as the media representation of women, sexual abuse of children, incest, rape, pornography, fashion, psychology, the idea of a feminist (rather than a feminine) aesthetic, and feminist films. The editors and writers gave advice and shared resources about publishing, finances, and the nascent computer technology. The editors tried to include a multitude of voices and viewpoints: rather than devoting a special issue of the magazine to topics such as feminist spirituality, Third World women, or lesbianism as did *Heresies,* every issue of *Chrysalis* included articles, stories, poems, and artwork by and about marginalized voices and topics. Their efforts did not satisfy all their readers, however: the editorial pages of the second issue included a letter from Patricia Jones, who opined: "I as a Black Woman am quite annoyed that there was only one text by a Black woman in the magazine, a poem by Audre Lorde. . . . I noted that there are three black women involved in an editorial capacity, but I feel that is not enough."[24] The editors responded by printing a poem by Jones in issue 3. By issue 10, the editors were still struggling to include more voices of Third World women: "So we ask readers, Third

World and white, to join us, to help us open the pages of *Chrysalis* to thinking about, exploring, confronting the issues of racism and, specifically, racism in the feminist movement."[25] The editorial board, many of whom identified as lesbians themselves, was even more forceful in their defense of a group of women who had previously had virtually no voice in the feminist movement. When an angry Janet Robinson in issue 9 requested to be unsubscribed because "I did not realize that *Chrysalis* is a Lesbian magazine of feminist arts," the editors responded that *Chrysalis* was "a feminist magazine that more truthfully reflects the sexual diversity of women."[26]

THE POLITICS OF FEMINIST SPIRITUALITY/ESSENTIALISM

In the pages of *Chrysalis,* feminist spirituality was inextricably linked with a radical feminist vision that emphasized inclusiveness and anti-violence—against the child, the woman, and the earth. Political action was sustained, rather than suppressed, through the invocation of Goddess spirituality. Charlene Spretnak, whose 1982 anthology *The Politics of Women's Spirituality* grew out of her work with *Chrysalis,* argues in the introduction to "Woman's Survival Catalogue: Women's Spirituality" that the Goddess was profoundly threatening because "anthropology tells us that the sex of the deity in a culture usually corresponds with the sex of those governing."[27] In issue 1, Edelson, in an article coauthored with Raven, reiterated her belief that feminist spirituality and radical politics were bound up in one another. "The Woman's spirituality movement has incredibly strong political overtones," she writes. "How it will evolve in action we don't know yet, but it will be a different kind of political action."[28] Many of the artists associated with the Woman's Building, including Suzanne Lacy, Cheri Gaulke, and Terry Wolverton, did agitprop performances that used feminist spirituality as a catalyst for imaging radical political change. Gaulke, for example, belonged to two activist collectives: the Feminist Art Workers, who created positive interactions with people, and the Sisters of Survival (S.O.S), who in the guise of feminist nuns protested against the desecration of the earth. Wolverton was instrumental in organizing *An Oral Herstory of Lesbianism,* one of the first collaborative performances about lesbian identity and subjectivity. The Waitresses, founded by Anne Gauldin and Jerry Allyn, used ideas culled from feminist spirituality—Gauldin's character copied the many-breasted Diana of Ephesus—to challenge the treatment of waitresses in various restaurants in the Los Angeles area.[29]

Given the close relationships among feminist spirituality/Goddess feminism, radical feminist politics, and activist art, a consideration of how feminist spirituality and politics were linked in the mid- to late '70s is long overdue. As Katherine Rountree has written, "the charge that 'embracing spirituality is an apolitical copout' seems unfair, based more on a Marxism-derived theory about the relationship between

NOTES

1. Mary Beth Edelson, "Pilgrimage/See for Yourself: A Journey to a Neolithic Goddess Cave, 1977, Grapceva, Hvar Island, Yugoslavia," in *Heresies #5: The Great Goddess*, rev. ed. (New York: Heresies Collective, 1978), 96–99. Also, Marija Gimbutas, *The Gods and Goddesses of Old Europe, 7000-3500 BC: Myths, Legends, and Cult Images* (London: Thames and Hudson, 1974).

2. Kathryn Rountree, "Goddess Pilgrims as Tourists: Inscribing the Body through Sacred Travel," *Sociology of Religion* 63, no.4 (2002): 475–96.

3. Lucy R. Lippard, *Overlay: Contemporary Art and the Art of Prehistory* (New York: Pantheon, 1983); Arlene Raven, *Crossing Over: Feminism and Art of Social Concern* (Ann Arbor, Mich.: UMI Research Press, 1988); Gloria Orenstein, "Recovering Her Story: Feminist Artists Reclaim the Great Goddess," in *The Power of Feminist Art*, ed. Norma Broude and Mary Garrard (New York: Abrams, 1994), 174–89; and Orenstein, *The Reflowering of the Goddess* (New York: Pergamon, 1990).

4. Gail Levin, *Becoming Judy Chicago* (New York: Harmony, 2007). *Wack! Art of the Feminist Revolution*, ed. Lisa Gabrielle Mark (Los Angeles: Museum of Contemporary Art, MIT Press, 2007). Published in conjunction with the exhibition *Wack!*, shown at the Museum of Contemporary Art, Los Angeles, the National Museum of Women in the Arts, Washington, D.C., and P.S. 1 Contemporary Art Center, New York. *Global Feminisms: New Directions in Feminist Art*, ed. Maura Reilly and Linda Nochlin (Brooklyn: Brooklyn Museum of Art, Merrell, 2007). Published in conjunction with the exhibition *Global Feminisms*, at the Brooklyn Museum of Art.

5. Mary Daly, *Beyond God the Father: Towards a Philosophy of Women's Liberation* (Boston: Beacon Press, 1973).

6. Merlin Stone, *When God Was a Woman* (New York: Harcourt Brace Jovanovich, 1976); Adrienne Rich, *Of Woman Born* (New York: Norton, 1976); Susan Griffin, *Woman and Nature* (New York: Harper and Row, 1978); Mary Daly, *Gyn/Ecology* (Boston: Beacon Press, 1978).

7. Mary Beth Edelson, "Self-Images of Strength and Wholeness," in *The Politics of Women's Spirituality*, rev. ed., ed. Charlene Spretnak (New York: Anchor, 1994), 314.

8. Jenni Sorkin, "Performance as Parody: Barbara T. Smith *in Situ*," in *The 21st Century Odyssey Part II: The Performances of Barbara T. Smith*, ed. Jennie Klein and Rebecca McGrew (Pomona, Calif.: Pomona College Museum of Art, 2005), 51.

9. Gimbutas, *Goddesses and Gods of Old Europe, 6500-3500 BC: Myths and Cult Images*, rev. ed. (Berkeley: University of California Press, 1982).

10. Joan Marler, "The Circle Is Unbroken," in *From the Realm of the Ancestors*, ed. Joan Marler (Manchester, Conn.: Knowledge, Ideas and Trends, Inc., 1997), 18–23.

11. Carol Christ, "Reading Marija Gimbutas," in *From the Realm of the Ancestors*, 169.

12. Gimbutas, *The Language of the Goddess: Unearthing the Hidden Symbols of Western Civilization* (San Francisco: Harper and Row, 1989); and *The Civilization of the Goddess* (San Francisco: HarperSanFrancisco, 1991).

13. Faith Wilding, *By Our Own Hands: The Women Artist's Movement in Southern California, 1970-1976* (Santa Monica, Calif.: Double X, 1977), 62.

14. See Michele Moravec, "Building Women's Culture: Feminism and Art at the Los Angeles Woman's Building" (Ph.D. diss., University of California, Los Angeles, 1998); Terry Wolverton, *Insurgent Muse: Life and Art at the Woman's Building* (San Francisco: City Lights, 2002).

15. Jennie Klein, "The Ritual Body as Pedagogical Tool: The Performance Art of the Woman's Building," in *From Site to Vision: The Los Angeles Woman's Building in Contemporary Culture*, ed. Sondra Hale and Terry Wolverton (Los Angeles: Woman's Building, 2007), 186–90, womansbuilding.org/fromsitetovision/. Accessed June 2011.

16. Terry Wolverton, "Lesbian Art Project," *Heresies #7* 2, no. 3 (Spring 1979): 18.

17. Laura Cottingham, "Shifting Signs: On the Art of Mary Beth Edelson," in *The Art of Mary Beth Edelson* (Gettysburg, Penn.: Gettysburg College, 2001), 26.

18. Carrie Rickey, "Writing (and Righting) Wrongs: Feminist Art Publications," in *The Power of Feminist Art*, 126.

19. Charlene Spretnak, "Preface: The First 20 Years," *The Politics of Women's Spirituality*, xi–xii.

20. Linda Palumbo, Maurine Renville, Charlene Spretnak, and Terry Wolverton, "Women's Survival Catalogue: Spirituality," *Chrysalis* 6 (1978): 77–99.

21. Lucy R. Lippard, "Quite Contrary: Body, Nature, and Ritual in Women's Art," *Chrysalis* 2 (1977): 31–49; Mary Daly, "Sparking: The Fire of Female Friendship," *Chrysalis* 6 (1978): 27–37; and Adrienne Rich, "Disloyal to Civilization: Feminism, Racism, Gynephobia," *Chrysalis* 7 (1978): 9–28.

22. Susan Griffin, "Gyn/Ecology: The Metaethics of Radical Feminism by Mary Daly," *Chrysalis* 7 (1978): 109–12; Mary Daly, "*Women and Nature: The Roaring Inside Her* by Susan Griffin," *Chrysalis* 7 (1978): 112–15.

23. Rickey, "Writing (and Righting) Wrongs," 126.

24. Patricia Jones, Letters to the Editor, *Chrysalis* 2 (1977): 5.

25. Editors, "Dear Readers," *Chrysalis* 10 (1979): 5.

26. Janet Robinson, Letters to the Editor, "Lesbianism in *Chrysalis*," *Chrysalis* 9 (1979): 8.

27. Spretnak, "Introduction to Woman's Survival Catalogue: Spirituality," 77–78.

28. Mary Beth Edelson and Arlene Raven, "Happy Birthday America," *Chrysalis* 1 (1977): 51.

29. Cheri Gaulke, "Acting Like Women: Performance Art of the Woman's Building," first published in *High Performance Magazine* (Fall/Winter 1980).

30. Kathryn Rountree, "The Politics of the Goddess: Feminist Spirituality and the Essentialism Debate," *Social Analysis* 43, no. 2 (July 1999): 140.

31. Rita Felski, *The Gender of Modernity* (Cambridge, Mass.: Harvard University Press, 1995), 59.

32. Lippard, "Quite Contrary," 32.

33. Debra Michals, "From 'Consciousness Expansion' to 'Consciousness Raising'": Feminism and the Countercultural Politics of the Self," in *Imagine Nation: The American Counterculture in the 1960s and '70s*, ed. Peter Braunstein and Michael William Doyle (New York: Routledge, 2002), 45.

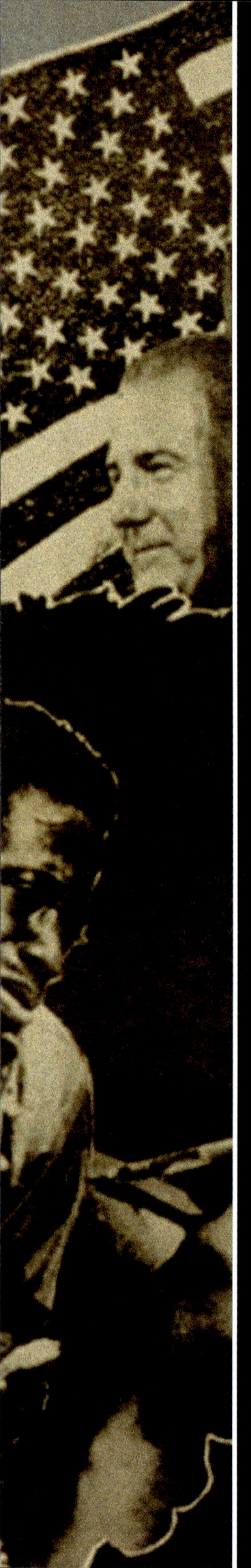

CHAPTER 14
THE REVOLUTION WILL BE VISUALIZED: BLACK PANTHER ARTIST EMORY DOUGLAS

Colette Gaiter

The revolution will not be right back
after a message about a white tornado, white lightning, or
white people.
You will not have to worry about a dove in your
bedroom, a tiger in your tank, or the giant in your toilet
bowl.
The revolution will not go better with Coke.
The revolution will not fight the germs that may cause bad
breath.
The revolution will put you in the driver's seat.

The revolution will not be televised, will not be televised,
will not be televised, will not be televised.
The revolution will be no re-run brothers;
The revolution will be live.

—Gil Scott-Heron, "The Revolution Will Not Be Televised"

The revolution to which Gil Scott-Heron's lyrics refer was the mid-to-late-twentieth-century worldwide fight against Western imperialism, racism, and capitalist economic domination.[1] Most people in the United States thought the Western powers were fighting against Communism, in a continuation of the cold war on new fronts. In 1966, following the acquittal by an all-white jury of the men accused of killing Samuel Younge, a black student at Tuskegee Institute, for using a whites-only restroom in an Alabama filling station, the Student Nonviolent Coordinating Committee (SNCC) issued a statement. Among other points, SNCC declared: "We maintain that our country's cry of 'preserve freedom in the world' is a hypocritical mask behind which it squashes the liberation movements which . . . refuse to be bound by the expediencies of the United States cold war policies."[2]

On the West Coast the same year, the Black Panther Party for Self Defense formed in Oakland, California, allying itself with revolutionary activity in Vietnam, Cuba, Angola, Nicaragua, and other countries around the globe. Even though there were riots and armed skirmishes associated with the struggle for black liberation in the United States, the resistance battles never escalated into all-out war as they did elsewhere. The Panthers were also distinguished from other Third World liberation movements by virtue of their belief that the most important battle in the fight against racist oppression was for the minds of the people. The revolutionaries in the Black Panther Party believed that if they could change "the people's" thinking, developing the tools to actively change their lives would naturally follow. The slogan "All power to the people" constantly reinforced the idea of ending complicity in racist oppression through self-actualization.

The Black Panther Party formed in direct response to rampant police brutality in San Francisco Bay Area black neighborhoods—the same activity against black people that sparked urban riots in other regions of the United States. The newspaper they published, the *Black Panther,* had appeared once, in 1967, when a young man barely in his twenties, the artist Emory Douglas, met Panther Party leaders Bobby Seale and Huey Newton at a meeting in San Francisco. That same year Douglas was named Minister of Culture for the Panther Party, a post he held until the early 1980s. Douglas's visual skills, combined with the Panther leaders' sharp verbal rhetoric, resulted in the graphically explosive *Black Panther* newspaper that embodied the group's concept of revolution through self-empowerment. That fortuitous meeting also started a visual movement that would help transform black consciousness, extending far beyond California. Over the course of his tenure as Minister of Culture, Douglas used revolutionary art to empower African Americans in a post–Civil Rights Act, everyday-in-the-streets struggle.[3] These years were among the most volatile of the late twentieth century, as the established American political, social, and economic ideologies were challenged on several fronts.

In a 1969 editorial, managing editor Frank Jones stated that Douglas had "thrown himself with full force into the world liberation movement, and had done so with consummate skill and highly developed revolutionary concepts. His combination of ability and ideology makes him a complete revolutionary man." Jones went on to say that "if not for the directness of Emory's work, many of the ideas of the revolutionary movement would have escaped the attention and awareness of a large number of active revolutionary advocates."[4] In concert with the goals of the Panther Party, Douglas's body of work played a major role in two formations that continue to grow—black cultural liberation and the increasing dominance of images over words in cultural production. His work used a graphically bold visual style to inspire, instruct, and confront.

REVOLUTIONARY ART AS AN ESSENTIAL PART OF LIBERATION

Douglas visualized working and poor black people as they had never been seen before in American mass media. His was a revolution of representation, giving visual expression to the conditions and feelings of oppression in black communities. As he explained, "Before a correct visual interpretation of the struggle can be given, we must recognize that Revolutionary Art is an art that flows from the people. It must be a whole and living part of the people's lives and their daily struggle to survive."[5] Many of his images were also hopeful, illustrating the perseverance and integrity of black people in the face of adversity. Children were among his favorite subjects, and their presence in his compositions was meant to suggest a changed future.

The use of the child in the poster titled "We Shall Survive without a Doubt" is typical of Douglas's inspirational work (Figure 14.1). The smiling boy wears glasses that metaphorically see a brighter future. One of Douglas's favorite devices was to embed images within images, like those in the boy's glasses and in the button on his hat. A woman instructs a child in one lens, and the other shows the Panthers' breakfast program, one of their most notable achievements. Other formal devices used in the image are bold, black lines that signify strength, confidence, and purpose. The textures in the boy's hat are created out of peel-off, rubdown vinyl sheets, one of the graphic tools of the time that helped artists fill in large areas quickly. These two methods and processes were used throughout Douglas's body of work and represent a central element of his signature style.

The red rays emanating from the boy's head are typical of Douglas's "beatification" of some subjects. Like the gold halos around the heads of saints in early Renaissance paintings, these rays came to be part of revolutionary iconography in 1960s poster art. In other images by a range of artists, the heads of Fidel Castro, murdered Black Panthers, and international high-profile figures were surrounded by these rays, indicating that the subjects deserved special respect. In the pages of the *Black Panther*

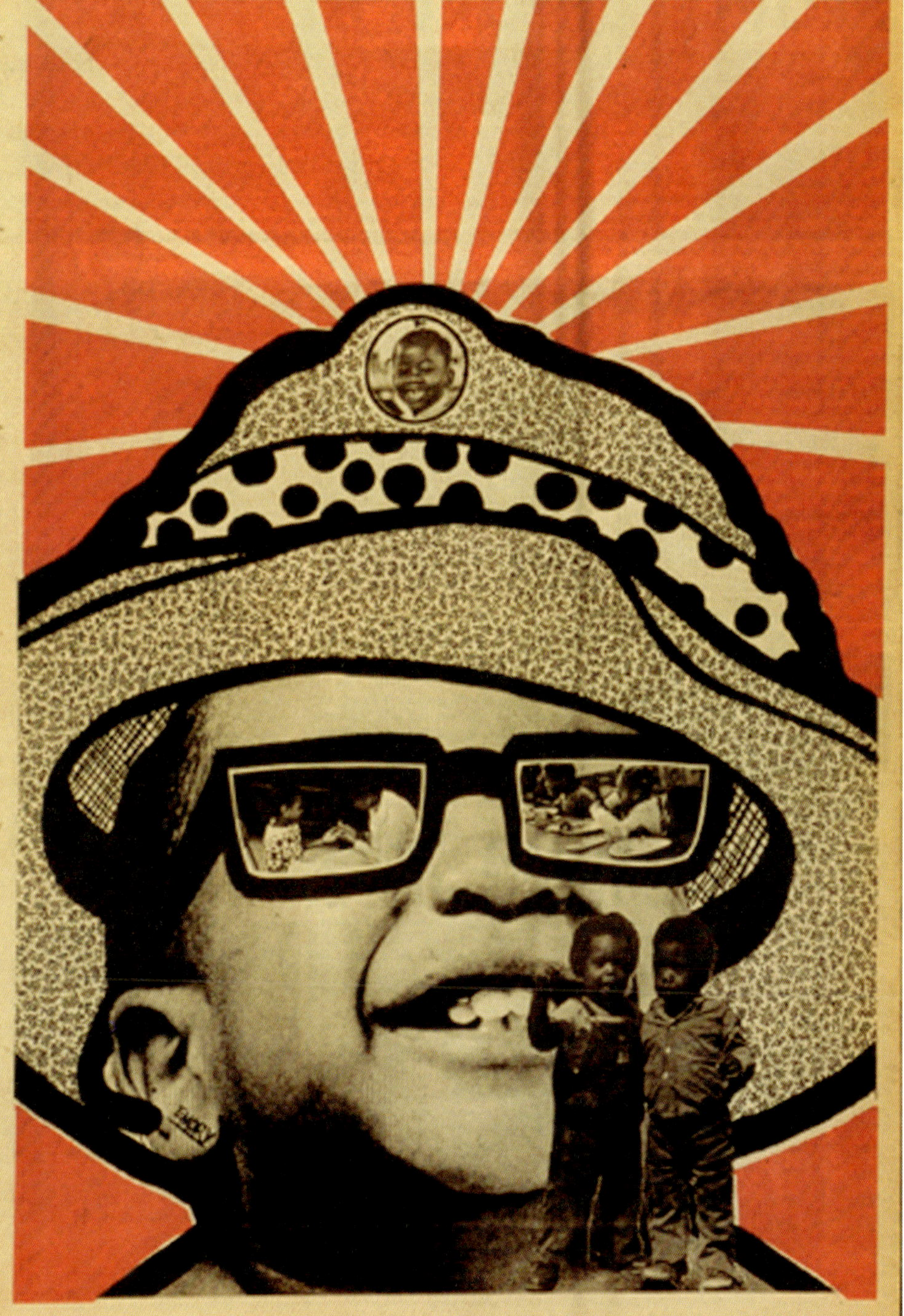

WE SHALL SURVIVE, WITHOUT A DOUBT

newspaper, Huey Newton and ordinary black people were represented in this way on front and back covers. In line with the Panthers' valorization of everyday people, Douglas made them heroes along with the highest leaders and revered martyrs of the party.

Douglas's stylized illustrations of dark-skinned, full-lipped, broad-nosed African-featured people visualized blackness in a way that was virtually absent from mainstream media in the 1960s. In 1963, Bell Telephone ran the first ad featuring a black person representing "Everyman."[6] Before that time, blacks in the media were almost exclusively portrayed in stereotypical racial roles as servants, workers, athletes, or entertainers. The importance of Douglas's work in redressing the violence of racial stereotypes is also connected to the distribution of his images far outside the elite centers of the art world. Although his work was part of the larger Black Arts and Black Power movements, the images Douglas produced for the Black Panther Party and its newspaper enjoyed widespread circulation, especially among audiences without access to or suspicious of institutions of high culture, including black people in urban communities, college students, and members of the counterculture. As such, Douglas's work was regarded as connected to rather than remote from the everyday life of black people. According to the artist, "the community became the gallery of the art itself. In the early morning when they took the papers out, they took posters and wheat paste and plastered these things all over the community. The artwork became part of the community, reflecting the feelings of the community."[7]

According to Donald Bogle, author of the classic review of black cinema *Toms, Coons, Mulattoes, Mammies, and Bucks*, the 1960s brought a challenge to assimilationist and watered-down stories: "No longer were sad-eyed black people trying to prove their worth in order to fit into white worlds. No longer were submissive, patient Negroes pleading for acceptance. Instead, the headstrong militants appeared."[8] A 1969 *Ebony* magazine editorial made this assessment of the Black Power movement's effect on all African Americans: "The constant striving to measure oneself by white standards is out. The constant acceptance of 'white is right' is out. Black people are finding a freedom that they never had before—the freedom to be themselves."[9] The *Black Panther* was the antithesis of the mainstream black press, which they accused of guiding African Americans toward assimilating the white "American Dream" and aspiring to those values and goals.

The 1970s also changed black cinema, and no one gets more credit from the Panthers than Melvin Van Peebles and his *Sweet Sweetback's Baadasssss Song:* "Van Peebles' depiction of the renegade black man, violent and sexual but noble still, resonated with black audiences—male and female—who wanted an image of themselves as active and resistant."[10] When Huey Newton devoted an entire issue of the *Black Panther* to Van Peebles's film, Douglas used its title graphics and a still image to create a cover that graphically matched the film's bravado. Applying huge, bold letters in red that simply stated "SWEET SWEET BACK" to a red-tinted black-and-white photograph of the title character on the run, the front page clearly conveyed the Panthers' vision of the liberated, self-actualized black man.

Douglas further made revolutionary art an integral part of black life by designing images to function as performative instructions and a means of communicating ideas. Experiencing his work was a visual exercise that made even imagined events seem possible. His incorporation of slogans and directives, like visual mantras, were meant to foster liberated thinking and reinforce new cognitive habits. As Douglas has explained about the Panthers' concept of revolutionary art, his was a practice that "enlightens the party to continue its vigorous attack against the enemy, as well as educate the masses of black people—we do this by showing them through pictures."[11]

Douglas's job as the party's Minister of Culture went beyond producing the newspaper. He was also charged with cultivating the Panthers' overall visual and public image, which included organizing fund-raisers and directing theater productions. About his expanded duties, Douglas recalls, "I used to procure the entertainment [for fund-raisers], like Santana and the Grateful Dead. When we had any kind of activity, we had to set up and do banners. All that became part of my responsibility at the same time that I was working on the newspaper." He goes on to describe a particular kind of culture clash at these events that illustrates the Panthers' unique style of politics that directly served the black community and reached additional audiences by incorporating forms of countercultural expression such as music and lightshows: "We knew that in the African American community, the older folks did not like the hemp smoking—marijuana smoking. We understood that. We were giving away five or ten thousand bags of groceries. We worked it out so that the seniors would come in and get their groceries and leave, then all the Deadheads came in to hear the music."[12]

Douglas recalls that the theater productions the Panthers put on in black communities in Oakland invited participation from audiences. Like his posters and illustrations for the *Black Panther,* these plays were instructive in helping people change their personal consciousness about their place in the world.[13] In concert with other political theater groups of the time, the Panther productions "meshed some combination of the everyday life, arts, popular entertainment, ritual, and play aspects of performance," according to Bradford D. Martin. As Martin has asserted about countercultural forms of performance, these kinds of free and open public performances, "spectacles in public places where no admission is charged and spectators are invited to participate, [conveyed] symbolic messages about social and political issues to audiences who might not have encountered them in traditional venues." Like other guerrilla theaters of the counterculture such as the Diggers or the Living

 THE REVOLUTION WILL BE VISUALIZED

Theatre, the Panthers "agitated for radical social change in both personal behavior and political institutions, pointing out the many connections between the two."[14]

FORM AND MEANING IN DOUGLAS'S GRAPHIC WORK

Douglas created a distinctive and recognizable style that became part of the Panthers' visual identity. There are a number of ways to analyze the formal aspects of his graphic work for the Panthers and their newspaper. Complicating any analysis is Douglas's use of a wide range of styles and working methods, including line drawing, photographic collage, pencil, and ink for the production of cartoons, posters, newspaper layouts, and advertisements. In addition to using multiple techniques, Douglas liked to combine narrative threads, often in the same image. Although routine today, Douglas's style required a high level of involvement on the part of the viewer in deciphering the image's message. In his own way, Douglas was an early postmodernist, using pastiche, collage, and "crowded space and multiple messages" to create works that were like prisms, refracting several ideas at once.[15]

Collage was one of Douglas's most favored techniques. In the Richard Nixon/Spiro Agnew image, he juxtaposed a photograph of the Republican nominees celebrating their ticket (from the cover of *Time* magazine on August 16, 1968) with images of anguished black people (Figure 14.2). Douglas was not interested in making dreamlike or metaphorical collaged images in the style of the Dadaists or surrealists. Instead, he wanted to tell specific stories and direct people to politically conscious thinking. In this image, the American flag blankets the background of the image to represent that the majority, who eventually elected them in November 1968, supported Nixon and Agnew's conservative agenda. Douglas's collage alludes to controversial perceptions that the Nixon administration neglected problems of the urban, mostly black, poor.

Since the *Black Panther* paper was on a tight budget and deadline, Douglas often reused images. The Nixon/Agnew image appeared in another edition of the paper without the flag and with the elected men's faces and upraised clasped hands colored red, representing the "heat that was turned on them" in reaction to their policies (Figure 14.3). The absence of the flag brings the viewer's attention to the people at the bottom of the composition. Here, Douglas collaged the image of a hand shooting a needle into an arm, the knuckles forming a silhouetted profile—a juxtaposition that symbolizes a drug addict's anonymity and loss of identity. Douglas's image suggests that the person has been replaced by the habit. The other two figures in the collage, showing direct expressions of pain and anguish, also serve as metonyms, personifying the pervasive struggles of African Americans. The implication of the entire image is that Nixon and Agnew are publicly reveling in a victory that is widely mediated, while black people suffer in obscurity. In these two images, there is the obvious reference to Nixon and Agnew being

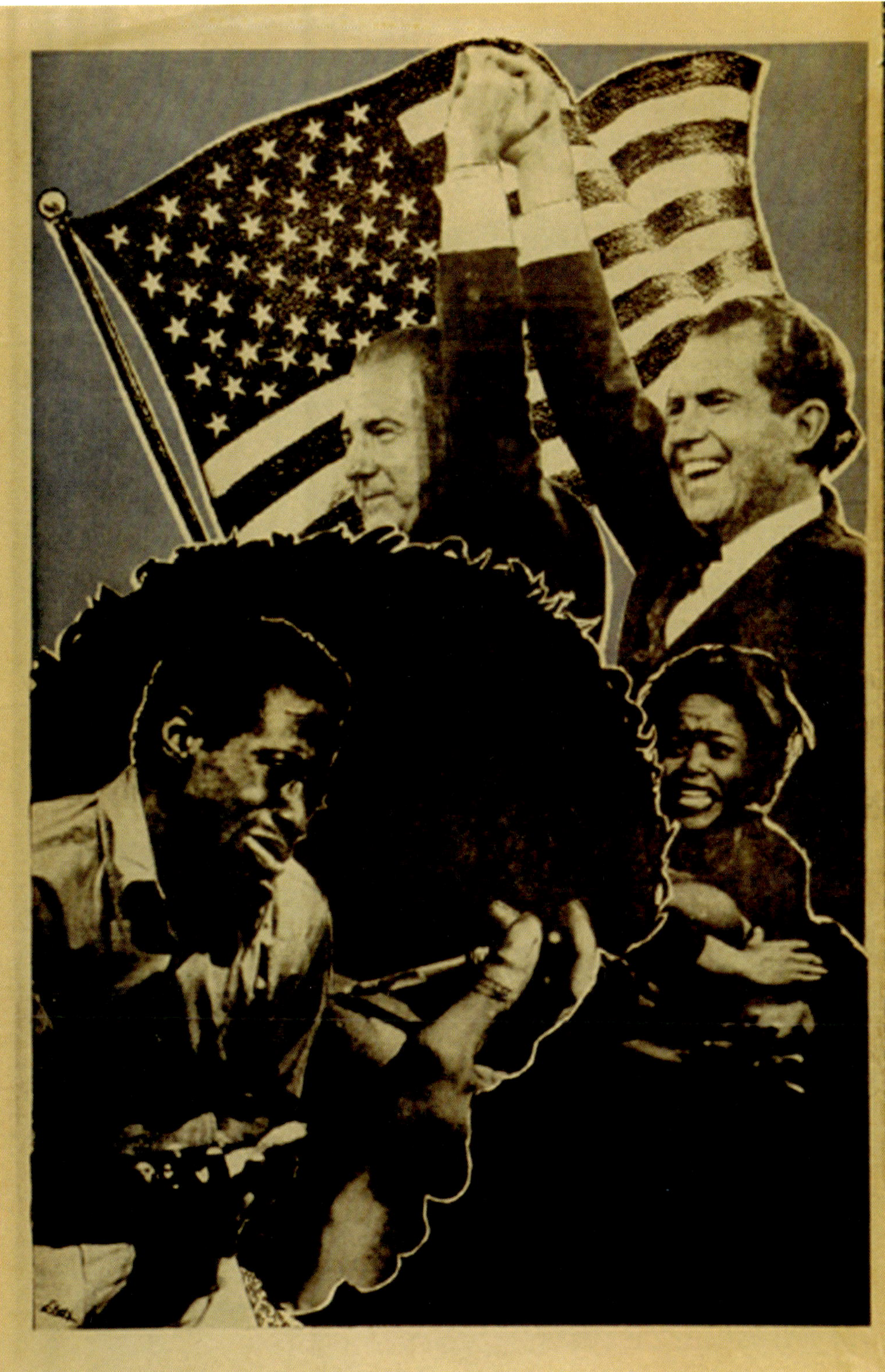

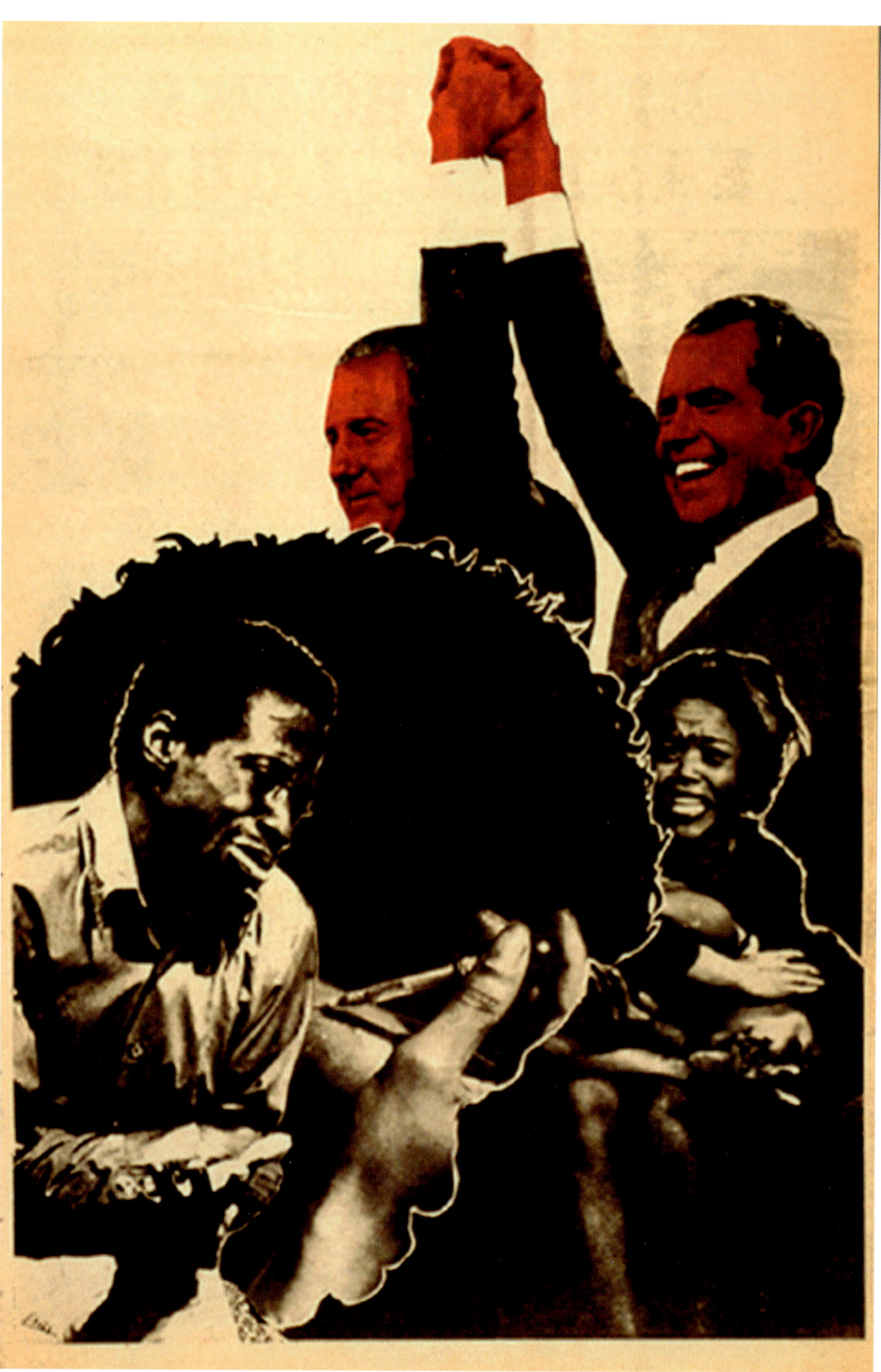

"up" while the black people are "down." The American flag in the background adds irony and suggests that the flag represents only the people at the top and not those at the bottom. The gaze of the two white men at the top of the image points away from the "tired, the poor, . . . and the wretched refuse" to a future that continues an established American mythology of endless prosperity and good fortune.[16]

One of Douglas's strongest skills was his ability to combine form and meaning without sacrificing either. In both images, the faces create a circle, starting with Agnew and completing the circle at Nixon. Even without the flag, the triumphant hands fill the empty space. Adding the flag at an angle creates a strong diagonal line that aids the composition's circular flow. The images of suffering people on the bottom of the page, however, interrupt the joy of victory and literally insert themselves between the pair.

Collage was just one of Douglas's illustration styles. He also favored pop art stylization of the human form over a style of drawing associated with classical Western fine art or that which privileged the artist's work as a form of personal expression. In addition, Douglas incorporated the florid art nouveau–inspired typography favored by psychedelic poster artists working for 1960s rock music promoters such as Bill Graham.

Douglas's distinctive bold, black lines and stylized drawings also functioned to make production faster and easier for the cheaply printed *Black Panther* paper. Former *New York Times* reporter Earl Caldwell, who covered the Panthers as a correspondent in San Francisco, called the Panthers' newspaper "brilliant" and said their deployment of rhetoric and art was nothing short of shooting a gun: "I had met Emory and at first I thought his art was so crude," Caldwell recalls. "But they [the Panthers] knew it worked in that it became a signature thing. People gravitated to it. I came to see how effective it was."[17] The bold outlines of Douglas's images and the violence of his cartoons translated into visual form the outrageousness he and the other Panther leaders believed was necessary to accomplish the movement's goals. As Caldwell's comments suggest, Douglas's drawings had the same mainstream cultural effect that African tribal art had when Westerners first encountered it. What was initially dismissed as primitive and too abstracted, due to a presumed lack of skill or sophistication, eventually came to be appreciated as deliberate manipulation of form for a communicative purpose. The abstract forms of tribal art were part of a visual language of specific meaning, just as Douglas's "crudeness" had intention.

REVOLUTIONARY ART AS A WEAPON OF SELF-DEFENSE

Although the Black Panthers and other Black Power groups differed on some important concepts, like cultural nationalism, in 1969, Black Arts movement poet, editor, and writer Larry Neal pointed out that the spiritual survival of black people in America depended as much on building cultural institutions as on guns. Neal went on to say that "the Black Arts

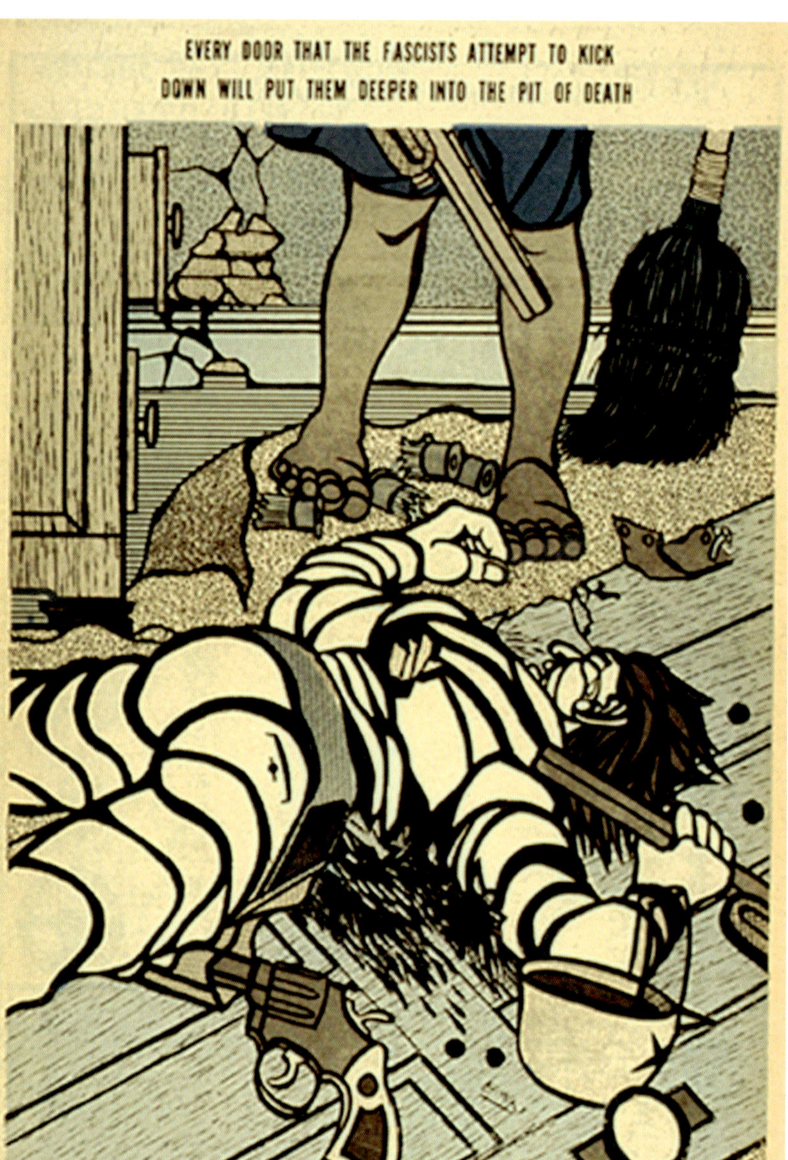

SHOOT TO KILL

movement supplies the brothers with an arsenal of feelings, images, and myth."[18] These are the weapons created by Douglas, who explained: "We try to create an atmosphere for the vast majority of black people—who aren't readers but activists. . . . through their observation of our work, they feel they have the right to destroy the enemy."[19] Douglas's images metaphorically fought back, through cartoons of eviscerated police as pigs or drawings of armed black revolutionaries. In his cartoons and illustrations, he created images that did not exist but that allowed people to reimagine what they had known as reality. Douglas's skillful deployment of semiotics helped him use art as a weapon and a tool.

The people in Douglas's drawings controlled their lives and destinies in their own homes and communities. His work showed armed women protecting their families from police, and children studying black history in all-black schools. Douglas's art helped black people imagine an alternate reality that was partially realized by Panther Party programs. For instance, in *Shoot to Kill* Douglas used his signature style of bold outlines and flat areas of color and texture to illustrate an incident of self-defense (Figure 14.4). This poster is representative of those by Douglas meant to be instructional—in this case, illustrating defense against unlawful entry by police or other authorities. Using exaggeration, Douglas made the intruder a storm trooper, wearing a suit of body armor that functions like an insect skin. The uniform/costume resembles (and predates) the *Star Wars* movies' storm troopers, who were dressed in similar suits. In this drawing, the room's isometric perspective makes it easier to read the story behind objects strewn on the floor. The indexical crumbling plaster indicates disrepair and poverty. Spent ammunition and the barrel of a shotgun illustrate how the storm trooper came to be lying on the floor with blood pouring from his center. He was heavily armed, with a shotgun still clenched in his hand and a pistol falling out of its holster around his hip. A broken door hinge shows that the "fascist" (so named in Douglas's text at the top of the poster) forced his way in. Indicated by just her bare legs and feet under a dress, a black woman, educated in self-defense by the Panthers, has successfully defended her impoverished home against the white storm trooper, who represents all abusive authority figures in uniform. As the image's title reads, "Every door that the fascists attempt to kick down will put them deeper into the pit of death." Hyperbole, melodrama, and sensationalism in the form of strong imagery are essential to Douglas's messages of self-empowerment. Like this example, the anger in his images seems directly relational to the perceived damage of oppression through a history of white supremacy in the United States. "Shoot to Kill," the text at the bottom of the poster, needs to be framed in this context.

Douglas's cartoons are the most controversial of his work for the *Black Panther*. They are disturbing or inspiring, depending on the audience's perception. While back-page posters in the newspaper often featured empathic portraits of the black people Douglas knew in the

San Francisco Bay Area, other pages of the paper contained startling cartoons of aggressive attacks on policemen, politicians, and businessmen (identified as enemies of the people) in response to their power abuses. Douglas characterized them as anthropomorphic pigs, which could be generic "everypigs" or representative of specific people, such as San Francisco Mayor Joseph Alioto, California Governor Ronald Reagan, or President Richard Nixon. The pigs usually had flies buzzing around them and wavy lines that indicated an unpleasant odor. Douglas used these indexical devices to make the characters as visually repulsive as most leftists viewed their politics and policies. Referring to his pig cartoons, Douglas writes: "This is revolutionary art—pigs lying in alley ways of the colony dead with their eyes gouged out—autopsy showing cause of death: 'They fail to see that majority rules.' Pictures we draw show them choking to death from their inhuman ways—these are the kinds of pictures revolutionary artists draw."[20]

In his iconic representations of avengers, Douglas gave the revolutionaries a creative arsenal of imaginary weapons, including machetes, acid, heavy boots, dynamite, and guns. Douglas created images that could be used to imagine fighting back (literally and metaphorically) against police brutality, racism, and economic oppression. The virtual attacks on police, public officials, and politicians in the *Black Panther*'s pages were taken seriously enough by the FBI to cause an all-out war on the organization, mobilizing the bureau's vast resources after its director, J. Edgar Hoover, declared the Panthers the "greatest threat to national security."[21]

The FBI saw the Panthers simply as public enemies and a law enforcement problem. In a much broader context, Emory Douglas's work represented the complexities of urban black life shown through his California Bay Area counterculture lens. Disparate elements coexist in Douglas's work: protest and political commentary, bold graphic style, instructive calls to action, cartoon violence, and poignant drawing. Together, these elements embody the ethos of their particular time, place, and subculture.

Emory Douglas's lasting influence on art and artists is easier to assess than the Panthers' influence on black consciousness. Douglas and other protest artists of the 1960s initiated the contemporary practice of activist art, which remains a strong element of black visual culture. One important African American artist whose work has been affected by Douglas's populist activism is the photographer Dawoud Bey. He describes Douglas's work as "giving visual form to [Black Panther] programs and beliefs" and "clearly establishing a function for art." He continues: "Much like other artists I was drawn to early on—Romare Bearden, Charles White and Jacob Lawrence—Douglas's work affirmed that the lives of ordinary everyday people *do* matter and that their experiences and representations can be the foundation for a meaningful and sustained art practice."[22]

NOTES

1. Gil Scott-Heron, "The Revolution Will Not Be Televised." Vinyl recording, 1970. Used by permission of Bienstock Publishing Company.

2. Quoted in Milton Viorst, *Fire in the Streets: America in the 1960s* (New York: Simon and Schuster, 1979), 364.

3. David Hilliard, ed., *Black Panther Intercommunal News Service* (New York: Atria, 2007), xxiii. Douglas created most of the artwork for the paper, but there were others who worked with him, including the artists known as "Malik" and "Matilaba" (Joan Lewis).

4. Quoted in G. Louis Heath, ed., *Black Panther Leaders Speak: Huey P. Newton, Bobby Seale, Eldridge Cleaver and Company Speak Out through the Black Panther Party's Official Newspaper* (Metuchen, N.J: Scarecrow, 1976), 2.

5. Emory Douglas, "Revolutionary Art/Black Liberation," in *The Black Panthers Speak*, ed. Philip S. Foner (New York: Da Capo, 2002), 16.

6. Marilyn Kern-Foxworth, *Aunt Jemima, Uncle Ben, and Rastus: Blacks in Advertising, Yesterday, Today, and Tomorrow* (Westport, Conn.: Greenwood Press, 1994).

7. Emory Douglas, interview by author, 12 July 2004.

8. Donald Bogle, *Toms, Coons, Mulattoes, Mammies, and Bucks: An Interpretive History of Blacks in American Films,* 4th ed. (New York: Continuum, 2001), 195.

9. "The Unity of Blackness," *Ebony* (August 1969): 42.

10. Aymar Jean Christian, "'Precious' Isn't the First Naughty Black Film," *TELEVISUAL*, 16 November 2009.

11. Douglas, "Revolutionary Art/Black Liberation," 16.

12. Douglas, interview by author.

13. Ibid.

14. Bradford D. Martin, *Theater Is in the Street: Politics and Performance in Sixties America* (Amherst: University of Massachusetts, 2004), 4, 51.

15. Philip B. Meggs and Alston W. Purvis, *Meggs' History of Graphic Design,* 4th ed. (Hoboken, N.J.: Wiley, 2006), 389.

16. The images at the bottom of the collage echo the words of Emma Lazarus's now-famous poem, "The New Colossus," inscribed on the Statue of Liberty, at Liberty State Park and Ellis Island: "Give me your tired, your poor, / Your huddled masses yearning to breathe free, / The wretched refuse of your teeming shore. / Send these, the homeless, tempest-tost to me, / I lift my lamp beside the golden door!"

17. Quoted in Jane Rhodes, *Framing the Black Panthers: The Spectacular Rise of a Black Power Icon* (New York: New Press, 2007), 102.

18. Larry Neal, "Any Day Now: Black Art and Black Liberation," *Ebony* (August 1969): 54–62.

19. Douglas, quoted in Foner, ed., *The Black Panthers Speak,* 16.

20. Douglas, "Revolutionary Art/Black Liberation," 16.

21. As cited by Ward Churchill, "To Disrupt, Discredit and Destroy: The FBI's Secret War against the Black Panther Party," in *Liberation, Imagination and the Black Panther Party,* ed. Kathleen Cleaver and George Katsiaficas (New York: Routledge, 2001), 83.

22. Dawoud Bey, "Emory Douglas—Forty Years and Larry Sultan, R.I.P." *What's Going On?,* 15 December 2009 (blog post), whatsgoingon-dawoudbeysblog.blogspot.com/.

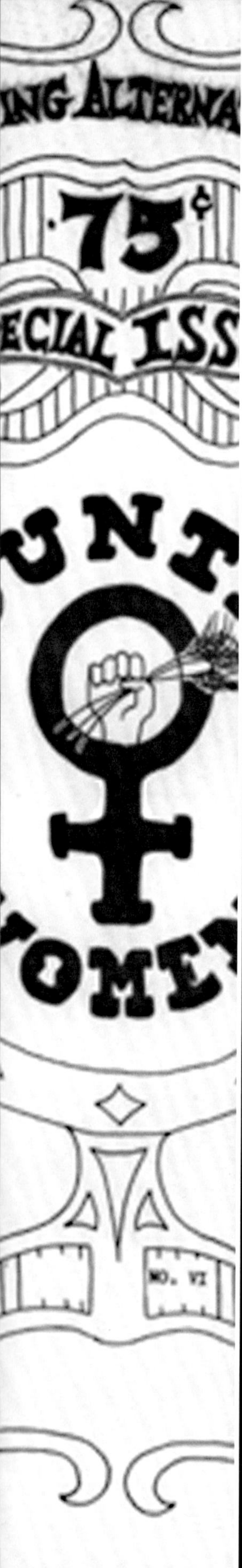

CHAPTER 15

OUT OF THE CLOSETS, INTO THE WOODS: THE POST-STONEWALL EMERGENCE OF QUEER ANTI-URBANISM

Scott Herring

At first glance, a communal-living farmhouse in Grinnell, Iowa, seems
an unlikely spot for a sustained campaign against the normalization of
white, urban, gay male identity in the post-Stonewall United States. But
consider this recollection of one winter in 1973:

For Christmas that year I had bought Julia, one of my housemates, a subscription
to *Country Women,* a rural feminist journal out of Mendocino. Reading and loving
Country Women, I wondered why there wasn't a similar magazine for gay men. I
just *knew* that I couldn't be the only gay man who liked rural life, though it sure
seemed that way. The six other inhabitants of our it's-not-a-commune-we-just-
live-together farmhouse were straight but lovable. The available gay publications
were all urban-oriented full of the latest news of cha cha palaces in San Francisco,
shows off-off Broadway, trendy fashions from West Hollywood, Gloria Gaynor's
latest album, and how to make a killing in the real estate market. As for rural magazines like *Mother Earth News,* well, let's just call these adamantly heterosexual.[1]

Julia's subscription to *Country Women*'s rural lesbian-separatism, it
turns out, became the inspiration for the *RFD* (once referred to as "Rural
Fairy Digest") quarterly. *RFD* was one of the first antiheteronormative,
anti-urbanist, and countersubcultural journals for queers to appear as a
challenge to and a critique of newly nationalized "cha cha" gay publications such as the Los Angeles—based glossy *Advocate*. It was thus one
of the first queer journals to extend the non-normative intersectional
politics of the Gay Liberation Front (GLF) to nonmetropolitan U.S. audiences.

Nearly two decades later, however, the Midwesterners who founded
RFD would have been somewhat hard-pressed to find critiques of normalizing urban gay culture in the pages of the journal they established.
Take a spring 2000 issue, when a different set of *RFD* editors published
"From Hippie to Fairy at Short Mountain Sanctuary," a historical retrospective of *RFD* that makes no mention of the Grinnell farmhouse or of
Country Women's influence. Located near the small town of Liberty, Ten-
nessee, the Short Mountain Sanctuary had been a gathering place for
radical—not necessarily rural-identified—faeries since 1979, the year
that former Mattachine Society founder Harry Hay published "A Call to
Gay Brothers" for a "Spiritual Conference" in RFD. The 2000 *RFD* essay
traces a genealogy of this neoprimitivist gay male collective, a counterculture known for its festivals in rural Appalachian mountains, Minnesota north woods, Arizona deserts, and elsewhere across the globe.[2] The
article glossed Short Mountain Sanctuary and presented a truncated
history of its origins:

Hippies knew how to wear flowing clothes, embrace dirt, and worship the goddess. Gay men knew how to have lots of sex, when to wear black, and why to
be attractive. They were all familiar with mind-altering substances. Community
values and spiritual inspiration married marijuana and sex: the earth mother and

pan. The offspring was the radical faeries, a term coined in the 1970s to reflect the need for a counter-cultural queer presence.[3]

There is much to question in this succinct history—its sketch of a historically complex countercultural movement assumed to "embrace dirt"; its unspoken assumption that all "hippies" are male; and its spurious cross-identifications with spiritually inspired cultures that many radical faeries stereotypically located in the Native figure of the two-spirit.[4] What is also curious about 2000 *RFD*'s unreflective equation between *hippie, gay,* and *radical faerie* is its unacknowledged reliance on the "values" of a communal "presence" that the journal was originally founded to push against—a sexual group identity that appears exclusively gay, exclusively male, and, ironically enough, exclusively urbanized. With allusions to leisure culture ("marijuana and sex"), style and sophistication ("when to wear black," "why to be attractive"), and knowingness ("gay men knew," "they were all familiar"), the history that late-nineties *RFD* offers here seems more the offspring of metro-oriented gay male cosmopolitanism than the issue of a radical, regionalized, and intersectional queer counterculture.

"From Hippie to Fairy at Short Mountain Sanctuary" thus confirms ethnographer Scott Morgensen's claim that many present-day U.S. radical faerie gatherings have erased portions of their political history, "outpaced" "rural men's participation," and now consist primarily of

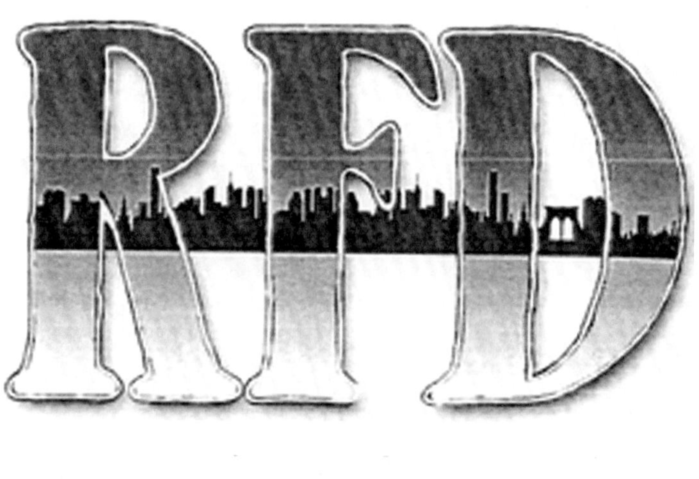

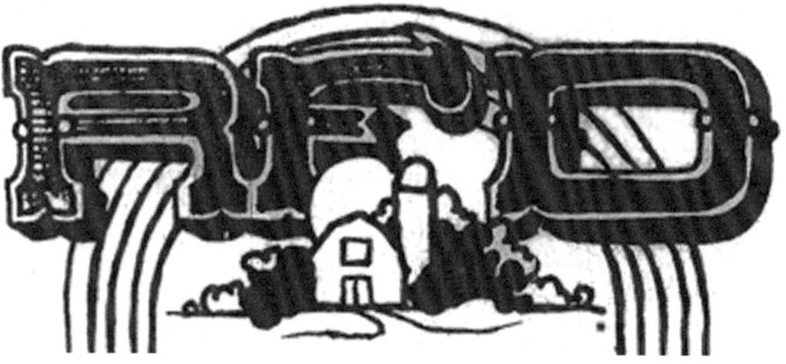

middle-class "urban gay men, who [frequent] gatherings as temporary rural retreats for the cultivation of a new cultural identity and spiritual insight for transport back to urban life."[5] When seen in this light, the amnesiac histories that late-1990s faeries tell themselves about their mid-to-late-1970s origins promote the mainstream "community values" that they like to think they dance, sing, worship, and write against. And though recent *RFD* articles have imagined and welcomed male readers who are "not interested in being 'bar clones', but who . . . explore their uniqueness and spirituality," the current publication may sometimes be closer to an urbanized version of U.S. gay male "bar clone" identity than it likes to presume (Figure 15.1).[6] In a telling moment, one disgruntled *RFD* reader lamented in 2000 that the journal is "quite a contrast from the early issues of *RFD* that came out in the mid-70s." He demanded: "Please cancel my subscription immediately! I thought your magazine was 'a country journal for gay men everywhere' but it's not! The 'RFD' connotation used to stand for those living a rural lifestyle, country affairs, small town life, etc. but not any more! Apparently your mag is now completely (90%+) a Radical Faery Digest."[7]

In the following pages I revisit *RFD*'s early-to-mid-1970s "rural lifestyle" to argue that the quarterly did not initially stand in or stand for a radical faerie digest that leisurely cosmopolites enjoyed as an armchair rural retreat (Figure 15.2). Rather, several working-class white males who politically affiliated with the Gay Liberation Front founded the journal in 1974, and they imagined themselves as the antithesis of what many metropolitan-based radical faeries now consider themselves to be. Quoting a sexological glossary titled "The Language of Homosexuality," historian Jonathan Ned Katz notes in his *Gay/Lesbian Almanac: A New Documentary* that "R.F.D." initially connoted the transcontinental sweep of the U.S. Postal Service, or "Rural Free Delivery." In the late 1940s and 1950s, pre-Stonewall white middle-class urban gay U.S. males appropriated this postal term to disparage what Katz describes as the "R.F.D. queen—a homosexual who lives in the country or in a small town, and who has homosexual impulses and desires, but who does not understand the argot and ways, or know the habits and places of congregation of the homosexual fraternity in cities and metropolitan centers."[8] In the 1970s, however, these so-called RFD queens reappropriated this regional slur to express dissatisfaction with the "argot and ways" of an emergent white gay male "ghetto" culture felt to be inherently normalizing rather than inherently oppositional. Far removed from the sophistication and knowingness that marks the late-nineties *RFD* (and many late-nineties post-Stonewall urban U.S. cultures), early-seventies *RFD* begins as a riposte to these "habits and places of congregation"—one that critiques by way of the unsophisticated, the anti-urban, the anti-urbane, and the anticosmopolitan, and one keen to distance itself geographically, materially, and aesthetically from a big-city "homosexual fraternity" through unexpected print alignments with small-town rural lesbians.[9] Through

     OUT OF THE CLOSETS, INTO THE WOODS

such critiques, *RFD* enabled the queer subjects in its pages and elsewhere to imagine and to inaugurate critical horizons that engaged with those bodies and consciousnesses that were often excluded from the matrix of urbane schemas, even as the journal's non-normative engagements were sometimes incompletely realized.

RFD, that is to say, was one of the first post-Stonewall print media to offer a ruralized counter to what Judith Halberstam has termed U.S.-based metronormativity. By *metronormativity,* Halberstam references a dominant "story of migration from 'country' to 'town,'" "a spatial narrative within which the subject moves to a place of tolerance after enduring life in a place of suspicion, persecution, and secrecy" and embraces a flight to the city that imagines the metropolis as the only sustainable space for queers.[10] To this compulsory narrative of rural-to-urban lesbian and gay migration, I add that racial, socioeconomic, and aesthetic norms inform metronormativity, including what José Esteban Muñoz terms the "normative ideal" of whiteness, "an image of ideality and normativity that structures gay male [and lesbian] desires and communities" and "is reproduced transnationally through print advertising."[11] To the racial and corporeal norms of such privileged whiteness, we could add the socioeconomic norms of the middle classes and the aesthetic norms of urbanity, sophistication, and cosmopolitanism, or what is often referred to as "trendy fashion," "chic," "style," or "lifestyle." Together these four interlocking aspects of metronormativity—the narratological, the racial, the socioeconomic, and the aesthetic—reproduce the imaginary geographic ideals of post-Stonewall urbanism for men and women, an urbanism that facilitates the ongoing commodification and depoliticization of U.S.-based queer cultures. Taken as story, style, or both, metronormativity thus buttresses the narratives, customs, and presumptions of many modern U.S. urban gays and lesbians while it simultaneously enables these gays and lesbians to govern the aesthetic, erotic, material, and affective imaginaries of many modern queers, irrespective of country, town, or somewhere in between.

That said, I stress that the cosmopolitan middle-class styles of U.S. metronormativity have always been countered by stylistic metrosubversions within and without the U.S. metropolis. The radical sexual politics of the Gay Liberation Front, to take but one example, were integral rejoinders to the racial, gendered, and class-based codes of homonormativity that emerged in the early 1970s, even as the GLF oftentimes promoted one aspect of metronormativity—rural-to-urban migration—in its emphasis on an urban-based politics of coming out in San Francisco, Los Angeles, New York City, and other major cities.[12] Homonormativity may facilitate metronormativity, but the two are not always coterminous. Likewise, outside the U.S. metropolis, a complementary form that metrosubversions have taken is a deliberately queer anti-urbanism that marks journals such as *RFD* and *Country Women.* Though *anti-urbanism* historically refers to a conservative, urbanoid, and heteronormative "white flight" from the city that marked post–World War II middle-class Anglo-American migrations to the suburbs, I here redeploy the term to describe a mode of queer critique that counters the normative ideals (the "argot and ways") of homonormative and metronormative post-Stonewall urban gay lifestyles.[13]

This essay, then, extends recent historical scholarship on 1970s lesbian and gay U.S. print cultures to analyze the anti-urban politics of *RFD*'s early stylistics. It offers an aesthetic archaeology of what one initial contributor, Donald Engstrom, later termed *RFD*'s "separatist fag community," and what one historian of regional U.S. cultures, James T. Sears, sees as the quarterly's "anarcho-effeminism."[14] Extending their findings, the essay explores how a particular version of gay male urbanity began to reprint itself as a normalizing print style in 1970s glossy magazines, and how *RFD*, alongside *Country Women,* responded to this historical packaging with oppositional stylistics of its own. Hence it examines the visual culture and stylistic productions of rural-based queer print culture that speak volumes about the calcification of U.S. metronormativity over the course of the 1970s. Interrogating these paratextual layouts will enable critics to witness how stylistics function as points of political and cultural contestation for gay urbanites and their detractors in several post-Stonewall U.S. literary public spheres. The layouts will also show how a rustic 1974 *RFD* logo tried to slow the historical march of what would gradually become the urban sprawl of *RFD*'s 2005 logoscape.

To accomplish these tasks, I return to a pivotal moment in U.S. sexual history that saw the fraught convergence of nationalizing glossies such as the "cha cha" *Advocate,* regionalizing radical lesbian mimeographs such as *Country Women,* and anti-urbane counterparts such as the Iowa-based *RFD*. I start in Los Angeles with an explosion of lifestyle publications that enabled aesthetic standards of gay urbanity in the post-Stonewall United States. I next explore rural-based California critiques launched against these stylistic ideals by lesbian separatists disenchanted with male "ghetto" publications. I finally return to where this essay began—a Grinnell, Iowa, farmhouse—to chart how *RFD* bounces on *Advocate* and builds on *Country Women*'s stylistics to advance what I theorize as critical rusticity. By *critical rusticity,* I mean an intersectional opportunity to geographically, corporeally, and aesthetically inhabit non-normative sexuality that offers new possibilities for the sexually marginalized outside the metropolis as well as inside it. Both of these journals, we will see, exhibited complicated, sometimes flawed, sometimes divisive gender and racial politics as they critiqued the *Advocate*'s metronormativity. Acknowledging their respective complexities, I show how a working-class "country journal for gay men everywhere" tried to present alternative aesthetic opportunities to dominant U.S. gay lifestyles through rural U.S. women's alternative lifestyles. These countercultural aesthetics were resistant to the "trendy fashions from West

   OUT OF THE CLOSETS, INTO THE WOODS

Hollywood," but they were nevertheless indebted to the antifashion cultural politics of *Country Women.*

RFD emerged at a pivotal moment in post–World War II U.S. lesbian and gay print cultures, one marked by a rising tide of consumer-oriented urban prints such as the *Advocate;* an increasing emphasis on world cities such as New York, Los Angeles, and San Francisco as the final destinations of internal U.S. lesbian and gay migrations; and an increasing bifurcation of queer print culture into distinct lesbian and gay literary public spheres.[15] I offer an overview of some aspects of U.S. lesbian separatist print culture in the next section of this essay. First, I explore the inchoate literary fields that *RFD* and its counterpart *Country Women* worked through and against.

Recounting the publishing climate that led to *RFD*'s first issue in 1974, Stuart Scofield, a founder of the journal alongside Donald Engstrom, recalled that

at the same time that *RFD* was being born, the third generation of gay magazines began to appear: the heavily-capitalized "slicks" such as *Blueboy, HONCHO,* and the new Goodstein version of the *Advocate.* Giving Gay Lib, at best lip service, they have grown and prospered since 1974 by avoiding political controversy, selling sex and catering to the so-called affluent "gay lifestyle." Unlike all the preceding publications, these new ones are money-making ventures—from Gay Liberation to a Gay Lifestyle, from attempts to define and establish a separate gay culture and identity to the selling of advertisers' products in just five years.[16]

In his mention of "preceding publications" and other "generations," Scofield references major 1950s and 1960s homophile publications such as the Los Angeles–based *ONE: The Homosexual Magazine* and the San Francisco–based *Mattachine Review* and the *Ladder: A Lesbian Review.* Each of these journals tried to politicize a "national gay and lesbian community," although none fully achieved this goal.[17]

Scofield then notes that "earlier prints" like *ONE* and the *Ladder* were supplanted by local-based newspapers and journals such as "*Gay Sunshine* (San Francisco), *Gay* (NYC), *Gay Alternative* (Philadelphia), the pre-Goodstein *Advocate* (Los Angeles), and *Gay Community News* and *Fag Rag* (Boston)."[18] As I mentioned earlier, many of these metropolitan-based prints were committed to intersectional Gay Liberation Front politics that engaged with concurrent critiques of racial, imperial, and capitalist norms, or what one GLF member (and subsequent founder of *RFD*) praised in the San Francisco *Free Press* as the interconnections of "women's liberation," "black [or Third World] liberation," Chicano liberation, and "white radical and ideologues" working against global capital and "Amerikan" imperialism.[19] Likewise, part of the multifront political aims of these queer prints was to critique the homonormative white gay male ghettos that were developing in Los Angeles and San Francisco.

As one GLF manifesto noted, "ghetto institutions are still part of our lives. . . . The prices are notoriously high, and the practices are often racist, sexist, and anti-working-class. This materially oppresses female, black, and poor homosexuals and also reinforces the false consciousness (racism, sexism, class-chauvinism) which divides us as a group and, in the end, oppresses us all."[20]

The *Advocate*, however, dismissed the intersectional ideals of these Gay Liberation prints and affirmed what Scofield sees as a depoliticized "Gay Lifestyle." By the early 1970s journals such as the *Mattachine Review* were either financially destitute or out of print, and antihomonormative prints such as Boston's *Fag Rag* were nationally (if not locally) eclipsed by the Los Angeles–based *Advocate*.[21] Emerging at the historical upswing of gay ghettoization, the *Advocate* paradoxically began as an offshoot of U.S. homophile monthlies and as a complement to urban-oriented gay liberation prints such as *Gay Community News* and *Gay Sunshine*. By the mid-1970s, it surpassed both of these constituencies and "made a killing" as a "gay lifestyles magazine" that promoted "trendy fashions."[22] Historians have often charted the *Advocate*'s devolution into an "affluent" lifestyle weekly as a refusal to maintain previous allegiances to post-Stonewall intersectional politics.[23] Yet even before Wall Street investment banker David Goodstein purchased the publication in 1974, overhauled it into a slick glossy, and added the subtitle "Touching Your Lifestyle" to its inside cover, the *Advocate* confirmed a white middle-class cosmopolitanism that marked norms of cultural and economic capital for many gay men and lesbians, metropolitan or not, and that *RFD* and *Country Women* would later try to counteract.

To do so, the *Advocate* imagined its gay readers as "heavily capitalized" consumers and interpellated them into a normalized racial and class identity by way of an aesthetics of chic and fashionability. Scanning the layout of early 1970s issues of the *Advocate,* one is struck by the relentless promotion of this cosmo-urbanism, an endless sea of ads for Persian rugs in Melrose, or skimpy swimwear, or Art World, or swank nightclubs, or Eye Mystic jewelry, or David's Divine Dining Nightly in Melrose, or Glendon's fine crystal, or Dresden kennels for your beagle, or advice for buying your perfect boat, or hat stores, or New Look loungewear, or glass tabletops. There are weekly columns with titles such as "BODY Buddy," "Fashionation," and "The Fine Art of Dining Out." To be more theoretical, there are ample opportunities for what Muñoz, in his overview of mainstream New York City gay nightlife, terms "the dominant imprint," "a blueprint of gay male desire and desirability that is unmarked and thus universally white," or what I see as the inchoate cultivation of U.S. metronormativity grounded in an *Advocate* Los Angeles ghetto yet extending beyond this print metropolis to encompass a globalizing U.S. nation-state.[24] As one March 1970 "Exclusive to the Homophile Society from Coast to Coast" advertisement for "specially designed" Eye Mystic 10K white-gold blue sapphire rings promises,

"We predict that the Eye Mystic will become the symbol of the Homo-sexual Society the world over."[25]

If not yet "the world over" (that would come soon enough), then certainly the transcontinental United States as the stylish imprint that fast became the *Advocate:* "Touching Your Lifestyle" matched the stylish commodified bodies offered between its pages. Witness the following 1970 gray-balance graphic that records a shift from Gay Liberation to Gay Lifestyle within an 8½ x 11 format (Figure 15.3). In its obsession with the duplication of leisure-oriented white gay male ghetto bodies, this ad erases lesbians and queers of color. Six clustered scenes repro-duce approximately thirty-eight persons, all white and none recogniz-able as female. Potential subscribers instead view exact replications of stylish men who dress the same, share similar chiseled features, and look at the same copy of *Advocate* newsprint, whose front page reads "Groovy Guy Gala Goes Ga-Ga" and whose back page reads "What do 70,000 gay people have in common? *The Advocate,* that's what!" In this ad for subscription, a developing apolitical urban clone culture becomes a uniform print culture, and unlike earlier publications such as *Mat-tachine* and *ONE* or later prints such as *RFD* or *Country Women,* lesbi-ans are nowhere in sight. Thus the buff body of a slim white male, hair coiffed, jean cuffs hemmed, calf muscles bulging, occupies a good third of the ad's frame. The epitome of "trendy fashion," this clean-cut reader presents himself as a sophisticated cosmopolite for interested subscrib-ers, and if his tight-fitting T-shirt and deliberately placed locks don't alert you to this, a quick semiotics of his sidekick poodle—another eager *Advocate* reader—certainly will.

This poodle, in fact, is key to decoding how the *Advocate*'s visual culture stylizes U.S. gay metronorms to record a shift in male-centered U.S. metronormativity. While most of the ad appears sleek, modern, and bulging—from the skyscrapers to the *Advocate* reader's crotch—the poodle appears somewhat removed from this glossy beefiness. With a bow on its head, it appears diminutive and effeminized. Yet the fact that the subscription aligns the marginalized poodle with the *Advocate* reader is noteworthy, since the dog functions as a representative carry-over from pre-Stonewall metropolitan stylistics, one in which a classed version of white gay male identity was registered through "fancy frills, froufrou, bric-a-brac, and au courant kitsch."[26] That the poodle is also an avid *Advocate* reader (note its cotton-ball tail wagging like a metro-nome) is just as significant, given that this pre-Stonewall dog reads a post-Stonewall lifestyle magazine rather than politicized prints such as the contemporaneous Gay Liberation Front journal *Fag Rag.* A recent historical shift in lesbian and gay U.S. print cultures becomes aestheti-cized as a recent historical realignment, and one effeminized mode of gay metrostyle is incorporated into—and made subservient to—a more masculinized other.

What the *Advocate*'s visual culture accomplishes here and through-

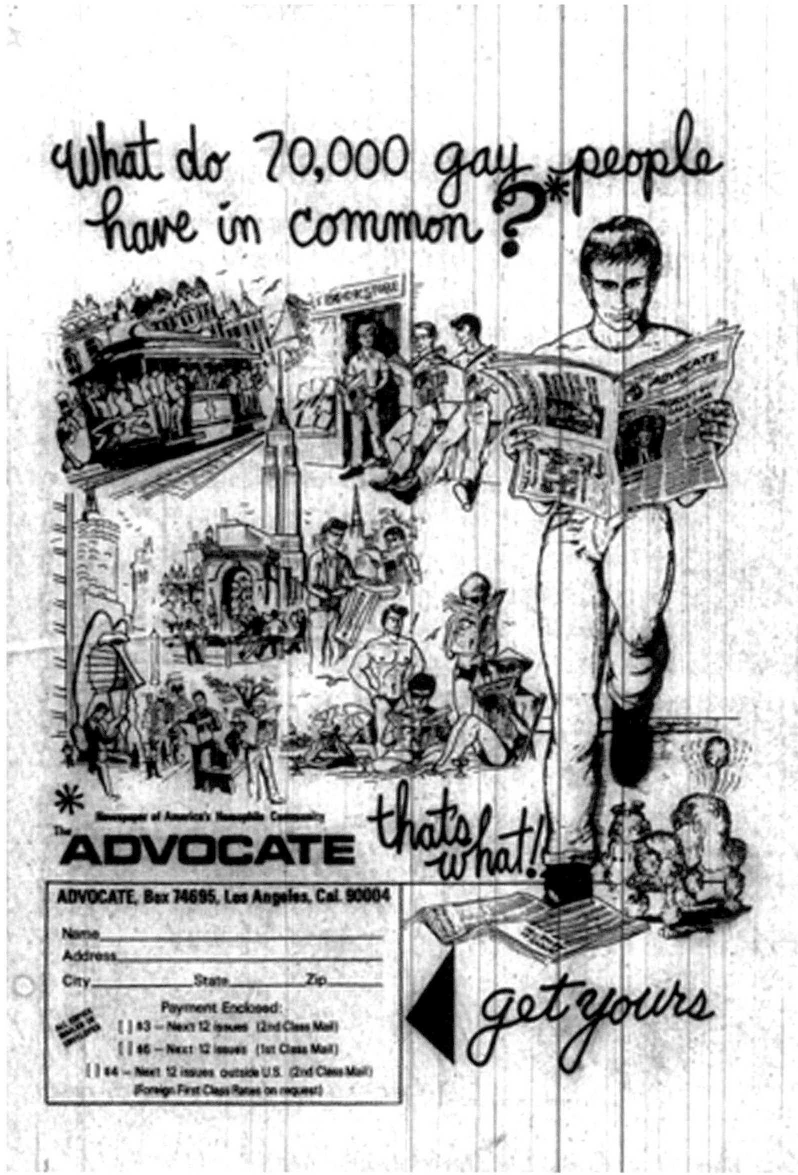

out its pages is impressive. Its images translate the gendered, racial,
and class biases of one pre-Stonewall generation of middle-class white
urban gay men—what a male GLF proponent criticized as a "bygone era
of their fantasy world of poodle dogs and Wedgwood tea cups and chan-
deliers and all the fancy clothes and home furnishings that any queen
could ever desire"—into the hypermasculinist norms of ghetto visibility.[27] This historical move is condensed into the spectacle of an apolitical
Advocate reader and his dog, and together these two come to epitomize a
certain legend of homosexuality in the post-Stonewall U.S. city, a guidebook of sophistication too often presumed to be intrinsic to Western
gay men regardless of historical specificities. Notes queer theorist
Joseph Litvak: "We have learned from gay, lesbian, and queer theorists

that gay people—especially gay men—have traditionally functioned as objects of such distinguished epistemological and rhetorical aggressions as urbanity and knowingness. But, in the Western *imaginaire,* gay people also function as subjects of sophistication."[28] To extend Litvak, "Western" gay men—especially Western lesbians and queers of color—within and without the city are "traditionally" subjected to sophistication as an aggressive communal standard not only from outside queer group identity but also from inside it. The 1970 *Advocate* image bears this out as it turns the "rhetorical aggressions" of an earlier U.S. cosmo-stylishness into an aestheticized norm that ideologically imagines itself to be "America's Homophile Community."

To confirm its representative claim, the *Advocate* nationalizes metronormativity by condensing an imaginary homosexual society into four U.S. cities. The *Advocate* ad is thus one of the first of its historical kind to illustrate another normalizing impulse that early issues of *RFD* and *Country Women* work against: bicoastality.[29] By *bicoastality,* I refer to an idealizing metropolitan scenario akin to "the flight to the city" that constructs intranational, national, and transcontinental queer identities by imagining the evacuation of the regional and the rural into global cities such as New York, Los Angeles, and San Francisco. The *Advocate* ad thus translates localized imaginaries of urban cosmopolitanism into a national readership that it assumes applies universally to all queers, irrespective of their geographic particulars. To do so, it subjects readers to an imagined Homophile Community bookended by geographic stereotypes of New York City, San Francisco, and Los Angeles with one token Midwestern city—Chicago, a Second (or Fourth) City—tacked on for good measure.

Left of the anonymous reader and his canine are six scenes. One depicts *Advocate* subscription space. Another depicts leisurely *Advocate* readers outside an unnamed bookstore. The remaining scenes—metonymies of a phantasmatic gay U.S. literary public sphere—figure specific geographic locales. The Golden Gate Bridge, hillside Victorians, and a trolley overflowing with clones signify San Francisco and its growing Castro district. The Washington Square arch, several raised water towers, and the Empire State Building register New York City or, perhaps, Greenwich Village. Los Angeles figures as a day at the beach accompanied by seagulls. And Chicago is condensed into a building from the Marina City complex as well as the Pablo Picasso statue in front of the Richard J. Daly Center (formally the Chicago Civic Center).

These "extra-regional" metropolitan centers are geographically distinct, but the *Advocate* ad pools them together through a gray-scale graphic layout of cosmopolitan nationalism.[30] Near the center of the ad, the Empire State Building's lightning rod penetrates the Golden Gate Bridge, and one standing *Advocate* reader at the Los Angeles beach blurs into another standing *Advocate* reader in Washington Park. All told, we view leisurely San Francisco readers, leisurely New York City readers,

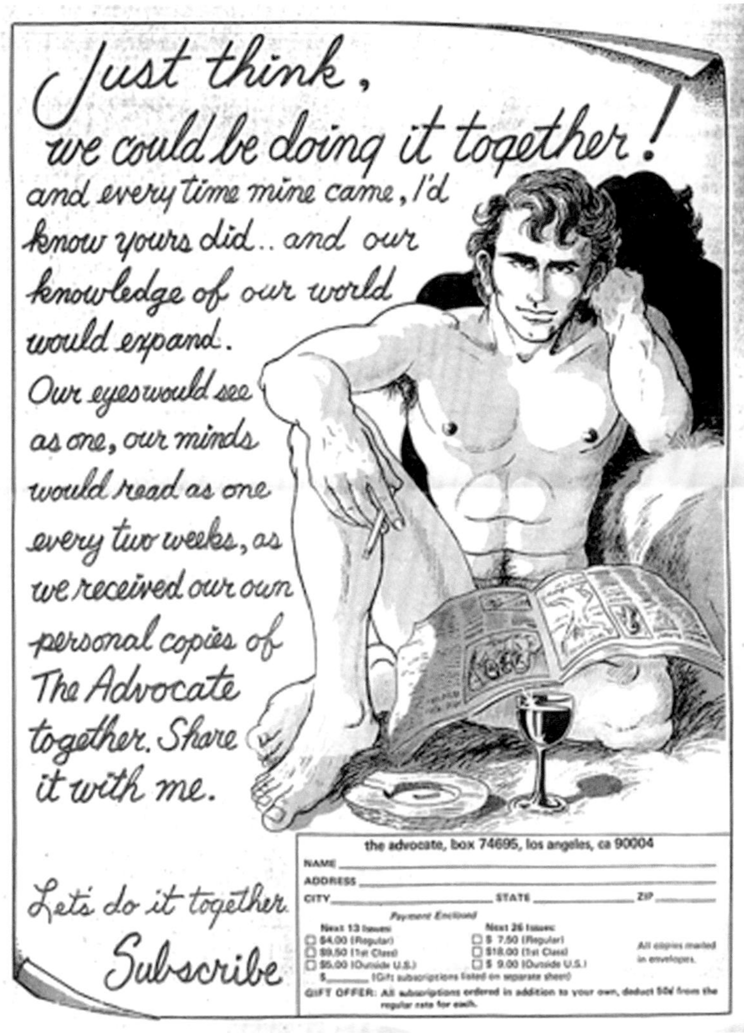

leisurely Chicago readers, and leisurely Los Angeles readers, all joined
through the *Advocate* subscription as a collective "America." In antici-
pation of later U.S. lifestyle slicks such as *Out* and *MetroSource,* these
metropolitan localities confirm an *Advocate* imaginary that figures the
urban white gay male ghetto as the locus of a nationalizing and nationalized queer U.S. identity. This *Advocate* ad thus represents the urban as
a geographic and homogenized space of leisure, wealth, and consumption, which works to replace the notion—and the politics—of the U.S.
city as a place of racially, corporeally, and socioeconomically diverse
queers as well as the urban as a space of political contestation, uprising,
and revolution that marked numerous metropoles in the late 1960s and
early 1970s.[31] This exemplary image is also one among the hundreds of
such images published in metropolitan gay lifestyle glossies in the decades after Stonewall, and its bicoastal focus on "trendy" contexts produced forms of exclusion that *RFD* and *Country Women* pushed against
(see Figure 15.4, with its shag carpeting and red wineglass).

If the *Advocate*'s "70,000 gay people" subscription notice erased women in general and lesbians in particular, there were numerous rejoinders to this oversight from white lesbian organizations, and they were blistering. Most notably, Del (Dorothy) Martin, a former editor of the *Ladder*, revoked her membership in the early 1970s homophile community and denounced white urban gay male publications in a manifesto titled "If That's All There Is." First published by the *Advocate* under the tongue-in-cheek title "Female Gay Blasts Men, Leaves Movement" in 1970 and later reprinted in the 1971 racially diverse and interclass collection *Lesbians Speak Out* by the Oakland-based Women's Press Collective, Martin's article bids "goodbye to all the 'representative' homophile publications that look more like magazines for male nudist colonies" and "goodbye to the gay bars that discriminate against women." In their place, she contends, "it is a revelation to find acceptance, equality, love, and friendship—everything we sought in the homophile community—not there, but in the women's movement."[32]

With this farewell to the *Advocate*, Martin joined a rising number of women's movement coalitions such as the National Organization of Women to launch critiques against misogyny, male-oriented capitalism, male-oriented aesthetics, and gay-male-oriented ghetto print cultures.[33] In fact, Martin became a member of NOW's board after breaking with nationalized homophile publications such as the *Advocate*, and soon after, she emerged as a key spokeswoman for radical lesbian separatism, a "lodestar of [largely white] Lesbian America in the 1970s" that encouraged political and cultural breaks from straight-male-identified (and gay-male-identified) cultures to promote women-centric lifestyles.[34]

While there were numerous critiques launched against the racial norms of lesbian separatism by queer of color/Third World feminists such as the Boston-based Combahee River Collective, Cherríe Moraga, Rosario Moralas, Audre Lorde, Chrystos, and Gloria Anzaldúa, I want to explore the visual culture and paratextual print culture of lesbian separatism to see how it stylized its racial norms even as it critiqued homonormative ideals. Manifestos such as "Leaving the Gay Men Behind" by New York City's Radicalesbians launched intersectional attacks on economic inequality, gender bias, and sophisticated stylistics—in brief, U.S. homonormativity—"as a form of oppression" that these critics sensed many white urban gay male middle-class publics typified.[35] As self-identified lesbian separatist Karla Jay writes in her influential essay of 1978, "No Man's Land":

I talk of women/lesbian culture and not gay male culture. I believe that culture is one area in which lesbians have greatly diverged from gay men, perhaps because, as I have pointed out, gay men have somewhat different roots, and, after all, they are men. . . . This is true, as I've said, in part because gay men, being men, with greater stake in the ruling culture, have relied heavily on already established institutions and forms for their "new" culture. Lesbians, twice removed and thoroughly alienated, have started from scratch.[36]

As many white lesbian separatists produced this "women/lesbian culture and not gay male culture," some (not all) lesbian separatists launched negative critiques through a politicized anti-aesthetic, a calculated stylization of the "not gay male" that "greatly diverged" from a gay male metronormativity symbolized by the *Advocate*. In fact, there was a significant strain of metropolitan-based 1970s lesbian separatism that promoted "antifashion" aesthetics for those "who were striking out against the *Hollywood–Madison Avenue–Playboy* ideal" as well as for those, like Martin, who were striking out against dominant publications that felt to be more like "magazines for male nudist colonies."[37] Or, as historian Robert Streitmatter explains, "lesbians did not write so colorfully about their culture" as white gay ghetto males did, primarily, he assumes, because urban U.S. gay men were thought to place more "value on physical beauty."[38]

I have no desire to assess the truth-value of this specious last claim. Nor am I invested in defining radical lesbians of any color or class solely as antisophisticates. Nor am I eager to reproduce stereotypes of 1970s lesbian separatism as unsophisticated.[39] A quick glimpse into the historical complexities of pre- or post-Stonewall U.S. lesbian cultures immediately proves otherwise, and a materialist critique that attends to white gay men's access to capital and publishing centers would also inform our understanding of these anti-aesthetic discourses. Yet when a prominent lesbian separatist such as Jay cautions that "we do not become the women of gay men," I am nevertheless intrigued by how a particular strain of white lesbian separatism, implicitly or explicitly, challenges the norms of America's Homophile Community with its own aesthetic critiques, and how such critiques functioned as both anti–Madison Avenue and anti-*Advocate*.[40]

Likewise, I am interested in how stylistics of the nonurban often informed these politics, and how these cultivations facilitated *RFD*'s critically queer anti-urbanism. One anti-middle-class journal of white-based lesbian separatism—*Country Women*—did just this as it aestheticized Jay's "No Man's Land" into a unique form of cultural criticism that signified on the *Advocate*'s bicoastal ideals. In her negative vision, Jay makes mention of "the proliferation of lesbian media after the Stonewall uprising" (63). Among the numerous journals that she catalogs (*Lesbian Tide, Big Mama Rag, Lesbian Connection,* and *her-self,* among many others) she highlights *Country Women*'s dedication to "rural living" and its critique of gay male "ruling culture" (63). Within this growing schism of radical lesbian separatism and gay male ghettoization—a schism that AIDS activism of the 1980s and 1990s would later somewhat bridge—*Country Women* introduced geographic separatism as a possible strategy against middle-class male culture as well as the gendered bias of bi-

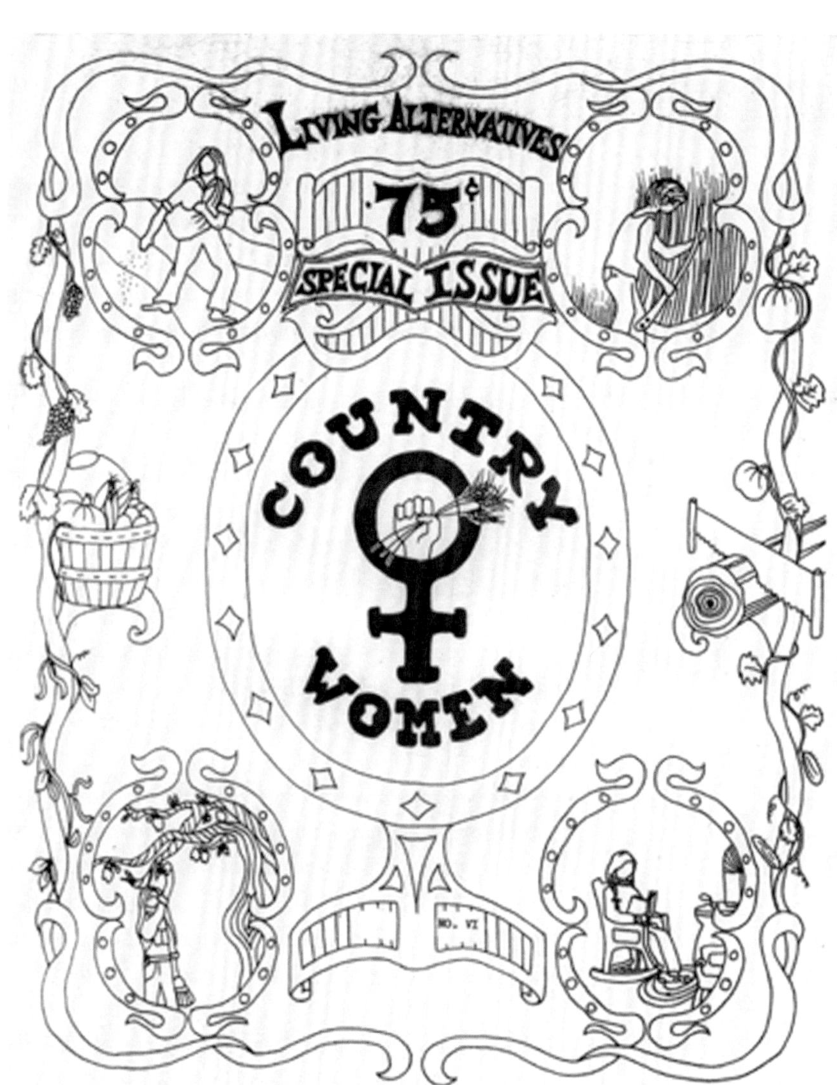

LIVING ALTERNATIVES
75¢
SPECIAL ISSUE
COUNTRY
WOMEN
NO. VI

Carmen Goodyear, front page
of *Country Women,* June 1973.
Courtesy of the artist.

coastal aesthetic norms. It "developed a critical view of urbanity," argues historian Martin Meeker, as it "struggl[ed] to build . . . outside of/and or independent of America's largest cities where gay [male] ghettoes were located."[41]

First published in the rural community of Albion, California, *Country Women* situated itself 147 miles north of San Francisco's developing gay ghetto. Printing the journal from 1973 to 1979, with an Anchor Press/ Doubleday compilation released in 1976, *Country Women*'s collective was composed of working-class and lower-middle-class women who sometimes addressed the sexual politics of opposite-sex rural communal living as they also invoked a back-to-the-land ideology, a countercultural ideology that often emphasized organic farming, communal activity, and eco-activism.[42] More often than not, members of the collective concerned themselves with publishing the principles of radical white lesbian separatism, "which whilst not exclusively anti-urban, could perhaps best be enacted away from man-made cities."[43] *Country Women* readers and writers thus imagined themselves as a countercultural antidote to male-oriented urban print cultures in general and gay-male-oriented urban print cultures such as the *Advocate* represented in particular. Much of the journal was separatist—or "woman-identified"—in its back-to-the-land politics.[44]

While this countercultural rural lesbian separatism was often dependent on strategic essentialism, utopian impulses critiqued by queer of color/Third World feminists, and an unquestioned reliance on racial normativity, it is clear that *Country Women* journal tried to advance "alternative (non-urban, non-industrial, non-consumerist) lifestyles" at levels of both content and form.[45] The journal was founded by white blue-collar and lower-middle-class feminists in low-wage occupations—one was a secretary, another a waitress—who were quick to respond to the socioeconomic difficulties of rural living and who were eager to instruct other separatist-minded feminists in the complexities of everyday land cultivation. "Unless you have inherited money," readers are informed, "buying land means saving money—either one or two people saving a lot of money (several thousand dollars anyway) or a group of people saving smaller amounts."[46] Though it recognized that rural communal living was not an affordable option for a majority of feminists, *Country Women* earnestly cultivated a nonurban reading public that it felt offered a "living alternative" to dominant middle-class lifestyles that would influence *RFD*. And if its working-class readers could not finance a move away from cities (or if they questioned the political value of a countercultural back-to-the-land movement), some could afford a *Country Women* subscription that enabled them to imagine themselves as members of a nonurbanist collective.

As we see from the front cover of a special issue dedicated to "Living Alternatives," *Country Women* figured itself as a counter to supposedly "man-made cities" and the aesthetic, socioeconomic, and narrative trap-

   OUT OF THE CLOSETS, INTO THE WOODS

pings that these environments were ideologically thought to entail for women, lesbian or not (Figure 15.5). Fighting what it saw as the aesthetic and socioeconomic norms of metropolitan leisure classes, this front page sketches an alternative to these ideals with idealizations of its own. What is most obvious about this front cover is its separatist erasure of men. Four clustered scenes reproduce approximately four persons, none recognizable as male. Moving clockwise, we see one female harvesting hay. Another reads in front of a wood-burning stove. Another picks apples. And another sows a field. Though each female is singular, these women are braided together through an illustrated border of grape and pumpkin vines. None of these females has a recognizable face since they are blank, though each is unmarked as white. None is wearing particularly "trendy" fashions. None participates in a capitalist economy. And none, to my knowledge, is beholden to ideals of "physical beauty" that stereotypically marked 1970s gay male cultures and that some strains of lesbian-separatist critique fought against. They are instead opposed to—and geographically distanced from—a stylistics of cosmo-urbanism that marks dominant homosocial publications such as *Playboy,* and dominant homophile publications such as the *Advocate.* This utopian scene presents potential subscribers with an alternative collective, a rusticity that "naturally" separates from the man-made institutions of urban gay print cultures by cloning white female anticlones. The print styles of *Country Women,* original founders Sherry Thomas and Jeanne Tetrault noted, "were simple and funky and plain crude."[47]

To rephrase these last claims: *Country Women*'s simple, funky, and plain crude stylistics work against the bicoastal male sophistications of "Hollywood–Madison Avenue" and the *Advocate* with a strategic aesthetic of womanly ruralism. Though the journal did promote an unquestioned emphasis on the white female body, the front cover also shows two-dimensional pumpkins figuratively overwriting slick Gay Lifestyle designs. This is the textual reproduction of Jay's woman/lesbian culture as "not gay male culture," and it occurs throughout *Country Women*'s paratextual "No Man's Land" during the mid- to late 1970s. As we see with the front page to "Living Alternatives," covers of the quarterly were always hand drawn. Captions to articles were often scribbled or written in bubble letters. And its nonindustrial, nonconsumerist politics refused capitalist advertisements. Through such stripped-down imaginaries, the journal naturalizes its critiques of cosmopolitanism through a woman-identified countercultural politics of coastal separatism.

Country Women also flaunts these female-dominated stylistics with invocations of graphic design that were anything but graphically designed, that were more akin to a handwritten do-it-yourself (DIY) print for those who could not afford typewriters (Figure 15.6). As opposed to the leisurely "fashionation" that saturated mainstream and middle-class ghetto print culture, the journal offers a space where metronormative stylistics—or a particular body type, if not a particular body's gender or racial identity—don't really enter into the picture. In keeping with these principles and its anticapitalist critiques, the quarterly published creative writings such as "A Fat Women's Journal" as well as how-to guides for collecting shellfish, sowing fields, raising sheep, chopping wood, bartering, understanding welfare rights, building hot beds, and raising calves. In the journal's first statement of purpose we are told: "Each issue will be regular columns plus articles about a central theme. Regular columns will include gardening, raising animals, how to use tools, building, food, country skills, alternatives (life styles), women's health, and reviews of women's literature." In brief, *Country Women* ruralized a strain of anti-middle-class white lesbian separatist critique into a distinctive version of counterculturalism. And though it may have reinforced racial norms in its neglect of metropolitan or nonmetropolitan Third World/ queer feminists, its visual culture nonetheless dismissed burgeoning gay male metro print norms.

In lieu of the *Advocate*'s nationalizing boutiques, then, *Country Women* offered readers a critical rusticity that encouraged a "lack of cultural sophistication and a preference for practical know-how."[48] By using the term *critical rusticity,* I follow anthropologist Gerald W. Creed and cultural critic Barbara Ching, who emphasize "the possibility of a culturally valuable rusticity" and note that "identities" stereotypically "based in the country can be considered *rustic* while those associated

OUT OF THE CLOSETS, INTO THE WOODS

with the city are *urbane,* or, more vernacularly, *sophisticated."*[49] And by
this term, I refer not only to an actual geographic space removed from
the metropolitan such as Albion, California. I also refer to an antagonistic mode of queer critique and a novel structure of feeling, a rhetorical
and affective engagement with U.S.-based metronormativity that critiques any representation of the rural as a pastoral space removed from
conditions of conflict and inequality, as it also supports the representational politics of those (such as the rural working classes) often typed as
"rustic."

By accomplishing these tasks, such critical rusticity, notes one
Country Women contributor in a self-reflexive "Retrospective" about
an unnamed "rural commune in the northern Midwest," would be an
anarchic queer "state" that is adamantly not a commodifying urban gay
nation-state. "This allows us to live together in a state of what I'd call
loving anarchy, and what a friend rephrased as 'responsible anarchy,'"
she tells readers. "We need neither structure nor rules to live together.
We find ourselves sharing work freely."[50] It is precisely this "responsible
anarchy" of countercultural nonurbanism that so intrigued *RFD* founder
Stuart Scofield, who was unimpressed by the "cha cha palaces" and
"trendy fashions" of the *Advocate*'s metronormativity, and who, "reading
and loving *Country Women*" in the winter of 1973, was inspired to print a
complementary quarterly for "country men everywhere."[51]

First published during the autumnal equinox in August 1974 with a
print run of seven hundred copies, *RFD* in its inaugural issue made clear
that the journal extended the rural stylistics of *Country Women,* that the
working-class editors imagined themselves as non-normative alternatives to bicoastal U.S. gay lifestyle. The journal was published by the
lesbian-run Iowa City Women's Press and strove to include lesbians of
any color—separatist or not—in its pages. In the quarterly's first issue,
the collective published an introduction titled "Rustic Fairy Dreams,"
which confessed that "no women have contributed material for this first
issue, but we hope it is not so male-oriented/dominated to prevent Lesbians from using this magazine for communication with each other. And
perhaps, with the Earth as our common ground, we can begin a much
needed dialogue between gay women and men."[52]

This intersectional emphasis on cross-gender alliance was complemented by *RFD*'s countercultural critique of U.S.-based capitalism. Much
like *Country Women, RFD* too advocated a critical rusticity as it offered
readers an anticosmopolitanism that undid *Advocate* ideals of middle-
class culture and corporeality. Using language that strikingly mirrors
Country Women editorials, the first issue included a tongue-in-cheek
advertisement for the Hop Brook Commune in rural Massachusetts:

We share most of the values that you would expect from an alternative society—
steering clear of consumerism, commercialism, T.V., A.M., affection, competition,

intellectualized bullshit, egoism, role-playing, meritocracy and the rest of that bourgeois. We are multi-uni-racial. WE RECOGNIZE NOT LESS THAN ONE SEX AMONG HUMAN BEINGS.

Rules. We have no rules. If we were to draw up a rule, it would be that no one here will objectify another (which is also to be objectified). We don't want this commune to be a crash pad—a homosexual motel—a place to bring the individual and collective falseness of "self"-hate and of "self"-love of either the major cultures or of the gay subcultures. But we have no fixed structures or systems for ourselves.[53]

With rhetoric that echoes *Country Women*'s claim that one "needs neither structure nor rules to live together," *RFD* situates itself outside the rules of heteronormative ("major") culture and an increasingly homonormative gay male subculture. Refusing to become the print equivalent of a bourgeois "homosexual motel" or an armchair urban gay rural retreat that would characterize later radical faerie gatherings, the journal distances itself from the consumerism and the commercialism thought to characterize mid-1970s urban gay lifestyle publications as it, like *Country Women*, merges countercultural and back-to-the-land ideologies. Though initially founded by white men, it also refuses gay-ghetto aesthetic norms with what one contributor called "its agony under the tinsel, dealing out death to the spirit but surfaced with glamour,"[54] and it tries to reach readers less settled into the "collective falseness" of capitalist homonormativity and less indebted to what was becoming a slick mainstream subculture.[55] In this focus on "multi-uni-racial," gender, and capitalist oppression, *RFD* extends the political aims of metropolitan-based Gay Liberation Fronts as it also critiques a dominant U.S. gay lifestyle. Recounting the journal's economic critiques of ghetto prints, one initial editor recalled that "we were poor and knew that many readers were poor, and 75¢ seemed the upper limit of what we personally could afford to spend for a magazine and it seemed what our collective political consciousness would allow."[56]

Thus the working-class editors of *RFD*—a journal under perpetual financial strain—imagined themselves as an extension of antihomonormative urban-produced gay liberation magazines such as Boston's *Fag Rag*: "*RFD* was the last Gay Liberation magazine to begin, in many ways quite fittingly. Just as some of the counter culture people were choosing the quiet organic life, gay people began to see rural life as a real option to the urban ghettos."[57] But I also highlight that *RFD* was adamantly not urban oriented, nor did it participate in the rural-to-urban metronormativity that marked even the most politically radical queer prints of the 1970s. Like its predecessor *Country Women*, *RFD* instead offered what one issue termed a "reader-participatory adventure" for nonbourgeois readers that details foraging for edible wild violets, paper cutting, goat dairying, water dowsing, basket making, and cooking with bark.[58] It also functioned as a "de-isolating connection" for queer readers who could not afford a move to a city, or who could not participate in the imaginary metropolitan flight that I detailed earlier.[59] Such an antimetronormative and antihomonormative agenda builds from rural lesbian separatism in particular, but it also refuses to separate itself from lesbians in general, as the first issue of *RFD* stressed. Explained one self-identified *RFD* queen: "I felt very alienated from the faggot scene and found myself constantly surrounded by Lesbians I was close to. I hardly used the city at all for things I had in the past."[60]

I emphasize that these anti-urban dismissals do not fall under the rubric of a conventional and racist "white flight" from the city since they are literally a flight from racially normative metropolitan gay culture. Like *Country Women, RFD* was more interested in defining itself against these metronorms, as both the journal's rhetoric and print aesthetics suggest. Compare the 1974 *RFD* subscription ad (Figure 15.7) to the 1970 *Advocate* subscription ad previously shown (Figure 15.3). What is note-worthy is how the *RFD* composition lays itself out as a nonbourgeois "faggot separatist" offshoot of rural lesbian separatist print culture and gay liberation, how it reprints itself below a subscription to *Country Women* by grafting itself onto *Country Women*. What also stands out is how these subscriptions are scrawled in chicken-scratch type rather than set in a "Groovy Ga Ga" metro type. Unlike the *Advocate*'s imposing and crisp logo font, shown in the bottom left-hand corner, here we have the aesthetic negation of such cosmo-stylization. In the *RFD* subscrip-tion, the typography slants. The initials are wobbly. Bold-typed abbre-viations appear to tumble off their lines. There is no uniform typeset. The ad jerks from lowercase cursive to uppercase print. And the spacing is skewed. That this double ad is not, in *RFD*-speak, "surfaced in glam-our" cuts to the chase of the quarterly's anarchic attempt to undermine U.S. metronormativity. It is not glossy. It is not full of flair. It is not beholden to male physical beauty. It is not a sophisticated style. It is not fashionable. It is instead critically rustic, a textual repetition of *Country Women*'s hyperfeminized, anti-middle-class rusticity. And this alterna-tive literary public sphere functions as both a negative and a positive counter to the *Advocate*'s mass-produced counterpublic. It is "the rural feminist experience," the subscription suggests, which is also the radical rural experience of reading, writing, and participating in early *RFD*.

Indebted to *Country Women*, these stylistics also owe an unacknowl-edged debt to the working-class white rural cultures that refused to assimilate into the middle-class metronormativity of the mid-1970s (and that did not participate in dominant white-flight narratives or styles of straights, lesbians, or gays). Given that the journal's editors were economically impoverished, rural based, and resistant to self-iden-tifications as urbanites, some came to embrace not only the subcultural slur of the "R.F.D. queen" but also the regional slur of the working-class hillbilly. As one anonymous *RFD* contributor from rural Massachusetts noted about Boston's metronormative climate in 1976: "Every time I

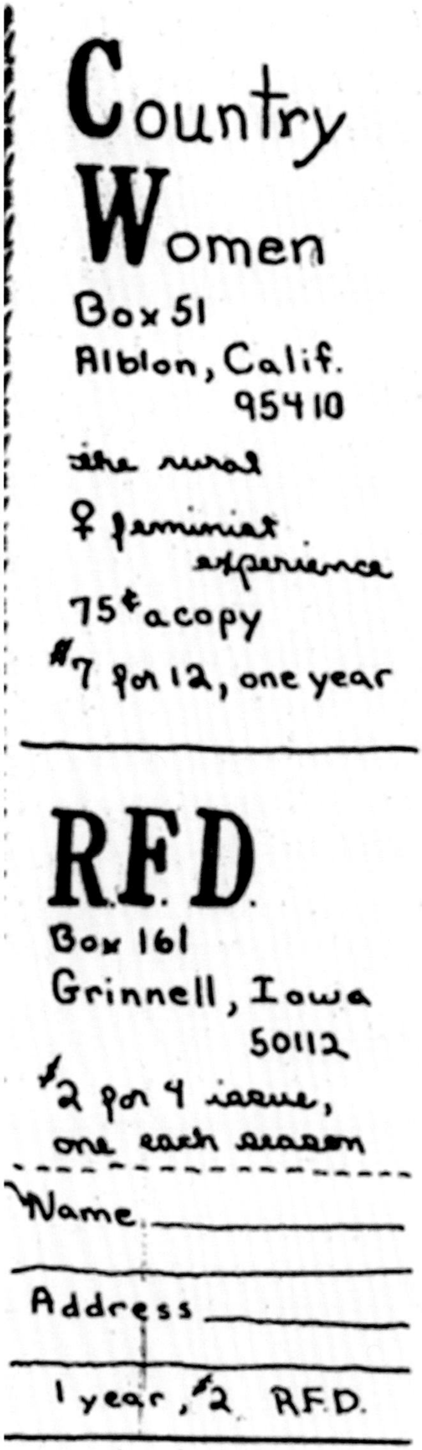

Figure 15.7

RFD/Country Women subscription advertisement, *RFD* issue 1 (Autumnal Equinox 1974): 11. Courtesy of Sr. Soami for the *RFD* Collective.

RFD is a magazine for country faggots to
Break down their isolation and fulfill their
needs for

R.F.D. is a magazine for country faggots so
they can share their lives.
isolation, ~~special needs not met~~ by
~~regualar~~

RFD is for

RFD is the expression of rural faggots in
~~the need to~~ come into contact with other
~~faggot men to speak~~ to their pleasure joys
and sorrows they share

RFD is the expression of country faggot men
to share their work, pleasure, joys and
sorrow with other rural fairies ~~whoever~~
~~where ever they live what ever their situation~~

RFD is an expression of country men to share
their faggot dreams and fairy delights

RFD is the Fairy Dreams and faggot delights
of country men

go to the city, there's less and less there that I can relate to at all, even meeting people who are there. . . . I don't know what I'd relate to them about. It's really hard." And his partner added: "I just feel funny going into a bar in Boston and walking up to someone and saying, 'How's your bean plants, baby?' I don't have much to talk with people there, it seems. We've become such lovely hillbillies. When we go into town, we get dressed up, but it's not getting dressed up like people in Boston do. Like we put on a pretty flannel shirt."[61] Though the term *hillbilly* historically refers to the rural, impoverished white populations of Appalachia, this comment suggests that many RFD readers, writers, and artists in nonurban areas embraced (or, just as likely, reappropriated) a hillbilly working-class style as a way to affirm the possibility of a culturally valuable—and culturally critical—rusticity that questioned the normative ideals that were crystallizing in the post-Stonewall United States.[62]

Though this hillbilly representation may be racially normative, *RFD* nevertheless deploys the stereotypically white working-class aesthetic to imagine something other than the masculinist bar-clone style that saturates the *Advocate* and other nationalizing gay male slicks. The handwritten ad presents mirror-image calligraphy for both Albion's *Country Women* and Grinnell's *RFD,* which amounts to a duplication of the former's nonurban, nonconsumerist aesthetics that extends into a unique form of queer anti-urbanism. Deploying the translocalities of Albion and Grinnell against the bicoastal U.S. metropolis, *RFD* resists incorporation—inscription—into the stylized aesthetics that is the *Advocate*'s nationalizing ghetto culture as it imagines itself to be what cultural historian Beth Bailey elsewhere terms "the antithesis of bicoastal sophistication."[63]

In so doing, disparaged "R.F.D. queens" transform into bumpkinfied RFD faeries; Scofield, Engstrom, and other *RFD* editors conjure an alternative print culture for reading publics removed from "the latest news of cha cha palaces in San Francisco, shows off-off Broadway, trendy fashions from West Hollywood, [and] Gloria Gaynor's latest album"; and *RFD* quarterly becomes an aesthetic reprint of *Country Women* quarterly as well as a political reprint of "country women" the countercultural rural collective. As it seeks independence from the national norms of America's Homophile Community, what *RFD* imagines here is nothing less than a Gay Liberation Front—an aesthetic dislocation—that unhinges itself from the domineering stylistics of normative urban gay male U.S. print culture. And much like the Advocate's pervasive bicoastal cosmopolitanism, this strategy of critical rusticity recurs through the entirety of early *RFD* issues (Figure 15.8).

As I noted in my introduction, *RFD*'s early efforts were soon complicated by a neoprimitivism that gradually overtook the journal once it was dominated by the radical faerie movement in the early 1980s, but its initial issues can be historically recuperated. The first instances of *RFD*'s

          OUT OF THE CLOSETS, INTO THE WOODS

critical rusticity let us imagine alternative possibilities for belonging within the sexual boundaries of the geographic U.S. nation-state, as well as for imaginatively extracting one's self from metronormativity at the moment of its historical inception in post-Stonewall queer cultures. And though predominantly anti-middle-class white men dissatisfied with the homonorms of the bicoastal metropolis first deployed its strategies, the journal's tactics today reverberate for many queers of any color and class regardless of where they might be geographically situated, metropolitan areas or not. As *RFD* moved its publication base from rural Iowa to the rural Northwest to rural North Carolina in the half decade following its first issue in 1974, we see how self-identified working-class "country men" aligned themselves with self-identified anti-middle-class "country women" to replace an *Advocate*-inspired "gay nationality" with a small-town queer regionality, how *RFD* undercut the urbanity of gay U.S. print culture with a mimeographed insistence on the intranational.[64]

As this hand-drawn 1974 image of transcontinental U.S. *RFD* readership suggests, the journal not only advanced *Country Women*'s aesthetics to counter the *Advocate*'s bicoastal cosmopolitanism. At times it also signified on the *Advocate*'s nationalist impulses to offer readers a regionalized queer country (Figure 15.9). Like much of the typescript and many of the images featured in early *RFD*, this drawing is somewhat poorly drawn and crude. Missing the sleekness that defined concurrent metro-oriented gay lifestyle magazines, we instead have a map of the United States on which many of the state lines appear scribbled or blurred, and it looks as if the artist has traced the outline of the continental U.S. border from a standardized map and then loosely delineated the states. Printed over these boilerplate states are 149 dots, each signi-

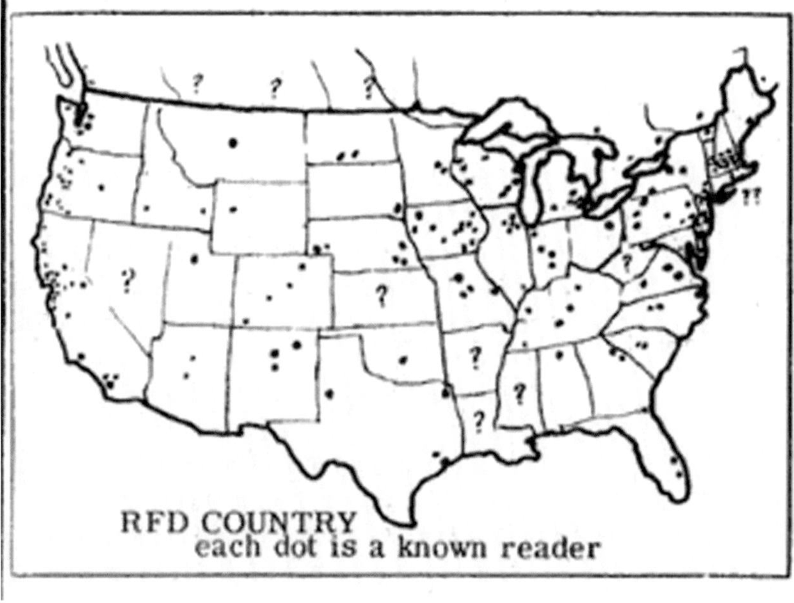

fying an *RFD* reader or subscriber, with question marks in states where readership cannot be verified.

This map could be critiqued for its unexamined national emphasis (Mexico and other hemispheric nation-states in North and South America are notably absent). Likewise, compared to *Advocate*'s "70,000" readers in 1970, these scattered *RFD* dots may seem insignificant for political mass mobilization, and they certainly did not stop the onslaught of cosmo-urbanisms that confirmed metronormativity. But reading this "RFD Country" map in an alternative light, we might follow Lisa Lowe and David Lloyd's advice that "resistances are more and more articulated through linkings of localities that take place across and below the level of the nation-state, and not by way of a politics that moves at the level of the national or modern institutions."[65] If such is the case, then these hand-drawn mimeographed dots might best be seen as tiny DIY pinpricks in the nationalizing U.S. imaginary that was *Advocate* urban visual print culture, as micropolitical interventions in the massive public literary sphere that the Los Angeles–based magazine came to exemplify.

Though *RFD* only had seven hundred or so subscribers by 1979, we might best read these dots as microinterventions that reestablish the regional, the rural, and the nonmetropolitan in order to blast open the bicoastal ideals of a normalizing U.S. gay print culture for antimetronormative and antihomonormative audiences of any color or class. As the *Advocate* obliterated other possible U.S. geographies with its emphasis on the bicoastal, the white, the male, the fashionable, and the middle class, RFD Country insists on reintroducing the very local and regional and often working-class styles and states that are rendered inconsequential. The caption below this cartography of RFD Country reads: "At this moment, RFD is being read in Vida, Nampa, Monona, Louisa; Philo, Solon, Malmo, Garnavillo; in River Rouge, Rogue River; Fall Creek, Clear Creek, and Cross Creek . . . Camp Verde, Junction City, Liberty and Independence; Honeydew and Orange; Alpine, Bunceton, Caspar, Dearing and right where you're sittin.'"[66]

These localities are the supposedly unsophisticated or rustic regions forgotten, dismissed, and disavowed in the forging of 1970s U.S. gay ghetto culture. They are also the geographic and imaginary spaces where a collective and critical lesbian and gay anti-urbanism emerged even as national urban prints championed a bicoastal "flight to the city." As *RFD* readers reworked U.S. metronormativity with a consideration of queer spaces "right where you're sittin,'" the initial issues of the quarterly fought subscription with subscription, and the journal separated from the cosmopolitan typing and the ideological geographies of metronormativity with a typography that resisted urbane stylistics.

Through these countersubcultural strategies, early *RFD* presented readers with the visual challenge of a regionalized alternative literary public sphere that connected rural queers outside the subcultural homonormative ghettos in New York City, San Francisco, and Los Angeles.

It wrote over the *Advocate*'s national ideals with rural lesbian separatist "living alternatives" inspired by *Country Women*. It circulated a novel imaginary of U.S. sexual citizenship and national belonging, one that might have been complicit in advancing a national and Westernized identity, but one that nevertheless thinks itself a regionalized alternative to the stylized homophilia found in imaginary white urban geographies. And while later *RFD* and early *Country Women* issues may have both instantiated racial norms, the journal's early collectives nevertheless intended to be comprehensive, intersectional, and politically antiassimilationist as they advocated a Gay Liberation Front—inspired capitalist critique for ruralized queers. With help from *Country Women, RFD* fantasized that it was a Rural Free Delivery from the stylistics of a metronormative U.S. identity that, in countless regions, many refused to purchase, since the price of ghetto institutions was notoriously high. The aftershocks of such metronormativity, it bears repeating, continue to try and to tax queer cultures and queer studies, no matter where they might be geographically "sittin'," to this present day.

NOTES

1. Stuart Scofield, *"RFD* History," *RFD* 9, no. 3 (1983): 9.

2. For detailed accounts of the rise of the radical faeries, see Harry Hay, *Radically Gay: Gay Liberation in the Words of Its Founder* (Boston: Beacon Press, 1996); Stuart Timmons, *The Trouble with Harry Hay: Founder of the Modern Gay Movement* (Boston: Alyson Publications, 1990); Elizabeth Povinelli, *The Empire of Love: Toward a Theory of Intimacy, Genealogy, and Carnality* (Durham, N.C.: Duke University Press, 2006); and Peter Hennen, *Faeries, Bears, and Leathermen: Men in Community Queering the Masculine* (Chicago: University of Chicago Press, 2008).

3. Olmo Eric Ganther and Frank S. Grant, "From Hippie to Fairy at Short Mountain Sanctuary," *RFD* 26, no. 3 (Spring 2000): 24.

4. Mitch Walker's *Visionary Love: A Spirit Book of Gay Mythology* (San Francisco: Treeroots Press, 1980) and the collected essays in *Gay Spirit: Myth and Meaning,* ed. Mark Thompson (New York: St. Martin's, 1987), present suspect analogies between gay male faeries and the Native American two-spirit.

5. Scott Morgensen, "Rooting for Queers: A Politics of Performativity," *Women & Performance: A Journal of Feminist Theory* 15, no. 1 (2005): 257.

6. B., "Ooo-h-h-h It's One of Those! Reflections and Projections of Faerie Past, Present and Future," *RFD* 30, no. 3 (Spring 2004): 20.

7. Anonymous, "Letter," *RFD* 26, no. 2 (Spring 2000): 4.

8. Gershon Legman, "The Language of Homosexuality," in *Sex Variants: A Study of Homosexual Patterns, with Selections Contributed by Specialists in Particular Fields,* ed. George B. Henry (New York: P. B. Hoeber, 1948). Reprinted in Jonathan Ned Katz, *Gay/Lesbian Almanac: A New Documentary* (New York: Harper & Row, 1983), 582.

9. I here invoke and extend Lauren Berlant and Elizabeth Freeman's readings of normative and non-normative queer print cultures in their essay "Queer Nationality," in *The Queen of America Goes to Washington City: Essays on Sex and Citizenship,* ed. Lauren Berlant (Durham, N.C.: Duke University Press, 1997), 169.

10. Judith Halberstam, *In a Queer Time and Place: Transgender Bodies, Subcultural Lives* (New York: New York University Press, 2005), 36–37.

11. José Esteban Muñoz, "Dead White: Notes on the Whiteness of the New Queer Cinema," *GLQ* 4, no. 1 (1998): 129, 131.

12. See Lisa Duggan, *The Twilight of Equality? Neoliberalism, Cultural Politics, and the Attack on Democracy* (Boston: Beacon Press, 2003), 50, 65, for an outline of U.S.-based homonormativity's relation to global consumption, corporate capitalism, and neoliberal ideals of privitization.

13. For detailed analyses of white flight, see Eric Avila, *Popular Culture in the Age of White Flight: Fear and Fantasy in Suburban Los Angeles* (Berkeley: University of California Press, 2004); William H. Frey, "Central City White Flight: Racial and Non-Racial Causes," *American Sociological Review* 44, no. 3 (1979): 425–48; and Steve Macek, *Urban Nightmares: The Media, the Right, and the Moral Panic over the City* (Minneapolis: University of Minnesota Press, 2006).

14. Donald L. Engstrom, telephone interview by the author, 12 January 2006; and James T. Sears, *Rebels, Rubyfruits, and Rhinestones: Queering Space in the Stonewall South* (New Brunswick, N.J.: Rutgers University Press, 2001), 306. Framing my argument in this manner, I join Michael Warner, "The Mass Public and the Mass Subject," in *Habermas and the Public Sphere,* ed. Craig Calhoun (Cambridge, Mass.: MIT Press, 1992), 377–401; Lisa Duggan, *Sapphic Slashers: Sex, Violence, and American Modernity* (Durham, N.C.: Duke University Press, 2000); Berlant and Freeman, "Queer Nationality"; Martin Meeker, *Contacts Desired: Gay and Lesbian Communications and Community, 1940s–1970s* (Chicago: University of Chicago Press, 2006); Richard Meyer, "Gay Power circa 1970," *GLQ* 12, no. 3 (2006): 441–64; and Margo Hobbs Thompson, "'Dear Sisters': The Visible Lesbian Presence in Community Arts Journals," *GLQ* 12, no. 3 (2006): 405–23. Each has written on the complex interconnections between collective U.S. lesbian and gay identity and modern print culture.

15. On urban destinations of gay and lesbian migration, see Halberstam, *In a Queer Time,* 35. On distinct lesbian and gay literary public spheres, see Rodger Streitmatter, *Unspeakable: The Rise of the Gay and Lesbian Press in America* (Boston: Faber and Faber, 1995), 154–55.

16. Scofield, *"RFD* History," 13.

17. Streitmatter, *Unspeakable,* 50.

18. Scofield, *"RFD* History," 13.

19. Carl Wittman, "A Gay Manifesto," in *Out of the Closets: Voices of Gay Liberation,* ed. Karla Jay and Allen Young (New York: New York University Press, 1992), 340–41. Originally published in 1972.

20. Chicago Gay Liberation, "Working Paper for the Revolutionary People's Constitutional Convention," in *Out of the Closets,* ed. Jay and Young, 349.

21. Streitmatter, *Unspeakable,* 150.

22. Ibid., 87. Allan Bérubé, in *Coming Out under Fire: A History of Gay Men and Women in World War Two* (New York: Free Press, 1990), and John D'Emilio, *Sexual Politics, Sexual Communities: The Making of a Homosexual Minority in the United States, 1940–1970* (Chicago: University of Chicago Press, 1983) provide the most detailed account to date on the rise of white lesbian and gay ghettos in major post–WWII U.S. cities. Martin P. Levine, *Gay Macho: The Life and Death of the Homosexual Clone* (New York: New York University Press, 1998), 31–43, provides a concise sociology of middle-class white male urban clone cultures in the 1970s. For contemporary critiques of this ideal by non-normative urban gay men, see Charles P. Thorp, "I.D., Leadership and Violence," in *Out of the Closets,* ed. Jay and Young, 352–63. For a complementary twenty-first-century critique, see Charles I. Nero, "Why Are the Gay Ghettoes White?" in *Black Queer Studies: A Critical Anthology,* ed. E. Patrick Johnson and Mae G. Henderson (Durham, N.C.: Duke University Press, 2006), 228–45.

23. One exception, however, is Michael Bronski, *Culture Clash: The Making of Gay Sensibility* (Boston: South End Press, 1984), 144–59, who viewed *Advocate* as a consumable sex object geared toward middle-class gay white men.

24. For critiques of globalizing lesbian and gay lifestyle in commodity capitalism, see José Esteban Muñoz, "The Future in the Present: Sexual Avant-Gardes and the Performance of Utopia," in *The Futures of American Studies,* ed. Donald E. Pease and Robyn Wiegman (Durham, N.C.: Duke University Press, 2002), 101; Rosemary Hennessy, *Profit and Pleasure: Sexual Identities in Late Capitalism* (New York: Routledge, 2000); Sharon Zukin, "Urban Lifestyles: Diversity and Standardisation in Spaces of Consumption," *Urban Studies* 35, no. 5–6 (1998): 825–40; and Ann Pellegrini, "Consuming Lifestyle: Commodity Capitalism and Transformations in Gay Identity," in *Queer Globalizations: Citizenship and the Afterlife of Colonialism,* ed. Arnaldo Cruz-Malavé and Martin F. Manalansan IV (New York: New York University Press, 2002), 134–45. For critiques of the *Advocate's* commodity capitalism in particular as well as its cosmopolitanism, see Katherine Sender, "Gay Readers, Consumers, and a Dominant Gay Habitus: 25 Years of the *Advocate* Magazine," *Journal of Communication* 51, no. 1 (March 2001): 73–99; as well as Sender's *Business, Not Politics: The Making of a Gay Market* (New York: Columbia University Press, 2004).

25. *Advocate,* February 1970, 40. My critical overview of Advocate

confirms Streitmatter's claim that "style and flair . . . has always been synonymous with the community" (103), and that "many gay men" "possess the high level of taste and style" (23). However, he assumes these "high" levels to be an essentialized component of gay "community" and (white) gay male print culture in the United States, rather than a historicized and compulsory urban norm.

26. Quoted in Levine, *Macho*, 56.

27. Craig Alfred Hanson, "The Fairy Princess Exposed," *Gay Sunshine*, 10 January 1972, 10. Reprinted in *Out of the Closets*, ed. Jay and Young, 266–69.

28. Joseph Litvak, *Strange Gourmets: Sophistication, Theory, and the Novel* (Durham, N.C.: Duke University Press, 1997), 4. Queer theorizations of cosmopolitanism, urbanity, style, and sophistication are ample and often disagree as to the value of these ideals. See D. A. Miller, "Sontag's Urbanity," in *The Lesbian and Gay Studies Reader*, ed. Henry Abelove, Michèle Aina Barale, and David M. Halperin (New York: Routledge, 1993), 212–20; and Susan Sontag, "Notes on 'Camp,'" in her *Against Interpretation and Other Essays* (New York: Picador, 1966), 275–92, or what she sees as "a variant of sophistication" that is "something of a private code, a badge of identity even, among small urban cliques" (275) or "a vision of the world in terms of style" (279). For more recent critiques of such gay cosmopolitanism, see Dereka Rushbrook, "Cities, Queer Space, and the Cosmopolitan Tourist," *GLQ* 8, no. 1–2 (2002): 183–206; Hiram Perez, "You Can Have My Brown Body and Eat It, Too!" *Social Text* 84–85 (2005): 171–91; and, especially, Karen Tongson, "Metronormativity and Gay Globalization," in *Quer durch die Geisteswissenschaften: Perspecktiven der Queer Theory* (Berlin: Querverlag, 2005), 40–52.

29. William J. Spurlin, "Remapping Same-Sex Desire: Queer Writing and Cultures in the American Heartland," in *De-Centring Sexualities: Politics and Representations Beyond the Metropolis*, ed. Richard Phillips, Diane Watt, and David Shuttleton (London: Routledge, 2000), 183–92; Michael Moon, "Whose History? The Case of Oklahoma," in *A Queer World: The Center for Lesbian and Gay Studies Reader*, ed. Martin Duberman (New York: New York University Press, 1997), 24–34; and, especially, John Howard, *Men Like That: A Southern Queer History* (Chicago: University of Chicago Press, 1999) offer trenchant critiques of what Howard terms the "bicoastal bias" (12).

30. For more on cities such as Chicago as "'extra-regional' exceptions" to geographies such as the U.S. Midwest, see Victoria Johnson, *Heartland TV: Prime Time Television and the Struggle for US Identity* (New York: New York University Press, 2008), 36.

31. Two exemplary works that tackle the political complexities of the U.S. metropolis in the 1960s and 1970s are Cynthia A. Young's *Soul Power Culture, Radicalism, and the Making of a U.S. Third World Left* (Durham, N.C.: Duke University Press, 2006), and Laura Pulido's *Black, Brown, Yellow, and Left: Radical Activism in Los Angeles* (Berkeley: University of California Press, 2006).

32. Del Martin, "If That's All There Is," *Advocate*, October 28–November 10, 1970, 74, 75.

33. See Saralyn Chesnut and Amanda C. Gable, "'Women Ran It': Charis Books and More and Atlanta's Lesbian-Feminist Community, 1971–1981," in *Carryin' On in the Lesbian and Gay South*, ed. John Howard (New York: New York University Press, 1997), 241–84; Karla Jay, "No Man's Land," in *Lavender Culture*, ed. Karla Jay and Allen Young, rev. ed. (New York: New York University Press, 1994), 63; Stephanie Foote, "Deviant Classics: Pulps and the Making of Lesbian Print Culture," *Signs* 31, no. 1 (2005): 169–90; and Streitmatter, *Unspeakable*, 155–58, for catalogs of lesbian print published during the 1970s and earlier.

34. Streitmatter, *Unspeakable*, 167.

35. Ibid., 161.

36. Jay, "No Man's Land," 53. See also Jill Johnston, *Lesbian Nation:*

The Feminist Solution (New York: Simon and Schuster, 1973); Charlotte Bunch, "Learning from Lesbian Separatism," in *Lavender Culture*, ed. Jay and Young, 433–44; Adrienne Rich, "Compulsory Heterosexuality and Lesbian Existence," in *The Lesbian and Gay Studies Reader*, ed. Abelove, Barale, and Halperin, 227–54; Alice Echols, *Daring to Be Bad: Radical Feminism in America, 1967–1975* (Minneapolis: University of Minnesota Press, 1989); Anna Lee, "For the Love of Separatism," in *Lesbian Philosophies and Cultures*, ed. Jeffner Allen (Albany: State University of New York Press, 1990), 143–55; Radicalesbians, "Leaving the Gay Men Behind," in *Out of the Closets*, ed. Jay and Young, 290–93; Berlant and Freeman, "Queer Nationality," on the "separatist withdrawal into safe territory" (168); Streitmatter, *Unspeakable*, 154–82; Audre Lorde, *Zami: A New Spelling of My Name* (Freedom, Calif.: Crossing Press, 1982); Ann Snitow, "A Gender Diary," in *Conflicts in Feminism*, ed. Marianne Hirsch and Evelyn Fox Keller (London: Routledge, 1990), 9–43; Linda Garber, *Identity Poetics: Race, Class, and the Lesbian-Feminist Roots of Queer Theory* (New York: Columbia University Press, 2001); and Cherríe Moraga, "Preface," in *This Bridge Called My Back: Writings by Radical Women of Color*, ed. Cherríe Moraga and Gloria Anzaldúa (Watertown, Mass.: Persephone Press, 1981), xiii–xix, for personal accounts and critical histories of U.S. radical lesbian feminisms in the 1970s.

37. See Streitmatter, *Unspeakable*, 161–63.

38. Ibid., 105, 192.

39. For discussions of this stereotype, see Garber, *Identity Poetics*; and Sender, "Gay Readers," 85.

40. Jay, "No Man's Land," 53. Further page references to this source will appear parenthetically in the text.

41. Meeker, *Contacts Desired*, 232.

42. For more on the cultural politics of the radical back-to-the-land movement as well as the countercultural strains that influenced *Country Women*, see Bennett M. Berger, *The Survival of a Counterculture: Ideological Work and Everyday Life among Rural Communards* (Berkeley: University of California Press, 1981); Jeffrey C. Jacob, "The North American Back-to-the-Land Movement," *Community Development Journal* 31, no. 3 (1996): 241–49; Alice Echols, *Shaky Ground: The '60s and Its Aftershocks* (New York: New York University Press, 2002); Van Gosse and Richard Moser, eds., *The World the Sixties Made: Politics and Culture in Recent America* (Philadelphia: Temple University Press, 2003); and Avital H. Bloch and Lauri Umansky, eds., *Impossible to Hold: Women and Culture in the 1960s* (New York: New York University Press, 2005).

43. David Bell and Gill Valentine, "Queer Country: Rural Lesbian and Gay Lives," *Journal of Rural Studies* 11, no. 2 (1995): 118.

44. See Angela R. Wilson, "Getting Your Kicks on Route 66! Stories of Gay and Lesbian Life in Rural America, c. 1950–1970," in *De-Centring Sexualities*, ed. Phillips, Watt, and Shuttleton, 199–216; Gill Valentine, "Introduction: From Nowhere to Everywhere: Lesbian Geographies," in *From Nowhere to Everywhere: Lesbian Geographies*, ed. Gill Valentine (Binghamton, N.Y.: Harrington Park, 2000), 1–9; Gill Valentine, "Making Space: Lesbian Separatist Communities in the United States," in *Contested Countryside Cultures: Otherness, Marginalization, and Rurality*, ed. Paul Cloke and Jo Little (London: Routledge, 1997), 109–22; and Sherry Thomas, *We Didn't Have Much, But We Sure Had Plenty: Stories of Rural Women* (Garden City, N.Y.: Anchor, 1981), 149–63, for more on the emancipatory politics as well as the ideological problematics of rural feminist/lesbian separatism.

45. Bell and Valentine, "Queer Country," 119.

46. Sherry Thomas and Jeanne Tetrault, "Introduction," *Country Women: A Handbook for the New Farmer* (Garden City, N.Y.: Anchor Press/Doubleday, 1976), 13.

47. Ibid., xiii.

48. Gerald W. Creed and Barbara Ching, "Introduction: Recognizing Rusticity: Identity and the Power of Place," in *Knowing Your Place: Rural Identity and Cultural Hierarchy,* ed. Barbara Ching and Gerald W. Creed (New York: Routledge, 1997), 10.

49. Ibid., 4.

50. Barbara, "Retrospective: Feminism and the Unconscious Collective," *Country Women* 2 (1973): 34.

51. Scofield, *"RFD* History," 9.

52. *RFD* Collective, "Rustic Fairy Dreams," *RFD* 1 (Autumnal Equinox 1974): 3.

53. "Hop Brook Commune," *RFD* 1 (Autumnal Equinox 1974): 11.

54. Lee Mintz, "The Gays—Who Are We? Where Do We Come From? What Are We For?" *RFD* 5 (Autumn 1975): 41.

55. I borrow the phrase *mainstream subculture* from Lauren M. E. Goodlad and Michael Bibby, "Introduction," in *Goth: Undead Subculture* (Durham, N.C.: Duke University Press, 2007), who use the term to describe contemporary goth group identities.

56. Scofield, *"RFD* History," 11.

57. Ibid., 13.

58. *RFD* Collective, "Rustic Fairy Dreams," 3.

59. Scofield, *"RFD* History," 9.

60. Lee Mintz, "City/Country," *RFD* 3 (Spring Equinox 1975): 9.

61. "As the Butter Churns," *RFD* 7 (Vernal Equinox 1976): 16.

62. Critical analyses of "hillbilly" or working-class white representations can be found in Matt Wray, *Not Quite White: White Trash and the Boundaries of Whiteness* (Durham, N.C.: Duke University Press, 2006); Constance Penley, "Crackers and Whackers: The White Trashing of Porn," in *White Trash: Race and Class in America,* ed. Matt Wray and Annalee Newitz (New York: Routledge, 1997), 89–112; Wendell Ricketts, "Passing Notes in Class: Some Thoughts on Writing and Culture in the Ga(y)ted Community," in *Everything I Have Is Blue: Short Fiction by Working-Class Men about More-or-Less Gay Life,* ed. Wendell Ricketts (San Francisco: Suspect Thoughts Press, 2005), 216–42; J. W. Williamson, *Hillbillyland: What the Movies Did to the Mountains and What the Mountains Did to the Movies* (Chapel Hill: University of North Carolina Press, 1995); and John Hartigan Jr., *Odd Tribes: Toward a Cultural Analysis of White People* (Durham, N.C.: Duke University Press, 2005).

63. Beth Bailey, *Sex in the Heartland* (Cambridge, Mass.: Harvard University Press, 1999), 4.

64. Meeker, *Contacts Desired,* 214.

65. Lisa Lowe and David Lloyd, "Introduction," in *The Politics of Culture in the Shadow of Capital,* ed. Lisa Lowe and David Lloyd (Durham, N.C.: Duke University Press, 1997), 25.

66. *RFD* 2 (Winter Solstice 1974): 3.

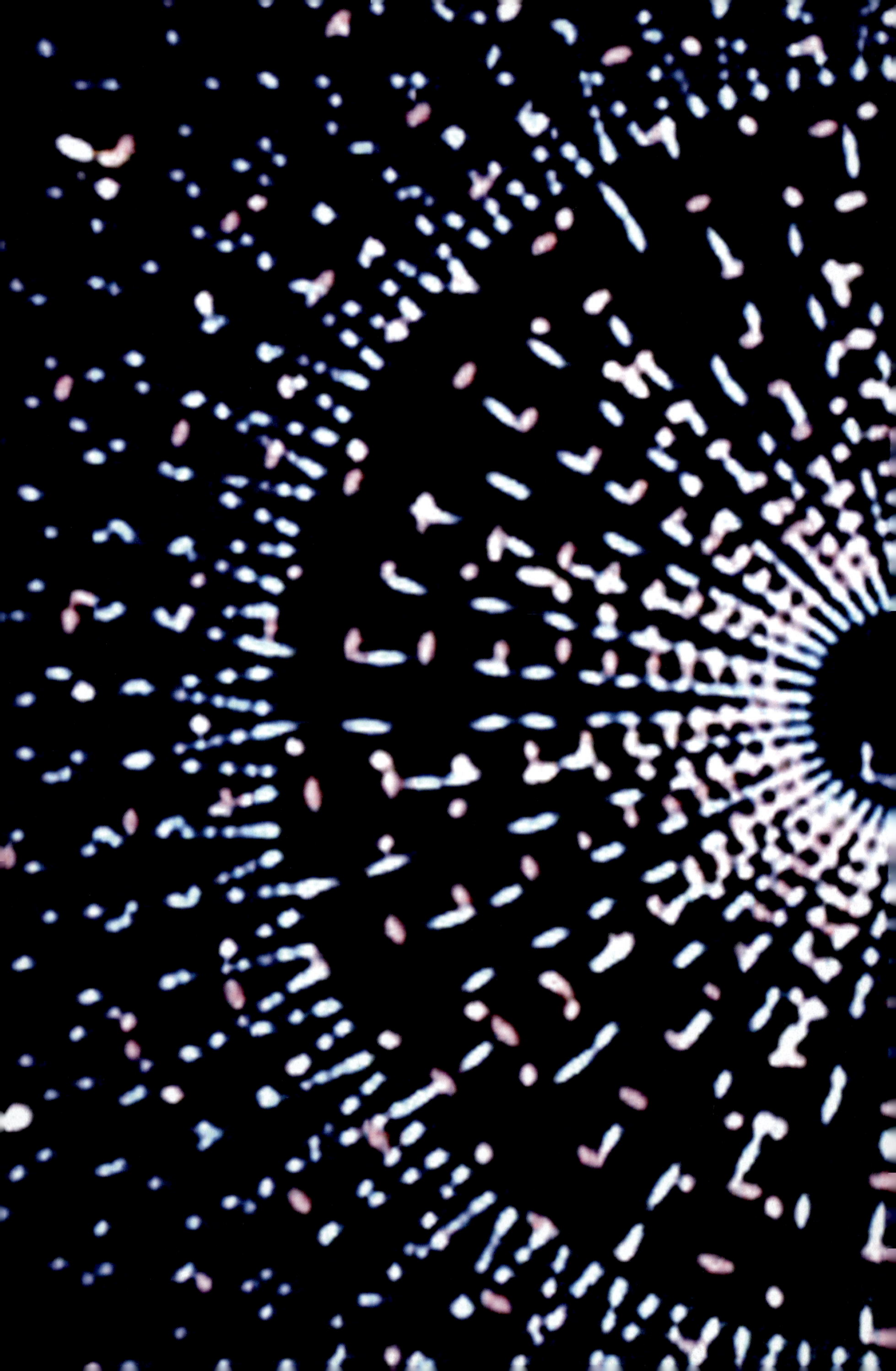

PART IV

ALTERED CONSCIOUSNESS

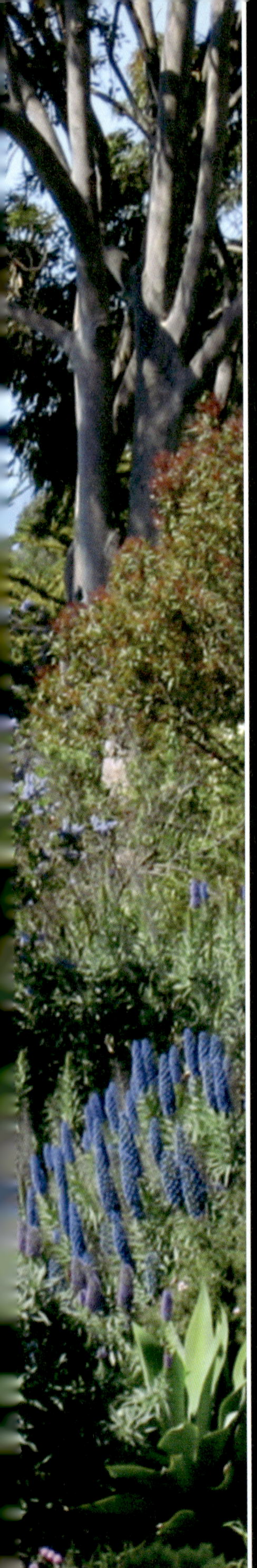

Suzanne Hudson

In the fall of 1963, Ansel Adams convened a three-day seminar on the work of his colleague, Edward Weston, who had died of Parkinson's disease some five years earlier (Figure 16.1). As listed in the wee brochure for the newly founded Big Sur Hot Springs, "The Eye of Edward Weston" (which ran September 20–22) encompassed an exhibition, a film screening of *The Photographer* (Willard Van Dyke's twenty-five-minute black-and-white reel about Weston), and round tables co-led by Adams and photographers Imogen Cunningham, Brett Weston, and Jack Welpott. As the publicity announced:

Since his death, the stature of Edward Weston has continued to increase. His particular vision has influenced art and artists outside America and outside the realm of photography. But as his reputation grows, his photographs become harder to see in the simplicity and clarity with which he made them. In this seminar his old friends, who are themselves artists of stature, will recall the man and the original impact of his photographs and will explore the nature of his influence.[1]

In certain respects, that Adams would organize these weekend events—in this setting—is unremarkable: Adams and Weston had been friends for decades, formalizing their allegiance in the 1932 founding of Group f/64, a clique unified around an eschewal of pictorialist mandates.

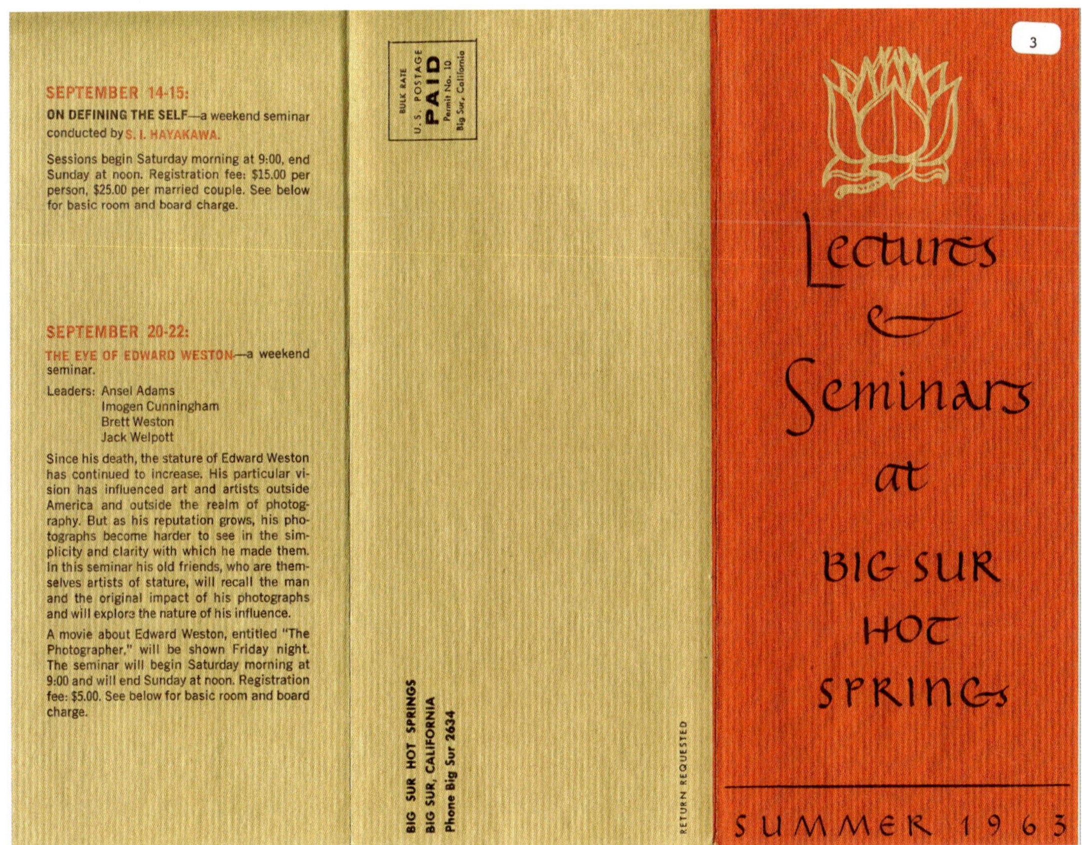

     NAKED PICTURES

Esalen Institute Hot Springs bath, Big Sur, California. Copyright Kat Wade/*San Francisco Chronicle*/Corbis.

Their pursuit of technical precision—as manifest in the crisply delineated forms the namesake aperture afforded—came to be synonymous with a brand of straight photography put to use chiefly on inanimate objects and the natural scene. As well, both men readily identified with the West Coast. An erstwhile midwesterner, Weston had arrived in Los Angeles in 1906 and quickly habituated himself to the place, becoming "a devotee of the local rites of sunbathing," among other indigenous pursuits.[2] Like Adams, a San Francisco native—he often waxed poetic about his misshapen nose, the result of a childhood fall during the 1906 earthquake—who had just built a new home and studio in Carmel Highlands, Weston had long lived in Carmel, a Monterey Peninsula hamlet whose physical proximity to Big Sur Hot Springs made this venue a potential choice for surveying his deeds. Plus, Weston had photographed extensively on the property's grounds.

Still, the legacy of Big Sur Hot Springs, an artist colony, alternative education complex, spa, and epicenter of the human potential movement, also suggests an incompatibility. Rechristened as Esalen Institute the subsequent year, it was populated by professors, prophets, healers, and too many others to reductively categorize. It is most likely remembered by many for its hot tubs, and the variously coupled naked bodies that have floated in them (Figure 16.2). The baths in particular would come to occupy an increasingly large place in the American cultural imaginary, though the whole Esalen enterprise was unfortunately satirized routinely in the popular media (even as salutary experiences partaken of therein were reported in publications as diverse as *Ladies' Home Journal,* the *New Yorker,* the *Harvard Crimson,* and *Life* magazine).[3]

More recently lampooned in a *New York Times* byline as "Sex, Drugs and Hot Tubs," Esalen's connection to the Summer of Love still casts an inescapably hedonistic shadow.[4] Even by the 1970s, Esalen had become a victim of its own wanton success, prompting numerous like communities devoted to intellectual, mystical, and bodily renovation and splintering off the much-maligned est training program founded by Werner H. Erhard in 1971. More generally, it spawned what Todd Gitlin acidly has named "a virtual transcendence industry whose crucibles were 'workshops' in therapeutic and spiritual technique: confrontational 'encounter,' gestalt therapy, bioenergetics, meditation, massage, breathing—and, not least, easy, recreational sex."[5] Its early, frequently Apollonian, reading-intensive courses and public programs were supplanted in a few years' time by more visceral (group and individual) pursuits. It was hard to talk about things like integral practice and bliss without the participants wanting to rehearse them for themselves. Spirituality was recast—if perhaps unwittingly—as self-actualization, and creativity renovated into the least emancipatory of narcissisms.

All of this to say that, at the very least, Adams's association with Esalen raises gainfully discomfiting questions about an artist all too quickly circumscribed by his technocratic mastery of a medium, as

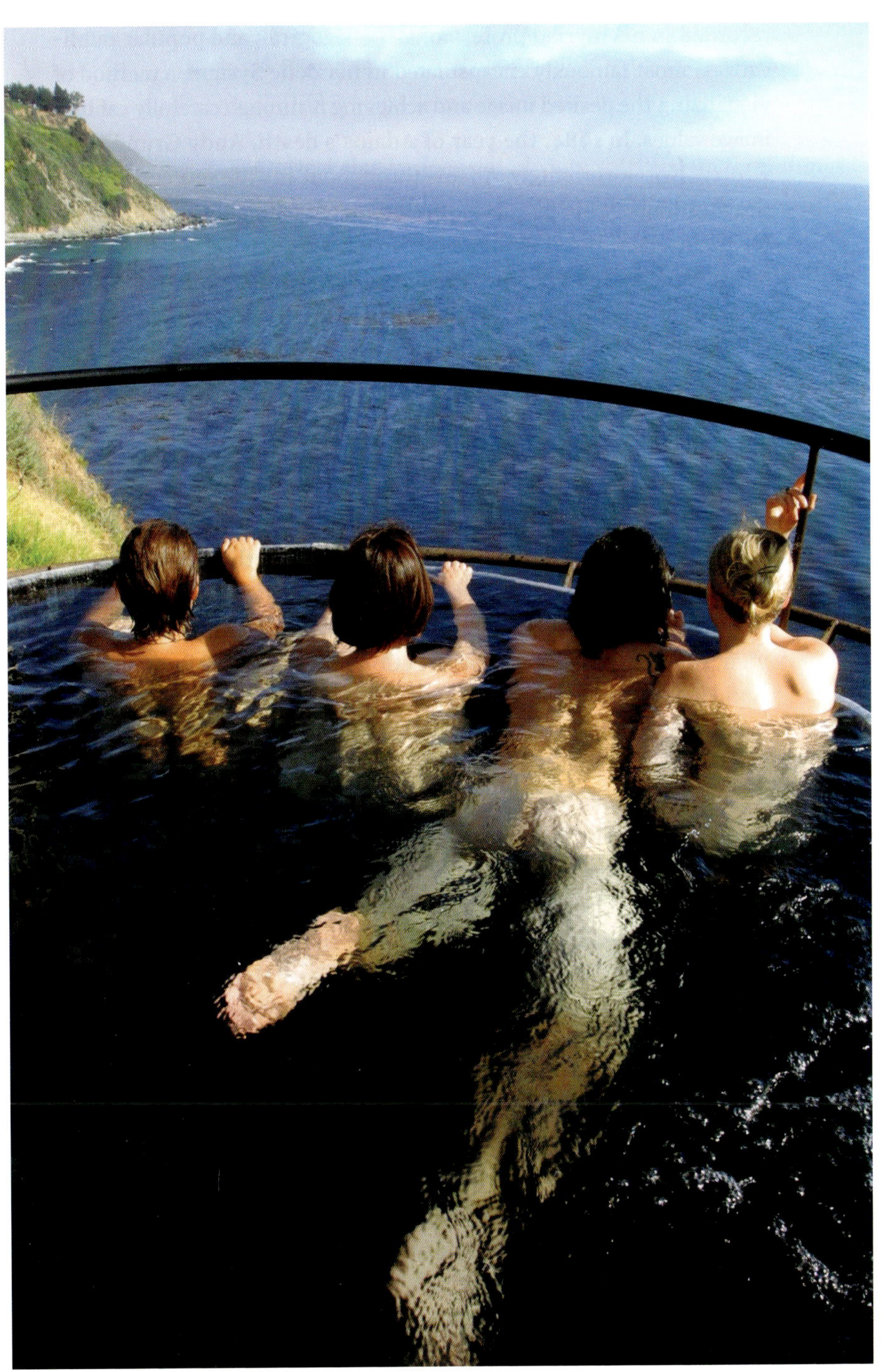

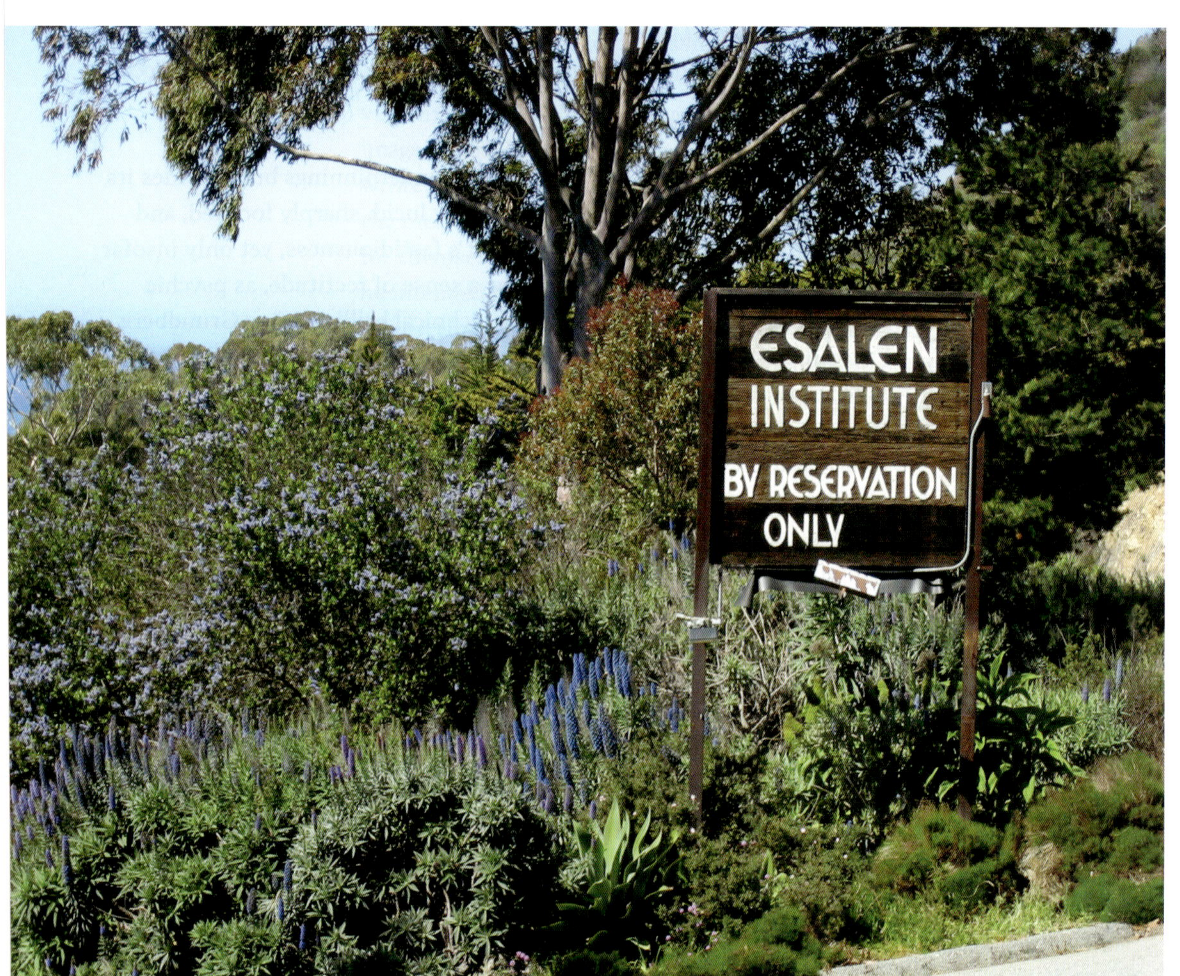

ESALEN
INSTITUTE
BY RESERVATION
ONLY

Figure 16.3
Esalen Institute entrance, Big
Sur, California. Photograph by
Suzanne Hudson.

the foundation for broader community action and social service. This is
to assert that, though I superficially am echoing Szarkowski, and agree-
ing especially with his maintenance of Adams's art as a form of "private
worship," I am also insisting that the context in which to appreciate
Adams's production is neither the modern museum nor the modernist photographic discourse that often justified it, but the ostensible
"counterculture" on the other side of the country—a counterculture
recurrently grasped in terms coeval with its most easily satirized iconography (of nudists, stoned musicians, etc.). Adams's images offer an
instance whereby artworks might look nothing like the milieu in which
they find their theoretical justification but are rendered legible through
it in a way otherwise obscured. In this case, thinking about Adams together with Esalen recommends his images as manifestations of sensate
connection with the land, itself privileged as the site of, and often the
very vehicle for, personal revolution.

ESALEN INSTITUTE, CIRCA 1963

Henry Miller once called Big Sur a "religion where extremes meet," and
anyone who has seen its verdant forest spilling headlong into the Pacific
cannot help but agree. For Miller, a resident of the area as of 1944, Big
Sur's attraction lay in its almost Edenic satiety, but also—or as much—
in its remoteness. A hundred-mile stretch of central California coast
between Carmel and San Simeon, Big Sur is situated some 120 miles
south of San Francisco and 250 miles north of Los Angeles. Inhabited for
thousands of years by nomadic tribes—the Esselen gave the site its
name despite having perished upon the advent of white settlers—the
land was known for its natural mineral springs, assumed to have med-
icinal powers. The modern Esalen Institute sits squarely on the site that
was once the tribe's burial ground (Figure 16.3).[13]

Miller appreciated Big Sur as the edge of the frontier—and literally
so, which remains part and parcel of its attraction. The land surrounding
Esalen was homesteaded in 1882 by a Missouri native, Thomas Benton
Slate, who had come from San Francisco decades earlier to take the waters
as a cure for his arthritis. He eventually sold the property, and in 1910,
it was sold, in turn, to Dr. Henry Murphy, a Salinas doctor with the objective of opening a European-style spa. The prospect of bringing in
bathtubs highlighted the place's inaccessibility, however, as no highways
existed at this time. Around 1918, the highways started creeping north
from Los Angeles, and a decade later, prison crews began toiling to open
the stretch of Big Sur, blasting only sixty miles in ten years and killing
many workers in the process. They left behind both public infrastructure
and a legacy of criminality, which was determinate of the ruggedly individualistic culture that would soon thrive there, with its stylized licen-
tiousness and game antiauthoritarianism predicated on the location's
physical isolation. So the spa would have to wait some decades, which is
where Big Sur Hot Springs comes into this chronicle more explicitly.

     NAKED PICTURES

Figure 16.4
Ansel Adams along Big
Sur coast. Copyright Roger
Ressmeyer/Corbis.

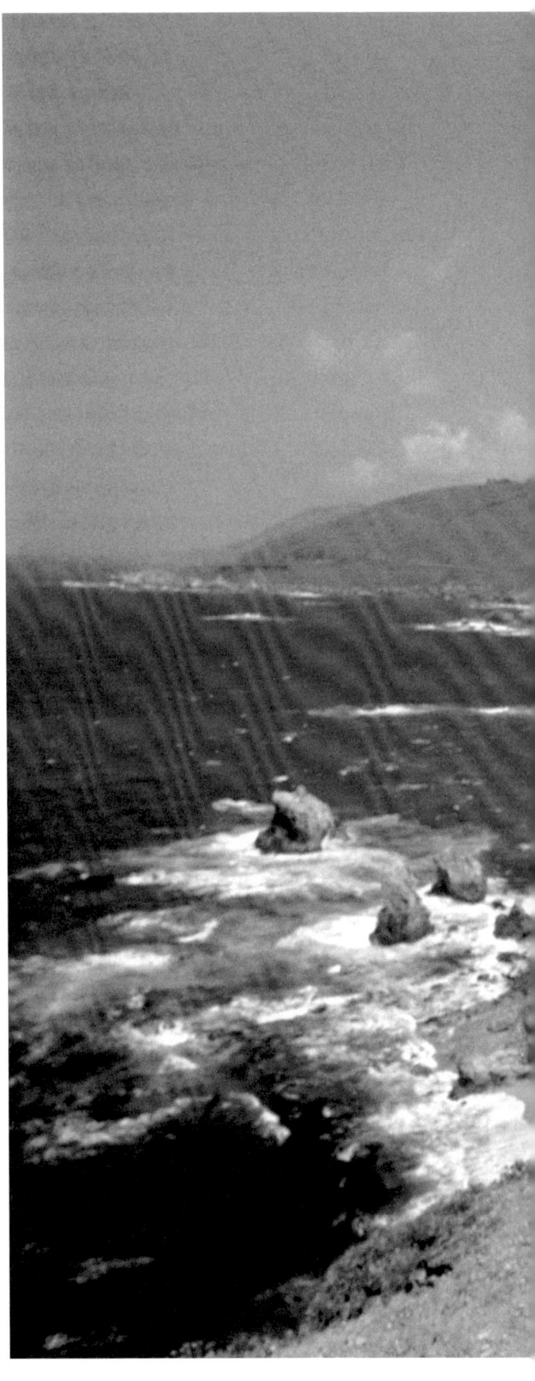

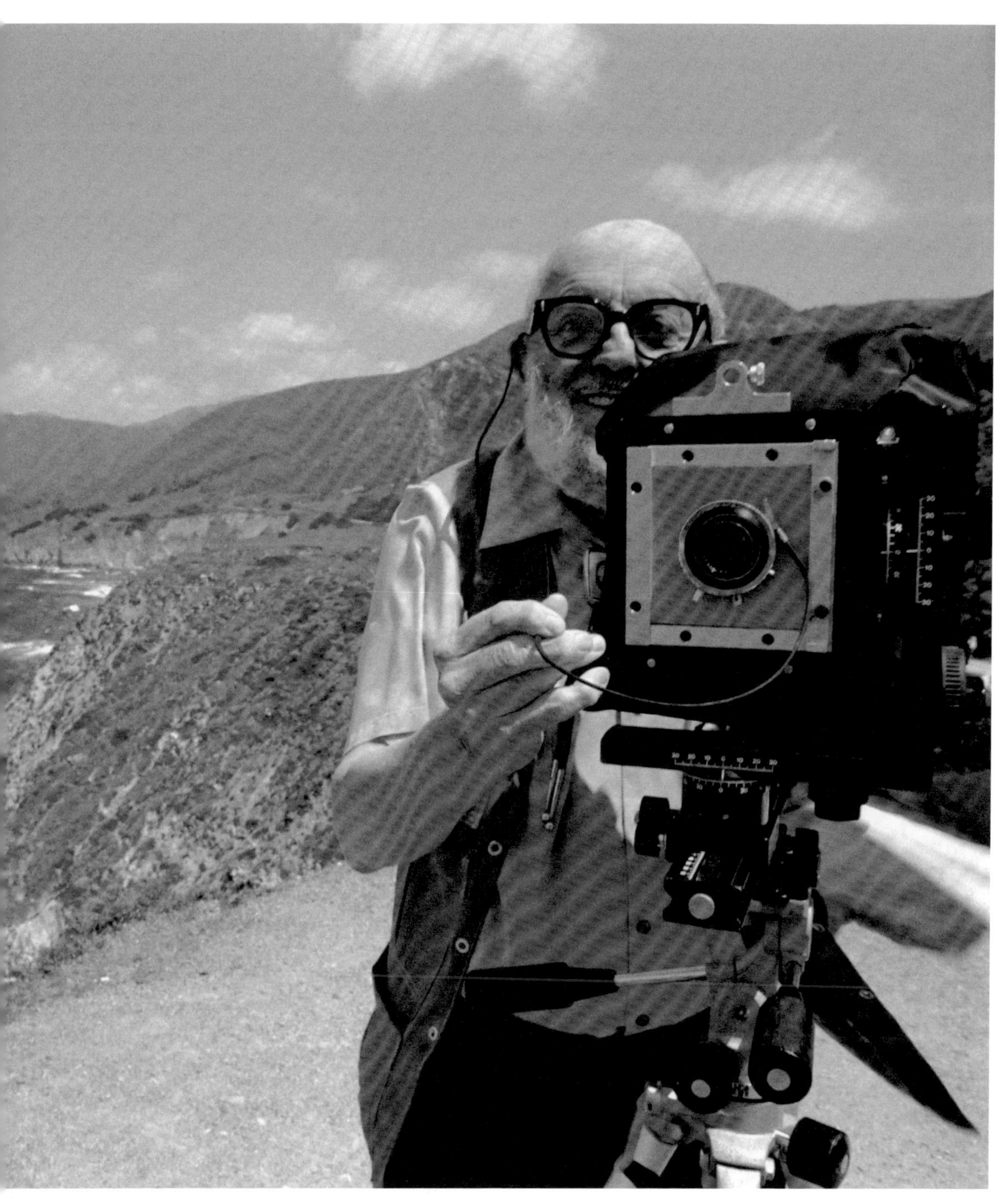

one particular, sublime night, "the stars loomed with terrifying brilliance, the darkness beyond them throbbed with unseen light."[27]

However sincere, Adams's union with nature is not unprecedented—nor did he pretend the contrary. There is a well-established mountaineering literature that places a premium on a Buckean cosmic consciousness, where an individual communes with nature to such an extent that he is dissolved into it or subsumed by it. In much of this writing, which Adams knew thoroughly, the physical challenge of reaching the summit is also psychic, and success brings illumination and a loss of fear—mountain as crucible.[28] Hence does his language of the unutterable find its muse. Ultimately Adams returned the favor, publishing photographs with passages culled from 1916 editions of John Muir's *The Mountains of California* and *My First Summer in the Sierra* and attesting to Muir's authority in disclosing that "on first reading his [Muir's] texts on the Sierra I became more confident of my own experience in nature."[29] As well, from his first engagement with *In the Heart of the Sierra,* Adams had been exposed to Yosemite's visual iconography, and the work of photographers (Carleton Watkins, for one) and painters (Albert Bierstadt) were proximate sources.

Adams's elation could not be sustained; it could only punctuate the quotidian, even under the best of circumstances, which is what made these occasional ecstatic states momentous. Without dwelling on Adams's biography, it is nonetheless important to know that Adams met his future wife, Virginia Best, at her father's Yosemite concession in 1921. Married in 1928, Adams had at least one noteworthy affair in the 1930s, the dissolution of which—following domestic strain and compounded by the general disenchantment that accompanied his residence in San Francisco and the failure of his center for creative photography—precipitated a collapse and hospitalization in 1936. Returning to Yosemite full time soon thereafter affected a change in his mentality and photography. As David Peeler characterizes: "Scenes that had earlier been rendered as mystical were now also described as curative. For Adams, photography became charged not only with enlightenment but also therapy."[30] Whether one abides by this reading (so that, for instance, *Rainbow over Yosemite Valley* [c. 1938] emblematizes his newfound sanguinity) or fixes it so punctually, Peeler's account of Adams's move to a curative understanding of the creative act convinces and finds its evidence in numerous contemporaneous images and words.

Additionally, the ground for this turn had been laid by Alfred Stieglitz, with whom Adams became better acquainted in these same years, and on whose model Adams had opened his failed San Francisco gallery.[31] Anne Hammond encapsulates:

As a master of these spiritual experiments, Stieglitz assisted Adams in his epistemic turn from objectivist to subjectivist. Transcendence for the objectivist lay in the revelation of essence, a quality derived from the object itself. . . .

Transcendence for the subjectivist came through the creation of an equivalent, a term Stieglitz explained to Adams as follows: "I perceive something of interest and significance; I recognize a photograph; I make the photograph. I show it to you as an equivalent of something that I felt and responded to." If, having experienced such an equivalent, the viewer was moved to create a work of art himself or herself, Stieglitz was doubly satisfied.[32]

Equally, Stieglitz's praise, which Adams took as critique, inadvertently consolidated his thinking. When Adams sent Stieglitz his *Sierra Nevada: The John Muir Trail,* Stieglitz congratulated his "perfect photography . . . [and] perfect workmanship."[33] A defensive Adams replied that he had to illustrate specified sites along the trail. At stake was not technical facility per se but the authenticity and vividness of the mountain experience—Adams's version of Stieglitz's equivalent—that he wanted his photographs to share. At his best, say, in images like *Monolith, The Face of Half Dome, Yosemite Valley* (1927), he accomplished this.

The problem was that most people, especially as the years passed and Adams contributed mightily to a growing corpus of technical manuals and instructional guides, saw the perfect photography alone. By 1963, Adams was forced to assess his work wholesale, as he prepared for a major retrospective at San Francisco's de Young Museum organized by Nancy Newhall. With more than five hundred prints in various sizes, spanning 1923 to 1963, *The Eloquent Light* was a testament to Adams's career as well as a moment of explicit consolidation. John Szarkowski—again, one of Adams's most perceptive if inhospitable critics—contends that "the act of selecting (with Newhall) the 1963 exhibition was perhaps the last time that Adams ever looked and thought hard about the meaning of his work and the definition of his oeuvre."[34] He is arguing this from a considerably later vantage, with the knowledge that Adams spent the better part of his elder years reprinting negatives taken decades before, but salient in the present context is the fact that Adams was involved in his own retrospection alongside that of Edward Weston.

If *The Eloquent Light* marks the end of Adams's creative output, it also reminds us of the other pursuits that followed. After 1963, Adams devoted much of his time to environmental activism and writing, culminating in his deathbed autobiography (activities that are neither Szarkowski's purview nor concern). These pursuits mark a more sustained mode of veneration than do his photographs. Where the latter attempt to pin down the near-ecstatic first flush of wilderness communion—with the face of granite, the luminescent moon—the former organize sensations into programs for future work. He was, in Esalen-speak appropriated from Abraham Maslow, a self-actualizing person, realizing his potential, socially. A fixture at Esalen from the time he stumbled onto the grounds in 1962 (his contemporaneous *Toward a Psychology of Being* was already being assimilated), Maslow was instrumental in humanistic psychology and, like Frederic Spiegelberg, deeply interested in the mystical experiences that form a common denominator among the world's religions while remaining apart from the institutionalization of any of them.[35]

A seminar on "The Theories of Abraham Maslow," followed directly on the heels of "The Eye of Edward Weston," but, more generally, Maslow's ideas circulated freely and provided a way to articulate mystical encounters (his so-called peak experiences), among other contributions. In 1964, he published *Religions, Values, and Peak-Experiences*, which collected his ideas on these moments of transcendental unity, with the hope of convincing his public that anyone could have a peak experience (that would, in turn, lead to personal betterment), and that these flashes of insight were not the jurisdiction of oracles alone. Maslow regretted the disproportionate emphasis on the individual his early readers adopted and the cult of the self that his writing seemed to warrant. In a 1970 edition he made his intentions clear: this was a form of individual seeking, but Maslow also strenuously called for civil responsibility:

The empirical fact is that self-actualizing people, our best experiencers, are also our most compassionate, our great improvers and reformers of society, our most *effective* fighters against injustice, inequality, slavery, cruelty, exploitation (and also our best fighters *for* excellence, effectiveness, competence). And it becomes clearer and clearer that the best "helpers" are the most fully human persons. What I may call the bodhisattvic path is an *integration* of self-improvement and social zeal, i.e., the best way to become a better "helper" is to become a better person. But one necessary aspect of becoming a better person is via helping other people. So one can and must do both simultaneously.[36]

In this way, Maslow encouraged the cultivation of the person, who would turn to others after finding his own salvation. The promotion of lifestyle as agent of subjectivity that has emerged in the wake of ideas such as this is perhaps a success of the worst possible kind—as the author himself acknowledged—but that neither diminishes Maslow's objectives nor wholly vitiates his conclusions.

Recall Szarkowski's condemnation of Adams: "Adams did not photograph the landscape as a matter of social service, but as a form of private worship. It was his own soul he was trying to save." It takes Maslow to reveal what this might actually mean, even if such language also echoes Stieglitz on his own prized equivalents. Adams's is a model of self-exploration as a politics of transformation from the inside out, which makes it a politics that often does not look like a politics at all. He found the consolation of nature, uplift in the natural scene, peak experiences that could, sometimes, find their expression, and that might induce others to seek comparable happenings for themselves in the national parks and other vast spaces that Adams worked to preserve. How we judge Adams— as a photographer, environmentalist, or citizen—does not interest me so much as how we might come to understand the complexities that his project admits.

It is worth noting, and not just parenthetically, that the lack of images of Adams's work in the present context accords with a reproduction prohibition on the part of the Ansel Adams Publishing Rights Trust, who believed that the printing of such classic photographs here would implicitly endorse my thesis—a thesis that they found not only objectionable but also abhorrent in its association of Adams with the counterculture. By way of conclusion, then, I wonder how we might recast a modernism—not to say an even more autonomous photographic history, so often kept at some remove from it—whose telling allows for practitioners who circulated in populations hopeful about the salutary, even curative, implications of the creative act? Besotted with the possibility of spiritual transcendence predicated on the land and one's corporal, cognitive, and aesthetic responses to it, Adams and Esalen chart points in this narrative, points that, though seemingly distinct, from certain vantages become impossible to tell apart.

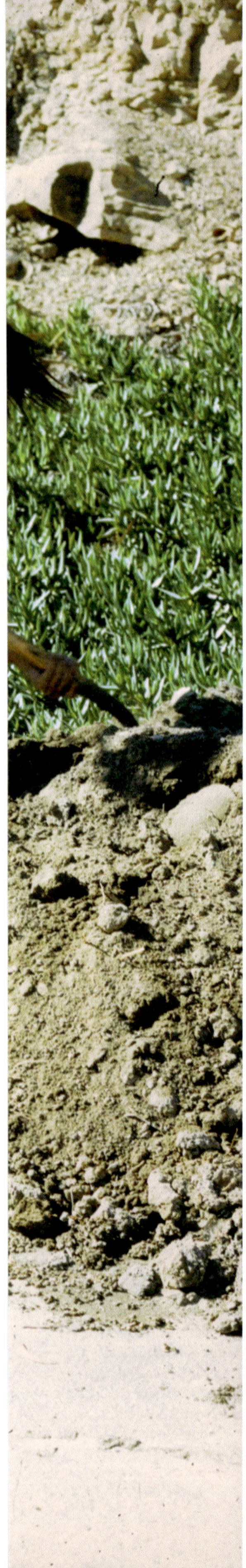

CHAPTER 17
TECHNIQUES OF SURVIVAL:
THE HARRISONS AND THE
ENVIRONMENTAL COUNTERCULTURE

Amanda Boetzkes

Technique integrates everything. . . . Man is not adapted to a world of steel; technique adapts him to it. It changes the arrangement of this blind world so that man can be a part of it without colliding with its rough edges, without the anguish of being delivered up to the inhuman.

—Jacques Ellul, 1967

To bring the sun, the wind, the earth, indeed the world of life, back into technology, into the means of human survival, would be a revolutionary renewal of man's ties to nature.

—Murray Bookchin, 1971

The statements above, by the French philosopher Jacques Ellul and the American political philosopher and ecologist Murray Bookchin, summarize a deep polarity that emerged within the early environmental movement.[1] On the one hand, Ellul's quote echoes the sentiment of many environmentalists who were vehemently opposed to the dehumanizing effects of global industrialization and a world seemingly overtaken by machines. On the other hand, there was a growing belief that technology was in fact the backbone of a new ecological society. As Bookchin describes, "an organic mode of life deprived of its technological component would be as nonfunctional as a man deprived of his skeleton."[2] This also became the conviction of artists who were exploring the points of convergence between ecology and art. While a rejection of technology came to be viewed as an unrealistic goal, environmentalists and artists alike sought new ways to bring the earth back to technology. Significantly, then, they did not aim at a return to nature but, rather, at a *return to technology,* suggesting that technology itself was the a priori condition of human societies.

The coextensiveness of political and ecological imperatives made environmental activism one of the most influential forces of the American counterculture. Not only did environmentalists protest resource depletion, toxic dumping, and other large-scale forms of environmental degradation, they generated an impetus to question the effects of everyday activity, such as patterns of consumption and waste, the widespread use of pollutants, and the living conditions of other species. It is within this context that the field now known as "eco-art" entered the domain of contemporary art. For the artist duo Newton and Helen Mayer Harrison, the project of fostering an ecological orientation involved acquiring specialized scientific knowledge of how ecosystems function, and developing technological strategies to create a symbiosis between the natural world and human systems of food and energy production. Thus, rather than strictly rejecting the technological underpinning of modern industry that was (and still is) largely geared toward stripping the planet of resources, their work operated in and through that apparatus, bridging the domains of activism and technology, aesthetic experience and scientific experimentation, in order to spearhead new ways of conceptualizing and inhabiting the planet.

Originally from New York, the Harrisons worked briefly at the University of New Mexico before relocating to California in 1967 to work at University of California at San Diego, with Newton taking a position as one of the founding members of the visual arts department, while Helen accepted a position as director of educational programs. There, the Harrisons moved to the heart of the countercultural movement, where they were introduced to Rachel Carson's *Silent Spring,* had heated exchanges with proponents of the New Left, including Herbert Marcuse, and initiated a number of controversial works that galvanized debates about how best to integrate an ecological consciousness into everyday life.

   TECHNIQUES OF SURVIVAL

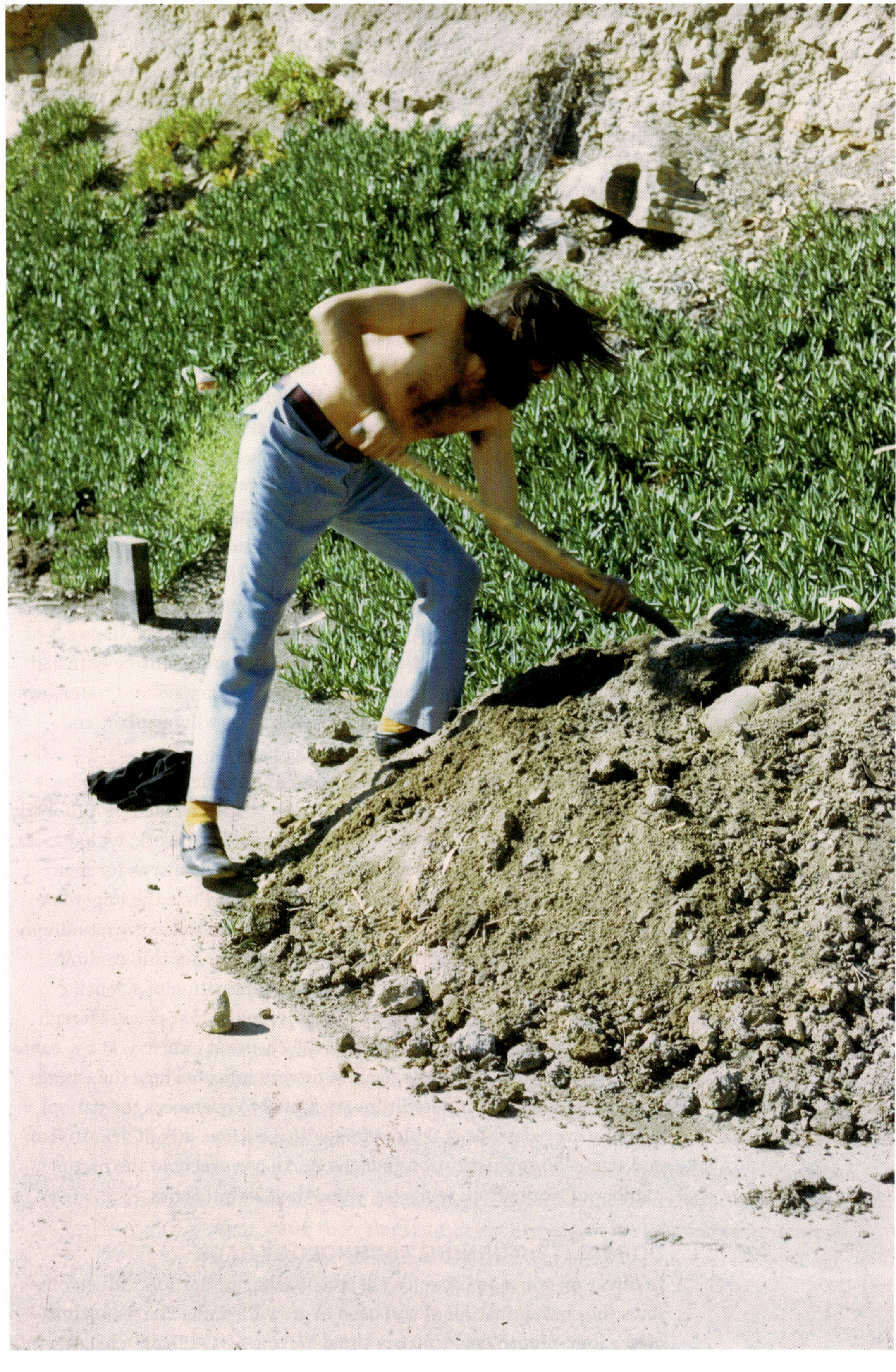

work, they gathered sand, clay, sewage sludge, leaf material, and animal manures, which they watered and turned repeatedly until their mixture had a rich "forest-floor smell" and could actually be tasted. What cannot be understated is the extent to which they transformed the act of composting into ritual behaviors that could themselves be conceived as "ecological output." Newton Harrison explains the performance in detail:

The mixture combines with time, and our touch, becoming literally a living element, a medium for growth. . . . every morning I spend ten minutes of my time with a shovel, ten with a hoe, ten with my hands—and one minute with a hose. . . . I notice that I breathe in when I pick up a shovel full of earth and breathe out when emptying it. I notice that I make three hoe strokes on inward breathing and three strokes on outward breathing. . . . In the beginning when the mixture smells vile, I take very deep breaths, drawing in air slowly, but letting it out quickly. At that point my behavior is almost gluttonous. I become very possessive, running my hands through the earth to break up small lumps. This behavior seems compulsive to me. Yet it is very necessary that I touch the soil all over, as a form of ornamentation.[9]

The art critic Jack Burnham astutely observes that the compulsive regularity of the Harrisons' performance is patterned by the ecosystem, thereby assuming the qualities of a natural event. Interestingly, here the human touch is understood as ornamentation, a word that presumes that this contact is a superfluous addition to the earth, and hence a technique. Through habit and ritual, the superadded action of forming base material produces and naturalizes the earth itself.

This naturalizing effect of the Harrisons' practice could be considered in terms of what the theorist David Wills calls a "dorsal" turn.[10] For Wills, as for Heidegger, the essence of technology is revealed through a return, that is to say, through an interrogation that leads to its origin. In contrast to the belief that technological development is a drive forward, a straight linear progress, Wills suggests that technology is paradoxically anterior in time. Technology is always already before and ahead of us: our sense of its vanguard position is always predetermined by its essential posteriority, or dorsality. Technology comes forward as alien or other to ourselves, emerging from our "natural state" or prehistory, but casting off its primordial origin to appear as the future. In its radical departure and subsequent disavowal of nature, technology cannot be foreseen and governed by humans but, rather, appears to anticipate our becoming *before* we arrive, therefore it does so seemingly *from behind*.

More subtly, Wills formulates the form of critical interrogation of technology that Heidegger initiates, as a return to its dorsality. In other words, it is an ethical imperative to recognize the implicit dorsality of the technological age. Thus, the dorsality of technology is not a literal return to a pretechnological state (as though that were possible) but,

   TECHNIQUES OF SURVIVAL

rather, a "turn back" to discover the condition from which it has sprung forward. The Harrisons first performance of the *Survival Series* encapsulates the double trajectory of technology: it deconstructs the earth, the basic support of natural life, by demonstrating its coextensiveness with the advanced scientific model that reduces it to its biochemical components. The performance as technique enacts the naturalization of an alternative agricultural technology through its return to a fundamental bodily relationship with earth, forged through a concentration on primary sensations of taste and touch.

The dorsal drive at play in the performance was by no means restricted to the Harrisons, nor was its trajectory exclusively environmental. Rather, it responded to a widely felt distrust of the modernist ideal of progress, and a desire to get back to base substance, precisely as a way to explore new possibilities of art and push the limits of its institutions. On the East Coast, one such rejection of modernism's tenets took the form of the earthworks movement, an offshoot of post-minimalism. Ranging from monumental sculptures embedded in the land such as Robert Smithson's *Spiral Jetty* and Michael Heizer's *Double Negative,* to more ephemeral markings such as those made by Richard Long during his long walks in remote landscapes, earthworks artists aimed to broaden the parameters of the artwork and situate it within the volatile conditions of the natural world. Despite their reliance on external nature, these works were not overtly ecological and were in no way invested in a return to Eden. For example, Smithson adamantly insisted that nature itself was a fiction. The ethical impetus of his works lay in their persistent examination of industrial technologies. Indeed, the artist was openly disparaging of reckless environmental practices such as strip-mining. Yet while some of his projects attempted to restore abandoned mines, his most powerful works confronted the bleak consequences of industrial society with neither utopian idealism nor nostalgia.

In his 1970 work the *Spiral Jetty,* Smithson explored the inherent posteriority of industrial machinery. Filming the construction of the fifteen-hundred-foot basalt rock spiral built into the Great Salt Lake in Utah, the artist paid special attention to the raucous presence of machines at the site, including the buzzing noise of the helicopter from which he filmed aerial views of the sculpture, the dinosaur-like teeth of the loader as it pierced the ground, and the laborious struggle of the dump truck as it clumsily navigated the rocky surface. The notable disharmony between the machines and the site foregrounds their historicity in such a way as to denaturalize industry and challenge the presumption that industrial technologies signaled progressive advancement. Indeed, Smithson positioned the entire process of construction as a sequence of backward movements. For example, he filmed the approach to the site pointing the camera behind his vehicle showing the recession of the road; he included extended cuts of the dump truck moving in reverse to unload another pile of rock; and he also had himself filmed running the spiral toward its endpoint, a movement in counterclockwise circles that clearly reference a move back in time.

Smithson's trenchant portrayal of industrial society and its impact on the land cannot be boiled down to accepting or rejecting the machines of progress. Rather, it positions this industrial landscape in the past, to see it by way of a turn back to (and against) it. In the artist's terms, the artwork stood as a bridge between the prehistoric and the posthistoric. In the no-man's-land where progression and regression are indistinguishable, the operations of industrial technologies are not omnipotent but are instead reduced to their rudimentary origins. Correspondingly, the momentum of technology is neutralized and laid bare.

Though Smithson and his contemporaries involved in the earthworks movement have occasionally been denounced for espousing an industrial aesthetic, and for the implicit aggressiveness of their interventions in the land, a return to nature in and of itself was not a viable avenue of criticism, whether for earth artists or emerging eco-artists.[11] Through Smithson's lens, industrial society was both an undeniable fact and an antiquated history. The machine exists in an agonistic relationship with the earth, by which it is ruined by the passage of time and the toll of the elements. In this respect, the earth remains irreducible to the processes of mining and refining resources. Yet where one might argue that Smithson staged the ultimate triumph of the earth over human labor, the Harrisons' *Making Earth* performance suggests a far more distressing paradigm of technological determinism, with which theorists of the New Left grappled in the early years of the counterculture. Where earthworks artists traveled to deserted sites to effect a sense of an earth that has outstripped the tremendous impact of human intervention, the prospect of an earth reduced to its biological makeup in *Making Earth* speaks to the sense of fundamental entanglement between nature and technology, the outcome of which was the principle of ecology itself. Despite their obvious differences, then, the Harrisons' practice is akin to Smithson's in its dorsal positioning of industry. Both rerouted the initial presumption of a return to nature as a return to technology. It is this subtle alteration that is most crucial for understanding the course of the environmental movement and its impact on the art world.

RECONCEIVING THE WHOLE EARTH THROUGH LIBERATORY TECHNOLOGIES

The Harrisons' work was highly consonant with a broader move in the late sixties and early seventies to rediscover basic tools and techniques of survival. The technological turn of the environmental movement was largely driven by Steward Brand, best known as the founder and editor of the *Whole Earth Catalog* and *CoEvolution Quarterly*.[12] Originally a biologist who graduated from Stanford University, Brand also trained as a designer and photographer. In 1962, he crossed paths with the author

     TECHNIQUES OF SURVIVAL

Ken Kesey and joined Kesey's group of Merry Pranskters, whose travels and escapades are recounted in Tom Wolfe's famous novel *The Electric Kool-Aid Acid Test*.[13] Brand's *Whole Earth Catalog*, which he launched in 1968, consolidated the democratic and pragmatic approach to environmentalism that Rachel Carson had begun in her insistence that science be accountable to the public. However, Brand espoused a kind of technological idealism that was alarming for theorists of the New Left such as Jacques Ellul, Lewis Mumford, and Herbert Marcuse, all of whom were insistently critical of centralized technological systems.[14] Ultimately, though, Brand's vision impacted the New Left and resulted in creative alternatives to the "megamachine" model that had presided over the early twentieth century.

In 1966, Brand campaigned to have NASA release a satellite image of the whole earth from space, which had never been shown to the public.[15] The campaign was so persistent, it ultimately succeeded, and it was this image that Brand chose for the first issue of the catalog in 1968, signifying its multifaceted aim of reconceptualizing the earth from an entirely new and outside perspective—from a higher consciousness, so to speak (Figure 17.2). At the same time, this perspective was a jarring reminder of the limits of the planet and pictured it as an enclosed organism, or as an isolated spacecraft, a metaphor pursued by the British economist and writer Barbara Ward in her 1966 book *Spaceship Earth*, and later by the architect and designer Buckminster Fuller in his *Operating Manual for Spaceship Earth* in 1969.[16] Interestingly, though, the goal of the *Whole*

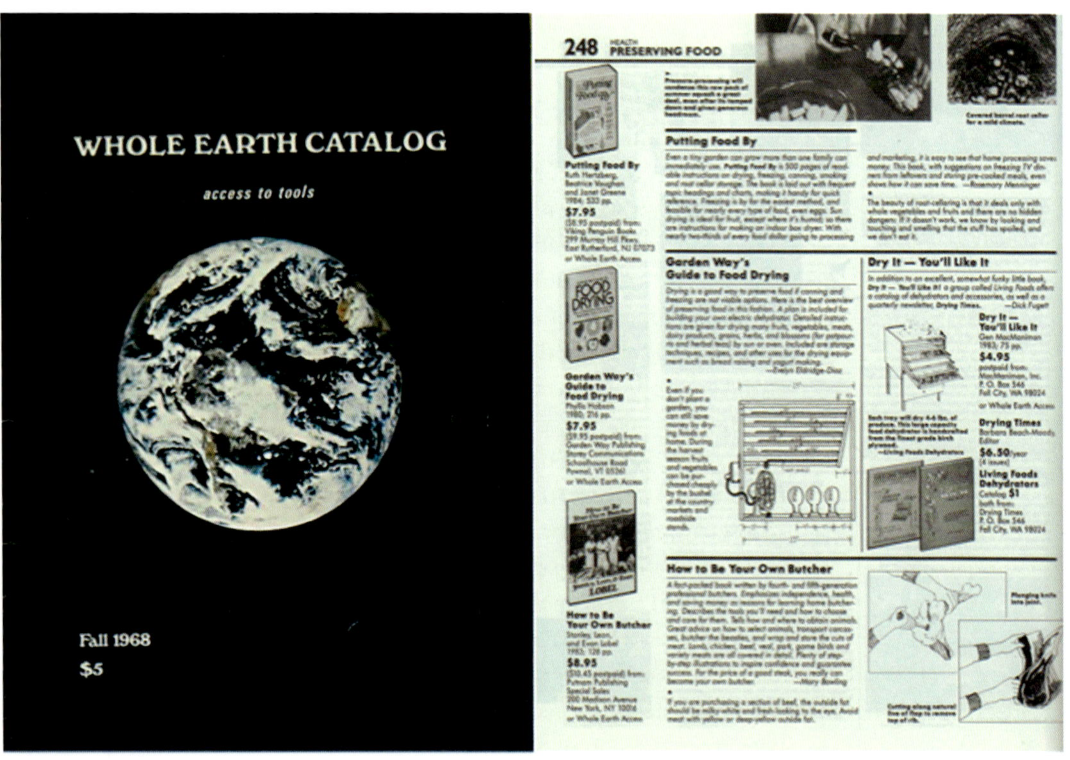

  TECHNIQUES OF SURVIVAL

Earth Catalog was, as its subtitle suggests, to provide its readers with access to tools. Tools here were broadly conceived as everything from garden implements, utensils, and construction equipment, to alternative materials, handbooks, and book reviews of how-to guides that might be employed to create sustainable communes. Its index gathered information into such varied categories as "whole systems," "land use," and "community," to "health," "nomadics," and "communications." Essentially, it launched an alternative vision of a technological future that was practical, accessible, and ecological.

The kind of low-tech tools Brand advertised in the *Whole Earth Catalog* could be understood as *intermediate technologies,* a term forwarded by the economist E. F. Schumacher in his popular book *Small Is Beautiful,* in which he advocated for individuals to regain control of their economy and environment and establish a middle ground between traditional and modern technology.[17] However, Murray Bookchin offered a more politically charged notion of a "liberatory technology" in his 1971 book *Post-Scarcity Anarchism,* which provided an appealing critical framework for the environmentalist counterculture. Like Schumacher's notion of appropriating traditional technologies, Bookchin suggested that technology itself could be reclaimed and deployed for a more democratic and free society. Not only this, but he insisted that technology could be used ecologically to "reawaken man's sense of dependence upon the environment."[18] Central to his vision were technologies of agriculture. Bookchin declared, for example, that "agriculture will become a living part of human society, a source of pleasant physical activity and, by virtue of its ecological demands, an intellectual, scientific and artistic challenge."[19] Here, he writes of a turn of technology against its own forward drive toward an imagined future in which society is a centrally governed industrial civilization. He thereby insists on a decentralized community-based appropriation of technology that would galvanize ecology and position it as the engine of intellectual and artistic life. It is the dorsality of Bookchin's notion of liberatory technology that best explains the Harrisons' work from 1971, *Portable Fish Farm.*

THE DILEMMA OF TECHNOLOGICAL ART

Portable Fish Farm was the third piece in the *Survival Series* and was commissioned by the Hayward Gallery in London, for a show titled *11 Los Angeles Artists,* which also featured works by Bruce Nauman, Ed Ruscha, Robert Irwin, and William Wegman. The Harrisons designed an installation of six rubber-lined tanks, measuring 8 feet × 20 feet × 3 feet, each containing in its respective tank catfish, brine shrimp, oysters, and lobsters. The artwork implemented what the artists termed "backyard fish harvesting," a self-enclosed small-scale system for producing a crop of catfish, alongside populations of brine shrimp and oysters, to eat the algae generated by the catfish tank, and lobsters, to feed on the catfish entrails.

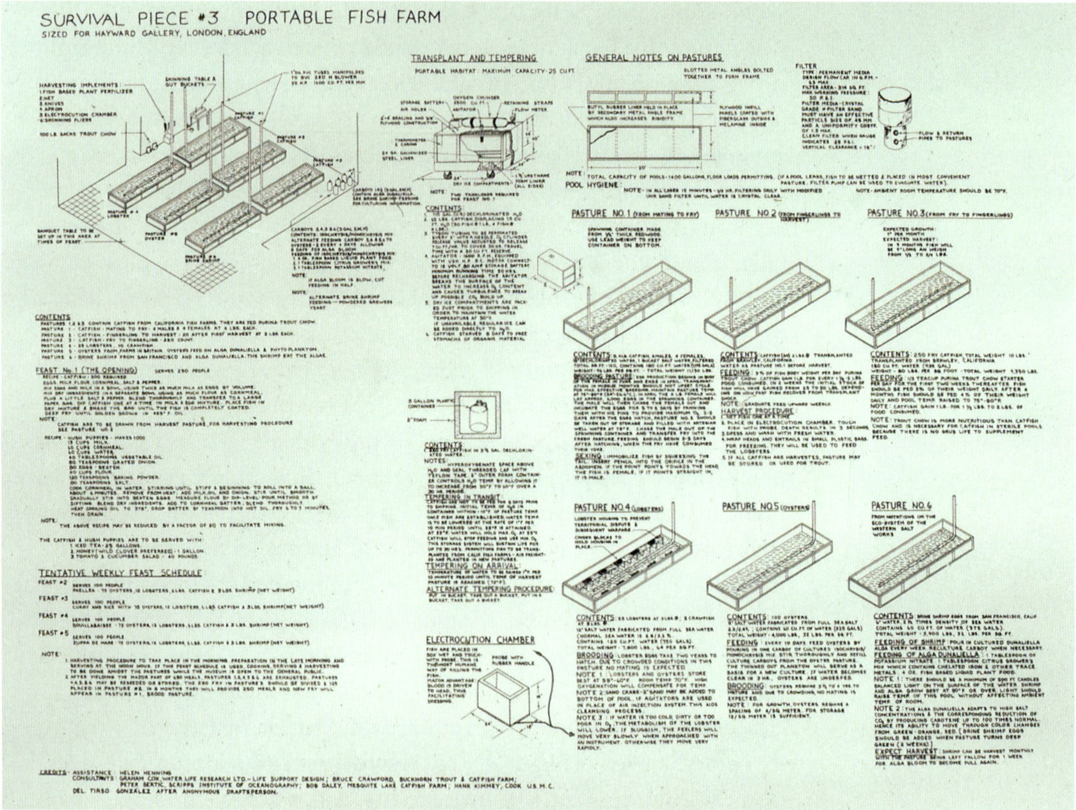

SURVIVAL PIECE #3 PORTABLE FISH FARM
SIZED FOR HAYWARD GALLERY, LONDON, ENGLAND

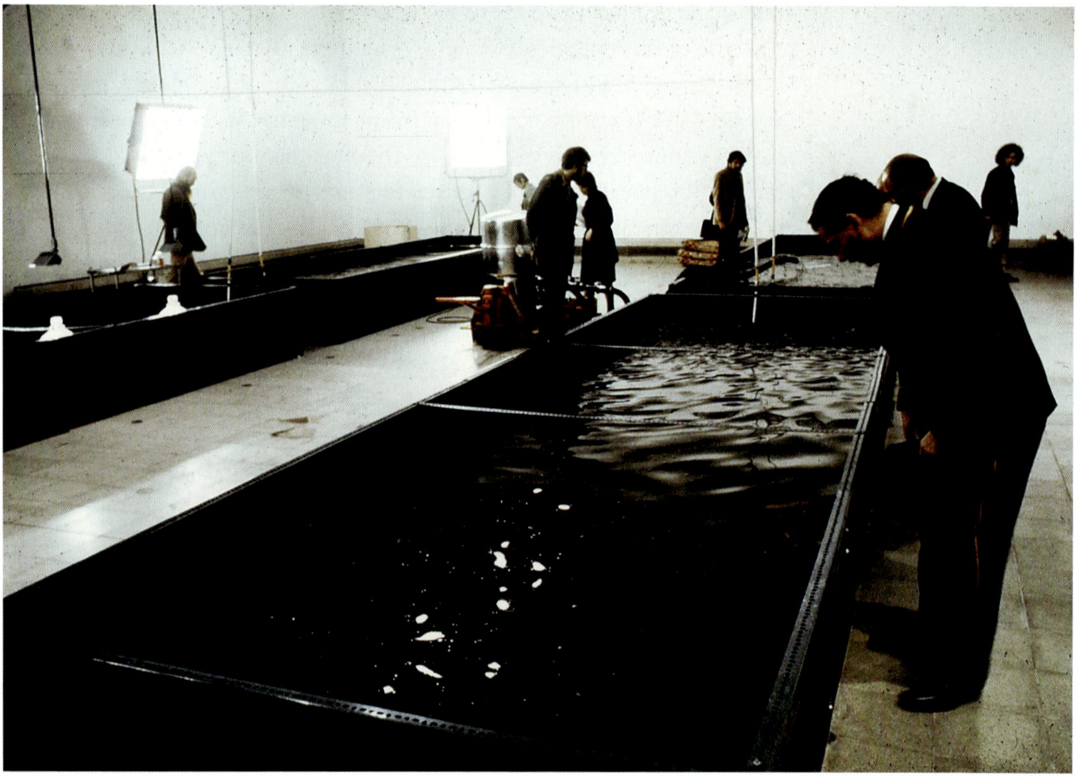

The catalog entry for the installation was a four-page layout of instructions for the construction and maintenance of the tanks, as well as how to raise and breed the fish (Figure 17.3). As though straight from the pages of the *Whole Earth Catalog,* the instructions included diagrams, measurements, temperatures, and other useful information about the upkeep of the tanks. Most crucial for the Harrisons, though, was that they also planned five feasts to accompany the installation, the first consisting of fried catfish and hush puppies for 250 people at the opening of the Hayward exhibition.[20] A recipe for the feast was included as part of the catalog entry. Herein lay the controversy.

The Harrisons planned a performance of the harvesting, skinning, and preparation of the fish as part of the artwork. Newton Harrison had learned from professional fish farmers in California that the most humane way to kill catfish was by electrocution, though it was standard practice to allow the fish to suffocate for up to four hours in the open air. After the installation at the gallery, a drawing of the electrocution system was published. It was not long before strong objections from the Royal Society for the Prevention of Cruelty to Animals, animal rights activists, other artists, and the general public appeared in news media, radio, television, and journals across the United Kingdom. The situation culminated when Lord Goodman, chairman of the British Arts Council, was sent to the museum to inform them that their funding would be removed if any catfish were killed. Newton Harrison recalls that Goodman arrived at the gallery and said, "We have a problem that needs to be ironed out," to which Harrison replied, "You think we're the problem and you're the iron?"[21]

After much deliberation, a compromise was met by which the electrocution of the catfish took place behind closed doors, and then the feast opened to its invited public. What is so curious about the exhibition is the way in which the work carried out a series of reversals between a liberatory technology born of the environmentalist counterculture and a new malignant form of modern agricultural technologies. The work began as a grassroots appropriation of marine agriculture that emphasized a small-scale, self-sustaining ecosystem, and the ritualization of food production and consumption. However, when presented as a work of art in a gallery, it came to signify the inevitable barbarism of human progress. From the perspective of animal rights activists, the ritualization of the harvest and feast was not an excessive and celebratory activity fueled by the spirit of political liberation but, rather, a sadistic and punitive action that was disturbingly complicit with the insidious forms of technological intervention that were being critiqued by environmentalists. The anthropologist Jonathan Benthall wrote to *Studio International,* commenting on the problematic nature of making killing into a symbolic rite.[22] More specifically, he noted the potential slippage between the electrocution of the catfish and the use of electrocution for judicial murder. Astutely, Benthall associated the Harrisons' perfor-

and response between the two artists. Specifically, the ecotechnological discourse is figured as a dialogue between two dominant voices: the Lagoonmaker, the engineer of the project performed by Newton, and the Witness, performed by Helen, a poet figure who counters the hubris and presumption of the Lagoonmaker, challenging him with the resistance and utterances that seemingly ensue from the lagoon itself. Significantly, the back-and-forth between the two voices moves in a kind of cycling forward and rounding back, a drive toward experimentation and knowledge, and an undoing and questioning of that drive. One of the panels of the second cycle features an image of the Harrisons with their crab tank, a simulacrum of the Sri Lankan lagoon (Figure 17.4). Alongside the image appears a written exchange between the Lagoonmaker and the Witness, each with distinctive handwriting:

But
The tank is not a lagoon
nor is it a tidal pond
nor does the mixing of fresh and salt water
make it an estuary. . . .

    But
    the tank is part of an experiment
    and the experiment is a metaphor for a lagoon
    if the metaphor works
    the experiment will succeed
    and the crabs will flourish. . . .

But
a metaphor can be a fragile idea
an improvisation born of discourse
of observation
and anyone may change or reinterpret it
for any reason

    Yet the metaphor for nature is a strong metaphor
an arrogant metaphor
    a useful metaphor
an improbable metaphor
    a playful metaphor
a dangerous metaphor that draws attention away
from the destruction of habitat
    a valuable metaphor that will lead
    to the regeneration of habitat. . . .[25]

The dorsal movement of the dialogue ultimately mobilizes the outcome and ethical potential of the Harrisons' early works in the *Survival*

TECHNIQUES OF SURVIVAL

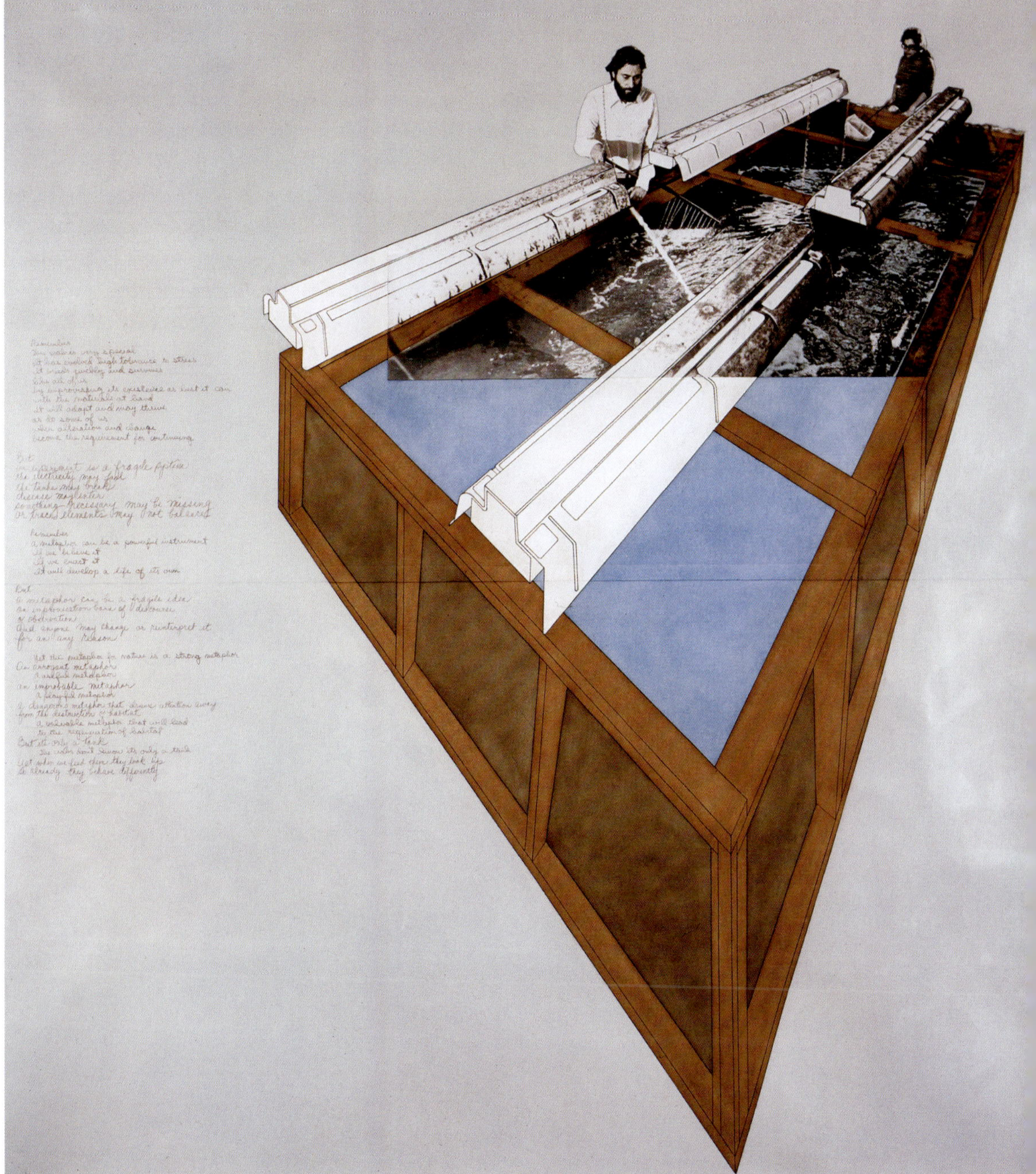

Remember
the water is very special
it has evolved high tolerance to stress
it heals quickly and survives
Like all of us
by improvising its existence as best it can
with the materials at hand
it will adapt and may thrive
as do some of us
when alteration and change
become the requirement for continuing

But
our experiment is a fragile system:
the electricity may fail
the tanks may break
disease may enter
something necessary may be missing
or trace elements may not balance

Remember
a metaphor can be a powerful instrument
if we believe it
if we enact it
it will develop a life of its own

But
a metaphor can be a fragile idea
an improvisation born of discourse
of abstraction
And anyone may change or reinterpret it
for any reason

Yet this metaphor for nature is a strong metaphor
An arrogant metaphor
A artful metaphor
an improbable metaphor
A fearful metaphor
A dangerous metaphor that draws attention away
from the destruction of habitat
A valuable metaphor that will lead
to the regeneration of habitat
But it's only a tank
The water won't know it's only a tank
Yet when we feed them they look up
& already they behave differently

Series. Despite their ambivalence towards ecotechnologies, the Harrisons deploy art as an arena of criticism that would spur the kinds of community-based discussions necessary for a grassroots appropriation of the technological apparatus. In this way, *The Lagoon Cycle* speaks to the multiple diverging trajectories within the environmentalist counterculture in the seventies, particularly with regard to the role of technology in addressing ecological imperatives. The artists responded neither by being straightforwardly oppositional nor simply by embracing the eco-utopian optimism of Stewart Brand. Rather, they accept both stances with equanimity, setting them into a motion that is neither straightforwardly progressive nor regressive but that, in its formulation of a dialectic between technology and nature, generates an ethical force and a future for ecology.

NOTES

1. Jacques Ellul, *The Technological Society* (New York: Vintage, 1967), 6; Murray Bookchin, *Post-Scarcity Anarchism* (Berkeley, Calif.: Ramparts, 1971), 129.

2. Bookchin, *Post-Scarcity Anarchism*, 87.

3. Ellul, *Technological Society*, 6.

4. Slavoj Žižek, *In Defense of Lost Causes* (New York: Verso, 2008), 441.

5. Martin Heidegger, "The Question Concerning Technology," in his *The Question Concerning Technology and Other Essays* (New York: Garland, 1977), 34.

6. Rachel Carson, *Silent Spring* (Boston: Houghton Mifflin, 1962).

7. Sarah L. Thomas, "A Call to Action: *Silent Spring*, Public Disclosure and the Rise of Modern Environmentalism," in *Natural Protest: Essays on the History of American Environmentalism*, ed. Michael Egan and Jeff Crane (New York: Routledge, 2009), 188.

8. Quoted in Jon Hughes, "What If Life Imitated Art," *Ecologist* (December/January 2008): 33.

9. Newton Harrison, quoted in Jack Burnham, *Great Western Salt Works: Essays on Post-Formalist Art* (New York: George Braziller, 1973), 164.

10. David Wills, *Dorsality* (Minneapolis: University of Minnesota Press, 2008).

11. For a succinct examination of the variety of ethical critiques of earthworks, see Suzanne Boettger, "Earthworks' Contingencies," in *Ethics and the Visual Arts*, ed. Elaine A. King and Gail Levin (New York: Allworth Press, 2006).

12. Stuart Brand, ed., *Whole Earth Catalog* (Menlo Park, Calif.: Portola Institute, 1968-72); and *CoEvolution Quarterly*, a journal edited and published by Brand from 1974 to 1984.

13. Tom Wolfe, *The Electric Kool-Aid Acid Test* (New York: Farrar, Straus, and Giroux, 1968).

14. Andrew G. Kirk, *Counterculture Green: The* Whole Earth Catalog *and American Environmentalism* (Lawrence: University Press of Kansas, 2007), 27.

15. Ibid., 40–41.

16. Barbara Ward, *Spaceship Earth* (New York: Columbia University Press, 1966); Buckminster Fuller, *Operating Manual for Spaceship Earth* (Carbondale: Southern Illinois University Press, 1969).

17. E. F. Schumacher, *Small Is Beautiful: Economics As If People Mattered* (New York: Harper and Row, 1973).

18. Bookchin, *Post-Scarcity Anarchism*, 114.

19. Ibid., 118.

20. Subsequent feasts that were planned included paella, curry, bouillabaisse, and *zuppa de mare*, each to feed a hundred people. After yielding 650 meals, the instructions read, "the pastures are exhausted and must be reseeded."

21. Quoted in Hughes, "What If Life Imitated Art?" 32.o

22. Jonathan Benthall, "Newton Harrison: Big Fish in a Small Pool," *Studio International* 182, no. 939 (December 1971): 230.

23. Burnham, *Great Western Salt Works*, 163

24. Newton and Helen Mayer Harrison, *The Lagoon Cycle* (Ithaca, N.Y.: Herbert F. Johnson Museum of Art, Cornell University, 1985), 26.

25. Ibid., 44–45.

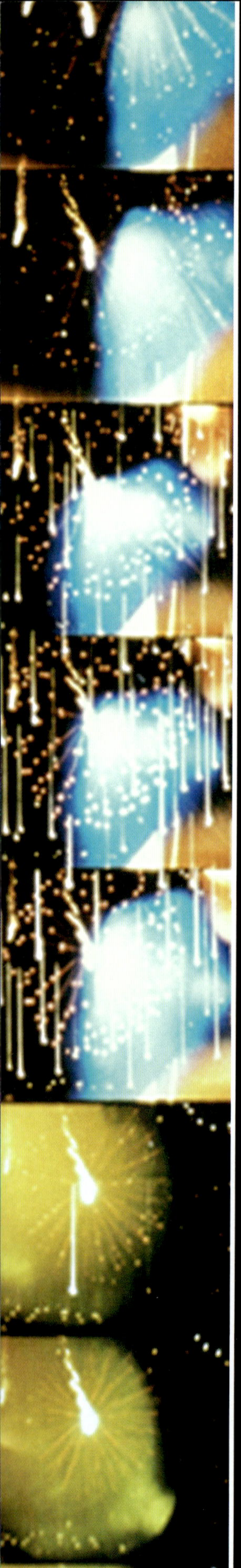

CHAPTER 18
COUNTERCULTURAL INTOXICATION: AN AESTHETICS OF TRANSFORMATION

Mark Harris

In the 1960s, negotiating psychedelic drugs became a categorical and predetermined undertaking for those seeking immersion in contemporary life. Experimentation with hallucinogens like LSD, peyote, and mescaline accessed a new world of alternatives to established social behavior. LSD in particular was taken as an agent enabling the change in awareness for hidden qualities of the world to be revealed and for new social and political practices to evolve. LSD was understood as the tool to accelerate the process by which lives could be made meaningful in an environment of rapidly changing possibilities. Recognition of the opportunities for engagement with this new world exponentially increased as the LSD advocacy campaigns by Timothy Leary and Ken Kesey attracted coverage in national media. By the mid-'60s the qualities of this new reality were being continuously redrawn by the communities of the counterculture, often in reaction to the distortions of mainstream media representations. From the start of that decade, artists, filmmakers, and writers were making innovative cultural productions to represent and interpret that evolving world for their own communities. Recalling her first acid trip taken in San Francisco in 1965, where a hallucinated panorama including every friend and family member presented itself for her scrutiny, poet Anne Waldman treasured its vision of a branching tree whose buds opened colorfully onto future lives: "My perspective now is that my first LSD experience was a partial blueprint or paradigm for the actions and karma of my life so far. . . . [it] did much to forge my commitment to *Sangha,* community, both Buddhist and poetic."[1] This essay discusses features of such adaptation to reveal how psychedelics influenced transformations of image and language in representing new possibilities for living. Often defined against the priorities of a previous generation, these features included new community and family structures, an appreciation of inner states of mind and self-knowledge, and responsibility placed on the full experience of the present as a means of transforming the future.

An influential advocate of such immediacy, Alan Watts, in his 1958 essay "The New Alchemy," provided criteria for understanding the value of his LSD experiences in terms that later became important for the counterculture.[2] The subtlety of his reflections on the functions of LSD was due to his prior extensive writing on Zen Buddhism in which he argued against sacrificing a wonder at daily existence to long-term career goals. Watts's account represented an early informal and open evaluation of LSD experiences that by the mid-1960s of Leary's Millbrook-based proselytizing would become more prescriptive and goal-driven under the instruction that *The Tibetan Book of the Dead* become the guidebook for tripping. Watts valued his acid trips for their removal of repressive perceptual routines that diminished our attunement to the world. He saw that LSD held at a distance the habitual assignation of things according to their purpose and instead permitted "the mind to organize its sensory impressions in new patterns."[3] These new patterns

and ideas, as in this first part of "Fusion," address a call to account for the transformative experience of psychedelics:

                Riddled
like a   body with a   submachine
gun
BLAST the night   is full of   radios
exclamation   marks and   words like
                    FLASH
bulbs and champagne corks   POPPING   pills and
prices SLASHED and   DROPPING   bombs and
SMACK and windows   CRASHING Jesus   SAVES and
SPEED   freaks FLASHING sirens   and revolving
lights on   SHINING RED and   Black & White
cars careening   toward the   spot
where I remember   I've been   SHOT[11]

Both poets write to the charge that the world revealed by the drug must stimulate newly configured poetic imagery. Gunn's body dissolves among undifferentiated stimuli while Randall's is assaulted by the intensified synesthesia of recognizable urban phenomena.

Such distinctions also mark the vocabulary of West Coast experimental film. Located primarily in San Francisco and New York, experimental filmmakers constituted a community of informal collaborators focused on innovative representations of contemporary experience. A number of films possess unusual liminal status as issuing from social events or becoming projections for Be-Ins and Acid Tests.[12] By participating freely in the milieu of new kinds of social gatherings, these artists tried to circumvent the difficulties facing other filmmakers, discouraged by the small audiences for experimental film. Scott Bartlett's 1967 psychedelic film *OffOn* grew from work on rock concert light shows and experiments with Glenn McKay and Tom DeWitt. Immersed in East Coast experimental film culture, Jud Yalkut's 1966 *Turn Turn Turn,* in partnership with the collective USCO, is a psychedelic interpretation of kinetic sculptures. Yalkut, then based in New York, worked with Nam June Paik on video works like *Beatles Electroniques* (1966–69), as well as helping Carolee Schneemann to find a printer for *Fuses* (1964–66) when its sexual content and heavily worked film stock proved too much for many companies. Intending the celebration of Schneemann's erotic life, the film's materiality (degraded by the application of heat, scratches, acids, and dyes), the complexity of its image overlays, and its acceleration convey a state of intoxication equivalent to that evidenced in contemporaneous films that directly address hallucinogens.

Living in a remote location in Colorado, filmmaker Stan Brakhage nevertheless maintained close contact with the New York and West

Coast experimental film milieus. Brakhage assisted in the archiving and printing of Wallace Berman's *Aleph,* which he termed a key depiction of 1960s counterculture. The film of Brakhage's most closely resembling a hallucination is the nine-second *Eye Myth* from 1967, in which a hovering central figure is enveloped and dissolved by detailed hand-painted spots and lines of color. Where Schneemann and Brakhage engaged in direct and visceral manipulation of filmed images for intense somatic effect, filmmakers James Whitney and Jordan Belson developed both mechanical and handmade techniques for manipulating abstract images into intricate visionary animations. Whitney's film *Lapis,* completed in Southern California in 1966, generates complex mandala dissolves composed of masses of points of light that are continually reforming concentric circles of green and gold in reference to Yogic meditation states. Equally engaged with representing heightened inner states of mind, San Francisco–based filmmaker Belson linked his abstract films to Yoga practice as well as to experiences of hallucinogens. Some of Belson's early work, like *Allures* (Figure 18.1) from 1961 and *Re-Entry* from 1964, conceptualized images of outer space, although he maintained his imagery related internal visions to concrete objective reality,

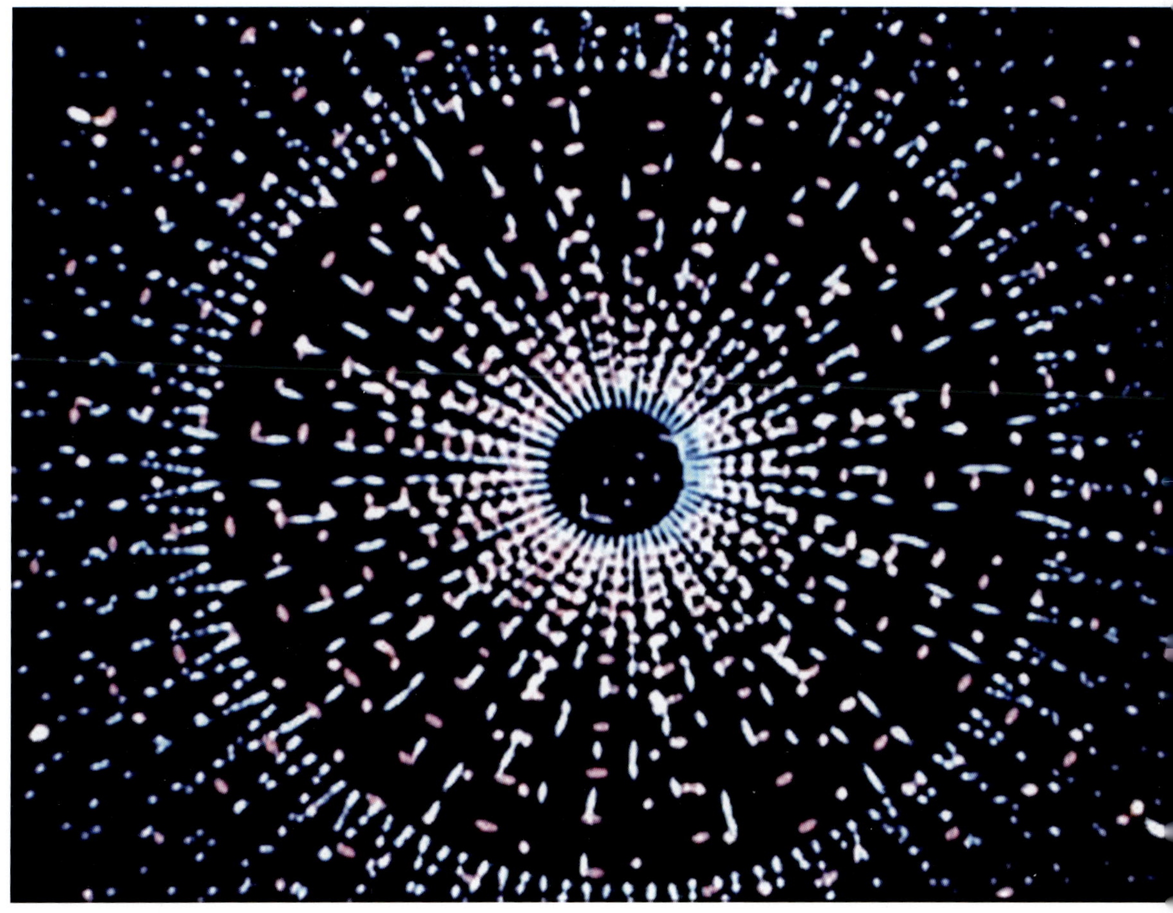

in that sense similar to Gunn's endeavor to account for correspondence between inner realizations and external events. Gunn's poem "The Fair in the Woods" (which has as its coda *"LSD, San Rafael Woods: 'Renaissance Fair'"*) approaches Belson's cinematic visions:

Landscape of acid:
                              where on fern and mound
The lights fragmented by the roofing bough
Throbbed outward, joining over broken ground
To one long dazzling burst; as even now
Horn closes over horn into one sound.[13]

While the configurations of light in Belson's *Allures* reprise mandala-like motifs from earlier work, the overall design is of movement into space rather than laterally. By the time of *Phenomena* (1965) and *Samadhi,* Belson was drawing primarily on sutra philosophy while incorporating evaluations of extensive early experimentation with peyote and other hallucinogens. Although Belson had declared unsatisfactory an earlier film titled *LSD,* he continued to acknowledge how helpful his drug experiences had been to the development of his work. His title *Re-Entry,* after all, referred in common usage to the process of reimprinting, or the reattunement, of awareness. Speaking in 1970, Belson explained:

Early in life I experimented with peyote, LSD, and so on. But in many ways my films are ahead of my own experience. [*Samadhi*] is way ahead of anything I've experienced on a continuing basis. And the same had been true of the drug experiences. They somehow set the stage for the insights. I had peyote fifteen years ago but I didn't have any cosmic or *Samadhic* experiences. That remained for something to happen through development on different levels of consciousness.[14]

For other artists and writers, however, their first encounters with LSD were sufficiently transformative. Even though hallucinogens remained a hidden agent in her poems, Belle Randall's first trip convinced her to become an active advocate for the LSD church, Fellowship of the Clear Light: "And yes, for people used to controlling experience with language, like us, it was an enormous eye-opener, just by being so intense—showing possibilities in experience we hadn't known before. I wept, I felt that I died and was reborn. I came back to earth vowing to savor every moment and to love everyone from now on."[15] "Genesis," part II of the poem "101 Different Ways of Playing Solitaire," is a section that communicates, as if describing a Belson film, the revelation and conviction behind such advocacy:

I push the beaded curtains back
And Genesis occurs:

The Mysteries of Creation sift
And tumble past me in a blurred

Profusion on the papered walls,
Dwindle and resolve themselves
In scattered, gleaming stars.[16]

The commune movement generated the greatest variety of new forms of community, experiments in living made more arduous by the frequent visitors and public official scrutiny. Lou Gottlieb's Sonoma County Morning Star Ranch hosted Haight-Ashbury LSD activists like Ramón Sender following Ken Kesey's Acid Test events in the mid-1960s.[17] Kesey's Acid Test occasions for mass induction to LSD use grew out of the Magic Bus tour that he and his band or family of followers, calling themselves the Merry Pranksters, initiated in 1964. Traveling from La Honda, California, to New York and back, the Pranksters staged outdoor music festivals and LSD promotional events along the way. Upon their return, the Acid Test events were organized. As David Farber has argued, "the Acid Tests pointed toward the creation of enclaves, social spaces in which visionaries played out new collective games. . . . the Pranksters took their acid visions as a sign of the immensely entertaining, challenging, and occasionally enlightening free spaces people could create if they cared to."[18]

Starting in the San Fernando Valley, the Hog Farm community under Hugh Romney (once a Prankster himself) launched their own bus tour in the late 1960s, traveling in large convoys of decorated vehicles and facilitating free concerts and light shows across the country in temporarily erected structures. As Romney explains, in this context psychedelics intermittently alleviated the trials of keeping buses running and the community fed: "Somewhere around that time the peyote arrived. From the Texas Plains with bulging gunny sacks came Federal Fred our Psychedelic Santa Claus to kick off the *Great Peyote Geeze*."[19]

The 1966 San Francisco Trips Festival, organized by Stewart Brand and others, concluded Kesey's Acid Test events. Speaking on a Trips Festival reunion panel in 2007, filmmaker Ben Van Meter described the sense of complete experiential integration of that 1966 event from the perspective of an imagined attendee, enveloped by projected lights and dancing crowd, feeling that "there is no point where he ends and everything else begins," as if paraphrasing Gunn's acid poems.[20] Van Meter's film *S.F. Trips Festival* was made across the Festival's three nights, edited in camera, and then assembled as one continuous piece. Referencing the acid-spiked drink provided by Kesey's Merry Pranksters, he explained how he "exposed each roll once each of the three nights. The resulting impressionistic vision can best be described as a documentary from the point of view of a goldfish in the Kool-Aid bowl."[21] Following that notion of entities without boundaries, Van Meter's camera films sideways and upside-down, often inverting figures over one another and superimposing them over light show images. With the sequences sped up and the mesh of imagery frequently indecipherable, a vividly chaotic and decentered kineticism conceptualizes hallucination as the overwhelming accumulation of unremitting external stimuli. This is the experience to which City Lights Bookstore founder Lawrence Ferlinghetti's imagery refers in "LSD, Big Sur," the second part of the 1966 poem "Through the Looking Glass":

Intolerable arabesques
    coming & coming & coming
        on & on
            toward me
      onto me
          over me
Relentless
    Ineffable!
      Coming down now
          re-echoing
        gliding down
           those landscapes
         & arabesques of earth
      seas reglitterized
    seen thru a silkscreen overlay
sun stricken![22]

Although the bad trip left few traces in experimental film, it dominated commercial cinema's categorization of LSD, reducing psychic transformation to a dead-end of personal disintegration. Supplying sensationalist movies for drive-in audiences, this approach fed off public anxiety in the wake of the criminalization of LSD in 1966. A handful of films did, however, represent LSD use with due complexity, without ever quite shaking off negative connotations. Conrad Rooks's 1966 film *Chappaqua,* reenacting a Swiss clinic cure for his drug and alcohol addiction, is an unlikely advocate for LSD experiences, yet the complex facture of its hallucination imagery, both beatific and morbid, connects this work to the celebratory middle period of 1960s counterculture history. Convincing as the cinematic representation of a bad trip is the scene in Dennis Hopper's *Easy Rider* where protagonists drop acid in a New Orleans cemetery. San Francisco artist and filmmaker Bruce Conner was a consultant for that sequence, which applies lens flare, hand-held pans, and rapid cross-cuts of naturalistic with hallucinatory imagery to portray an intensely bleak hallucination signaling the downturn in counterculture ebullience that was well under way by the time of the film's release in 1969. Both these movies adopted multiple exposure techniques that were a staple for experimental films of the counterculture.

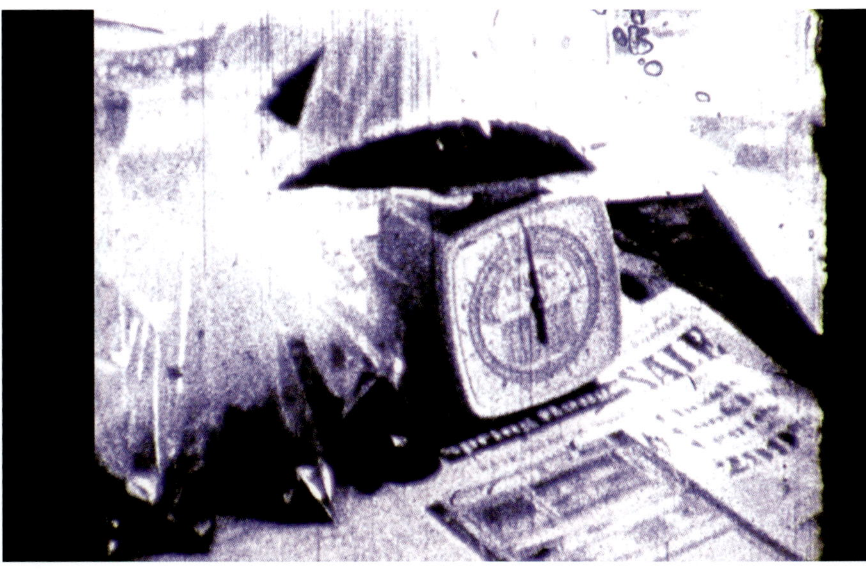

The layered, multiple-exposure imagery of Wallace Berman's *Aleph* (Figure 18.2), Brakhage's *Dog Star Man* (1961–64), Bruce Conner's *Looking for Mushrooms* (Figure 18.3), Van Meter's *S.F. Trips Festival* (Figure 18.4), and Jerry Abrams's *Be-In* (1967) intended to evoke new techniques of seeing and feeling. Of several variations of Conner's *Looking for Mushrooms,* the one from 1967 used the Beatles' psychedelic "Tomorrow Never Knows" as its sound track. It was only much later, in 1996, that he made the apt substitution of a 1968 recording of West Coast musician Terry Riley's work for an extended version.[23] Starting with depictions of a journey through rural Mexico, Conner's film features scenes of work and recreation, as well as close-ups of plants and flowers, weathered masonry, and hands holding hallucinogenic mushrooms, after which the footage becomes bleached out and progressively obscured. The film concludes in San Francisco, with in-camera superimpositions of up to eight layers of imagery. Edenic scenes of interiors, women, lights, a cat, a chair, and Christmas decorations are exposed over fireworks that fill the screen with exploding light. This sense of an ecstatic outcome is emphasized in scenes of faces superimposed on "found" mandalas of white-wall tires, light fixtures, clocks, and circular advertisements. Among Conner's varied artwork were illustrations of mandala-like compositions of circles for the *San Francisco Oracle* (an outspoken advocate for LSD use), notably the monochrome centerpiece of issue 2 from October 1966, and the colored cover of issue 9 from December 1967 (Figure 18.5).

Conner's film imagery anticipates a very different kind of LSD representation appearing in some European commercial films about drug subcultures. Barbet Schroeder's 1968 *More* includes a thirty-second sequence of close-ups representing entrancement with nature under the influence of LSD. Images of stratified rock, fossilized plants, butterfly wing, purple dahlia, and cowrie shell give way to writhing maggots and

  COUNTERCULTURAL INTOXICATION

Figure 18.3
Bruce Conner, film still from
Looking for Mushrooms, 1959–
65. 16 mm film, color, sound, 3
minutes. Courtesy of Walker Art
Center, Minneapolis, Minnesota.
Photography by Dan Dennehy.
Copyright Conner Family Trust,
San Francisco.

Figure 18.4
Film still sequence from Ben Van
Meter, *S.F. Trips Festival,* 1966.
16 mm film, color, sound, 9
minutes. Courtesy of the artist.

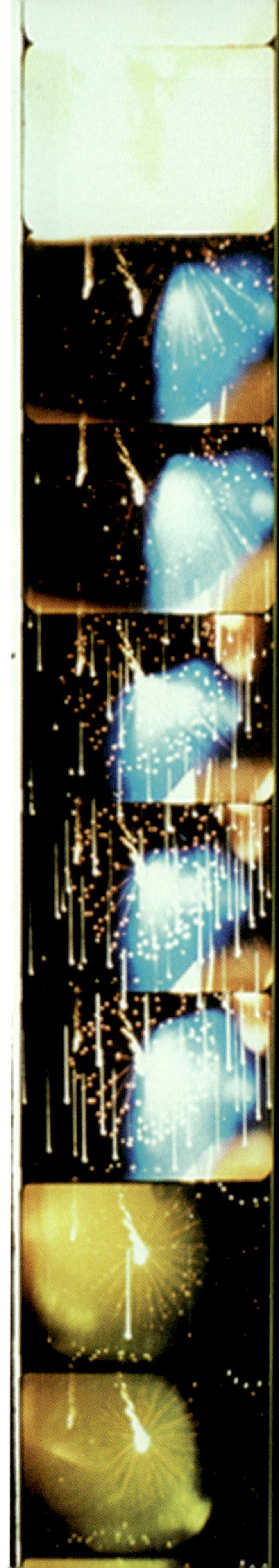

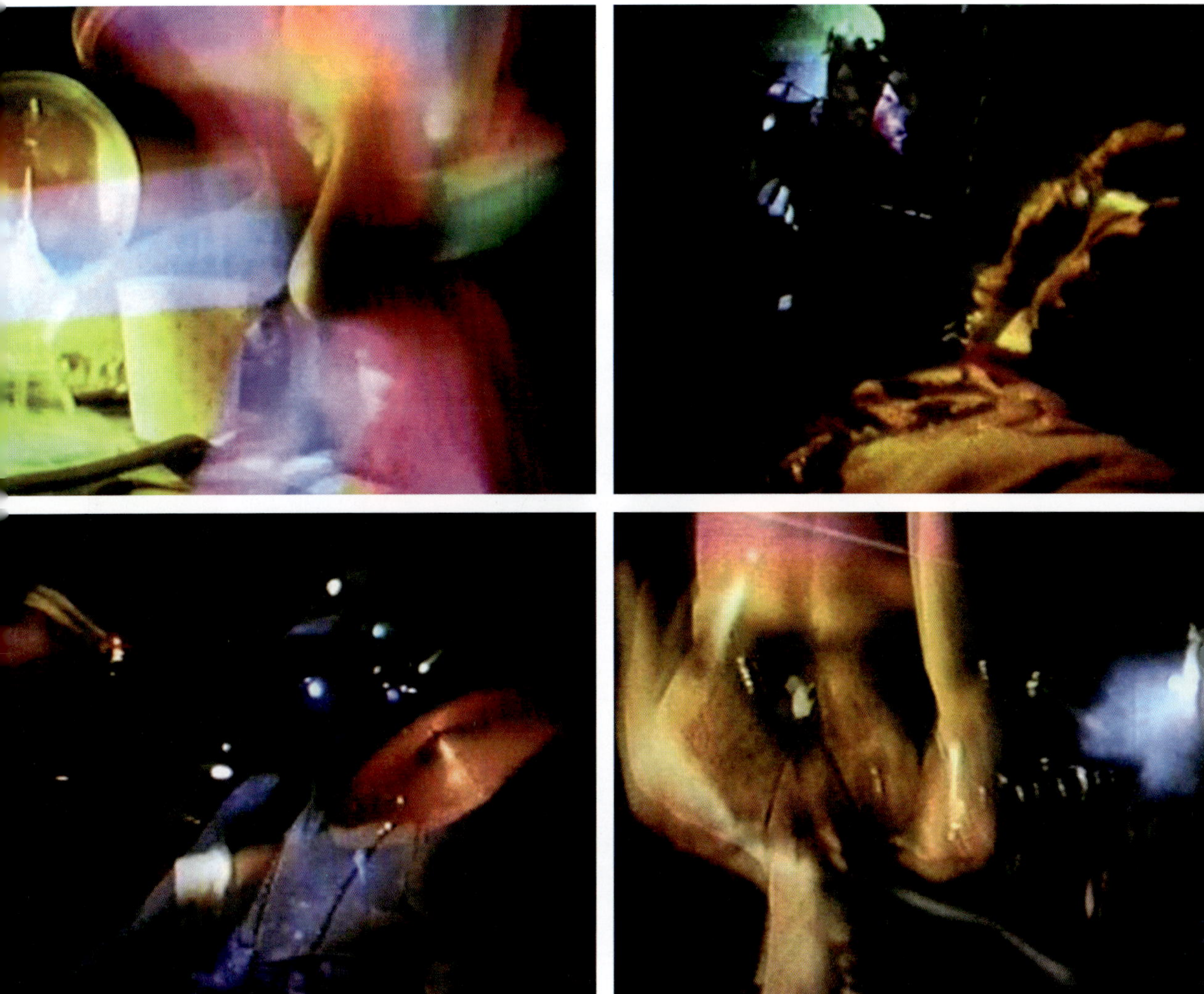

❖ ORACLE ❖

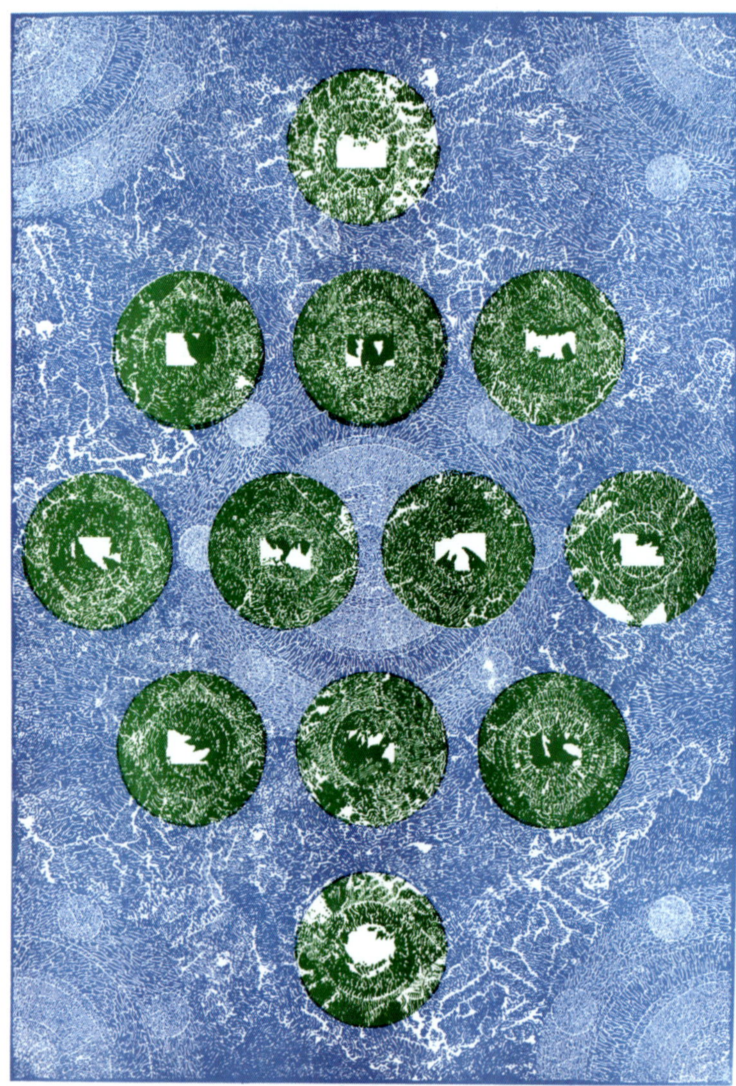

THE CITY OF SAINT FRANCIS
THE CITY OF SAINT FRANCIS
VOLUME ONE, NUMBER NINE
25
in state
(c) 1967 SAN FRANCISCO ORACLE ✦ AUGUST
35
out of state
245

the pupil of an eye. Nicholas Roeg and Donald Cammell use this same device in *Performance,* released in 1970, where the speckled surfaces of magic mushrooms are scrutinized in extreme close-up, taking the form of a psychedelic representation that, like the sequence in *More,* presages the grim denouements of both films.

By comparison, the indeterminacy of drug-related experimental film is more effectively analogous to hallucinogens. As a psychedelic film deeply preoccupied with the relation of private to public life, Berman's *Aleph* includes sampled images alongside footage of family and friends. Moving at a frenetic pace, its materiality altered by paint, scratches, and applied Letraset, *Aleph* includes scans of television shows, of Mick Jagger singing, of photos of dancers, baseball players, the Pope, and Bob Dylan, alternating with images of Berman's own studio work. Scenes are successively repeated as if they were melodic elements in a composition. The film opens on the torso and arm of artist Robert Alexander shooting up and closes similarly by showing the whole figure of a man applying a tourniquet. Toward the start of the film are images of marijuana plants and grass being sorted and weighed. Berman's son Tosh views these as reflections of what was going on in the artist's milieu: "Wallace greatly admired the Surrealists for their sense of adventure in traveling and being immersed through art and narcotics. . . . for these artists drugs were a tool for art making—which is a narcotic in itself."[24] The drug reference is underlined in a brief penultimate image of the John Tenniel illustration titled "Alice after drinking the first potion," showing the character's elongated neck and startled face from *Alice in Wonderland,* of which Berman had made a life-sized cardboard cutout version that stood around his house. That Berman was a committed advocate of psychedelics is seen in correspondence with close friend David Meltzer: "Sunday was LSD day & i fared very cool" (May 1962 letter) and "was peyoted out last week first time in a year   beautiful" (an undated letter).[25] Although in private Berman opposed his friends' use of heroin, the representation of drugs in his handmade journal *Semina* and in *Aleph* present, without obvious judgment, a contest between hallucinogens and narcotics. Berman was convinced that the heroin use of friends like John Alexander, Philip Lamantia, Alexander Trocchi, and Stuart Perkoff impaired their creative work. In *Semina 4* (1959) under the pseudonym Pantale Xantos, Berman included a poem (excerpted here): "Morphine mother / Heroin mother / Yage mother / Benzidrine mother / Peyote mother / Marijuana mother / Cocaine mother / Hashish mother / Mushroom mother / Opium mother / Mescalin mother."[26] This had been preceded in *Semina 3* (1958) by Michael McClure's "Peyote Poem," the affirmative account of a more agreeable experience than the one he was to have in 1961:

> there is a golden bed radiating all light
> the air is full of silver hangings and sheathes
> I smile to myself. I know

all that there is to know. I see all there
is to feel. . . .[27]

It was Berman's encouragement of McClure to take peyote in 1958 that
initiated this event. Richard Cándida Smith explains that Berman's opposition of hallucinogens to narcotics defined his utopian perspectives:
"Experimentation with drugs did not mean removal from the world, but
could, at least theoretically, lead to a sense of social obligation and a
desire to change the world as it exists. . . . Drug taking was not an unfortunate irrelevancy but an essential element in formulating the social
ideology of the Californian avant-garde."[28]

By 1963 McClure was maturing into his drug experiences to the point
that his *Meat Science Essays* could become a hybrid guidebook and testament to the best that hallucinogens had to offer. Very different from the
image intoxication of that later celebratory prose, his 1961 "Lines from a
Peyote Depression" experiments with inarticulacy and imageless verse
to convey the intensity of these challenging experiences:

        and I can't go on.
! Or go on—that this is not a mood! But the way
that matter is—and love
AND I DON'T KNOW WHAT TO SAY FROM HERE
There are stars far away and cold   to eyes so hot
      we measure them. In space and cold
     COLD COLD COLD COLD COLD COLD
     COLD COLD COLD AND FAR AWAY. . . .[29]

    Moving to San Francisco in 1956 as a guest of fellow poet Ed Dorn,
Robert Creeley immediately immersed himself in Beat poetry circles,
befriending Allen Ginsberg, Jack Kerouac, Philip Whalen, and McClure.
Creeley's poetry critically examined his own subjectivity, and encouraged by Ginsberg, he explored writing in different cognitive states.
In his 1965 essay "Introduction to New Writing in the USA," Creeley
recognizes McClure's "Peyote Poem" as an experiment with the translation into unconventional poetic form of a newly intensified exploration
of self, driven by hallucinogens.[30] Written from 1968–71 and split into
prose and verse halves, *A Day Book* embeds Creeley's own intense self-
reflection among prosaic biographical details on family, sex, drugs, and
friendships in the poem "On Acid," exposing an exhausted intellect and
fractured subjectivity:

And had no actual
 hesitancies, always
(flickering) minds'
sensations: here, here, *here**

philo-tro-

bic-port-

a-bil-ity?

End, end, end, end, end, end
Next? Next who/ who/ they we
                   for she me
*or there?   is not we'll
                 be. . . .[31]

Whalen was one of those participating in the landmark Beat poetry reading on October 7, 1955, at San Francisco's Six Gallery, where Ginsberg introduced "Howl" to enthusiastic acclaim. Following Gary Snyder, another poet reading that night, Whalen was to move to Japan in 1967, becoming increasingly involved in Zen Buddhism and developing an intimate, witty poetry of intercultural contextualization of Japanese asceticism and West Coat secular sensuality. In "Stolen and Abandoned," from the collection *The Kindness of Strangers: Poems 1969–1974*, Whalen moves from autobiographical asides to Zen teaching, linking deliberations on anxiety and death to experiences with hallucinogens:

                     Pattern
     without words equals 'mandala' which is one
     single troublesome image? (But recall five
     several personal body images during Kyoto
     psilocybin trip. Have I been seeing some-
     thing backwards or upside down?)
O sharp cumbersome Death!
Most of us tire of thinking and feeling
We fall asleep. Reb is asleep
Head in a tiger's mouth.[32]

However, the most extreme example of bad trips, and of the language and imagery brought to their depiction, came from Allen Ginsberg, who understood the overwhelmingly negative imagery of his 1959–60 experiments with hallucinogens to be caused by his own prescriptive expectations for drug-enabled personal enlightenment. In these poems that flourish as explicit commentary on sexuality, spirituality, and mortality, Ginsberg was overwhelmed with visions of death and incessant violence. "Lysergic Acid" (San Francisco, 1959) sees the poet connected to the universe by an extensive web, embedded as prey yet remaining "sensitive to the infinite minutest vibration of eternal harmony." The imagery here describes the desubjectivized trance state in ways suggestive of Belson's films:

It is a Ghost Trap, woven by priest in Sikkim or Tibet
a crossframe on which a thousand threads of differing color
are strung, a spiritual tennis racket
in which when I look I see aethereal lightwaves radiate
bright energy passing round on the threads as for billions of years
the thread-bands magically changing hues one transformed to another as if the
Ghost Trap
were an image of the Universe in miniature[33]

Like other acid intellectuals in the '60s, Ginsberg was intent on mapping expanded consciousness onto political change. It seems likely that the presence of such predetermined expectations throws his trips into a realm of negative accomplishments. Ginsberg's poems are cosmic in scale, unfettered by the mundane. Recording visions experienced while taking the Amazon plant-based hallucinogen ayahuasca, the last three poems retrieve the shamanic origins of that intoxicant as devastating rounds of self-realization. The imagery is apocalyptic, whether concerning the poet's body ("Invade my body with the sex of God, choke up my nostrils with corruption's infinite caress") or mass populations ("Volcanos of flesh over London, on Paris a rain of eyes—truckloads of angelhearts besmearing Kremlin walls—the skullcap of light to New York") or animal aggression ("Gnarl Moth," "warmouth doveling," "slimy worms," "Eyeless Squid," "pack of heavy dogs"). With terse resignation Ginsberg concludes in a postscript: "The message is: Widen the area of consciousness."[34]

Creeley's 1966 view of Ed Dorn's poetry as revealing "the dry, tough, drawn, harsh *unrelieved* experience of the world . . . attentive to the specific qualities and quantities it manifests" points to a transformation in the latter's writing in the hallucinogenic and narcotic allegory *Gunslinger*.[35] From the vantage point of London in the late '60s, and Chicago and San Francisco in the early '70s, Books I and II of Dorn's *Gunslinger* flamboyantly draw together the routes of transformation activated by LSD experiences. Dorn's invitation from Ginsberg and Waldman to speak at Boulder, Colorado's Naropa Institute would later lead to a university position. Ideals of richer community life, enlightenment, innovative political advocacy, ease of movement, and a new aesthetic radicality are narrated as archetypal, if quixotic, contemporary pursuits. Dorn's verse conflates cultural archetypes to get at what was significant about the 1960s. Magic Bus odysseys like Kesey's and Hog Farm's are transposed to a cowboy burlesque where an unlikely alternative community of a gunslinger, a poet, Claude the "Turned On Horse," Lil the cabaret manager, and "I" embark by stagecoach from Mesilla to Las Vegas, "across / two states / of mind." Police hassles and suspicious locals are replayed as the imagery of epic Westerns, while the poem is replete with references to hallucinogens:

Huh!? Oh that.
well thats, uh,
Acid.

How pure is it?

Straight man.

1000 percent,
nothin but molecules.[36]

For literary critic Michael Davidson, "Dorn is . . . interested in the *mind* of an era, and the mind of the sixties was considerably affected by the context of drugs. The fact that 'I' is preserved in Kool Everything's batch of acid represents the entire transformation of the ego made possible through hallucinogens."[37] Dorn's concept of the "Literate Projector" suggests experimental film's innovations—estrangement of image from sound, absence of narrative, and willful treatment of subject:

Well, There's a Literate Projector,
which, when a 35 mm strip is put thru it
turns it into a Script
Instantaneously!
and projects that—the finished script
onto the virgin screen

Shake a circus up and down
put funny music next to Death
or document something
about military commitment
and let woodchucks play the parts[38]

The projector, we are told, was made for "the stix / but works best in University towns," where the audiences most likely to be sympathetic to such films are found.[39]

It is easily overlooked that the counterculture's history of hallucinogens often concerns a family affair, a case of domestic revolution where trips transformed existing nuclear families and inspired the creation of new communities. Ginsberg's 1952 account of a peyote experience at his parents' home in Paterson, New Jersey, reveals a suburban utopia with family life benignly swirling around him.[40] In 1964, Belle Randall was turned on by her mother who had resorted to clinical LSD treatment after fifteen years of ineffective psychotherapy. So important was the experience that Randall's mother immediately paid for her daughter to undergo the same treatment.[41] Berman's extended family was particularly intimate, where *Semina* relied on contributions from friends for its contents and, distributed only as a gift, offered up an intellectual and psychedelic portrait of that community in return. McClure described this particular symbiotic relationship as "on the lip exactly between love and generosity and selfish appetite: Wallace's appetite for art and for friendship and for spirituality."[42] Berman's *Aleph* and Conner's *Looking for Mushrooms* drew together the strands of their communities as a commitment driven by psychedelic experiences. Under the influence of hallucinogens, countercultural artists and writers and the transformation of imagery and text in their work indeed represented the desire for new possibilities for living that in some milieus were successfully achieved. In carrying through the directives realized through peyote, mescalin, and LSD visions, these poets and filmmakers developed innovative languages celebrating a new agency of hallucinogens and presenting challenging propositions for a socially engaged aesthetics whose complexities have been historically underacknowledged.

NOTES

1. Anne Waldman is quoted in Charles Hayes, *Tripping: An Anthology of True-Life Psychedelic Adventures* (New York: Penguin, 2000), 72–73.

2. Alan Watts, "The New Alchemy," in his *This Is It and Other Essays on Zen and Spiritual Experience* (New York: Pantheon Books, 1960), 127–53.

3. Alan Watts, "Beat Zen, Square Zen, Zen," in *This Is It*, 135.

4. Ibid., 143–44.

5. Editorial, *Psychedelic Review* 1 (Summer 1963): 2. Further page references to this editorial appear parenthetically in the text.

6. Timothy Leary, "Languages: Energy Systems Sent and Received," *ETC.: A Review of General Semantics* 22, no. 4 (1965): 441.

7. Ibid., 454, 459.

8. Thom Gunn is quoted in Mike Jay, ed., *Artificial Paradises* (London: Penguin, 1999), 169.

9. Thom Gunn, *Moly and My Sad Captains* (New York: Farrar, Straus and Giroux, 1973), 40.

10. Belle Randall, correspondence with author, 2009.

11. Belle Randall, *101 Different Ways of Playing Solitaire* (Pittsburgh: University of Pittsburgh Press, 1973), 60.

12. Perhaps the most direct engagement of this kind was Ben Van Meter's *S.F. Trips Festival* (later discussed more extensively) comprising layered imagery filmed during the three-night-long 1966 San Francisco Trips Festival. Ronald Nameth's 1967 *Exploding Plastic Inevitable* had been filmed in Andy Warhol's club of the same name. It consists of modified footage of Factory associates like Gerald Malanga and Ingrid Superstar dancing to music by the Velvet Underground, in front of Warhol's film and slide projections. The experimental montage of Jerry Abrams's *Be-In* derives from footage taken of the January 1967 San Francisco Human Be-In. Working in 1967 with the North American Ibis Alchemical Light Company, Bruce Conner incorporated segments of his earlier work, as well as introducing entirely new films, in light shows at the Avalon Ballroom in San Francisco. See Peter Boswell, "Bruce Conner: Theater of Light and Shadow," in *2000 BC: The Bruce Conner Story Part II* (Minneapolis: Walker Art Center, 1999). Glenn McKay incorporated Scott Barlett's films in light show performances before the latter's production of *OffOn*. Jon Stehura was one filmmaker who collaborated with light show artists in generating projections for audiences outside cinemas: "Stehura's film footage was also used by the Single Wing Turquoise Bird light show, a large-scale performance on which a dozen artists might collaborate simultaneously, using film projections, slide projections, color wheels, liquid projections, calibrated-speed flicker mechanisms, etc. to modulate dazzling breath-taking visuals parallel to a variety of music and sound phenomena." See William Moritz, "Making the Soul Visible," iotaCenter Web site, www.iotacenter.org/visualmusic/articles/kinetica4/soulvisible.

13. Thom Gunn, *Moly and My Sad Captains*, 29.

14. Belson is quoted in Gene Youngblood, *Expanded Cinema* (New York: Dutton, 1970), 174.

15. Randall, correspondence with author.

16. Randall, *101 Different Ways*, 34.

17. In 1961 Sender had founded the San Francisco Tape Music Center with Morton Subotnik, joined soon after by Pauline Oliveros. Intended to enable production of new music and the development of early synthesizers, the center notably premiered Terry Riley's *In C* in 1965. See Thom Holmes, *Electronic and Experimental Music* (New York: Routledge, 2002), 206–7.

18. David Farber, "The Intoxicated State/Illegal Nation: Drugs in the Sixties Counterculture," in *Imagine Nation: The American Counterculture of the 1960s and '70s*, ed. Peter Braunstein and Michael William Doyle (New York: Routledge, 2002), 26.

Published in 1968, Tom Wolfe's *The Electric Kool-Aid Acid Test* was a supportive journalistic account of Kesey's itinerant activism with the Merry Pranksters. It remains one of the most compelling accounts of this social experiment. Wolfe, *The Electric Kool-Aid Acid Test* (New York: Farrar, Straus, and Giroux, 1968).

19. Hugh Romney, *countdown2* (New York: New American Library, 1970), 75.

20. Van Meter's film *S.F. Trips Festival* and the panel discussion from 2007 are featured on the *The Trips Festival Movie*, DVD (Trips Festival, LLC, 2007).

21. Van Meter is quoted in Wheeler Winston Dixon, *The Exploding Eye: A Re-Visionary History of 1960s American Experimental Cinema* (Albany: State University of New York Press, 1997), 175.

22. Lawrence Ferlinghetti, *The Secret Meaning of Things* (New York: New Directions, 1968), 29.

23. Conner used a 1968 live performance of Riley's "Poppy Nogood and the Phantom Band." Besides his involvement in West Coast psychedelic culture, Riley's inclusion becomes particularly appropriate because of his 1960–62 composition "Mescaline Mix." As he explains, "This piece Mescaline Mix also came about because I had been taking peyote at the time—a form of natural mescaline—and I wanted to recreate a kind of atmosphere in the music which could resemble the altered states of consciousness induced by the drug." From a 2006 interview with Jacqueline Caux, reprinted in *Looking for Mushrooms: Beat Poets, Hippies, Funk, Minimal: Art San Francisco 1955–68* (Köln: Museum Ludwig and Verlag der Buchhandlung Walther König, 2008), 225.

24. Tosh Berman, *Wallace Berman* (Amsterdam: Institute of Contemporary Art, 1992), 75–76.

25. Correspondence is quoted in Michael Duncan, *Semina Culture: Wallace Berman and His Circle* (New York: DAP, 2005), 362–68.

26. Quoted in ibid., 58.

27. Quoted in the *Beat Patrol* blog, beatpatrol.wordpress.com/2008/09/09/michael-mcclure-peyote-poem-part-1/.

28. Richard Cándida Smith, *Utopia and Dissent: Art, Poetry, and Politics in California* (Berkeley: University of California Press, 1995), 251–52.

29. Michael McClure, *Huge Dreams: San Francisco and Beat Poems* (New York: Penguin Poets, 1999), 16–17.

30. Robert Creeley, *A Quick Graph: Collected Notes and Essays* (San Francisco: Four Seasons Foundation, 1970), 50.

31. Robert Creeley, "In London 2," in his *A Day Book* (New York: Scribner's, 1972), n.p.

32. Philip Whalen, "Stolen and Abandoned," in his *The Kindness of Strangers: Poems 1969–74* (Berkeley: Four Seasons Foundation, 1976), 33.

33. Allen Ginsberg, "Lysergic Acid," in his *Kaddish and Other Poems 1958–1960* (San Francisco: City Lights Books, 1961), 68.

34. Ibid., 92–93.

35. Robert Creeley, "Ed Dorn's Geography," in *A Quick Graph*, 218.

36. Ed Dorn, *Slinger* (Berkeley, Calif.: Wingbow Press, 1975), n.p.

37. Michael Davidson, "'To Eliminate the Draw': Narrative and Language in Slinger," in *Internal Resistances: The Poetry of Edward Dorn*, ed. Donald Weslin (Berkeley: University of California Press, 1985), 126.

38. Dorn, *Slinger*, n.p.

39. Ibid.

40. Allen Ginsberg, untitled 1952 account, later published in *Birth No. 3, 1960*, in *The Drug Experience*, ed. David Elbin (New York: Orion Press, 1961), 304.

41. Randall, correspondence with author.

42. McClure is quoted in T. Berman, *Wallace Berman*, 61.

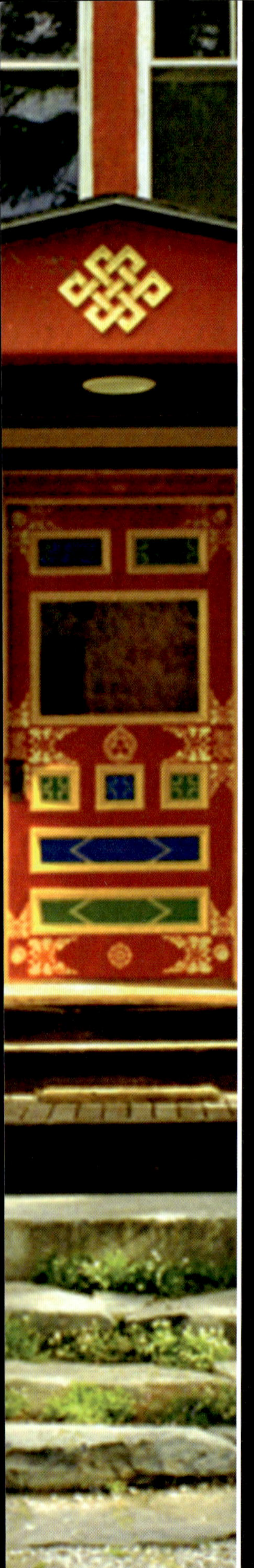

CHAPTER 19

EVERYWHERE PRESENT YET NOWHERE VISIBLE: CHÖGYAM TRUNGPA RINPOCHE AND DHARMA ART AT THE NAROPA INSTITUTE

Bill Scheffel

Chögyam Trungpa Rinpoche was a shaper and icon of the counterculture and its embrace of Buddhist teachings and practice (Figure 19.1).
He arrived in America in 1970, an ideal guru for the times—a lama,
poet, calligrapher, painter, photographer, and playwright with an intense
interest in the culture and psychology of the West, a place he'd dreamed
of encountering since he was a child. Born in Geje, a Tibetan community
of scattered yak tents, to a mother whose first husband had abandoned
her, Trungpa, the infant son of two of the poorest residents in the area,
appeared in a dream to the Gyalwa Karmapa, the supreme head of one of
Tibet's four major Buddhist lineages. Trungpa (whose family name was
Mukpo) was found as the instructions of the dream specified, installed,
and enthroned as a *tulku*—an incarnate lama—and when he grew older
became the spiritual and temporal leader of Surmang monastery and its
surrounding local population, the same desolate region of eastern Tibet
where he was born.[1] In 1959, as the Chinese "liberation" of Tibet became
in reality an eradication of its spiritual culture and heritage, Trungpa
led a handful of compatriots across the Himalayas and into exile. They
nearly starved on the way and were once reduced to eating shoe leather.
Having already lived a life of both enchantment and grueling discipline,
Trungpa arrived in India as a twenty-one-year-old incarnate lama, the
first step of his journey to the West completed.

As a bright and gifted young monk with a series of modest fellow-
ships and a good fortune that was both uncanny and unpredictable,
Trungpa over the next decade met, among others, Thomas Merton, R. D.
Laing, and David Bowie (who was for a time his student). He fathered a
son, received a scholarship to study at Oxford, founded Samye Ling, a
meditation center in Scotland, crashed an automobile into a junk shop,
traded his monastic robes for Western attire, eloped with a sixteen-
year-old English girl, Diana Pybus, and set off virtually penniless with
his new wife for North America in 1970. Without his status in the
twenty-five-hundred-year-old lineage of Gautama Buddha, he could
have been just another hippie.

At that time, Jack Niland, a young aspiring artist from suburban New
Jersey, was about to become one of Trungpa's first students. Niland, after countless LSD trips and a pilgrimage to San Francisco's Haight-Ashbury district, still had no satisfying insight into the striking moments
of perception he'd experienced as a child—how, for instance, an electric fan clipped afternoon sunlight to produce mesmerizing geometric
designs inside his eyes. Even the beauty of a schoolgirl in his first-grade
class lingered as a haunting pinnacle of insight into the nature of reality.
Niland wanted not only to reproduce such moments but also to understand them. Academic studies left him bored and feeling sidelined; Niland wanted personal access to "the doors of perception." He was about
to embark on yet another road trip when his sister mentioned to him
that the Dalai Lama had moved to Vermont. "Cool!" Niland responded.
"We'll visit him on our way to Canada!"[2]

   EVERYWHERE PRESENT YET NOWHERE VISIBLE

Allen Ginsberg (left) and Chögyam Trungpa Rinpoche reading poetry together. Photograph by Bob Morehouse.

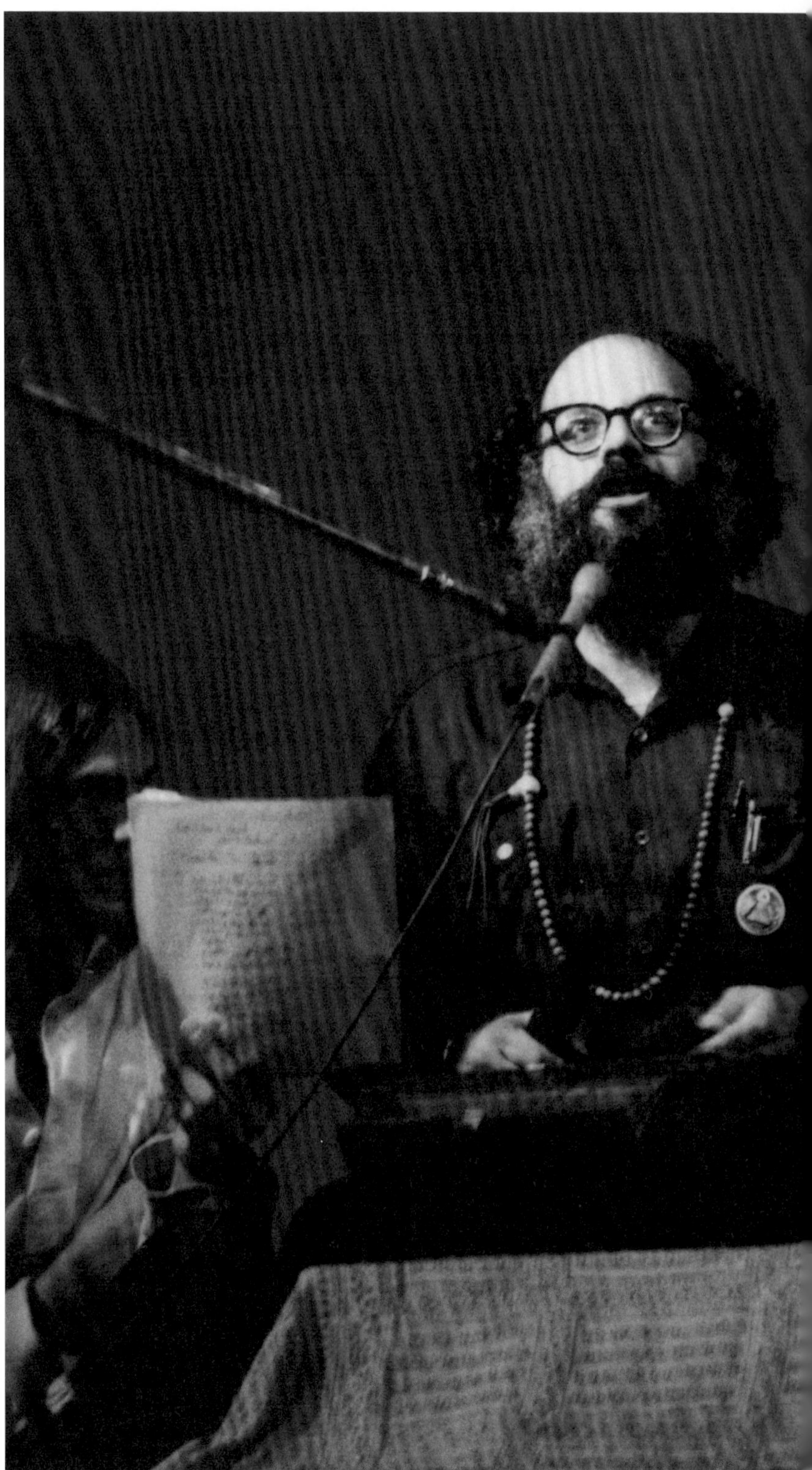

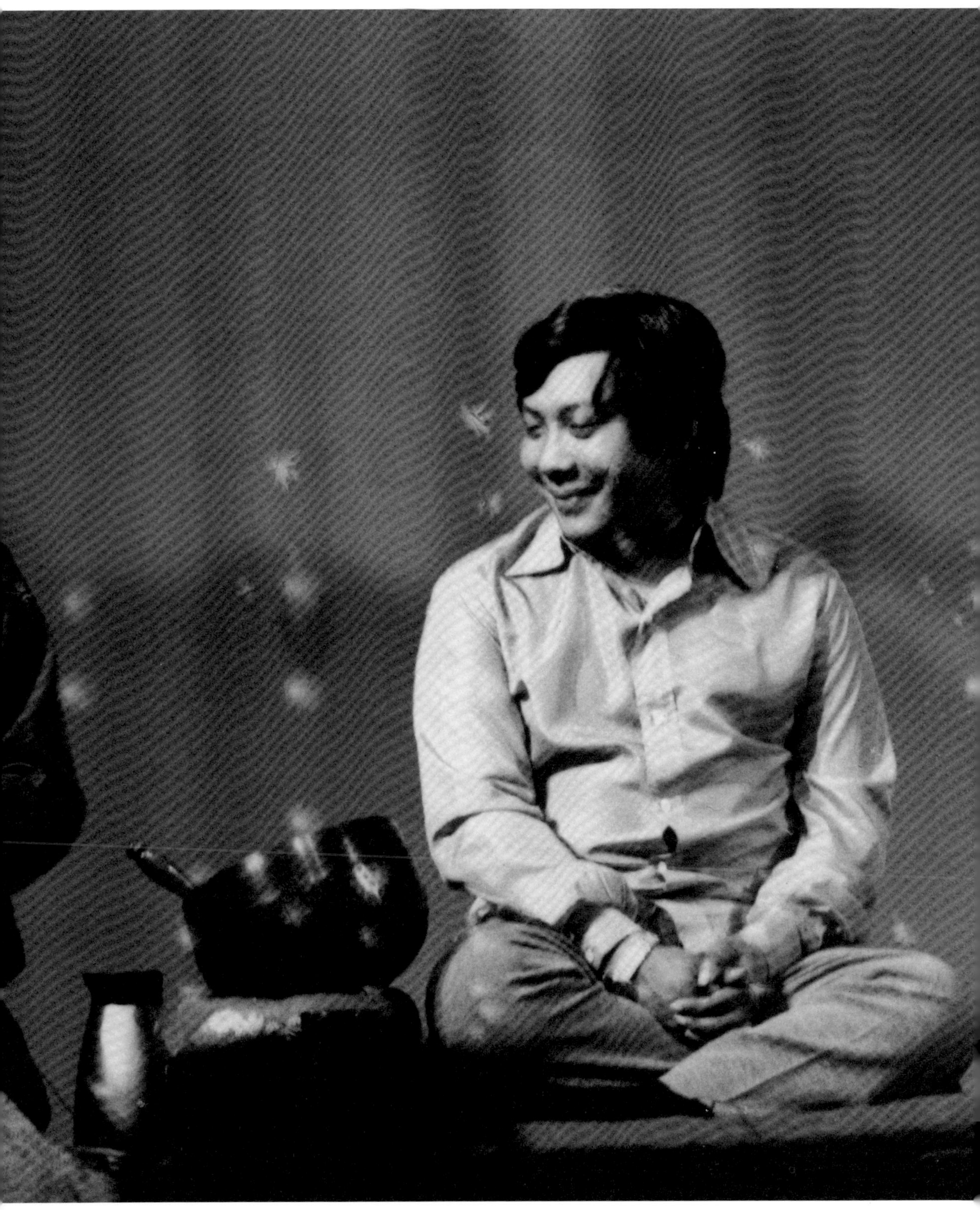

A few days later, Niland found his way to Tail of the Tiger, a fledgling, semi-impoverished spiritual community in northern Vermont with a young Tibetan teacher in residence, a lama who, of course, was not the Dalai Lama but thirty-year-old Trungpa. Niland knocked on the front door of the farmhouse, which was the living quarters of the community, and was quickly ushered to a small room where Trungpa sat by a table with a pad of drawing paper, a brush, and a bottle of India ink. "There was this little Tibetan hippie guy, this cherubic guy with long hair and a huge grin," Niland recalled, "who looked up and said, 'Oh, I've been waiting for you!'" Trungpa, with "radiant energy and unbelievable charisma," immediately enlisted Niland to assist him in making his "very first work of art in North America," a calligraphy of the Tibetan syllable *Ah*.[3] As he drew the syllable, Trungpa called attention to the "dot," the first moment when pencil, pen, or brush meets paper, which is not only the beginning of any line but also the moment form materializes from space. Trungpa called Niland's attention again and again to the significance of the dot, how the dot is the first moment of arising in space, how the dot is in our hearts, how our mind is a dot. The splash of India ink is really the center of the cosmos, Trungpa insisted.

As he listened to Trungpa, Niland realized he had found someone who understood the phenomenology of perception. When he mentioned his experience with the fan, Trungpa replied, "Sure, sure, I understand, those colors come from the rods and cones in the eye. Tibetan *thangkas* are all based on that." For Niland, Trungpa was the opposite of art history lectures and theories. Sitting in that room with him, Niland had no idea who Trungpa was. But he knew this lama wasn't simply explaining electricity to him but handing him the current. The syllable *Ah*, Trungpa added, means what it sounds like, a baby's sense of wonder. If the *Ah*, a prethought and innocent moment of surprise, astonishment, or even shock, was Trungpa's first work of art in North America, it was also at the core of his behavior, his artistic philosophy, and what it felt like to encounter him personally.

That Trungpa was indispensable to bringing Tibetan Buddhism to North America is widely known and well documented.[4] Within a matter of a few years, Trungpa went from being a notoriously informal *tulku* to wearing a three-piece suit as the president of the first Buddhist-inspired college in the West, Naropa Institute in Boulder, Colorado, founded in 1974. Trungpa was also the spiritual director of the Shambhala Meditation Centers that sprung up in the 1970s in nearly every major U.S. and Canadian city—the result of the constant teaching and traveling he pursued until the end of his life.[5] Trungpa brought the hippies with him and pursued with them—and all the hundreds of students who followed—an intense creative collaboration, one in which he was as much artist as teacher, as much social engineer as guru.

Trungpa was a spiritual teacher who shattered the clichés Westerners expected of a holy man. He also took art very seriously and argued that it might be the only way to save the world. For him, *saving* not only meant the individual spiritual process of awakening—as simple as noticing the beauty of a rose and as arduous as relinquishing everything ego-centered—but also initiating a collective energy that could turn back what he called the "setting sun," the Moloch, or mindless consumption the counterculture found so appalling and degraded. Art could restore a sense of wonder and "subjugate aggression." To this end, he offered manifestos such as this one:

To create an Enlightened Society
We must change the culture
To change the culture
We must change the art
To change the art
We must change how art is taught
To change how art is taught
We must present the dharma art principles
And then make them popular
Throughout the whole world
Especially to children[6]

That art underlies culture and is therefore the way to change it underscores a belief and understanding that human beings are *aesthetic* creatures and that most of our decisions, the decisions we make a thousand times a day, are aesthetic ones. Even where we set down the toothpaste cap is a complex and aesthetically sensitive gesture. Potentially. Often we are too much in a hurry, or trapped in our compulsive ideation, to pay much attention, to appreciate. Could simple attention to detail lead to major social, political, and environmental changes? And if so, how to get there? How to enact that change of consciousness? To that end, Trungpa articulated the "dharma art principles."[7] Curiously, these principles were really one principle: nonaggression, a concept that has less to do with anger and rage and more to do with the obstacles that prevent one from achieving perceptual clarity. What does that look like? Trungpa would argue that the foundation of nonaggression—and of nonaggressive art—is simply curiosity and a willingness to communicate. He established his own commitment to this foundation:

Upon my arrival in the West, I felt strongly that a meeting of the two minds—culturally, spiritually, metaphysically—could be realized by means of "first thought, best thought" the uncontaminated first glimpse of one another. . . . I applied myself to examine Western wisdom and uncover the nature of occidental insight. I found that I had to immerse myself thoroughly in everything from the doctrines of Western religion up to the way people tied their shoelaces. I was intensely curious to discover in all this where were the true heart and the true brain. And I was determined to find these matters out by personal experience, rather than by second-hand account.[8]

During Trungpa's first years in North America, he hung out with his students—an intense period of mutual curiosity and communication. He drank, smoked cigarettes, and tried their mind-altering drugs (which he criticized for producing ersatz enlightenment experiences and dissociative states of self-absorption). His students called him Chogyie and for a while had nearly unlimited access to him, though the pleasure of his enlightened charisma also meant encountering an almost feral honesty that did not accommodate "masks." His "first thought best thought" could be a sharp instrument on which those he encountered often found themselves impaled. Allen Ginsberg, an early collaborator and cofounder of the creative writing department at Naropa Institute, describes such a meeting with Trungpa in 1972:

We were comparing our travels and our poetry. He [Trungpa] had a heavy schedule and a long itinerary and I said I was getting fatigued with mine. He said, "That's probably because you don't like your poetry." So I said, "What do you know about poetry? How do you know I don't like my poetry?" He said, "Why do you need a piece of paper? Don't you trust your own mind? Why don't you do like the classic poets? [Buddhist poet-saint] Milarepa made up his poems on the spot.[9]

Insulted at first, Ginsberg recovered quickly and eventually went on to retell anecdotes like these whenever he could. Magnetized by his honesty, Ginsberg incorporated Trungpa's advice to be more spontaneous when he performed. Frank Berliner, another early student who worked in an administrative role for Chögyam Trungpa, once spent a week along with his staff, refurbishing their office suite in response to comments by Trungpa that the place looked "funky." Trungpa arrived, looked around, and sat down at Berliner's desk. "I stood in the doorway," Berliner recalls, "looking at him expectantly, as if he might now award a small ribbon to me for how impeccably pristine the national office of Shambhala Training looked. Behind me stood my colleagues, craning their necks in hopes they might see whatever I was seeing." Trungpa's response was to cast a sharp glance in Berliner's direction, then attach a paper clip to his lower lip and let it dangle there. Nonaggression, it seems, is not always nice.[10]

It was this lively, edgy, and unpredictable atmosphere that brought Trungpa and his students together, and the results were mutually transformative. After his conversation with Trungpa, Ginsberg not only revised his approach to performing his poetry but also eventually became Trungpa's student—a relationship that was also a demanding friendship of collaboration and mutual influence. On a four-hour drive from New York City to Karmê Chöling (the renamed retreat center Niland had earlier happened on), Ginsberg read long passages of Jack Kerouac's *Mexico City Blues* to Trungpa:

The wheel of the quivering meat
conception
Turns in the void expelling human beings,
Pigs, turtles, frogs, insects, flits
Mice, lice, lizards, rats' roan. . . .

All the endless conception of living
beings
Gnashing everywhere in Consciousness.[11]

Lines such as these echoed the mordant humor and scathing explications of human suffering that characterized Trungpa's own lectures, and he laughed out loud as Ginsberg read them on their drive through rural Vermont. When Ginsberg asked Trungpa what he thought of Kerouac's writing, he replied, "It's a perfect exposition of mind."[12]

Ten years later, Trungpa published his own book of poetry, *First Thought Best Thought: 108 Poems,* and Ginsberg wrote the introduction. Trungpa had, in recent years, put aside the lofty, devotional poetry that he wrote in Tibet or as a young exile in exchange for a bebop American modernism. Ginsberg called the transition a journey from the "absolute truth expressed through symbols" to a "relative truth" that was the expression of Trungpa's devotion to his American students and to the meeting of East and West that so intrigued him. Ginsberg concluded his introduction to *First Thought Best Thought* with a question: "The author Chögyam with all his Vajra Perfections is the drunk poet on his throne in the Rockies proclaiming 'Chogyie is yours.' What will Walt Whitman's expansive children do faced with such a person?"[13]

When Trungpa showed up in North America penniless with a teenage wife, he had a copy of the *I Ching* with him. Soon after calligraphing the *Ah* syllable, Trungpa enlisted Niland—who had stayed on to join the Tail of the Tiger community—to help him create his "second work of art," which required Niland to paint the front door and porch of the community farmhouse according to Trungpa's design. For this, Trungpa consulted his *I Ching,* the same Wilhelm-Baynes translation with the yellow hardcover familiar to any educated hippie. The trigram of the Joyous Lake can be easily recognized in the center of the front door, painted in striking primary colors (Figure 19.2).[14] Trungpa told Niland that he "used the *I Ching* for everything," though only occasionally opened the book. "Read it, memorize it, then throw it away," Trungpa suggested to Niland, "because there are hexagrams everywhere if you can see them."

Moments of life are self-symbols, not of something else but of the truth of the moment. Each moment's truth is *potential* and contains the

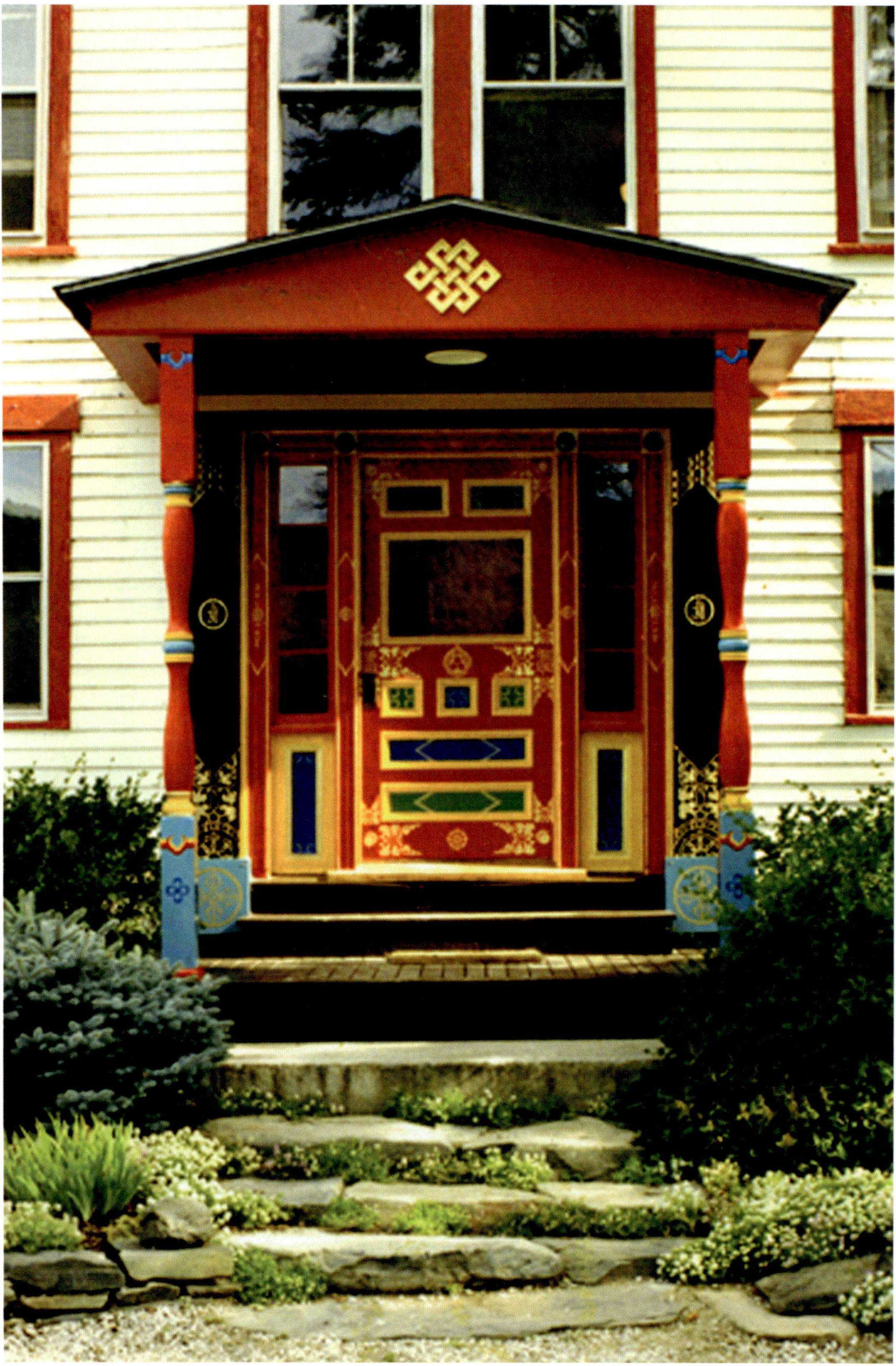

seed of what to do next. This is the truth of the *I Ching,* of Trungpa's Kagyu Buddhist lineage (whose highest teaching epitome is *mahamudra* or "great symbol") and of the dharma art teachings he was beginning to share with his students. The community of Tail of the Tiger and the other communities Trungpa founded, taught at, and often resided in were always living, evolving, hands-on expressions of his dynamic exchanges with his students. Some communities were devoted exclusively to the arts and included Padma Jong in northern California and the Boulder Craft House, the first artists' cooperative in the Boulder, Colorado, area.

Within less than ten years, Trungpa's creative output and influence evolved from the painted front door of Karmê Chöling (an early expression of his desire to combine the vivid colors of Tibetan art with a Japanese sense of spaciousness and an American sense of scale) to the founding of Naropa Institute, whose first formal degree programs included a BA in Buddhist studies, an MA in psychology, an MFA in visual arts, and expressive arts certificates in dance, theater, and poetics. At Naropa, Trungpa presented a series of seminars on his conception of dharma art and produced numerous large-scale installations based on its principles with his students in Boulder, Los Angeles, and San Francisco.[15]

The dharma art seminars conducted at Naropa and elsewhere included lectures, discussions, meditation practice, art installations, flower arrangement, and spontaneous demonstrations of calligraphy characterized by directness, unselfconsciousness, and nonaggression (Figure 19.3). Trungpa's teachings on dharma art centered on accessing the qualities inherent in a first flash of perception prior to the clumsy fracturing of the world into seer and seen, object and audience. He explained his own installations and flower arrangements as embodying the principle of "inherent richness, called *yün* in Tibetan."[16] Trungpa's teachings led to the formation of cadres of practitioners called Explorers of the Richness of the Phenomenal World (Figure 19.4), whose meditative practice consisted of "aimless wandering" with the paradoxical goal of discovering objects in the immediate environment that exuded one of the five "buddha qualities" (self-existing richness/fertility, spaciousness, spontaneous action, freely radiating passion, or mirror-like wisdom).[17] Enormous installations of these objects would be temporarily assembled in various spaces around Boulder and elsewhere. As Kimberley Lueck has explained, the work of the Explorers "points to a central teaching of Shambhala Buddhism offered by Trungpa. He emphasized the power of awareness to awaken persons to the sacred world and its inherent richness, which is the world we are already part of when we actually take notice."[18] Regarding our availability to sacredness through awareness, Trungpa writes:

You experience a vast realm of perceptions unfolding. There is unlimited sound, unlimited sight, unlimited taste, unlimited feeling and so on. The realm of per-

   EVERYWHERE PRESENT YET NOWHERE VISIBLE

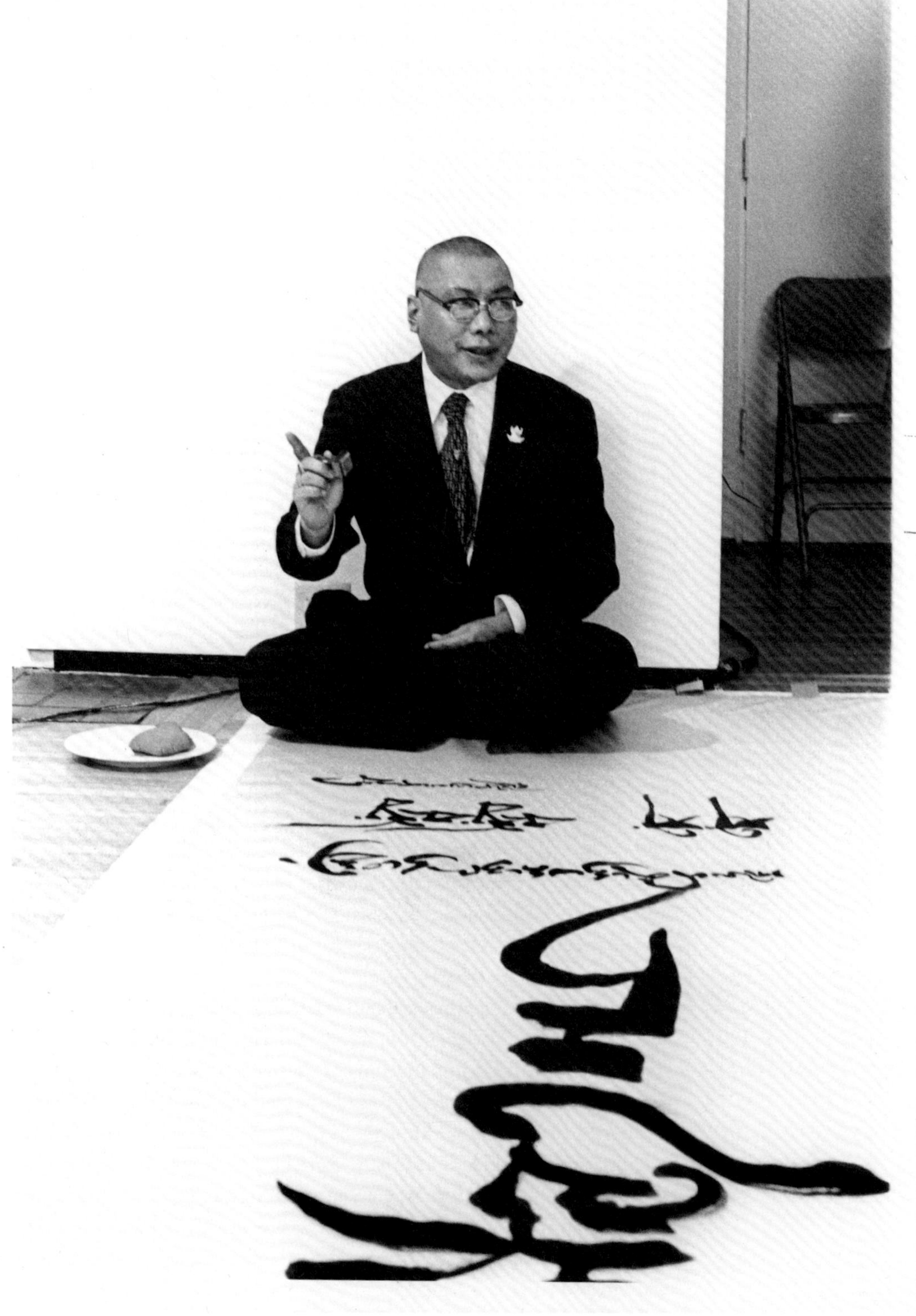

ception is limitless, so limitless that perception itself is primordial, unthinkable, beyond thought. There are so many perceptions that they are beyond imagination. There are a vast number of sounds. There are sounds that you have never heard. There are sights and colors you have never seen. There are feelings that you have never experienced before. There are endless fields of perception.[19]

Dharma art was an extension of meditative practice. Many of those who came face to face with Trungpa, including myself, began to *sit*— a three-letter vernacular for the traditions of meditation (*samatha* or "calm abiding," and *vipassana* or "penetrating insight") that Trungpa had inherited and introduced to his students. He explained that sitting is what supported the open communication of nonaggression and allowed it to evolve, adding that meditation "is the only way." Later it became clear to his students, zealous as we were, that the meditation we were beginning to do was not the only way to meditate and that meditation occurs in many contexts. Trungpa agreed that great artists like Mozart certainly "sat." With the introduction of Shambhala Training, a program of Buddhist meditation designed to reach a secular audience, we began to talk about meditation in a way that revealed it for what it is: an innate human activity, the natural way of becoming aware of who we are. As Gary Snyder writes, "Traditions of deliberate attention to consciousness

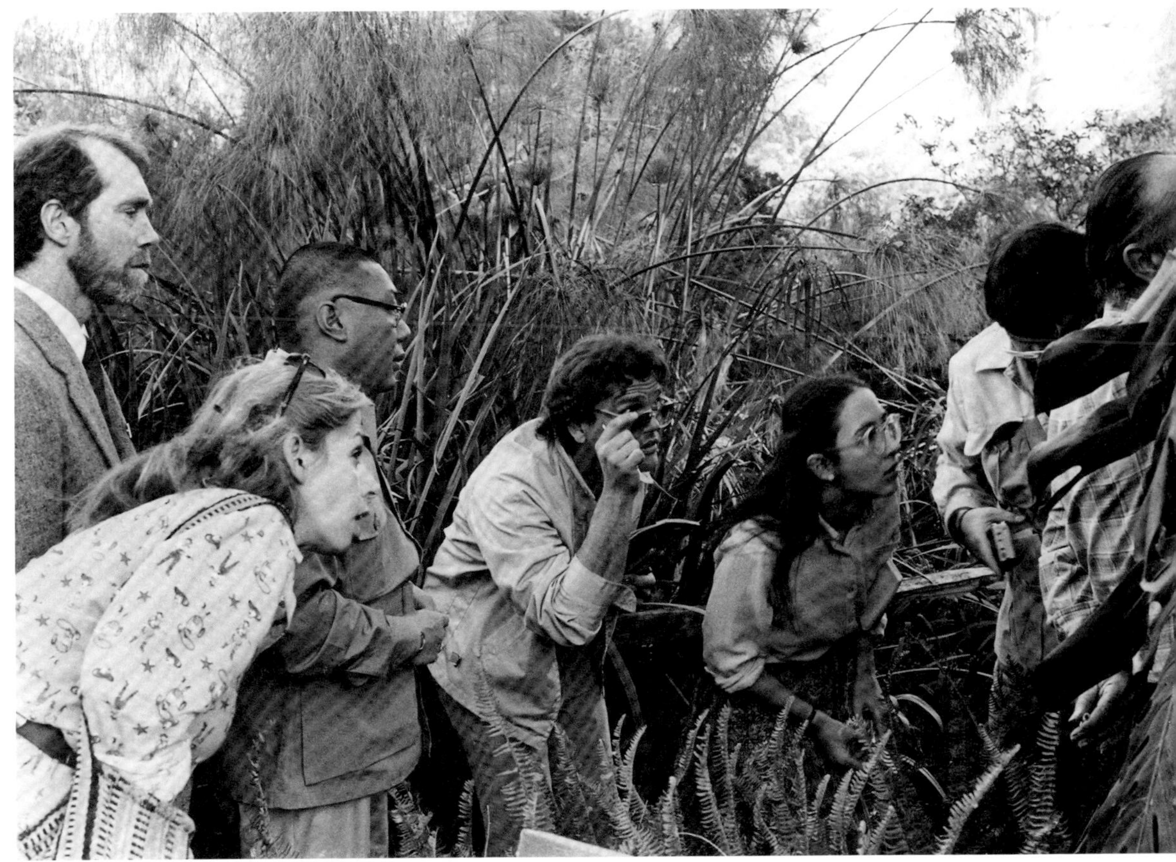

    EVERYWHERE PRESENT YET NOWHERE VISIBLE

art teachings were intended to bring these principles into the world without any "-isms" at all.

Relating to the world directly is more than simply becoming receptive to it, since in every instance of life we must also act, even if only to fix a meal or get dressed in the morning. Before we act we must decide. What breakfast cereal, what shirt to wear? Trungpa said, *first we look, then we see*—first, direct perception, then knowing. The practice of dharma art was meant to highlight and heighten this process. Art asks us to become greatly disciplined in this process, and it punishes when we ignore it, try to speed it up—or deny the reality of our own response. Robert Motherwell pointed out that a successful painting is the result of "ten-thousand brush strokes" and the crucial decisions that go into each one. He said the decision came from "one's gut" and for him, "a heavy, awkward, clumsy man," he preferred his painting to come with something similar, a kind of weight or earthboundness. If a painting veered from this sensibility, it lost its genuineness.[27]

Trungpa articulated an entire toolbox of principles for the artist— some of them more method, some more of sensibility. The principles were a blade that on one side cut, on the other empowered. He said it was a problem if you considered yourself an artist, the problem of egoism, and there was a problem if you didn't—a demeaning of one's human birthright, since there was no way, in Trungpa's understanding, that a human being was anything less than an artist. The dharma art principles were not so much unique in themselves as uniquely understood by Trungpa and uniquely suited to the aspirations of his audience, romantic to the core, sensibility descendants of Percy Bysshe Shelley and Lord Byron, J. M. W. Turner and Eugene Delacroix. John Keats's well-known poetic dictum of "Negative Capability"—"when man is capable of being in uncertainties, Mysteries, doubts, without any irritable reaching after fact & reason"—is the necessary state of aesthetic toughness needed to endure direct perception, which of course includes all the feelings and emotions that jolt and bombard us and tempt us to take sides with something so that we can get out of feeling them.[28] Trungpa liked nothing more than stirring up uncertainties, which was part of the rub: art is not escape but engagement.

Trungpa's artistic influence on the counterculture is similar to the influence of the counterculture on our life today: a manifold and perennial influence that must be taken up again each year, by each generation. Trungpa's legacy is a collection of creative though urgent inspirations, present this very moment, available for any of Walt Whitman's expansive children to recognize and manifest.

NOTES

1. Trungpa was the eleventh in the line of Trungpa *tulkus,* important figures in the Kagyu lineage, one of the four main schools of Tibetan Buddhism with a strong emphasis on meditative practice. Trungpa was also trained in the Nyingma tradition, the oldest of the four schools, and was an advocate of the nonsectarian (sometimes referred to as the "secular") ecumenical movement within Tibetan Buddhism, which sought to make available all the teachings of the different schools free of sectarian rivalry.

2. Unless otherwise noted, quotations from Jack Niland come from conversations with the author, March–April 2010.

3. Trungpa's religious training in Tibet included the study of traditional artistic practices, including monastic dance, calligraphy, *thangka* painting, and poetry. In England he pursued photography, painting, theater, and music and studied the arts of Japanese calligraphy and flower arranging. In North America, upon settling in Boulder, Colorado, Trungpa added filmmaking to his repertoire and established the Mudra Theater Group, among other pursuits.

4. On the subject see Fabrice Midal, *Chögyam Trungpa: His Life and Vision* (Boston: Shambhala, 2004); Stephen Batchelor, *The Awakening of the West: The Encounter of Buddhism and Western Culture* (Berkeley, Calif.: Parallax, 1994); and Rick Fields, *How the Swans Came to the Lake: A Narrative History of Buddhism in America* (Boston: Shambhala, 1992).

5. Today, there are 165 Shambhala Meditation Centers presided over by Sakyong Mipham Rinpoche. Shambhala Buddhism, a unique path created by Trunpga for his Western followers, is based on his own model for an Enlightened Society, the so-called Kingdom of Shambhala, and the teachings of his Kagyu and Nyingma Buddhist lineage. Asian legend records a kingdom called Shambhala, also known in the West as Shangri-la. "According to the legends, this was a place of peace and prosperity, governed by wise and compassionate rulers. The citizens were equally kind and learned, so that, in general, the kingdom was a model society." Chögyam Trungpa, *Shambhala: Sacred Path of the Warrior* (Boston: Shambhala, 1983), 17.

6. As recalled by Jack Niland. "The day my mother died in 1985, Trungpa called (how did he know?!), told me a very funny joke, and then suddenly [recited this]."

7. *Dharma,* the Sanskrit term for "carrying" or "holding," is central to Buddhist practice. There are several applications of the term, including Buddha dharma or the teachings of the Buddha, the phenomena around us, and the law underlying the whole of existence.

8. Chögyam Trungpa, *First Thought Best Thought: 108 poems* (Boulder, Colo.: Shambhala Publications, 1983), xix.

9. Trungpa asked poets Allen Ginsberg, Anne Waldman, John Cage, and Diane di Prima to found the creative writing program at Naropa, which they named the Jack Kerouac School of Disembodied Poetics. For this anecdote, see Allen Ginsberg, "Meditation and Poetics," lecture delivered to students at Naropa in 1978. Transcribed by Christian M. Katt and revised by Ide Hintz and Juergen Berlakovich. See http://sfd.at/english/texts/meditation.pdf. Accessed June 2011.

10. Frank Berliner, conversation with author, around 1980.

11. Jack Kerouac, "Chorus 211," in *Mexico City Blues: 242 Choruses* (New York: Grove, 1959).

12. Allen Ginsberg, in Peter Barry Chowka, "Interview with Allen Ginsberg," reprinted from *New Age Journal* (April 1976). See http://www.english.illinois.edu/maps/poets/g_l/ginsberg/interviews.htm.

13. Ginsberg, "Introduction," in Trungpa, *First Thought Best Thought,* xi, xii.

14. *I Ching,* 3rd ed., Bollingen Series XIX, trans. Richard Wilhelm and Cary F. Baynes (Princeton, N.J.: Princeton University Press, 1967). The *I Ching* consists of sixty-four hexagrams formed by combining eight core trigrams in different combinations.

15. For Trungpa's lectures on dharma art, see Chögyam Trungpa, *Dharma Art,* ed. Judith L. Lief (Boston: Shambhala, 1996); a revised edition of this is Trungpa, *True Perception: The Path of Dharma Art,* ed. Judith Lief (Boston: Shambhala, 2008); and volume 7 of *The Collected Works of Chögyam Trungpa: The Art of Calligraphy, Dharma Art, Visual Dharma, Selected Poems, Selected Writings,* ed. Carolyn Rose Gimian (Boston: Shambhala, 2004).

16. Judith L. Lief, "Editor's Introduction," in *Dharma Art,* xiii. An exhibition by Trungpa was installed at the Los Angeles Institute for Contemporary Art in 1981 and is documented in the film *Discovering Elegance,* directed by Chögyam Trungpa Rinpoche (16mm, 28 minutes).

17. For a contemporary demonstration of one aspect of this practice, see the video documentation of the 2010 Shambhala Art Intensive Seminar under "Resources—Media Library," Shambhala Art home page, www.shambhalaart.org/.

18. Kimberely Lueck, "Joining Heaven and Earth: Chögyam Trungpa and the Dharma Arts of Shambhala Buddhism," http://www.shambhala-mn.org/documents/Dotarticles_002.pdf. Accessed June 2011.

19. Chögyam Trungpa, *Shambhala: The Sacred Path of the Warrior* (Boston: Shambhala, 1983), 101.

20. See Gary Snyder, *Beneath a Single Moon: Buddhism in Contemporary American Poetry* (Boston: Shambhala, 2001), 2; and *The Real Work* (New York: New Directions, 1969), 83.

21. Further subdivisions of the three main traditions, Hinayana, Mahayana, and Vajrayana, subsumed within Tibetan Buddhism.

22. Gertrude Stein, "What Are Masterpieces and Why Are There So Few of Them?" (1936), reprinted in *Context 5,* www.dalkeyarchive.com/book/?GCOI=15647100034260&fa=details.

23. Robert Irwin, as quoted by Lawrence Weschler, "When Fountainheads Collide," *New Yorker,* 8 December 1997, 60.

24. Chögyam Trungpa, *Shambhala: The Sacred Path of the Warrior,* ed. Carolyn Rose Gimian (Boston: Shambhala, 1988), 53.

25. Chögyam Trungpa, *Journey without Goal* (Boulder, Colo.: Prajna, 1981), 59.

26. Robert Irwin, as quoted by Lawrence Weschler, *Seeing Is Forgetting the Name of the Thing One Sees* (Berkeley: University of California Press, 2008), 70.

27. Robert Motherwell, as quoted by Anna Held Audette, *The Black Canvas* (Boston: Shambhala, 1993), 81.

28. John Keats, Letter to George and Thomas Keats, 21, 27 December 1817, in his *Selected Poems and Letters,* ed. Douglas Bush (Boston: Houghton Mifflin, 1959), 261.

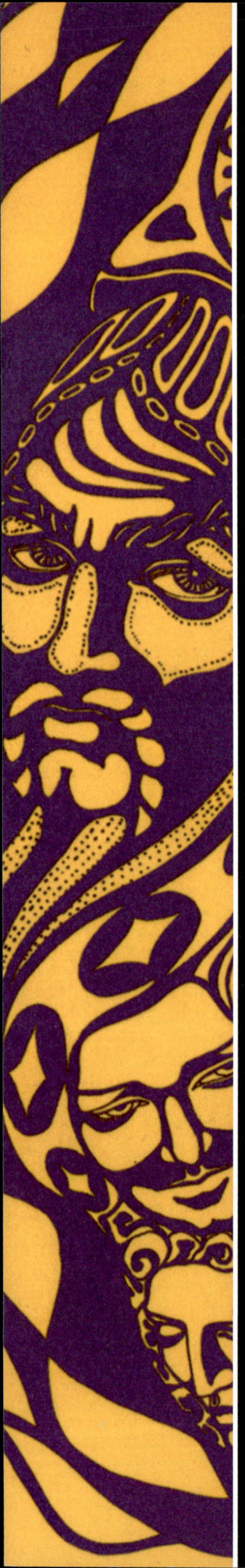

CHAPTER 20
SIGNIFYING THE INEFFABLE: ROCK POSTER ART AND PSYCHEDELIC COUNTERCULTURE IN SAN FRANCISCO

Scott B. Montgomery

In his 1849 essay "Das Kunstwerk der Zukunft," Richard Wagner conceived an interplay of the arts as a *Gesamtkunstwerk*

that has to embrace all genres of art, in order to consume, to destroy each one of these genres to some extent as resources for the sake of achieving the overall purpose of them all, in other words the unconditional, direct representation of perfect human nature—this great Gesamtkunstwerk it (i.e., our spirit) recognizes not as the arbitrary possible deed of the individual, but as the necessarily conceivable joint work of the people of the future.[1]

Both as a fusion of art forms and a utopian ideal based on notions of transcendent or forward-looking culture, this concept seems to prefigure the multimedia environments of San Francisco dance concerts involving music, light shows, dancing, and graphic arts all working to melt the divide between audience and performer, distinct individuals, as well as the various media utilized. Wagner's own articulation of a desired return to the intertwining of dance, tone (music), and poetry, as conceived in ancient Greece, also seems to suggest an antecedent philosophical basis to the melting of barriers between various arts as practiced by the San Francisco counterculture of the 1960s. Wagner's philosophical template resonates with the psychedelic tribal sensibilities that the dance concerts expressed a century later, beginning in 1965 and fully manifest by 1966.[2] Wagner casts his aesthetic formulation in a cultural context of a popular *(Volk)* sense of community that feels a collective identity and desires to fashion art to express, and even define, that cultural cohesion. While it would be easy to posit a stark contrast between Wagner's Apollonian conception of this phenomenon and the more obviously Dionysian manifestations of the counterculture dance concert, this would reflect a superficial understanding of the importance of the dance concert *Gesamtkunstwerk* in the formulation and articulation of a distinct cultural identity. As such, the very Dionysian elements of the countercultural performance are equally Apollonian, as an elevated conception of cultural ideals was thereby expressed. Much of this cultural conception was doubtless subconscious, but it was nonetheless deeply ensconced within the expression, or even performance, of the San Francisco counterculture.[3] The counterculture was not only happening in San Francisco; it was itself a Happening in the Haight.

In 1968, performance art pioneer Allan Kaprow remarked that "happenings are a medium, let's face it: they've become an art form. Fundamentally, what a happening does, which the other historic arts don't do, is permit you a number of moves through different media and, moreover, through times and places that you have to filter through another medium in the other arts."[4] Kaprow's notion of "eliminating the audience altogether," removing the boundaries between performer and audience, and facilitating an intermingling of diverse media has been lauded as a significant aspect of the artistic avant-garde in the 1960s.

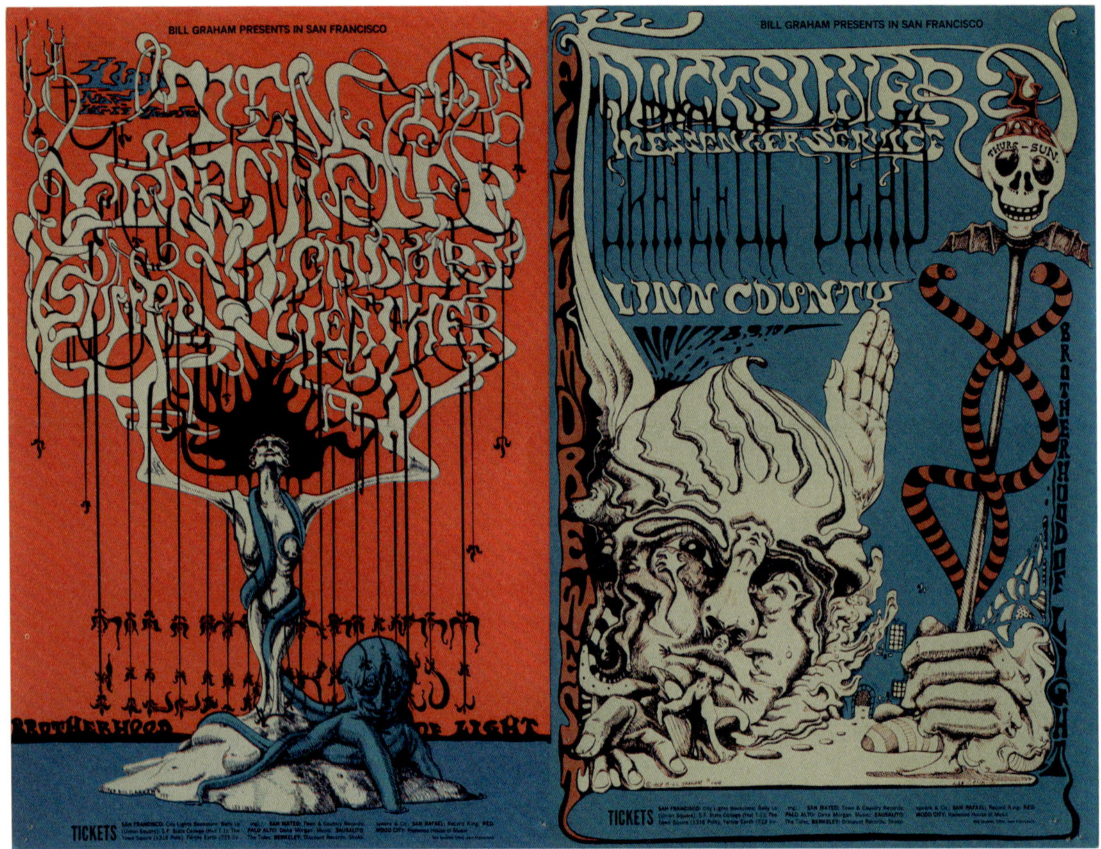

Curiously, we have tended to downplay this phenomenon in terms of its relationship to the contemporaneous rise of a countercultural sensibility in San Francisco. Though they were more chaotic and spontaneous than Kaprow's carefully orchestrated Happenings, dance concerts in San Francisco involved at least some degree of organization of musical acts, liquid light shows, and striking graphic art to fashion a context in which this multimedia spectacle could spontaneously unfold in "an overpowering simultaneity."[5] Let us take as an example a series of dance concerts held at the Fillmore West in mid-November of 1968. The posters for the events, designed by Lee Conklin, advertise performances by Quicksilver Messenger Service, the Grateful Dead, and Linn County on November 7–10, and Ten Years After, Country Weather, and Sun Ra on November 14–17 (Figure 20.1).[6] While the double-billing of San Francisco musical siblings—the Grateful Dead and Quicksilver—on the first weekend is hardly unusual, what are we to make of the surprising contrast of the English heavy-blues rock of Ten Years After with the Neptunian Nubian jazz explorations of Sun Ra? Such a billing, not unlike the pairings of the Butterfield Blues Band with the Charles Lloyd Quartet, or the Grateful Dead with the Preservation Hall Jazz Band, reveals Bill Graham's desire to provide a venue for contrast and fusion of musical forms, and the countercultural audience in experiencing these juxtapositions.[7] The

Lee Conklin, BG-144: Quicksilver Messenger Service, Grateful Dead, Linn County, Lights by Brotherhood of Light, November 7–10, 1968, Fillmore West, San Francisco. BG-145: Ten Years After, Country Weather, Sun Ra, Lights by Brotherhood of Light, November 14–17, 1968, Fillmore West, San Francisco. Copyright Wolfgang's Vault.

inclusion of liquid light projections by the Brotherhood of Light on both posters reveals a conscious acknowledgment of the multimediation of the advertised events, as they are essentially billed as performers.[8]

The images themselves, fashioned in Conklin's magnificently hallucinogenic surrealism, add further dimension to the events by visualizing them as psychedelic, morphic happenings that endeavor to transcend, or at least question, the seeming absolutes of conscious reality. Furthermore, the juxtaposition of Conklin's two images in the double-flyer distributed in advance of the concerts fashions a connection between the two seemingly self-standing concert runs. Despite the differences in compositional axes, both images are united by the same quadripartite color scheme—silver, blue, red, and black. The dynamic epigraphy and melting anthropomorphic/zoomorphic forms are picked out in bold silver, visually connecting the two images coloristically and formally. While the aggressive red of BG-145 contrasts sharply with the receding blue of BG-144, each image is punctuated with its blue or red contrast, thereby bringing the two images further into dialogue. The boldly advancing reds and recessional blues create a spatial discord as the juxtaposed images seem to beat back and forth across the two-dimensional picture plane and a coloristically implied, nebulously three-dimensional space. Poster design, musical juxtaposition, and psychedelic light shows are all part of an endeavor to both formulate and articulate an ineffable counterculture aesthetic that was happening both within and without the walls of the Fillmore West.

The multimediated, performative event was not a new development in San Francisco with the onset of the psychedelic dance concert at the Avalon Ballroom and Fillmore Auditorium. Already in the 1950s, San Francisco's Six Gallery had fostered the blending of poetry, art, and dramatic performance, presaging the Happenings of the 1960s, as discussed by Kaprow. As ground zero for the Beat counterculture, the Six Gallery witnessed the first public reading of Allen Ginsberg's watershed poem "Howl" on October 7, 1955.[9] The West Coast was always outside the view that New York abstract expressionism was the primary (or only) significant factor in the rise of the American artistic avant-garde, as defined by theorists such as Clement Greenberg. Despite the significance of the San Francisco Poetry Renaissance, championed by Allen Ginsberg, Lawrence Ferlinghetti, Michael McClure, and others, the West Coast was essentially ignored and marginalized by the art world.[10] Thus, the San Francisco counterculture was distinct, separate, and even counter to both the dominant mainstream culture of the United States, and the artistic avant-garde as defined on the East Coast. Perhaps it was this very autonomy that fostered the development of a rich, self-directed, multimedia counterculture aesthetic.[11]

Addressing the increasingly polymediated nature of the psychedelic dance concert poster, Christopher Gair notes both its links to earlier multimedia art forms as well as its more intricate fusing of media: "The

   SIGNIFYING THE INEFFABLE

artists responsible for these posters . . . belonged to a more obviously inter-disciplinary counterculture than that of the 1940s and '50s, in which art, music and poetry, for example, were often brought together as part of a single 'happening' or 'experience.'"[12] Ultimately developing out of North Beach Beat Happenings, such seminal events as the Merry Prankster's Acid Tests (1965–66), the Trips Festival (January 21–23, 1966; flyer by Wes Wilson), and the Human Be-In (January 14, 1967; poster by Stanley Mouse and Michael Bowen) amplified these ideas to a degree that they embodied a northern Californian counterculture that sought its own articulation and shifting patterns of identity in the very matrix of the musical happenings that became its culturally unifying and defining rituals. By 1966, its cathedrals were consecrated—the Fillmore, the Avalon, the Matrix.

Pulsing liquid light shows projected on screens and dancers alike and expansive improvisational musical formats wrestling raga-derived modalities out of the vestiges of blues traditions all melded together through the melting ministrations of lysergic acid diethylamide (LSD-25). Such was the ocean of signifiers that bombarded a visitor to a dance concert in San Francisco circa 1966–67: a Wagnerian *Gesamtkunstwerk* of epically and joyfully chaotic proportions. Whether one came to see the Grateful Dead, the Jefferson Airplane, the Butterfield Blues Band, or simply arrived to be a part of the scene, handing in one's ticket and crossing the threshold led one like Alice down a rabbit hole into a new realm of reality and cognition. While this may be difficult to nail down in our academic definitions of culture, it is precisely this penchant toward avoiding overt circumscription—by script or scripture—that gave the psychedelic Happening its raison d'être. Similarly, both the events and the posters intentionally blur the distinctions between high and low art, fashioning a quotidian aesthetic that transgresses such purportedly elitist distinctions.[13] From 1966 onward, these occurrences were less concerts than expressions of countercultural identity. The spontaneous was its creed and its ritual. The indescribable, ineffable, and intangible were part and parcel of this swirling cultural milieu, and thus need to be considered in any endeavor to formulate an explanation or exegesis of this cultural phenomenon. In her study of the "anti-disciplinary politics" of the counterculture, Julie Stephens explores the ways in which the counterculture cultivated practices that could be neither described in language nor circumscribed with absolute taxonomy. This denial of absolute categorization, an embrace of cultural ineffability, constituted a form of radical politics in its conscious deviation from what it perceived as mainstream cultural practices of prescription and description, defying even the New Left's embrace of these same mainstream political conventions.[14] This was a polymediated event intended to both transform and enlighten (in a personal, spiritual, psychological, and cultural sense).[15] Within this vortex of seemingly ever-shifting sound and vision lay the very kernel of this countercultural self-identification—to be a

part of an organically cohesive culture outside the confines of normative, straight America.

To some degree, countercultural identity was based on ideas and ideals of cultural separateness, essentially more concerned with asserting a
divergent, parallel culture than with changing the dominant, established
cultural norms.[16] However, these very ideals were ultimately geared
toward inverting the relationship with mainstream culture, replacing it
with a more "real" set of values and practices, and thus being essentially
revolutionary and political.[17] Despite obvious links to and even dependence on mainstream capitalist institutions, counterculture communities in San Francisco, such as the Diggers and the Grateful Dead, actively
strove to create a distinct cultural infrastructure independent of what
they deemed to be mainstream culture.[18] Though it is common to scoff
at the naïveté of this cultural experiment and snidely lambaste it for its
failures and hypocrisies, such jaded cynicisms do little to explain the
very real sense of idealism that spawned countercultural philosophy. Recent scholarship has examined the notion of countercultural concepts of
personal and group identity as inherently political, challenging assumptions of a divide between culture and politics.[19] Theodore Roszak astutely outlines the political aspect of psychedelic culture, as an intended
cognitive change in the way we look at, and interact with, the world.[20]
As Nick Bromwell remembers, the counterculture youth "was concerned
above all to enlarge the possibilities of existence, to create a social order
more tolerant of alternative visions of reality."[21] In 1967, Ralph Gleason
observed that hippies "are not just dropping out in Limbo or Nirvana.
They are building a new set of values, a new structure, a new society."[22]
In being self-aware, largely in rejection of normative beliefs and practices, the counterculture ipso facto constructs its own culture. Similarly,
we also must be careful to not clump together nonrelated subcultures
within an ideal construct of a mythologized sixties. The counterculture
was extremely heterogeneous and pluralistic, not only across different locations within the United States and beyond, but even within the
rather tight geographic parameters of the San Francisco area.[23] One of
the distinct qualities of this particular countercultural identity was a
sense of heterogeneity, perhaps most visible in the eclectic fashion and
widespread appropriation of visual signifiers recontextualized within
psychedelic poster art. Nonetheless, an overarching sense of confluence seems to have simultaneously circumscribed the identity of this
counterculture while allowing for manifold manifestations of aesthetic
and philosophic variation.[24]

The counterculture embraced an aesthetic of amassed exoticism, a
rich nexus of widespread referents loosely drawn together to fashion
a heterogeneous though nebulously cohesive group identity. Concert
events were not only polymediated but also comprised a rich weave of
historical and cultural indicators, all reshaped to fit the counterculture's self-image. The cultural cocktail concocted with the fusion of

these disparate elements seems to have been embraced as an alternative version of the American tapestry: an idealized construct of a new, alternate world order. What was envisioned was not only a mash-up of global cultural appropriations but also a blurring of temporal and historical boundaries. This was manifest in the concert event, as singer and counterculture figurehead Grace Slick describes: "As you walk onto the dance floor, you have the feeling you've just entered seven different centuries all thrown together in one room. . . . . Electronics and Indians, disco balls and medieval flutes, Day-Glo space colors and Botticelli sprites, the howl of an amplifier and the tinkling of ankle bracelets. . . . . This is the American dream."[25] If not that of mainstream America, it certainly was the dream of this alternate American culture. Nadya Zimmerman observes, "no one image reveals, in itself, who is and isn't countercultural, yet taken together, they lay claim to a shared sense of nonconformity."[26]

Though much in the way that visual signifiers and motifs of the psychedelic counterculture were adopted, adapted, and popularized by more commercial media and culture from the Summer of Love onward, it is important to recall that the style was already well established as an aesthetic associated with the San Francisco counterculture. From 1965 to at least 1967, the dynamic potpourri of varied motifs, epigraphy, and psychedelic stylings were the primary visual signifiers of countercultural identity. Despite the gradual mainstream absorption (and eventual bastardization or trivialization) of the visual referents of psychedelia, they remained inextricably linked to the self-fashioning of the counterculture. From within, the mainstream embrace of the style was seen not so much as a sell-out on the part of the countercultural players as much as it was a facet of cultural colonialism associated with dominant or mainstream consumer America. To be sure, the potency of the referents may have been diluted in terms of the associations comprehended by the majority of the populace. However, within the matrix of the San Francisco counterculture, there remained a close relationship between psychedelic style and countercultural self-identification.[27]

Due to its appropriation by the music industry (evidence of this already appearing at the Monterey Pop Festival, June 16–18, 1967), the countercultural developments of the second half of the 1960s in San Francisco are largely relegated to discussions of musical style—specifically tropes of psychedelic rock. Such historic myopia misses the profoundly polymediating nature of the culture, with its experimental fascination with synesthesia and performativity not limited to the aural aspects of music.[28] Contrary to the delusional assertions of certain music critics, this was not all about the music. Indeed, the very notion of media exclusivity ran counter to the fluid tenets of this tribal idealism. In 1968, Sandy Darlington articulated the interconnected nature of music and social philosophy within the counterculture: "This music is more than entertainment. It describes and helps us define a way of life we believe

in."[29] The counterculture's embrace of newly maturing rock music as a
cultural flashpoint was manifest not only aurally but also through visual
and other cognitive means. The conception of the performance as a true
concert, in which all elements literally played together, was not an ancil-
lary attribute but, rather, a central aspect of the counterculture. This
sense of communal and aesthetic convergence is articulated by John Rocco:
"San Francisco's secret was not the dancing, the lightshows, the posters,
the long sets, or the complete lack of a stage act, but the ideal that all of
them together were the creation and recreation of a community."[30] As
pioneer poster designer Wes Wilson described the 1966 Trips Festival:
"There was music, there was drama, there were costumed people, there
was Ken Kesey and the Pranksters, light shows, weird sound equipment.
It was like this big 'happening' for me."[31] Today, many see the posters
created for the concert events as secondary—servants made to advertise
a musical performance. As such, they are often cataloged by musical
performer. While understandable, given the overarching control exerted
by the music industry in the intervening decades, this band-directed
taxonomy misses the intent of the early psychedelic posters, which did
not so much advertise concerts as they heralded events, cultural happenings, manifestations of the ineffable aspects of fluid unity that nebulously circumscribed the psychedelic counterculture.[32]

The challenge for artists charged with fashioning advertisements for
these dance concerts involved addressing their very bifold nature: heralding a distinct countercultural event while seeking to convey something of its spirit, which was by definition undefined and possibly inde-
finable. This broader, cultural aspect of the psychedelic poster is noted
by John Barnicoat: "The Hippy Poster is used to create an environment—in itself another manifestation of total art, as was Art Nouveau.
. . . the true effect is achieved only if an entire environment is created:
indeed, it is a way of life."[33] More succinctly, artist Bob Fried observed
that "the posters were just a part of a much larger cultural event."[34] Naturally, in addition to signifying a philosophical-cultural outlook, these
posters also included such staples of event advertising as date, time,
location, and performer. It is in their efforts to convey precise, specific
information as well as more nebulous allusions to cultural identity that
the artists of these posters expanded the art of graphic poster design,
exploding it into a technicolor self-referential matrix of meanings often
only legible to the initiated.[35] While many of these artworks revel in
chaos, they strive to manifest the patterns and subcurrents that course
within that chaos—formatting formless form. In developing new and
increasingly illegible lettering and fantastic, optically challenging figural
and color formats, the artist of the dance concert posters explored the
means of signifying the ineffable. As such, the posters that advertised
these events were signifiers of culture.[36] Whether stapled to telephone
poles, plastered on the windows of head shops, or tacked to the wall of
a house, these images frequently defined the bounds of the culture, as

on the corner, as suggested by the packages in the prospector's bag and possibility that he might be cleaning seeds from the very gold acquired on the site. Understanding this image involves an acknowledgment that all work together simultaneously to fashion a complex, layered image of cultural identity: the New Wild West continues the voyage of discovery of the Old Wild West, though the gold standard may have changed to more musical and hallucinogenic currencies.

While the artists of these psychedelic posters seem to have been as omnivorous as the music and dress codes, no art movement was as influential on the major players as art nouveau. Doubtless inspired by the November 1965 exhibition of *Jugendstil and Expressionism in German Posters* at the University of California, Berkeley Art Gallery, many of the poster artists responded to the undulating lines, bold patterns, and spatial discrepancies seen in these earlier designs.[48] It didn't hurt that the aesthetic of art nouveau had earlier made a strong impact on San Francisco and as such was already a part of the quotidian heritage of the City by the Bay. Whether the undulating sensuousness of Wes Wilson's BG-29 ("The Sound") or Victor Moscoso's floral décor on FD-36, motifs, colors, and linear design principles of art nouveau were drawn on both to form something visually arresting and to fashion an aesthetic identity.[49] Stanley Mouse and Alton Kelley's Alphonse Mucha–derived design for FD-29 most explicitly reveals the enormity of the debt to the graphic traditions of art nouveau (Figure 20.2).[50] Directly appropriating Mucha's smoking girl from an 1896 poster for Job cigarettes, in all her undulating, linear glory, Mouse and Kelley connect their poster to the elegant, unbridled associations of art nouveau.[51] The stylistic connection with San Francisco's past conjures up both the romance of nostalgia and the excitement of the frontier. The notion of an unbridled, wild frontier is processed through the psychedelic countercultural mind frame with its connotations of pioneers of the New Wild West "exploring mental frontiers," as even the cigarette held by Mucha's woman appears to be transformed into a joint, the association of which is subtly suggested by the poster's use of colors commonly occurring in marijuana—green, red, and purple. And so our smoking woman, let us call her Mary Jane, smoothly glides between historic associations and contemporary recreations to fashion a visual suggestion of culture—a psychedelic experience in which time, space, and artistic media interact in the creation of a Wagnerian *Gesamtkunstwerk* gone happily hallucinogenic.

Like Mucha's designs, the psychedelic counterculture posters do not just advertise a product or event but also fashion a unified image of culture, by way of a visual relationship to one another, as the posters can be seen not in isolation but as collective aspects of an endeavor to articulate the ineffable qualities of palpable mutability with which the counterculture defined, amused, and recreated (and re-created) itself. The creation of a period style, intended to be viewed with a period eye, makes these images quintessential artistic visions of their culture. Like

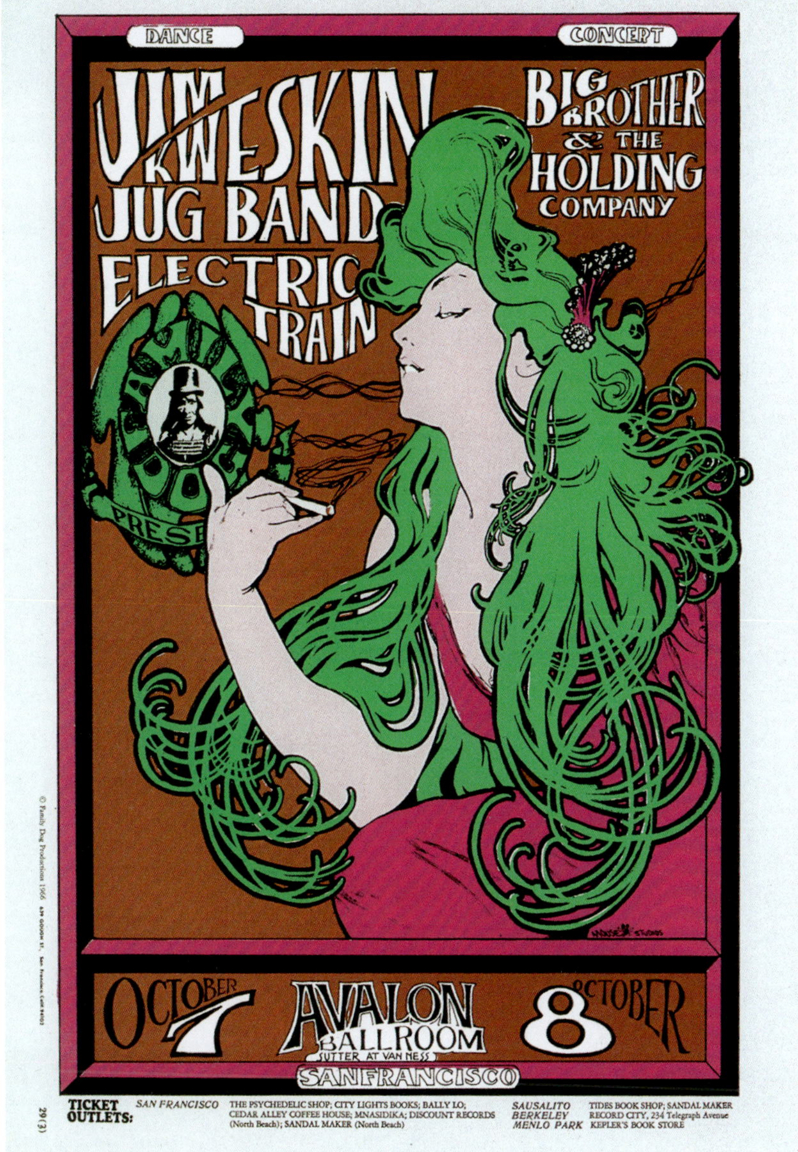

Figure 20.2

Stanley Mouse and Alton Kelley, FD-29: Jim Kweskin Jug Band, Big Brother and the Holding Company, Electric Train, October 7–8, 1966, Avalon Ballroom, San Francisco. Copyright 2011 Rhino Entertainment, a Warner Music Group Company.

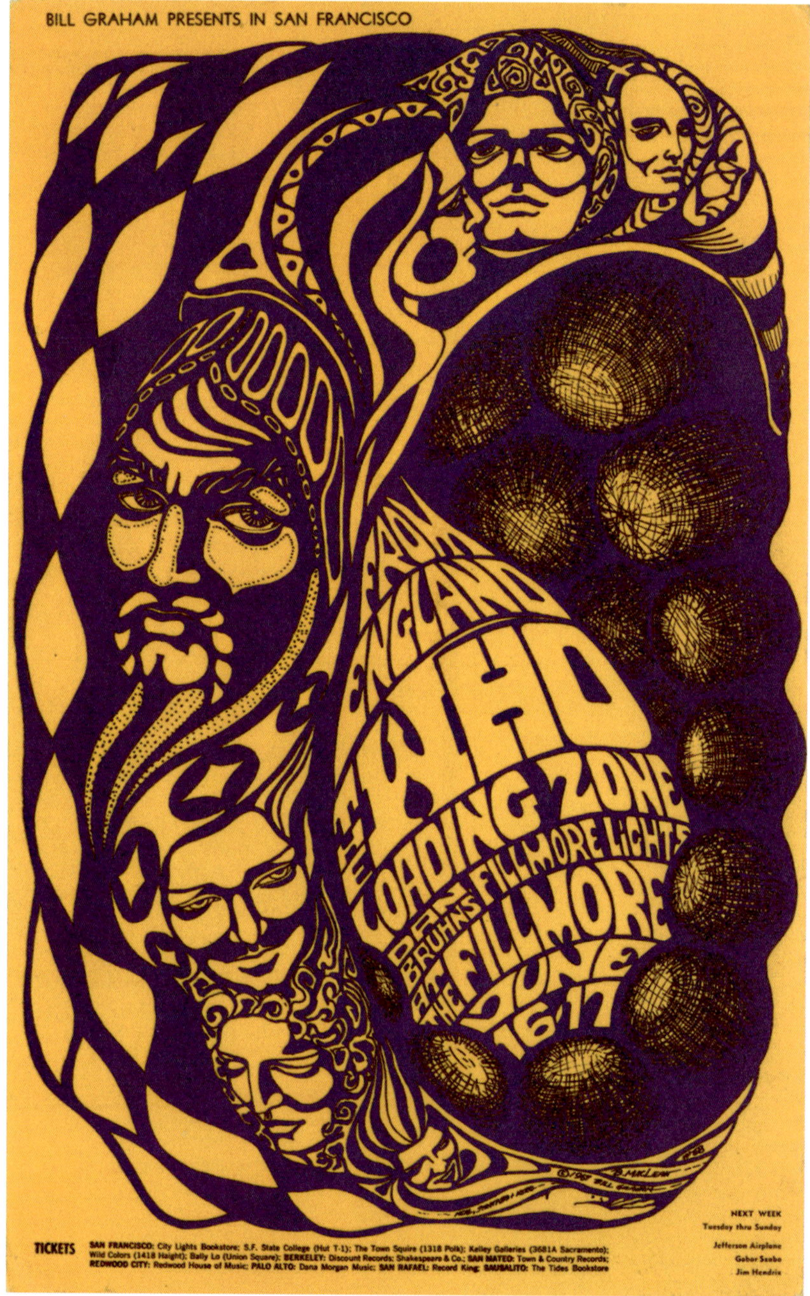

Figure 20.3

Bonnie MacLean, BG-68: The Who, Loading Zone, Lights by Dan Bruhn's Fillmore Lights, June 16–17, 1967, Fillmore Auditorium, San Francisco. Copyright Wolfgang's Vault.

art historian Michael Baxandall's churchgoing banker with a taste for dancing admiring Botticelli's *Cestello Annunciation,* we might posit the ideal existence of a concert-going young hippie with a taste for LSD taking in the meaning and associations of the swirling protuberance of faces and flowing linear forms that grace Bonnie MacLean's poster (BG-68) announcing the arrival "from England" of The Who (Figure 20.3).[52]

This overt appeal to a hallucinogenic or psychedelic visual frame of reference is something of a leitmotif in much of the poster artwork from San Francisco and the greater Northwest. Certainly psychotropic substances were part of the equation, but to focus exclusively on them as the motivating force behind psychedelic imagery is to miss the larger context, one of consciousness expanding that eclipses the substances that are often taken to enhance this broader melting of barriers—cognitive, psychic, social, moral, musical, artistic. It would be historically inaccurate to either deny or overemphasize the purely Dionysian recreational facets of drug use within the counterculture. As David Farber notes, "those academicians who have written about the 1960s without any attempt to seriously or analytically relate drug consciousness to the events of the 1960s have done so at the cost of warping and misconstructing much of what went on."[53] While Farber's admonition is largely directed toward those who cast nascent psychedelic drug culture as separated from political actions and motivations, it could also be levied at those who seek to denigrate or ignore any such relation. Psychedelics were part of a more complex countercultural endeavor to question accepted social and cognitive norms as well as to (however naively) explore new frontiers. This was, after all, the New, REALLY Wild West. That the substances that were initially most commonly used—marijuana and hallucinogens (particularly LSD)—involve essentially social or communally directed experiences suggests a common cultural quest, or at least endeavor.[54] Nick Bromwell notes: "When psychedelics are taken out of specific cultural practices and rituals and disseminated indiscriminately to adolescents coming of age in a modern . . . world, consequences will follow."[55] Indeed, they did, and some of these consequences seem to have been the questioning of established, traditional notions of reality, truth, and social norms. Rather than deritualizing psychedelics, as Bromwell implies, it would seem as though the youthful counterculture sought to fashion its own rituals, embracing hallucinogens and marijuana with an almost sacramental zeal. Hence the quasi-religious ritualization of the dance concert event as a psychedelic countercultural signifier. The ineffable is inherently counter to established norms that seek to regularize and minimize ambiguity and cognitive destabilization. Ineffability is therefore inherently countercultural, and LSD and marijuana both fostered and forced exploration of the ineffable lightness of being.[56] This was part and parcel of a larger sociopolitical philosophy of flirting with the liminality of the Doors of Perception.

Artists have stated that one of their goals in designing posters was to somehow express something of the experience of a hallucinatory acid trip.[57] But even this experience occurred within a broader cultural and aesthetic matrix of references. Consider Lee Conklin's BG-101 and BG-134, with their finely delineated yet surrealistically metamorphic forms.[58] The pulsating protoplasmic epigraphy in Conklin's BG-143 and ethereal iron human gate of his BG-145 phase in and out of clarity like hallucinogenic beats of lucidity and befuddlement.[59] Fantastic melting forms and Boschian landscapes provide shifting visual referents in Conklin's BG-138, BG-144, BG-149, and BG-173.[60] At times, Conklin's rougher, looser line and disturbingly hallucinatory forms feel more akin to a mind-battering bad trip than the swirling happiness of the graceful linearity of Bonnie MacLean's BG-89 and BG-90.[61] Nonetheless, Conklin's and MacLean's work, as well as those of most of the other artists associated with the movement, revels in a dynamic, linear (and often coloristic) intensity that most frequently manifests the artists' desire to create something that would extol and exalt cognitive, even precognitive, expansion. This could extend to pushing the barriers of visual perception by offset color printing, as done with Lee Conklin's BG-139, or simultaneously emphasizing multiple planar views, as in Conklin's BG-127.[62] While it would be dishonest to state that hallucinogenic substances did not play a powerful role in the conceptualization of these posters, it would be equally myopic to aver that these alone explain them. It was all part of a larger calling into question of notions of a fixed nature of reality and perception that was at the very core of countercultural philosophy and practice.

Psychedelics were not the only ingredients in the particularly coloristic intensity of some of these posters, most dramatically those by Victor Moscoso, who developed some of the most eyeball-melting Day-Glo designs ever envisioned. Already visible in the earliest Neon Rose posters from December 1966 to January 1967, such as NR-1 and NR-2, the color juxtapositions are pulsatingly bold.[63] Implying, if not actually depicting, movement, the color palette and design seem to swell and breathe as though seen while under the influence of hallucinogens. By overlaying boldly color-contrasting layers of linear design elements, he creates a veil-like reality that must be peeled away as though removing so many damask-thin covers of the doors of perception, as seen in NR-10, appropriately announcing a stint at the Matrix by the Doors.[64] The sheer optical intensity of the rich, hypersaturated Day-Glo colors in images such as FD-47 and FD-49 seem to serve as coloristic overloads intended to shock the viewer out of any visual complacency vis-à-vis normative perceptions of reality.[65]

Not only were form and color the improvisatory playground of these artists, but so too was epigraphy—the very shape of language. Wes Wilson dramatically expanded the possibilities of lettering and its ability to signify beyond its traditional linguistic and formal constraints, developing much of the template and basic aesthetic for the psychedelic poster design.[66] Early Fillmore posters, from 1966, tend toward focusing on the text, with little to no image. Bonnie MacLean's BG-0 resembles a carnival flyer, an association furthered by Peter Bailey's biplane/horse contraption on BG-1 and BG-1A.[67] Already in BG-3, Wilson is beginning to tentatively explore both dynamic lettering and the fusion of figure and text.[68] Though still very much legible, the letters form both structure and surface detail of the face, which looks downward, askew from the picture plane, while the curving letters of "Jefferson Airplane" seem to form an upward glancing third eye on the forehead. Subsequently, Wilson produced a number of posters that utilized only the text and some color patterns, yet arranged in dynamic spatial compositions that seem to bulge and flow with a palpable life force. BG-5 further develops this intertwining of text and image.[69] Forms and letters swell and move to merge, creating disorienting and shifting perceptions of space and form. Is it an eyeball, or are they lips that swell forth from the now-violated picture plane? BG-18 sees the words turned into vibrant red flames that dance against the solid green background, animating the text into a visual association beyond the textual.[70] BG-48 and BG-54 utilize vibrant, swelling text that visually entrains with the melting, anthropomorphic, and decorative forms, essentially becoming another part of the pulsating aesthetic mélange.[71] The structurally and visually integrated lettering that spells "Truth Search" in BG-54 sums it up: viewing these works is a process not only of searching for Truth but also of accepting the very ineffably shifting quality of this established countercultural truth (Figure 20.4).

But Wilson was not alone in this endeavor to "blow the mind" of text. In addition to his influential championing of Day-Glo palettes, Victor Moscoso was also among the most daring pioneers of epigraphic mutation. Moscoso's designs for FD-51 (Figure 20.5), FD-81, and FD-86 incorporate text into the structure of the image, so that the two fuse in such a way as to abjure any perceptible division between word and picture.[72] Moscoso also employed circular text, dramatically visible in FD-53, forming a coloristically pulsating eyeball, the words reading around as iris and cornea, while the pupil is occupied by the Family Dog logo.[73] This opens up an entirely new means of visual communication, as it cannot be read in any traditional way from a single vantage point. Nor can it be actually read as a poster, in that a single viewing perspective is more or less inherently fixed for a poster. Can the poster be "read" without being read? Perhaps this is the litmus test—a visual signifier asking if one is in the know or not—if one is a part of the counterculture or the mainstream culture. It is an epigraphic rite of initiation. As we have seen, over the course of time, as the notion of a self-identifying and self-literate counterculture became more broadly articulated, the need to signify outside of this culture was occasionally ignored completely. I do not propose that this brief discussion is anything other than an introduction to some countercultural facets of San Francisco psyche-

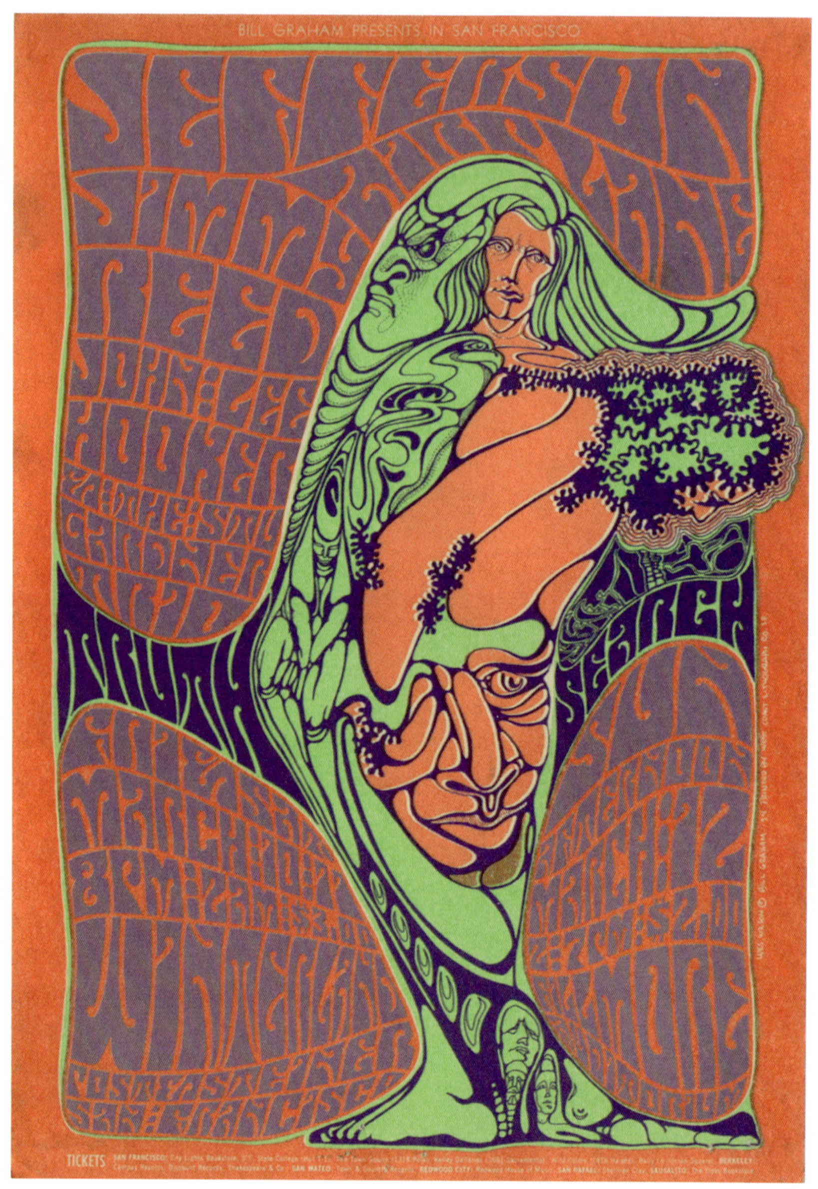

Figure 20.4

Wes Wilson, BG-54: Jefferson Airplane, Jimmy Reed, John Lee Hooker, Stu Gardner Trio, March 10–11, 1967, Winterland, San Francisco, and March 12, 1967, Fillmore Auditorium, San Francisco. Copyright Wolfgang's Vault.

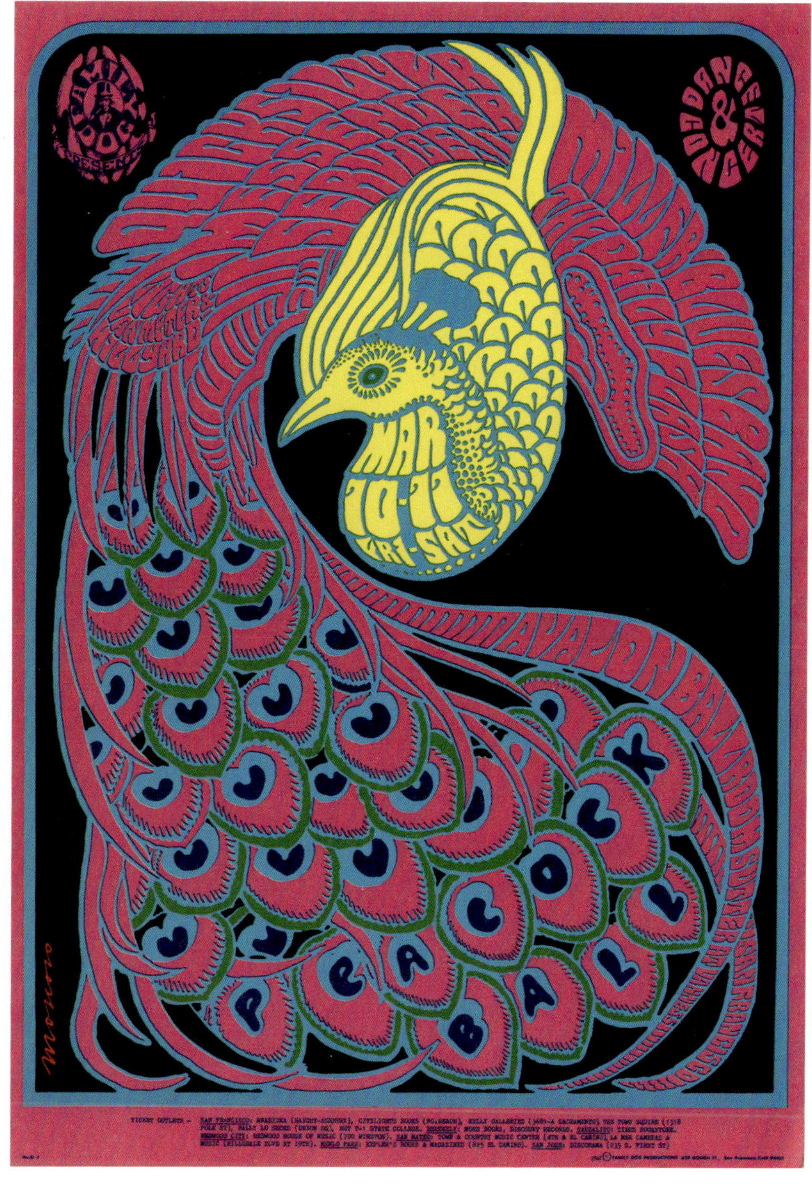

TICKET OUTLETS — SAN FRANCISCO: BRAVERMA (HAIGHT-ASHBURY), CITYLIGHTS BOOKS (NO.BEACH), KELLY GALLERIES (3681-A SACRAMENTO) THE TOWN SQUIRE (1318 POLK ST), BALLY LO SHOES (UNION SQ), 827 7-1 STATE COLLEGE. BERKELEY: MOES BOOKS, DISCOUNT RECORDS. SAUSALITO: TIDES BOOKSTORE. REDWOOD CITY: REDWOOD HOUSE OF MUSIC (700 WINSTON). SAN MATEO: TOWN & COUNTRY MUSIC CENTER (4TH & EL CAMINO) LA KEN CAMERAS & MUSIC (HILLSDALE BLVD ST 19TH). MENLO PARK: KEPLER'S BOOKS & MAGAZINES (825 EL CAMINO). SAN JOSE: DISCORAMA (235 S. FIRST ST)

delic poster art. There is no discernible priority placed on text, pattern, or figural allusion. All are formed and reformed together in a perpetual state of becoming—the essentials of a style that is laden with psychedelic countercultural signification. The embrace of this shifting, intertwined open-endedness was itself a politically charged aesthetic. Ineffably manifest and manifestly ineffable, these images convey the very essence of the countercultural aesthetic ideal. The rich intertwining of historical and cultural signifiers, as well as the interplay between fixed meaning and ineffability, is by its very nature impossible to categorically elucidate. Nonetheless, I hope to have convincingly demonstrated some of the ways in which this art form conveyed complex messages and degrees of meaning within the formulation and performance of countercultural identity. If, as has been noted, one cannot realistically separate rock music from countercultural politics and identity, it would be problematic at best to ignore the ways in which other media were inextricable aspects of this same larger cultural phenomenon.[74] Psychedelic rock posters were very much part of a larger terrain of shifting cultural and cognitive signifiers that played within, without, and across distinct media and senses. Indeed, their most potent power was to transgress barriers, fixity, and perceived conventions—the signifying basis for countercultural *Gesamtkunstwerk*.

 SIGNIFYING THE INEFFABLE

NOTES

This essay stems from a much larger research project on art historical and cultural facets of San Francisco psychedelic poster art. Some of these ideas were first formulated in a paper delivered at the University of Colorado, Boulder, in February 2009. I thank Bob Nauman and Maria DeFilippo in particular for affording me this opportunity to develop and present these ideas. For including the essay in this fine volume, I thank Elissa Auther and Adam Lerner. For their kindness, generosity, and patience in putting up with my enthusiastic inquiries, I owe tremendous gratitude to Lee Conklin, Wes Wilson, and Stanley Mouse. For inimitable editorial assistance, insight, and all-around support, Alice Bauer deserves more thanks and praise than I can offer with these meager words of appreciation. (Summer of) Love to Alice, Francesca, Gabriella, and Bloopy, who make the trip worthwhile.

1. Richard Wagner, *The Art-Work of the Future, and Other Works,* trans. and ed. W. Ashton Ellis (Lincoln: University of Nebraska Press, 1993).

2. Regarding the use and meaning of the term *tribal* within the counterculture, see Mark Watson's article in this volume.

3. I use the *San Francisco counterculture* to refer to a broader geographical region of the San Francisco Bay Area. Dance concerts, Acid Tests, and other countercultural events in Berkeley, Palo Alto, Virginia City, Santa Rosa, and elsewhere were very much connected to, and part of, this distinct countercultural formulation.

4. See Allan Kaprow, *Essays on the Blurring of Art and Life,* ed. Jeff Kelley (Berkeley: University of California Press, 1993).

5. Charles Perry, quoted in Barney Hoskyns, *Beneath the Diamond Sky: Haight-Ashbury 1965–1979* (New York: Simon and Schuster, 1997), 75.

6. In this essay I use the standardized nomenclature to identify posters. For instance, in the literature on the psychedelic rock poster, the images referenced here are known as BG-144 (Quicksilver) and BG-145 (Ten Years After), referring to its number in the Bill Graham Fillmore series. The issue of cataloging these images is itself problematic, as the determination of the primary identifier is often arbitrary. While many authors and viewers focus attention on the musical performers, I believe that the artists responsible for the designs are more significant. That said, my argument here is that the posters are so intertwined with their related performances as to render such delineations somewhat misleading vis-à-vis the polymediation of the cultural performance. Though cataloging by promoter—Bill Graham—is equally (if not more) misleading, it does have the advantage of distinct numeration enabling absolute clarity.

7. See BG-46: Wes Wilson—Butterfield Blues Band, Charles Lloyd Quartet, January 20–22, 1967, Fillmore Auditorium, San Francisco. BG-134: Lee Conklin—Steppenwolf, Staple Singers, Santana; lights by Holy See; August 27–29, 1968, Fillmore West. Grateful Dead, Preservation Hall Jazz Band, Sons of Champlin; lights by Holy See; August 30–September 1, 1968, Fillmore West.

8. The invention of projecting light through moving liquid pigments in 1952 by San Francisco State University art professor Seymour Locks would prove to be exceptionally influential in the development of the visual language of the psychedelic dance concert. Initially accompanying poetry readings and experimental theater, lights became increasingly tied to countercultural dance concerts in the aftermath of their success in augmenting the chaotic polymediation of the Merry Prankster's Acid Tests and events at the Longshoreman's Hall in San Francisco in 1965–66. The rise of the liquid light show as an important, performing element is evidenced by the emergence of individual lighting personalities with distinctive styles, such as Glen McKay's Head Lights, Holy See, and Little Princess 109, as advertised on the posters.

9. The Six Gallery was founded by five artists (Wally Hedrick, Hayward King, Deborah Remington, John Allen Ryan, and David Simpson) and a poet (Jack Spicer). See Christopher Gair, *The American Counterculture* (Edinburgh: Edinburgh University Press, 2007), 91. Ginsberg's performance of "Howl" was part of a reading by five poets—Ginsberg, Gary Snyder, Philip Whalen, Michael McClure, and Philip Lamantia. See Gair, *American Counterculture,* 28. See also Preston Whaley Jr., *Blows Like a Horn: Beat Writing, Jazz, Style, and Markets in the Transformation of U.S. Culture* (Cambridge, Mass.: Harvard University Press, 2004), 24.

10. Gair, *American Counterculture,* 93.

11. In its "mesh between poetry and music in the visual arts," the North Beach Beat movement was tremendously influential in the concepts of polymediation in subsequent psychedelic dance concerts. Regarding the Beat fusion of art forms, see Colin Gardner, "The Influence of Wallace Berman on the Visual Arts," in *Wallace Berman: Support the Revolution* (Amsterdam: Institute of Contemporary Art, 1992), 79.

12. Gair, *American Counterculture,* 184.

13. Ibid., 191–92. Peter Seltz's *Art of Engagement: Visual Politics in California and Beyond* (Berkeley: University of California Press, 2006) contains one essay surveying California's countercultural art scene but favors so-called high art over the graphic rock poster. In doing so, Seltz misses the egalitarian ideals resonating within the counterculture and its visual culture.

14. Julie Stephens, *Anti-Disciplinary Protest: Sixties Radicalism and Postmodernism* (Cambridge: Cambridge University Press, 1998).

15. Several years later, Ralph Gleason noted this quasi-religious ritual: "The Family Dog called their first dance 'A Tribute to Dr. Strange.' And the very concept of giving a dance a name like a celebration implied the mildly religious nature of the whole idea. It was like a feast day or a saint's birthday and I thought at the time that a new religion was in the process of evolving." Ralph J. Gleason, *The Jefferson Airplane and the San Francisco Sound* (New York: Ballantine, 1969), 4.

16. See Nadya Zimmerman, *Counterculture Kaleidoscope: Musical and Cultural Perspectives on Late Sixties San Francisco* (Ann Arbor: University of Michigan Press, 2008), 5.

17. Theodore Roszak, *The Making of a Counter Culture* (Berkeley: University of California Press, 1995), originally published in 1969; J. Milton Yinger, *Countercultures: The Promise and Peril of a World Turned Upside Down* (New York: Free Press, 1982).

18. Gair, *American Counterculture,* 143.

19. See Peter Braunstein and Michael William Doyle, eds., *Imagine Nation: The American Counterculture of the 1960s and '70s* (London: Routledge, 2001) for a savvy critical response to the notion of cultural radicalism as essentially apolitical and related to traditional American consumerism.

20. Roszak, *Making of a Counter Culture,* 1995.

21. Nick Bromwell, *Tomorrow Never Knows: Rock and Psychedelics in the 1960s* (Chicago: University of Chicago Press, 2000), 86.

22. Ralph Gleason, "The Power of Non-Politics or the Death of the Square Left," *Evergreen Review* (September 1967). Quoted in Jesse Kornbluth, *Notes from the New Underground: Where It's At and What's Up* (New York: Ace, 1968), 216. See also Stephens, *Anti-Disciplinary Protest.*

23. For a discussion of the mythologizing tendency to reduce the complexity of the counterculture to a simple reading, particularly in terms of its reduction to music and lifestyle, see Zimmerman, *Counterculture Kaleidoscope,* especially 3ff.

24. Certainly, it is ironic that this very ideal of egalitarian inclusivity was not actually practiced by the counterculture, as can be seen

73. FD-53: Victor Moscoso and Fred Roth (photographer)—"From the Plains of Quicksilver"—Quicksilver Messenger Service, John Lee Hooker, Miller Blues Band; lights by Van Meter & Hillyard; March 22-23, 1967, Avalon Ballroom. One might also note the Western theme suggested by the title, presumably intended to evoke the outlaws of the New Wild West image, most obviously promulgated by QMS and the Charlatans.

74. See, for example, Simon Frith, *Music for Pleasure: Essays in the Sociology of Pop* (New York: Routledge, 1988), 75; Bromwell, *Tomorrow Never Knows*.

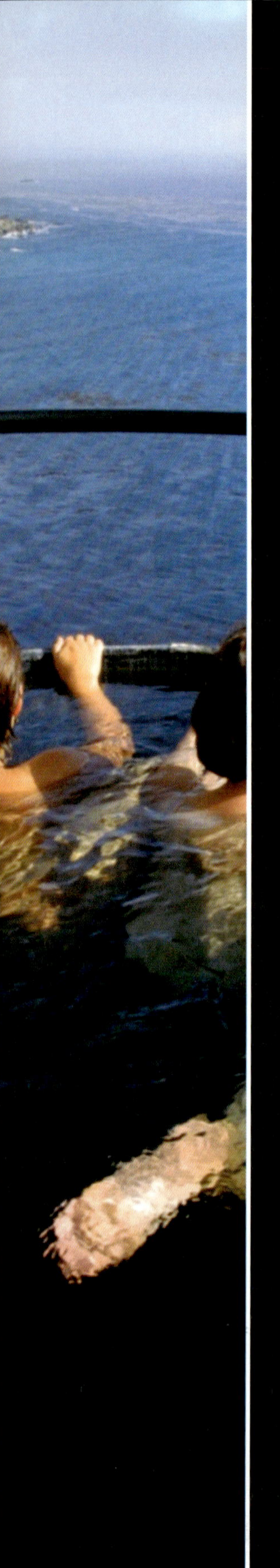

ACKNOWLEDG

The ideas in this book first saw the light of day at the College Art Association conference in 2009 in Los Angeles, and we are grateful to Michel Oren, Suzanne Hudson, Eva J. Friedberg, Robin Oppenheim, and Amy Azzarito for participating on our panel then. Research for the introduction was supported by a fellowship in the fall of 2009 from the Georgia O'Keeffe Museum Research Center. The stunning beauty of Santa Fe, New Mexico, combined with the scholarly and collegial atmosphere fostered at the center provided the perfect retreat. To Richard Morrison, our editor at the University of Minnesota Press, we owe our sincere gratitude for his unwavering support and enthusiasm for the project from its earliest stages. Of course, we would be nowhere without the contributions of our authors, all of whom were a delight to work with and from whom we learned a tremendous amount about the American counterculture. We thank Kathy O'Dell and the anonymous readers of the manuscript, whose comments and criticism were crucial to the development and full realization of our introductory essay. We are grateful to Kourosh Larizadeh and Luis Pardo for opening their home to us and sharing their enthusiasm for the Cockettes. We are enormously grateful to Mark Falcone and the boards of trustees of, first, the Laboratory of Art and Ideas at Belmar, then the Museum of Contemporary Art Denver, for encouragement and support. We are deeply grateful to the many artists who shared their stories, work, and personal archives, including Clark Richert, Richard Kallweit, Linda Fleming, Roberta Price, Jack Fulton, Anna Halprin, Chip Lord, Curtis Scheirer, Paolo Soleri, Fayette Houser, Rumi Missabu, Roger Anderson, Billy Bowers, Peter Mays, Michael Scroggins, David LeBrun, and Lawrence Janss: their openness and generosity greatly aided our conceptualization of this project and inspired us at every turn. We would like to thank the staff of MCA Denver who assisted with the exhibition and research, especially Tricia Robson and Nick Silici. We would like to thank exhibition designer Ben Griswold for his insight into the material. Finally, Adam wants it to be acknowledged that the origins of this endeavor can be traced back a long way, probably to Elissa's childhood identification with Gloria on *All in the Family*. This project may even owe something to her admiration for the television character Maude and other strong women who found their voices amid the uproar of the 1960s and 1970s.

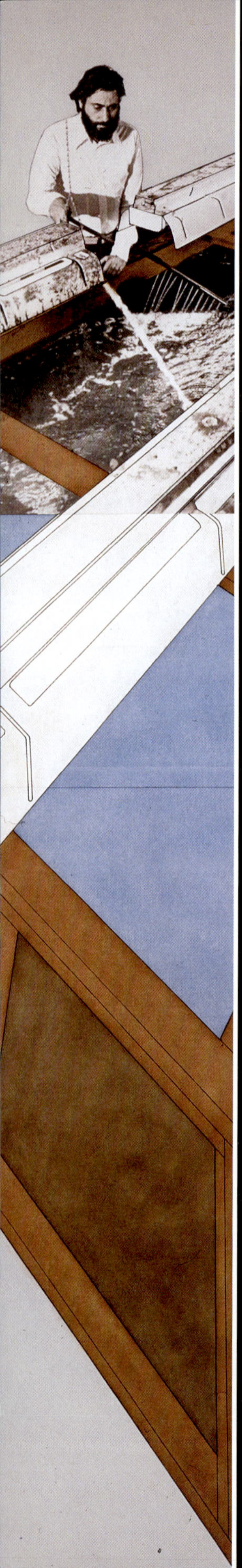

CONTRIBUTORS

ELISSA AUTHER is associate professor of contemporary art at the University of Colorado, Colorado Springs. Her book *String, Felt, Thread: The Hierarchy of Art and Craft in American Art* (Minnesota, 2010) examines the innovative use of fiber in American art and the impact of its elevation on the conceptual boundaries distinguishing "art" from "craft" in the postwar era. She is codirector of Feminism & Co.: Art, Sex, Politics at the Museum of Contemporary Art Denver.

AMY AZZARITO received her master's degree in the history of decorative arts and design at Parsons, New School for Design, Cooper-Hewitt National Design Museum. She is senior editor of the popular design blog Design*Sponge.

JANA BLANKENSHIP is curator at the CCA Wattis Institute for Contemporary Arts in San Francisco. She is also assistant curator of the Twelfth Istanbul Biennial and director of the People's Gallery in San Francisco. Her master's thesis in curatorial studies at California College of the Arts was a study of Bonnie Ora Sherk's early works and her environmental performance sculpture *Crossroads Community (The Farm)*.

AMANDA BOETZKES is assistant professor in the Department of History of Art at Ohio State University. Her book *The Ethics of Earth Art* (Minnesota, 2010) deals with the relationship between ecological ethics and the aesthetic strategies of earth art from the late 1960s to the present.

JULIA BRYAN-WILSON is author of *Art Workers: Radical Practice in the Vietnam War Era.* She is a frequent contributor to *Artforum,* and her writing has appeared in *Art Bulletin, Art Journal, Frieze, Grey Room, Modern Painters, October,* and the *Journal of Modern Craft.* Her current project investigates the politics of handmaking in contemporary art.

KAREN MARY DAVALOS is chair and associate professor of Chican@ studies at Loyola Marymount University in Los Angeles. Her book *Yolanda M. López* (Minnesota, 2008) brings together her research and teaching interests in Chicana feminist scholarship, spirituality, art, exhibition practices, and oral history.

ERIN ELDER is an independent curator, writer, and teacher interested in collaboration, sense of place, and expanded notions of culture. She has worked with a variety of institutions, including Yerba Buena Center for the Arts, Württembergischer Kunstverein, Creative Time, and the Center for Land Use Interpretation. In 2009, she cofounded PLAND, an off-the-grid residency program in northern New Mexico.

EVA J. FRIEDBERG received her Ph.D. in visual studies from the University of California at Irvine, where her dissertation examined Lawrence

Halprin's development of the RSVP Cycles as an alternative architectural practice in the 1960s. She lectures in the Department of Art, Architecture, and Art History at the University of San Diego.

COLETTE GAITER is associate professor of visual communication in the art department at the University of Delaware. She is a contributing author to *Black Panther: The Revolutionary Art of Emory Douglas,* and in 2008 her video about Douglas and his work was included in the exhibition *Cinema Remixed & Reloaded: Black Women and the Moving Image since 1970.*

MARK HARRIS is professor of art at the University of Cincinnati. Recent exhibitions of his artwork include *State Fare* at the Wexner Center, Columbus; *Morning Star* at Country Club Gallery, Cincinnati; and *High Society* at the Wellcome Collection, London. He is the author of *Pipilotti Rist's Music, Marcia Farquhar: Chelsea Hotel, March 14, 2008, Heather Phillipson: The City Sings,* and *Marcia Hafif: Glaze Painting.*

SCOTT HERRING is associate professor of English at Indiana University. He is author of *Queering the Underworld: Slumming, Literature, and the Undoing of Lesbian and Gay History* and, most recently, *Another Country: Queer Anti-Urbanism.*

SUZANNE HUDSON is assistant professor of modern and contemporary art at the University of Illinois, Urbana–Champaign. She is cofounder of the Contemporary Art Think Tank and president of the Society of Contemporary Art Historians, an affiliate society of the College Art Association. She is author of *Robert Ryman: Used Paint* and is working on a manuscript about abstraction and spirituality in 1960s America.

DAVID E. JAMES, professor in the School of Cinema–Television at the University of Southern California, is author of *Power Misses: Essays across (Un)Popular Culture, Allegories of Cinema: American Film in the Sixties,* and *The Most Typical Avant-Garde: History and Geography of Minor Cinemas in Los Angeles,* among other titles.

JENNIE KLEIN is an associate professor of art history at Ohio University. Her research focuses on contemporary feminist art and performance.

ADAM LERNER is director of the Museum of Contemporary Art Denver and chief animator in the Department of Fabrications. He was the founder and executive director of the Laboratory of Art and Ideas at Belmar until the lab merged with the Museum of Contemporary Art Denver in March 2009. His writing projects can be found at AdamLernerInAmerica.com.

LUCY R. LIPPARD is a writer, activist, and curator. She is the author of twenty-one books on contemporary art. She is a contributing editor for

Art in America and was a columnist for the *Village Voice, In These Times,* and *Z Magazine.*

SCOTT B. MONTGOMERY is associate professor of art history at the University of Denver. A medievalist, he has published articles on figural reliquaries and imagery related to relic claims and the cult of saints in a wide array of locations across medieval Europe. He has written two books, *Saint Ursula and the Eleven Thousand Virgins of Cologne: Relics, Reliquaries, and the Visual Culture of Group Sanctity in Late Medieval Europe* and *Casting Our Own Shadows: Recreating the Medieval Pilgrimage to Santiago de Compostela,* coauthored with Alice A. Bauer. He is currently working on a monograph on psychedelic poster artist Lee Conklin.

DEANNE PYTLINSKI is assistant professor and coordinator of art history, theory, and criticism at Metropolitan State College of Denver, where she is assistant chair of the Department of Art. Her research focuses on women in early video art and video collectives in upstate New York.

BILL SCHEFFEL is a poet, writer, documentary filmmaker, and teacher of meditation who began studies in the Buddhist/Shambhala tradition in 1976 with Chögyam Trungpa Rinpoche. Beginning in 1991, Bill taught classes in poetry, creative writing, and meditation at Naropa University for the following thirteen years. In 2007, he made the documentary *Cambodia: Lord Mukpo's Dream Time* as an homage to the people of Cambodia. His second film, *Denise: Circle of Blessing,* chronicles the spiritual aspects of death and dying. Bill is the author of *Loving-kindness Meditation.*

JENNI SORKIN is assistant professor of critical studies, media, and design at the University of Houston. Her research focuses on the intersection of gender and material culture within modern and contemporary art. Her writing has appeared in the *New Art Examiner, Art Journal, Art Monthly, Frieze, NU: The Nordic Art Review, Modern Painters,* and *Third Text,* as well as numerous exhibition catalogs.

MARK WATSON is a Ph.D. candidate in the Department of Art History and Archeology at Columbia University. He specializes in modern American and Native American art.

TOM WILSON is a freelance curator and lecturer. He works for the Design Museum in London, where he supports the management and development of the museum's permanent collection, and he teaches design history at London Metropolitan University and Brighton University. His current research interests focus on graphic design in Cuba from 1955 to 1975.

WEST OF CENTER

Published by the University of Minnesota Press
in cooperation with the Museum of Contemporary Art Denver

Editorial Director: Richard Morrison
Production and Design Manager: Daniel Ochsner
Managing Editor: Laura Westlund

Copyediting by Louisa Castner
Book design and composition by Jena Sher
Printing and binding by Friesens Corp., Altona, Manitoba, Canada